Historic Documents
of 2012

Historic Documents
of 2012

Heather Kerrigan, Editor

Los Angeles | London | New Delhi
Singapore | Washington DC

Los Angeles | London | New Delhi
Singapore | Washington DC

FOR INFORMATION:

CQ Press

SAGE Publications, Inc.

2455 Teller Road

Thousand Oaks, California 91320

E-mail: order@sagepub.com

SAGE Publications Ltd.

1 Oliver's Yard

55 City Road

London EC1Y 1SP

United Kingdom

SAGE Publications India Pvt. Ltd.

B 1/I 1 Mohan Cooperative Industrial Area

Mathura Road, New Delhi 110 044

India

SAGE Publications Asia-Pacific Pte. Ltd.

3 Church Street

#10-04 Samsung Hub

Singapore 049483

Developmental Editor: Andrew Boney

Managing Editor: Heather Kerrigan

Contributors: Brian Beary, Anastazia Clouting, Hilary
Ewing, Linda Fecteau, Melissa Feinberg,
Jessica Heffner, Heather Kerrigan, Roger K.
Smith

Editorial Assistant: Josh Benjamin

Production Editor: David C. Felts

Copy Editor: Patrice J. Sutton

Typesetter: C&M Digitals (P) Ltd.

Proofreader: Talia Greenberg

Indexer: Shapiro Indexing Services

Cover Designer: Michael Dubowe

Marketing Manager: Carmel Schrire

Cover image © AP Images/Pablo Martinez Monsivais

"Assange (Appellant) v The Swedish Prosecution Authority (Respondent), [2012] UKSC 22," May 30, 2012. © Crown Copyright 2013.

"Observation of a New Particle With a Mass of 125 GeV." July 4, 2012. © Copyright CERN, for the benefit of the CMS Collaboration. Used with permission.

"Breaking News: CTU Files Notice of Intent to Strike." August 29, 2012. Used with permission from the Chicago Teachers Union Department of Communications.

"Opening Ceremony of the Games of the XXX Olympiad." July 27, 2012. Used with permission from the International Olympic Committee.

"Presentation Speech by Thorbjørn Jagland, Chairman of the Norwegian Nobel Committee." December 10, 2012 © The Nobel Foundation 2012. Used with permission.

Printed in the United States of America.

A catalog record of this book is available from the Library of Congress.

ISBN 978-1-4522-8206-0 (cloth)

This book is printed on acid-press paper.

13 14 15 16 17 10 9 8 7 6 5 4 3 2 1

Contents

JANUARY

FEBRUARY

MARCH

APRIL

MAY

JUNE

JULY

AUGUST

SEPTEMBER

OCTOBER

NOVEMBER

and three documents written and released by the new president of Mexico on December 1, 2012, detailing the goals for his new administration and announcing proposals submitted to various agencies for consideration.

DECEMBER

Thematic Table of Contents

AMERICAN LIFE

BUSINESS, THE ECONOMY, AND LABOR

ENERGY, ENVIRONMENT, SCIENCE, TECHNOLOGY, AND TRANSPORTATION

GOVERNMENT AND POLITICS

HEALTH AND SOCIAL SERVICES

INTERNATIONAL AFFAIRS
AFRICA

INTERNATIONAL AFFAIRS
ASIA

INTERNATIONAL AFFAIRS
EUROPE

INTERNATIONAL AFFAIRS
LATIN AMERICA AND THE CARIBBEAN

INTERNATIONAL AFFAIRS
MIDDLE EAST

INTERNATIONAL AFFAIRS
RUSSIA AND FORMER SOVIET REPUBLICS

INTERNATIONAL AFFAIRS
GLOBAL ISSUES

NATIONAL SECURITY AND TERRORISM

RIGHTS, RESPONSIBILITIES, AND JUSTICE

List of Document Sources

CONGRESS

EXECUTIVE DEPARTMENTS, AGENCIES, AND COMMISSIONS

INTERNATIONAL GOVERNMENTAL ORGANIZATIONS

JUDICIARY

NONGOVERNMENTAL ORGANIZATIONS

NON-U.S. GOVERNMENTS

U.S. STATE AND LOCAL GOVERNMENTS

WHITE HOUSE AND THE PRESIDENT

Preface

A United States presidential election with unprecedented campaign spending, continued measures to boost the economies of European Union (EU) member states, a newly elected president of Egypt, a devastating hurricane in the northeastern United States, new political leadership in China, and significant Supreme Court rulings on police use of GPS technology, immigration, prison terms for juveniles, and strip searches are just a few of the topics of national and international significance chosen for discussion in *Historic Documents of 2012*. This edition marks the forty-first volume of a CQ Press project that began with *Historic Documents of 1972*. This series allows students, librarians, journalists, scholars, and others to research and understand the most important domestic and foreign issues and events of the year through primary source documents. To aid research, many of the lengthy documents written for specialized audiences have been excerpted to highlight the most important sections. The official statements, news conferences, speeches, special studies, and court decisions presented here should be of lasting public and academic interest.

Historic Documents of 2012 opens with an "Overview of 2012," a sweeping narrative of the key events and issues of the year, which provides context for the documents that follow. The balance of the book is organized chronologically, with each article comprising an introduction and one or more related documents on a specific event, issue, or topic. Often, an event is not limited to a particular day. Consequently, readers will find that some events include multiple documents that may span several months. Their placement in the book corresponds to the date of the first document included for that event. The event introductions provide context and an account of further developments during the year. A thematic table of contents (p. xvii) and a list of documents organized by source (p. xxi) follow the standard table of contents and assist readers in locating events and documents.

As events, issues, and consequences become more complex and far-reaching, these introductions and documents yield important information and deepen understanding about the world's increasing interconnectedness. As memories of current events fade, these selections will continue to further understanding of the events and issues that have shaped the lives of people around the world.

How to Use This Book

Each of the seventy entries in this edition consists of two parts: a comprehensive introduction followed by one or more primary source documents. The articles are arranged in chronological order by month. Articles with multiple documents are placed according to the date of the first document. There are several ways to find events and documents of interest:

By date: If the approximate date of an event or document is known, browse through the titles for that month in the table of contents. Alternatively, browse the tables of contents that appear at the beginning of each month's articles.

By theme: To find a particular topic or subject area, browse the thematic table of contents.

By document type or source: To find a particular type of document or document source, such as the White House or Congress, review the list of document sources.

By index: The index allows researchers to locate references to specific events or documents as well as entries on the same or related subjects.

An online edition of this volume, as well as an archive going back to 1972, is available and offers advance search and browse functionality.

Each article begins with an introduction. This feature provides historical and intellectual contexts for the documents that follow. Documents are reproduced with the original spelling, capitalization, and punctuation of the original or official copy. Ellipsis points indicate textual omissions (unless they were present in the documents themselves indicating pauses in speech), and brackets are used for editorial insertions within documents for text clarification. The excerpting of Supreme Court opinions has been done somewhat differently from other documents. In-text references and citations to laws and other cases have been removed when not part of a sentence to improve the readability of opinions. In those documents, readers will find ellipses used only when sections of narrative text have been removed.

Full citations appear at the end of each document. If a document is not available on the Internet, this too is noted. For further reading on a particular topic consult the "Other Historic Documents of Interest" section at the end of each article. These sections provide cross-references for related articles in this edition of *Historic Documents* as well as in previous editions. References to articles from past volumes include the year and page number for easy retrieval.

Overview of 2012

In the United States, 2012 was dominated by the presidential election and the continuing economic recovery. President Barack Obama and former Massachusetts governor Mitt Romney faced off in the general election campaign, each trying to lure voters to his side with promises to prop up the ailing middle class with new jobs and tax relief. It was ultimately Obama who won reelection, with 51 percent of the popular vote. The ongoing economic recovery continued in 2012, and by the end of the year, the unemployment rate had fallen to 7.8 percent; but the recovery nearly stalled as Republicans and Democrats in Congress debated whether to maintain tax cuts that affected 98 percent of Americans. The two parties also struggled to reach a consensus on gun control legislation following the December shooting at an elementary school in Connecticut in which twenty-seven were killed, including twenty six- and seven-year-olds. While Democrats promised to introduce legislation to reinstate the assault weapons ban and called for the closing of background check loopholes, Republicans, led by the powerful National Rifle Association (NRA), argued that tougher gun control would not stop these kinds of acts.

Internationally, the continuing debt crisis in the European Union dominated headlines, as Greece requested another bailout to support its ailing economy and faced continuing unrest among its citizens in response to new austerity measures meant to help put the nation's fiscal house in order. North Korea and Iran brought renewed attention to their ongoing nuclear ambitions. Under the watch of its new leader, North Korea launched two satellites in April and December, defying international sanctions. Iran continued to enrich uranium, much to the dismay of Israel, which proposed possible military action and called on the international community for support. Two nations that experienced a revolution during the 2011 Arab Spring—Egypt and Libya—made attempts in 2012 to reform their governments under democratic principles and draft new constitutions. By late in the year, Egypt had succeeded in electing a new president and approving a constitution; however, massive protests continued over discontent with the new leader, who opponents accused of trying to establish authoritarian rule. In Libya, the transitional government struggled to hold elections and maintain security, and on September 11, a terrorist attack at the U.S. consulate compound in Benghazi killed four Americans, including the ambassador. In Syria, a nation that had its own round of Arab Spring uprisings, the autocratic ruler, Bashar al Assad, maintained his grip on power as the country devolved into a civil war. The international community struggled to determine how to respond.

DOMESTIC ISSUES

The dominant issue in the presidential election and public life in 2012 was the state of the economy. By most measurements, the economy was continuing to improve—by the end of 2012, the unemployment rate had dropped to 7.8 percent, and the private sector was adding tens of thousands of jobs per month (the public sector, however, was shedding jobs, but at a slower pace). The economic uptick had a positive impact on many Americans, as evidenced in the U.S. Census Bureau's report on poverty released in September 2012. The report reviewed data from 2011 and noted that there was not a statistically significant change in the poverty rate from 2010 to 2011, the first time the rate had not increased in four years. The supplemental report on poverty, released by the U.S. Census Bureau in November—which, unlike the official report, takes into account some household spending and government support systems—also did not note a statistically significant change in year-to-year poverty levels.

Although the official Census Bureau poverty report indicated that the poverty rate in 2011 had remained steady at 15 percent, it did show the growing gap between the rich and poor and, perhaps more significant, the financial impact being experienced by the middle class. In 2011, the Gini index, the measure of inequality used by the Census Bureau, marked its first annual increase since 1993. According to the Census Bureau, this change was largely due to declining income for the middle class while income rose for top earners. As of 2012, the second and third quintile of Americans hold only 23.8 percent of the nation's total income.

While the middle class struggled to recover from the recession, Congress debated how to avoid the *fiscal cliff*, a term that entered common parlance in late 2012 and described a simultaneous increase in tax rates and decrease in government spending (known as the sequester), set to go into effect in January 2013. The Congressional Budget Office (CBO) reported that if Congress allowed the United States to go over the cliff, it would almost certainly lead to another recession, mainly because a tax hike would hit 98 percent of Americans. However, the CBO estimated, by allowing the spending cuts and tax increases to go into effect, the federal deficit could be cut by hundreds of billions of dollars.

Republicans and Democrats in Congress and the White House offered various proposals to stop or delay some of the most significant impacts of the fiscal cliff. It was not until shortly before midnight on December 31, 2012, that the Senate announced that it had reached an agreement to maintain some of the tax cuts while delaying the mandatory budget cuts until at least March 2013. The compromise deal left open a number of questions, such as how the government will deal with the recurring debt ceiling issue, or how the mandatory budget cuts will be divided among federal agencies.

Throughout 2012, women's health issues were fiercely debated, starting in January with President Obama's decision to exempt all churches from a provision of his Affordable Care Act (ACA) that required employers to provide contraceptive or sterilization services without a co-pay in its health insurance policy. This portion of the ACA had sparked significant outcry from religious institutions, which claimed that it infringed on the separation of church and state. In response to critics who said his January announcement was insufficient because it did not cover nonchurch religious institutions, such as hospitals or charities, on February 10, Obama announced that all religiously affiliated institutions would be exempt from providing contraceptive services to female employees as part of its health insurance plan. However, these employees would be able to obtain no-cost contraceptives directly from the company's insurance provider.

In response, the House and Senate each proposed legislation to entirely block the women's contraception rule. The House Committee on Oversight and Government Reform held a hearing that featured witnesses including Lutheran and Baptist clergy, an Orthodox rabbi, and a Roman Catholic bishop. The choice of witnesses, all of whom expressed that Obama's new rule was insufficient to protect religious organizations, was attacked by Democrats, especially because the panel did not include any women. On February 23, House Democrats held their own hearing, calling only one witness, Georgetown law student Sandra Fluke. Fluke, the former president of her school's Students for Reproductive Justice Group, described hearing from a number of students and others who worked for religious organizations that they had been emotionally and financially impacted by their inability to obtain contraceptive coverage.

While the Fluke testimony drew criticism from pundits on the right, including Rush Limbaugh, who later apologized for telling his radio audience that Fluke "wants to be paid to have sex," Republicans were facing their own backlash from the left, especially in the wake of controversial comments made about rape by two Republican candidates for the Senate. In August, Rep. Todd Akin, R-Mo., told a television station that he opposes abortion in all instances because "if it's a legitimate rape, the female body has ways to try and shut that whole thing down." In October, Indiana State Treasurer Richard Mourdock said in a debate that "even when life begins in that horrible situation of rape, that is something God intended to happen." Democrats used the remark as an indication of overall Republican sentiment toward women. Both Akin and Mourdock lost their Senate elections.

The divide among Americans on various social issues including same-sex marriage and recreational marijuana use was clear in 2012, even though public opinion polls showed a slight majority of Americans supporting both issues. Maine, Maryland, and Washington became the first states in the nation to approve same-sex marriage by popular vote, while in Minnesota, voters rejected an amendment to the state constitution that would define marriage as between one man and one woman. North Carolina, however, became the thirtieth state to ban same-sex marriage in its constitution, when voters approved the measure by more than 20 percentage points. Two federal courts struck down the 1996 Defense of Marriage Act (DOMA), a hotly contested law that defines marriage in the eyes of the federal government as between one man and one woman and does not require the federal government or states to recognize same-sex marriages and thus does not guarantee federal benefits to legally married same-sex couples. The Justice Department had already stopped defending the law in federal cases in 2011 under an order from President Obama.

Following the growing number of states approving marijuana for medicinal purposes, in November, Colorado and Washington became the first states to legalize marijuana for recreational use. Marijuana use, whether medicinal or recreational, is still illegal under federal law, and the Justice Department said it would review the two new laws. Arkansas, Massachusetts, and Montana had medical marijuana on their November ballots— Massachusetts voters approved medical marijuana use while Arkansas voters rejected a similar proposal, and in Montana, voters added restrictions to their current medical marijuana laws.

Labor rights were at the forefront again in 2012. After signing into law a highly unpopular budget repair bill that restricted the rights of collective bargaining for state employees, Wisconsin Governor Scott Walker faced a recall election against his 2010 Democratic opponent, Milwaukee Mayor Tom Barrett. Walker was ultimately able to retain his seat, and the election revealed a stark divide in support for labor union rights, as 36 percent of those who voted to keep Governor Walker were from a household with at least one union member. The Indiana and Michigan legislatures also flexed their muscles against collective bargaining, becoming the twenty-third and twenty-fourth states to pass right-to-work laws that bar employees from being required to join or pay dues to a union as a condition of employment.

In Chicago, a stalwart pro-union city, the Chicago Teachers Union went on a seven-day strike, leaving 350,000 students out of the classroom. The strike pitted the powerful union against Mayor Rahm Emanuel, who argued that the union was in violation of state law, which prohibits striking for noneconomic issues. The city courts, however, were unable to hear the case before the union came to an agreement with the city on a new contract that included a 7 percent raise over three years, a longer school day and school year, a new teacher evaluation system that will judge teachers at least partially on student performance, and a complicated hiring and firing system that takes into account both seniority and performance.

Throughout 2012, a series of mass shootings elevated the issues of gun control and gun rights. In February, three students were killed by a teenager at their Chardon, Ohio, high school; in April, an Oikos University dropout killed seven students at the school's Oakland, California, campus; in July, twelve were killed at a movie theater in Colorado; in August, an army veteran who associated himself with the white supremacist movement killed seven, including himself, at a Sikh temple in Oak Creek, Wisconsin; and in September, a disgruntled ex-employee killed six people and then took his own life at his former office. The shooting that sparked the greatest public outcry for tougher gun control laws occurred at a Connecticut elementary school on December 14, when twenty-year-old Adam Lanza shot and killed twenty six- and seven-year-old students and six adults before killing himself.

Almost immediately following the Sandy Hook Elementary School shooting, the gun control debate was revived on Capitol Hill, and speculation grew as to whether the president would push for new regulations, including a renewal of the assault weapons ban that expired in 2004. On December 17, Sen. Dianne Feinstein, D-Calif., said she would introduce a new assault weapons ban during the next session of Congress in January 2013, but many Republicans argued that stricter gun laws were not the answer to stopping such horrific events. The NRA led the anti–gun law charge, with its executive vice president arguing one week after the Newtown shootings that "the only thing that stops a bad guy with a gun is a good guy with a gun." The organization called instead for armed police officers in every school, which drew criticism from school associations that said such a tactic would put students at even greater risk. On December 19, President Obama called on lawmakers to reinstate the assault weapons ban, restrict high-capacity magazine clips, and close background check loopholes. In addition, the president announced that he would form a task force to review all possible gun violence solutions including gun restrictions, mental health programs, and societal issues such as entertainment. That task force is set to make recommendations in January 2013.

As it struggled with the gun control debate, Congress was also dealing with how to respond to Hurricane Sandy, which had ravaged the East Coast and done more than $70 billion in damage, mainly in New Jersey and New York. The storm killed at least 100, left millions without power, and destroyed tens of thousands of homes and businesses. The power outages led to gas rationing in New Jersey and New York, and shut down most mass transit along the Eastern Seaboard. New York's subway system experienced the heaviest damage, with seven of its tunnels completely flooded and requiring extensive repair. In late December, the Senate passed a more than $50 billion emergency appropriations bill to aid in Sandy recovery, but Speaker of the House John Boehner, R-Ohio, decided not to hold a vote before Congress recessed because the most fiscally conservative in his party wanted to offset any recovery spending. Both Republican and Democratic legislators from the affected areas were critical of Boehner's decision. It was not until January 15, 2013, that the House passed its own $50 billion recovery package, which the Senate approved on January 28.

THE 2012 PRESIDENTIAL ELECTION

The 2012 presidential election kicked off in early 2011 as a large field of candidates vied for the Republican nomination. As the year drew to a close, the field was narrowed to four front-runners—Romney, former Pennsylvania senator Rick Santorum, former Speaker of the House Newt Gingrich, and Texas Representative Ron Paul. Polling and early primary results in 2012 revealed a divided Republican Party. Financially, Romney was the strongest candidate, but he faced criticism from many mainstream Republicans for his sometimes moderate stance on a number of issues, particularly during his time as governor. This included the Massachusetts universal health care plan he implemented as governor that served at least in part as a blueprint for Obama's controversial health care legislation. Romney was forced to become increasingly more conservative in his positions, a bold move because, although it would appeal to mainstream Republicans, it had the potential to alienate undecided voters, a crucial portion of the electorate for winning the election.

It was not until April that the Republican National Committee (RNC) announced Romney as the presumed nominee, and in August, he was officially selected as the Republican presidential candidate at the party's nominating convention. Romney chose Rep. Paul Ryan, R-Wis., the chair of the House of Representatives Budget Committee as his running mate. Ryan was well known as a rising star within the Republican Party, but his only foray onto the national stage prior to his nomination came when he unveiled a budget that would turn Medicare into a voucher-like program. The choice of Ryan was important for solidifying the Republican base of economic conservatives, but his critics argued that Ryan's budget plan would be a hard sell for swing voters.

The general election campaign between Romney and Obama was mainly a face-off over who would be better at continuing the economic recovery and, more specifically, bolstering the middle class, which had been hardest hit during the recession. The president used the ongoing economic turnaround as evidence of why he deserved a second term. To his critics who said he had not done enough, Obama cited evidence of the job and tax legislation that he had pushed in Congress, but which had been blocked by Republicans. The Romney-Ryan team proposed a five-point economic plan that they said would create 12 million jobs in the next four years. The plan was criticized for not offering enough specifics as to how Romney planned to reach this goal. During the three presidential debates, and on the campaign trail, Romney explained the lack of detail, saying that it was to serve as a blueprint from which bipartisan legislation could develop in Congress.

The 2012 general election highlighted the increasing importance of the 2010 Supreme Court decision in *Citizens United v. Federal Election Commission*, which gave corporations and labor unions nearly unlimited power to indirectly support candidates. This decision gave rise to a new generation of political action committees (PACs) known as super PACs. Throughout the 2012 campaign season, these super PACs lent most of their support to Republicans and spent a total of $567 million. The biggest spender was Restore Our Future, which spent more than $142 million in support of Romney and in opposition to his opponents. The next biggest spender was Priorities USA Action, which spent more than $64 million against Romney. A significant portion of the millions spent by super PACs went toward running television ads that blanketed battleground states.

Ultimately, on November 6, Obama came out on top, winning 51 percent of the popular vote to Romney's 47 percent. Obama was victorious in nine of ten swing states. He won the most important battleground state, Ohio—no Republican has ever won the White House without Ohio—and won Virginia, a former Republican stronghold, for a second time. The only swing state Obama did not win was North Carolina. Despite attempts by Romney to make inroads with young and Hispanic voters, both groups overwhelmingly supported Obama. Areas with higher unemployment generally supported Romney, an unsurprising trend given that a majority of Americans polled leading up to the election thought Romney would be better on the economy than the president.

FEDERAL COURT DECISIONS

The 2011–2012 Supreme Court term featured important decisions in the areas of First, Fourth, and Eighth Amendment rights, but the two most highly anticipated decisions dealt with Obama's health care law and a controversial Arizona immigration law.

Perhaps the most closely watched of the Supreme Court's decisions in 2012 was the case of *National Federation of Independent Business v. Sebelius*, which brought before the Court the issue of the constitutionality of the enactment of President Obama's 2010 health care law. Since passage, the ACA faced a number of challenges both in lower courts and in Congress, where Republican lawmakers made many attempts to nullify it. Most of the criticism of the law was related to the individual mandate, which required all U.S. citizens (with some exceptions) to purchase health insurance or pay a penalty. The provision was intended to reduce health care costs across the board and help offset the cost of expanding health insurance to millions of low-income Americans. In their ruling, the Supreme Court justices focused on whether the individual mandate was constitutional, whether they could rule on the mandate before it went into effect, whether the provision could be removed with the rest of the ACA intact, and whether another provision related to Medicaid expansion was constitutional. Ultimately, on June 28, 2012, the justices ruled 5–4 to uphold the individual mandate, but the majority decided that the Medicaid expansion was unconstitutional. Chief Justice John Roberts cast the deciding vote, calling the individual mandate a legitimate use of Congress's taxation power.

U.S. immigration policy remained in the national spotlight in 2012—in June, without congressional agreement on a new, comprehensive immigration policy, President Obama issued an executive order giving temporary legal protection to illegal immigrants who were brought to the United States as children and who met a number of conditions. That same month, the Supreme Court ruled on one of the most controversial immigration issues in recent history in the case of *Arizona v. United States*, determining whether four provisions of the state's anti–illegal immigration law were in direct conflict with federal immigration policy and therefore in violation of the Supremacy Clause of the Constitution. The most controversial provision of the law is referred to as "show me your papers"; it requires law enforcement to verify the immigration status of anyone they stopped, detained, or arrested on some other legitimate basis, if the officer had a reasonable suspicion that the person might be in the country illegally. In its 5–3 ruling, the Court upheld the "show me your papers" provision. Three other challenged provisions of the law— including an authorization for state police to arrest aliens for possible deportation, making it a state crime for an illegal immigrant to work in the state, and making failure to comply with the federal alien-registration requirements a state misdemeanor—were overturned because of federal preemption.

Fourth Amendment rights were also on the docket for the Supreme Court's 2011–2012 term. In the case of *United States v. Antoine Jones*, the Court reviewed the constitutionality of search and seizure as it relates to digital devices. The question in the case was whether evidence obtained from a secretly placed global positioning system (GPS) tracking device could be used to try and convict D.C. drug kingpin Antoine Jones, who was sentenced to life in prison. Although the justices differed on their rationale, on January 26, 2012, the Court ruled unanimously that the GPS device constituted a search under the Fourth Amendment, and because no warrant was obtained to place it, the use of the device was therefore unconstitutional. Although the Court ruled narrowly, the decision indicates that it will likely review the connection between privacy and advancing technology in the future.

The Court also ruled on the Fourth Amendment principle of unreasonable searches and seizures in the case of *Florence v. Board of Chosen Freeholders of the County of Burlington*. In a divided 5–4 decision, the Court upheld the constitutionality of strip searches for all new prison inmates who will be introduced to the general jail population, even those charged with minor offenses who are ultimately not incarcerated. The majority found that security concerns among corrections officers outweighed the privacy concerns of those who had been arrested.

The Supreme Court made a groundbreaking ruling on the division of church and state on January 11, 2012. In a unanimous decision in the case of *Hosanna-Tabor Evangelical Lutheran Church and School v. EEOC*, the Court ruled that the First Amendment of the Constitution protects churches and religious schools from discrimination suits brought by employees who perform religious duties. Without such a "ministerial exception," the Court found, discrimination lawsuits would interfere with church internal governance and decisions as to who should be the public face of the religion.

The 2011–2012 term also included a First Amendment case on decency in broadcasting. In the case of *FCC v. Fox Television Stations, Inc.*, the Court ruled unanimously to overturn fines that were imposed on two television networks, ABC and Fox, because the Federal Communications Commission (FCC) had not given the networks advance notice as to what would be considered indecent under its revised regulations. The ruling was narrow, however, and did not review the overall issue of the FCC's ability to levy fines, especially in light of the growing cable, satellite, and Internet markets, which are free of governmental regulation of indecent content.

In 2012, the Supreme Court again took on the constitutionality of mandatory sentencing guidelines for juvenile offenders. In 2005, the Court found that the Eighth Amendment prohibits capital punishment for underage offenders, and in 2011, it ruled that life imprisonment without parole for nonhomicide offenses is unconstitutional for minors. In the 2012, the Court reviewed the case of *Miller v. Alabama*, in which two fourteen-year-old offenders had, in separate incidents, been convicted of murder and sentenced to life in prison without parole. In each case, the presiding judge was bound by mandatory sentencing guidelines. In a 5–4 ruling, the majority ruled that such a conviction violated the Eighth Amendment prohibition on "cruel and unusual punishments." The decision, however, did not ban all such convictions but required that when choosing a sentence, a judge must consider the age and maturity of the defendant.

Two cases of note were decided by federal circuit courts in 2012—*Texas v. Holder*, which reviewed the constitutionality of a state voter identification law, and *Coalition to Defend Affirmative Action v. Regents of the University of Michigan*, which determined whether a Michigan ban on the use of affirmative action in state college and university admissions was unconstitutional. Under Section 5 of the Voting Rights Act, Texas is one of five states with a history of voter discrimination required to receive preclearance from the U.S. Justice Department before making any changes to its election laws. In March 2012, the Justice Department denied preclearance of a Texas law to require specific types of identification to be presented at a polling location before a person would be allowed to cast a vote, determining that the state could not provide enough evidence to prove that the law would not have a discriminatory effect. Seeking to have the decision reversed, the state filed suit, and on August 30, 2012, a three-judge panel of the U.S. District Court for the District of Columbia ruled 2–1 that the Texas law would disproportionately affect minorities and the poor and therefore struck down the law.

In Michigan, the case before the Sixth Circuit Court of Appeals dealt with a voter-approved ban on using affirmative action in college and university acceptance decisions. On November 15, 2012, in an 8–7 decision, the court ruled that the Michigan ban violated the Equal Protection Clause of the Constitution because it disproportionately affected the ability of black students to change school admissions policy. The court chose to rule narrowly and avoided the issue of whether affirmative action itself is constitutional or unconstitutional.

SCIENTIFIC DISCOVERIES

On July 4, 2012, scientists at the European Organization for Nuclear Research (CERN) announced the discovery of a new particle matching the description of the long-sought universe particle. The universe particle, or Higgs boson, is what scientists use to describe how elements gained mass following the Big Bang and led to the creation of the universe as people know it today. Without the magnetic force field created by a collection of Higgs bosons, particles would zoom about the atmosphere never gaining mass and therefore never creating atoms, the building blocks of life. Media outlets hailed the finding as a "breakthrough," but CERN scientists were hesitant to use such language because they still have years of necessary research to determine if the new particle is in fact the Higgs boson, as they suspect, or an impostor. CERN scientists said that an imposter particle would still help them unlock many mysteries of the universe that they have been trying to solve for decades, such as what dark matter is or why the universe is made up of matter rather than antimatter.

Another significant scientific occurrence came in August 2012, when the National Aeronautics and Space Administration (NASA) celebrated a historic achievement when it successfully landed the Curiosity rover, an unmanned space vehicle, on Mars. The rover came a year after the end of the space shuttle program, and followed years of research and development of what became the largest rover to date. The intent of the Curiosity mission was, over the course of twenty-three months, to expand on previous Mars missions to determine whether the planet had once and could again support life. By the close of 2012, the rover had sent more than 23,000 images back to NASA and analyzed its first soil sample, which found evidence of water and sulfur and chlorine-containing substances. The rover is expected to lay the groundwork for two future unmanned Mars missions.

FOREIGN AFFAIRS

The year 2012 was highlighted by unrest in a number of countries. Libya, where longtime leader Col. Muammar el-Qaddafi was deposed during the 2011 Arab Spring uprisings, was in a state of turmoil as its interim government struggled to maintain security and set up elections. Although the July 2012 vote to choose a government was deemed an overall success, the new prime minister was unable to seat his cabinet and shortly after taking office was ousted. His replacement faced the daunting task of determining how best to represent the diverse Libyan population on the panel that will draft the nation's new constitution. The new Libyan government also faced continuing pressure from the United

States to find and bring to justice those responsible for the September 11, 2012, terrorist attack on the U.S. consulate compound in Benghazi that killed Ambassador Chris Stevens and three other consulate employees.

Syria experienced its own Arab Spring uprising that began on March 15, 2011, and President Assad's government violently cracked down on protesters. Rebel groups formed to fight the government for control of towns and cities around the country, and early on, the government easily beat back any such attempts. But by 2012, the government had been somewhat worn down—members of Assad's security forces defected in greater numbers and the government's equipment, which had been its major strength in 2011, was failing to keep up with the constant fighting. With more than 25,000 thought to have been killed and millions displaced or otherwise in need of aid, the United Nations declared the situation a civil war. The international community, however, struggled to determine how to properly respond. Some countries worried that, given the interconnectedness of the region, intervention could spark a larger war. The United Nations attempted on multiple occasions to take action, but Russia and China thwarted any attempt. A six-point ceasefire negotiated by the UN's special envoy to Syria, former secretary general Kofi Annan, went into effect in April; however, the Assad government failed to follow through on most of the agreement. In August, President Obama announced that military force could be used if there was any indication that Assad was moving his stocks of chemical or biological weapons with intent to use them against civilians. As of the end of 2012, the United States has not yet taken unilateral action but had increased aid to rebels.

A third nation that experienced significant political change during the Arab Spring, Egypt, experienced its own difficulties in forming a new government. The government of autocratic ruler Hosni Mubarak was overthrown in February 2011, and power was handed over to the military. Despite promising to give control to a democratically elected government, in late 2011, the military announced that it would allow the elections to take place but would retain executive power. When Mohamed Morsi was elected in June 2012, he forced three key military leaders to resign and took back executive power for himself. In November, Morsi issued a presidential decree making all of his decisions above judicial review. The announcement brought protesters back to Tahrir Square, the site of the 2011 revolution. The protesters believed that Morsi was trying to make himself the sole leader and impose sharia law. In response to the protests, Morsi rescinded his order in December, although it was not retroactive. That same month, Egyptian voters approved a new constitution, drafted by a largely Islamic constitutional assembly. The new constitution paves the way for parliamentary elections in 2013.

The nuclear-ambitious nations of Iran and North Korea made headlines in 2012. The UN's International Atomic Energy Agency (IAEA) announced that Iran was enriching uranium beyond what would be needed for peaceful energy generation needs. The European Union responded by placing an embargo on Iranian oil and caused oil production in Iran to fall to its lowest level in twenty-five years. The United States imposed its own financial sanctions against Iran in February, July, and October. Iran's continuing nuclear program increased tension with Israel, which raised the possibility of taking unilateral military action against Iran to protect itself from any possible nuclear attack. In September, Prime Minister Benjamin Netanyahu spoke at a meeting of the UN General Assembly, calling for the international community to draw a "red line" after which point the United States would no longer permit Iran to enrich uranium and would take military action itself.

Under the leadership of its new ruler, Kim Jong-un, who came to power in late 2011 after the death of his father, Kim Jong-il, North Korea launched two satellites in April and

December 2012. The buildup to the April launch was celebrated in North Korea, and marking the importance of the occasion, the official launch date was set on the birthday of the nation's founder, Kim Il-sung. The North Korean government even invited international media to the launch, in an effort to prove that its test was for peaceful purposes. Approximately one minute after launch, the satellite broke apart and never entered orbit. Undeterred by the failure and disregarding international condemnation and promises of additional sanctions, in December, North Korea launched a second satellite, which successfully entered orbit, although its tumbling pattern indicated that it was nonfunctioning. Few nations believed that it was the intent of North Korea to launch a peaceful meteorological satellite, and many attempts were made at the United Nations to impose sanctions in response to the launches. However, China and Russia blocked anything more than a statement of condemnation against the North's actions.

In November, North Korea's main ally, China, went through its once-in-a-decade leadership transition. There was little expectation that the nation's newest Communist leaders would bring any reform or open up relations with the West, as many of them are closely linked to former hard-line leaders. However, the new president said he did intend to tackle the Communist Party's corruption problem and the nation's economic struggles.

In Africa, four nations faced violent coup attempts, including Guinea-Bissau, the Democratic Republic of the Congo (DRC), the Central African Republic (CAR), and Mali. In Guinea-Bissau, a coup was staged after the sitting prime minister won a majority of votes in the first round of the country's presidential elections. A body headed by the army chief of staff arrested the prime minister and interim head of government, and a new government was installed.

In the DRC, in November, a rebel group called the March 23 Movement (M23) formed with the intent of overthrowing the government. The group first took control of the capital of the North Kivu region but returned the region to the central government without much struggle. As of the end of 2012, the rebels remain engaged in occasional peace talks with the central government.

Opposition groups who claimed the sitting president had not followed through on a 2007 agreement that ended the country's bush war led a rebellion in the CAR. The rebels moved slowly toward the CAR capital, but they agreed to enter negotiations with the central government. Those negotiations broke down in January 2013, when the sitting president was overthrown.

In Mali, a rebel group in the northern portion of the country took up arms and overthrew the central government. The rebel movement was supported by Islamists, including those with ties to al Qaeda. The Islamists soon began imposing strict sharia law against the will of the citizens of northern Mali and took back cities captured by the original rebel movement. In December, the United Nations announced its support for an African-led international military mission to drive the Islamists out of the country. As of the end of 2012, despite the work of forces from France and some African nations, the Islamist militants have not yet been defeated.

During a year of celebration for the United Kingdom's monarchy, London hosted the 2012 Summer Olympic Games in July and August. The city received much acclaim for its third Olympic Games, although it was criticized over the complicated lottery process for allocating tickets, which left many seats at key events, such as gymnastics, empty. A number of world records were set during the course of the seventeen-day event, including U.S. swimmer Michael Phelps becoming the most decorated competitor in Olympic history.

EU Continuing Financial Crisis

Following the 2008 global recession that led to a financial crisis in a number of its twenty-seven member states, the European Union partnered with the International Monetary Fund (IMF) and European Central Bank (ECB) to form a troika that would provide bailout funds to ailing nations and enforce stricter monetary policy, specifically for the seventeen eurozone nations. Although it accepted a $147 billion bailout in 2010, Greece required even more financial assistance in 2012. Greece's debt had been steadily increasing since 2001, when the country adopted the euro as its currency, but EU leaders were interested in helping the Mediterranean nation in order to prevent the country from exiting the eurozone, which would likely cause a ripple effect in other European markets. On February 21, the European Union agreed to give the country an additional $165 billion, while calling on creditors to write off a large portion of Greek debt. In return, the Greek government instituted public spending cuts and structural reforms, including cutting the minimum wage by 22 percent, reducing pensions by more than $700 million, and cutting thousands of jobs in the public sector. These austerity measures sparked fury and violent protests among the Greek public. By the end of 2012, there was little evidence that the second Greek bailout was working as hoped. The economy shrank by 6 percent in 2012, and unemployment reached over 25 percent. The structural changes in Greece put pressure on the closely linked market of Cyprus, which requested a $22.65 billion EU bailout in June 2012 that has not yet been approved.

In an effort to stall the continuing economic slump, the ECB decided in July to cut interest rates to their lowest-ever level. In addition, in September, the European Commission, the executive body of the European Union, proposed that the ECB be given a supervisory role of the 6,000 EU banks. This would give the ECB the ability to remove banking licenses and investigate banks. This proposal was being considered as of the end of 2012.

Although the EU's actions throughout 2012 did have some stabilizing effect, the heavily indebted nations of Cyprus, Greece, Ireland, Italy, Portugal, and Spain were still in precarious fiscal situations, which were being closely monitored from around the world. The financial status of Italy and Spain, the EU's second- and third-largest economies, were most closely watched because there was general agreement that the European Union did not have the financial ability to bail out the two countries. In July, fears mounted about Italy's stability when Moody's reduced the country's credit rating to two notches above junk status after the Italian economy slid back into recession. In Spain, the situation was dire. Many of its banks were near collapse, the public deficit was 7 percent of GDP in 2012, unemployment stood at 25 percent, and billions of dollars in spending cuts by the government triggered massive demonstrations. To shore up its economy, Spain requested a $48 billion bailout, to which the eurozone members agreed, but attached many conditions.

One bright point for the European Union came in October 2012, when the Norwegian Nobel Committee announced that the organization had been awarded the year's Nobel Peace Prize. Although the European Union was still struggling financially, the committee stressed that its decision was one based on the EU's history of forging bonds through peace, a trait that would serve it well as it works through its current financial crisis.

—Heather Kerrigan

January

State of the Union Address and Republican Response

President Obama Releases New Defense Strategy

JANUARY 5, 2012

Following Congress's 2011 decision to cut the defense budget by at least $487 billion, on January 5, 2012, President Barack Obama made a rare visit to the Pentagon to unveil the details of a new defense strategy that would take into account both the budgetary constraints and the changing face of threats to the United States going forward. The president's plan placed a greater focus on the Asia-Pacific and Middle East regions, meaning a likely troop drawdown in Europe, and will include more work in the areas of intelligence, surveillance, cybersecurity, and counterterrorism. Although trade-offs will be made, the president and defense leaders said the United States would be no less secure and no less combat ready than it is today.

LEANER, STREAMLINED MILITARY FORCE

On January 5, 2012, flanked by Defense Secretary Leon Panetta and Chairman of the Joint Chiefs of Staff Gen. Martin Dempsey, President Obama released his eight-page defense strategy titled "Sustaining U.S. Global Leadership: Priorities for 21st Century Defense." "Yes, the tide of war is receding," the president said. "But the question that this strategy answers is what kind of military will we need after the long wars of the last decade are over. And today, we're fortunate to be moving forward, from a position of strength." In laying out his new strategy, which offered few specific details, the president noted that the future military will be smaller, leaner, and more flexible, but he insisted that this will not mean reduced security or a weakened U.S. military. "Yes, our military will be leaner, but the world must know—the United States is going to maintain our military superiority with Armed Forces that are agile, flexible and ready for the full range of contingencies and threats," Obama said.

Obama's new strategy takes into account the $487 billion in cuts over the next decade that Congress added to 2011's Budget Control Act. According to the Pentagon, while the budget cuts make the strategy changes necessary, so does the evolving nature of threats against the United States, including cybersecurity issues, violent extremism, nuclear weapons, rising powers in Asia, and ongoing instability in North Korea and Iran. Savings will come from a variety of places. Although no specifics were offered on the size of troops in the future, the Army and Marine Corps are set to cut forces beginning in 2015. Panetta expects additional cost savings to come from pay and health care benefit changes. The defense budget for fiscal year (FY) 2013 is expected to be $662 billion—$27 billion less than Obama had requested and $43 billion less than Congress allocated to the Pentagon in FY 2012. These cuts will continue each year, with the expectation that more than $480 billion will be cut over the next decade, $261 billion of which will be cut through 2017. While confident in the military's future strength and effectiveness, Secretary Panetta did express concern about an additional $500 billion in budget cuts starting in January 2013, mandated by the failure of 2011's congressional super committee to reach an agreement on deficit reduction. These cuts, Panetta said, "would result in a demoralized and hollowed out force."

Changing Priorities

Under the new defense strategy, no current missions will be canceled, and the United States will continue on its current trajectory to draw down troops in Afghanistan, with an aim of ending the U.S. mission by 2014. Two major changes will be made moving forward. First, the U.S. military will be a smaller force overall, making it ready to move quickly. This will bring an end to the sixty-five-year-old policy of a joint force that is capable of fighting two major wars at the same time and will be replaced with a strategy that allows the United States to combat one adversary directly while holding back another. This change has faced a lot of criticism, with complaints surfacing about the trade-offs and decisions that might need to be made. "Suppose there is a threat from Iran and threat from Korea," said Dov Zakheim, former Pentagon comptroller under President George W. Bush and adviser to 2012 Republican presidential candidate Mitt Romney. "What are we going to do? Ignore Iran or ignore North Korea?" Zakheim asked. In response to critics, Panetta said, "There's no question that we have to make some trade offs . . . some level of additional but acceptable risk." But, Panetta added, "With this joint force, I am confident we can effectively defend the United States of America."

The second major change involves a shift to focus more on the Asia-Pacific region and the Middle East. This will mean less involvement in Europe. Though the United States will maintain its commitment to the North Atlantic Treaty Organization (NATO) and other alliances, it will likely draw down troops on the continent. Panetta, Dempsey, and Obama all stressed that this shift does not mean there will be a military conflict in these regions in the near future. "All of the trends—demographic trends, geopolitical trends, economic trends and military trends—are shifting toward the Pacific," said Dempsey, echoing Panetta, who told those gathered that the "region is growing in importance to the future of the United States' economy and our national security." The new focus is partly driven by concern over China's rapid economic growth, its defense buildup and continued tension with Taiwan over China's desire to have it reunite with the mainland, and China's claim of territories in the South China Sea. In an effort to maintain stability in the region and the free flow of commerce, the new defense plan states, "The growth of China's military power must be accompanied by greater clarity of its strategic intentions in order to avoid causing friction in the region." The United States also plans to work collaboratively with Asian allies to keep tensions low on the Korean peninsula. The United States also plans to place a greater focus on Persian Gulf security and work with Saudi Arabia and other allies in the region, especially as it pertains to the instability of Iran and its drive to develop nuclear weapons. "To support these objectives, the United States will continue to place a premium on U.S. and allied military presence in—and support of—partner nations in and around this region," the plan states. Other changes that will be made under the new defense plan include a budget that will grow more slowly than it has in the past—an acceptable trade-off, according to the president, because the U.S. defense budget is larger than the spending on defense in the next ten countries combined. The new plan also calls for bigger investments in cybersecurity and space-based intelligence. This will mean eliminating "outdated cold war–era systems so that we can invest in the capabilities we need for the future," said Obama.

The proposals made on January 5 are not new. In fact, former Defense Secretary Donald Rumsfeld made similar proposals when he called for a "transformation agenda" after being appointed to the position by then-president George W. Bush, following the 2000 election. "We need rapidly deployable, fully integrated joint forces capable of reaching distant theaters quickly and working with our air and sea forces to strike adversaries swiftly, successfully, and with devastating effect," he said in January 2002. Rumsfeld faced little opposition to his plan, even on Capitol Hill, but after the 9/11 attacks and facing two wars, his plan was derailed. In 2012, Republicans were critical of Obama's defense strategy, saying that it cut too much from the Defense Department budget and put the United States at risk, especially as more nations consider developing nuclear weapons. "An honest and valid strategy for national defense can't be founded on the premise that we must do more with less, or even less with less," said Rep. Howard McKeon, R-Calif., chairman of the House Armed Services Committee.

Pentagon Opens Some Positions to Women

One month after the president unveiled his new defense strategy, on February 9, 2012, the Pentagon announced that women would officially be permitted to undertake some dangerous jobs close to the front lines of combat. The move came after a year-long study ordered by Congress that found the old job policy for women "has become irrelevant given the modern battlespace with its nonlinear boundaries," which often puts women close to the front lines. Women, who make up 15 percent of active duty military personnel, can now be assigned on a permanent basis to a battalion in a number of positions, including radio operator, medic, tank mechanic, and fire detection specialist. In total, the policy will open 14,000 new positions to female troops. The new policy eliminates rules that allowed women to serve only with units bigger than a brigade, or 3,500 troops, as well as the ban on women being attached to any unit close to the front lines. Women have been performing these newly opened jobs for a number of years, but, to circumvent the rules barring them from these positions, have been considered "temporary attachments" to the battalions. This terminology has been used increasingly over the past decade because of the need for troops in these positions in Iraq and Afghanistan. The impact will be felt mostly in the Army and Marines because the Air Force already allows women to serve in 99 percent of its positions.

Despite this opening of positions, women will still be barred from serving in the infantry, in combat tanks, or in Special Operations units. This presents a problem for women when it comes to promotions. Combat positions are key for career advancement, and without access to the infantry or other front-line positions, women are often unable to move through the ranks to top positions like men do. And although some women in Iraq and Afghanistan served in the newly opened positions as temporary attachments, they did not receive the service credit needed for advancement.

Reaction to the new policy was mixed. "It's a really, really tiny step forward," said Anu Bhagwati, a former Marine Corps captain and the executive director of the Service Women's Action Network, a group that advocates for women in the military. "We're not talking about opening up the infantry to every woman, but the women who do want to try these jobs, who are we to say that they can't? A lot of women will leave service early when they know their career path is limited," said Bhagwati. Others applauded the Pentagon for keeping women out of the infantry, expressing concern that they might not be able to overcome the physical and psychological demands.

Regarding the new policy, Panetta said it would be the beginning and not the end of the process and that the Pentagon will continue to review which jobs should be open to women. These reviews may include other issues raised in the report to Congress, including sleeping arrangements and privacy, limits on physically demanding jobs for women, and restrictions on joining the Special Forces.

The Marines are already exploring some of these questions. According to Marine officials, there are few data on whether women should be allowed in close-to-combat jobs, so they have placed forty-four women in positions that are normally unavailable to female troops to study how they perform. "This has a lot [to do] with physical standards," said Maj. Shawn Haney, a spokesperson for the Marine Corps. "We've got to make sure we're doing the right thing for the institution and the individual."

—Heather Kerrigan

Following are two statements delivered on January 5, 2012, by President Barack Obama and Secretary of Defense Leon Panetta on the nation's changing defense strategy.

DOCUMENT

President Obama Speaks on a Leaner Military

January 5, 2012

Good morning, everybody. The United States of America is the greatest force for freedom and security that the world has ever known. And in no small measure, that's because we've built the best trained, best led, best equipped military in history, and as Commander in Chief, I'm going to keep it that way.

Indeed, all of us on this stage—every single one of us—have a profound responsibility to every soldier, sailor, airman, marine, and coast guardsman who puts their life on the line for America. We owe them a strategy with well-defined goals, to only send them into harm's way when it's absolutely necessary, to give them the equipment and the support that they need to get the job done, and to care for them and their families when they come home. That is our solemn obligation.

And over the past 3 years, that's what we've done. We've continued to make historic investments in our military—our troops and their capabilities, our military families, and our veterans. And thanks to their extraordinary service, we've ended our war in Iraq. We've decimated Al Qaida's leadership. We've delivered justice to Usama bin Laden, and we've put that terrorist network on the path to defeat. We've made important progress in Afghanistan, and we've begun to transition so Afghans can assume more responsibility for their own security. We joined allies and partners to protect the Libyan people as they ended the regime of Muammar Qadhafi.

Now we're turning the page on a decade of war. Three years ago, we had some 180,000 troops in Iraq and Afghanistan. Today, we've cut that number in half. And as the transition in Afghanistan continues, more of our troops will continue to come home. More broadly, around the globe we've strengthened alliances, forged new partnerships, and served as a force for universal rights and human dignity.

In short, we've succeeded in defending our Nation, taking the fight to our enemies, reducing the number of Americans in harm's way, and we've restored America's global leadership. That makes us safer, and it makes us stronger. And that's an achievement that every American, especially those Americans who are proud to wear the uniform of the United States Armed Forces, should take great pride in.

This success has brought our Nation once more to a moment of transition. Even as our troops continue [to] fight—to fight in Afghanistan, the tide of war is receding. Even as our forces prevail in today's missions, we have the opportunity and the responsibility to look ahead to the force that we are going to need in the future.

At the same time, we have to renew our economic strength here at home, which is the foundation of our strength around the world. And that includes putting our fiscal house in order. To that end, the Budget Control Act passed by Congress last year, with the support of Republicans and Democrats alike, mandates reductions in Federal spending, including defense spending. I've insisted that we do that responsibly. The security of our Nation and the lives of our men and women in uniform depend on it.

And that's why I called for this comprehensive defense review to clarify our strategic interests in a fast-changing world and to guide our defense priorities and spending over the coming decade, because the size and the structure of our military and defense budgets have to be driven by a strategy, not the other way around. Moreover, we have to remember the lessons of history. We can't afford to repeat the mistakes that have been made in the past, after World War II, after Vietnam, when our military was left ill prepared for the future. As Commander in Chief, I will not let that happen again. Not on my watch.

We need a start—we need a smart, strategic set of priorities. The new guidance that the Defense Department is releasing today does just that. I want to thank Secretary Panetta and General Dempsey for their extraordinary leadership during this process. I want to thank the service secretaries and chiefs, the combatant commanders, and so many defense leaders—military and civilian, active, Guard, and Reserve—for their contributions. Many of us met repeatedly, asking tough questions, challenging our own assumptions, and making hard choices. And we've come together today around an approach that will keep our Nation safe and our military the finest that the world has ever known.

This review also benefits from the contributions of leaders from across my national security team, from the Departments of State, Homeland Security, and Veterans Affairs, as well as the intelligence community. And this is critical, because meeting the challenges of our time cannot be the work of our military alone or the United States alone. It requires all elements of our national power, working together in concert with our allies and our partners.

So I'm going to let Leon and Marty go into the details. But I just want to say that this effort reflects the guidance that I personally gave throughout this process. Yes, the tide of war is receding. But the question that this strategy answers is what kind of military will we need long after the wars of the last decade are over. And today, we're fortunate to be moving forward from a position of strength.

As I made clear in Australia, we will be strengthening our presence in the Asia-Pacific, and budget reductions will not come at the expense of that critical region. We're going to continue investing in our critical partnerships and alliances, including NATO, which has demonstrated time and again—most recently in Libya—that it's a force multiplier. We will stay vigilant, especially in the Middle East.

As we look beyond the wars in Iraq and Afghanistan and the end of long-term nation-building with large military footprints, we'll be able to ensure our security with smaller conventional ground forces. We'll continue to get rid of outdated cold war–era systems so that we can invest in the capabilities that we need for the future, including intelligence, surveillance, and reconnaissance, counterterrorism, countering weapons of mass destruction, and the ability to operate in environments where adversaries try to deny us access.

So yes, our military will be leaner, but the world must know the United States is going to maintain our military superiority with Armed Forces that are agile, flexible, and ready for the full range of contingencies and threats.

We're also going to keep faith with those who serve by making sure our troops have the equipment and capabilities they need to succeed and by prioritizing efforts that focus on wounded warriors, mental health, and the well-being of our military families. And as our newest veterans rejoin civilian life, we'll keep working to give our veterans the care, the benefit—the benefits, and job opportunities that they deserve and that they have earned.

Finally, although today is about our defense strategy, I want to close with a word about the defense budget that will flow from this strategy. The details will be announced in the coming weeks. Some will no doubt say that the spending reductions are too big; others will say that they're too small. It will be easy to take issue with a particular change in a particular program. But I'd encourage all of us to remember what President Eisenhower once said, that "each proposal must be weighed in the light of a broader consideration: the need to maintain balance in and among national programs." After a decade of war, and as we rebuild the source of our strength at home and abroad, it's time to restore that balance.

I think it's important for all Americans to remember, over the past 10 years, since 9/11, our defense budget grew at an extraordinary pace. Over the next 10 years, the growth in the defense budget will slow, but the fact of the matter is this: It will still grow, because we have global responsibilities that demand our leadership. . . .

SOURCE: Executive Office of the President. "Remarks at the Pentagon in Arlington, Virginia." January 5, 2012. *Compilation of Presidential Documents* 2012, no. 00004 (January 4, 2012). http://www.gpo.gov/fdsys/pkg/DCPD-201200004/pdf/DCPD-201200004.pdf.

Defense Secretary Panetta on the New Military Strategy

DOCUMENT

January 5, 2012

Let me begin by thanking President Obama for coming here to the Pentagon this morning, and also in particular to thank him for his vision and guidance and leadership as this department went through a very intensive review that we undertook to try to develop the new strategic guidance that we're releasing today.

And in my experience, this has been an unprecedented process, to have the President of the United States participate in discussions involving the development of a defense strategy, and to spend time with our service chiefs and spend time with our combatant commanders to get their views. It's truly unprecedented.

This guidance that we are releasing today, and which has been distributed now throughout the department—it really does represent a historic shift to the future. And it recognizes that this country is at a strategic turning point, after a decade of war and after large increases in defense spending.

As the president mentioned, the U.S. military's mission in Iraq has now ended. We do have continued progress in Afghanistan. It's tough, and it remains challenging, but we are beginning to enable a transition to Afghan security responsibility. The NATO effort in Libya has concluded with the fall of Qadhafi. And targeted counterterrorism efforts have significantly weakened al-Qaida and decimated its leadership.

And now, as these events are occurring . . . the Congress has mandated, by law, that we achieve significant defense savings. So clearly, we are at a turning point.

But even as our large-scale military campaigns recede, the United States still faces [a] complex and growing array of security challenges across the globe. And unlike past drawdowns when oftentimes the threats that the country was facing went away, the fact is that there remain a number of challenges that we have to confront, challenges that call for reshaping of America's defense priorities: focusing on the continuing threat of violent extremism, which is still there and still to be dealt with; proliferation of lethal weapons and materials; the destabilizing behavior of nations like Iran and North Korea; the rise of new powers across Asia; and the dramatic changes that we've seen unfold in the Middle East.

All of this comes at a time when America confronts a very serious deficit and debt problem here at home, a problem which is itself a national security risk that is squeezing both the defense and domestic budgets. Even as we face these considerable pressures, including the requirement of the Budget Control Act to reduce defense spending by what we have now as the number of $487 billion over 10 years, I do not believe—and I've said this before—that we have to choose between our national security and fiscal responsibility. The Department of Defense will play its part in helping the nation put our fiscal house in order.

The president has made clear, and I've made clear, that the savings that we've been mandated to achieve must be driven by strategy and must be driven by rigorous analysis, not by numbers alone.

Consequently, over the last few months, we've conducted an intensive review to try to guide defense priorities and spending over the coming decade, all of this in light of the strategic guidance that we received in discussions with the president and the recommendations of this department's both senior military and civilian leadership. Both of them provided those kinds of recommendations. This process has enabled us to assess risk, to set priorities and to make some very hard choices.

Let me be clear again. The department would need to make a strategic shift regardless of the nation's fiscal situation. We are at that point in history. That's the reality of the world we live in. Fiscal crisis has forced us to face the strategic shift that's taking place now.

As difficult as it may be to achieve the mandated defense savings, this has given all of us in the Department of Defense the opportunity to reshape our defense strategy and force structure to more effectively meet the challenges of the future—to deter aggression, to shape the security environment and to decisively prevail in any conflict.

From the beginning, I set out to ensure that this strategy review would be inclusive. Chairman Dempsey and I met frequently with department leaders, including our undersecretaries, the service chiefs, the service secretaries, the combatant commanders, our senior enlisted advisers. We also discussed this strategy and its implications, obviously, with the president, his national security advisers, with members of Congress and with outside experts.

There are four over-arching principles that have guided our deliberations, and I've said this at the very beginning as we began this process. One, we must maintain the world's finest military, one that supports and sustains the unique global leadership role of the

United States in today's world. Two, we must avoid hollowing out the force—a smaller, ready, and well-equipped military is much more preferable to a larger, ill-prepared force that has been arbitrarily cut across the board.

Third, savings must be achieved in a balanced manner, with everything on the table, including politically sensitive areas that will likely provoke opposition from parts of the Congress, from industry and from advocacy groups.

That's the nature of making hard choices. Four, we must preserve the quality of the all-volunteer force and not break faith with our men and women in uniform or their families. With these principles in mind, I'll focus on some of the significant strategic choices and shifts that are being made.

The United States military—let me be very clear about this—the United States military will remain capable across the spectrum. We will continue to conduct a complex set of missions ranging from counterterrorism, ranging from countering weapons of mass destruction, to maintaining a safe, secure and effective nuclear deterrent. We will be fully prepared to protect our interests, defend our homeland and support civil authorities.

Our goal to achieve the U.S. force for the future involves the following significant changes.

First, the U.S. joint force will be smaller, and it will be leaner. But its great strength will be that it will be more agile, more flexible, ready to deploy quickly, innovative, and technologically advanced. That is the force for the future.

Second, as we move towards this new joint force, we are also rebalancing our global posture and presence, emphasizing the Pacific and the Middle East.

These are the areas where we see the greatest challenges for the future. The U.S. military will increase its institutional weight and focus on enhanced presence, power projection, and deterrence in [the] Asia-Pacific.

This region is growing in importance to the future of the United States in terms of our economy and our national security. This means, for instance, improving capabilities that maintain our military's technological edge and freedom of action. At the same time, the United States will place a premium in maintaining our military presence and capabilities in the broader Middle East. The United States and our partners must remain capable of deterring and defeating aggression while supporting political progress and reform.

Third, the United States will continue to strengthen its key alliances, to build partnerships and to develop innovative ways to sustain U.S. presence elsewhere in the world. A long history of close political and military cooperation with our European allies and partners will be critical to addressing the challenges of the 21st century. We will invest in the shared capabilities and responsibilities of NATO, our most effective military alliance.

The U.S. military's force posture in Europe will, of necessity, continue to adapt and evolve to meet new challenges and opportunities, particularly in light of the security needs of the continent relative to the emerging strategic priorities that we face elsewhere. We are committed to sustaining a presence that will meet our Article 5 commitments, deter aggression, and the U.S. military will work closely with our allies to allow for the kinds of coalition operations that NATO has undertaken in Libya and Afghanistan.

In Latin America, Africa, elsewhere in the world, we will use innovative methods to sustain U.S. presence, maintaining key military-to-military relations and pursuing new security partnerships as needed. Wherever possible, we will develop low-cost and small-footprint approaches to achieving our security objectives, emphasizing rotational deployments, emphasizing exercises—military exercises with these nations, and doing other innovative approaches to maintain a presence throughout the rest of the world.

Fourth, as we shift the size and composition of our ground, air and naval forces, we must be capable of successfully confronting and defeating any aggressor and respond to the changing nature of warfare. Our strategy review concluded that the United States must have the capability to fight several conflicts at the same time. . . .

In accordance with this construct, and with the end of U.S. military commitments in Iraq and the drawdown that is already under way in Afghanistan, the Army and Marine Corps will no longer need to be sized to support the kind of large-scale, long-term stability operations that have dominated military priorities and force generation over the past decade.

Lastly, as we reduce the overall defense budget, we will protect, and in some cases increase, our investments in special operations forces, in new technologies like ISR and unmanned systems, in space—and, in particular, in cyberspace—capabilities, and also our capacity to quickly mobilize if necessary.

These investments will help the military retain and continue to refine and institutionalize the expertise and capabilities that have been gained at such great cost over the last decade.

And most importantly, we will structure and pace the reductions in the nation's ground forces in such a way that they can surge, regenerate and mobilize capabilities needed for any contingency. Building in reversibility and the ability to quickly mobilize will be key. That means re-examining the mix of elements in the active and Reserve components. It means maintaining a strong National Guard and Reserve. It means retaining a healthy cadre of experienced NCOs and mid-grade officers and preserving the health and viability of the nation's defense industrial base.

The strategic guidance that we're providing is the first step in this department's goal to build the joint force of 2020, a force sized and shaped differently than the military of the Cold War, the post–Cold War force of the 1990s, or the force that was built over the past decade to engage in large-scale ground wars.

This strategy and vision will guide the more specific budget decisions that will be finalized and announced in the coming weeks as part of the president's budget. In some cases, we will be reducing capabilities that we believe no longer are a top priority.

But in other cases, we will invest in new capabilities to maintain a decisive military edge against a growing array of threats. There's no question—there's no question—that we have to make some trade-offs and that we will be taking, as a result of that, some level of additional but acceptable risk in the budget plan that we release next month. These are not easy choices.

We will continue aggressive efforts to weed out waste, reduce overhead, to reform business practices, to consolidate our duplicative operations. But budget reductions of this magnitude will inevitably impact the size and capabilities of our military. And as I said before, true national security cannot be achieved through a strong military alone. It requires strong diplomacy. It requires strong intelligence efforts. And above all, it requires a strong economy, fiscal discipline and effective government.

The capability, readiness and agility of the force will not be sustained if Congress fails to do its duty and the military is forced to accept far deeper cuts, in particular, the arbitrary, across-the-board cuts that are currently scheduled to take effect in January of 2013 through the mechanism of sequester. That would force us to shed missions and commitments and capabilities that we believe are necessary to protect core U.S. national security interests.

And it would result in what we think would be a demoralized and hollow force. That is not something that we intend to do.

And finally, I'd like to also address our men and women in uniform, and the civilian employees who support them, whom I—who I know have been watching the budget debates here in Washington with concern about what it means for them and for their families. You have done everything this country has asked you to do and more.

You have put your lives on the line, and you have fought to make our country safer and stronger. I believe the strategic guidance honors your sacrifice and strengthens the country by building a force equipped to deal with the future. I have no higher responsibility than fighting to protect you and to protect your families. And just as you have fought and bled to protect our country, I commit to you that I will fight for you and for your families.

There is no doubt that the fiscal situation this country faces is difficult, and in many ways we are at a crisis point. But I believe that in every crisis there is opportunity. Out of this crisis, we have the opportunity to end the old ways of doing business and to build a modern force for the 21st century that can win today's wars and successfully confront any enemy, and respond to any threat and any challenge of the future.

Our responsibility—my responsibility as secretary of defense—is to protect the nation's security and to keep America safe. With this joint force, I am confident that we can effectively defend the United States of America.

Thank you.

SOURCE: U.S. Department of Defense. Office of the Assistant Secretary of Defense (Public Affairs). "Statement on Defense Strategic Guidance." January 5, 2012. http://www.defense.gov/speeches/speech .aspx?speechid=1643.

OTHER HISTORIC DOCUMENTS OF INTEREST

FROM THIS VOLUME

FROM PREVIOUS *HISTORIC DOCUMENTS*

Supreme Court Rules on Discrimination in Religious Organizations

---

On January 11, 2012, in a groundbreaking church-state ruling, the Supreme Court held that the First Amendment to the Constitution protects churches from employment discrimination suits brought by employees who perform religious duties. Chief Justice John Roberts wrote for the unanimous Court in *Hosanna-Tabor Evangelical Lutheran Church and School v. EEOC,* recognizing for the first time a so-called ministerial exception to federal, state, and local laws against employment discrimination. Without such an exception, Justice Roberts wrote, lawsuits would interfere impermissibly with the "internal governance of the church, depriving the church of control over the selection of those who will personify its beliefs." Considered by some legal scholars to be the Court's most important religious liberty decision in two decades, this decision extended the principle of church-state separation to shield churches and religious schools nationwide from employment discrimination lawsuits brought by teachers and other employees who are found to be "ministers" of the faith.

Teacher With Narcolepsy Fired

Hosanna-Tabor Evangelical Lutheran Church and School is a member congregation of the Lutheran Church–Missouri Synod, the second largest Lutheran denomination in America. It operates a small school in Redford, Michigan, where Cheryl Perich served as a teacher. She taught first as a lay teacher and then received extensive training to become "called"—that is, a teacher regarded as having been called to the vocation by God through the congregation. Once called, she received the formal title Minister of Religion, Commissioned. She primarily taught secular subjects, including math, language arts, social studies, science, gym, art, and music, but also taught a religion course four days a week, led the students in prayer each day, and led a chapel service twice a year. She estimated that the "religious" part of her responsibilities encompassed about forty-five minutes per day.

In 2004, Perich became ill with narcolepsy and went on disability leave. When her doctor cleared her to return to work, her employer, Hosanna-Tabor, told her that it had contracted with a lay teacher to fill her position and offered her a "peaceful release" from her call, whereby the congregation would pay a portion of her health insurance premiums in exchange for her resignation. She refused to resign and attempted to return to work. When she was asked to leave, she responded that she had spoken with an attorney and intended to assert her legal rights. "Their response," Perich said, "was to fire me." The Hosanna-Tabor Church agreed that it had terminated her because she had "threatened to take legal action," but maintained that part of its faith required that such disputes must be resolved internally within the church.

The Equal Employment Opportunity Commission (EEOC) brought suit on Perich's behalf, alleging that she had been fired in violation of the Americans with Disabilities Act (ADA), which prohibits an employer from discriminating against a qualified individual on the basis of a disability and also prohibits an employer from firing an employee in retaliation for threatening to file an ADA lawsuit.

Unanimous Supreme Court Ruling

When this case reached the Supreme Court, the question it presented was whether the First Amendment—which provides, in part, that "Congress shall make no law respecting an establishment of religion, or prohibiting the free exercise thereof"—bars employment discrimination suits over claims of wrongful termination when the employer is a religious group and the employee is one of the group's ministers.

Before answering this question, Justice Roberts first provided a detailed overview of the history of church and state tensions, spanning from 1215 and the Magna Carta, through the history of colonists seeking the opportunity to choose their own ministers in a new world, and finally resulting in a constitution designed to guard against political interference with religious affairs. He also noted that, since the passage of the Civil Rights Act, nearly fifty years ago, the appellate courts had uniformly recognized the existence of a "ministerial exception" to the application of those laws, grounded in the First Amendment, which served to keep government out of employment matters concerning religious institutions and their ministers. This case presented the Supreme Court for the first time with the question of whether such an exception exists, and the Court unanimously found that it did and made the ministerial exception the law of the land, exempting religious organizations from discrimination lawsuits brought by their "ministers."

While underscoring the societal importance of enforcing employment discrimination laws, Justice Roberts noted that more is at stake when the law requires a church to retain an unwanted minister or punishes a church for failing to do so. Interfering with the internal governance of a religion by usurping control over who the church chooses to personify its beliefs violates both provisions of the First Amendment. First, he wrote, "By imposing an unwanted minister, the state infringes the Free Exercise Clause, which protects a religious group's right to shape its own faith and mission through its appointments." And second, "According the state the power to determine which individuals will minister to the faithful also violates the Establishment Clause, which prohibits government involvement in such ecclesiastical decisions."

After recognizing this ministerial exception to employment discrimination laws, the Court next had to determine whether the exception applied to Perich, the fired teacher. The justices rejected the argument of the appellate court that, because her religious duties took only forty-five minutes each workday, they were inadequate to qualify her as a minister under the exception. "The issue before us," Justice Roberts wrote, "is not one that can be resolved by a stopwatch." Declining to adopt a rigid formula for deciding when an employee qualifies as a minister, the Court looked instead to several factors. It particularly noted that after completing an ecclesiastical course of study at a Lutheran college and passing an exam, she was given the formal title of minister and held herself out by that title and also that she performed important religious functions for the church, such as leading students in daily prayer, escorting them to chapel, and teaching a religious class. These factors taken together, the Court held, qualify Perich as a minister within the meaning of the exception and require that her employment discrimination suit against the church, which employed her, be dismissed.

Justice Clarence Thomas wrote a concurring opinion, indicating that he would have gone a step further in resolving this case. He objected to the Court's attempting to determine who qualifies for the ministerial exception, whether through a bright-line test or a multifactor analysis. The question of "whether an employee is a minister is itself religious in nature," he wrote. He argued that the Court should look only to whether the church sincerely considered the employee a minister, and no further: "Judicial attempts to fashion a civil definition of 'minister' through a bright-line test or multi-factor analysis risk disadvantaging those religious groups whose beliefs, practices, and membership are outside of the 'mainstream' or unpalatable to some."

In a second concurring opinion, Justice Samuel Alito, joined by Justice Elena Kagan, wrote separately to clarify that what was important in this case was not the word *minister*, which is a designation commonly used by Protestant denominations. The exception at issue in this case would apply equally to Catholics, Jews, Muslims, Hindus, or Buddhists, who rarely if ever use the term *minister*. Courts, rather than focusing on the term, should pay attention instead to the function performed by the people who work for religious bodies.

REACTION TO THE COURT'S DECISION

After the ruling was announced, University of Virginia constitutional law professor Douglas Laycock, who represented the Hosanna-Tabor Church, described it as "a huge win for religious liberty." The Court held that "the church need not explain its [employment] decision, because the reasons are none of the court's business." Bishop William E. Lori, chairman of the United States Conference of Catholic Bishops' ad hoc committee for religious liberty, agreed that the ruling is "a great day for the First Amendment." In a statement, he described the decision as making "resoundingly clear the historical and constitutional importance of keeping internal church affairs off limits to the government—because whoever chooses the minister chooses the message."

Others were disappointed with the result. The Rev. Barry W. Lynn, executive director of Americans United for Separation of Church and State, felt the Court took the concept of a ministerial exception too far. Allowing a house of worship to fire a minister for reasons unrelated to religion would, he feared, deny recourse in the courts, for example, to a pastor fired for objecting to being sexually harassed. "Clergy who are fired for reasons unrelated to matters of theology—no matter how capricious or venal those reasons may be—have just had the courthouse door slammed in their faces," Lynn said.

Future cases will determine how broad and far-reaching this ministerial exception is. The Court opinion discounted the "parade of horribles" that the EEOC predicted would follow recognition of the exception to employment discrimination suits. These included use of the exception to protect religious organizations from liability for retaliating against employees for reporting criminal misconduct. Would the ruling protect a church that fired a minister for reporting sexual abuse to the police? The Court did not address this beyond noting that the exception would not bar criminal prosecutions from interfering with law enforcement proceedings. The Court also made clear that it was leaving open whether the exception would bar other kinds of suits beyond employment discrimination, including breach of contract or for damages arising from some wrongful conduct by the religious organization.

—Melissa Feinberg

Following is the edited text of the unanimous Supreme Court ruling in Hosanna-Tabor Evangelical Lutheran Church and School v. EEOC, *in which the Court ruled on January 11, 2012, that the First Amendment of the Constitution protects churches from employment discrimination suits brought by employees who perform religious duties.*

Hosanna-Tabor Evangelical Lutheran Church and School v. EEOC

January 11, 2012

No. 10–553

Hosanna-Tabor Evangelical
Lutheran Church and School,
Petitioner

v.

Equal Employment Opportunity
Commission Et Al.

On writ of certiorari to
the United States Court
of Appeals for the Sixth
Circuit

[January 11, 2012]

[Footnotes and stand-alone references have been omitted.]

CHIEF JUSTICE ROBERTS delivered the opinion of the Court.

Certain employment discrimination laws authorize employees who have been wrongfully terminated to sue their employers for reinstatement and damages. The question presented is whether the Establishment and Free Exercise Clauses of the First Amendment bar such an action when the employer is a religious group and the employee is one of the group's ministers.

I

[Section I A, containing background information on the details of the case, has been omitted.]

B

Perich filed a charge with the Equal Employment Opportunity Commission, alleging that her employment had been terminated in violation of the Americans with Disabilities Act, 104 Stat. 327, 42 U. S. C. §12101 *et seq.* (1990). The ADA prohibits an employer from discriminating against a qualified individual on the basis of disability. It also prohibits an employer from retaliating "against any individual because such individual has opposed any act or practice made unlawful by [the ADA] or because such individual made a charge, testified, assisted, or participated in any manner in an investigation, proceeding, or hearing under [the ADA]."

The EEOC brought suit against Hosanna-Tabor, alleging that Perich had been fired in retaliation for threatening to file an ADA lawsuit. Perich intervened in the litigation, claiming unlawful retaliation under both the ADA and the Michigan Persons with Disabilities Civil Rights Act, Mich. Comp. Laws §37.1602(a) (1979). The EEOC and Perich sought Perich's reinstatement to her former position (or frontpay in lieu thereof), along with backpay, compensatory and punitive damages, attorney's fees, and other injunctive relief.

Hosanna-Tabor moved for summary judgment. Invoking what is known as the "ministerial exception," the Church argued that the suit was barred by the First Amendment because the claims at issue concerned the employment relationship between a religious institution and one of its ministers. According to the Church, Perich was a minister, and she had been fired for a religious reason—namely, that her threat to sue the Church violated the Synod's belief that Christians should resolve their disputes internally.

The District Court agreed that the suit was barred by the ministerial exception and granted summary judgment in Hosanna-Tabor's favor. The court explained that "Hosanna-Tabor treated Perich like a minister and held her out to the world as such long before this litigation began," and that the "facts surrounding Perich's employment in a religious school with a sectarian mission" supported the Church's characterization. In light of that determination, the court concluded that it could "inquire no further into her claims of retaliation."

The Court of Appeals for the Sixth Circuit vacated and remanded, directing the District Court to proceed to the merits of Perich's retaliation claims. The Court of Appeals recognized the existence of a ministerial exception barring certain employment discrimination claims against religious institutions—an exception "rooted in the First Amendment's guarantees of religious freedom." The court concluded, however, that Perich did not qualify as a "minister" under the exception, noting in particular that her duties as a called teacher were identical to her duties as a lay teacher. Judge White concurred. She viewed the question whether Perich qualified as a minister to be closer than did the majority, but agreed that the "fact that the duties of the contract teachers are the same as the duties of the called teachers is telling."

We granted certiorari.

II

The First Amendment provides, in part, that "Congress shall make no law respecting an establishment of religion, or prohibiting the free exercise thereof." We have said that these two Clauses "often exert conflicting pressures," *Cutter* v. *Wilkinson,* 544 U. S. 709, 719 (2005), and that there can be "internal tension . . . between the Establishment Clause and the Free Exercise Clause," *Tilton* v. *Richardson,* 403 U. S. 672, 677 (1971) (plurality opinion). Not so here. Both Religion Clauses bar the government from interfering with the decision of a religious group to fire one of its ministers.

[Sections II A and II B, containing a historical discussion of the separation of church and state, have been omitted.]

C

Until today, we have not had occasion to consider whether this freedom of a religious organization to select its ministers is implicated by a suit alleging discrimination in employment. The Courts of Appeals, in contrast, have had extensive experience with this issue. Since the passage of Title VII of the Civil Rights Act of 1964, 42 U. S. C. §2000e *et seq.*, and other employment discrimination laws, the Courts of Appeals have uniformly recognized the existence of a "ministerial exception," grounded in the First Amendment, that precludes application of such legislation to claims concerning the employment relationship between a religious institution and its ministers.

We agree that there is such a ministerial exception. The members of a religious group put their faith in the hands of their ministers. Requiring a church to accept or retain an unwanted minister, or punishing a church for failing to do so, intrudes upon more than a mere employment decision. Such action interferes with the internal governance of the church, depriving the church of control over the selection of those who will personify its beliefs. By imposing an unwanted minister, the state infringes the Free Exercise Clause, which protects a religious group's right to shape its own faith and mission through its appointments. According the state the power to determine which individuals will minister to the faithful also violates the Establishment Clause, which prohibits government involvement in such ecclesiastical decisions.

The EEOC and Perich acknowledge that employment discrimination laws would be unconstitutional as applied to religious groups in certain circumstances. They grant, for example, that it would violate the First Amendment for courts to apply such laws to compel the ordination of women by the Catholic Church or by an Orthodox Jewish seminary. According to the EEOC and Perich, religious organizations could successfully defend against employment discrimination claims in those circumstances by invoking the constitutional right to freedom of association—a right "implicit" in the First Amendment. The EEOC and Perich thus see no need—and no basis—for a special rule for ministers grounded in the Religion Clauses themselves.

We find this position untenable. The right to freedom of association is a right enjoyed by religious and secular groups alike. It follows under the EEOC's and Perich's view that the First Amendment analysis should be the same, whether the association in question is the Lutheran Church, a labor union, or a social club. That result is hard to square with the text of the First Amendment itself, which gives special solicitude to the rights of religious organizations. We cannot accept the remarkable view that the Religion Clauses have nothing to say about a religious organization's freedom to select its own ministers. . . .

III

Having concluded that there is a ministerial exception grounded in the Religion Clauses of the First Amendment, we consider whether the exception applies in this case. We hold that it does.

Every Court of Appeals to have considered the question has concluded that the ministerial exception is not limited to the head of a religious congregation, and we agree. We are reluctant, however, to adopt a rigid formula for deciding when an employee qualifies as a minister. It is enough for us to conclude, in this our first case involving the ministerial exception, that the exception covers Perich, given all the circumstances of her employment.

To begin with, Hosanna-Tabor held Perich out as a minister, with a role distinct from that of most of its members. When Hosanna-Tabor extended her a call, it issued her a "diploma of vocation" according her the title "Minister of Religion, Commissioned." She was tasked with performing that office "according to the Word of God and the confessional standards of the Evangelical Lutheran Church as drawn from the Sacred Scriptures." The congregation prayed that God "bless [her] ministrations to the glory of His holy name, [and] the building of His church." In a supplement to the diploma, the congregation undertook to periodically review Perich's "skills of ministry" and "ministerial responsibilities," and to provide for her "continuing education as a professional person in the ministry of the Gospel."

Perich's title as a minister reflected a significant degree of religious training followed by a formal process of commissioning. To be eligible to become a commissioned minister, Perich had to complete eight college-level courses in subjects including biblical interpretation, church doctrine, and the ministry of the Lutheran teacher. She also had to obtain the endorsement of her local Synod district by submitting a petition that contained her academic transcripts, letters of recommendation, personal statement, and written answers to various ministry related questions. Finally, she had to pass an oral examination by a faculty committee at a Lutheran college. It took Perich six years to fulfill these requirements. And when she eventually did, she was commissioned as a minister only upon election by the congregation, which recognized God's call to her to teach. At that point, her call could be rescinded only upon a supermajority vote of the congregation—a protection designed to allow her to "preach the Word of God boldly."

Perich held herself out as a minister of the Church by accepting the formal call to religious service, according to its terms. She did so in other ways as well. For example, she claimed a special housing allowance on her taxes that was available only to employees earning their compensation " 'in the exercise of the ministry.' " ("If you are not conducting activities 'in the exercise of the ministry,' you cannot take advantage of the parsonage or housing allowance exclusion" (quoting Lutheran Church–Missouri Synod Brochure on Whether the IRS Considers Employees as a Minister (2007)). In a form she submitted to the Synod following her termination, Perich again indicated that she regarded herself as a minister at Hosanna-Tabor, stating: "I feel that God is leading me to serve in the teaching ministry. . . . I am anxious to be in the teaching ministry again soon."

Perich's job duties reflected a role in conveying the Church's message and carrying out its mission. Hosanna-Tabor expressly charged her with "lead[ing] others toward Christian maturity" and "teach[ing] faithfully the Word of God, the Sacred Scriptures, in its truth and purity and asset forth in all the symbolical books of the Evangelical Lutheran Church." In fulfilling these responsibilities, Perich taught her students religion four days a week, and led them in prayer three times a day. Once a week, she took her students to a school-wide chapel service, and—about twice a year—she took her turn leading it, choosing the liturgy, selecting the hymns, and delivering a short message based on verses from the Bible. During her last year of teaching, Perich also led her fourth graders in a brief devotional exercise each morning. As a source of religious instruction, Perich performed an important role in transmitting the Lutheran faith to the next generation.

In light of these considerations—the formal title given Perich by the Church, the substance reflected in that title, her own use of that title, and the important religious functions she performed for the Church—we conclude that Perich was a minister covered by the ministerial exception.

In reaching a contrary conclusion, the Court of Appeals committed three errors. First, the Sixth Circuit failed to see any relevance in the fact that Perich was a commissioned minister. Although such a title, by itself, does not automatically ensure coverage, the fact that an employee has been ordained or commissioned as a minister is surely relevant, as is the fact that significant religious training and a recognized religious mission underlie the description of the employee's position. It was wrong for the Court of Appeals—and Perich, who has adopted the court's view—to say that an employee's title does not matter.

Second, the Sixth Circuit gave too much weight to the fact that lay teachers at the school performed the same religious duties as Perich. We express no view on whether someone with Perich's duties would be covered by the ministerial exception in the absence of the other considerations we have discussed. But though relevant, it cannot be dispositive that others not formally recognized as ministers by the church perform the same functions—particularly when, as here, they did so only because commissioned ministers were unavailable.

Third, the Sixth Circuit placed too much emphasis on Perich's performance of secular duties. It is true that her religious duties consumed only 45 minutes of each workday, and that the rest of her day was devoted to teaching secular subjects. The EEOC regards that as conclusive, contending that any ministerial exception "should be limited to those employees who perform exclusively religious functions." We cannot accept that view. Indeed, we are unsure whether any such employees exist. The heads of congregations themselves often have a mix of duties, including secular ones such as helping to manage the congregation's finances, supervising purely secular personnel, and overseeing the upkeep of facilities.

Although the Sixth Circuit did not adopt the extreme position pressed here by the EEOC, it did regard the relative amount of time Perich spent performing religious functions as largely determinative. The issue before us, however, is not one that can be resolved by a stopwatch. The amount of time an employee spends on particular activities is relevant in assessing that employee's status, but that factor cannot be considered in isolation, without regard to the nature of the religious functions performed and the other considerations discussed above.

Because Perich was a minister within the meaning of the exception, the First Amendment requires dismissal of this employment discrimination suit against her religious employer. The EEOC and Perich originally sought an order reinstating Perich to her former position as a called teacher. By requiring the Church to accept a minister it did not want, such an order would have plainly violated the Church's freedom under the Religion Clauses to select its own ministers. . . .

The EEOC and Perich suggest that Hosanna-Tabor's asserted religious reason for firing Perich—that she violated the Synod's commitment to internal dispute resolution—was pretextual. That suggestion misses the point of the ministerial exception. The purpose of the exception is not to safeguard a church's decision to fire a minister only when it is made for a religious reason. The exception instead ensures that the authority to select and control who will minister to the faithful—a matter "strictly ecclesiastical," *Kedroff,* 344 U. S., at 119—is the church's alone.

IV

The EEOC and Perich foresee a parade of horribles that will follow our recognition of a ministerial exception to employment discrimination suits. According to the EEOC and Perich, such an exception could protect religious organizations from liability for retaliating against employees for reporting criminal misconduct or for testifying before a grand jury or in a criminal trial. What is more, the EEOC contends, the logic of the exception would confer on religious employers "unfettered discretion" to violate employment laws by, for example, hiring children or aliens not authorized to work in the United States.

Hosanna-Tabor responds that the ministerial exception would not in any way bar criminal prosecutions for interfering with law enforcement investigations or other proceedings. Nor, according to the Church, would the exception bar government enforcement of general laws restricting eligibility for employment, because the exception applies only to suits by or on behalf of ministers themselves. Hosanna-Tabor also notes that the ministerial exception has been around in the lower courts for 40 years, see *McClure* v. *Salvation Army*, 460 F. 2d 553, 558 (CA5 1972), and has not given rise to the dire consequences predicted by the EEOC and Perich.

The case before us is an employment discrimination suit brought on behalf of a minister, challenging her church's decision to fire her. Today we hold only that the ministerial exception bars such a suit. We express no view on whether the exception bars other types of suits, including actions by employees alleging breach of contract or tortuous conduct by their religious employers. There will be time enough to address the applicability of the exception to other circumstances if and when they arise.

* * *

The interest of society in the enforcement of employment discrimination statutes is undoubtedly important. But so too is the interest of religious groups in choosing who will preach their beliefs, teach their faith, and carry out their mission. When a minister who has been fired sues her church alleging that her termination was discriminatory, the First Amendment has struck the balance for us. The church must be free to choose those who will guide it on its way.

The judgment of the Court of Appeals for the Sixth Circuit is reversed.

It is so ordered.

[The concurring opinions of Justices Thomas and Alito have been omitted.]

SOURCE: U.S. Supreme Court. *Hosanna-Tabor Evangelical Lutheran Church and School v. EEOC,* 565 U.S.__(2012). http://www.supremecourt.gov/opinions/11pdf/10–553.pdf.

CDC Releases Reports on Obesity in the United States

JANUARY 17 AND AUGUST 13, 2012

Today's fast-food culture has not been kind to America's waistline, according to a trio of reports released by the Centers for Disease Control and Prevention (CDC) in 2012. In January, the CDC reported that more than one third of adults and 17 percent of children in the United States are obese, a number that overall has remained flat since 2003 but with increases seen in men, young boys, and African American and Hispanic females. By May, the CDC predicted that by 2030, even in spite of local and nationwide wellness initiatives and wider availability of healthy foods, 42 percent of Americans will be obese. In August, the CDC released state-specific data on current obesity rates, painting a clearer picture of how geography and demographics play a role in obesity prevalence. Obesity does not just harm individuals; it also puts a strain on the health care system overall. As obesity levels creep up, so do cases of Type 2 diabetes, some cancers, heart disease, stroke, and osteoarthritis. CDC experts predict that by 2030, the United States could have spent an extra $550 billion on obesity-related health issues. Although it is not easy to reverse obesity trends now that they are ingrained in American culture, some public officials are taking on the challenge.

OVERALL FLATTENING OF OBESITY RATE

In a report titled "Prevalence of Obesity in the United States, 2009–2010," released on January 17, 2012, the CDC reported that in 2009 to 2010, more than 35 percent of adults were obese, or more than 78 million Americans. The CDC defines obesity as having a body mass index (BMI) greater than thirty, which for someone measuring five feet nine inches would be 203 pounds or more. The biennial study, which included nearly 6,000 adults and 4,000 children, also suggested that 13 million children aged two to nineteen also fit into the obesity category. When the number of overweight Americans is taken into account, 69 percent of Americans are either overweight or obese—73.9 percent of men and 63.7 percent of women. The obesity figures rose from 30.5 percent of adults in 2000. Since 2003, however, growth has remained relatively flat. "There is really a slowing down of the rapid increase in the prevalence of obesity that we saw in the 1980s and 1990s," said Cynthia Ogden, one of the lead CDC researchers on the study. "It's good that we didn't see increases," but "on the other hand, we didn't see any decreases in any group," she said.

Because most obesity prevention efforts are relatively recent, it will take some time before these efforts yield results. Dr. William Dietz, director of the Division of Nutrition, Physical Activity, and Obesity at the CDC, likens it to antismoking campaigns that began in the 1950s. There was little movement in the number of smokers until nearly three decades later, when smoking bans and cigarette taxes came into play. "Nutrition programs and physical activity efforts have only just begun to kick in, and haven't had much time to operate. It takes time before the effects of policy change begin to show benefit in terms of behavior changes," said Dietz. "I believe we're not yet at the place with obesity where tobacco was when cigarette use started to drop," he said.

Whether obesity rates increase or remain stable, health care costs linked to obesity-related diseases like Type 2 diabetes, some cancers, heart disease, osteoarthritis, sleep apnea, and stroke will continue to rise. In 2012, the cost of treating these conditions came to approximately $147 billion, according to the CDC.

DIRE PREDICTIONS

On its current trajectory, 42 percent of Americans will be obese by 2030, according to a CDC projections report released in May. This increase means that 32 million more Americans will be considered obese. Those considered severely obese, weighing eighty pounds more than their ideal weight, will double to comprise 11 percent of the population in less than two decades. If current growth trends revert back to the fast growth rates seen from the 1980s to the early 2000s, the United States would be on track to have 51 percent of its population considered obese by 2030. However, the report authors admit that projecting the growth of obesity is difficult. "This and other forecasts likely overstate future obesity prevalence given the recent evidence of slower growth," the report states.

The projections report described several factors that impact obesity: eating and exercise habits, cost of groceries, number of restaurants, unemployment, the price of gas, Internet access, and the average age of the population. The report provided some explanation as to why the obesity rate will continue increasing. Three significant reasons are the growing population of Latino adults whose culture does not stigmatize obesity, obese children becoming obese adults, and an aging population.

OBESITY BY STATE AND DEMOGRAPHICS

In August, the CDC released the results of its national Behavioral Risk Factor Surveillance System phone survey, comprising 400,000 Americans in 2011. The survey asks participants their height and weight and uses the data to create a picture of obesity rates by state. With the data from this year's survey, the CDC was able to determine that the South has the highest prevalence of obesity, with Mississippi having the highest rate in the nation at 34.9 percent. In 1995, Mississippi led the nation at 19.4 percent. University of Alabama at Birmingham biostatistics professor George Howard equated this to culture. "There's not a social stigma attached to being fat in the South," he said. In twelve states at least 30 percent of the population was obese in 2011, including Alabama, Arkansas, Indiana, Kentucky, Louisiana, Michigan, Mississippi, Missouri, Oklahoma, South Carolina, Texas, and West Virginia. Colorado had the lowest obesity rate at 20.7 percent, and no state had an obesity rate under 20 percent. Two decades ago, no state had an obesity rate above 15 percent.

Because no real measurements are taken as part of this study, some question how reliable the results are. Additionally, the data from this survey cannot be easily compared to previous studies because a new methodology was used that included cell-phone-only households. The 2011 survey will be used as the new baseline for all future reports.

Using CDC data to create a state-by-state picture of obesity rates in 2030, the Robert Wood Johnson Foundation and the Trust for America's Health released their own report, *F as in Fat*, which concluded that half of U.S. adults will be obese by 2030. According to this report, in every state, the obesity rate will be at least 44 percent, and in thirteen states, it will be over 60 percent, with Mississippi remaining the highest at 66.7 percent and Colorado the lowest at 44.8 percent. Based on these projections, the report predicts an increase in obesity-related health problems, including 7.9 million new diabetes cases each year compared with 1.9 million now and 6.8 million new cases of chronic heart disease and stroke compared to 1.3 million now. "[If] we stay on the current track, we're going to see unacceptably high rates of obesity, and more importantly, unacceptably high rates of diabetes, heart disease, stroke, obesity-related cancers, arthritis, that will really place a huge burden on our health care system," said Jeff Levi, executive director of the Trust for America's Health.

Critics of the *F as in Fat* report say the future obesity rates are overstated because the report assumes that past trends in obesity growth will continue. "This is a strong assumption," said Justin Trogdon, a health economist at RTI International, a nonprofit organization that provides research to government and corporate clients. "Recent evidence from other surveys suggest obesity rates may be leveling off," he said.

The trio of 2012 CDC reports revealed a clear delineation between demographic groups in terms of those who are more predisposed to obesity. In the 1999 to 2000 study, more women than men were obese—27.5 percent of men and 33.4 percent of women—whereas today, that number is almost identical—35.5 percent of men and 35.8 percent of women. For teenagers, the obesity rate among boys has continued to rise, while that of girls has leveled off and remains stable. Regardless of whether the rapid increases seen in the 1980s and 1990s for girls has tapered off, "We're plateauing at an unacceptably high prevalence rate," says Dr. David Ludwig, director of the Obesity Prevention Center at Boston Children's Hospital.

One possible reason for the increase in obesity rates among boys but not girls is the prevalence of video games, the Internet, and other electronic devices. Boys spend more time playing these games while girls have become increasingly self-conscious about their bodies, according to Jacob Warman, the chief of endocrinology at Brooklyn Hospital Center in New York. Another reason may be fast-food restaurants, which target men and boys more than girls. "Marketers encourage boys and young men to eat and drink as much as they can as part of macho lifestyles," said Marion Nestle, a professor of nutrition and food studies at New York University. "The bigger the portions, the more the calories, and the bigger the person."

Age also plays a role, as obesity tends to become more common as one gets older, a dangerous trend considering that Type 2 diabetes also becomes more common with age. In the CDC's 2009 to 2010 obesity study, women aged sixty and older had the highest obesity rate, at 42.3 percent.

The *F as in Fat* report found links between obesity and education and finances. One third of those without a high school diploma are obese, compared with one fifth of those with a college or technical school degree. Financially, one third of those who earn less than $15,000 per year are obese while one quarter of those who earn $50,000 or more per year are obese. The *F as in Fat* report says the link between poverty and obesity is likely caused by a number of factors. These include poor neighborhoods being less likely to have playgrounds, sidewalks, or other outdoor activities that encourage exercise, and less likely to have grocery stores—making unhealthy fast food a cheap and convenient option.

PREVENTION EFFORTS

"Unless we see declining rates of obesity the impact on society will continue to mount for many years to come," says Ludwig. According to the *F is for Fat* report, if the average body mass index (BMI) was lowered by 5 percent by 2030, then 100 cases of obesity-related cancers per 100,000 people would be avoided, 800,000 diabetes cases in California could be prevented, and most states would see health care savings between 6.5 percent and 7.9 percent. The authors of the report recommend increased physical activity in schools, new standards for school meals, and better promotion of preventative care to help reach this 5 percent goal.

The federal government is doing its part to help encourage healthy habits, with the Department of Health and Human Services giving more than $119 million to states for obesity prevention efforts since 2009. Additionally, First Lady Michelle Obama's Let's Move! initiative targets school-aged children with an exercise and healthy eating message because studies show that obese children tend to become obese adults. Around the country, two dozen states have banned soda and sugary drinks from vending machines and lunch lines, and restaurant chains are increasingly committed to trimming calories from their menu options.

In New York City, schools are encouraging healthier eating and more physical activity for students. Those efforts helped the obesity rate in grade school children drop 5.5 percent between 2006 and 2010. In September 2012, the city passed a ban on the sale of sugary drinks of more than sixteen ounces at restaurants, fast-food chains, theaters, delis, and a number of other food establishments that are regulated by the city's Board of Health to further encourage residents to make healthier decisions.

In Philadelphia, the CDC reported that the obesity rate among school-aged children dropped from 21.5 percent to 20.5 percent after the city removed all soda and sugary drinks from schools, got rid of deep fryers, and offered free breakfast to all students. "The city achieved the greatest achievements in [body mass index] among African-American males and Hispanic females, two groups that historically have experienced higher rates of obesity and related health problems," said Michelle Larkin, the assistant vice president and deputy director for the Robert Wood Johnson Foundation's Health Group. The city is also working with the nonprofit group The Food Trust to bring grocery stores to communities lacking them and to ensure that food stamps can be used at farmer's markets. There are important steps in lowering obesity rates because, according to the CDC's Dietz, "People need to make healthy choices, but the healthy choices must first be available and accessible in order to make them."

—Heather Kerrigan

Following is the edited text of a report released by the Centers for Disease Control and Prevention (CDC) on January 17, 2012, on the level of obesity among adults and children in the United States, and a table on obesity prevalence by state, released by the CDC on August 13, 2012.

CDC Findings on Obesity in the United States

January 17, 2012

[All sidebars, graphics, and footnotes—and references to them—have been omitted.]

Obesity increases the risk of a number of health conditions including hypertension, adverse lipid concentrations, and type 2 diabetes. The prevalence of obesity in the United

States increased during the last decades of the 20th century. More recently there appears to have been a slowing of the rate of increase or even a leveling off. Given the health risks of obesity and its high prevalence, it is important to continue to track the prevalence of obesity among U.S. adults and children. This report presents the most recent national estimates of obesity in the United States based on measured weight and height.

In 2009–2010, 35.7% of U.S. adults were obese.

More than 35% of U.S. men and women were obese in 2009–2010. There was no significant difference in prevalence between men and women at any age. Overall, adults aged 60 and over were more likely to be obese than younger adults. Among men there was no significant difference in obesity prevalence by age. Among women, however, 42.3% of those aged 60 and over were obese compared with 31.9% of women aged 20–39.

In 2009–2010, 16.9% of U.S. children and adolescents were obese.

The prevalence of obesity was higher among adolescents than among preschool-aged children. The prevalence of obesity was higher among boys than girls (18.6% of boys and 15.0% of girls were obese).

In 2009–2010, over 78 million U.S. adults and about 12.5 million U.S. children and adolescents were obese.

Almost 41 million women and more than 37 million men aged 20 and over were obese in 2009–2010. Among children and adolescents aged 2–19, more than 5 million girls and approximately 7 million boys were obese.

Between 1999–2000 and 2009–2010, the prevalence of obesity increased among men but not among women.

In 1999–2000, 27.5% of men were obese, and by 2009–2010 the prevalence had increased to 35.5%. Among women, 33.4% were obese in 1999–2000 with no significant change in 2009–2010 (35.8%). In 1999–2000, the prevalence of obesity was higher in women than in men. Between 1999–2000 and 2009–2010, the prevalence of obesity in men was virtually equal to that in women. There was no significant change in the prevalence of obesity from 2007–2008 to 2009–2010 overall or among men or women.

Between 1999–2000 and 2009–2010, there was an increase in the prevalence of obesity among boys but not among girls.

The prevalence of obesity among boys increased from 14.0% in 1999–2000 to 18.6% in 2009–2010. There was no significant change among girls: the prevalence was 13.8% in 1999–2000 and 15.0% in 2009–2010. There was no significant change in obesity prevalence from 2007–2008 to 2009–2010 overall or among boys or girls.

SUMMARY

The most recent national data on obesity prevalence among U.S. adults, adolescents, and children show that more than one-third of adults and almost 17% of children and adolescents were obese in 2009–2010. Differences in prevalence between men and women diminished between 1999–2000 and 2009–2010, with the prevalence of obesity among men reaching the same level as that among women.

Age differences in obesity prevalence varied between men and women. The prevalence of obesity was higher among older women compared with younger women, but there was no difference by age in obesity prevalence among men. Among children and adolescents, the prevalence of obesity was higher among adolescents than among pre-school-aged children.

There has been no change in obesity prevalence in recent years; however, over the last decade there has been a significant increase in obesity prevalence among men and boys but not among women and girls overall. The Healthy People 2010 goals of 15% obesity among adults and 5% obesity among children were not met.

[The remainder of the report, including the definition of obesity, data source, methods, author information, and references, has been omitted.]

SOURCE: Centers for Disease Control and Prevention. National Center for Health Statistics (NCHS). "Prevalence of Obesity in the United States, 2009–2010." January 17, 2012. NCHS Data Brief no. 82 (January 2012). http://www.cdc.gov/nchs/data/databriefs/db82.pdf.

DOCUMENT

Prevalence of Self-Reported Obesity Among U.S. Adults, 2011

August 13, 2012

State	2011 Prevalence	2011 Confidence Interval
Alabama	32.0	(30.5, 33.5)
Alaska	27.4	(25.3, 29.7)
Arizona	24.7	(22.7, 26.9)
Arkansas	30.9	(28.8, 33.1)
California	23.8	(22.9, 24.7)
Colorado	20.7	(19.7, 21.8)
Connecticut	24.5	(23.0, 26.0)
Delaware	28.8	(26.9, 30.7)
District of Columbia	23.7	(21.9, 25.7)
Florida	26.6	(25.4, 27.9)
Georgia	28.0	(26.6, 29.4)
Hawaii	21.8	(20.4, 23.4)
Idaho	27.0	(25.3, 28.9)
Illinois	27.1	(25.4, 28.9)
Indiana	30.8	(29.5, 32.3)
Iowa	29.0	(27.6, 30.3)
Kansas	29.6	(28.7, 30.4)
Kentucky	30.4	(28.9, 31.9)
Louisiana	33.4	(32.0, 34.9)
Maine	27.8	(26.8, 28.9)
Maryland	28.3	(26.9, 29.7)
Massachusetts	22.7	(21.8, 23.7)

(Continued)

(Continued)

State	2011 Prevalence	2011 Confidence Interval
Michigan	31.3	(30.0, 32.6)
Minnesota	25.7	(24.6, 26.8)
Mississippi	34.9	(33.5, 36.3)
Missouri	30.3	(28.6, 32.0)
Montana	24.6	(23.3, 26.0)
Nebraska	28.4	(27.6, 29.2)
Nevada	24.5	(22.5, 26.6)
New Hampshire	26.2	(24.7, 27.7)
New Jersey	23.7	(22.7, 24.8)
New Mexico	26.3	(25.1, 27.6)
New York	24.5	(23.2, 25.9)
North Carolina	29.1	(27.7, 30.6)
North Dakota	27.8	(26.3, 29.4)
Ohio	29.6	(28.3, 31.0)
Oklahoma	31.1	(29.7, 32.5)
Oregon	26.7	(25.2, 28.3)
Pennsylvania	28.6	(27.3, 29.8)
Rhode Island	25.4	(23.9, 27.0)
South Carolina	30.8	(29.6, 32.1)
South Dakota	28.1	(26.3, 30.1)
Tennessee	29.2	(26.8, 31.7)
Texas	30.4	(29.1, 31.8)
Utah	24.4	(23.4, 25.5)
Vermont	25.4	(24.1, 26.8)
Virginia	29.2	(27.5, 30.9)
Washington	26.5	(25.3, 27.7)
West Virginia	32.4	(30.9, 34.0)
Wisconsin	27.7	(25.8, 29.7)
Wyoming	25.0	(23.5, 26.6)

NOTE: Prevalence reflects BRFSS (Behavioral Risk Factor Surveillance System) methodological changes in 2011, and these estimates should not be compared to previous years.

SOURCE: Centers for Disease Control and Prevention, Behavioral Risk Factor Surveillance System. "Prevalence of Self-Reported Obesity Among U.S. Adults: BRFSS 2011." August 13, 2012. http://www .cdc.gov/obesity/downloads/DNPAO_State_Obesity_Prevalence_Map_2011_508.pdf.

OTHER HISTORIC DOCUMENTS OF INTEREST

FROM PREVIOUS HISTORIC DOCUMENTS

State Department, President Deny Keystone XL Pipeline Application

JANUARY 18 AND MARCH 22, 2012

With gas prices near and above $4 in many locations around the country in 2012, President Barack Obama received heavy criticism when he rejected the application to build a $7 billion, 1,700-mile pipeline to connect the oil sands in western Canada to refineries in Texas and the Gulf of Mexico. Known as the Keystone XL Pipeline, the plan had been in the works for many years to help bring more Canadian oil to the United States to reduce the nation's dependence on oil from unfriendly foreign countries. Canada is already the United States' biggest foreign oil supplier, and supporters say the proposed pipeline would provide much-needed jobs. Opposition to the pipeline comes mainly from environmentalists who worry about its impact on Nebraska's Sandhills and the Ogallala Aquifer, which provides water to much of the Great Plains. Because the pipeline crosses international borders, it requires the approval of the president, who makes his determination based on the recommendation of the State Department. Department officials had rejected the project in January 2012, arguing that a 2011 congressional mandate that a decision be made on the pipeline by February 21 did not allow enough time to review the builder's application and the environmental impact. The president promised that the January rejection was not final, and he encouraged the builder, TransCanada, to reapply with a new pipeline route that would alleviate the concerns of those in Nebraska. TransCanada did so in May 2012, and without releasing specifics, the State Department said the company included a revised route. A decision on the application would likely come by April 2013.

KEYSTONE XL

Since the initial proposal to build this transcontinental pipeline from Canada to the United States first surfaced in 2008, it has been a contentious issue with passionate debate on both sides, raising a multitude of economic concerns important to Americans. The proposed pipeline would carry more than 500,000 barrels of heavy crude oil from Canada's oil sands each day. The United States stands to gain a significant amount of oil from the pipeline—in 2010, the oil sands production was at 1.5 million barrels of oil per day, and Canada hopes it will be 2.2 million barrels by 2015 and 3.7 million barrels by 2025. But questions have been raised about the pipeline's necessity—a 2010 study by the State Department found that the oil from Canada's oil sands would reach the United States whether the pipeline was built or not.

The key issue in building the pipeline is its potential environmental impact. As presented by TransCanada, one of North America's largest gas storage providers and the builder of the pipeline, the originally proposed route would run the pipeline through the Ogallala Aquifer in Nebraska. This source supplies water to a majority of farmers in the Great Plains region. If the pipeline were to leak, this water could be contaminated, affecting a wide swath of the middle of the country. Nebraska's governor, Dave Heineman, and some of the state's congressional delegation do not support the original route of the pipeline. In 2011, Heineman called a special session of the state legislature, during which it passed a law to require the pipeline to be routed away from the state's Sandhills, which sit on top of the Ogallala Aquifer. TransCanada agreed to comply in April 2012 when it released a possible plan for a revised route.

INITIAL APPLICATION REJECTED

In late 2011, Congress reached an agreement for a temporary extension of the payroll tax deduction. In the agreement, Republicans added a sixty-day window for the president to decide whether the Keystone project would be allowed to move forward. Prior to the February 21, 2012, sixty-day deadline, on January 18, President Obama said that he was not given enough time to review all the information necessary to make a decision. The president was facing pressure from environmentalists and those along the pipeline's proposed route, specifically those in Nebraska, to make a critical review of the potential environmental impact. In denying TransCanada's application, the president said it was not the end of the line, and encouraged the company to reapply with a new route that would bypass the aquifer. "This announcement is not a judgment on the merits of the pipeline, but the arbitrary nature of a deadline that prevented the State Department from gathering the information necessary to approve the project and protect the American people," the president said. Following Obama's announcement, TransCanada Chief Executive Russ Girling said, "While we are disappointed, TransCanada remains fully committed to the construction of Keystone XL." He added that he expected a future permit request to be expedited and that the pipeline could be functioning by 2014.

The State Department recommended that the president refuse to issue a permit for the project, deeming the initial application not in the nation's best interest given the limited time frame for study. The Canadian government responded to the decision, expressing its discontent and desire to seek business elsewhere. The "decision by the Obama administration underlines the importance of diversifying and expanding our markets, including the growing Asian market," said Joe Oliver, Canada's natural resources minister.

TransCanada responded to the State Department's decision in February, saying that it would reapply. It also requested immediate approval to build the southern portion of the pipeline from Cushing, Oklahoma, to the Gulf Coast. Because this portion of the pipeline did not cross international borders, it would not require the State Department's approval. According to TransCanada, this portion of the pipeline could be in operation by 2013 and would create 4,000 jobs at a cost of $2.3 billion.

SUPPORT COMES MAINLY FROM REPUBLICANS

Republicans were relatively united on the Keystone issue and used it throughout the 2012 election season to back their key areas of concern: jobs, energy independence, and competition with China. Republicans asserted that if the United States does not come to an agreement with TransCanada, the company will send its oil to China, which will reap the economic benefit. Republicans were critical of the January decision, claiming that the president was standing in the way of job creation and in helping to lower gas prices across the country. Supporters say the pipeline would create 10,000 construction jobs over the two-year build, add $5 billion in property tax revenue, and add a total $20 billion to the U.S. economy over the pipeline's expected 100-year life span.

The Obama administration responded to critics, saying that the expected number of jobs was inflated and that because of the process of moving the oil, refining it, and getting it back to the market, it would be a long time before gas prices would be impacted. On jobs, the Obama administration pointed to TransCanada's own estimates that the pipeline would create 20,000 job years, not jobs—13,000 for construction and 7,000 for supply manufacturers. Over two years, the number of construction workers would be 6,500 per year according to TransCanada. The number of supply jobs created could be lower than the estimate because TransCanada already purchased a number of the necessary parts for the pipeline build.

Despite this, U.S. Chamber of Commerce President Thomas Donohue, a pipeline supporter, said, "This political decision offers hard evidence that creating jobs is not a high priority for this administration." He continued, "The President's decision sends a strong message to the business community and to investors: keep your money on the sidelines, America is not open for business." The decision has also drawn criticism from a number of trade unions, including the International Union of Operating Engineers, whose president, James Callahan, called the decision "a blow to America's construction workers" in "the sector hardest hit by the recession."

Environmentalists firmly oppose the pipeline build. They are concerned about the impact of a possible pipeline leak, which they say is likely because the oil sands crude is more corrosive than typical crude. A Cornell University study found that Keystone could produce up to ninety-one significant spills in fifty years. Environmentalists have also expressed concern that by allowing the pipeline to go ahead, rather than building a renewable energy source, the United States is continuing to support and promote finite, dirty forms of fuel and might cut jobs in the green economy. Additionally, they say the mining tactics used to pull oil from the oil sands often causes water pollution along with deforestation. A large amount of energy is required to separate the sand from the oil, meaning more greenhouse gas, estimated to be 5 percent to 30 percent greater than that from typical oil drilling.

"President Obama put the health and safety of the American people and our air, lands and water—our national interest—above the interests of the oil industry," said Frances Beinecke, president of the National Resources Defense Council. "His decision represents a triumph of truth over Big Oil's bullying tactics and its disinformation campaign with wildly exaggerated job claims," she said. In an attempt to alleviate environmental concerns, TransCanada has agreed to fifty-seven provisions to keep the pipeline secure from leaks.

Partial Pipeline Go-Ahead

The Senate tried again on January 30 to get the pipeline project approved, proposing legislation that would begin construction immediately but would allow for a redrawing of the proposed route to circumvent Nebraska's sensitive lands. "Clearly we can make this decision. Clearly after more than three years of study it doesn't make sense to not move forward. Particularly when we're talking about tens of thousands of jobs [that] today we need, not only will it not cost our federal government revenue, it will generate hundreds of millions in revenue back to local, state, and federal government," said Sen. John Hoeven, R-N.D. The bill would invoke the Commerce Clause of the Constitution, meaning that presidential approval of the project would not be necessary. However, the president would still have the option of vetoing the Senate's legislation. Forty-four Republican senators backed the measure, but only one Democrat—Sen. Joe Manchin, D-W.Va.—supported it. "As our country continues to need oil, common sense tells me I'd rather buy it from our friends in Canada, not countries around the world that seek to do us harm," said Manchin, calling the pipeline a benefit for labor and business.

In a nod to pipeline supporters, on March 22, at a press conference in Oklahoma, Obama gave the go-ahead to fast-track the southern portion of the pipeline. "Today I'm directing my administration to cut through the redtape, break through the bureaucratic hurdles, and make this project a priority," Obama said, calling it part of his "all-of-the-above" energy strategy that supports both renewables and fossil fuels. The Army Corps of Engineers granted the permits needed to move forward on the build in July. The 500-mile section of the pipeline will relieve a bottleneck in Cushing, Oklahoma, that was created by new oil production in North Dakota, which creates a massive oil buildup. This buildup that feeds Midwest oil refineries, however, has helped keep gas prices low in the Midwest, and there are now questions as to whether gas prices will rise. TransCanada has estimated that the southern portion could add $4 billion each year to the total U.S. fuel bill.

—Heather Kerrigan

Following is a statement released by the U.S. Department of State on January 18, 2012, announcing its recommendation to President Barack Obama to deny the initial Keystone XL Pipeline application; the text of an announcement by President Obama on January 18, 2012, regarding the denial of the application to build the Keystone XL Pipeline; and an additional statement by President Obama on March 22, 2012, concerning his administration's intent to fast-track the building of the southern portion of the pipeline.

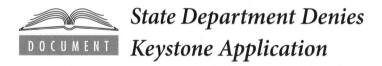

State Department Denies Keystone Application

DOCUMENT

January 18, 2012

Today, the Department of State recommended to President Obama that the presidential permit for the proposed Keystone XL Pipeline be denied and, that at this time, the TransCanada Keystone XL Pipeline be determined not to serve the national interest. The President concurred with the Department's recommendation, which was predicated on the fact that the Department does not have sufficient time to obtain the information necessary to assess whether the project, in its current state, is in the national interest.

Since 2008, the Department has been conducting a transparent, thorough, and rigorous review of TransCanada's permit application for the proposed Keystone XL Pipeline project. As a result of this process, particularly given the concentration of concerns regarding the proposed route through the Sand Hills area of Nebraska, on November 10, 2011, the Department announced that it could not make a national interest determination regarding the permit application without additional information. Specifically, the Department called for an assessment of alternative pipeline routes that avoided the uniquely sensitive terrain of the Sand Hills in Nebraska. The Department estimated, based on prior projects of similar length and scope, that it could complete the necessary review to make a decision by the first quarter of 2013. In consultations with the State of Nebraska and TransCanada, they agreed with the estimated timeline.

On December 23, 2011, the Congress passed the Temporary Payroll Tax Cut Continuation Act of 2011 ("the Act"). The Act provides 60 days for the President to determine whether the Keystone XL pipeline is in the national interest—which is insufficient for such a determination.

The Department's denial of the permit application does not preclude any subsequent permit application or applications for similar projects.

SOURCE: U.S. Department of State. Office of the Spokesperson. "Denial of the Keystone XL Pipeline Application." January 18, 2012. http://www.state.gov/r/pa/prs/ps/2012/01/181473.htm.

President Obama Announces Keystone Application Denial

January 18, 2012

Earlier today I received the Secretary of State's recommendation on the pending application for the construction of the Keystone XL Pipeline. As the State Department made clear last month, the rushed and arbitrary deadline insisted on by congressional Republicans prevented a full assessment of the pipeline's impact, especially the health and safety of the American people, as well as our environment. As a result, the Secretary of State has recommended that the application be denied. And after reviewing the State Department's report, I agree.

This announcement is not a judgment on the merits of the pipeline, but the arbitrary nature of a deadline that prevented the State Department from gathering the information necessary to approve the project and protect the American people. I'm disappointed that Republicans in Congress forced this decision, but it does not change my administration's commitment to American-made energy that creates jobs and reduces our dependence on oil. Under my administration, domestic oil and natural gas production is up, while imports of foreign oil are down. In the months ahead, we will continue to look for new ways to partner with the oil and gas industry to increase our energy security—including the potential development of an oil pipeline from Cushing, Oklahoma, to the Gulf of Mexico—even as we set higher efficiency standards for cars and trucks and invest in alternatives like biofuels and natural gas. And we will do so in a way that benefits American workers and businesses without risking the health and safety of the American people and the environment.

SOURCE: Executive Office of the President. "Statement on Keystone XL Pipeline." January 18, 2012. *Compilation of Presidential Documents* 2012, no. 00031 (January 18, 2012). http://www.gpo.gov/fdsys/pkg/DCPD-201200031/pdf/DCPD-201200031.pdf.

President Obama Gives Green Light to Southern Portion of Keystone XL Pipeline

March 22, 2012

. . . It is good to be back in Oklahoma. I haven't been back here since the campaign, and everybody looks like they're doing just fine. Thank you so much for your hospitality. It is wonderful to be here.

Yesterday, I visited Nevada and New Mexico to talk about what we're calling an all-of-the-above energy strategy. It's a strategy that will keep us on track to further reduce our dependence on foreign oil, put more people back to work, and ultimately help to curb the spike in gas prices that we're seeing year after year after year.

So today I've come to Cushing, an oil town, because producing more oil and gas here at home has been and will continue to be a critical part of an all-of-the-above energy strategy.

Now, under my administration, America is producing more oil today than at any time in the last 8 years. Over the—[*applause*]—that's important to know. Over the last 3 years, I've directed my administration to open up millions of acres for gas and oil exploration across 23 different States. We're opening up more than 75 percent of our potential oil resources offshore. We've quadrupled the number of operating rigs to a record high. We've added enough new oil and gas pipeline to encircle the Earth and then some.

So we are drilling all over the place right now. That's not the challenge. That's not the problem. In fact, the problem in a place like Cushing is that we're actually producing so much oil and gas in places like North Dakota and Colorado that we don't have enough pipeline capacity to transport all of it to where it needs to go, both to refineries, and then eventually all across the country and around the world. There's a bottleneck right here because we can't get enough of the oil to our refineries fast enough. And if we could, then we would be able to increase our oil supplies at a time when they're needed as much as possible.

Now, right now a company called TransCanada has applied to build a new pipeline to speed more oil from Cushing to state-of-the-art refineries down on the Gulf Coast. And today I'm directing my administration to cut through the redtape, break through the bureaucratic hurdles, and make this project a priority, to go ahead and get it done.

Now, you wouldn't know all this from listening to the television set. This whole issue of the Keystone pipeline has generated obviously a lot of controversy and a lot of politics. And that's because the original route from Canada into the United States was planned through an area in Nebraska that supplies some drinking water for nearly 2 million Americans and irrigation for a good portion of America's croplands. And Nebraskans of all political stripes, including the Republican Governor there, raised some concerns about the safety and wisdom of that route.

So to be extra careful that the construction of the pipeline in an area like that wouldn't put the health and the safety of the American people at risk, our experts said that we needed a certain amount of time to review the project. Unfortunately, Congress decided they wanted their own timeline. Not the company, not the experts, but Members of

Congress, who decided this might be a fun political issue, decided to try to intervene and make it impossible for us to make an informed decision.

So what we've said to the company is, we're happy to review future permits. And today we're making this new pipeline from Cushing to the Gulf a priority. So the southern leg of it we're making a priority, and we're going to go ahead and get that done. The northern portion of it we're going to have to review properly to make sure that the health and safety of the American people are protected. That's common sense.

But the fact is that my administration has approved dozens of new oil and gas pipelines over the last 3 years, including one from Canada. And as long as I'm President, we're going to keep on encouraging oil development and infrastructure, and we're going to do it in a way that protects the health and safety of the American people. We don't have to choose between one or the other. We can do both.

So I just—if you guys are talking to your friends, your neighbors, your coworkers, your aunts, or your uncles and they're wondering what's going on in terms of oil production, you just tell them anybody who suggests that somehow we're suppressing domestic oil production isn't paying attention. They are not paying attention.

What you also need to tell them is anybody who says that just drilling more gas and more oil by itself will bring down gas prices tomorrow or the next day or even next year, they're also not paying attention. They're not playing it straight. Because we are drilling more, we are producing more. But the fact is, producing more oil at home isn't enough by itself to bring gas prices down.

And the reason is we've got an oil market that is global, that is worldwide. And I've been saying for the last few weeks, and I want everybody to understand this, we use 20 percent of the world's oil; we only produce 2 percent of the world's oil. Even if we opened up every inch of the country, if I put a[n] oil rig on the South Lawn—if we had one right next to the Washington Monument, even if we drilled every little bit of this great country of ours, we'd still have to buy the rest of our needs from someplace else if we keep on using the same amount of energy, the same amount of oil.

The price of oil will still be set by the global market. And that means every time there's tensions that rise in the Middle East, which is what's happening right now, so will the price of gas. The main reason the gas prices are high right now is because people are worried about what's happening with Iran. It doesn't have to do with domestic oil production. It has to do with the oil markets looking and saying, you know what, if something happens, there could be trouble, and so we're going to price oil higher just in case.

Now, that's not the future that we want. We don't want to be vulnerable to something that's happening on the other side of the world somehow affecting our economy or hurting a lot of folks who have to drive to get to work. That's not the future I want for America. That's not the future I want for our kids. I want us to control our own energy destiny. I want us to determine our own course.

So yes, we're going to keep on drilling. Yes, we're going to keep on emphasizing production. Yes, we're going to make sure that we can get oil to where it's needed. But what we're also going to be doing as part of an all-above—all-of-the-above strategy is looking at how we can continually improve the utilization of renewable energy sources, new clean energy sources, and how do we become more efficient in our use of energy.

That means producing more biofuels, which can be great for our farmers and great for rural economies. It means more fuel-efficient cars. It means more solar power. It means more wind power, which, by the way, nearly tripled here in Oklahoma over the past 3 years, in part because of some of our policies.

We want every source of American-made energy. I don't want the energy jobs of tomorrow going to other countries. I want them here in the United States of America. And that's what an all-of-the-above energy strategy is all about. That's how we break our dependence on foreign oil.

Now, the good news is we're already seeing progress. Yesterday I went, in Nevada, to the largest solar plant of its kind anywhere in the country. Hundreds of workers built it. It's powering thousands of homes, and they're expanding to tens of thousands of homes more as they put more capacity online.

After 30 years of not doing anything, we've finally increased fuel efficiency standards on cars and trucks, and Americans are now designing and building cars that will go nearly twice as far on the same gallon of gas by the middle of the next decade. And that's going to save the average family $8,000 over the life of a car. And it's going to save a lot of companies a lot of money, because they're hurt by rising fuel costs as well.

All of these steps have helped put America on the path to greater energy independence. Since I took office, our dependence on foreign oil has gone down every single year. Last year, we imported 1 million fewer barrels per day than the year before. Think about that. America, at a time when we're growing, is actually importing less oil from overseas because we're using it smarter and more efficiently. America is now importing less than half the oil we use for the first time in more than a decade.

So the key is to keep it going, Oklahoma. We've got to make sure that we don't go backwards, that we keep going forwards. If we're going to end our dependence on foreign oil, if we're going to bring gas prices down once and for all, as opposed to just playing politics with it every single year, then what we're going to have to do is to develop every single source of energy that we've got, every new technology that can help us become more efficient.

We've got to use our innovation. We've got to use our brain power. We've got to use our creativity. We've got to have a vision for the future, not just constantly looking backwards at the past. That's where we need to go. That's the future we can build.

And that's what America has always been about, is building the future. We've always been at the cutting edge. We're always ahead of the curve. Whether it's Thomas Edison or the Wright Brothers or Steve Jobs, we're always thinking about what's the next thing. And that's how we have to think about energy. And if we do, not only are we going to see jobs and growth and success here in Cushing, Oklahoma, we're going to see it all across the country.

All right? Thank you very much, everybody. God bless you. God bless the United States of America.

SOURCE: Executive Office of the President. "Remarks at the TransCanada Pipe Storage Yard in Stillwater, Oklahoma." March 22, 2012. *Compilation of Presidential Documents* 2012, no. 00204 (March 22, 2012). http://www.gpo.gov/fdsys/pkg/DCPD-201200204/pdf/DCPD-201200204.pdf.

OTHER HISTORIC DOCUMENTS OF INTEREST

FROM THIS VOLUME

FROM PREVIOUS *HISTORIC DOCUMENTS*

Congressional Response to Internet Piracy Protests

JANUARY 20, 2012

For years, congressional Republicans and Democrats tried to take action to curb online piracy, which is thought to cost copyright owners and producers billions of dollars each year. There is general agreement between the two parties that something must be done to stop foreign copyright infringement and some consensus on how to do so. In 2011, the House and Senate introduced separate bills aimed at stopping foreign copyright infringement and the piracy of copyrighted works. Both bills gained support from Hollywood movie studios, recording labels, and pharmaceutical companies that lose profit to counterfeit Internet drug sales, but the larger force in the fight turned out to be Internet giants like Google and Wikipedia, which garnered support with online protests that suspended consideration of both bills.

House and Senate Bills

Both the Stop Online Piracy Act (SOPA), introduced in the House of Representatives in late October 2011 by House Judiciary Committee Chairman Rep. Lamar Smith, R-Texas, and the Protect Intellectual Property (IP) Act (PIPA), introduced in the Senate on May 12, 2011, by Sen. Patrick Leahy, D-Vt., proposed relatively similar actions to combat foreign copyright infringement and online piracy.

Both SOPA and PIPA would have given law enforcement entities greater power to combat online piracy and foreign copyright infringement by shutting down foreign websites and services that pirate content from U.S. firms or offer counterfeited content. In addition, anyone who streams copyrighted works without permission could be punished with five years in prison for a first offense, considered to be illegally downloading ten pieces of music or movies over a six-month period.

The bills also took aim at websites that link to, or otherwise interact with, the websites of suspected infringers. A copyright holder could request that a payment processor or advertising network stop supporting one of these sites. If the site does not comply, the copyright holder could seek a court order to take action. But should a copyright holder obtain a court order against a site through a false claim, that copyright holder is liable for damages. As originally written, SOPA and PIPA would require Internet service providers (ISPs) to block access—once requested to do so by the Department of Justice—to sites infringing on copyrights. Domain registrars would be required to take reasonable action to shut down a website suspected of infringement.

In reality, neither bill had much power to shut down foreign websites, only to block access to them. The larger issue, according to those in Congress who support the bill, is stopping money flowing from credit card processors or advertising networks to these sites.

To encourage this, Sens. Darrell Issa, R-Calif., and Ron Wyden, D-Ore., proposed an alternative bill that would give the International Trade Commission the responsibility for stopping money and ads from going to sites that violate copyright laws and pirate music, movies, and other copyrighted products. The Online Protection and Enforcement of Digital Trade Act (OPEN Act) would not allow the Justice Department to seek court orders to stop ISPs from linking to such sites, as SOPA and PIPA do, but would instead stop fund transfers to offshore websites accused of piracy. The OPEN Act was meant to address critics who thought the House and Senate bills allowed too much policing of the Internet.

Content Producers Back the Bill

Support for the two bills came mainly from content producers and providers, including music recording labels, pharmaceutical companies, the electronic and automotive industries—the latter of which is concerned with the buying and selling of counterfeit parts that would hinder a car's performance—the Better Business Bureau, law enforcement agencies, the National Consumers League, some state attorneys general, and some public employee unions. Those in support of the bills argued that online piracy kills jobs and causes billions of dollars in losses each year. Creative America, a coalition of Hollywood studios, networks, and unions and a supporter of the two bills, estimated the cost of online piracy to U.S. workers at $5.5 billion per year. The U.S. Chamber of Commerce, another supporter, estimated that movie studios, record labels, and publishing companies lose $135 billion each year to online piracy. Tighter regulation of the Internet, supporters argued, would help eliminate these losses. "Millions of American jobs hang in the balance, and our efforts to protect America's intellectual property are critical to our economy's long-term success," said Rep. John Conyers, D-Mich.

On October 26, 2011, the guilds and unions representing movie makers, teamsters, musicians, and a number of other content and service providers released a statement saying, "Without proactive measures like the STOP Online Piracy Act, rogue sites will continue to siphon away wages and benefits from members of the creative community, greatly compromising our industry's ability to foster creativity, provide opportunities, and ensure good jobs."

Opposition Likens Bills to Censorship

Web giants, such as Google, Twitter, Wikipedia, Facebook, Yahoo, Amazon, and eBay, strongly opposed both PIPA and SOPA as written. During a November 2011 hearing, Markham Erickson, the executive director of NetCoalition, the group representing these companies, called SOPA "a full-on assault against lawful U.S. Internet companies." The Business Software Alliance, made up of companies such as Microsoft, Intel, Adobe, and Apple, initially supported SOPA but pulled their support in November 2011, saying that the bill "needs work" and has "unintended consequences."

Critics of the bills alleged that, because federal law enforcement could stop search engines from linking to these suspected sites, require ISPs to block access to these sites, or make the domain registrars take the website down, these bills would have a significant impact on Internet freedom and could potentially increase cybersecurity risks. "SOPA represents the flawed proposition that censorship is an acceptable tool to protect rights owners' private interests in particular media," wrote Geoff Brigham, general counsel for the Wikimedia Foundation. NetCoalition and congressional representatives from Silicon

Valley argued that it would be difficult for websites to link to or write about sites suspected of violating the bills, which would hamper free speech. "If the *LA Times* runs an article in their online paper, and they're talking about a site that promotes piracy . . . we would have to look and say, 'Well, Google's going to have to cut off the links to the *LA Times* page because that link has a link,'" said Issa. He continued, "Once you begin to cut off links—once you become China-esque—you start a snowball effect from which there is no end." Some opponents of the two bills have also expressed concern that social media would be in jeopardy because all user-generated comments would need to be prescreened. They argue that, as written, the legislation would allow copyright holders to seek court injunctions against legitimate websites that contain user-generated content, such as YouTube, Facebook, and Twitter.

In an open letter to lawmakers in December 2011, groups including Twitter, Google, and Yahoo expressed their opinion that SOPA and PIPA were akin to Internet censorship in China and Iran. This allegation drew reaction from the White House, which has pushed those countries and others to loosen restrictions. In a January 14 blog post, the president's chief technology officials expressed the concern of the Obama administration. "Let us be clear," the authors said, "online piracy is a real problem that harms the American economy, threatens jobs for significant numbers of middle class workers and hurts some of our nation's most creative and innovative companies and entrepreneurs." The authors went on to explain that while the administration supported legislation to curb foreign piracy, it would not support anything that affects free speech, increases the cybersecurity risk, or harms online innovation. It was the hope of the Obama administration that any such legislation would instead promote "voluntary measures and best practices." The post did not threaten a presidential veto.

ONLINE PROTESTS

In response to criticism, in January 2012, Rep. Smith announced that he would remove the provision requiring ISPs to block access to sites to "further examine the issues surrounding this provision." The Senate subsequently reworked SOPA to remove a similar provision.

The redaction of that aspect of the bills was not enough for opponents, and a number of website owners chose January 18 as a day of protest. WordPress, Reddit.com, Wikipedia, and Craigslist blacked out their sites, presenting users with a screen encouraging them to contact their senators and representatives. Wikipedia's page displayed a message stating, "For over a decade, we have spent millions of hours building the largest encyclopedia in human history. Right now, the U.S. Congress is considering legislation that could fatally damage the free and open Internet. For 24 hours, to raise awareness, we are blacking out Wikipedia." Some Wikipedia editors argued that the protest was like fighting censorship with censorship and that the site was going against its promise to remain neutral and avoid advocacy. Wikipedia founder Jimmy Wales rebutted critics, saying that the site can be neutral even if the company takes a position on a public issue. "The encyclopedia will always be neutral. The community need not be, not when the encyclopedia is threatened," he said in a tweet.

Twitter, Facebook, and Google chose not to black out, although each did express opposition to the bills. Twitter CEO Dick Costolo said that while he did not want to see the bills pass, "closing a global business in reaction to single-issue national politics is foolish." In a Facebook post, founder Mark Zuckerberg said, "We can't let poorly thought out laws get in the way of the Internet's development." Google placed a black bar over its logo, and the home page featured a link to sign a petition telling Congress, "Please don't censor the Web." According to the search engine, it collected 7 million signatures. "There are smart, targeted ways to shut down foreign rogue websites without asking American companies to censor the Internet," said Google spokesperson Samantha Smith.

Supporters of SOPA and PIPA blasted websites for shutting down or otherwise protesting the bills. "This publicity stunt does a disservice to its users by promoting fear instead of facts," said Rep. Smith, noting that the bill would not harm domestic websites and social media outlets. Chris Dodd, former Connecticut senator and current chair of the Motion Picture Association of America, said the protest was an "abuse of power given the freedoms these companies enjoy in the marketplace today." He continued, "It's a dangerous and troubling development when the platforms that serve as gateways to information intentionally skew the facts to incite their users in order to further their corporate interests." Regardless, the protests had an impact. According to the spokesperson for the House Chief Administrator's Office, traffic to House member websites doubled on January 18.

ACTION SUSPENDED

Following the web protests, a number of lawmakers began withdrawing their support, including thirteen cosponsors of the House and Senate measures, who said the bills needed to be reworked before they could support them. On January 20, Senate Majority Leader Harry Reid, D-Nev., who once called the bill "too important to delay," canceled a January 24 procedural vote, stating, "There is no reason that the legitimate issues raised by many about this bill cannot be resolved" and noting that he was optimistic that a compromise would be reached. Sen. Leahy criticized the delay, arguing that those who sell counterfeit products "are smugly watching how the United States Senate decided it was not even worth debating how to stop the overseas criminals from draining our economy." Leahy said it would not be long before senators would realize that they made a mistake. In response to the Senate decision, Rep. Smith postponed consideration of SOPA in the House Judiciary Committee. Smith admitted that compromise needed to be reached but that "Congress cannot stand by and do nothing while American innovators and job creators are under attack."

—Heather Kerrigan

Following is a statement by Senate Majority Leader Harry Reid, D-Nev., postponing the vote on the Protect IP Act on January 20, 2012, and a statement by Rep. Lamar Smith, R-Texas, January 20, 2012, postponing debate on the Stop Online Piracy Act.

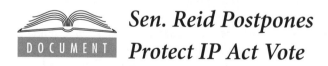

Sen. Reid Postpones
Protect IP Act Vote

January 20, 2012

Nevada Senator Harry Reid released the following statement today on the Senate's PROTECT I.P. Act:

"In light of recent events, I have decided to postpone Tuesday's vote on the PROTECT I.P. Act.

"There is no reason that the legitimate issues raised by many about this bill cannot be resolved. Counterfeiting and piracy cost the American economy billions of dollars and thousands of jobs each year, with the movie industry alone supporting over 2.2 million jobs. We must take action to stop these illegal practices. We live in a country where people rightfully expect to be fairly compensated for a day's work, whether that person is a miner in the high desert of Nevada, an independent band in New York City, or a union worker on the back lots of a California movie studio.

"I admire the work that Chairman Leahy has put into this bill. I encourage him to continue engaging with all stakeholders to forge a balance between protecting Americans' intellectual property, and maintaining openness and innovation on the internet. We made good progress through the discussions we've held in recent days, and I am optimistic that we can reach a compromise in the coming weeks."

SOURCE: Office of Senator Harry Reid. Newsroom. "Reid Statement on Intellectual Property Bill." January 20, 2012. http://www.reid.senate.gov/newsroom/pr_012012_reidstatementonintellectualpropertybill.cfm.

DOCUMENT

Rep. Smith Postpones Stop Online Piracy Act Debate

January 20, 2012

House Judiciary Committee Chairman Lamar Smith (R-Texas) today issued the following statement in response to the Senate decision to postpone consideration of legislation to help combat online piracy.

Chairman Smith: "I have heard from the critics and I take seriously their concerns regarding proposed legislation to address the problem of online piracy. It is clear that we need to revisit the approach on how best to address the problem of foreign thieves that steal and sell American inventions and products.

"The problem of online piracy is too big to ignore. American intellectual property industries provide 19 million high-paying jobs and account for more than 60 percent of U.S. exports. The theft of America's intellectual property costs the U.S. economy more than $100 billion annually and results in the loss of thousands of American jobs. Congress cannot stand by and do nothing while American innovators and job creators are under attack.

"The online theft of American intellectual property is no different than the theft of products from a store. It is illegal and the law should be enforced both in the store and online.

"The Committee will continue work with both copyright owners and Internet companies to develop proposals that combat online piracy and protect America's intellectual property. We welcome input from all organizations and individuals who have an honest difference of opinion about how best to address this widespread problem. The Committee remains committed to finding a solution to the problem of online piracy that protects American intellectual property and innovation."

The House Judiciary Committee will postpone consideration of the legislation until there is wider agreement on a solution.

SOURCE: Office of Rep. Lamar Smith. News Releases. "Statement From Chairman Smith on SOPA." January 20, 2012. http://lamarsmith.house.gov/news/documentsingle.aspx?DocumentID=275770.

OTHER HISTORIC DOCUMENTS OF INTEREST

FROM PREVIOUS HISTORIC DOCUMENTS

Supreme Court Rules on Privacy

JANUARY 23, 2012

On January 23, 2012, the U.S. Supreme Court decided *United States v. Jones,* one of its first major cases to interpret the reach of the Fourth Amendment's ban on unreasonable searches and seizures in the digital era. Given recent, rapid advances in monitoring technology, this case attracted much attention and the term *Big Brother* was evoked repeatedly in the oral arguments. At issue was alleged District of Columbia drug-kingpin Antoine Jones, who had been sentenced to life imprisonment based in large part on the evidence obtained from a global positioning system (GPS) tracking device surreptitiously placed on his vehicle and tracking its every movement for twenty-eight days. While they differed on the rationale, all the justices unanimously agreed that placing the GPS was a search and, therefore, without a valid search warrant, violated Jones's Fourth Amendment rights. The majority opinion, written by Justice Antonin Scalia, relied on very narrow grounds and ducked some of the harder questions the Court will undoubtedly face going forward, as increased sophistication of wireless electronic monitoring devices is expected to trigger a flood of privacy cases. When viewed together, however, the three opinions in this case signal that a majority of the Court is prepared to rethink and overhaul how it applies the privacy principles of the Fourth Amendment to the rapidly advancing technology of the twenty-first century.

New Technology Raises Constitutional Questions

Technological advances making it possible for the government to easily gather vast quantities of detailed and highly private information have, in recent years, been speeding on a collision course with the Constitution's privacy protections. Specifically, the Fourth Amendment to the U.S. Constitution provides that "the right of the people to be secure in their persons, houses, papers and effects against unreasonable searches and seizures, shall not be violated." Such a search can occur lawfully only after a court has found probable cause and issued a valid search warrant. New technologies that have become available to law enforcement raise questions of when something that bears no resemblance to anything imagined by the founders qualifies as a "search" and therefore triggers this constitutional protection. Judges across the country have been reaching divergent opinions on such matters as whether police need a search warrant to inspect cell phones for text messages or require cell phone providers to turn over location records.

In *United States v. Jones,* the Supreme Court was asked whether the police's attaching a GPS device on a suspect's vehicle and then tracking its movements over a prolonged period of time was a search that required first obtaining a search warrant from a court. The district court had permitted the evidence, holding the data admissible because "a person traveling in an automobile on public thoroughfares has no reasonable expectation of privacy in his movements from one place to another." The jury returned a guilty verdict, and Jones was sentenced to life imprisonment. The appellate court reversed the conviction because it held the admission of the evidence obtained by the warrantless use of the GPS device to be unconstitutional. The Supreme Court agreed to hear the government's appeal.

THE FOURTH AMENDMENT AND THE GPS: THREE OPINIONS

Justice Scalia, writing the majority opinion, joined by Chief Justice John Roberts Jr. and Justices Anthony Kennedy, Clarence Thomas, and Sonia Sotomayor, ruled that the placement of the GPS constituted a search. They resolved this case by looking to the roots of the Fourth Amendment in the eighteenth-century common law of trespass. At its most basic level, this was a case, according to the majority, where "the Government physically occupied private property for the purpose of obtaining information." Justice Scalia wrote that he had "no doubt that such a physical intrusion would have been considered a 'search' within the meaning of the Fourth Amendment when it was adopted." The violation, according to this opinion, was with the placement of the device on the vehicle, which was private property.

Justice Samuel Alito, while agreeing with the result in this case, wrote a separate concurring opinion faulting the majority for deciding a case rooted in twenty-first-century technology "based on 18th-century tort law." Among other problems with this approach, Justice Alito wrote, it would "present particularly vexing problems in cases involving surveillance that is carried out by making electronic, as opposed to physical, contact with the item to be tracked." He proposed instead analyzing the case under a standard first enunciated in the 1967 case *Katz v. United States*. In the *Katz* case, the Court rejected the warrantless attachment of a wiretap to a public phone booth, finding that a violation occurs when government officers violate a person's "reasonable expectation of privacy." Justice Alito wrote that he would analyze the current case by "asking whether respondent's reasonable expectations of privacy were violated by the long-term monitoring of the movements of the vehicle he drove."

Alito's concurrence, joined by Justices Ruth Bader Ginsburg, Stephen Breyer, and Elena Kagan, argued that the lengthy monitoring that occurred in this case did intrude on a contemporary reasonable expectation of privacy, but he indicated that this is not an easy analysis in all cases. The relationship between advancing technology and people's privacy expectations can be circular such that "dramatic technological change may lead to periods in which popular expectations are in flux and may ultimately produce significant changes in popular attitudes."

Justice Alito discussed the emergence of new devices that all impact our privacy, including ubiquitous closed-circuit television video monitoring and EasyPass automatic toll collection systems that create a record of a motorist's movements. Most important on this list, he said, were the more than 322 million cell phones and other wireless devices now in use in the United States, which permit wireless carriers to track and record the location of their users. The convenience and availability of devices like these and other new devices will "shape the average person's expectations about the privacy of his or her daily movements."

Justice Scalia, in the majority opinion, did not shut the door on the "reasonable expectation of privacy" analysis for which Justice Alito advocated in his concurrence, but he felt "no reason for rushing forward" to resolve issues that weren't necessary for resolving this case. "It may be," he wrote, "that achieving the same result through electronic means, without an accompanying trespass, is an unconstitutional invasion of privacy." But, he found, "the present case does not require us to answer that question."

Although she joined in the majority opinion, Justice Sotomayor also wrote a separate concurring opinion. She agreed with the majority that the government's trespass on Antoine Jones's vehicle without a valid warrant violated long-recognized Fourth Amendment rights. "When the Government physically invades personal property to gather information," she wrote, "a search occurs. The reaffirmation of that principle suffices to decide this case." But she felt the need to write separately to make clear that the Fourth Amendment is concerned with much more than trespass and applies when the "government violates a subjective expectation of privacy that society recognizes as reasonable." This will become particularly important going forward, she noted, as "physical intrusion is now unnecessary to many forms of surveillance." The majority opinion, rooted as it is in physical trespass, would provide little guidance if the police wanted to get the same information but, rather than rely on the physical placement of a GPS, instead enlisted the factory- or owner-installed vehicle tracking devices or GPS-enabled smartphones.

Justice Sotomayor added that future cases will require reconsidering the "3rd party doctrine," which holds that an individual has no reasonable expectation of privacy in information that is voluntarily disclosed to third parties. She noted that "people disclose the phone numbers that they dial or text to their cellular providers; the URLs that they visit and the e-mail addresses with which they correspond to their Internet service providers; and the books, groceries and medications they purchase to online retailers." Despite these voluntary disclosures, she wrote, "I for one, doubt that people would accept without complaint the warrantless disclosure to the government of a list of every Web site they had visited in the last week, or month, or year."

Together, the five justices who signed onto the two concurring opinions in this case have signaled that a dramatic revision of our Fourth Amendment understanding may be necessary to protect privacy going forward, as the courts will inevitably have to rule on cases involving an invasion of privacy that does not require any physical trespass.

IMPACT OF *UNITED STATES V. JONES*

In the wake of the *Jones* ruling, the Federal Bureau of Investigation (FBI) reported that it pulled the plug on 3,000 GPS-tracking devices that had been in active use without a search warrant, primarily in major narcotics investigations. In its place, Wired.com reported that the government has turned to relying even more on warrantless mobile phone GPS tracking. The courts that have evaluated this kind of tracking have come to split decisions over whether people have a reasonable expectation of privacy in data that mobile phone companies possess that can detail the location of a cell phone. Prosecutors argue that such records are not protected because they are in the possession of a third party, the mobile phone company. Cell phone companies testified before Congress that, in 2011, they responded to 1.3 million demands from law enforcement agencies for information about subscribers.

It is clear that many very difficult decisions lie ahead for the Supreme Court and, in his concurring opinion, Justice Alito suggested that the courts might be the wrong forum to resolve these issues. The best solution, he wrote, may instead be legislative. Legislatures, he reasoned, are better able to "gauge changing public attitudes, to draw detailed lines, and to balance privacy and public safety in a comprehensive way." After the Supreme Court first faced issues regarding the privacy concerns raised by wiretapping in the 1960s, Congress enacted a comprehensive statute, regulating the complex subject. Since that time, the regulation of wiretapping has been governed primarily by statutes created by legislatures and not case law created by judges. While the Supreme Court has now made it clear that a warrant is needed for planting a GPS tracker, only a few states such as Delaware, Maryland, and Oklahoma have proposed legislation that would require police to get a warrant before demanding location records from cell phone carriers. There is, as yet, no clear federal statute to govern location records, and in the absence of such legislation, the courts are coming to contradictory decisions, setting the issue up for the Supreme Court in the near future.

—Melissa Feinberg

Following is the edited text of the U.S. Supreme Court's decision in United States v. Jones, *in which the Court ruled unanimously on January 23, 2012, that attaching a GPS device to someone's car and using that device to track the movement of that person constitutes a search under the Fourth Amendment of the Constitution.*

DOCUMENT   *United States v. Antoine Jones*

January 23, 2012

No. 10–1259

United States, Petitioner		On writ of certiorari
v.	⎱	to the United States Court of Appeals for the District of Columbia Circuit
Antoine Jones		

[January 23, 2012]

[Footnotes and stand-alone references have been omitted.]

JUSTICE SCALIA delivered the opinion of the Court.

We decide whether the attachment of a Global Positioning System (GPS) tracking device to an individual's vehicle, and subsequent use of that device to monitor the vehicle's movements on public streets, constitutes a search or seizure within the meaning of the Fourth Amendment.

[Section I, containing background on the case of Antoine Jones, has been omitted.]

II

A

The Fourth Amendment provides in relevant part that "[t]he right of the people to be secure in their persons, houses, papers, and effects, against unreasonable searches and seizures, shall not be violated." It is beyond dispute that a vehicle is an "effect" as that term is used in the Amendment. We hold that the Government's installation of a GPS device on a target's vehicle, [*footnote omitted*], and its use of that device to monitor the vehicle's movements, constitutes a "search."

It is important to be clear about what occurred in this case: The Government physically occupied private property for the purpose of obtaining information. We have no doubt that such a physical intrusion would have been considered a "search" within the meaning of the Fourth Amendment when it was adopted. *Entick* v. *Carrington,* 95 Eng. Rep. 807 (C. P. 1765), is a "case we have described as a 'monument of English freedom' 'undoubtedly familiar' to 'every American statesman' at the time the Constitution was adopted, and considered to be 'the true and ultimate expression of constitutional law'" with regard to search and seizure. In that case, Lord Camden expressed in plain terms the significance of property rights in search-and seizure analysis:

> "[O]ur law holds the property of every man so sacred, that no man can set his foot upon his neighbour's close without his leave; if he does he is a trespasser, though he does no damage at all; if he will tread upon his neighbour's ground, he must justify it by law." *Entick, supra,* at 817.

The text of the Fourth Amendment reflects its close connection to property, since otherwise it would have referred simply to "the right of the people to be secure against unreasonable searches and seizures"; the phrase "in their persons, houses, papers, and effects" would have been superfluous.

Consistent with this understanding, our Fourth Amendment jurisprudence was tied to common-law trespass, at least until the latter half of the 20th century. Thus, in *Olmstead* v. *United States,* 277 U. S. 438 (1928), we held that wiretaps attached to telephone wires on the public streets did not constitute a Fourth Amendment search because "[t]here was no entry of the houses or offices of the defendants," *id.,* at 464.

Our later cases, of course, have deviated from that exclusively property-based approach. In *Katz* v. *United States,* 389 U. S. 347, 351 (1967), we said that "the Fourth Amendment protects people, not places," and found a violation in attachment of an eavesdropping device to a public telephone booth. Our later cases have applied the analysis of Justice Harlan's concurrence in that case, which said that a violation occurs when government officers violate a person's "reasonable expectation of privacy."

. . . At bottom, we must "assur[e] preservation of that degree of privacy against government that existed when the Fourth Amendment was adopted." As explained, for most of our history the Fourth Amendment was understood to embody a particular concern for government trespass upon the areas ("persons, houses, papers, and effects") it enumerates. *Katz* did not repudiate that understanding. Less than two years later the Court upheld defendants' contention that the Government could not introduce against them conversations between *other* people obtained by warrantless placement of electronic surveillance devices in their homes. The opinion rejected the dissent's contention that there was no Fourth Amendment violation "unless the conversational privacy of the homeowner himself is invaded." "[W]e [do not] believe that *Katz,* by holding that the Fourth Amendment protects persons and their private conversations, was intended to withdraw any of the protection which the Amendment extends to the home. . . ."

[Further discussion of past cases related to the Fourth Amendment has been omitted.]

B

The concurrence begins by accusing us of applying "18th-century tort law." That is a distortion. What we apply is an 18th-century guarantee against unreasonable searches, which we believe must provide *at a minimum* the degree of protection it afforded when it was adopted. The concurrence does not share that belief. It would apply *exclusively Katz*'s reasonable-expectation-of-privacy test, even when that eliminates rights that previously existed.

The concurrence faults our approach for "present[ing] particularly vexing problems" in cases that do not involve physical contact, such as those that involve the transmission of electronic signals. We entirely fail to understand that point. For unlike the concurrence, which would make *Katz* the *exclusive* test, we do not make trespass the exclusive test. Situations involving merely the transmission of electronic signals without trespass would *remain* subject to *Katz* analysis.

In fact, it is the concurrence's insistence on the exclusivity of the *Katz* test that needlessly leads us into "particularly vexing problems" in the present case. This Court has to date not deviated from the understanding that mere visual observation does not constitute a search. We accordingly held in *Knotts* that "[a] person traveling in an automobile on public thoroughfares has no reasonable expectation of privacy in his movements from one place to another." 460 U. S., at 281. Thus, even assuming that the concurrence is correct to say that "[t]raditional surveillance" of Jones for a 4-week period "would have required a large team of agents, multiple vehicles, and perhaps aerial assistance," our cases suggest that such visual observation is constitutionally permissible. It may be that achieving the same result through electronic means, without an accompanying trespass, is an unconstitutional invasion of privacy, but the present case does not require us to answer that question.

[The remainder of the opinion has been omitted.]

* * *

The judgment of the Court of Appeals for the D. C. Circuit is affirmed.

It is so ordered.

JUSTICE SOTOMAYOR, concurring.

I join the Court's opinion because I agree that a search within the meaning of the Fourth Amendment occurs, at a minimum, "[w]here, as here, the Government obtains information by physically intruding on a constitutionally protected area." . . .

Nonetheless, as JUSTICE ALITO notes, physical intrusion is now unnecessary to many forms of surveillance. With increasing regularity, the Government will be capable of duplicating the monitoring undertaken in this case by enlisting factory- or owner-installed vehicle tracking devices or GPS-enabled smartphones. In cases of electronic or other novel modes of surveillance that do not depend upon a physical invasion on property, the majority opinion's trespassory test may provide little guidance. But "[s]ituations involving merely the transmission of electronic signals without trespass would *remain* subject to *Katz* analysis." As JUSTICE ALITO incisively observes, the same technological advances that have made possible nontrespassory surveillance techniques will also affect the *Katz* test by shaping the evolution of societal privacy expectations. *Post*, at 10–11. Under that rubric, I agree with JUSTICE ALITO that, at the very least, "longer term GPS monitoring in investigations of most offenses impinges on expectations of privacy."

In cases involving even short-term monitoring, some unique attributes of GPS surveillance relevant to the *Katz* analysis will require particular attention. GPS monitoring generates a precise, comprehensive record of a person's public movements that reflects a wealth of detail about her familial, political, professional, religious, and sexual associations. See, *e.g., People* v. *Weaver,* 12 N. Y. 3d 433, 441–442, 909 N. E. 2d 1195, 1199 (2009) ("Disclosed in [GPS] data . . . will be trips the indisputably private nature of which takes little imagination to conjure: trips to the psychiatrist, the plastic surgeon, the abortion clinic, the AIDS treatment center, the strip club, the criminal defense attorney, the by-the-hour motel, the union meeting, the mosque, synagogue or church, the gay bar and on and on"). The Government can store such records and efficiently mine them for information years into the future. And because GPS monitoring is cheap in comparison to conventional surveillance techniques and, by design, proceeds surreptitiously, it evades the ordinary checks that constrain abusive law enforcement practices: "limited police resources and community hostility."

Awareness that the Government may be watching chills associational and expressive freedoms. And the Government's unrestrained power to assemble data that reveal private aspects of identity is susceptible to abuse. The net result is that GPS monitoring—by making available at a relatively low cost such a substantial quantum of intimate information about any person whom the Government, in its unfettered discretion, chooses to track— may "alter the relationship between citizen and government in a way that is inimical to democratic society."

I would take these attributes of GPS monitoring into account when considering the existence of a reasonable societal expectation of privacy in the sum of one's public movements. I would ask whether people reasonably expect that their movements will be recorded and aggregated in a manner that enables the Government to ascertain, more or less at will, their political and religious beliefs, sexual habits, and so on. I do not regard as dispositive the fact that the Government might obtain the fruits of GPS monitoring through lawful conventional surveillance techniques. I would also consider the appropriateness of entrusting to the Executive, in the absence of any oversight from a coordinate branch, a tool so amenable to misuse, especially in light of the Fourth Amendment's goal to curb arbitrary exercises of police power to and prevent "a too permeating police surveillance," *United States* v. *Di Re,* 332 U. S. 581, 595 (1948).

More fundamentally, it may be necessary to reconsider the premise that an individual has no reasonable expectation of privacy in information voluntarily disclosed to third parties. This approach is ill suited to the digital age, in which people reveal a great deal of information about themselves to third parties in the course of carrying out mundane tasks. People disclose the phone numbers that they dial or text to their cellular providers; the URLs that they visit and the e-mail addresses with which they correspond to their Internet service providers; and the books, groceries, and medications they purchase to online retailers. Perhaps, as JUSTICE ALITO notes, some people may find the "tradeoff" of privacy for convenience "worthwhile," or come to accept this "diminution of privacy" as "inevitable," and perhaps not. I for one doubt that people would accept without complaint the warrantless disclosure to the Government of a list of every Web site they had visited in the last week, or month, or year. But whatever the societal expectations, they can attain constitutionally protected status only if our Fourth Amendment jurisprudence ceases to treat secrecy as a prerequisite for privacy. I would not assume that all information voluntarily disclosed to some member of the public for a limited purpose is, for that reason alone, disentitled to Fourth Amendment protection.

Resolution of these difficult questions in this case is unnecessary, however, because the Government's physical intrusion on Jones' Jeep supplies a narrower basis for decision. I therefore join the majority's opinion.

JUSTICE ALITO, with whom JUSTICE GINSBURG, JUSTICE BREYER, and JUSTICE KAGAN join, concurring in the judgment.

This case requires us to apply the Fourth Amendment's prohibition of unreasonable searches and seizures to a 21st-century surveillance technique, the use of a Global Positioning System (GPS) device to monitor a vehicle's movements for an extended period of time. Ironically, the Court has chosen to decide this case based on 18th-century tort law. . . .

I would analyze the question presented in this case by asking whether respondent's reasonable expectations of privacy were violated by the long-term monitoring of the movements of the vehicle he drove.

[Sections I–IVA have been omitted and contain information on the Court's decision and past related cases.]

IV

B

Recent years have seen the emergence of many new devices that permit the monitoring of a person's movements. In some locales, closed-circuit television video monitoring is becoming ubiquitous. On toll roads, automatic toll collection systems create a precise record of the movements of motorists who choose to make use of that convenience. Many motorists purchase cars that are equipped with devices that permit a central station to ascertain the car's location at any time so that roadside assistance may be provided if needed and the car may be found if it is stolen.

Perhaps most significant, cell phones and other wireless devices now permit wireless carriers to track and record the location of users—and as of June 2011, it has been reported, there were more than 322 million wireless devices in use in the United States. For older phones, the accuracy of the location information depends on the density of the tower network, but new "smart phones," which are equipped with a GPS device, permit more precise tracking. For example, when a user activates the GPS on such a phone, a provider is able to monitor the phone's location and speed of movement and can then report back real-time traffic conditions after combining ("crowd sourcing") the speed of all such phones on any particular road. Similarly, phone-location-tracking services are offered as "social" tools, allowing consumers to find (or to avoid) others who enroll in these services. The availability and use of these and other new devices will continue to shape the average person's expectations about the privacy of his or her daily movements.

V

In the pre-computer age, the greatest protections of privacy were neither constitutional nor statutory, but practical. Traditional surveillance for any extended period of time was difficult and costly and therefore rarely undertaken. The surveillance at issue in this case—constant monitoring of the location of a vehicle for four weeks—would have required a large team of agents, multiple vehicles, and perhaps aerial assistance. Only an investigation of unusual importance could have justified such an expenditure of law enforcement resources. Devices like the one used in the present case, however, make long-term monitoring relatively easy and cheap. In circumstances involving dramatic technological change, the best solution to privacy concerns may be legislative. A legislative body is well situated to gauge changing public attitudes, to draw detailed lines, and to balance privacy and public safety in a comprehensive way.

To date, however, Congress and most States have not enacted statutes regulating the use of GPS tracking technology for law enforcement purposes. The best that we can do in this case is to apply existing Fourth Amendment doctrine and to ask whether the use of GPS tracking in a particular case involved a degree of intrusion that a reasonable person would not have anticipated.

Under this approach, relatively short-term monitoring of a person's movements on public streets accords with expectations of privacy that our society has recognized as reasonable. But the use of longer term GPS monitoring in investigations of most offenses impinges on expectations of privacy. For such offenses, society's expectation has been that law enforcement agents and others would not—and indeed, in the main, simply could not—secretly monitor and catalogue every single movement of an individual's car for a very long period. In this case, for four weeks, law enforcement agents tracked every movement that respondent made in the vehicle he was driving. We need not identify with precision the point at which the tracking of this vehicle became a search, for the line was surely crossed before the 4-week mark. Other cases may present more difficult questions. But where uncertainty exists with respect to whether a certain period of GPS surveillance is long enough to constitute a Fourth Amendment search, the police may always seek a warrant. We also need not consider whether prolonged GPS monitoring in the context of investigations involving extraordinary offenses would similarly intrude on a constitutionally protected sphere of privacy. In such cases, long-term tracking might have been mounted using previously available techniques.

* * *

For these reasons, I conclude that the lengthy monitoring that occurred in this case constituted a search under the Fourth Amendment. I therefore agree with the majority that the decision of the Court of Appeals must be affirmed.

SOURCE: U.S. Supreme Court. *United States v. Antoine Jones,* 565 U.S. __ (2012). http://www.supreme court.gov/opinions/11pdf/10–1259.pdf.

OTHER HISTORIC DOCUMENTS OF INTEREST

FROM PREVIOUS *HISTORIC DOCUMENTS*

Europe, Israel Respond to Rising Tensions With Iran

JANUARY 23 AND SEPTEMBER 27, 2012

Tensions between Iran and Israel over Iran's nuclear program continued to escalate in 2012, fueled in part by accusations that each country was involved in violent plots to undermine the other. Iran alleged that Israel was responsible for the assassination of a nuclear scientist, while Israel claimed Iran was behind a series of bombings targeting Israelis. Meanwhile, the European Union and the United States imposed new sanctions on Iran, seeking to impede the country's economy and, by extension, its nuclear program, by restricting oil and other exports.

ISRAEL-IRAN RELATIONS

The hostility between Israel and Iran has its beginnings in the Islamic Revolution of 1979, when Ayatollah Ruhollah Khomeini overthrew Iran's sitting shah. Khomeini called Israel an "enemy of Islam" and later severed all diplomatic and commercial ties to the country. For its part, Israel considers Iran to be a dangerous adversary, primarily because of its suspected nuclear program, possession of missiles capable of hitting Israeli targets, and its support for Palestinian militant groups.

Their relationship became more strained when Mahmoud Ahmadinejad, who has denied the Holocaust occurred and called for Israel to be "wiped off the map," was elected as Iran's president in 2005. Then, in 2009, Benjamin Netanyahu became Israel's prime minister. After taking office, Netanyahu claimed, "Iran is seeking to obtain a nuclear weapon and constitutes the gravest threat to our existence since the war of independence" and said stopping the Iranian threat was his top priority. Since then, Netanyahu has raised the possibility of taking unilateral military action against Iran if Western countries— namely, the United States—do not move first. Meanwhile, the two countries have engaged in what some U.S. intelligence officials describe as a "shadow war" against each other.

A RASH OF BOMBINGS

On January 11, 2012, Iranian nuclear scientist Mostafa Ahmadi Roshan was killed in Tehran when a magnetic bomb that had been attached to his car detonated. Roshan was a deputy director for commercial affairs at Iran's Natanz uranium enrichment facility. Just two days before, the International Atomic Energy Agency (IAEA) announced that Iran was enriching uranium to 20 percent purity. Iran has long claimed that its nuclear program is intended for peaceful purposes, primarily to generate electricity for its citizens, but 20 percent purity is beyond the level needed for civilian uses.

The bombing followed the pattern of four previous attacks against Iranian scientists since 2010. Iranian officials immediately blamed U.S. intelligence agencies and Israel for the attack and suggested the country's Islamic Revolutionary Guards Corps may conduct revenge assassinations. "The bomb used in the explosion was a magnetic bomb, the same kind that were used in previous assassinations of Iranian scientists. And the fact is that this is the work of the Zionists," said Tehran Deputy Governor Safarali Baratloo. Israeli officials did not comment on their alleged role in the incidents, but U.S. Secretary of State Hillary Rodham Clinton categorically denied "any United States involvement in any kind of act of violence inside Iran."

U.S. intelligence officials later confirmed that the attacks were carried out by the People's Mujahedin of Iran (MEK), an Iranian dissident group that the United States has designated as a terrorist organization and accused of killing American servicemen and contractors in the 1970s. Importantly, officials also stated that Mossad, Israel's secret service, had financed, trained, and armed the MEK for the attacks.

Shortly thereafter, Israel blamed Iran for a series of incidents that began in late January, when three Azerbaijani nationals were intercepted before they could attack Israeli Ambassador Michael Lotem, a rabbi, and his wife at the Chabad center in Baku. Then in February, Israeli officials blamed Iran for an attack against Israeli Embassy personnel in New Delhi, India, which involved a sticky bomb placed on an embassy vehicle. Four people were injured in the February 13 bombing, including an Israeli diplomat's wife. The same day, a similar bomb was found on an Israeli car in Tbilisi, Georgia, but the device was defused. The attacks escalated further in July, when a suicide bomber killed five Israelis who were traveling on a tour bus in Burgas, Bulgaria. Israel claimed Hezbollah, a Lebanese militia backed by Iran, was responsible.

New Sanctions

As tensions rose between Israel and Iran, the broader international community took new steps to further isolate Iran's economy and pressure officials into a diplomatic wind down of the country's nuclear program.

On January 23, the European Union (EU) approved a round of new sanctions against Iran, which included an embargo on Iranian oil. The embargo was set to go into effect on July 1 to allow countries some time to make alternate import arrangements, and EU officials said they would provide special exemptions to ease the embargo's impact on certain countries. Since European countries purchase approximately 20 percent of Iranian oil, officials hoped the embargo would force Iran to sell its oil to other customers at steep discounts, thereby reducing the government's income.

The new sanctions also included restrictions on exports of gold, technology, and "sensitive dual-use goods"; a ban on dealing with the Central Bank of Iran; measures intended to prevent investment in Iran's oil and gas sector; and a ban on using Iranian insurance. The latter included a ban on Iranian ship insurance, which later resulted in a decision by major supertanker companies to stop loading Iranian cargo. The European Union also named an additional 180 individuals and entities, including some owned by the Islamic Revolutionary Guards Corps that were linked directly to Iran's nuclear program.

The EU's action was motivated in part by a November 2011 IAEA report that laid out the agency's concerns that there were military dimensions to Iran's nuclear activities. While the report did not provide evidence of a fully constructed nuclear weapon, it cited activities such as high-explosives testing and the development of atomic bomb triggers as indicators of possible ongoing weapons research. Iran raised additional concerns when it announced in early January 2012 that it was on the verge of beginning production at its second major uranium enrichment site, the Fordo facility.

Some critics warned the new sanctions would backfire on Europe, arguing that it could cause oil prices to rise even higher as supply shrank and could further weaken an already fragile global economy. Others suggested Iran would simply find new customers to replace Europe's purchases, causing only a temporary disruption. Notably, the value of the rial, Iran's currency, immediately fell by 10 percent following the embargo announcement. The same day the sanctions were approved, Iranian officials responded by threatening to close the Strait of Hormuz, a critical waterway through which roughly 20 percent of the world's oil supply is transported, and warned the United States against attempts to break such a blockade. "If any disruption happens regarding the sale of Iranian oil, the Strait of Hormuz will definitely be closed," Mohammad Kossari, deputy head of the Iranian Parliament's foreign affairs and national security committee, told Fars News Agency. "If America seeks adventures after the closure of the Strait of Hormuz, Iran will make the world unsafe for Americans in the shortest possible time."

The United States, which praised the European Union for its oil embargo, soon imposed its own new sanctions, moving in February to freeze all U.S. property owned by the Central Bank of Iran, other Iranian financial institutions, and the Iranian government. Then, on March 17, the Society for Worldwide Interbank Financial Telecommunications (SWIFT), a Belgium-based consortium critical to the global banking industry, agreed to disconnect Iranian banks that were not operating in accordance with EU sanctions from its services. The move, an effort to ensure SWIFT was in full compliance with EU law, denied Iranian institutions their ability to receive revenue from banks abroad. On June 28, measures approved by the U.S. Congress in December 2011 that were intended to punish foreign countries for buying Iranian oil went into effect. Congress approved yet another round of sanctions on Iran's energy, shipping, and financial industries on August 1 in an effort to close loopholes that made it possible for some companies to circumvent international sanctions.

Signs that the various sanctions were having an impact on Iran began showing in February. Iran engaged China in discussions about finding an alternative to dollars as payment for Chinese purchases of crude oil, given the weakness of the rial. Reports surfaced that Malaysian palm oil exporters stopped shipments to Iran, that Ukrainian wheat exporters cut shipments in half due to payment issues, and that Iran had not been able to pay for rice imported from India. Western medicines also became more difficult to obtain due to U.S. Treasury Department rules, requiring vendors of medicines and medical equipment to obtain a special license before selling merchandise in Iran. By the summer, European purchases of Iranian oil had already been reduced by half from the previous year, and China had negotiated significant discounts on its oil purchases. In July, Kenyan officials announced they had canceled plans to import Iranian oil, fearing repercussions from the U.S. sanctions. Angola, Iraq, Libya, and Saudi Arabia had all begun increasing their oil production, helping to compensate for lost Iranian oil.

Netanyahu Calls for a "Red Line"

In late September, Netanyahu, Ahmadinejad, and U.S. President Barack Obama were all scheduled to speak at a meeting of the United Nations General Assembly. In an unusual move, the White House said Obama would not meet with Netanyahu while the prime minister was in the United States, citing scheduling conflicts. Though the two later spoke by phone, some claimed the president was snubbing Netanyahu, causing speculation that the prime minister's intensifying pressure on the United States to consider military action against Iran had motivated the decision. The announcement followed Netanyahu's declaration that "those in the international community who refuse to put red lines before Iran don't have a moral right to place a red light before Israel." Netanyahu had increasingly called for the United States to set a "red line" on Iran's nuclear program, such as a cap on the level and amount of enriched uranium Iran would be permitted to stockpile. If the program progressed beyond that line, the United States would take military action.

Netanyahu continued to argue the need for such a red line in his speech to the General Assembly on September 27, claiming that "nothing could imperil the world more than the arming of Iran with nuclear weapons" and that assuming a nuclear-armed Iran could be deterred was dangerous. He warned that Iran's uranium enrichment capabilities must be stopped by the spring or early summer of 2013, the point at which the country would allegedly have enough material to produce a nuclear bomb. He also noted that the goal of preventing a nuclear-armed Iran had unified the United States and Israel as well as other nations, and he cited Obama's speech from two days before in which he said a "nuclear-armed Iran is not a challenge that can be contained." Ahmadinejad did not reference Iran's nuclear program during his speech but complained that "an arms race and intimidation by nuclear weapons and weapons of mass destruction by the hegemonic powers have become prevalent" and that Iran was now under threat.

Domestic Turmoil and a Chance for Talks

In the week following the General Assembly meeting, the rial fell in value by another 40 percent, feeding fears of a severe inflationary spiral in Iran and prompting many Iranians to sell their rials for dollars. That same week, Iran's labor minister received a petition signed by 10,000 Iranian workers complaining about the decline in their purchasing power and other economic issues. On October 3, a protest broke out in central Tehran after riot police attempted to crack down on black-market money changers who were profiting on Iranians' desire to sell their rials. The money changers were joined by merchants in Tehran's Grand Bazaar and others demanding economic relief and complaining that Iran's government should have spent less money on helping to keep Syrian President Bashar al-Assad in power and more money on domestic issues. Just over a week later, the IAEA reported that daily oil production in Iran fell in September to the weakest level in nearly twenty-five years and forecast declines in the country's long-term production capability if international sanctions were not lifted.

Then, on October 20, *The New York Times* reported that U.S. and Iranian officials had agreed in principle to direct talks. Officials later denied that any final agreement had been reached, but the news suggested openness on both sides to return to the negotiating table.

—Linda Fecteau

Following is the text of the conclusion reached by the Council of the European Union to place an oil embargo on Iran on January 23, 2012; and a summary of the speech delivered before the United Nations General Assembly on September 27, 2012, by Israeli Prime Minister Benjamin Netanyahu on peace in the Middle East and Iran's nuclear ambition.

European Union Imposes Iranian Oil Embargo

January 23, 2012

The Council adopted the following conclusions:

"1. Recalling the European Council conclusions of 9 December 2011 and the Foreign Affairs Council Conclusions of 1 December, the Council reiterates its serious and deepening concerns over the Iranian nuclear programme and in particular over the findings on Iranian activities relating to the development of military nuclear technology, as reflected in the latest IAEA report. The recent start of operations of enrichment of uranium to a level of up to 20% in the deeply buried underground facility in Fordow near Qom further aggravates concerns about possible military dimensions to Iran's nuclear programme. Iran's acceleration of enrichment activities is in flagrant violation of six UNSC Resolutions and eleven IAEA Board resolutions and contributes to increasing tensions in the region. The Council calls upon Iran to fully cooperate with the IAEA, including in the context of the planned visit by its Deputy Director General for Safeguards.

2. Iran continues to refuse to comply with its international obligations and to fully co-operate with the IAEA to address the concerns on its nuclear programme, and instead continues to violate those obligations. In this context and in accordance with the Council conclusions of 1 December 2011, the Council has agreed [to] additional restrictive measures in the energy sector, including a phased embargo of Iranian crude oil imports to the EU, in the financial sector, including against the Central Bank of Iran, in the transport sector as well as further export restrictions, notably on gold and on sensitive dual-use goods and technology, as well as additional designations of persons and entities, including several controlled by the Islamic Revolutionary Guards Corps (IRGC).

3. The Council again reaffirms the longstanding commitment to work for a diplomatic solution to the Iranian nuclear issue in accordance with the dual-track approach. The Council stresses that the restrictive measures agreed today are aimed at affecting the funding of Iran's nuclear programme by the Iranian regime and are not aimed at the Iranian people. The Iranian regime itself can act responsibly and bring all sanctions to an end.

4. The Council reaffirms that the objective of the EU remains to achieve a comprehensive and long-term settlement which would build international confidence in the exclusively peaceful nature of the Iranian nuclear programme, while respecting Iran's legitimate rights to the peaceful uses of nuclear energy in conformity with the NPT. Supporting the ongoing efforts by the EU High Representative and reaffirming the importance of close co-operation with the E3+3, the Council urges Iran to reply positively to the offer for substantial negotiations, as set out in the High Representative's letter of 21 October 2011, by clearly demonstrating its readiness to engage in confidence building measures and, without preconditions, in meaningful talks to seriously address existing concerns on the nuclear issue."

SOURCE: Council of the European Union. "Council Conclusions on Iran." January 23, 2012. http://www
.consilium.europa.eu/uedocs/cms_data/docs/pressdata/EN/foraff/127446.pdf.

Summary of Netanyahu Statement
Before the United Nations

September 27, 2012

[The statements of other world leaders have been excluded from the excerpt here, which pertains only to the statements of the Israeli prime minister.]

BENJAMIN NETANYAHU, Prime Minister of Israel, told the Assembly that, three thousand years ago, King David had reigned over the Jewish State in its eternal capital, Jerusalem. In saying that, he addressed, in particular, those who proclaimed that the Jewish State had no roots in the region, and that it would soon disappear. The Jewish people had lived on, and "the Jewish State will live forever," he said. Even after it was exiled from Israel, the Jewish people never gave up the dream of returning to their ancient homeland; over time, they had restored independence and rebuilt their national life. "The Jewish people have come home, and we will never be uprooted again," he stressed.

Yesterday, on the holiest day of the Jewish year, Yom Kippur, Jews had taken stock of the past, prayed for the future, and remembered the sorrows of persecution, including the extermination of a third of its people—6 million—during the Holocaust. But, at the end of the day, they had celebrated the heroism of their people and the marvel of the "flourishing, modern" Jewish State. "We walk the same paths tread by our patriarchs," but "we blaze new trails in science, technology, medicine and agriculture," he said, adding that the past and the future found common ground in his nation. Unfortunately, that was not the case in many other countries, as a great battle was being waged between the modern and the medieval. Modernity sought a bright future in which the rights of all were protected and life was precious. The forces of medievalism sought a world in which women were subjugated, and in which rights were suppressed and death, not life, was glorified. Nowhere was that more stark than in the Middle East, he said.

Israel stood firmly with the forces of modernity. Its exceptional creativity was matched by its remarkable compassion, he said, describing Israeli humanitarian efforts during recent crises in Haiti, Japan, Tunisia and elsewhere. Israel treated thousands of Palestinian Arabs in its hospitals. Indeed, it was because Israel so cherished life that it also cherished and sought peace. It sought to preserve historic ties with Egypt and Jordan, and to forge a lasting peace with the Palestinian People. However, he emphasized, "we won't solve our conflict with libellous speeches at the United Nations" or with "unilateral declarations of statehood." Instead, the parties must sit together to negotiate a solution in which a demilitarized Palestinian State recognized the one and only Jewish State.

Israel wanted to see the three great religions that had sprung from its region coexist in peace and mutual respect, he went on. But, the forces of radical Islam, which sought supremacy over all of Islam, wanted to extinguish freedom and "end the modern world." It had many branches, from the rulers of Iran to Al-Qaida terrorists to the radical cells lurking in every part of the world. They were all rooted in the same "bitter soil of intolerance," he said, and they were directed at their fellow Muslims, at Christians, and Jews, at secular people and at anyone who did not submit to their creed. However, he stressed that "ultimately, they will fail . . . ultimately light will penetrate the darkness." Ignorance had given way to enlightenment in the past, and so, too, would the Middle East once again be guided not by fanaticism and conspiracy, but by reason and curiosity. The question was not whether fanaticism would be defeated, but how many lives would be lost before it was defeated.

In the past, those who opposed fanaticism had waited too long to act, at a "horrific cost." That could not happen again. "Nothing could imperil the world more than the arming of Iran with nuclear weapons." Likening a nuclear-armed Iran to a nuclear-armed Al-Qaida, he said that both were fired "by the same hatred, and driven by the same lust for violence." He pointed to the actions of Iran to date, even without nuclear weapons: it had brutally put down protests for democracy in its own country in 2009, and abetted the killing of American soldiers in Iraq. It had turned Lebanon and Gaza into terrorist strongholds, embedding thousands of rockets and missiles. Thousands of those had been fired at Israel by their terrorist proxies. It had even plotted to blow up a restaurant a few blocks from the White House, and continued to deny the Holocaust, as it had done again this week at the United Nations. Given that record of Iranian aggression, he asked the Assembly to imagine its actions with nuclear weapons. In that context, "Who among you would feel safe in the Middle East?" Who would feel safe in Europe, in America or anywhere?

Some believed that a nuclear-armed Iran could be deterred, as the Soviet Union had once been. But, that was a dangerous assumption. Secular Marxists were very different from a country with suicide bombers, he warned. For Iran, in fact, mutually assured destruction was not a deterrent, it was an inducement. One of their leaders had said that using a nuclear weapon on Israel would destroy everything, but it would only "harm" the Islamic world, and, thus, it was not irrational to contemplate such a reality. And that was coming from a so-called moderate.

He had been speaking about the need to prevent Iran from acquiring a nuclear weapon for 15 years, but now "the hour is getting very late." Diplomacy had not worked, as Iran had used those negotiations to bide time to advance its nuclear programme. Strong sanctions had had an effect on the Iranian economy, but they had not stopped the country's nuclear programme. At this late hour, there was one way to prevent a nuclear-armed Iran, and that was to "place a clear red line" on its nuclear programme, he said. "Red lines don't lead to war, red lines prevent war," he said in that respect, describing several incidents in history where that rule had been proven true; for example, the North Atlantic Treaty Organization (NATO)'s red line had prevented war in Europe for half a century, and the invasion of Kuwait by Iraq and other conflicts might have been avoided with a clear red line.

To be credible, he said, such a line must be drawn, first and foremost, on Iran's efforts to enrich uranium. Producing a diagram of a bomb and a fuse, he demonstrated how much enriched uranium was needed to produce a nuclear weapon, and showed the three stages that Iran would go through in order to do it. It was currently well into the second stage and, at current enrichment rates, it would finish the second stage by next spring or summer. That information was not as secret; it was based on IAEA reports that anyone can read online. "If these are the facts—and they are—where should a red line be drawn?" he asked, and answered that it should be drawn before Iran completed the second stage of nuclear enrichment. "Each day, that point is getting closer," he stressed, and everyone should, therefore, have a sense of urgency.

Some claimed that even if they crossed that line, intelligence services would be able to find where and when they were making the fuse and preparing the bomb and warhead. Yet, while no one had more respect for intelligence services than Israel's Prime Minister and they had saved many lives, they were not foolproof. For longer than two years they had not known that Iran was building a huge uranium enrichment plant under a mountain. Should the security of the world rest on the assumption that a small workshop somewhere in a country half the size of Europe can be found in time? The red line must be drawn on the enrichment facilities because those were the only facilities that could be definitely seen and credibly targeted. He believed that, "faced with a clear red line, Iran will back down."

Just days ago at the United Nations, United States President Barack Obama had reiterated that a nuclear-armed Iran could not be contained. Indeed, the goal to prevent such a reality united Israelis and Americans, as well as others around the world. "Together we can chart a course forward," he said. The Jewish people had always looked towards the future and worked to expand liberty, promote equality and defend human rights. "Let us commit ourselves to defend those values, and protect our common civilization," he concluded.

SOURCE: United Nations. General Assembly. Department of Public Information. "Shared Goal of Middle East Peace at Centre of General Assembly Debate, But Leaders Chart Divergent Paths to its Achievement." September 27, 2012. http://www.un.org/News/Press/docs/2012/ga11295.doc.htm.

OTHER HISTORIC DOCUMENTS OF INTEREST

FROM THIS VOLUME

FROM PREVIOUS *HISTORIC DOCUMENTS*

State of the Union Address and Republican Response

JANUARY 24, 2012

When President Barack Obama stood before a joint session of Congress to deliver his third State of the Union address, he had a number of factors working to his benefit, including an economy that was continuing to recover and an approval rating on the rise. The *Washington Post*–ABC News poll taken before the speech showed the president with an approval rating of approximately 50 percent and a majority of independent voters now viewing his time in office favorably, the latter an important point in an election year. However, the president was also facing a weak housing market and 8.5 percent unemployment, two facts Republican Governor Mitch Daniels of Indiana was unwilling to let him forget in his response.

In his nearly one-hour speech, considered to be the kickoff to his reelection campaign, the president proposed few new initiatives and mainly stuck to themes from his previous addresses before Congress. The proposals the president did make were mainly ones he could use executive power to enact, while other, more lofty proposals, such as revising the tax code, were unlikely to see any movement. The speech was dominated by the economy, with only a small nod to foreign affairs and national security.

Throughout his speech, the president struck an optimistic tone. "Think about the America within our reach: a country that leads the world in educating its people. An America that attracts a new generation of high-tech manufacturing and high-paying jobs. A future where we're in control of our own energy, and our security and prosperity aren't so tied to unstable parts of the world. An economy built to last, where hard work pays off, and responsibility is rewarded," Obama said. "The defining issue of our time is how to keep that promise alive."

While Obama, as he had in the past, said that he would "work with anyone in this chamber" to continue improving the economy and creating jobs, in his response, Daniels blamed the president for an unwillingness to compromise with Republicans.

ECONOMY BUILT TO LAST

Reminding the audience that he inherited a bad economy but that economic policies that he helped put in place were keeping the economic recovery going, Obama promised that the United States "will not go back to an economy weakened by outsourcing, bad debt and phony financial profits," adding that he wants "an economy built on American manufacturing, American energy." Harkening back to his 2008 campaign theme, Obama said that helping the middle class get a fair shot is not about "Democratic values or Republican values, but American values."

Obama made clear in his speech his belief that the middle class was being negatively affected by the growing gap between the rich and everyone else, a belief that Republicans criticize as "class warfare." To reverse this trend, Obama proposed seven steps: eliminating tax incentives for companies that outsource, lowering taxes for companies that create jobs in the United States and manufacture in the United States, training and placing 2 million skilled workers, making college more affordable, helping homeowners refinance their mortgages, extending the payroll tax cut, and asking the wealthy to pay a higher tax rate.

On the latter point, Obama reiterated a proposal first made in September 2011 that those making more than $1 million should pay a tax rate of no less than 30 percent. During his State of the Union address, Obama highlighted what he dubbed the "Buffett rule" by inviting Warren Buffett's secretary, Debbie Bosanek, to sit with First Lady Michelle Obama. Bosanek gained attention when it was revealed that she paid a higher effective federal tax rate than her boss, the third wealthiest person in the world. "It's time to apply the same rules from top to bottom: no bailouts, no handouts, and no cop-outs. An America built to last insists on responsibility from everybody," Obama said. The president said changing the tax rate will help create jobs and would replace the alternative minimum tax (AMT), put in place to ensure that wealthy taxpayers cannot avoid taxes by using a myriad of deductions. The tax proposals made by the president were politically charged and came the same day Republican presidential candidate Mitt Romney released his tax returns, which showed an effective federal income tax rate in 2010 of 13.9 percent although his income fell into the top one tenth of one percent of all taxpayers.

House Speaker John Boehner, R-Ohio, said Obama's plans "are just going to double down on what hasn't worked." He continued, "The politics of envy, the politics of dividing our country is not what our country is all about." It is unlikely that these tax hikes or deduction eliminations would pass because Republicans in Congress had already said they'd reject new revenue while they try to find $1.5 trillion in cuts agreed to in 2011. Neither the new tax rate nor the deductions were added to his fiscal year 2013 budget proposal released in February.

Domestic Politics

Although the economy dominated the speech, the president did touch on a few other domestic issues, including the housing market, education, and domestic energy. To continue to shore up the housing market, Obama called on Congress to make it easier for homeowners to refinance, which he said would save the average American approximately $3,000 per year. This proposal was similar to programs already available for homeowners with loans guaranteed by Fannie Mae and Freddie Mac, but what the president wanted to do in this instance was also include loans guaranteed by private companies. Obama also said he would create a financial crimes unit to investigate what lenders did to contribute to the financial crisis. This unit, he said, "will hold accountable those who broke the law, speed assistance to homeowners and help turn the page on an era of recklessness that hurt so many Americans."

On education, Obama renewed his themes from previous years about rewarding good teachers, getting rid of bad ones, and giving teachers more flexibility instead of forcing them to teach to a test. He called on states to pass laws that would keep students in high school until they graduate or turn eighteen, aimed at reducing the 25 percent national dropout rate. To encourage more Americans to pursue higher education, and to make it more affordable to do so, the president asked Congress to continue the tuition tax credit and stop interest rates on student loans from rising as they were set to do in July. And he put colleges and universities on notice that they were in danger of losing their federal funding if they allowed tuition prices to continue to climb.

Coming into his State of the Union address, Obama faced criticism from Republicans for his rejection of the Keystone XL oil pipeline application one week earlier. The president had indicated then that it was not an outright rejection of the project but rather a rejection of the current proposed route of the transcontinental pipeline through sensitive lands in Nebraska. In his State of the Union address, Obama did not mention Keystone by name; instead, he promoted safely developing America's natural gas, creating clean energy jobs, reducing of dependence on foreign oil, giving incentives to manufacturers for energy upgrades, and opening up more federal lands to develop green energy, such as wind farms and solar plants.

NATIONAL SECURITY AND DEFENSE

Calling the United States the world's "one indispensible nation," the president listed the foreign policy gains of the past year: the end of the Iraq War, the assassination of Osama bin Laden, an increase in strikes against al-Qaeda, and the troop drawdown in Afghanistan where the president said he would work to build an "enduring partnership" with the Afghan people. The president called these gains "a testament to the courage, self-lessness and teamwork of America's armed forces. At a time when too many of our institutions have let us down, they exceed all expectations. They're not consumed with personal ambition. They don't obsess over their differences. They focus on the mission at hand. They work together," he said. With the end of the Iraq War and continuing drawdown in Afghanistan, the president proposed splitting the anticipated savings from ending the two wars, expected to be approximately $200 billion over six years, and giving half to infra-structure projects in the United States, while using the other half to reduce the deficit.

On the heels of releasing a new defense strategy with Pentagon leaders on January 5, Obama spoke briefly about the changing focus of the military and renewed his commitment to cut $487 billion from the defense budget over the next decade, a move he said would not hurt national security or the continued excellence of the U.S. military. The president offered no specifics in his speech on where cuts would be made or how he would ensure minimal impact from the shrinking budget. The new defense strategy would shift more focus to the Asia-Pacific region and the Middle East, where Obama said he would work with U.S. allies to keep peace and stability in nations like Iran. President Obama has faced criticism for not being tougher on Iran, but he did not use his State of the Union address to give in to critics. Instead, he said he would take "no options off the table" to stop Iran from building a nuclear weapon, but said he believed "peaceful resolution of this issue is still possible, and far better." The president had been criticized for not taking a tougher stance on China, a nation long known to artificially deflate its currency to compete with American goods, but in his 2012 address, the president mentioned the country by name and said he would create a trade enforcement unit that would pursue unfair trade practices.

REPUBLICAN RESPONSE

Republicans chose Indiana Governor Daniels, a former budget director under President George W. Bush, to deliver the rebuttal to the president's address. The governor was in his last term due to term limits and had ruled out a bid for the White House in late 2011. "On these evenings, presidents naturally seek to find the sunny side of our national condition," Daniels said. "But when President Obama claims that the state of our union is anything but grave, he must know in his heart that this is not true." Daniels took issue with the proposals Obama made to help the middle class by making the wealthy pay more, saying "no feature of the Obama presidency has been sadder than its constant efforts to divide us, to curry favor with some Americans by castigating others. . . . We Americans are all in the same boat."

Daniels also took aim at the president's assertion that he had worked with Republicans to help turn around the economy. Daniels said the president had done nothing to fix the economy; rather, it was Republicans who had worked to do so, only to be stopped by Obama. "It's not fair and it's not true for the president to attack Republicans in Congress as obstacles on these questions. They and they alone have passed bills to reduce borrowing, reform entitlements and encourage new job creation, only to be shot down time and time again by the president and his Democratic Senate allies," he said.

Daniels worked throughout his speech to paint Republicans as the party determined to bring jobs to America and lift people out of poverty, looking specifically at the Keystone XL pipeline as an example of the president's unwillingness to follow a "pro-growth approach" to creating jobs, lowering utility bills, and reducing American dependence on foreign oil. "As Republicans, our first concern is for those waiting tonight to begin or resume the climb up life's ladder," he said. "We do not accept that ours will ever be a nation of haves and have-nots; we must always be a nation of haves and soon-to-haves."

—Heather Kerrigan

Following is the full text of President Barack Obama's State of the Union address and the Republican response given by Indiana Governor Mitch Daniels, both on January 24, 2012.

DOCUMENT   *State of the Union Address*

January 24, 2012

Mr. Speaker, Mr. Vice President, Members of Congress, distinguished guests, and fellow Americans: Last month, I went to Andrews Air Force Base and welcomed home some of our last troops to serve in Iraq. Together, we offered a final, proud salute to the colors under which more than a million of our fellow citizens fought and several thousand gave their lives.

We gather tonight knowing that this generation of heroes has made the United States safer and more respected around the world. For the first time in 9 years, there are no Americans fighting in Iraq. For the first time in two decades, Usama bin Laden is not a threat to this country. Most of Al Qaida's top lieutenants have been defeated. The Taliban's momentum has been broken, and some troops in Afghanistan have begun to come home.

These achievements are a testament to the courage, selflessness, and teamwork of America's Armed Forces. At a time when too many of our institutions have let us down, they exceed all expectations. They're not consumed with personal ambition. They don't obsess over their differences. They focus on the mission at hand. They work together.

Imagine what we could accomplish if we followed their example. Think about the America within our reach: a country that leads the world in educating its people; an America that attracts a new generation of high-tech manufacturing and high-paying jobs; a future where we're in control of our own energy and our security and prosperity aren't so tied to unstable parts of the world; an economy built to last, where hard work pays off and responsibility is rewarded.

We can do this. I know we can, because we've done it before. At the end of World War II, when another generation of heroes returned home from combat, they built the strongest economy and middle class the world has ever known. My grandfather, a veteran of Patton's army, got the chance to go to college on the GI bill. My grandmother, who worked on a bomber assembly line, was part of a workforce that turned out the best products on Earth.

The two of them shared the optimism of a nation that had triumphed over a depression and fascism. They understood they were part of something larger, that they were contributing to a story of success that every American had a chance to share, the basic American promise that if you worked hard, you could do well enough to raise a family, own a home, send your kids to college, and put a little away for retirement.

The defining issue of our time is how to keep that promise alive. No challenge is more urgent. No debate is more important. We can either settle for a country where a shrinking number of people do really well while a growing number of Americans barely get by. Or we can restore an economy where everyone gets a fair shot and everyone does their fair share and everyone plays by the same set of rules. What's at stake aren't Democratic values or Republican values, but American values. And we have to reclaim them.

Let's remember how we got here. Long before the recession, jobs and manufacturing began leaving our shores. Technology made businesses more efficient, but also made some jobs obsolete. Folks at the top saw their incomes rise like never before, but most hard-working Americans struggled with costs that were growing, paychecks that weren't, and personal debt that kept piling up.

In 2008, the house of cards collapsed. We learned that mortgages had been sold to people who couldn't afford or understand them. Banks had made huge bets and bonuses with other people's money. Regulators had looked the other way or didn't have the authority to stop the bad behavior.

It was wrong, it was irresponsible, and it plunged our economy into a crisis that put millions out of work, saddled us with more debt, and left innocent, hard-working Americans holding the bag. In the 6 months before I took office, we lost nearly 4 million jobs. And we lost another 4 million before our policies were in full effect.

Those are the facts. But so are these: In the last 22 months, businesses have created more than 3 million jobs. Last year, they created the most jobs since 2005. American manufacturers are hiring again, creating jobs for the first time since the late 1990s. Together, we've agreed to cut the deficit by more than $2 trillion. And we've put in place new rules to hold Wall Street accountable so a crisis like this never happens again.

The state of our Union is getting stronger. And we've come too far to turn back now. As long as I'm President, I will work with anyone in this Chamber to build on this momentum. But I intend to fight obstruction with action, and I will oppose any effort to return to the very same policies that brought on this economic crisis in the first place.

No, we will not go back to an economy weakened by outsourcing, bad debt, and phony financial profits. Tonight I want to speak about how we move forward and lay out a blueprint for an economy that's built to last, an economy built on American manufacturing, American energy, skills for American workers, and a renewal of American values.

Now, this blueprint begins with American manufacturing.

On the day I took office, our auto industry was on the verge of collapse. Some even said we should let it die. With a million jobs at stake, I refused to let that happen. In exchange for help, we demanded responsibility. We got workers and automakers to settle their differences. We got the industry to retool and restructure. Today, General Motors is back on top as the world's number-one automaker. Chrysler has grown faster in the U.S. than any major car company. Ford is investing billions in U.S. plants and factories. And together, the entire industry added nearly a hundred and sixty thousand jobs.

We bet on American workers. We bet on American ingenuity. And tonight, the American auto industry is back.

What's happening in Detroit can happen in other industries. It can happen in Cleveland and Pittsburgh and Raleigh. We can't bring every job back that's left our shore. But right now it's getting more expensive to do business in places like China. Meanwhile, America is more productive. A few weeks ago, the CEO of Master Lock told me that it now makes business sense for him to bring jobs back home. Today, for the first time in 15 years, Master Lock's unionized plant in Milwaukee is running at full capacity.

So we have a huge opportunity at this moment to bring manufacturing back. But we have to seize it. Tonight my message to business leaders is simple: Ask yourselves what you can do to bring jobs back to your country, and your country will do everything we can to help you succeed.

We should start with our Tax Code. Right now companies get tax breaks for moving jobs and profits overseas. Meanwhile, companies that choose to stay in America get hit with one of the highest tax rates in the world. It makes no sense, and everyone knows it. So let's change it.

First, if you're a business that wants to outsource jobs, you shouldn't get a tax deduction for doing it. That money should be used to cover moving expenses for companies like Master Lock that decide to bring jobs home.

Second, no American company should be able to avoid paying its fair share of taxes by moving jobs and profits overseas. From now on, every multinational company should have to pay a basic minimum tax. And every penny should go towards lowering taxes for companies that choose to stay here and hire here in America.

Third, if you're an American manufacturer, you should get a bigger tax cut. If you're a high-tech manufacturer, we should double the tax deduction you get for making your products here. And if you want to relocate in a community that was hit hard when a factory left town, you should get help financing a new plant, equipment, or training for new workers.

So my message is simple: It is time to stop rewarding businesses that ship jobs overseas, and start rewarding companies that create jobs right here in America. Send me these tax reforms, and I will sign them right away.

We're also making it easier for American businesses to sell products all over the world. Two years ago, I set a goal of doubling U.S. exports over 5 years. With the bipartisan trade agreements we signed into law, we're on track to meet that goal ahead of schedule. And soon there will be millions of new customers for American goods in Panama, Colombia, and South Korea. Soon there will be new cars on the streets of Seoul imported from Detroit and Toledo and Chicago.

I will go anywhere in the world to open new markets for American products. And I will not stand by when our competitors don't play by the rules. We've brought trade cases against China at nearly twice the rate as the last administration, and it's made a difference.

Over a thousand Americans are working today because we stopped a surge in Chinese tires. But we need to do more. It's not right when another country lets our movies, music, and software be pirated. It's not fair when foreign manufacturers have a leg up on ours only because they're heavily subsidized.

Tonight I'm announcing the creation of a trade enforcement unit that will be charged with investigating unfair trading practices in countries like China. There will be more inspections to prevent counterfeit or unsafe goods from crossing our borders. And this Congress should make sure that no foreign company has an advantage over American manufacturing when it comes to accessing financing or new markets like Russia. Our workers are the most productive on Earth, and if the playing field is level, I promise you, America will always win.

I also hear from many business leaders who want to hire in the United States, but can't find workers with the right skills. Growing industries in science and technology have twice as many openings as we have workers who can do the job. Think about that: openings at a time when millions of Americans are looking for work. It's inexcusable, and we know how to fix it.

Jackie Bray is a single mom from North Carolina who was laid off from her job as a mechanic. Then Siemens opened a gas turbine factory in Charlotte and formed a partnership with Central Piedmont Community College. The company helped the college design courses in laser and robotics training. It paid Jackie's tuition, then hired her to help operate their plant.

I want every American looking for work to have the same opportunity as Jackie did. Join me in a national commitment to train 2 million Americans with skills that will lead directly to a job. My administration has already lined up more companies that want to help. Model partnerships between businesses like Siemens and community colleges in places like Charlotte and Orlando and Louisville are up and running. Now you need to give more community colleges the resources they need to become community career centers, places that teach people skills that businesses are looking for right now, from data management to high-tech manufacturing.

And I want to cut through the maze of confusing training programs so that from now on, people like Jackie have one program, one web site, and one place to go for all the information and help that they need. It is time to turn our unemployment system into a reemployment system that puts people to work.

These reforms will help people get jobs that are open today. But to prepare for the jobs of tomorrow, our commitment to skills and education has to start earlier.

For less than 1 percent of what our Nation spends on education each year, we've convinced nearly every State in the country to raise their standards for teaching and learning, the first time that's happened in a generation. But challenges remain, and we know how to solve them.

At a time when other countries are doubling down on education, tight budgets have forced States to lay off thousands of teachers. We know a good teacher can increase the lifetime income of a classroom by over $250,000. A great teacher can offer an escape from poverty to the child who dreams beyond his circumstance. Every person in this Chamber can point to a teacher who changed the trajectory of their lives. Most teachers work tirelessly, with modest pay, sometimes digging into their own pocket for school supplies, just to make a difference.

Teachers matter. So instead of bashing them or defending the status quo, let's offer schools a deal. Give them the resources to keep good teachers on the job and reward the best ones. And in return, grant schools flexibility to teach with creativity and passion, to stop teaching to the test, and to replace teachers who just aren't helping kids learn. That's a bargain worth making.

We also know that when students don't walk away from their education, more of them walk the stage to get their diploma. When students are not allowed to drop out, they do better. So tonight I am proposing that every State—every State—requires that all students stay in high school until they graduate or turn 18.

When kids do graduate, the most daunting challenge can be the cost of college. At a time when Americans owe more in tuition debt than credit card debt, this Congress needs to stop the interest rates on student loans from doubling in July.

Extend the tuition tax credit we started that saves millions of middle class families thousands of dollars and give more young people the chance to earn their way through college by doubling the number of work-study jobs in the next 5 years.

Of course, it's not enough for us to increase student aid. We can't just keep subsidizing skyrocketing tuition; we'll run out of money. States also need to do their part by making higher education a higher priority in their budgets. And colleges and universities have to do their part by working to keep costs down.

Recently, I spoke with a group of college presidents who have done just that. Some schools redesign courses to help students finish more quickly. Some use better technology. The point is, it's possible. So let me put colleges and universities on notice: If you can't stop tuition from going up, the funding you get from taxpayers will go down. Higher education can't be a luxury. It is an economic imperative that every family in America should be able to afford.

Let's also remember that hundreds of thousands of talented, hard-working students in this country face another challenge: the fact that they aren't yet American citizens. Many were brought here as small children, are American through and through, yet they live every day with the threat of deportation. Others came more recently, to study business and science and engineering, but as soon as they get their degree, we send them home to invent new products and create new jobs somewhere else. That doesn't make sense.

I believe as strongly as ever that we should take on illegal immigration. That's why my administration has put more boots on the border than ever before. That's why there are fewer illegal crossings than when I took office. The opponents of action are out of excuses. We should be working on comprehensive immigration reform right now.

But if election-year politics keeps Congress from acting on a comprehensive plan, let's at least agree to stop expelling responsible young people who want to staff our labs, start new businesses, defend this country. Send me a law that gives them the chance to earn their citizenship. I will sign it right away.

You see, an economy built to last is one where we encourage the talent and ingenuity of every person in this country. That means women should earn equal pay for equal work. It means we should support everyone who's willing to work and every risk taker and entrepreneur who aspires to become the next Steve Jobs.

After all, innovation is what America has always been about. Most new jobs are created in startups and small businesses. So let's pass an agenda that helps them succeed. Tear down regulations that prevent aspiring entrepreneurs from getting the financing to grow. Expand tax relief to small businesses that are raising wages and creating good jobs. Both parties agree on these ideas. So put them in a bill and get it on my desk this year.

Innovation also demands basic research. Today, the discoveries taking place in our federally financed labs and universities could lead to new treatments that kill cancer cells, but leave healthy ones untouched, new lightweight vests for cops and soldiers that can stop any bullet. Don't gut these investments in our budget. Don't let other countries win the race for the future. Support the same kind of research and innovation that led to the computer chip and the Internet, to new American jobs and new American industries.

And nowhere is the promise of innovation greater than in American-made energy. Over the last 3 years, we've opened millions of new acres for oil and gas exploration, and tonight I'm directing my administration to open more than 75 percent of our potential offshore oil and gas resources. Right now—right now—American oil production is the highest that it's been in 8 years. That's right, 8 years. Not only that, last year, we relied less on foreign oil than in any of the past 16 years.

But with only 2 percent of the world's oil reserves, oil isn't enough. This country needs an all-out, all-of-the-above strategy that develops every available source of American energy, a strategy that's cleaner, cheaper, and full of new jobs.

We have a supply of natural gas that can last America nearly 100 years. And my administration will take every possible action to safely develop this energy. Experts believe this will support more than 600,000 jobs by the end of the decade. And I'm requiring all companies that drill for gas on public lands to disclose the chemicals they use. Because America will develop this resource without putting the health and safety of our citizens at risk.

The development of natural gas will create jobs and power trucks and factories that are cleaner and cheaper, proving that we don't have to choose between our environment and our economy. And by the way, it was public research dollars, over the course of 30 years, that helped develop the technologies to extract all this natural gas out of shale rock, reminding us that Government support is critical in helping businesses get new energy ideas off the ground.

Now, what's true for natural gas is just as true for clean energy. In 3 years, our partnership with the private sector has already positioned America to be the world's leading manufacturer of high-tech batteries. Because of Federal investments, renewable energy use has nearly doubled, and thousands of Americans have jobs because of it.

When Bryan Ritterby was laid off from his job making furniture, he said he worried that at 55 no one would give him a second chance. But he found work at Energetx, a wind turbine manufacturer in Michigan. Before the recession, the factory only made luxury yachts. Today, it's hiring workers like Bryan, who said, "I'm proud to be working in the industry of the future."

Our experience with shale gas, our experience with natural gas, shows us that the payoffs on these public investments don't always come right away. Some technologies don't pan out, some companies fail. But I will not walk away from the promise of clean energy. I will not walk away from workers like Bryan. I will not cede the wind or solar or battery industry to China or Germany because we refuse to make the same commitment here.

We've subsidized oil companies for a century. That's long enough. It's time to end the taxpayer giveaways to an industry that rarely has been more profitable and double down on a clean energy industry that never has been more promising. Pass clean energy tax credits. Create these jobs.

We can also spur energy innovation with new incentives. The differences in this Chamber may be too deep right now to pass a comprehensive plan to fight climate change. But there's no reason why Congress shouldn't at least set a clean energy standard that creates a market for innovation. So far, you haven't acted. Well, tonight I will. I'm directing my administration to allow the development of clean energy on enough public land to power 3 million homes. And I'm proud to announce that the Department of Defense, working with us, the world's largest consumer of energy, will make one of the largest commitments to clean energy in history, with the Navy purchasing enough capacity to power a quarter of a million homes a year.

Of course, the easiest way to save money is to waste less energy. So here's a proposal: Help manufacturers eliminate energy waste in their factories and give businesses incentives to upgrade their buildings. Their energy bills will be a hundred billion dollars lower over the next decade, and America will have less pollution, more manufacturing, more jobs for construction workers who need them. Send me a bill that creates these jobs.

Building this new energy future should be just one part of a broader agenda to repair America's infrastructure. So much of America needs to be rebuilt. We've got crumbling roads and bridges, a power grid that wastes too much energy, an incomplete high-speed broadband network that prevents a small-business owner in rural America from selling her products all over the world.

During the Great Depression, America built the Hoover Dam and the Golden Gate Bridge. After World War II, we connected our States with a system of highways. Democratic and Republican administrations invested in great projects that benefited everybody, from the workers who built them to the businesses that still use them today.

In the next few weeks, I will sign an Executive order clearing away the redtape that slows down too many construction projects. But you need to fund these projects. Take the money we're no longer spending at war, use half of it to pay down our debt, and use the rest to do some nation-building right here at home.

There's never been a better time to build, especially since the construction industry was one of the hardest hit when the housing bubble burst. Of course, construction workers weren't the only ones who were hurt. So were millions of innocent Americans who've seen their home values decline. And while Government can't fix the problem on its own, responsible homeowners shouldn't have to sit and wait for the housing market to hit bottom to get some relief.

And that's why I'm sending this Congress a plan that gives every responsible homeowner the chance to save about $3,000 a year on their mortgage by refinancing at historically low rates. No more redtape. No more runaround from the banks. A small fee on the largest financial institutions will ensure that it won't add to the deficit and will give those banks that were rescued by taxpayers a chance to repay a deficit of trust.

Let's never forget: Millions of Americans who work hard and play by the rules every day deserve a Government and a financial system that do the same. It's time to apply the same rules from top to bottom. No bailouts, no handouts, and no copouts. An America built to last insists on responsibility from everybody.

We've all paid the price for lenders who sold mortgages to people who couldn't afford them and buyers who knew they couldn't afford them. That's why we need smart regulations to prevent irresponsible behavior. Rules to prevent financial fraud or toxic dumping or faulty medical devices, these don't destroy the free market. They make the free market work better.

There's no question that some regulations are outdated, unnecessary, or too costly. In fact, I've approved fewer regulations in the first 3 years of my Presidency than my Republican predecessor did in his. I've ordered every Federal agency to eliminate rules that don't make sense. We've already announced over 500 reforms, and just a fraction of them will save business and citizens more than $10 billion over the next 5 years. We got rid of one rule from 40 years ago that could have forced some dairy farmers to spend $10,000 a year proving that they could contain a spill, because milk was somehow classified as an oil. With a rule like that, I guess it was worth crying over spilled milk.

Now, I'm confident a farmer can contain a milk spill without a Federal agency looking over his shoulder. Absolutely. But I will not back down from making sure an oil company can contain the kind of oil spill we saw in the Gulf 2 years ago. I will not back down from protecting our kids from mercury poisoning or making sure that our food is safe and our water is clean. I will not go back to the days when health insurance companies had unchecked power to cancel your policy, deny your coverage, or charge women differently than men.

And I will not go back to the days when Wall Street was allowed to play by its own set of rules. The new rules we passed restore what should be any financial system's core purpose: getting funding to entrepreneurs with the best ideas and getting loans to responsible families who want to buy a home or start a business or send their kids to college.

So if you are a big bank or financial institution, you're no longer allowed to make risky bets with your customers' deposits. You're required to write out a "living will" that details exactly how you'll pay the bills if you fail, because the rest of us are not bailing you out ever again. And if you're a mortgage lender or a payday lender or a credit card company, the days of signing people up for products they can't afford with confusing forms and deceptive practices, those days are over. Today, American consumers finally have a watchdog in Richard Cordray, with one job: to look out for them.

We'll also establish a financial crimes unit of highly trained investigators to crack down on large-scale fraud and protect people's investments. Some financial firms violate major antifraud laws because there's no real penalty for being a repeat offender. That's bad for consumers, and it's bad for the vast majority of bankers and financial service professionals who do the right thing. So pass legislation that makes the penalties for fraud count.

And tonight I'm asking my Attorney General to create a special unit of Federal prosecutors and leading State attorney[s] general to expand our investigations into the abusive lending and packaging of risky mortgages that led to the housing crisis. This new unit will hold accountable those who broke the law, speed assistance to homeowners, and help turn the page on an era of recklessness that hurt so many Americans.

Now, a return to the American values of fair play and shared responsibility will help protect our people and our economy. But it should also guide us as we look to pay down our debt and invest in our future.

Right now our most immediate priority is stopping a tax hike on a hundred and sixty million working Americans while the recovery is still fragile. People cannot afford losing $40 out of each paycheck this year. There are plenty of ways to get this done. So let's agree right here, right now. No side issues. No drama. Pass the payroll tax cut without delay. Let's get it done.

When it comes to the deficit, we've already agreed to more than $2 trillion in cuts and savings. But we need to do more, and that means making choices. Right now we're poised to spend nearly $1 trillion more on what was supposed to be a temporary tax break for the wealthiest 2 percent of Americans. Right now because of loopholes and shelters in the Tax Code, a quarter of all millionaires pay lower tax rates than millions of middle class households. Right now Warren Buffett pays a lower tax rate than his secretary.

Do we want to keep these tax cuts for the wealthiest Americans? Or do we want to keep our investments in everything else, like education and medical research, a strong military and care for our veterans? Because if we're serious about paying down our debt, we can't do both.

The American people know what the right choice is. So do I. As I told the Speaker this summer, I'm prepared to make more reforms that rein in the long-term costs of Medicare and Medicaid and strengthen Social Security, so long as those programs remain a guarantee of security for seniors. But in return, we need to change our Tax Code so that people like me, and an awful lot of Members of Congress, pay our fair share of taxes.

Tax reform should follow the Buffett rule. If you make more than a million dollars a year, you should not pay less than 30 percent in taxes. And my Republican friend Tom Coburn is right: Washington should stop subsidizing millionaires. In fact, if you're earning a million dollars a year, you shouldn't get special tax subsidies or deductions. On the other hand, if you make under $250,000 a year, like 98 percent of American families, your taxes shouldn't go up. You're the ones struggling with rising costs and stagnant wages. You're the ones who need relief.

Now, you can call this class warfare all you want. But asking a billionaire to pay at least as much as his secretary in taxes? Most Americans would call that common sense.

We don't begrudge financial success in this country. We admire it. When Americans talk about folks like me paying my fair share of taxes, it's not because they envy the rich. It's because they understand that when I get a tax break I don't need and the country can't afford, it either adds to the deficit or somebody else has to make up the difference, like a senior on a fixed income or a student trying to get through school or a family trying to make ends meet. That's not right. Americans know that's not right. They know that this generation's success is only possible because past generations felt a responsibility to each other and to the future of their country, and they know our way of life will only endure if we feel that same sense of shared responsibility. That's how we'll reduce our deficit. That's an America built to last.

Now, I recognize that people watching tonight have differing views about taxes and debt, energy and health care. But no matter what party they belong to, I bet most Americans are thinking the same thing right about now: Nothing will get done in Washington this year or next year or maybe even the year after that, because Washington is broken.

Can you blame them for feeling a little cynical?

The greatest blow to our confidence in our economy last year didn't come from events beyond our control. It came from a debate in Washington over whether the United States would pay its bills or not. Who benefited from that fiasco?

I've talked tonight about the deficit of trust between Main Street and Wall Street. But the divide between this city and the rest of the country is at least as bad, and it seems to get worse every year.

Now, some of this has to do with the corrosive influence of money in politics. So together, let's take some steps to fix that. Send me a bill that bans insider trading by Members of Congress. I will sign it tomorrow. Let's limit any elected official from owning stocks in industries they impact. Let's make sure people who bundle campaign contributions for Congress can't lobby Congress and vice versa, an idea that has bipartisan support, at least outside of Washington.

Some of what's broken has to do with the way Congress does its business these days. A simple majority is no longer enough to get anything—even routine business—passed through the Senate. Neither party has been blameless in these tactics. Now both parties should put an end to it. For starters, I ask the Senate to pass a simple rule that all judicial and public service nominations receive a simple up-or-down vote within 90 days.

The executive branch also needs to change. Too often, it's inefficient, outdated, and remote. That's why I've asked this Congress to grant me the authority to consolidate the

Federal bureaucracy so that our Government is leaner, quicker, and more responsive to the needs of the American people.

Finally, none of this can happen unless we also lower the temperature in this town. We need to end the notion that the two parties must be locked in a perpetual campaign of mutual destruction, that politics is about clinging to rigid ideologies instead of building consensus around commonsense ideas.

I'm a Democrat, but I believe what Republican Abraham Lincoln believed: That Government should do for people only what they cannot do better by themselves and no more. That's why my education reform offers more competition and more control for schools and States. That's why we're getting rid of regulations that don't work. That's why our health care law relies on a reformed private market, not a Government program.

On the other hand, even my Republican friends who complain the most about Government spending have supported federally financed roads and clean energy projects and Federal offices for the folks back home.

The point is, we should all want a smarter, more effective Government. And while we may not be able to bridge our biggest philosophical differences this year, we can make real progress. With or without this Congress, I will keep taking actions that help the economy grow. But I can do a whole lot more with your help. Because when we act together, there's nothing the United States of America can't achieve.

That's the lesson we've learned from our actions abroad over the last few years. Ending the Iraq war has allowed us to strike decisive blows against our enemies. From Pakistan to Yemen, the Al Qaida operatives who remain are scrambling, knowing that they can't escape the reach of the United States of America.

From this position of strength, we've begun to wind down the war in Afghanistan. Ten thousand of our troops have come home. Twenty-three thousand more will leave by the end of this summer. This transition to Afghan lead will continue, and we will build an enduring partnership with Afghanistan so that it is never again a source of attacks against America.

As the tide of war recedes, a wave of change has washed across the Middle East and North Africa, from Tunis to Cairo, from Sana'a to Tripoli. A year ago, Qadhafi was one of the world's longest serving dictators, a murderer with American blood on his hands. Today, he is gone. And in Syria, I have no doubt that the Asad regime will soon discover that the forces of change cannot be reversed and that human dignity cannot be denied.

How this incredible transformation will end remains uncertain. But we have a huge stake in the outcome. And while it's ultimately up to the people of the region to decide their fate, we will advocate for those values that have served our own country so well. We will stand against violence and intimidation. We will stand for the rights and dignity of all human beings: men and women; Christians, Muslims, and Jews. We will support policies that lead to strong and stable democracies and open markets, because tyranny is no match for liberty.

And we will safeguard America's own security against those who threaten our citizens, our friends, and our interests. Look at Iran. Through the power of our diplomacy, a world that was once divided about how to deal with Iran's nuclear program now stands as one. The regime is more isolated than ever before. Its leaders are faced with crippling sanctions, and as long as they shirk their responsibilities, this pressure will not relent.

Let there be no doubt: America is determined to prevent Iran from getting a nuclear weapon, and I will take no options off the table to achieve that goal. But a peaceful resolution of this issue is still possible, and far better. And if Iran changes course and meets its obligations, it can rejoin the community of nations.

The renewal of American leadership can be felt across the globe. Our oldest alliances in Europe and Asia are stronger than ever. Our ties to the Americas are deeper. Our ironclad commitment—and I mean ironclad—to Israel's security has meant the closest military cooperation between our two countries in history.

We've made it clear that America is a Pacific power, and a new beginning in Burma has lit a new hope. From the coalitions we've built to secure nuclear materials, to the missions we've led against hunger and disease, from the blows we've dealt to our enemies, to the enduring power of our moral example, America is back.

Anyone who tells you otherwise, anyone who tells you that America is in decline or that our influence has waned, doesn't know what they're talking about. That's not the message we get from leaders around the world who are eager to work with us. That's not how people feel from Tokyo to Berlin, from Cape Town to Rio, where opinions of America are higher than they've been in years. Yes, the world is changing. No, we can't control every event. But America remains the one indispensable nation in world affairs, and as long as I'm President, I intend to keep it that way.

That's why, working with our military leaders, I've proposed a new defense strategy that ensures we maintain the finest military in the world, while saving nearly half a trillion dollars in our budget. To stay one step ahead of our adversaries, I've already sent this Congress legislation that will secure our country from the growing dangers of cyber threats.

Above all, our freedom endures because of the men and women in uniform who defend it. As they come home, we must serve them as well as they've served us. That includes giving them the care and the benefits they have earned, which is why we've increased annual VA spending every year I've been President. And it means enlisting our veterans in the work of rebuilding our Nation.

With the bipartisan support of this Congress, we're providing new tax credits to companies that hire vets. Michelle and Jill Biden have worked with American businesses to secure a pledge of 135,000 jobs for veterans and their families. And tonight I'm proposing a veterans jobs corps that will help our communities hire veterans as cops and firefighters, so that America is as strong as those who defend her.

Which brings me back to where I began. Those of us who've been sent here to serve can learn a thing or two from the service of our troops. When you put on that uniform, it doesn't matter if you're Black or White, Asian, Latino, Native American; conservative, liberal; rich, poor; gay, straight. When you're marching into battle, you look out for the person next to you or the mission fails. When you're in the thick of the fight, you rise or fall as one unit, serving one nation, leaving no one behind.

You know, one of my proudest possessions is the flag that the SEAL team took with them on the mission to get bin Laden. On it are each of their names. Some may be Democrats, some may be Republicans, but that doesn't matter. Just like it didn't matter that day in the Situation Room, when I sat next to Bob Gates, a man who was George Bush's Defense Secretary, and Hillary Clinton, a woman who ran against me for President.

All that mattered that day was the mission. No one thought about politics. No one thought about themselves. One of the young men involved in the raid later told me that he didn't deserve credit for the mission. It only succeeded, he said, because every single member of that unit did their job: the pilot who landed the helicopter that spun out of control, the translator who kept others from entering the compound, the troops who separated the women and children from the fight, the SEALs who charged up the stairs. More than that, the mission only succeeded because every member of that unit trusted each other, because you can't charge up those stairs into darkness and danger unless you know that there's somebody behind you, watching your back.

So it is with America. Each time I look at that flag, I'm reminded that our destiny is stitched together like those 50 stars and those 13 stripes. No one built this country on their own. This Nation is great because we built it together. This Nation is great because we worked as a team. This Nation is great because we get each other's backs. And if we hold fast to that truth, in this moment of trial, there is no challenge too great, no mission too hard. As long as we are joined in common purpose, as long as we maintain our common resolve, our journey moves forward, and our future is hopeful, and the state of our Union will always be strong.

Thank you, God bless you, and God bless the United States of America.

SOURCE: Executive Office of the President. "Address Before a Joint Session of Congress on the State of the Union." January 24, 2012. *Compilation of Presidential Documents* 2012, no. 00048 (January 24, 2012). http://www.gpo.gov/fdsys/pkg/DCPD-201200048/pdf/DCPD-201200048.pdf.

Republican Response to the State of the Union Address

January 24, 2012

"The status of 'loyal opposition' imposes on those out of power some serious responsibilities: to show respect for the Presidency and its occupant, to express agreement where it exists. Republicans tonight salute our President, for instance, for his aggressive pursuit of the murderers of 9/11, and for bravely backing long overdue changes in public education. I personally would add to that list admiration for the strong family commitment that he and the First Lady have displayed to a nation sorely needing such examples.

"On these evenings, Presidents naturally seek to find the sunny side of our national condition. But when President Obama claims that the state of our union is anything but grave, he must know in his heart that this is not true.

"The President did not cause the economic and fiscal crises that continue in America tonight. But he was elected on a promise to fix them, and he cannot claim that the last three years have made things anything but worse: the percentage of Americans with a job is at the lowest in decades. One in five men of prime working age, and nearly half of all persons under 30, did not go to work today.

"In three short years, an unprecedented explosion of spending, with borrowed money, has added trillions to an already unaffordable national debt. And yet, the President has put us on a course to make it radically worse in the years ahead. The federal government now spends one of every four dollars in the entire economy; it borrows one of every three dollars it spends. No nation, no entity, large or small, public or private, can thrive, or survive intact, with debts as huge as ours.

"The President's grand experiment in trickle-down government has held back rather than sped economic recovery. He seems to sincerely believe we can build a middle class out of government jobs paid for with borrowed dollars. In fact, it works the other way: a government as big and bossy as this one is maintained on the backs of the middle class, and those who hope to join it.

"Those punished most by the wrong turns of the last three years are those unemployed or underemployed tonight, and those so discouraged that they have abandoned the search for work altogether. And no one has been more tragically harmed than the young people of this country, the first generation in memory to face a future less promising than their parents did.

"As Republicans our first concern is for those waiting tonight to begin or resume the climb up life's ladder. We do not accept that ours will ever be a nation of haves and have nots; we must always be a nation of haves and soon to haves.

"In our economic stagnation and indebtedness, we are only a short distance behind Greece, Spain, and other European countries now facing economic catastrophe. But ours is a fortunate land. Because the world uses our dollar for trade, we have a short grace period to deal with our dangers. But time is running out, if we are to avoid the fate of Europe, and those once-great nations of history that fell from the position of world leadership.

"So 2012 is a year of true opportunity, maybe our last, to restore an America of hope and upward mobility, and greater equality. The challenges aren't matters of ideology, or party preference; the problems are simply mathematical, and the answers are purely practical.

"An opposition that would earn its way back to leadership must offer not just criticism of failures that anyone can see, but a positive and credible plan to make life better, particularly for those aspiring to make a better life for themselves. Republicans accept this duty, gratefully.

"The routes back to an America of promise, and to a solvent America that can pay its bills and protect its vulnerable, start in the same place. The only way up for those suffering tonight, and the only way out of the dead end of debt into which we have driven, is a private economy that begins to grow and create jobs, real jobs, at a much faster rate than today.

"Contrary to the President's constant disparagement of people in business, it's one of the noblest of human pursuits. The late Steve Jobs—what a fitting name he had—created more of them than all those stimulus dollars the President borrowed and blew. Out here in Indiana, when a businessperson asks me what he can do for our state, I say 'First, make money. Be successful. If you make a profit, you'll have something left to hire someone else, and some to donate to the good causes we love.'

"The extremism that stifles the development of homegrown energy, or cancels a perfectly safe pipeline that would employ tens of thousands, or jacks up consumer utility bills for no improvement in either human health or world temperature, is a pro-poverty policy. It must be replaced by a passionate pro-growth approach that breaks all ties and calls all close ones in favor of private sector jobs that restore opportunity for all and generate the public revenues to pay our bills.

"That means a dramatically simpler tax system of fewer loopholes and lower rates. A pause in the mindless piling on of expensive new regulations that devour dollars that otherwise could be used to hire somebody. It means maximizing on the new domestic energy technologies that are the best break our economy has gotten in years.

"There is a second item on our national must-do list: we must unite to save the safety net. Medicare and Social Security have served us well, and that must continue. But after half and three quarters of a century respectively, it's not surprising that they need some repairs. We can preserve them unchanged and untouched for those now in or near retirement, but we must fashion a new, affordable safety net so future Americans are protected, too.

"Decades ago, for instance, we could afford to send millionaires pension checks and pay medical bills for even the wealthiest among us. Now, we can't, so the dollars we have should be devoted to those who need them most.

"The mortal enemies of Social Security and Medicare are those who, in contempt of the plain arithmetic, continue to mislead Americans that we should change nothing. Listening to them much longer will mean that these proud programs implode, and take the American economy with them. It will mean that coming generations are denied the jobs they need in their youth and the protection they deserve in their later years.

"It's absolutely so that everyone should contribute to our national recovery, including of course the most affluent among us. There are smart ways and dumb ways to do this: the dumb way is to raise rates in a broken, grossly complex tax system, choking off growth without bringing in the revenues we need to meet our debts. The better course is to stop sending the wealthy benefits they do not need, and stop providing them so many tax preferences that distort our economy and do little or nothing to foster growth.

"It's not fair and it's not true for the President to attack Republicans in Congress as obstacles on these questions. They and they alone have passed bills to reduce borrowing, reform entitlements, and encourage new job creation, only to be shot down time and time again by the President and his Democratic Senate allies.

"This year, it falls to Republicans to level with our fellow citizens about this reality: if we fail to act to grow the private sector and save the safety net, nothing else will matter much. But to make such action happen, we also must work, in ways we Republicans have not always practiced, to bring Americans together.

"No feature of the Obama Presidency has been sadder than its constant efforts to divide us, to curry favor with some Americans by castigating others. As in previous moments of national danger, we Americans are all in the same boat. If we drift, quarreling and paralyzed, over a Niagara of debt, we will all suffer, regardless of income, race, gender, or other category. If we fail to shift to a pro-jobs, pro-growth economic policy, there will never be enough public revenue to pay for our safety net, national security, or whatever size government we decide to have.

"As a loyal opposition, who put patriotism and national success ahead of party or ideology or any self-interest, we say that anyone who will join us in the cause of growth and solvency is our ally, and our friend. We will speak the language of unity. Let us rebuild our finances, and the safety net, and reopen the door to the stairway upward; any other disagreements we may have can wait.

"You know, the most troubling contention in our national life these days isn't about economics, or policy at all. It's about us, as a free people. In two alarming ways, that contention is that we Americans just can't cut it anymore.

"In word and deed, the President and his allies tell us that we just cannot handle ourselves in this complex, perilous world without their benevolent protection. Left to ourselves, we might pick the wrong health insurance, the wrong mortgage, the wrong school for our kids; why, unless they stop us, we might pick the wrong light bulb!

"A second view, which I admit some Republicans also seem to hold, is that we Americans are no longer up to the job of self-government. We can't do the simple math that proves the unaffordability of today's safety net programs, or all the government we now have. We will fall for the con job that says we can just plow ahead and someone else will pick up the tab. We will allow ourselves to be pitted one against the other, blaming our neighbor for troubles worldwide trends or our own government has caused.

"2012 must be the year we prove the doubters wrong. The year we strike out boldly not merely to avert national bankruptcy but to say to a new generation that America is still the world's premier land of opportunity. Republicans will speak for those who believe in the dignity and capacity of the individual citizen; who believe that government is meant to serve the people rather than supervise them; who trust Americans enough to tell them the plain truth about the fix we are in, and to lay before them a specific, credible program of change big enough to meet the emergency we are facing.

"We will advance our positive suggestions with confidence, because we know that Americans are still a people born to liberty. There is nothing wrong with the state of our Union that the American people, addressed as free-born, mature citizens, cannot set right. Republicans in 2012 welcome all our countrymen to a program of renewal that rebuilds the dream for all, and makes our 'city on a hill' shine once again."

SOURCE: Office of the Governor of Indiana. "Republican Address to the Nation." January 24, 2012. http://indiana.gov/gov/3628.htm.

OTHER HISTORIC DOCUMENTS OF INTEREST

FROM THIS VOLUME

FROM PREVIOUS *HISTORIC DOCUMENTS*

February

United Nations Fails to Take Action in Syria

FEBRUARY 4, 2012

The Arab Spring uprisings that swept through the Middle East and North Africa reached Syria on March 15, 2011, when residents in a southern city protested the torture of students accused of antigovernment graffiti. When President Bashar al Assad's government responded, it violently cracked down on the protest, garnering attention from the rest of the country and causing the demonstrations to spread. While other government opposition groups in Arab Spring nations largely experienced some form of success by the end of 2011, Syria's ongoing uprising had yet to reach a conclusion by the end of 2012. The international community struggled throughout the year to decide how to properly respond and faced criticism for failing to intervene in what the United Nations now considers a civil war.

PROTESTS BEGIN AND OPPOSITION FORMS IN 2011

When protests began in Syria, Assad moved between offering reform and using force to crack down on protesters. In April 2011, he lifted the country's state of emergency, only to call for his security forces to violently halt demonstrations. Demonstrators considered any offer of reform as empty promises. As the conflict dragged on into the summer of 2011, some of Assad's soldiers began defecting and joining the opposition.

To bring some organization to the anti-Assad movement, an opposition government was formed in exile called the Syrian National Council. The goal of the group is to overthrow Assad's government, and it is made up of representatives from the Damascus Declaration Group, Syrian Muslim Brotherhood, Kurdish factions, Local Coordination Committees, and other independent and tribal groups, and led by human rights activist Ammar al Qurabi. The group failed to gain formal support from Western and Arab nations due in part to its own internal division, which the group is unable to resolve. "Negotiating or having dialogue with any one opposition faction is against the will of the people and the Syrian revolution," the council said in a statement. Under pressure from Western governments, in November 2012, the Syrian National Council was absorbed into the National Coalition of Syrian Revolutionary and Opposition Forces, a body now recognized as the legitimate representative of Syria by the United States.

Through the fall and winter of 2011, the conflict grew deadlier and Assad seemed willing to stop at nothing to maintain his stranglehold on power. In December, the United Nations said the nation was on the brink of civil war.

WAVERING CONTROL

The opposition's biggest setback is that it remains poorly organized and is made up of many factions without a cohesive political agenda, despite the formation of the Syrian National Council and subsequent National Coalition. Infighting has grown within the group, and influence from al Qaeda and Muslim jihadists is increasing. The opposition has been easily swayed to take on jihadist agendas because it helps the group attract more financing. In February 2012, U.S. counterterrorism analysts reported that Sunni militants connected to al Qaeda were operating in Syria against Assad's government. Since al Qaeda tied itself to the opposition movement, the number of suicide bombings, a key tactic it has used in Iraq, increased.

One attempt at bringing some order to the opposition forces came in the creation of the Free Syrian Army, which is organizing inside of Turkey and attacking Syrian government targets from across the border. The group is small and unlikely to overthrow Assad's government, and it lacks political leadership. Although it operates from inside of Turkey, the Turkish government says it has not given the group weapons or military support and that no such requests have been made. However, weapons, money, and medical supplies have made their way into Syrian opposition hands from refugee camps in Turkey.

Neither the government nor opposition has been able to maintain control of cities and towns around the country, and in response, Assad's forces shifted tactics to destroy towns instead of making an attempt to regain control. The opposition has used the weakening of Assad's government to its advantage and has gained control of some military equipment, including helicopters. Meanwhile, the Assad government, which has waged a massive air assault across the country, has struggled to keep all of its weaponry and heavy machinery functioning.

CIVILIAN IMPACT

Civilians have been hard hit by the ongoing violence in Syria. By the fall of 2012, more than 25,000 people, mostly civilians, are thought to have been killed and tens of thousands arrested. Advocacy groups report that this marks a significant increase in violence since 2011, noting that 400 were killed in June 2011 but 3,000 were killed in the same month in 2012. The United Nations estimates that as of September 2012, 2.5 million within Syria are in need of some form of aid, while another 1.2 million are displaced within Syria.

A number of Syrian civilians have chosen to flee the violence. According to the United Nations, by September 2012, although 234,000 refugees had registered in nearby countries, tens of thousands were thought to have fled without registering. About half of these registered refugees left Syria in August 2012. In September, 20,000 refugees entered Jordan, many describing to aid workers their destroyed villages, lack of power and water, and shelling by government forces. By early 2013, Jordan and nearby Lebanon reported receiving 3,000 to 4,000 refugees per day. Opposition troops have helped Syrian civilians escape under the cover of darkness, but some have been stopped by Assad's forces or killed during their attempt. Women and children make up the greatest portion of those in refugee camps, as men often leave their families to return to the fight. The conditions in the camps are poor, and supplies are minimal. Aid workers report that those they've spoken to were driven out by a governmental effort to eliminate anyone supporting the opposition.

Effect on the Region

Given the interconnectedness of the Middle East, made clear during the Arab Spring uprisings, it is not surprising that the violence in Syria has sparked tension elsewhere. Instability has been seen among religious sects in Lebanon, where Sunnis and Alawites fought each other throughout 2012 in what has been attributed to violence in Syria.

A major concern for international observers is the relationship between Turkey and Syria, which were formerly allies. Turkey shelled locations inside Syria in October 2012 to retaliate against a Syrian mortar attack that killed five Turkish citizens. Because Turkey is a member of the North Atlantic Treaty Organization (NATO), concern has been raised that as it becomes ever more drawn into the skirmish in Syria, other Western nations might be drawn in as well.

Whether Assad's government stays in power could have a larger effect in places such as Lebanon, where the government is heavily controlled by Hezbollah, a group that stands to lose monetary and military support from Assad should his government fall. Russia also supports Syria's government, hoping to keep Assad in power or it risks losing both influence in the region and one of its large arms buyers. If a new government is formed, Russia's support of Assad will likely be taken into account by the new government, and this resentment could spread across the region, further weakening Russian influence.

Little International Intervention

Although the conflict had been going on for nearly two years, by the end of 2012, there was little international intervention. The reasons for staying out of the violence varied, from the risk of losing allies to the risk of sparking a larger, regional war. The Arab League, which revoked Syria's membership after it agreed to a ceasefire and subsequently stepped up its attacks on the opposition, has observers in Syria, but their presence has been relatively meaningless and has done nothing to quell the violence. The United Nations attempted on multiple occasions to take some form of action but has been thwarted by Syrian supporters Russia and China, who hold veto power on the Security Council. In February 2012, the General Assembly voted to condemn Assad's crackdown on protesters, but the United Nations remains unable to take any stronger action without the support of China and Russia, the latter of which believes that it is not the place of the international body to force the fall of a government or involve itself in internal politics.

The UN's special envoy to Syria, former secretary general Kofi Annan, helped to negotiate a ceasefire with Assad's government that was set to go into effect in April 2012. Although Assad had agreed to a six-point plan to end the violence, which would have allowed him to maintain power, he did not follow through on most if it. The United Nations suspended its ceasefire observer mission in June because of the continuing violence and ended the observer mission altogether in August, but a liaison office was left in the country. Frustrated by Assad's inaction and the inability of the two sides to reach an agreement, in early August, Annan left his position.

The United States has not yet taken unilateral action in Syria, and the Obama administration has come under fire from Republicans who think the nation should intervene militarily as it did in Libya in 2011. Instead of acting alone, or with a small group of partners as it initially did in Libya, the United States has tried to work through the Arab League and United Nations to bring about an end to the violence. Analysts say this tactic has a lot to do with Iran and the United States' desire to avoid any action that might encourage the nuclear-ambitious nation to become involved. President Obama was also facing reelection in November, making it even less likely that he would invoke military action.

On February 19, Sens. John McCain, R-Ariz., and Lindsey Graham, R-S.C., both members of the Senate Armed Services Committee, publicly spoke out to encourage the United States to arm the rebels to help combat Assad's forces, arguing that by doing so, the United States would have a greater chance to weaken Iran's influence in the region. Following their comments, Iran docked two warships in a Syrian port, in what the Iranian Fars News Agency called "a serious warning" to the United States. "The presence of Iran and Russia's flotillas along the Syrian coast has a clear message against the United States' possible adventurism," said Hossein Ebrahimi, a vice chair of the Iranian Parliament's national security and foreign policy commission. Because the opposition does not control enough secure areas to allow an influx of arms from the United States, the United States instead decided to provide intelligence support and also support of light weapons coming from other Arab countries to the opposition. According to *New York Times* reports, in July, the United States increased aid to rebels and tried to work outside of the United Nations to gather countries to help bring down Assad's government; however, the administration maintained that it would not directly supply the opposition with weapons. Saudi Arabia and Qatar have organized shipments of arms for opposition groups, but according to American and Middle Eastern officials, a number of these weapons are ending up in the hands of Islamic jihadists rather than the Syrian opposition the West supports.

In August, Obama announced that military action might be used if there were any evidence of Assad moving his stocks of chemical or biological weapons. "We cannot have a situation in which chemical or biological weapons are falling into the hands of the wrong people," the president said. "That's an issue that doesn't just concern Syria. It concerns our close allies in the region, including Israel. It concerns us." Assad, who is thought to possess some of the world's largest stocks of mustard gas, cyanide, and a nerve agent, said he would not use these weapons unless foreign nations intervened in the crisis. However, in December, the United Kingdom and the United States announced that they had intelligence that indicated Assad was moving his chemical weapons as a precursor to creating sarin gas. Russian Foreign Minister Sergey Lavrov, while expressing the nation's belief that such weapons should not be used, called the reports rumors, and cited information from the Syrian government that Assad has no intent to use chemical weapons.

Syria does have some supporters, including Iran, which, according to a Western intelligence report, has pushed the Iraqi government to allow it to use airspace and bases to send weapons into Syria. Because it is already economically isolated from the West for its desire to develop a nuclear weapon, Iran has been open about the military and financial support it sent to Syria. Given the relationship between Syria and Iran, if Assad's government falls, it could mean the rebirth of democratic protests in Iran.

—Heather Kerrigan

Following is a statement released by the United Nations Security Council on February 4, 2012, announcing that a veto by Russia and China prevented the UN body from adopting a resolution to demand that the Syrian government and opposition groups end the deadly violence in the country.

United Nations Resolution
on Syria Fails

February 4, 2012

The Russian Federation and China vetoed today a Security Council draft resolution that would have demanded that all parties in Syria—both Government forces and armed opposition groups—stop all violence and reprisals, ending days of intense negotiations in New York as diplomats laboured to bring a halt to the deadly 10-month crackdown on anti-Government protests in the Middle Eastern country.

Supported by the 13 other Council members, the text would have expressed grave concern at the deteriorating situation in Syria and profound concern over the deaths of thousands of people. It would have condemned widespread gross violations of human rights and "all violence, irrespective of where it comes from," while demanding that the Syrian Government implement, "without delay," the elements of a plan set out by the League of Arab States on 22 January.

That plan, outlined in the Council's text, would have demanded that Syria immediately cease all violence and protect its population; release all persons detained arbitrarily; withdraw all military and armed forces from cities and towns; and guarantee the freedom to hold peaceful demonstrations. It would have called for "an inclusive Syrian-led political process conducted in an environment free from violence, fear, intimidation ad extremism, and aimed at effectively addressing the legitimate aspirations and concerns of the Syrian people."

Explaining his negative vote, the representative of the Russian Federation said that the draft resolution sought to send an "unbalanced" message to Syria. Moreover, no proposal had been made to end attacks by armed groups, or their association with extremists. Stressing that the violence and bloodshed must end immediately, he announced that the Russian Government was taking direct action by sending high-level officials to meet with Syrian President Bashar al-Assad on 7 February. Yet, while the Russian Federation was committed to finding a solution, some influential members of the international community had been undermining the possibility of a peaceful settlement by advocating regime change, he said.

The Councils' three other permanent members—France, the United Kingdom and the United States—were outraged by the rejection of the text, believing it represented the best compromise position. "It is a sad day for the Council, a sad day for Syrians, and a sad day for all friends of democracy," said France's representative, who was among those speakers who noted that today marked the thirtieth anniversary of the Hama massacre. "What message is now being sent to the Syrian people and to all the victims of human rights violations?" Denouncing those who had obstructed action under the "obviously false" belief that the aim of the text was military intervention, he said history would judge harshly those who had prevented the Council from lending its support to the Arab League's efforts.

Saying that her delegation was "disgusted" that the text had been blocked, the representative of the United States explained that the Council had been held hostage for months while the same two members had held fast to "empty arguments and individual interests," trying to "strip bare" any measure that would call on the Syrian regime to change its tactics. The draft's co-sponsors had truly "gone the last mile" to accommodate the concerns of Council members regarding the use of force. Yet, "wrecking amendments" proposed at the last hour to delay action further were reprehensible, she said, especially because they had come as the Assad regime was ratcheting up its "horrific campaign" in Homs.

Against that backdrop, the international community must help to end "this abhorrent brutality," especially since some Council members continued to "sell out the Syrian people to shield a craven tyrant," she continued, warning that any further bloodshed would be on their hands. Applauding the growing number of Syrians who were taking to the streets to speak out against President Assad's regime, she said that, after today, they would be able to look at the Security Council and see clearly which nations had stood behind their calls for democracy and which had chosen to "prop up desperate dictators."

Syria's representative, taking the floor at the end of the meeting, said the statements made by some Council members betrayed their "true hostile intentions" against his country, and would "fan the flames" of violence and bloodshed. Indeed, Syria was in the midst of a crisis "manufactured" by States that did not wish it well, and which gave money, arms and media coverage to the armed terrorist groups that were killing, abducting and intimidating Syrian civilians. The draft resolution that had failed to pass today emphasized the importance of dialogue, which Syria supported, he said. However, some of the parties to the conflict refused to engage in dialogue as all Council members knew well.

He said that Syria sought dialogue that was inclusive of all parties, under "the roof of its homeland," emphasizing that such a dialogue would be developed in Syria and by Syrians. They did not need to await "instructions on democracy" from others. Saying that he had hoped that the situation would remain "in the Syrian household" and within the Arab structure, he stressed that the rush by some parties to bring the issue to the Council was a cause of great concern. The United Nations had indeed become an "instrument of war," he said, adding that those parties were waging wars in order to gain control of geographic locations and lucrative resources.

The Council's latest attempt at consensus followed days of intense negotiations in the wake of its ministerial-level briefing on Tuesday, when it heard from Hamad bin Jassim bin Jaber bin Muhammad Al-Thani, Prime Minister and Minister for Foreign Affairs of Qatar and Chairman of the Arab League's Ministerial Council, and Nabil Elaraby, the League's Secretary-General. While Council members were split over the path to action on Syria, those two regional officials had called for decisive action, with Sheik Hamad stressing: "Our efforts and initiatives have been in vain for the Syrian Government has not made any sincere effort to cooperate with our efforts, and, unfortunately, its only solution has been to kill its own people." . . .

Statements

[Statements by Morocco, France, and Germany, expressing regret at the Security Council's failure to pass the resolution, have been omitted.]

SUSAN RICE (*United States*) said her delegation was "disgusted" that two members continued to prevent the Council from fulfilling its sole purpose: addressing a deepening crisis in Syria and a growing threat to regional peace and security. Indeed, the Council had been held hostage for months while those members had held fast to empty arguments and individual interests. Their ongoing intransigence "is even more shameful when you consider that at least one of them continues to deliver weapons to Assad," she said, pointing out that, while many countries had imposed or called for tough targeted sanctions, "this text didn't even do that." It merely supported an Arab League plan for a peaceful solution to the crisis.

She went on to say that the draft's co-sponsors had truly "gone the last mile" to accommodate the concerns of Council members regarding the use of force. Yet, "wrecking amendments" proposed at the last hour to delay action further were reprehensible, especially because they had come as the Assad regime was ratcheting up its "horrific campaign" in Homs, murdering women [and] children. Moreover, Syrian forces continued to prevent innocent and injured civilians from seeking help. In light of all that, the international community must help, especially since some Council members had "sold out the Syrian people to shield a craven tyrant," she said. The United States, in contrast, stood "fully and irrevocably" with the people of Syria.

She recalled that, since the two members had vetoed earlier action, the Council had heard reports that the regime might be committing crimes against humanity. Since then, an estimated 3,000 more civilians had been killed, including an estimated 250 just yesterday. At the same time, a growing number of Syrians were taking to the streets to speak out against the Assad regime. After today, they would be able to see clearly which nations had stood for their legitimate rights and which had chosen to "prop up desperate dictators." Indeed, any further bloodshed in Syria would be on their hands, she said. The Governments that had stymied Council action must reverse course and heed the voices of the Syrian people, for their own sake, for the sake of Syria, and for the sake of the Council itself, she emphasized. . . .

[A statement by Portugal's representative to the Security Council has been omitted. It expressed the country's desire to send a forceful message to the Syrian regime.]

MARK LYALL GRANT (*United Kingdom*) said he was "appalled" by the decision of China and the Russian Federation to veto the widely supported draft resolution. It had been 10 months since the Syrian people had bravely demanded their rights, he said, adding that since then the regime had responded by killing its own people. The number of deaths had steadily increased, and today it stood at about 6,000, a number [that] had risen substantially during the last 24 hours. Those who had blocked the Council's action today should ask themselves how many deaths they were willing to tolerate before they supported "even modest action," he said.

Representatives of the Arab League had pleaded for the Council's support for their plan to end the violence, he continued, noting that Morocco's original draft had only backed that request. Yet some had argued that it advocated regime change. The same minority now argued about the language of the current text, which had been amended several times in order to ensure consensus. There was nothing in the text that should have incited the use of a veto, he stressed. The truth was that China and the Russian Federation had failed in their responsibility to support the peaceful resolution of the crises in Syria. "The regime must end the violence," he reiterated, warning that, if it continued on its "bloody trajectory," the issue would once again come before the Council. . . .

[Statements by the representatives from Colombia, Guatemala, and India have been omitted. Each explained the country's desire to end the conflict in Syria.]

VITALY CHURKIN (*Russian Federation*) said the bloodshed and violence in Syria must be ended immediately, adding that his country was taking direct action and planned to hold a meeting with President Bashar al-Assad on 7 February. While the Russian Federation was committed to finding a solution to the crisis, some influential members of the international community had been undermining the possibility of a peaceful settlement by advocating a change of regime. The draft resolution voted down today sought to send an "unbalanced" message to Syria, he said, adding that it did not accurately reflect the situation there. No proposal had been made to end attacks by armed groups, or their association with extremists, he said, adding that his delegation had, therefore, voted against the text. The Russian Federation greatly regretted the results of the Council's joint work, and hoped that a successful Syrian political process would take place, he said, emphasizing that the Russian Federation would continue to work towards that goal.

LI BAODONG (*China*), also calling for an immediate end to all violence in Syria, asked for the respect of the Syrian people for a reform process that was in their own interest. China supported the Arab League's "good office" efforts to restore stability in Syria, he said, adding that the international community should provide "constructive assistance" to achieve that goal. However, the country's sovereignty, independence and territorial integrity must be respected, he emphasized. The purposes and principles of the United Nations Charter must be respected, he added, citing the need to promote political dialogue and to defuse disputes "rather than complicate the issue." China had played an active part in the negotiations on the draft, and maintained that, under the current circumstances, placing "undue emphasis" on pressuring the Syrian Government would not help to resolve the crisis, but would further complicate the situation, he said. China supported the amendments to the text proposed by the Russian Federation, and noted that the latter would meet with the President of Syria next week. Pushing through a draft resolution while members of the Council were still "seriously divided" over the issue would not help to resolve it, he stressed, adding that it was in that context that China had voted against the text. Nonetheless, it would continue to work with the international community towards an appropriate end to the crisis, he said. . . .

[Statements from Pakistan, South Africa, Azerbaijan, and Togo have been omitted. Each expressed their opinion on the conclusion reached by the security council and concern for Syria.]

BASHAR JA'AFARI (*Syria*) said that, given his country's belief in the importance of its "pan-Arab role," he had hoped that the question of the situation there would remain "in the Syrian household," and within the Arab structure. The rush by some parties to bring the issue to the Council was a cause of great concern. The United Nations had indeed become an "instrument of war," he said, adding that those parties were waging wars in order to gain control of geographic locations and lucrative resources.

Pointing out that the Council had adopted only 690 resolutions between its inception and the year 1988, he said it had adopted three times that number in the following 20 years. That was an indication that the world was becoming less secure, less just and less fair. Syria, a founding member of the United Nations, was being targeted by some Powers, he said. Indeed, it was in the midst of a crisis "manufactured" by States that did not wish it well, and which gave money, arms and media coverage to the armed terrorist groups that were killing, abducting and intimidating Syrian civilians. Would any sensible person believe that a Government would commit massacres on a day when the Council was scheduled to hold a meeting to examine the situation in its territory? he asked.

The killings committed this morning were the most convincing proof of the criminal nature of those groups, he said, adding that they had been carried out to send a "misleading message" aimed at swaying Council members. The Council had not examined the Arab League's report, which noted that Syria had, in fact, fulfilled its obligations. The League had recently been "dragged" to the Council in an effort to influence it, he said, adding that some Council members sought to "internationalize" the crisis. Additionally, he cited support for allegations that forced regime change lay at the heart of such efforts.

The draft resolution that had failed to pass today emphasized the importance of dialogue, he noted, saying that Syria supported that. However, some of the parties to the conflict refused to engage in dialogue, as all Council members knew well. Syria sought dialogue that was inclusive of all parties, under "the roof of its homeland," he said, adding that . . . such a dialogue would be developed in Syria and by Syrians. They did not need to wait for "instructions on democracy" from others, he said, noting that the statements made by some Council members betrayed their "true hostile intentions" against Syria, and would "fan the flames" of violence and bloodshed.

SOURCE: United Nations. Security Council. Department of Public Information. "Security Council Fails to Adopt Resolution on Syria as Russian Federation, China Veto Text Supporting Arab League's Proposed Peace Plan." February 4, 2012. http://www.un.org/News/Press/docs/2012/sc10536.doc.htm.

OTHER HISTORIC DOCUMENTS OF INTEREST

FROM PREVIOUS *HISTORIC DOCUMENTS*

California and Washington Legalize Same-Sex Marriage

FEBRUARY 7 AND 13, 2012

The same-sex marriage debate heated up again in 2012 as a number of states added initiatives to the primary and general election ballots on legalizing same-sex marriage or defining marriage. Public opinion polls throughout the year showed a slight majority of Americans supporting gay marriage overall, but that did not stop voters in North Carolina from passing an amendment to define marriage as between one man and one woman or New Jersey's governor from vetoing legislation that would permit same-sex marriage in his state. In an indication of just how divided the country was on the issue, courts and voters in a number of other states chose to allow same-sex couples to marry.

CALIFORNIA REVIEWS PROPOSITION 8

In May 2008, the California state supreme court ruled that a same-sex marriage ban was in violation of the state constitution because domestic partnerships were not a legal substitution for marriage. This ruling legalized same-sex marriage in the Golden State. Opponents of the ruling pushed to have a referendum on the November 2008 ballot, titled Proposition 8, asking voters to overturn the court's decision and outlaw same-sex marriage. The measure passed by a margin of 52 to 48 percent, and immediately afterward, supporters of same-sex marriage pursued legal action. In May 2009, the state supreme court upheld the ban passed by voters while also allowing those couples that had married before voters approved the ban to remain married.

The two lawyers who represented opposing sides in the 2000 presidential election outcome filed a lawsuit in federal court known as *Perry v. Schwarzenegger* on behalf of two same-sex couples. In August 2010, the federal district judge assigned to the case, Vaughn Walker, ruled that Proposition 8 was in violation of the Equal Protection Clause of the U.S. Constitution. "Proposition 8 cannot survive any level of scrutiny under the Equal Protection Clause," wrote Judge Walker in his decision. "Excluding same-sex couples from marriage is simply not rationally related to a legitimate state interest." The ruling was appealed.

On February 7, 2012, a three-judge panel of the Ninth Circuit Court of Appeals agreed with Judge Walker, finding Proposition 8 in violation of the 14th Amendment because it discriminates against gay men and lesbians. The 2–1 ruling was narrow, because the court did not decide whether it was constitutional for same-sex couples to marry but rather whether the difference in treatment under the law of married couples and domestic partners violated the Equal Protection Clause. "Although the Constitution permits communities to enact most laws they believe to be desirable, it requires that there be at least a legitimate reason for the passage of a law that treats different classes of people differently," wrote Judge Stephen Reinhardt in the majority decision. "There was no such reason that Proposition 8 could have been enacted," he wrote. "All that Proposition 8 accomplished was to take away from same-sex couples the right to be granted marriage licenses and thus legally to use the designation 'marriage.'" He continued, "Proposition 8 serves no purpose, and has no effect, other than to lessen the status and human dignity of gay men and lesbians in California." Judge N. Randy Smith, who wrote the dissenting opinion, decided that it was not the place of the court to overturn a voter decision.

On December 7, 2012, the U.S. Supreme Court announced that it would take up the issue of same-sex marriage and review the Proposition 8 case. Proposition 8 supporters say the courts that have decided the case so far are liberal-leaning and that when the case goes to the U.S. Supreme Court, it would be decided in their favor. The Court's ruling, expected to come in June 2013, could accept or reject the constitutionality of same-sex marriage in all fifty states. However, the Court might instead choose to rule narrowly, in which case the decision would impact only California residents. Because of the Court's decision to review the case, the Proposition 8 ban will stay in place until the Court's ruling.

North Carolina Says "No"

Prior to 2012, North Carolina already had a law banning same-sex marriage, but Republicans in the state wanted the ban added to the state's constitution, fearful that a judge might strike down the law in the future. Conservatives had been working for years to get a referendum on the ballot to do so, but Democrats in the legislature thwarted any attempts. However, in 2010, Republicans took control of both houses of the state legislature for the first time since 1870.

On the 2012 primary ballot, the legislature included a referendum to add an amendment to the state constitution that would read thus: "Marriage between one man and one woman is the only domestic legal union that shall be valid or recognized in this state." The opposition, pointing to a similar referendum in Ohio that remained on the books only briefly, warned that the vagueness of the language could put in jeopardy the rights of opposite-sex couples who are unmarried but live together, for example, when it comes to issues such as domestic violence cases, child custody, and hospital visitation rights.

Although those opposing the amendment raised nearly twice as much money as supporters, the amendment passed by more than 20 percentage points, making North Carolina the thirtieth state in the country, and the last in the South, to ban gay marriage in its state constitution. In response, Tami Fitzgerald, chair of the executive committee for the pro-amendment Vote for Marriage NC, said, "We are not anti-gay—we are pro-marriage." She continued, "And the point, the whole point is simply that you don't rewrite the nature of God's design for marriage based on the demands of a group of adults."

Washington State Goes to the Ballot

In February 2012, Washington State's legislature passed a law granting same-sex couples the right to marry, and Governor Christine Gregoire quickly signed it. The law was set to take effect June 7, and it would make Washington the seventh state in the nation to legalize same-sex marriage. One day after the signing, opponents in the traditionally liberal state began working to get the issue on the November ballot. Referendum 74 collected enough signatures to appear on the ballot, as observers had anticipated, and asked voters whether they wanted to approve and maintain the legislature's decision or overturn it.

Supporters of the new law faced an uphill battle—in every state in which gay marriage has been added to the ballot, voters have rejected allowing same-sex couples to marry. Governor Gregoire was confident that the ballot measure opposing same-sex marriage would fail. "The state should not be in the business of discriminating against those who request a marriage license, and I believe a majority of Washington voters agree," she said. Those supporting traditional marriage came out strongly in support of Referendum 74. The Family Policy Institute of Washington said on its website, "Don't forget to continue to pray that the citizens of Washington State will be fearless in their support and defense of traditional marriage between one man and one woman."

On November 6, voters maintained the law as written in the legislature to allow same-sex marriage by a margin of 52–48.

DOMA REJECTED TWICE

In 1996, then-president Bill Clinton signed the Defense of Marriage Act (DOMA), now a hotly contested law that defines marriage in the eyes of the federal government as between one man and one woman; it does not require the federal government or states to recognize same-sex marriages, thus does not guarantee federal benefits to couples legally married in states that allow it. These benefits include such things as Social Security survivor benefits and joint tax filing. In a move to begin unraveling the law, the Obama administration in 2011 asked the Justice Department to stop defending DOMA federal cases. In May 2012, nine years after Massachusetts legalized same-sex marriage, a federal appeals court in Boston declared DOMA unconstitutional in a unanimous decision. The ruling came in regards to two separate but related cases, one brought by seven married same-sex couples and three surviving spouses of a same-sex marriage. The second case, brought by the state, argued that because the federal government has largely left the definition of marriage up to the states, it would be unconstitutional to deny benefits to someone in a state that recognizes same-sex marriage. "Under current Supreme Court authority, Congress' denial of federal benefits to same-sex couples lawfully married in Massachusetts has not been adequately supported by any permissible federal interest," wrote Judge Michael Boudin for the majority.

The second rejection of DOMA came in October when a federal appeals court in New York, where same-sex marriage was legalized in 2011, ruled in the case of Edith Windsor, an eighty-three-year-old lesbian who was charged more than $360,000 in federal estate taxes because she was not granted spousal deductions. A lower court ruled that these estate taxes violated the Equal Protection Clause of the Constitution, and the appeals court agreed in a 2–1 vote. In this case, the court used "heightened scrutiny" to reach its decision, an elevation from previous same-sex marriage cases in which judges must consider whether the group in question had suffered a history of discrimination. During its next term, the U.S. Supreme Court will take up the issue of DOMA as it relates to Windsor's case. The Court will decide whether federal benefits can be given to same-sex couples, but if it chooses to rule narrowly, the decision may affect only New York residents. The DOMA case is not expected to have as great a chance for nationwide impact as the Proposition 8 case.

NEW JERSEY

In 2006, New Jersey's supreme court ruled that both heterosexual and homosexual couples should have the same rights and benefits afforded to them. In response to the ruling, the legislature passed a law to legalize civil unions. Since passage of the law, supporters of gay marriage have argued that civil unions are confusing and unequal to marriage. In 2012, the state legislature took up the issue and passed a bill that would legalize same-sex marriage in the state, despite a veto threat from Republican Governor Chris Christie. Christie explained that he supports the state's civil union law, which he believes grants same-sex couples the same legal protection as heterosexual couples enjoy. Christie did in fact veto the bill in February. His conditional veto asked the legislature to change the language of the bill to instead set up a body that would handle complaints related to the civil union law, but it was noted that there had only been thirteen such complaints since that law took effect. The governor also told the legislature that it was not his place, nor theirs, to decide whether same-sex marriage should be legal. "An issue of this magnitude and importance, which requires a constitutional amendment, should be left to the people of New Jersey to decide," Christie said.

VOTERS DECIDE MARRIAGE'S FATE

In addition to the state of Washington, the states of Maine, Maryland, and Minnesota all had same-sex-marriage issues on their November 2012 ballots. In Maryland, the legislature had approved a bill in early 2012 to allow gay marriage, but enough signatures were collected to put the issue before voters. Ultimately, voters approved the measure 52–48 to allow same-sex couples to obtain civil marriage licenses, beginning on January 1, 2013. The law also protects members of the clergy from performing marriage ceremonies that conflict with their religious beliefs. In Minnesota, voters rejected an amendment to the state constitution that would define marriage as being between one man and one woman by a margin of 52 to 48 percent. And in Maine, in 2009, voters had approved a ban on same-sex marriage by overturning a law approved earlier in the year by the legislature. In 2012, voters overturned that 2009 decision, 53 to 47 percent. Maine, Maryland, and Washington became the first states in the nation to approve same-sex marriage by popular vote.

—Heather Kerrigan

Following is the edited text of the decision of the United States Court of Appeals for the Ninth Circuit on February 7, 2012, in the case of Perry v. Brown, *ruling 2–1 that California's ban on same-sex marriage is unconstitutional; and the text of a statement by Washington Governor Christine Gregoire on February 13, 2012, upon signing into law a bill allowing same-sex couples to marry legally in the state.*

DOCUMENT *Perry v. Brown*

February 7, 2012

[The names of the plaintiffs and defendants, and all footnotes, have been omitted.]

Appeal from the United States District Court for the Northern
District of California Vaughn R. Walker, Chief District Judge, Presiding
(No. 10–16696) James Ware, Chief District Judge, Presiding (No. 11–16577)

No. 10–16696: Argued and Submitted December 6,
2010 San Francisco, California Submission Withdrawn January
4, 2011 Resubmitted February 7, 2012

No. 11–16577: Argued and Submitted December 8, 2011
San Francisco, California

Filed February 7, 2012

Before: Stephen Reinhardt, Michael Daly Hawkins, and
N. Randy Smith, Circuit Judges.

Opinion by Judge Reinhardt; Partial Concurrence and
Partial Dissent by Judge N.R. Smith

[A list of the counsel in each case has been omitted.]

OPINION

REINHARDT, Circuit Judge:

Prior to November 4, 2008, the California Constitution guaranteed the right to marry to opposite-sex couples and same-sex couples alike. On that day, the People of California adopted Proposition 8, which amended the state constitution to eliminate the right of same-sex couples to marry. We consider whether that amendment violates the Fourteenth Amendment to the United States Constitution. We conclude that it does.

Although the Constitution permits communities to enact most laws they believe to be desirable, it requires that there be at least a legitimate reason for the passage of a law that treats different classes of people differently. There was no such reason that Proposition 8 could have been enacted. Because under California statutory law, same-sex couples had all the rights of opposite-sex couples, regardless of their marital status, all parties agree that Proposition 8 had one effect only. It stripped same-sex couples of the ability they previously possessed to obtain from the State, or any other authorized party, an important right—the right to obtain and use the designation of "marriage" to describe their relationships. Nothing more, nothing less. Proposition 8 therefore could not have been enacted to advance California's interests in child-rearing or responsible procreation, for it had no effect on the rights of same-sex couples to raise children or on the procreative practices of other couples. Nor did Proposition 8 have any effect on religious freedom or on parents' rights to control their children's education; it could not have been enacted to safeguard these liberties.

All that Proposition 8 accomplished was to take away from same-sex couples the right to be granted marriage licenses and thus legally to use the designation of "marriage," which symbolizes state legitimization and societal recognition of their committed relationships. Proposition 8 serves no purpose, and has no effect, other than to lessen the status and human dignity of gays and lesbians in California, and to officially reclassify their relationships and families as inferior to those of opposite-sex couples. The Constitution simply does not allow for "laws of this sort." "Broader issues have been urged for our consideration, but we adhere to the principle of deciding constitutional questions only in the context of the particular case before the Court." Whether under the Constitution same-sex couples may *ever* be denied the right to marry, a right that has long been enjoyed by opposite-sex couples, is an important and highly controversial question. It is currently a matter of great debate in our nation, and an issue over which people of good will may disagree, sometimes strongly. Of course, when questions of constitutional law are necessary to the resolution of a case, courts may not and should not abstain from deciding them simply because they are controversial. We need not and do not answer the broader question in this case, however, because California had already extended to committed same-sex couples both the incidents of marriage and the official designation of "marriage," and Proposition 8's only effect was to take away that important and legally significant designation, while leaving in place all of its incidents. This unique and strictly limited effect of Proposition 8 allows us to address the amendment's constitutionality on narrow grounds.

Thus, as a result of our "traditional reluctance to extend constitutional interpretations to situations or facts which are not before the Court, much of the excellent research and detailed argument presented in [this case] is unnecessary to [its] disposition." Were we unable, however, to resolve the matter on the basis we do, we would not hesitate to proceed to the broader question—the constitutionality of denying same-sex couples the right to marry.

Before considering the constitutional question of the validity of Proposition 8's *elimination* of the rights of same-sex couples to marry, we first decide that the official sponsors of Proposition 8 are entitled to appeal the decision below, which declared the measure unconstitutional and enjoined its enforcement. The California Constitution and Elections Code endow the official sponsors of an initiative measure with the authority to represent the State's interest in establishing the validity of a measure enacted by the voters, when the State's elected leaders refuse to do so. It is for the State of California to decide who may assert its interests in litigation, and we respect its decision by holding that Proposition 8's proponents have standing to bring this appeal on behalf of the State. We therefore conclude that, through the proponents of ballot measures, the People of California must be allowed to defend in federal courts, including on appeal, the validity of their use of the initiative power. Here, however, their defense fails on the merits. The People may not employ the initiative power to single out a disfavored group for unequal treatment and strip them, without a legitimate justification, of a right as important as the right to marry. Accordingly, we affirm the judgment of the district court.

We also affirm—for substantially the reasons set forth in the district court's opinion—the denial of the motion by the official sponsors of Proposition 8 to vacate the judgment entered by former Chief Judge Walker, on the basis of his purported interest in being allowed to marry his same-sex partner.

[The remainder of the decision—including background in each of the cases combined into Perry v. Brown, *a look at the state's history of same-sex marriage, the questions addressed by the court in its decision, same-sex marriage in other states and at the federal level, and greater detail of the court's decision—has been omitted. All related footnotes have also been omitted.]*

N. R. SMITH, Circuit Judge, concurring in part and dissenting in part:

I agree with the majority's analysis and decisions in parts III and VI of its opinion, determining that (1) the Proponents have standing to bring this appeal; and (2) the Motion to Vacate the Judgment should be denied. Because I do not agree with the majority's analysis of other topics regarding the constitutionality of Proposition 8, I have chosen to write separately. Ultimately, I am not convinced that Proposition 8 is not rationally related to a legitimate governmental interest. I must therefore respectfully dissent. . . .

[Sections I and II, outlining the arguments in the case and the judgments of past cases; Section III, outlining the majority decision; and Section IV, presenting the arguments of Proposition 8 proponents, have been omitted.]

V.

Given the presumption of validity accorded Proposition 8 for rational basis review, I am not convinced that Proposition 8 lacks a rational relationship to legitimate state interests. Precedent evidences extreme judicial restraint in applying rational basis review to equal protection cases.

Only by faithful adherence to this guiding principle of judicial review of legislation is it possible to preserve to the legislative branch its rightful independence and its ability to function. . . . [R]estraints on judicial review have added force where the legislature must necessarily engage in a process of line-drawing. Defining the class of persons subject . . . inevitably requires that some persons who have an almost equally strong claim to favored treatment be placed on different sides of the line, and the fact that the line might have been drawn differently at some points is a matter for legislative, rather than judicial, consideration.

Thus, the judiciary faces a conspicuous limit on our judicial role in applying equal protection to legislative enactments, because [t]he Court has held that the Fourteenth Amendment permits States a wide scope of discretion in enacting laws which affect some groups of citizens differently than others. The constitutional safeguard is offended only if classification rests on grounds wholly irrelevant to the achievement of the State's objective. State legislatures are presumed to have acted within their constitutional power despite the fact that, in practice, their laws result in some inequality. A statutory discrimination will not be set aside if any state of facts reasonably may be conceived to justify it.

A law must be upheld unless the government's judgment "is 'clearly wrong, a display of arbitrary power, [or] not an exercise of judgment.'"

Applying rational basis review in these circumstances also requires such restraint. As the Eighth Circuit said, in *Citizens for Equal Protection*, 455 F.3d at 870:

In the nearly one hundred and fifty years since the Fourteenth Amendment was adopted, to our knowledge no Justice of the Supreme Court has suggested that a state statute or constitutional provision codifying the traditional definition of marriage violates the Equal Protection Clause or any other provision of the United States Constitution. Indeed, in *Baker v. Nelson*, . . . when faced with a Fourteenth Amendment challenge to a decision by the Supreme Court of Minnesota denying a marriage license to a same-sex couple, the United States Supreme Court dismissed "for want of a *substantial* federal question." There is good reason for this restraint.

SOURCE: United States Court of Appeals for the Ninth Circuit. *Perry v. Brown*. February 7, 2012. http://www.ca9.uscourts.gov/datastore/opinions/2012/02/10/10-16696.pdf.

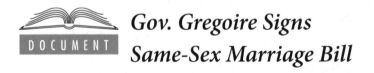

Gov. Gregoire Signs Same-Sex Marriage Bill

February 13, 2012

Good morning. Welcome! . . .

We are here to make history in Washington State!

I'm about to sign into law a bill making us the seventh state in the nation to give our gay and lesbian citizens marriage equality.

I'll explain and sign the bill in a few minutes, but first let me say that as governor for more than seven years, this is a very proud moment. . . .

. . . Most surely it is a proud day in the history of the Legislature and the state of Washington.

It is a day historians will mark as a milestone for equal rights. . . .

A day when we did what was right, we did what was just, and we did what was fair.

We stood up for equality and we did it together—Republicans and Democrats, gay and straight, young and old, and a number of religious faiths.

I'm proud of who and what we are in this state.

. . . I'm proud that our same-sex couples will no longer be treated as separate but equal. They will be equal.

I'm proud that children in our schools and neighborhoods will not have to wonder why their loving parents are considered different than other loving parents.

I'm proud of parents who have fought so fiercely for the rights of their much-loved gay and lesbian children. . . .

I'm proud that children who discover they are gay and lesbian can feel good about themselves. . . .

. . . Like the 16 year old girl who wrote to tell me her sexual orientation made her life hard, and that she had considered suicide. . . .

. . . But marriage equality would make her stronger and allow her to live and to dream of the day she would not have to get on bended knee and say: "Will you civil union me" but instead could say: "Will you marry me?"

I'm proud we live in a state where a six-year-old boy came to my office one day with his two Moms to deliver me a note written in neat little block letters that said:

"Please change the law so we can marry anyone we love."

I'm proud to live in a state where two women e-mailed me to say they have been together for 20 years this month, and can now look forward to the day they can vow their commitment and love in front of family and friends right here in their beloved Washington.

I'm proud to live in a state where, just last Thursday, a gay high-school senior wrote me to say he already has an associate's degree in computer science, and his future is so bright. . . . Except for one thing!

In his e-mail, he wrote:

"My biggest obstacle in life is clearly not my passion or intellect. It is my sexuality. I have grown up in a world where people are not accepted for who they are. . . .

"So I want you to know that I salute you and your government, because one day, as this nation continues to change, people like me will not have to be extraordinary to appear ordinary."

I am so very proud of our young people—including my two daughters—who tell us marriage equality is the civil-rights issue of their time, and who—pollsters say—are helping my generation to catch up.

I'm proud of so many who led the way—not just this year, but every hard step that came before.

And I'm proud of our legislators of both parties who stood up for what's right. Who fought against discrimination. Who took a personal journey—as I did—and voted their conscience.

I thank the Legislature not only for making history, but in the way they did it. Proponents and opponents were thoughtful and respectful! Marriage equality is a difficult issue, and feelings run high on both sides.

Yet, our Legislature conducted itself professionally and respectfully. Thank you, Speaker Chopp and Representative DeBolt in the House. Thank you, Majority Leader Brown and Senator Hewitt in the Senate. On this issue, you and your members showed the world the best of Washington State democracy.

And thank you to Reps. Jinkins, Moeller, Liias, and Upthegrove for your hard work.

And finally to Sen. Murray and Rep. Pedersen, thank you for your skilled leadership as prime sponsors of this marriage equality legislation.

We have been on a long journey together.

And the intelligence, care and patience you brought to this struggle over so many years defines what it means to be a great legislator.

We began in 2006 when we passed a law—too long in the making—to ban discrimination against members of our L-G-B-T community.

We said yes in 2007 and again in 2008 when we created and expanded domestic partnership rights.

Our voters said yes in 2009 to R-71 granting full domestic partner rights—and did so by a vote of 53 percent to 47 percent, the first time voters in any state upheld a domestic partnership law.

And now in 2012 our Senate said yes to this marriage equality bill by 28–21, and the House by 55–43.

The bill I'm signing today is simple and clear:

First, it gives same-sex couples the same right to a marriage license as heterosexual couples.

Second, churches or their affiliates do not have to perform same-sex marriages. The law provides an exemption and immunity for religious organizations, religiously affiliated educational institutions, ministers, priests, imams (ee-MOMS), rabbis and similar officials of religious organizations.

Third, no religious organization is required to provide accommodations, facilities, advantages, privileges, services, or goods related to the solemnization or celebration of a marriage.

In short, this bill preserves freedom of religion! For our churches—absolutely nothing changes!

Here in Washington, we've taken a long, difficult journey, and now the final step—the right step. We've finally said yes to marriage equality!

We join six other states and the District of Columbia in allowing same-sex marriage, and their experience proves that "the sky will fall" rhetoric is simply not true.

A recent University of New Hampshire poll found that a majority of New Hampshire citizens want to keep their marriage equality law partly because they realized it makes no difference in their own lives.

In Massachusetts, an economic study found that same-sex marriage improved the economy, and so did a similar study about same-sex marriage in Iowa.

The truth is, respectful, welcoming societies make a stronger economy. Thank you to companies like Microsoft and Starbucks, Google and Nike, Vulcan, Real Networks, Group Health, and Concur—who have already said yes to marriage equality in Washington.

And if asked, I believe the voters of Washington will say yes to marriage equality.

I believe Washingtonians will say yes because a family is a family—all facing the same challenges: Can we keep a roof over our heads, keep our jobs, and provide for our children's health, safety, education and happiness?

I believe Washingtonians will say yes because it is time to stand up for our sons and daughters, brothers and sisters, moms and dads, friends, and that couple just down the street.

I believe Washingtonians know it is time. . . . It is time to give loving gay and lesbian couples the right to a marriage license.

It is time to allow them to invite family and friends to witness their marriage.

I ask all Washingtonians to look into your hearts and ask yourselves:

Isn't it time?

Isn't it time to tell the children of same-sex couples that their parents are as loving and important as any others?

Isn't it time to support strong families, and make Washington stronger too?

And isn't it time to send a message to the world that Washington believes in equality for all—I believe if we ask ourselves those questions, our answers will be yes—marriage equality is right for Washington State. And the time is now.

Over the last month thousands of people have called and written from around our state, our nation and the world to say thank you to me. But I have to say that as I look out over this room, you are the ones to thank.

. . . You who have been fighting for this day for years. . . .

. . . You [who] took time to attend and testify at legislative hearings. . . .

. . . You who fought for your gay and lesbian children . . . and other family members. . . .

. . . You with your own loved ones [who] are giving back to your communities and making our state stronger.

This is your time. I'm just proud to stand with you at this great moment in our history. I'm proud to sign this bill bringing marriage equality to the great State of Washington.

And now I'll sign the bill.

SOURCE: Office of the Governor of Washington. Newsroom. "Marriage Equality Bill Signing." February 13, 2012. http://www.digitalarchives.wa.gov/GovernorGregoire/speeches/speech-view.asp?SpeechSeq=223.

OTHER HISTORIC DOCUMENTS OF INTEREST

FROM PREVIOUS *HISTORIC DOCUMENTS*

Federal Officials Announce
$26 Billion Mortgage Settlement

FEBRUARY 9, 2012

In 2010, it was revealed that some banks were using robo-signing techniques to fast-track foreclosure proceedings without checking that all of the paperwork was in order or ensuring that mortgage documents were not falsified. In September 2010, Ally Financial stopped foreclosure proceedings in twenty-three states after a lawsuit was filed alleging that an employee of the company was signing off on tens of thousands of foreclosures without looking at the documentation. Other banks followed suit, admitting their own robo-signing procedures, and on October 13, 2010, all fifty state attorneys general said they would look into mishandled documents and fraud in the foreclosure process. In 2011 alone, 1.9 million homes were foreclosed on with another 2 million in the foreclosure process as of late 2012. And over the past five years, home prices have fallen by one third, leaving 11 million homeowners holding mortgages that exceed the property value.

In an effort to alleviate some of the financial hardship experienced by homeowners and bring to justice those banks responsible for contributing to the failure of the housing market and financial crisis, forty-nine state attorneys general agreed to a $26 billion settlement with five mortgage servicers. Most of the settlement amount will go toward helping homeowners reduce mortgage debts or refinance their mortgages at a lower interest rate, while some of those foreclosed on between 2008 and 2011 will receive a small stipend. The settlement is not expected to help the housing market's recovery, and many homeowners are ineligible for assistance. However, President Barack Obama's administration considers it a starting point for homeowner aid and further economic recovery. Oklahoma was the only state that refused to commit to the deal, instead reaching a separate agreement with the five banks.

TERMS OF THE SETTLEMENT

It took more than a year for the states party to the $26 billion settlement to reach an agreement with Bank of America, Wells Fargo, JPMorgan Chase, Citigroup, and Ally. California, New York, and Oklahoma were the last holdout states, hoping to get a better deal that would provide more aid to homeowners, but in an all-night session shortly before the agreement was reached, California and New York came on board. The banks had agreed that without those two states, they would be unwilling to settle for the full $26 billion.

The five banks included in the February 2012 settlement will each pay a portion of the $26 billion. Bank of America will pay $11.8 billion; Wells Fargo is contributing $5.4 billion, JPMorgan Chase $5.3 billion, Citigroup $2.2 billion, and Ally $310 million. Bank of America will pay an additional $1 billion to the Federal Housing Administration (FHA) to settle claims that its subsidiary, Countrywide Financial, defrauded the FHA. These five banks handle the payments of 55 percent of all outstanding mortgages in the United States, or about 27 million mortgages. Out of the settlement amount, $20 billion will go toward reducing mortgage debts and refinancing mortgages for 1 million

Americans. Approximately $17 billion is expected to be used for principal reduction while the remainder goes toward refinancing. Given this, banks are more likely to work first with the loans on their own books, rather than those they are servicing for another company, because they will receive the largest credit to meet their minimum targets of borrowers assisted. Most of the homeowners who qualify for principal reductions will receive up to $20,000, and Bank of America customers can expect to receive up to $100,000. Approximately $1.5 billion of the deal total will give stipends of $1,500 to $2,000 to some 750,000 of the homeowners who were foreclosed on between 2008 and 2011, while the remainder of the funds will be sent from the banks to the states and federal government for foreclosure prevention. Homeowners in Florida and California will receive nearly half of the total settlement amount because of the greater number of delinquent and underwater loans—those with a value greater than the property's worth—in those states.

Oklahoma chose not to sign on to the deal, reaching instead an $18.6 million settlement with the five lenders on February 9, 2012. According to the Oklahoma attorney general's office, those in the state affected by unfair lending practices or robo-signing will receive more compensation than they would have under the federal settlement. Oklahomans are still eligible to participate in the principal reduction and refinancing portion of the national settlement; no portion of the $18.6 million will be used for these purposes.

Help for Homeowners and the Housing Market?

Banks are being given three years to distribute the aid and work with homeowners on principal reduction and refinancing, but the attorneys general have stated that they would like a bulk of the work to take place in the first twelve months after the deal was reached. The first step for the banks involved will be to figure out which homeowners are eligible and contact them. Based on the terms of the settlement, to be eligible for principal reduction or refinancing, a homeowner's loan must be serviced by one of the banks included in the deal. Mortgages owned but not serviced by these banks are ineligible. Qualified homeowners will be allowed to refinance only if they are underwater and current on their payments, while those seeking principal reduction must be at "imminent risk" of defaulting. "The settlement includes far-reaching relief that will help many of our customers and complement our already extensive efforts to improve our borrower assistance efforts and servicing processes," said Amy Bonitatibus, spokesperson for Chase.

Despite the rosy picture painted by banks, the settlement has many critics. "It is frankly a headline victory for both banks and attorneys general with a modest impact on the housing market," said Joshua Rosner, managing director of the investment firm Graham Fisher & Co. A majority of the criticism has focused on how many homeowners are ineligible for any relief under the settlement because it does not include anyone with a loan owned by Fannie Mae and Freddie Mac, or nearly half of all American homeowners, as well as mortgages held by private investors not party to the deal. Department of Housing and Urban Development Secretary Shaun Donovan said he hopes the settlement will help spur homeowner assistance through these government mortgage programs. "We do believe there should be principal reduction at Fannie Mae and Freddie Mac," he said, adding, "We've been disappointed that this hasn't happened thus far."

Others have criticized the settlement's time frame. Katherine Porter, a law professor at the University of California at Irvine, said the settlement lacks urgency. "That three-year window makes me really nervous because a lot of people could be out of their homes by then," Porter said. She also noted that, while the sum seems large, only a small number of those who have lost their homes would be impacted. Others are concerned about the danger that the settlement will encourage homeowners to default on their mortgages in an effort to receive aid.

Supporters of the settlement recognize its limitations. "No compensation, no amount of money, no measure of justice is enough to make it right for a family who's had their piece of the American dream wrongly taken from them," said President Obama. "And no action, no matter how meaningful, is going to by itself entirely heal the housing market. But this settlement is a start," he continued. With 2 million homes currently in the foreclosure process and $700 billion in underwater mortgage debt across the country, this agreement is a drop in the bucket. But, says Roy Cooper, North Carolina's attorney general, "This agreement is more important for the foreclosures we're hoping to prevent." And preventing future foreclosures is in the best interest of banks because foreclosure is often more costly than loan modification. Banks may benefit from the removal of some legal uncertainty that forced stock prices down and slowed lending; however, that is still unlikely to impact future mortgages. But, agree Donovan and Attorney General Eric Holder, this settlement will force banks to prevent and avoid future problems similar to those that collapsed the housing market. "With this settlement, we recover precious taxpayer resources, fix a broken system and lay a groundwork for a better future," said Holder. Donovan added, "No more lost paperwork. No more excuses. No more runaround."

Nine other mortgage servicers are in discussions with state attorneys general to come to a similar agreement, which could increase the total homeowner relief to $30 billion or more.

FUTURE SETTLEMENTS POSSIBLE

The five banks included in this settlement are not immune from future prosecution. Homeowners who receive assistance from the settlement still have the option to sue one of the banks. Lenders could also face criminal charges brought by state attorneys general for fraud in the loan process and packaging of mortgages into securities. However, if the five banks follow the terms of the settlement—including ending robo-signing; using legal procedures in the foreclosure process; stopping servicer abuses, such as harassing borrowers who are delinquent on payments; and offering more principal reductions in the mortgage modification processes—future state claims cannot be brought against them for foreclosure abuse from robo-signing. The New York attorney general has said that he will continue with his lawsuit against Bank of America, JPMorgan Chase, and Wells Fargo for an electronic mortgage database that the attorney general claims contributed to improper foreclosures.

—Heather Kerrigan

Following is the text of two statements—the first delivered by Attorney General Eric Holder and the second by Housing and Urban Development Secretary Shaun Donovan—from February 9, 2012, on the details of the $26 billion foreclosure settlement reached with five of the country's largest banks.

Attorney General Remarks on Housing Settlement

February 9, 2012

Good morning. I'm pleased to join with Secretary Shaun Donovan; Attorney General for the State of Iowa, Tom Miller; Associate Attorney General, Tom Perrelli; HUD Inspector General, David Montoya; and Attorney General for the State of Colorado, John Suthers—to announce our latest step forward in righting the wrongs that led to our nation's housing-market collapse and economic crisis.

Today, the Departments of Justice and Housing and Urban Development—along with 49 state attorneys general and other federal agencies—have reached a landmark $25 billion agreement with the nation's five largest mortgage servicers: Bank of America, JPMorgan Chase & Co., Wells Fargo & Company, Citibank, and Ally Financial, which was formerly GMAC.

This agreement reflects our commitment—at both the federal and state levels—to ensure justice, and to recover losses, for victims of reckless and abusive mortgage practices. In addition to addressing many of the most egregious mortgage loan servicing abuses that our investigations have uncovered, this agreement establishes significant new homeowner protections to help prevent future misconduct. It also provides substantial financial assistance to victim borrowers. In fact, it is the largest joint federal-state civil settlement in history.

Although every American can be encouraged by today's settlement and the progress it achieves, I realize more work must be done. That's why we have taken steps to ensure that the claims we are releasing through this settlement will not interfere with our ability to move current investigations and prosecutions forward—and to advance the work of the Financial Fraud Enforcement Task Force.

Let me be clear on this. While today's agreement resolves certain civil claims based on mortgage loan servicing activities, it does not prevent state and federal authorities from pursuing criminal enforcement actions. And it preserves extensive claims related to mortgage securitization activities, including the claims that will be the focus of the new Residential Mortgage-Backed Securities Working Group. Furthermore, the agreement does not prevent any claims by any individual borrowers who wish to bring their own lawsuits.

This agreement underscores a point that many of you heard me make here at the Justice Department, less than two weeks ago, when Secretary Donovan and I announced—and convened the first meeting of—the Financial Fraud Enforcement Task Force's new Residential Mortgage-Backed Securities Working Group. I noted that, by focusing on collaboration—and by bringing our government's full enforcement resources to bear—we can improve our ability to identify and prosecute misconduct in our financial markets, recover losses, prevent fraud, and hold those who violate the law accountable.

Today's settlement proves this—and is a remarkable example of cooperative law enforcement. Multiple federal agencies—including DOJ, HUD's Office of the Inspector General, the Federal Housing Administration, the Federal Housing Finance Agency, the

Board of Governors of the Federal Reserve System, the Federal Trade Commission, and the Special Inspector General for the Trouble Assets Relief Program—played key roles in achieving this settlement. And we partnered with state attorney general offices and state banking regulators from across the country, who brought valuable expertise—and unique, on-the-ground experience with those directly affected by the foreclosure crisis—to this resolution.

In particular, I want to recognize the outstanding work of the Justice Department's United States Trustees Program, and our United States Attorneys' Offices.

The U.S. Trustees Program, which serves as the watchdog of all bankruptcy court operations, was one of the first federal agencies to investigate mortgage servicer abuse of homeowners in financial distress. As part of their investigation, Trustees reviewed more than 37,000 documents filed by major mortgage servicers in federal bankruptcy court—and took discovery in more than 175 cases across the country. These efforts were advanced by several United States Attorneys, including U.S. Attorney Loretta Lynch from the Eastern District of New York, who is here with us. During a three-year investigation, her office issued multiple subpoenas, reviewed over two million documents, and interviewed numerous witnesses. They have worked tirelessly to seek justice for homeowners who were treated unfairly and taxpayers who footed the bill. And the information and evidence that these teams compiled—and the expertise they provided—was essential in reaching this historic settlement.

Similar large-scale reviews were also conducted by HUD, FHA, and others. Our investigations revealed disturbing practices. For instance, we saw that—far too often—servicers pushed borrowers into foreclosure, even though federal regulations required the servicers to try other alternatives first. These failures didn't just hurt borrowers who might have been able to afford modified mortgages. They fueled the downward spiral of our economy—and of communities nationwide. They eroded faith in our financial systems. And they punished American taxpayers, who have had to foot the bill for foreclosures that could have been avoided.

With this settlement, we are recovering precious taxpayer resources. And the state attorneys general will be establishing a fund to facilitate payments to borrowers who, as a result of improper lending practices, lost their homes during the foreclosure crisis. Mortgage servicers also will be required to dedicate substantial resources—approximately $20 billion—to provide relief and assistance to struggling homeowners and neighborhoods. And the agreement includes specific provisions that will enhance protections—and help ensure justice—for U.S. service members and their families.

I also want to note that, with this settlement, we aren't just holding mortgage servicers accountable for wrongs they committed. We are using this opportunity to fix a broken system, and to lay the groundwork for a better future. Our nation's leading mortgage servicers will be required to follow a new set of standards, which will be overseen by an independent monitor—and will be enforceable in federal court.

My colleagues will discuss some of the details of today's settlement more specifically—and I encourage anyone seeking addition[al] information to visit a new website that we've established: www.NationalMortgageSettlement.com.

I want to thank everyone who contributed to this achievement. And, now, I'd like to turn things over to one of the leaders of this important work—Secretary Shaun Donovan.

SOURCE: U.S. Department of Justice. Office of Public Affairs. "Attorney General Eric Holder Speaks at the Mortgage Servicers Settlement Press Conference." February 9, 2012. http://www.justice.gov/iso/opa/ag/speeches/2012/ag-speech-120209.html.

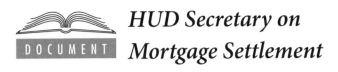

HUD Secretary on Mortgage Settlement

February 9, 2012

Thank you, Eric. I want to thank you and the whole bipartisan coalition who made this settlement possible—one, as you mentioned, only second in size to the tobacco settlement. And I want to thank Iowa's Attorney General Tom Miller as well.

This historic settlement will provide immediate relief to homeowners—forcing banks to reduce the principal balance on many loans, refinance loans for underwater borrowers, and pay billions of dollars to states and consumers.

And it comes not a moment too soon for homeowners, for our housing market and for our economy.

We all know how the housing bubble burst—how lenders sold loans to people who couldn't afford them and how they packaged those mortgages up to make profits that turned out to be nothing more than a mirage.

And we know these actions hurt millions of families—families who did the right thing but still lost their house or saw their home prices drop.

But as the banks acknowledge with this settlement—and as HUD, state attorneys general and banking regulators across the country heard from consumers across the country—those abuses didn't stop there. They continued long after people got the keys to their new homes.

We know this because in the summer of 2010, HUD initiated a large-scale review of the Federal Housing Administration's largest servicers.

Devoting thousands of hours to reviewing servicing files for thousands of FHA-insured loans, the scope of this review encompassed a long list of mortgage servicing issues, such as lost paperwork, long delays and missed deadlines for loan modifications.

As HUD's Office of the Inspector General found, the country's five largest loan servicers routinely signed foreclosure related documents without really knowing whether the facts they contained were even correct.

In effect, many of the very same financial institutions responsible for so much of this crisis were actually making it worse—harming families, neighborhoods and our economy.

This settlement holds those institutions accountable for their actions, to the tune of $25 billion—$30 billion if all 14 servicers join, and possibly billions more in relief for homeowners.

But this isn't just about punishing the banks for their irresponsible behavior.

It's also about requiring them to help the people they harmed—by funding to efforts to help homeowners stay in their homes.

And that's precisely what this settlement delivers, reducing the overall loan balance for approximately a million families who owe more on their mortgages than their homes are worth.

Principal reduction at this scale will not only help these underwater homeowners start building equity again—but also their neighbors, many of whom have watched their own property values plummet by $5,000–10,000 simply because they live on the same block as a foreclosed home.

The settlement will also help unemployed homeowners to catch up on late mortgage payments. It funds housing counseling services to connect at risk families to the help they need. And it helps communities struggling with vacant properties that drag down neighborhood home values.

And by instituting tough penalties and stringent timelines enforced by an independent monitor, banks have a strong incentive to provide this help quickly and effectively.

The settlement also provides cash payments to homeowners who were victims of deceptive servicing practices.

We all recognize that you cannot undo the pain of this crisis by writing a check. But these payments provide victims with welcome and needed relief.

One of the most important ways this settlement helps homeowners is that it forces the banks to clean up their acts and fix the problems uncovered during our investigations. And it does that by committing them to major reforms in how they service mortgage loans.

These new customer service standards are in keeping with the Homeowners Bill of Rights recently announced by President Obama—a single, straightforward set of commonsense rules that families can count on. And they require lenders and servicers in this settlement, which service nearly 2 out of every 3 mortgages, to follow a long list of rights for those facing foreclosure.

No more lost paperwork. No more excuses. No more runaround.

And this is just the first step. Indeed, last month, Attorney General Holder and I announced an investigation into the conduct of financial servicers that broke the law and led to the crash of the housing market, including securities- and origination-related cases.

So, while it isn't designed to address all the issues of the housing crisis, it is a historic agreement—and a very big victory for those who[m] it harmed the most.

And combined with the broad-based refinancing plan President Obama announced to help homeowners last month, it provides a path toward stability for our housing market and our broader economy.

Banks and mortgage servicers expect that homeowners will meet their obligations under a mortgage. Homeowners should have the same expectation of them.

Holding the banks accountable is what this servicing settlement is about—and it's why I'm proud to join my partners in announcing it today.

SOURCE: U.S. Department of Housing and Urban Development. Press Room. "Prepared Remarks of Secretary Shaun Donovan at a Press Conference Announcing the Mortgage Servicing Settlement." February 9, 2012. http://portal.hud.gov/hudportal/HUD?src=/press/speeches_remarks_statements/2012/Speech_02092012.

OTHER HISTORIC DOCUMENTS OF INTEREST

FROM THIS VOLUME

FROM PREVIOUS HISTORIC DOCUMENTS

President Obama on Contraception Compromise

FEBRUARY 10, 2012

Early in 2012, women's health emerged as one of the most fiercely debated issues in U.S. politics. In January and February, President Barack Obama fueled an ongoing debate over contraception with a series of decisions related to preventive care services covered by the Affordable Care Act, prompting congressional hearings on the matter. A controversial decision by Susan G. Komen for the Cure (a national charity) to cut its funding to Planned Parenthood, later reversed, and statements made by Republican candidates regarding rape and abortion also helped make women's health a key issue in the 2012 elections.

DEFINING "PREVENTIVE CARE" UNDER THE AFFORDABLE CARE ACT

Signed into law in 2010, the Affordable Care Act requires that all new health insurance plans cover certain preventive health services without a co-pay. For women, covered preventive services included mammograms, pap smears, and cancer screenings. Following an Institute of Medicine recommendation, this list was expanded to include contraceptive and sterilization services in August 2011. Because the law applies to the full range of contraceptive methods approved by the Federal Drug Administration, emergency contraceptives, such as Plan B, are also covered.

The move prompted an outcry from numerous religious groups and institutions. They claimed the Obama administration's decision infringed upon their religious liberty because, as employers, they had a religious objection to directly providing insurance that covers contraceptive services for their employees, particularly emergency contraceptives. The White House had allowed religiously affiliated organizations an additional year to comply with the mandate, meaning they would not need to offer contraceptive coverage until August 2013, but critics argued that that did not address their moral objections. On January 20, 2012, the administration responded by exempting all churches from the law's requirement. Critics claimed the church exemption was still insufficient, as it did not apply to other religiously affiliated institutions, but administration officials argued that no woman should be denied access to preventive care because of where she works.

On February 10, Obama announced a new rule on preventive care, intended to address the dispute. Under the rule, religiously affiliated nonprofit organizations, such as hospitals and charities, are not required to directly provide contraceptive services to female employees as part of their health plan. Instead, those employees can obtain contraceptive coverage directly from their insurance companies at no additional cost. Announcing the rule, Obama claimed, "Religious liberty will be protected, and a law that requires free preventive care will not discriminate against women."

Several religious groups immediately denounced the rule. The U.S. Conference of Catholic Bishops argued the proposal continues "to threaten government coercion of religious people and groups to violate their most deeply held convictions." The bishops and others claimed that religious and secular for-profit employers should also be protected from the mandate, meaning that if a sporting goods store owner believed birth control pills were immoral, he should be able to offer his employees health insurance that does not include contraception coverage. They also questioned what a religiously affiliated organization that self-insures and objects to contraception would do, as there would be no insurance company that could provide coverage directly to employees in that case.

Others praised the new rule. Sister Carol Keehan, leader of the Catholic Health Association of the United States, said, "The framework developed has responded to the issues we identified that needed to be fixed." Planned Parenthood President Cecile Richards said, "in the face of a misleading and outrageous assault on women's health," the rule "does not compromise a woman's ability to access these critical birth control benefits."

Republicans and Democrats adhered to their typical party positions, with Democrats applauding the move and Republicans claiming it was a threat to religious freedom. Republicans promised to pursue legislation that would repeal the health law's requirement for employers to cover contraception.

SUSAN G. KOMEN FOR THE CURE CUTS, RESTORES PLANNED PARENTHOOD FUNDING

In the midst of the contraception debate, a spokesperson for Susan G. Komen for the Cure, the nation's leading charity dedicated to breast cancer research and prevention, told the Associated Press on January 31 that it would cut its grant funding for breast cancer screening and education programs run by nineteen Planned Parenthood affiliates. As part of its broader programming, Planned Parenthood provides breast examinations and covers the costs of mammograms and ultrasounds for women who otherwise could not afford necessary diagnostic services.

A Komen spokesperson said the organization had adopted a new rule prohibiting grants to organizations under investigation by local, state, or federal authorities. Rep. Cliff Stearns, R-Fla., was conducting an inquiry into how Planned Parenthood spends and reports its funding; therefore, the organization was disqualified from receiving grants. Additionally, Komen officials said they were concerned that because of the investigation, they could lose credibility with their donors.

Conversely, Planned Parenthood representatives claimed Komen's decision was politically motivated, and it was caving in to long-standing pressure from antiabortion groups. Planned Parenthood is known to be the country's leading provider of abortion services. "There has been a years-long coordinated pressure campaign from right-wing organizations to get Komen to sever ties with Planned Parenthood," said Eric Ferrero, vice president for communications at Planned Parenthood. "The true culprits here are the organizations that bullied, harassed and pressured Komen for years on this."

Planned Parenthood had increasingly drawn scrutiny from Capitol Hill, with some conservative lawmakers arguing that, because it provides abortions, the group should not receive federal funding for other services such as contraceptives and preventive screenings. Planned Parenthood supporters suggested that Komen's new senior vice president for public policy, Karen Handel, made or directly influenced the funding decision. Handel is a Republican who, as a gubernatorial candidate in Georgia, previously called for an end to Planned Parenthood's funding.

The Komen decision generated a major backlash. Several of the organization's board members resigned, as did the executive director of its Los Angeles chapter.

Some Komen state chapters sent letters to the group's Texas headquarters, opposing the position, and the Connecticut chapter refused to defund that state's Planned Parenthood affiliate. Furthermore, twenty-two senators signed a letter calling for Komen to reverse its decision.

The Komen decision did, however, drive a tremendous increase in donations to Planned Parenthood, which received $650,000 for a new Breast Health Emergency Fund within twenty-four hours of Komen's announcement. New York Mayor Michael Bloomberg was among the contributors, pledging to match donations dollar for dollar, up to $250,000. By the end of the week, Planned Parenthood had raised nearly $3 million for breast cancer programs.

Under tremendous pressure, Komen reversed its decision to cut Planned Parenthood's funding on February 3. In a statement signed by Komen Founder Nancy Brinker and its board of directors, the organization apologized "for recent decisions that cast doubt upon our commitment to our mission of saving women's lives." It also said Komen would amend its new funding criteria to ensure politics was not involved in the grant process and to make clear that a group under investigation will be disqualified only if the probe "is criminal and conclusive in nature and not political." Planned Parenthood responded by saying it was "enormously grateful" that Komen amended the rules and looked forward "to continuing our partnership."

Republican Hearing on Obama Contraception Rule

Less than two weeks after Komen's reversal, the House Committee on Oversight and Government Reform, led by Rep. Darrell Issa, R-Calif., held a hearing on Obama's contraceptive coverage rule. Both the House and Senate were considering legislation that would block the rule, including an amendment proposed by Sen. Roy Blunt, R-Mo., that would permit employers and insurers to refuse to provide or pay for coverage of "specific items or services" if the coverage would be "contrary to the religious beliefs or moral convictions of the sponsor, issuer or other entity offering the plan."

Hearing witnesses included Lutheran and Baptist clergy, an Orthodox rabbi, and a Roman Catholic bishop. All expressed different views on contraception, but all agreed that Obama's rule was insufficient to address concerns about religious freedom. "The putative accommodation is no accommodation at all," said Meir Soloveichik of Yeshiva University and Congregation Kehilath Jeshurun in New York City. "Religious organizations would still be obligated to provide employees with an insurance policy that facilitates acts violating the organization's religious tenets," he continued.

Democratic lawmakers accused Issa of stacking the panel with witnesses who only shared the Republican perspective and for failing to include women, though two did testify. Several female members of Congress walked out of the hearing in protest, and a group of female Democratic senators protested the following day on the Senate floor, calling it an "assault on women." House Democrats also claimed Issa rejected their requested witness, Georgetown law student Sandra Fluke. Issa said he did not believe Fluke was an appropriate witness since she was not a member of the clergy and that Democrats did not submit her name in time for consideration. He also said Republicans initially invited Democratic witness Rev. Barry Lynn of Americans United for Separation of Church and State, but Democrats told Lynn not to attend the hearing.

On February 23, House Democrats held their own hearing on women's health and contraception, with only Democratic lawmakers present and featuring Fluke as the only witness. Fluke spoke of her experience as the former president of Georgetown Law's Students for Reproductive Justice Group and shared stories of Georgetown students who had not been able to obtain contraceptive services through the Jesuit-affiliated school's student health plans. "On a daily basis, I hear from yet another woman from Georgetown or from another school or who works for a religiously affiliated employer, and they tell me that they have suffered financially, emotionally and medically, because of this lack of coverage," she said.

Fluke's testimony drew the attention of conservative talk radio host Rush Limbaugh, who claimed on his show that Fluke "wants to be paid to have sex." Limbaugh continued making similar comments for several days and ultimately declared, "If we are going to pay for your contraceptives, and thus pay for you to have sex, we want something for it, and I'll tell you what it is. We want you to post the videos online so we can all watch." Limbaugh's comments were immediately criticized by political leaders and advocacy organizations on both the right and the left, and many advertisers discontinued their sponsorship of his show. He later apologized, saying he "did not mean a personal attack on Ms. Fluke."

The Senate ultimately voted against Senator Blunt's bill on March 1, and House Republicans shelved similar efforts, following the vote.

REMARKS ON RAPE BECOME ELECTION-SEASON FODDER

Republicans continued to draw criticism for their positions on women's health issues, particularly following controversial comments made by two Republican candidates for Senate.

In an August interview with St. Louis television station KTVI, Rep. Todd Akin, R-Mo., attempted to explain why he opposes abortion even when a pregnancy is the result of a rape. "First of all, from what I understand from doctors, [pregnancy from rape] is really rare," Akin said. "If it's a legitimate rape, the female body has ways to try and shut that whole thing down." The remarks sparked an immediate uproar, with critics questioning what Akin meant by "legitimate rape" and expressing concern that he did not understand scientific fact. Akin later issued a statement on August 19, saying he "misspoke" and that his remarks did "not reflect the deep empathy I hold for the thousands of women who are raped and abused every year." Republicans pressured Akin to drop out of the race, but he declined to withdraw. In November, he lost his race to Democrat Claire McCaskill.

In October, Indiana State Treasurer Richard Mourdock, who was running for U.S. Senate, said during a debate that "even when life begins in that horrible situation of rape, that is something God intended to happen." Democratic National Committee Chair Debbie Wasserman Schultz called Mourdock's remarks "outrageous and demeaning to women" and said such comments had become "part and parcel of the modern Republican Party's platform toward women's health, as Congressional Republicans like Paul Ryan have worked to outlaw all abortions and even narrow the definition of rape." Mourdock later said his comments had been "twisted" and that he meant nothing more than that he believes "life is precious." Mourdock lost the election in November to Democratic opponent Joe Donnelly.

Democratic leaders worked to tie Republican presidential candidate Mitt Romney to Akin and Mourdock, including pointing to Romney's previous endorsement of Mourdock. In both instances, Romney distanced himself from the candidates, declaring that their comments did not reflect his views. He also sought to reassure voters that, if elected, he and running mate Rep. Paul Ryan, R-Wis., would not oppose abortion in instances of rape, incest, or when the life of the woman is in danger.

—Linda Fecteau

Following is a statement by President Barack Obama on February 10, 2012, announcing a new preventive care rule that would allow religiously affiliated nonprofit organizations to deny contraceptive services to female employees, giving those employees the option instead to purchase these services directly from their insurance company at no additional cost.

President Obama on Contraception and Women's Health

February 10, 2012

... As part of the health care reform law that I signed last year, all insurance plans are required to cover preventive care at no cost. That means free checkups, free mammograms, immunizations, and other basic services. We fought for this because it saves lives and it saves money for families, for businesses, for Government, for everybody. And that's because it's a lot cheaper to prevent an illness than to treat one.

We also accepted a recommendation from the experts at the Institute of Medicine that when it comes to women, preventive care should include coverage of contraceptive services such as birth control. In addition to family planning, doctors often prescribe contraception as a way to reduce the risks of ovarian and other cancers and treat a variety of different ailments. And we know that the overall cost of health care is lower when women have access to contraceptive services.

Nearly 99 percent of all women have relied on contraception at some point in their lives—99 percent. And yet more than half of all women between the ages of 18 and 34 have struggled to afford it. So for all these reasons, we decided to follow the judgment of the Nation's leading medical experts and make sure that free preventive care includes access to free contraceptive care.

Whether you're a teacher or a small-business woman or a nurse or a janitor, no woman's health should depend on who she is or where she works or how much money she makes. Every woman should be in control of the decisions that affect her own health— period. This basic principle is already the law in 28 States across the country.

Now, as we move to implement this rule, however, we've been mindful that there's another principle at stake here, and that's the principle of religious liberty, an inalienable right that is enshrined in our Constitution. As a citizen and as a Christian, I cherish this right.

In fact, my first job in Chicago was working with Catholic parishes in poor neighborhoods, and my salary was funded by a grant from an arm of the Catholic Church. And I saw that local churches often did more good for a community than a government program ever could, so I know [the importance of] the work that faith-based organizations do and how much impact they can have in their communities.

I also know that some religious institutions, particularly those affiliated with the Catholic Church, have a religious objection to directly providing insurance that covers contraceptive services for their employees. And that's why we originally exempted all churches from this requirement—an exemption, by the way, that eight States didn't already have.

And that's why, from the very beginning of this process, I spoke directly to various Catholic officials, and I promised that before finalizing the rule as it applied to them, we would spend the next year working with institutions like Catholic hospitals and Catholic universities to find an equitable solution that protects religious liberty and ensures that every woman has access to the care that she needs.

Now, after the many genuine concerns that have been raised over the last few weeks, as well as, frankly, the more cynical desire on the part of some to make this into a political football, it became clear that spending months hammering out a solution was not going to be an option, that we needed to move this faster. So last week, I directed the Department of Health and Human Services to speed up the process that had already been envisioned. We weren't going to spend a year doing this, we're going to spend a week or two doing this.

Today we've reached a decision on how to move forward. Under the rule, women will still have access to free preventive care that includes contraceptive services, no matter where they work. So that core principle remains. But if a woman's employer is a charity or a hospital that has a religious objection to providing contraceptive services as part of their health plan, the insurance company—not the hospital, not the charity—will be required to reach out and offer the woman contraceptive care free of charge, without copays and without hassles.

The result will be that religious organizations won't have to pay for these services, and no religious institution will have to provide these services directly. Let me repeat: These employers will not have to pay for or provide contraceptive services. But women who work at these institutions will have access to free contraceptive services just like other women, and they'll no longer have to pay hundreds of dollars a year that could go towards paying the rent or buying groceries.

Now, I've been confident from the start that we could work out a sensible approach here, just as I promised. I understand some folks in Washington may want to treat this as another political wedge issue, but it shouldn't be. I certainly never saw it that way. This is an issue where people of good will on both sides of the debate have been sorting through some very complicated questions to find a solution that works for everyone. With today's announcement, we've done that. Religious liberty will be protected, and a law that requires free preventive care will not discriminate against women.

Now, we live in a pluralistic society where we're not going to agree on every single issue or share every belief. That doesn't mean that we have to choose between individual liberty and basic fairness for all Americans. We are unique among nations for having been founded upon both these principles, and our obligation as citizens is to carry them forward. I have complete faith that we can do that.

Thank you very much, everybody.

SOURCE: Executive Office of the President. "Remarks on Preventive Health Care Insurance Coverage and an Exchange With Reporters." February 10, 2012. *Compilation of Presidential Documents* 2012, no. 00091 (February 10, 2012). http://www.gpo.gov/fdsys/pkg/DCPD-201200091/pdf/DCPD-201200091.pdf.

OTHER HISTORIC DOCUMENTS OF INTEREST

FROM PREVIOUS *HISTORIC DOCUMENTS*

- Health Care Reform Signed Into Law, *2010,* p. 83

European Leaders Agree to New Greek Bailout

FEBRUARY 21, 2012

The efforts of Europe's leaders to prevent Greece from sliding into a disorderly default on its debt reached another milestone on February 21, 2012, when the European Union (EU) agreed to a new bailout worth $165 billion (€130B). Under the deal, private creditors agreed to write off a large chunk of Greek debt, and EU governments agreed to make more bailout money available, in return for which Greece committed to more public spending cuts and structural reforms. The agreement, clinched after hours of tense negotiations among EU finance ministers in Brussels, Belgium, gave much-needed respite to the eurozone, the single currency area comprising seventeen EU members, including Greece. However, tensions simmered throughout 2012 as the Greek public's fury over the seemingly endless rounds of austerity being forced upon them erupted into violent clashes. Meanwhile, other highly indebted EU countries like Spain and Italy struggled to ward off their own crises.

First Bailout Insufficient

The new rescue package was cobbled together after it became clear that the first EU bailout in 2010 worth $147 billion was insufficient to prevent a chaotic default by Greece on its debt. This situation had arisen as a result of the global financial crisis of autumn 2008 and subsequent recession, which caused tax revenues to decline across Europe just as stimulus spending, aimed at avoiding an even deeper economic slump, was taking effect. Sovereign debt levels spiked, with the problem especially acute in Mediterranean countries, Ireland, and Portugal. What turned an already worrying situation in Greece into a prolonged crisis were the myriad structural flaws in its economy and government.

Greece's debt had been increasing steadily since 2001, when the European Union agreed to allow it to adopt the euro as its currency. Being part of the eurozone gave Greece a sense of security, which encouraged it to spend and borrow beyond its means. Wages and pensions rose faster than the economy grew, and the government failed to tackle long-term endemic problems, such as tax evasion. When a new government took office in October 2009, it discovered that the country's finances were in worse shape than the previous government had acknowledged. As the scale of the problem became evident, the financial markets lost faith in Greece's ability to pay back its debts. In response, the European Union in May 2010 created both a Greek bailout fund and an even bigger fund worth $560 billion that all indebted eurozone countries could potentially dip into. In addition, the European Union put in place a troika structure, comprising the European Commission, European Central Bank (ECB), and International Monetary Fund (IMF), to oversee implementation of bailout agreements. The troika's mandate was to disburse bailout funds only after it had verified that the recipient was proceeding with the required reforms.

After the first Greek bailout, the European Union gave the green light to a $108 billion bailout for Ireland in November 2010 and a $102 billion bailout for Portugal in May 2011. In July 2011, the European Union fine-tuned the Greek bailout deal by lowering interest rates; giving Greece more time to pay back the loans; and persuading private creditors, such as banks and investment funds, to write off some of the debt Greece owed them. But there was still massive resentment among Greeks over the austerity measures they were being asked to adopt, which made it very difficult for the Greek government to make the necessary adjustments such as cuts in public sector employment and pensions. The other side of that coin was that resentment grew among the EU countries that were contributing the most to the Greek bailout, notably Germany, the Netherlands, and Finland. Many of their citizens doubted the wisdom of trying to save a country so resistant to change.

NEW DEAL REACHED

Despite these mutual resentments, all sides were united by a desire to do whatever it took to keep Greece in the eurozone. EU leaders feared that a Greek exit from the eurozone—a "Grexit," as the media dubbed it—would have a devastating domino effect, causing markets to target other vulnerable eurozone members like Spain and Italy. Spain's economy was vulnerable because of a severe crisis in its undercapitalized banking sector, coupled with a 25 percent unemployment rate, while Italy's debt-to-gross domestic product (GDP) ratio, at 120 percent, was double the maximum allowed under eurozone membership rules. The question the markets were asking was, Would these countries be able to continue to pay their debts? Greeks also wanted to stay in the eurozone even if they strongly disliked the medicine they were being forced to swallow. With this common goal, EU finance ministers meeting in Brussels managed to hammer out a deal after thirteen hours, emerging at 5 a.m. on February 21, 2012. Its core elements were an additional $172 billion funding program for Greece; interest rates on Greece's loans lowered by 1.5 percentage points; private bondholders agreeing to write off $127 billion of Greek debt; the ECB agreeing to pass on, to national central banks and ultimately back to Athens, profits made from Greek debt repayments; the troika more strictly monitoring how Greece implements the required reforms; and revised fiscal targets requiring Greece to return to a primary surplus by 2013 and reduce its debt from 150 percent to 120.5 percent of GDP by 2020.

In return for this financial lifebuoy, Greece agreed to such measures as more privatization of state assets and liberalization of its labor markets—for example, by allowing more competition in certain professions that previously had been closed off. The government slashed the country's minimum wage by 22 percent, reduced pensions by $763 million, and imposed 15,000 job cuts in the public sector. The private bondholders, which included banks, insurers, pension funds, and investment funds, were represented at the Brussels talks by Charles Dallara and Jean Lemierre of the Institute of International Finance. They agreed to increase the amount of privately held debt to be written off from 50 percent to 53.5 percent of the nominal value of the debt. This amounted to about 70 percent losses on the Greek bonds' net present value—a write-off they insisted was "exceptional and unique." The European Commission installed a permanently embedded task force in Greece to keep it on the right track.

The Brussels deal relieved pressure on other bond markets, in particular Spanish and Italian bonds, whose interest rates decreased by about 1.5 percentage points. That had been a major concern for EU leaders because many doubted that the larger EU bailout fund, which in March 2012 was increased to more than $1 trillion, would be big enough to bail out large economies, such as Spain's and Italy's, if the situation there deteriorated to the level of Greece. Meanwhile, the European Union made a slew of decisions aimed at harmonizing fiscal policy. For example, in March 2012, a fiscal treaty was signed, providing for countries that persistently maintained excessive public deficits to be automatically fined by the European Union. While twenty-five of the European Union's twenty-seven member countries signed that treaty, the United Kingdom and the Czech Republic declined to do so, objecting to the loss of national sovereignty that it entailed.

New Political Forces Emerge

The Greek government that signed on the February 2012 deal was a technocratic government of unity led by Prime Minister Lucas Papademos, the previous government of George Papandreou having collapsed in November 2011 under the strain of the debt crisis. It took seven months and two elections—held in May and June 2012—for a successor government to be formed. Led by Antonis Samaras of the center-right New Democracy Party, the coalition consisted of New Democracy, the center-left Panhellenic Socialist Movement (PASOK), and the smaller left-wing Democratic Left party. The crisis has caused a precipitous drop in support for the two parties that had dominated Greek politics for decades, New Democracy and PASOK. New political forces have emerged, notably the antibailout, left-wing Coalition of the Radical Left (SYRIZA) party, now the second largest in Greece's 300-seat parliament with 72 seats, and the neo-Nazi Golden Dawn party, which won 18 seats in the June 2012 ballot.

While Greece remained in the eye of Europe's debt storm, the fallout is felt continent-wide—both in highly indebted countries and in the less indebted ones that contribute most of the bailout funds. In the Netherlands, for instance, the government collapsed in April 2012 after the departure of a coalition party that had heavily criticized the Greek bailout. Because many were predicting that this anti-EU group, the Party for Freedom led by Geert Wilders, would surge in the September 2012 Dutch elections, there was some surprise when the party lost seats. But while the new Dutch government, led by Prime Minister Mark Rutte, is solidly pro–European Union, it also takes a tough line on Greece, insisting that Athens fully implement agreed-upon austerity measures before any new installment of the bailout can be handed over. The Dutch-Greek tensions are symptomatic of a north-south cultural divide in Europe that the debt crisis has laid bare, which has pitted countries such as Germany and Finland against Greece and Portugal. The more fiscally prudent northern European states are insisting that their southern EU partners put their fiscal houses in order. With all these countries now in a single monetary area, there is less willingness to tolerate divergent approaches to deficits and debts.

While speculation was rampant in early 2012 that Greece's days as a euro area country were numbered, Greece and the European Union somehow managed to muddle through the year with the eurozone intact. By late 2012, the situation remained delicately poised. There were frequent street riots in Greece over the austerity cuts, and the Greek government continued to squabble with the European Union over how to implement its bailout program. Some commentators viewed the glass as being half full, with Greece proceeding steadily with painful reforms that will eventually transform it into a more efficient, functional country that can compete in the global economy and pay off its debts. But for the glass-half-empty camp, the austerity policies foisted on Greece have been a dismal failure, plunging its economy into five successive years of recession, with unemployment now in excess of 25 percent and youth unemployment topping 50 percent.

The situation for the other two recipients of EU bailout funds, Ireland and Portugal, is somewhat better. Portugal has been praised by the European Union and IMF for meeting its structural reform and deficit reduction targets, although it has yet to register an uptick in GDP growth. Ireland has managed both to comply with the terms of its bailout and restore modest economic growth. Italy and Spain have avoided having to dip into the EU bailout fund, although they remain in choppy waters. By autumn 2012, the small Mediterranean island of Cyprus was in talks with the European Union over a potential bailout worth several billion dollars for Cyprus Popular Bank, which sustained massive losses in Greece's debt restructuring. The broader question on observers' minds was whether the debt crisis would ultimately forge a stronger, more integrated Europe (and Greece) or one that leaves Europe a weakened and fractured force.

—Brian Beary

Following is a statement by the members of the Eurogroup released on February 21, 2012, announcing a new $165 billion bailout to help Greece close its fiscal gap.

DOCUMENT

European Union Announces New Greek Bailout

February 21, 2012

The Eurogroup welcomes the agreement reached with the Greek government on a policy package that constitutes the basis for the successor programme. We also welcome the approval of the policy package by the Greek parliament, the identification of additional structural expenditure reductions of €325 million to close the fiscal gap in 2012 and the provision of assurances by the leaders of the two coalition parties regarding the implementation of the programme beyond the forthcoming general elections.

This new programme provides a comprehensive blueprint for putting the public finances and the economy of Greece back on a sustainable footing and hence for safeguarding financial stability in Greece and in the euro area as a whole.

The Eurogroup is fully aware of the significant efforts already made by the Greek citizens but also underlines that further major efforts by the Greek society are needed to return the economy to a sustainable growth path.

Ensuring debt sustainability and restoring competiveness are the main goals of the new programme. Its success hinges critically on its thorough implementation by Greece. This implies that Greece must achieve the ambitious but realistic fiscal consolidation targets so as to return to a primary surplus as from 2013, carry out fully the privatisation plans and implement the bold structural reform agenda, in both the labour market and product and service markets, in order to promote competitiveness, employment and sustainable growth.

To this end, we deem essential a further strengthening of Greece's institutional capacity. We therefore invite the Commission to significantly strengthen its Task Force for

Greece, in particular through an enhanced and permanent presence on the ground in Greece, in order to bolster its capacity to provide and coordinate technical assistance. Euro area Member States stand ready to provide experts to be integrated into the Task Force. The Eurogroup also welcomes the stronger on site-monitoring capacity by the Commission to work in close and continuous cooperation with the Greek government in order to assist the Troika in assessing the conformity of measures that will be taken by the Greek government, thereby ensuring the timely and full implementation of the programme. The Eurogroup also welcomes Greece's intention to put in place a mechanism that allows better tracing and monitoring of the official borrowing and internally-generated funds destined to service Greece's debt by, under monitoring of the troika, paying an amount corresponding to the coming quarter's debt service directly to a segregated account of Greece's paying agent. Finally, the Eurogroup in this context welcomes the intention of the Greek authorities to introduce over the next two months in the Greek legal framework a provision ensuring that priority is granted to debt servicing payments. This provision will be introduced in the Greek constitution as soon as possible.

The Eurogroup acknowledges the common understanding that has been reached between the Greek authorities and the private sector on the general terms of the PSI exchange offer, covering all private sector bondholders. This common understanding provides for a nominal haircut amounting to 53.5%. The Eurogroup considers that this agreement constitutes an appropriate basis for launching the invitation for the exchange to holders of Greek government bonds (PSI). A successful PSI operation is a necessary condition for a successor programme. The Eurogroup looks forward to a high participation of private creditors in the debt exchange, which should deliver a significant positive contribution to Greece's debt sustainability.

The Eurogroup considers that the necessary elements are now in place for Member States to carry out the relevant national procedures to allow for the provision by EFSF of (i) a buy back scheme for Greek marketable debt instruments for Eurosystem monetary policy operations, (ii) the euro area's contribution to the PSI exercise, (iii) the repayment of accrued interest on Greek government bonds, and (iv) the residual (post PSI) financing for the second Greek adjustment programme, including the necessary financing for recapitalisation of Greek banks in case of financial stability concerns.

The Eurogroup takes note that the Eurosystem (ECB and NCBs) holdings of Greek government bonds have been held for public policy purposes. The Eurogroup takes note that the income generated by the Eurosystem holdings of Greek [g]overnment bonds will contribute to the profit of the ECB and of the NCBs. The ECB's profit will be disbursed to the NCBs, in line with the ECB's statutory profit distribution rules. The NCBs' profits will be disbursed to euro area Member States in line with the NCBs' statutory profit distribution rules.

- The Eurogroup has agreed that certain government revenues that emanate from the SMP profits disbursed by NCBs may be allocated by Member States to further improving the sustainability of Greece's public debt. All Member States have agreed to an additional retroactive lowering of the interest rates of the Greek Loan Facility so that the margin amounts to 150 basis points. There will be no additional compensation for higher funding costs. This will bring down the debt-to-GDP ratio in 2020 by 2.8pp and lower financing needs by around 1.4 bn euro over the programme period. National procedures for the ratification of this amendment to the Greek Loan Facility Agreement need to be urgently initiated so that it can enter into force as soon as possible.

• Furthermore, governments of Member States where central banks currently hold Greek government bonds in their investment portfolio commit to pass on to Greece an amount equal to any future income accruing to their national central bank stemming from this portfolio until 2020. These income flows would be expected to help reducing the Greek debt ratio by 1.8pp by 2020 and are estimated to lower the financing needs over the programme period by approximately 1.8 bn euro.

The respective contributions from the private and the official sector should ensure that Greece's public debt ratio is brought on a downward path reaching 120.5% of GDP by 2020. On this basis, and provided policy conditionality under the programme is met on an ongoing basis, the Eurogroup confirms that euro area Member States stand ready to provide, through the EFSF and with the expectation that the IMF will make a significant contribution, additional official programme of up to 130 bn euro until 2014.

It is understood that the disbursements for the PSI operation and the final decision to approve the guarantees for the second programme are subject to a successful PSI operation and confirmation, by the Eurogroup on the basis of an assessment by the Troika, of the legal implementation by Greece of the agreed prior actions. The official sector will decide on the precise amount of financial assistance to be provided in the context of the second Greek programme in early March, once the results of PSI are known and the prior actions have been implemented.

We reiterate our commitment to provide adequate support to Greece during the life of the programme and beyond until it has regained market access, provided that Greece fully complies with the requirements and objectives of the adjustment programme.

SOURCE: Council of the European Union. "Eurogroup Statement." February 21, 2012. http://consilium .europa.eu/uedocs/cms_data/docs/pressdata/en/ecofin/128075.pdf.

OTHER HISTORIC DOCUMENTS OF INTEREST

FROM THIS VOLUME

FROM PREVIOUS *HISTORIC DOCUMENTS*

March

Mitt Romney and the RNC Remark on 2012 Presidential Primary

MARCH 6 AND AUGUST 31, 2012

As 2011 drew to a close, the Republican field of presidential candidates narrowed to four front-runners—former Massachusetts' Governor Mitt Romney, former Pennsylvania Senator Rick Santorum, former Speaker of the House Newt Gingrich, and Texas Congressman Ron Paul. Primary results in early 2012 revealed a divided Republican Party and sparked concern that the race for who would take on President Barack Obama in the November general election could stretch all the way to the party's August convention. "That will be very tough for the party if millions of dollars more are spent on Republicans attacking Republicans," said Al Cardenas, chair of the American Conservative Union. The four contenders jockeyed for the front-runner position throughout the first few months of the year, and it was not until April that the Republican National Committee (RNC) declared Romney the presumptive nominee and began its general election campaign work.

The 2012 Republican primary underscored the importance of the Supreme Court's landmark campaign finance ruling in *Citizens United v. Federal Election Commission* in 2010. That decision opened up the floodgates of nearly unlimited spending in indirect support of candidates by individuals, labor unions, and corporations. "Super PACs" rose out of the decision—these political action committees (PACs) can raise funds for, but cannot be legally tied to, any candidate and help circumvent the limitations imposed on direct support of a candidate. The *Citizens United* decision has been criticized for not just the amount now spent on campaigns—the pro-Romney super PAC Restore Our Future spent more than $142 million through November 30, 2012—but also for its ability to allow a small group of wealthy individuals to heavily influence the political landscape. For example, in the first two months of 2012, $50 million was funneled to pro-Republican super PACs from less than thirty individuals, couples, and corporations.

With super PAC ads flooding the airwaves, the candidates tried to reach a larger national audience when they met a total of twenty times for debates, with the final seven taking place in the first two months of 2012. The candidates used the debates to lay out their key issues, including health care, jobs and the economy, and federal spending. The candidates were united in many of their opinions, including the repeal of Obama's health care law, but used the debates as a way to gang up on the front-runner. In most cases, this left Romney defending himself against attacks on his universal health care law in Massachusetts and his time as a CEO. He used these attacks to turn the tables on his competitors, all three current or former members of Congress, to paint them as big spenders who did nothing to cut the deficit or rein in the size and scope of the federal government. In one debate, Romney said that during Santorum's time in the Senate, federal spending increased by 80 percent. Santorum used this point to attack Romney, claiming that Romney raised taxes during his time as governor of Massachusetts. Gingrich was a popular debate participant among Republicans, who appreciated his attacks against the moderators, whom he labeled the "elite media" and portrayed as supporters of Obama.

RICK SANTORUM

From the outset, the Santorum campaign tried to portray itself as the most socially conservative choice for Republican presidential nominee. Santorum promised to defund Planned Parenthood if elected, and his campaign platform included a ban on abortion in all instances, even rape or incest. The candidate explained to CNN that the woman should "make the best out of a bad situation." His social positions did backfire somewhat during the debates, as Romney accused Santorum of voting for an appropriations bill that in part helped fund Planned Parenthood.

Santorum gained momentum early in the year after winning the January 3 Iowa caucuses, where he visited all ninety-nine counties, a trademark of his campaign to directly reach voters. It was initially announced that Romney had won, but two weeks later the results were certified, putting Santorum ahead by thirty-four votes. Santorum went on to sweep the February 7 primaries in Colorado, Minnesota, and Missouri, dealing a blow to the Romney campaign as it tried to portray its earlier wins as a clear indication that it was on an unstoppable path to the nomination. The wins raised concerns in the Romney campaign about its candidate's ability to win swing states like Colorado if he were chosen as the nominee. Romney had won Colorado and Minnesota by a large margin when he sought the nomination in 2008, but he ran third in Minnesota in 2012, behind both Santorum and Paul.

The victories started to swing public opinion, and money, in Santorum's direction. "We're doing really well and we feel like going forward we're going to have the money we need to make the case we want to make," Santorum said. A Gallup poll conducted February 8 to 12 showed Romney and Santorum statistically tied for the nomination among registered voters, while Gingrich and Paul ran third and fourth, respectively. This represented a fourteen-point swing for Santorum in less than one week.

Santorum's campaign ran into a number of problems on Super Tuesday, all of which contributed to the candidate's downfall. In Ohio, Santorum did not appear on the ballot in some districts because he did not meet eligibility requirements. In Michigan, two at-large delegates were awarded to Romney, despite state party rules in which the delegates are awarded on a proportional basis based on the primary vote, which Romney won 41 percent to 38 percent. The state party had decided in February to award the two at-large delegates to the primary victor, but it sent a memo to the campaigns incorrectly explaining that decision. "We never thought the Romney campaign would try to rig the outcome of an election by changing the rules after the vote. This kind of backroom dealing political thuggery just cannot and should not happen in America," said Hogan Gidley, the national communications director for the Santorum campaign. Romney spokesperson Andrea Saul struck back, saying, "Because his strategy failed and Mitt Romney won, he is now attacking the Republican Party." Santorum also faced a problem in North Dakota, where he won the presidential caucus on Super Tuesday, whereas during the North Dakota party convention Romney had the most supporters, according to the Associated Press. The state party had informed the candidates that delegates were encouraged to respect caucus results but that delegates could vote with their conscience for whichever candidate they wanted at the national convention.

After winning eleven primary states, Santorum suspended his campaign on April 10, one day after his three-year-old daughter, who has Trisomy 18 disorder, was released from the hospital. "This was a time for prayer and thought over this past weekend," Santorum said. "Just like it was when we decided to get into this race . . . we were very concerned about our role of being the best parents we possibly could to our kids." Santorum did not mention Romney in his speech, but following the announcement, Romney called Santorum "an able and worthy competitor." In total, the Santorum campaign spent $18.7 million, the equivalent of what the Romney campaign spent in a thirty-one day period in January and February.

Newt Gingrich

Although Gingrich got off to a rocky start in 2011 when his senior staff quit en masse and questions were raised about an unpaid bill at a Tiffany jewelry store, by late in the year, he was considered to be the Republican front-runner for the nomination. By early 2012, however, following losses in the first two primary states, his campaign seemed all but over as millions of dollars were spent on attack ads against Gingrich by super PACs favoring Romney. Gingrich had his own secret weapon in casino mogul and billionaire Sheldon Adelson, who provided $5 million to a pro-Gingrich super PAC, Winning Our Future, just weeks before the South Carolina primary. The cash infusion shot Gingrich to the front of the pack in the southern state, where he claimed victory on January 21.

But his strong finish in South Carolina did little to bolster his waning national image. He went on to run second in Florida, Alabama, and Mississippi. As his performance in primary states petered out, so did the influx of money to his campaign and the super PACs that supported him. In March 2012, despite winning in the primary in his home state of Georgia, Gingrich's financial woes led him to lay off one third of his staff, and he said he would move forward on a limited campaign schedule. "We're focusing exclusively on what it'll take to win what we're going to be calling a big-choice convention in August," said Gingrich's communications director, Joe DeSantis. That same month, Adelson said Gingrich was "at the end of his line" and threw his support to Romney. Gingrich continued to visit states that had not yet held primaries, with an overall strategy of hoping that Romney would not get enough delegates before the convention to secure the nomination. Gingrich suspended his campaign on May 2, $4 million in debt. Both the RNC and the Romney campaign agreed to open their campaign donor networks to help him cover this amount.

Ron Paul

Representative Paul, who was retiring at the end of his current term in the House of Representatives, made his third bid for the presidency in 2012, first running in 1988 as the Libertarian Party nominee and then in 2008 as a Republican primary candidate. His campaign was considered a long shot because, while he was a standout among the candidates at drawing in young voters and raising money on the Internet, some of his policies, including legalizing marijuana and bringing the United States back to an isolationist position in global politics, did not appeal to mainstream Republican voters. He was, however, credited with helping to start the Tea Party movement, and his campaign stops often drew supporters dressed in colonial garb with "Don't Tread on Me" flags.

Paul's biggest primary victory came in New Hampshire, where he placed second to Romney, but with only 23 percent of the vote. On May 14, Paul announced that his campaign would no longer compete in the remaining primary elections. Instead, it would focus on states that had voted but had not yet held state conventions to choose delegates. "Moving forward . . . we will no longer spend resources campaigning in primaries in states that have not yet voted," Paul said. "Doing so with any hope of success would take many tens of millions of dollars we simply do not have." This decision left Romney without the delegates needed to secure the nomination but as the only active candidate.

Paul's campaign was officially suspended on July 15 because he did not receive enough delegates to allow his name to be submitted for consideration at the national party convention. He had 104 delegates at the time of his decision, and although support-ers said he could still win by making a play for additional delegates at the convention, many state primaries and caucuses have binding results, meaning he could not hope for those delegates to switch their candidate choice at the convention unless no candidate won on the first ballot.

MITT ROMNEY

From the outset of 2012, Romney's campaign had better financing and better organization than those of his opponents. This support was the driver behind the Romney campaign's claim that its candidate had made history by being the first nonincumbent Republican to win the first two primaries of the year in Iowa and New Hampshire. However, once all of the votes were tallied in Iowa, it was Santorum who came out ahead, in what Romney called a "virtual tie." Romney did, however, claim a large victory in New Hampshire.

Gingrich, Paul, and Santorum attacked Romney as being too moderate, as shown in developing a universal health care law in Massachusetts that is widely considered a blue-print for Obama's health care law, and they took aim at his time as the head of Bain Capital, an asset management firm that they said bought companies only to fire all of the workers, shut the companies down, and reap large profits for themselves. These Bain attacks both came out of President Obama's reelection campaign and made their way into the Republican advertisements. After his New Hampshire victory, Romney criticized this tac-tic, saying, "President Obama wants to put free enterprise on trial, and the last few days we've seen some desperate Republicans join forces with him." He continued, "This is such a mistake for our party." The "country already has a leader who divides us with the bitter politics of envy," Romney said.

Although the Republican Party hoped for a decisive victory for one of the candi-dates by Super Tuesday, March 6, it was not until April 25 that the RNC officially named Romney the presumptive nominee. "It's beyond an endorsement," said Reince Priebus, chair of the RNC. "It is a complete merger wherein the RNC is putting all of its resources and energy behind Mitt Romney to be the next president of the United States." The announcement was of benefit to the Republican Party because the Obama campaign had been working for months in the states, collecting money and establishing a ground game. "Our objective is to raise more money than we've ever raised in the history of the RNC, to communicate better than we've ever communicated, have social and digital reach that we've never seen before, and have a movement across this country that allows every person in America, no matter where you're from, to be able to tap into that move-ment," said Priebus. "Everything that the DNC is doing for Barack Obama, we are going to do times 10 for Mitt Romney."

Although the candidate for the Republican Party would not officially be chosen until the GOP's August convention, Romney claimed himself the official nominee after he won the Texas primary on May 29, because the victory gave him enough delegates to reach the 1,144 threshold needed to secure the nomination. "I am honored that Americans across the country have given their support to my candidacy and I am humbled to have won enough delegates," Romney said.

The national Republican convention was delayed by one day due to Hurricane Isaac, but when the time came, it was the New Jersey delegation that gave Romney the final del-egates he needed to get to 1,144. Upon accepting the nomination, Romney told conven-tion delegates, "I am running for president to help create a better future. A future where everyone who wants a job can find one. Where no senior fears for the security of their retirement. An America where every parent knows that their child will get an education that leads them to a good job and a bright horizon."

With the candidate for president officially chosen, Romney considered his choices for vice president, narrowing the field to former Minnesota governor Tim Pawlenty, Ohio Senator Rob Portman, and House Budget Committee Chair Paul Ryan of Wisconsin. In the end, it was the latter who was chosen as Romney's running mate, and the campaign dubbed the pair "America's comeback team." Romney said Ryan "has worked tirelessly leading the effort to rein in federal spending and increase accountability to taxpayers." While the choice of Ryan, a rising star in the Republican Party, would be good for pulling in the Republican base of economic conservatives, his critics argued that his budget plan would turn Medicare into a voucher program, an idea that divided some Republicans and would be a hard sell for independent voters, a key group needed to win in November.

—Heather Kerrigan

Following is the text of a statement by Republican National Committee Chair Reince Priebus on March 6, 2012, on the outcome of Super Tuesday; and an excerpt from a speech delivered by Republican presidential candidate Mitt Romney on August 31, 2012, accepting the Republican nomination for president.

DOCUMENT   ## RNC on Super Tuesday Results

March 6, 2012

WASHINGTON—As we await final results from Alaska, Republican National Committee (RNC) Chairman Reince Priebus released the following statement regarding the results of eight Super Tuesday contests:

"After three years of Barack Obama's failed policies and broken promises, Americans are ready for a new direction. At the primaries and caucuses held today, they made their voices heard," said RNC Chairman Reince Priebus.

"Under President Obama, America is suffering from reckless spending, record debt, high unemployment, and rising gas prices. Today voters sent a clear message: We cannot afford four more years of this administration that promises to bring us higher taxes, even higher debt and a weaker defense.

"As a country we are ready for Republican leadership that will bring us an America that will reap the benefits of fiscal responsibility, renewed economic opportunity, and a comprehensive energy policy.

"I want to congratulate Mitt Romney on winning Idaho, Ohio, Massachusetts, Vermont and Virginia. Rick Santorum's wins in Oklahoma and Tennessee and Newt Gingrich's win in Georgia.

"Republicans stand ready to lead, and with each primary contest, we add to our momentum, propelling us toward victory in November."

SOURCE: Republican National Committee. Press Releases. "RNC Chairman Reince Priebus Statement on Super Tuesday Results." March 6, 2012. http://www.gop.com/news/press-releases/rnc-chairman-reince-priebus-statement-on-super-tuesday-results.

Mitt Romney Accepts Republican Presidential Nomination

August 31, 2012

. . . To the majority of Americans who now believe that the future will not be better than the past, I can guarantee you this: if Barack Obama is re-elected, you will be right.

I am running for president to help create a better future. A future where everyone who wants a job can find one. Where no senior fears for the security of their retirement. An America where every parent knows that their child will get an education that leads them to a good job and a bright horizon.

And unlike the president, I have a plan to create 12 million new jobs. It has 5 steps.

First, by 2020, North America will be energy independent by taking full advantage of our oil and coal and gas and nuclear and renewables.

Second, we will give our fellow citizens the skills they need for the jobs of today and the careers of tomorrow. When it comes to the school your child will attend, every parent should have a choice, and every child should have a chance.

Third, we will make trade work for America by forging new trade agreements. And when nations cheat in trade, there will be unmistakable consequences.

Fourth, to assure every entrepreneur and every job creator that their investments in America will not vanish as have those in Greece, we will cut the deficit and put America on track to a balanced budget.

And fifth, we will champion SMALL businesses, America's engine of job growth. That means reducing taxes on business, not raising them. It means simplifying and moderniz- ing the regulations that hurt small business the most. And it means that we must rein in the skyrocketing cost of healthcare by repealing and replacing Obamacare. . . .

SOURCE: Republican National Committee. Press Releases. "ICYMI: Governor Mitt Romney Nomination Remarks Excerpts From Address at the Republican National Convention." August 31, 2012. http:// www.gop.com/news/press-releases/icymi-governor-mitt-romney-nomination-remarks-excerpts-from- address-at-the-republican-national-convention.

OTHER HISTORIC DOCUMENTS OF INTEREST

FROM THIS VOLUME

FROM PREVIOUS *HISTORIC DOCUMENTS*

Putin on His Reelection as President of Russia

MARCH 8, 2012

In December 2011, Russian voters went to the polls to elect members of the State Duma, the nation's lower house of parliament. The vote was wrought with widespread allegations of voter intimidation and fraud that included ballot-stuffing in favor of the ruling party, United Russia. In the end, United Russia was victorious, but it lost enough seats to no longer hold a majority. Antigovernment demonstrations broke out, calling for an investigation into the allegations of fraud and asking for reform of the political system.

Protesters also took issue with the announcement by then–prime minister Vladimir Putin that he intended to run for president for a third nonconsecutive term in 2012. Despite the protests, Putin was declared victorious in the March 2012 elections, and when he officially took office in May, he began undoing a number of reforms the former president and current prime minister, Dmitry Medvedev, had put in place. The state police force in turn cracked down on citizens who spoke out against the government. Internationally, Putin eroded diplomatic inroads made by his predecessor with the United States and at the United Nations, partly because of his fierce defense of the Syrian government even as it used deadly force against its own citizens.

Winning Campaign Brings Political Changes

Putin was reelected to his third six-year term in March 2012 with 64.7 percent of the vote. Similar to the December Duma elections, Putin's opponents and international election observers claimed that fraud put his election in question. Protesters came to the Kremlin after the election, shouting, "Putin is a thief; we are the government!" The day before Putin's inauguration in May, 20,000 demonstrators took to the streets outside of the Kremlin, where they were met with resistance from the Russian police force. More than 400 protesters were arrested. On the day of the inauguration, a new round of protests broke out, and 120 were arrested, according to Russian police.

With the presidency firmly in his hands, Putin appointed Medvedev to the position of prime minister and subsequently began overturning a number of Medvedev's initiatives that had been enacted during the previous six years, including raising the government employee retirement age and recriminalizing slander. One Medvedev law Putin did not overturn was the direct election of local governors. However, when these elections took place in October, independent observers again complained of vote rigging, and independent monitor Golos reported 1,000 vote irregularities. When the results were announced, it was Putin's United Russia that came out on top, with all five gubernatorial races producing candidates he supported as victors. Golos estimated that half of the votes for Putin's party were fake.

Not all of Putin's changes were viewed negatively. Bowing to pressure from his critics, Putin made it easier to form political parties by decreasing the number of members needed to register and run for office from 40,000 to 500. Although the size needed to register a political party was a sticking point for protesters during the December election, critics now say that Putin's decision will further fracture the opposition and essentially keep Putin and United Russia in power. In a rare move, Putin also fired the national defense minister to allow police to continue an investigation into wrongdoing at the ministry. The minister, Anatoly Serdyukov, was not charged with a crime, but the decision was significant, as Putin rarely fires those within his inner circle, even in cases of suspected illegal activity.

The relationship between Medvedev and Putin seemed to cool at the beginning of Putin's third term. Even as the leader of the ruling party, United Russia, Medvedev has always been seen as a more liberal leader, and a number of Putin's inner circle blamed Medvedev for the opposition movement that gained momentum following the Duma elections. In reversing some of Medvedev's decrees, Putin made clear that he is firmly in charge. Leaving no doubt about this fact, Putin worked to weaken Medvedev's national profile. On the fourth anniversary of the August 2008 war with Georgia, Putin's government released a documentary that portrayed Medvedev as an indecisive coward who required the consultation of Putin throughout the crisis, including allowing Putin to decide whether Russian troops should be sent to Georgia. Previously, Medvedev had touted himself as the decision maker who took solitary action throughout the conflict.

CRACKDOWN ON CITIZENS

After Putin announced his intent to seek another presidential term, protesters took to the streets. And following his victory, the opposition movement continued, although it lost some of its passion and momentum after December 2011 as both the number of protests and protesters decreased. In response, after taking office, Putin cracked down on protests and citizens who spoke out publicly against the government, even though one day after being elected he said his government's efforts would "be for the benefit of the entire Russian nation, regardless of party preference."

On June 8, 2012, Putin signed a new law to levy heavy fines on anyone who organizes or takes part in unsanctioned demonstrations. Fines include $9,000 for individual participants that cause harm to people or property; $18,000 for individual protest organizers; and $30,000 for groups or companies that organize rallies. The law also allows local authorities to decide where protests are prohibited. Citizens have already defied the ban. Less than one week after it was signed, 10,000 protesters gathered in Moscow and 16 were charged with hooliganism. Another protest took place in September, drawing upward of 14,000.

In July, Putin gave his government authority to shut down any websites publishing information deemed harmful to children. The bill also required nonprofit organizations to be labeled "foreign agents" if they engage in political activities and receive funding from outside Russia. The latter portion of the law got the attention of the United Nations High Commissioner for Human Rights, Navi Pillay. "I urge the government of the Russian Federation to avoid taking further steps backward to a more restrictive era," she said. In response, the Russian Foreign Ministry stated, "We consider Ms. Pillay's statement as unbefitting to her status as high commissioner and attempts to publicly accuse the leaders of the Russian state of failing to carry out some kinds of 'promises'—as outside the framework of diplomatic ethics."

Perhaps the most high-profile crackdown in Russia took place in May, when the three-member female band Pussy Riot was arrested after performing an anti-Putin song at the altar of the Cathedral of Christ the Savior. The trio was charged with inciting religious hatred and faced trial in July 2012. The band's lawyer, Violetta Volkova, read letters from each of the accused during the trial. "Our criminal case is political censorship from the side of the authorities, the start of a campaign of authoritarian, repressive measures aimed at lowering the level of political activism and provoking a feeling of fear among citizens who hold opposition views," Yekaterina Samutsevich wrote in her letter. The women apologized for their actions and said they did not intend to offend the Orthodox Church, but rather were speaking out against both Putin and the church's leader, who continuously supported Putin's actions. "I thought the church loved its children. It turns out the church only loves those children who believe in Putin," wrote Maria Alyokhina.

There was little question that the women would be found guilty because less than one percent of cases in Russia that go to trial end with a not guilty verdict. And on August 17, the band was convicted of hooliganism and sentenced to two years in prison. The verdict was criticized both in Russia and around the world. Even some government supporters questioned the ruling. Former finance minister Alexei Kudrin, a Putin ally, called the move "yet another blow to the court system and citizens' trust in it." Medvedev called for the group to be freed, saying, "In my view, a suspended sentence would be sufficient, taking into account the time they have already spent in custody." In October, Samutsevich was freed after the court agreed to arguments by her new lawyer that she had less of a role in the offending event. At the end of 2012, the other two band members remained in prison.

Given the changes imposed by Putin upon his return to office, questions are being raised about whether he can hold power for the full six years of his presidential term. "My forecast is the following: The regime we have now cannot last six years," said Kseniya Sobchak, a television host. "This movement will pick up force and eventually it may lead to quite tragic events, like revolution or a coup," she continued. Even members of United Russia agree that Putin must make some concessions to appear to be a more democratic leader. According to Olga Kryshtanovskaya, a sociologist and member of United Russia, Putin must do all he can to become more liberal, but if he does, he will be making that move "with his intellect, and not with his heart, and under pressure, because he is afraid." Putin's own efforts to change have been mixed. He has a loyal inner circle with which he surrounds himself, as though he fears outside influence; he promotes competition but fiercely criticizes those who oppose him as pawns and refuses to give up power.

RELATIONSHIP WITH THE UNITED STATES AND UNITED NATIONS

After years of improvement under Medvedev, with Putin back in power, the nation's relationship with the United States began to deteriorate, partly because of Russia's relationship with Syria, even in light of the civil war taking place in the country. Russia has been supplying Bashar al Assad's troops with weapons and providing diplomatic support at the United Nations. In June 2012, Secretary of State Hillary Rodham Clinton accused Russia of sending attack helicopters to Assad's government, and Russia struck back, criticizing the U.S. support of opposition forces in Syria.

In 2012, the U.S. Congress worked on two different bills with regard to U.S.-Russian relations. The first bill, named after Sergei Magnitsky, a lawyer who died in a Russian prison in 2009—accused of stealing from the government with the support of Russian officials—would block visas and freeze assets of Russian officials who abuse human rights. The second, strongly supported by the Obama administration, would repeal the Jackson-Vanik trade restrictions put in place in 1974 after Russia restricted the emigration of Jews. The restrictions have been waived every year since the fall of the Soviet Union, meaning they have no true effect. However, because Russia is now a member of the World Trade Organization (WTO), if this law, which violates WTO rules, remains on the books, Russia could place higher duties on U.S. goods. In November, the House attached the Magnitsky bill to the Jackson-Vanik bill, passing it 365–43. The Senate passed the combined House legislation, and President Obama signed it into law. Calling the bills an attempt to interfere with internal affairs, the Russian foreign minister and State Duma promised to retaliate.

On September 18, 2012, Russia ordered the U.S. Agency for International Development (USAID) to end all financial support of pro-democracy, public health, and other civil society programs because the Putin government believes the United States is trying to meddle in internal affairs. Aleksandr Lukashevich, a spokesperson for the Russian Foreign Ministry, said there were "serious questions" about the work USAID was doing in the country, which he said included "attempts to influence the political process through the distribution of grants." This will cut approximately $50 million in aid, but the move was not surprising. Last year, in anticipation of such a decision, the Obama administration proposed creating a fund of $50 million as an endowment for a private foundation, allowed by Russian law, for the continued support of democratic and civil society projects. Russia's USAID block will likely speed up work on this proposal.

In December, Putin dealt an additional blow to the United States, signing a law to prevent Americans from adopting Russian children. The law, which went into effect on January 1, 2013, stopped the proceedings on all pending adoptions; blocked the children from leaving the country; and left in question what would happen to the estimated 740,000 parentless Russian children, many of whom often end up in American homes.

At the United Nations, Russia has blocked, with the support of China, Security Council attempts to intervene in Syria or impose additional sanctions. Russia said it does not believe it is the job of the United Nations to interfere with domestic politics or force a change in leadership in any country. The Russian delegation was critical of the West for supporting the opposition to Assad's government and blamed it for Kofi Annan's departure as special envoy to Syria. Russia claimed that it tried to support Annan's ceasefire plan but that the West refused to work with it. Western nations have in turn argued that it was Russia that forced Annan's hand. In July 2012, Russia cast its third veto against a resolution to punish Syria.

—Heather Kerrigan

Following is the text of a meeting between Russian President Dmitry Medvedev and Prime Minister Vladmir Putin on March 8, 2012, discussing Putin's reelection to the presidency.

President Medvedev and Prime Minister Putin Discuss the Presidential Election

March 8, 2012

PRESIDENT OF RUSSIA DMITRY MEDVEDEV: Good afternoon, Mr. Putin.

First of all I would like to sincerely congratulate you on your victory in the presidential election. Yesterday, the Central Election Commission published the final results. The figures are absolutely convincing, and they show an indisputable fact: our citizens trust the policy implemented in our country in recent years.

Indeed, we have been working together on laying the foundation for a new economy, modernising the economy and promoting a technological overhaul. Naturally, a great deal of attention was paid to the development of the social sphere, although it is clear that there is still a wide range of outstanding problems. A major challenge facing our state is ensuring security and defence capability, as well as maintaining high-level relations with other nations around the globe.

I am confident that your future policy will cover all of these areas and would like to sincerely wish you every success. Once again, congratulations.

PRIME MINISTER OF RUSSIA VLADIMIR PUTIN: Thank you.

Mr President, I would like to address all Russian citizens today and thank everyone who participated in the presidential election.

It would be appropriate to point out that the President in our country is not affiliated with any particular party. Therefore, our efforts will be for the benefit of the entire Russian nation, regardless of party preference.

Just yesterday you held a meeting where we discussed economic development. Our main challenge in the economy is to maintain the macroeconomic indicators and the positive trends that we have reached in recent years, despite the economic crisis.

Together you and I have outlined our priority tasks in the social sphere and they can be addressed solely on the basis of strong economic growth. Yesterday we decided which aspects of this work we will tackle together. As we have agreed, today we will begin consultations on the issues related to shaping the future of the Russian Federation.

DMITRY MEDVEDEV: Agreed. Let's get down to work.

SOURCE: President of Russia. Speeches and Transcripts. "Meeting with Prime Minister Vladimir Putin." March 8, 2012. http://eng.kremlin.ru/transcripts/3523.

OTHER HISTORIC DOCUMENTS OF INTEREST

FROM PREVIOUS *HISTORIC DOCUMENTS*

Evolving Relationship Between the United States and Afghanistan

---

MARCH 15 AND JUNE 1, 2012

Since his election in 2008, President Barack Obama has worked to bring the war in Afghanistan to an end. In 2011, with the assistance of his senior defense officials, the president created a withdrawal timetable to remove all U.S. troops from Afghanistan by 2014. According to the president, this was feasible because the United States had achieved almost all of its goals, including the assassination of Osama bin Laden.

In 2012, the United States faced a difficult start to the year when Korans were burned, reportedly by accident, at a U.S. military base in Afghanistan and an American army sergeant killed seventeen Afghan civilians. Anti-American demonstrations took place after each incident and added to the already tenuous security situation for troops who were increasingly being attacked by their Afghan security counterparts. Because of these insider assaults, the Pentagon reworked its strategy in Afghanistan, maintaining the withdrawal timetable but changing its training methods.

Despite these difficulties, in May, President Obama reaffirmed his commitment to Afghanistan even beyond 2014, signing a development assistance agreement that would give nonmilitary support to the nation through 2024. And in September, just one month after the United States reached the grim milestone of 2,000 American soldiers killed since the war began in 2001, Obama began making good on his promise to bring the war to a close when the last of the 33,000 troops that made up the 2009 surge were withdrawn.

ANTI-AMERICAN DEMONSTRATIONS

Afghan opinion of American forces continued to deteriorate in 2012 after a series of incidents sparked violent protests and drew strong reactions from Afghan President Hamid Karzai, typically a supporter of U.S. action in the country. The first incident occurred in February, when copies of the Koran that were collected at a facility for suspected insurgents were accidentally incinerated. In response to the Koran burning, on February 25, two American soldiers were killed. The North Atlantic Treaty Organization (NATO) subsequently pulled its advisers out of the Afghan ministries in Kabul, where the soldiers were shot. On February 27, nine Afghans were killed and four NATO personnel wounded in dual suicide attacks. In total, at least four American troops and thirty-six others were killed while many were wounded, following the Koran burning. President Obama apologized to Karzai for the incident in a letter, writing, "The error was inadvertent," and "I assure you that we will take the appropriate steps to avoid any recurrence, to include holding accountable those responsible."

On March 11, Army Sergeant Robert Bales methodically went from house to house in southern Afghanistan, killing seventeen civilians, including nine children. The U.S. military arrested Bales and sent him back to the United States, angering Afghans who wanted the solider to be tried where the killings took place. Soon after the seventeen civilians were killed, Karzai ordered U.S. troops to be confined to major bases by 2013. At the end of 2012, Bales was still awaiting trial in Fort Leavenworth, Kansas.

Following Karzai's announcement, Taliban leaders, who had been working with the United States to reach a peace agreement, cut off any future talks, angered by the issues surrounding a potential prisoner swap. The United States had initially hoped to come to an agreement with the Taliban before 2014 but is now leaving that to the Afghans, and it is likely that negotiations will not take place until after American troops leave the nation.

In September, a trailer for the movie *Innocence of Muslims*, an anti-Islam film, was released and sparked violence across the Middle East. Although most of the attacks against Americans took place elsewhere, in Kabul on September 18, a suicide bomber killed fourteen, including ten foreigners.

QUESTIONS ABOUT AFGHAN LEADERSHIP

Afghanistan faces a number of challenges before it can be considered fully capable of maintaining its own security and running a stable government. Politically, elections have never been smooth since the U.S. invasion ushered in democratic elections, with widespread allegations of fraud and voter intimidation. In October 2012, Karzai announced that the next presidential election would be held on April 5, 2014. But given that the May 2009 presidential election was delayed until August of that year and that reported fraud called Karzai's victory into question, there are doubts about whether the date will be adhered to and whether the country can hold a free and fair election.

At the end of 2012, the United States still had about 65,000 troops in the country, following the August drawdown of the last of the 33,000 troops that were part of the 2009 surge. This drawdown received mixed reaction—some Afghan officials said it was clear that the nation was ready to lead, while others feared the beginning of the resurgence of the Taliban. The Afghan army numbers nearly 200,000 troops, but every year, approximately one third of the force must be replaced because desertions are high and reenlistments are low. Approximately 7 percent to 10 percent of the forces desert each year, while only about 75 percent reenlist after their initial three-year commitment, even though pay increases upon reenlistment. Deserters say the army is corrupt; that they get little food, equipment, and medical care; and that the Taliban threatens their families. Many share the belief that the military will not be able to resist the Taliban once U.S. and coalition forces leave. The process for recruiting Afghan troops remains on track, but there are no troops operating independently of NATO or U.S. forces. However, Afghan troops did give some indication of their readiness to take over security on April 15, when Taliban suicide bombers and gunmen attacked Kabul and a number of eastern provinces. The Afghan troops who responded to the incident required little assistance from their coalition counterparts. The attacks raised new concern about whether some of the Taliban networks, in this case the Haqqani network, have the ability to undertake such attacks on a regular basis and whether, after 2014, the Afghan forces would be able to repel them.

One of the greatest concerns for American and coalition troops in 2012 has been so-called insider assaults, or green-on-blue attacks, that occur when a member of the Afghan forces attacks a U.S. or coalition troop. From the outset, 2012 was a year rife with these attacks, and August and September were particularly violent months. On August 9 and 10, eight American and British soldiers were killed; six of the eight were shot inside bases with

Afghan troops. On August 13, two more insider attacks took place. In the first, no harm was done, and in the second, two coalition soldiers were injured. On August 17, an Afghan police recruit killed two American Special Forces members, and on the same day, another two American soldiers were wounded. In mid-September, six coalition troops were killed in insider assaults, marking the first time more than fifty international troops were killed by Afghan forces in this type of attack in a single year. In late September, a fight broke out between Afghan and American troops, resulting in the deaths of two Americans and three Afghans.

Evolving U.S. Strategy

The increasing number of insider assaults led to changes in U.S. and NATO strategy in Afghanistan. In early September, the training of local police and Special Operations Forces was put on hold until American troops could review the recruits and determine who posed a threat. There is now a strict process for accepting new recruits for military or police training in an attempt to try to root out those who might have insurgent tendencies.

By the middle of the month, the Pentagon announced that although U.S. troops will still train, advise, and fight with the Afghan units and prepare them for independence, in light of the insider assaults, a general's approval will now be required for joint work at the small-unit level. Two additional policies were put in place to combat rising insider attacks. First, coalition members are required to always carry a loaded magazine in their weapon. Second, a program called Guardian Angel was created, in which two anonymous coalition soldiers are present at every mission or meeting to monitor the Afghans and fire when necessary.

Changes were already made earlier in the year in an effort to continue transferring primary security responsibility to the Afghans. On February 1, 2012, Secretary of Defense Leon Panetta announced that as early as mid-2013, U.S. troops would no longer have a combat role in Afghanistan. He called the move a logical next step in the effort to withdraw all U.S. troops by 2014. In April, in an effort to reduce direct combat situations between coalition troops and insurgents, the United States handed over all Special Operations missions to Afghan forces, including the controversial night raids that American forces consider a key part of their strategy to combat the Taliban. In May, during the NATO summit, President Obama, along with other leaders of NATO nations in the Afghanistan coalition, ratified an agreement that would hand over primary security responsibility to the Afghans in the summer of 2013, though subsequently agreeing to support the nation beyond 2014.

Development Assistance Agreement

On May 1, President Obama made a secret trip to meet with President Karzai and sign an agreement to establish a roadmap for how Afghanistan and the United States will work together after 2014. The agreement was negotiated for twenty months and promises that the United States will continue to support Afghanistan in a nonmilitary capacity until 2024, although a residual American troop presence has been left in question. Approximately $2 billion per year will be spent in that decade after U.S. withdrawal, and it is likely that additional funds will be sent to Afghanistan for other forms of civil aid.

—Heather Kerrigan

Following is a press release from March 15, 2012, from Afghan President Hamid Karzai, requesting that foreign troops confine their operations to military bases and leave Afghan villages; and the edited text of the development assistance agreement between the United States and Afghanistan, released on June 1, 2012.

President Karzai Asks Foreign Troops to Leave Villages

March 15, 2012

President Hamid Karzai demanded in a meeting with Leone [*sic*] Panetta the US Defense Secretary Thursday afternoon that foreign troops pull back from their outposts in Afghan villages and confine their troops to military bases in Afghanistan.

In the meeting held in the Presidential Palace, President Karzai stressed that Afghan security forces are capable of protecting villages of Afghanistan.

The two sides then discussed Afghan-US strategic partnership and the transition of security responsibilities from the international troops to Afghan security forces.

The President said, the two sides should work on the transition so that the transfer of security responsibilities be completed in 2013 rather than 2014.

President Karzai added, Afghanistan is ready now to undertake full security responsibilities and the Afghan people demand that this transfer be accelerated as well as security responsibilities delegated to the Afghan government.

[The] US Defense Secretary offered his deepest condolences and sympathies once again to the President and people of Afghanistan on behalf of the US government and people over the tragic killings in Panjway district of Kandahar province.

Leone [*sic*] Panetta said, the United States wants to successfully transfer security responsibilities to the Afghan security forces a soon as possible.

President Karzai labeled the recent massacre cruelty on the people of Afghanistan and underscored that such incidents do not happen again.

The President said, such incidents have been a source of tension between the two countries, undermining the US-Afghan relationship for a long time and asked for serious actions to be taken for prevention of such tragedies.

President Karzai noted, these incidents have damaged public trust on the international forces[;] therefore foreign forces need to work on rebuilding public trust and confidence in the country.

The President added, this trust-building could be realized only if the foreign troops totally respect religious and cultural values of the Afghan people, avoid entering Afghan homes and focus on economic assistance to Afghanistan.

President Karzai called for transparent investigations on Panjway killings and punishment for those who are responsible for the incident and full cooperation by US side with the Afghan delegation.

Leone [*sic*] Panetta gave the President assurances of carrying out serious investigations and punishing those who perpetrated the crime.

SOURCE: Office of the President of the Islamic Republic of Afghanistan. "President Karzai: Foreign Troops Must Leave Afghan Villages." March 15, 2012. http://president.gov.af/en/news/7860.

United States and Afghanistan Agree to Strategic Partnership

June 1, 2012

I. Preamble

The Islamic Republic of Afghanistan ("Afghanistan") and the United States of America ("United States") have partnered closely since 2001 to respond to threats to international peace and security and help the Afghan people chart a secure, democratic, and prosperous future. As a result, Afghanistan is now on a path towards sustainable self-reliance in security, governance, economic and social development, and constructive partnership at the regional level.

The Parties express their appreciation for the November 2011 Traditional Loya Jirga, which declared: "Emphasizing the need to preserve the achievements of the past ten years, respect the Afghan Constitution, women's rights, freedom of speech, and taking into consideration the prevailing situation in the region, strategic cooperation with the United States of America, which is a strategic ally of the people and government of Afghanistan, is considered important in order to ensure political, economic and military security of the country. Signing a strategic cooperation document with the United States conforms with the national interest of Afghanistan and is of significant importance. . . . When signing this document Afghanistan and the United States must be considered as two sovereign and equal countries," in accordance with the Charter of the United Nations.

Emphasizing their shared determination to further advance the Afghan people's desire for a stable and independent Afghan state, governed on the basis of Afghanistan's Constitution and shared democratic values, including respect for the fundamental rights and freedoms of all men and women, Afghanistan and the United States ("the Parties") commit to strengthen long-term strategic cooperation in areas of mutual interest, including: advancing peace, security, and reconciliation; strengthening state institutions; supporting Afghanistan's long-term economic and social development; and encouraging regional cooperation. Recognizing the continued relevance of their commitments at the 2010 London and Kabul Conferences, as well as the 2011 Bonn Conference, the Parties affirm their resolve to strengthen Afghanistan's institutions and governance capacity to advance such areas of long-term strategic cooperation.

Cooperation between Afghanistan and the United States is based on mutual respect and shared interests—most notably, a common desire for peace and to strengthen collective efforts to achieve a region that is economically integrated, and no longer a safe haven for al-Qaeda and its affiliates.

Afghanistan and the United States go forward in this partnership with confidence because they are committed to seeking a future of justice, peace, security, and opportunity for the Afghan people.

Respect for the sovereignty and equality of states constitutes the foundation of this partnership.

Respect for the rule of law, as well as the sound and transparent adherence to Afghanistan's Constitution and all other operative laws, reinforces its foundation. The

Parties reaffirm their strong commitment to the sovereignty, independence, territorial integrity and national unity of Afghanistan.

Accordingly, the Parties agree to the following:

II. Protecting and Promoting Shared Democratic Values

1. The Parties agree that a strong commitment to protecting and promoting democratic values and human rights is a fundamental aspect of their long-term partnership and cooperation.

2. Underscoring the central importance of the values and principles of the Afghan Constitution, Afghanistan reaffirms its strong commitment to inclusive and pluralistic democratic governance, including free, fair, and transparent elections in which all people of Afghanistan participate freely without internal or external interference. Reaffirming its commitments made at the 2011 Bonn Conference, Afghanistan shall strengthen and improve its electoral process.

3. Afghanistan reaffirms its commitment to protecting human and political rights under its Constitution and international obligations, including the International Covenant on Civil and Political Rights. In this regard, Afghanistan shall strengthen the integrity and capacity of its democratic institutions and processes, including by taking tangible steps to further the efficiency and effectiveness of its three branches of state, within its unitary system of government, and supporting development of a vibrant civil society, including a free and open media.

4. Afghanistan reaffirms its commitment to ensuring that any kind of discrimination and distinction between citizens of Afghanistan shall be forbidden, and ensuring the rights and freedoms that are guaranteed to all Afghans under Afghan law and the Afghan Constitution. Consistent with its Constitution and international obligations, Afghanistan shall ensure and advance the essential role of women in society, so that they may fully enjoy their economic, social, political, civil and cultural rights.

III. Advancing Long-Term Security

1. The Parties affirm that the presence and operations of the U.S. forces in Afghanistan since 2001 are aimed at defeating al-Qaeda and its affiliates. The Parties acknowledge the great sacrifices and suffering that the Afghan people have endured in the struggle against terrorism and the continued threats to their desire for peace, security and prosperity. The Parties also pay tribute to the sacrifices made by the people of the United States in this struggle.

2. In order to strengthen security and stability and Afghanistan, contribute to regional and international peace and stability, combat al-Qaeda its affiliates, and enhance the ability of Afghanistan to deter threats against its sovereignty, security, and territorial integrity, the Parties shall continue to foster close cooperation concerning defense and security arrangements, as may be mutually determined.

   a. The Parties' respective obligations under this Agreement, and any subsequent arrangements, are without prejudice to Afghan sovereignty over its territory, and each Party's right of self-defense, consistent with international law.

b. The Parties shall, subject to their international procedures, initiate negotiations on a Bilateral Security Agreement. Negotiations should begin after the signing of this Strategic Partnership Agreement, with the goal of concluding within one year a Bilateral Security Agreement to supersede the *Agreement regarding the Status of United States Military and Civilian Personnel of the U.S. Department of Defense Present in Afghanistan in connection with Cooperative Efforts in Response to Terrorism, Humanitarian, and Civic Assistance, Military Training and Exercises, and Other Activities* (2003), and other such related agreements and understandings that are mutually determined to be contrary to the provisions of the Bilateral Security Agreement.

c. The conduct of ongoing military operations shall continue under existing frameworks, which include the Memorandum of Understanding on the Transfer of U.S. Detention Facilities (2012) and the Memorandum of Understanding on the Afghanization of Special Operations (2012), until superseded by the Bilateral Security Agreement or other arrangements, as mutually determined. This obligation is without prejudice to the status, commitments, and understandings of those frameworks, until superseded as noted above.

3. To help provide a long-term framework for mutual security and defense cooperation, the United States shall designate Afghanistan a "Major Non-NATO Ally."

4. The Parties underscore their strong support for Afghan efforts towards peace and reconciliation.

a. The necessary outcomes of any peace and reconciliation process are for individuals and entities to: break ties with al-Qaeda; renounce violence; and abide by the Afghan Constitution, including its protections for all Afghan women and men.

b. Afghanistan affirms that in all state actions and understandings with regard to peace and reconciliation, it shall uphold the values of the Afghan Constitution.

5. Beyond 2014, the United States shall seek funds, on a yearly basis, to support the training, equipping, advising, and sustaining of the Afghan National Security Forces (ANSF), so that Afghanistan can independently secure and defend itself against internal and external threats, and help ensure that terrorists never again encroach on Afghan soil and threaten Afghanistan, the region, and the world.

a. Such support should: (1) help build appropriate capabilities reflecting the evolving nature of mutually-recognized threats to Afghan stability; (2) support efforts to help the Afghan State attain a sustainable security structure; and (3) strengthen the capacity of security institutions of Afghanistan.

b. A U.S.-Afghanistan Working Group on Defense and Security, established under the framework of the Agreement, shall undertake regular assessments of the level of threat facing Afghanistan, as well as the country's security and defense requirements, and make specific recommendations about future cooperation in this field to the Bilateral Commission.

c. Assistance to the ANSF should have the goal of being consistent with NATO standards and promote interoperability with NATO forces.

d. The Parties further call on NATO member states to sustain and improve Afghan security capabilities beyond 2014, by taking concrete measures to implement the Declaration by NATO and the Government of the Islamic Republic of

Afghanistan on an Enduring Partnership concluded at the November 2010 NATO Lisbon Summit.

6. Afghanistan shall provide U.S. forces continued access to and use of Afghan facilities through 2014, and beyond as may be agreed in the Bilateral Security Agreement, for the purposes of combating al-Qaeda and its affiliates, training the Afghan National Security Forces, and other mutually determined missions to advance shared security interests.

   a. The United States emphasizes its full respect for the sovereignty and independence of Afghanistan. It reaffirms its commitment to the *Inteqal* framework, and a transition to full Afghan security responsibility. It further reaffirms that it does not seek permanent military facilities in Afghanistan, or a presence that is a threat to Afghanistan's neighbors.

   b. The United States further pledges not to use Afghan territory or facilities as a launching point for attacks against other countries.

   c. The nature and scope of the future presence and operations of U.S. forces in Afghanistan, and the related obligations of Afghanistan and the United States, shall be addressed in the Bilateral Security Agreement.

7. The Parties shall enhance information and intelligence sharing to counter common threats, including terrorism, narcotics trafficking, organized crime, and money laundering.

8. The Parties underscore their support to improve regional security cooperation and coordination. The Parties affirm that the production, trafficking, and consumption of illicit narcotics poses a major threat to ensuring security and the formation of a licit Afghan economy, as well as to regional security and a healthy world. They are determined to cooperate in Afghanistan, the region, and the world to eliminate this threat.

9. Recognizing that the stability of Afghanistan would contribute to the development and stability of South-Central Asia, the United States affirms that it shall regard with grave concern any external aggression against Afghanistan. Were this to occur, the Parties shall hold consultations on an urgent basis to develop and implement an appropriate response, including, as may be mutually determined, political, diplomatic, economic, or military measures, in accordance with their respective constitutional procedures.

IV. Reinforcing Regional Security and Cooperation

1. The Parties agree on the importance of Afghanistan having cooperative and friendly relations with its neighbors, and emphasize that such relations should be conducted on the basis of mutual respect, non-interference, and equality. They call on all nations to respect Afghanistan's sovereignty and territorial integrity, and to refrain from interfering in Afghanistan's internal affairs and democratic processes.

2. With a view to the importance of regional cooperation for the consolidation of security in the region, the Parties shall undertake earnest cooperation with the countries of the region, regional organizations, the United Nations, and other international organizations on mutually recognized threats, including: terrorist networks; organized crime; narcotics trafficking; and money laundering.

3. To enhance regional stability and prosperity, the Parties shall further cooperate in restoring Afghanistan's historic role as a bridge connecting Central and South Asia and the Middle East by:

   a. building on and facilitating implementation of exiting and future regional initiatives, including transit and trade agreements;
   b. strengthening border coordination and management between Afghanistan and its neighbors;
   c. expanding linkages to regional transportation, transit, and energy networks through the realization of projects, including infrastructure, throughout Afghanistan; and
   d. mobilizing international support for regional investments that facilitate Afghanistan's integration with the region.

V. Social and Economic Development

1. The Parties agree that developing Afghanistan's human and natural resources is crucial to regional stability, sustainable economic growth, and Afghanistan's recovery from more than three decades of war and that Afghanistan will have special, significant and continuing fiscal requirements that cannot be met by domestic revenues in the years following Transition. In this regard, the United States reaffirms its commitment made at the 2011 Bonn Conference to directing financial support, consistent with the Kabul Process, towards Afghanistan's economic development, helping Afghanistan address its continuing budget shortfall to secure the gains of the last decade, make Transition irreversible, and become self-sustaining.

2. In the economic sphere:

   a. The Parties shall pursue consolidation and growth of a market economy, and long-term cooperation for Afghanistan's sustainable economic growth, taking into consideration Afghanistan's Constitution, as well as its historical and social realities.
   b. Noting Afghanistan's priorities, the United States shall help strengthen Afghanistan's economic foundation and support sustainable development and self-sufficiency, particularly in the areas of: licit agricultural production; transportation, trade, transit, water, and energy infrastructure; fostering responsible management of natural resources; and building a strong financial system, which is needed to sustain private investment.
   c. To encourage trade and private sector development, the Parties shall undertake common efforts to increasingly use the Generalized System of Preferences. Further, to encourage investment, the United States intends to mobilize the Overseas Private Investment Corporation, U.S. Export-Import Bank, and U.S. Trade and Development Agency to encourage U.S. private sector activity in Afghanistan. Afghanistan shall augment its support for the development of its private sector through the relevant Afghan institutions.
   d. The Parties affirm their strong desire that the Afghan people should be the primary beneficiaries of Afghanistan's mineral wealth. The United States shall therefore support Afghanistan's efforts to govern its natural wealth through an accountable, efficient, effective and transparent framework that builds upon and surpasses international best practices.

3. In the social sphere, the Parties shall undertake sustainable joint efforts to help Afghanistan develop its human capacity through:
    a. access to and enhancing the quality of education, including higher education and vocational training in key areas for all Afghans; and
    b. access to basic health services and specialized care, including for women and children.

4. The Parties underscore the crucial importance of the fight against corruption.
    a. The Parties shall fight decisively against all forms of corruption.
    b. The Parties shall devise mechanisms to enhance aid effectiveness and avoid corruption through improved procurement practices, transparency, and accountability.
    c. Afghanistan shall strengthen its anticorruption institutions, and revise and enforce its laws, as necessary, in accordance with its national and international obligations.
    d. Afghanistan further shall safeguard and enhance the Afghan financial system by implementing recommendations from the Financial Action Task Force Asia Pacific Group (FATF/APG) regarding anti–money laundering and combating terrorist financing.

5. The United States and Afghanistan shall continue their cooperation to promote Afghanistan's development, including annual U.S. social and economic assistance to Afghanistan commensurate with the strategic importance of the U.S.-Afghan partnership.
    a. To achieve this goal, the United States shall seek on a yearly basis, funding for social and economic assistance to Afghanistan. The United States also supports Afghanistan's efforts to encourage international investment and support for the Afghan private sector, which is crucial to developing a secure, prosperous, peaceful Afghanistan and region.
    b. Building on its commitments at the 2010 Kabul and London Conference ("the Conferences"), the United States reiterates its commitment to channel at least 50 percent of such economic and social assistance to Afghanistan through Afghan government budgetary mechanisms. The Parties shall periodically review this commitment, through the Afghanistan–United States Bilateral Commission, established under this Agreement, with the goal of increasing the percentage of assistance channeled through Afghan Government budgetary mechanisms beyond 2012.
    c. The United States also reaffirms its 2010 Kabul Conference commitment to progressively align its development assistance behind Afghan National Priority Programs, as mutually determined by both Parties, with the goal of achieving 80 percent of alignment by the end of 2012. The United States agrees that any development assistance not aligned is to be fully transparent and consulted with the Government of Afghanistan.
    d. These commitments are contingent upon the Afghan government establishing mechanism and demonstrating agreed-upon progress to ensure financial transparency and accountability, increasing budget expenditures, improving revenue collection, enhancing public financial management systems, and other mutually determined measures of performance and progress, including those committed at the Conferences. . . .

VI. Strengthening Afghan Institutions and Governance

1. The Parties shall cooperate towards improving the human capacity of Afghanistan's crucial government institutions. U.S. assistance to Afghanistan should be based on the priorities of the Afghan Government and mutually identified needs.

2. Afghanistan shall improve governance by increasing the responsiveness [and] transparency of Afghan executive, legislative, and judicial institutions so that they better meet the civil and economic needs of the Afghan people. It shall promote efficiency and accountability at all levels of the government, consistent with Afghan law, and ensure that they provide services according to fair and objectively applied procedures and [are] consistent with national standards for minimum service delivery.

3. The United States shall support the Afghan Government in strengthening the capacity, self-reliance, and effectiveness of Afghan institutions and their ability to deliver basic services.

4. The Parties shall work cooperatively to eliminate "parallel structures," including Provincial Reconstruction Teams and District Stabilization Teams consistent with the *Inteqal* framework.

VII. Implementing Arrangements and Mechanisms

1. To advance cooperation and monitor progress towards implementing this Agreement, the Parties shall establish an Afghanistan–United States Bilateral Commission and associated implementation mechanisms.
   a. The Commission shall be chaired by the respective foreign ministers of Afghanistan and the United States, or their designees, and meet semi-annually in Kabul and/Washington on a rotational basis.
      i. Preexisting bilateral forums, such as the Afghanistan–United States Bilateral Security Consultative Forum, shall be incorporated into the framework of this new structure.
   b. A Joint Steering Committee shall guide and report to Ministers on the work of standing expert groups formed to implement this Agreement.
      i. These working groups shall be chaired by relevant ministers, or their designees, and are to constitute a forum for regular, senior-level consultations on issues of mutual concern. These issues include, but are not limited to, advancing long-term security, promoting social, democratic, and economic development, and strengthening Afghan institutions and governance.
   c. The Joint Steering Committee should also convene regularly to assess common threats and discuss regional issues of mutual concern.

2. Through the Bilateral Commission, Parties should establish mutually determined levels of support and assistance.

3. Afghanistan and the United States may enter into further arrangements or agreements, as necessary and appropriate, to implement this Agreement, subject to the relevant laws and regulations of both Parties. . . .

[Section VIII, detailing when the agreement enters into force and a recognition of following through on the agreement based on any other commitments under national or international law, and the signature section, have been omitted.]

Source: The White House. "Enduring Strategic Partnership Agreement Between the United States of America and the Islamic Republic of Afghanistan." June 1, 2012. http://www.whitehouse.gov/sites/default/files/2012.06.01u.s.-afghanistanspasignedtext.pdf.

OTHER HISTORIC DOCUMENTS OF INTEREST

FROM PREVIOUS *HISTORIC DOCUMENTS*

Florida Governor Responds to Trayvon Martin Shooting

March 22, 2012

On February 26, 2012, Trayvon Martin, a seventeen-year-old African American man, was shot and killed by George Zimmerman, a twenty-eight-year-old Hispanic man patrolling during a neighborhood watch in Sanford, Florida. The facts in the case are largely unknown or unverifiable because there were few witnesses. Questions have been raised about whether Zimmerman, or the police who did not arrest him at the scene, were motivated by racial bias. The shooting sparked a federal investigation into such allegations and also brought Florida's Stand Your Ground (SYG) self-defense law to the forefront of national debate. Opponents of the law argue that it has a clear racial bias and increases the number of justifiable homicides, while supporters say it protects law-abiding citizens from criminals. Following the Martin killing, Florida Governor Rick Scott created a task force designated to review the law and determine its merits and potential misuses.

Little Verifiable Evidence

In a Sanford, Florida, gated community on the evening of February 26, 2012, Martin, who was unarmed, was walking from a convenience store to his father's girlfriend's house, dressed in a gray hooded sweatshirt with the hood up, blocking the rain. Zimmerman, who formed a neighborhood watch in 2011 after concerns were raised about an increase in burglaries and suspicious people in the neighborhood, was patrolling the community in his sport utility vehicle (SUV). When Zimmerman spotted Martin, who was walking close to the homes rather than on the sidewalk, he followed Martin before calling 911, explaining to the dispatcher that Martin was "up to no good." The dispatcher warned Zimmerman against following Martin, but he disregarded the request.

What happened after Zimmerman hung up with the 911 dispatcher is unclear and is pieced together with information from various accounts. They included a series of 911 calls made by Zimmerman, neighbors, and other witnesses (none of whom saw the confrontation); Zimmerman's own testimony; information from Zimmerman's father based on the story he was told by his son; the police story; and the statements of Martin's girlfriend in Miami, who was on the phone with him at the time of the confrontation.

Initially, Zimmerman told police that he left his SUV but could no longer see Martin, who suddenly came up behind him asking if he had a problem. Martin then allegedly punched Zimmerman to the ground and slammed his head into the sidewalk. Zimmerman told the officers on the scene that he had called out for help. Zimmerman's statements released in June, the first after his April 11 arrest, said that he was ambushed by Martin and that his head "felt like it was going to explode." He also noted that Martin covered his nose and mouth and reached for Zimmerman's gun. A paramedic report from the night of the altercation noted a one-inch laceration on the back of Zimmerman's head.

Robert Zimmerman, George's father, who spoke with his son about the incident, gave a different story, saying that after losing sight of Martin, Zimmerman went back to his

SUV, where Martin appeared behind him and subsequently punched him in the nose and slammed his head into the sidewalk. Zimmerman tried to escape and in doing so made the gun in his waistband visible. Upon seeing the gun, Martin reportedly said to Zimmerman, "You are going to die tonight," after which Zimmerman shot Martin. Robert Zimmerman's story has been called into question because he gave a report to an Orlando news outlet that indicated that Zimmerman was punched by Martin as he was reaching for his cell phone to call for help, but he told the *New York Times* that he wasn't sure if Zimmerman reached for his phone or not and that he may have confused his son's description of the event with media reports he had heard.

The police story given to Martin's parents said that Martin approached Zimmerman on two occasions, asking why he was being watched. Martin walked away, but Zimmerman followed him, and Martin responded, "What's your problem, homie?" before pinning Zimmerman to the ground and beating him. Zimmerman then grabbed his gun and shot Martin, who said, "You got me," before falling backward. The official police report called the incident an "unnecessary killing to prevent an unlawful act."

According to Martin's girlfriend, as told to the Martin family lawyer, Martin told her on the phone that someone was watching him and that he was going to walk fast to get away from him. Martin then asked Zimmerman why he was being followed, Zimmerman asked Martin what he was doing in the community, and then the girlfriend said she heard what sounded like an altercation before the phone went dead. Follow-up calls to Martin's phone by his girlfriend went unanswered.

The final side of the story comes from two witnesses, roommates Selma Mora Lamilla and Mary Cutcher, who ran out of their home after hearing a gunshot. The pair reported seeing Zimmerman on top of Martin with his knees straddling his sides, but they said Zimmerman didn't appear to be helping Martin, who had just been shot. Cutcher reported that she hadn't heard a struggle prior to the gunshot but that a whining noise she heard did stop immediately afterward.

CHARGES, A CIVIL RIGHTS INVESTIGATION, AND A TASK FORCE

Because he invoked Florida's SYG law at the scene, police did not arrest Zimmerman. However, prosecutors rejected that claim, and Zimmerman was arrested on April 11, charged with second-degree murder. He pleaded not guilty and claimed that he shot Martin in self-defense with a licensed, 9-mm handgun. On April 20, Zimmerman had a bond hearing, during which his wife, Shellie, and other family members told the court that the family had no money. Zimmerman did not correct this statement, even though he had $130,000 between his checking account and those of his wife and sister. This money was raised through a website for his legal defense. Believing Shellie's story to be true, the judge released Zimmerman on a $150,000 bond. Shellie was charged with perjury in June, and Zimmerman was subsequently arrested, but he was released in July on a $1 million bond. Zimmerman's trial is set for June 2013, and a conviction would carry a maximum sentence of life in prison.

Because allegations were raised that Zimmerman was acting on a racial bias when he shot Martin, the Federal Bureau of Investigation (FBI) opened a civil rights case. The FBI conducted interviews with Zimmerman's friends, coworkers, and neighbors, none of whom were willing to state that Zimmerman had any racial bias. Conflicting information came from Zimmerman's 911 calls in the weeks leading up to the shooting, in which he was complaining about suspicious African Americans roaming the neighborhood. On the night of the shooting, Zimmerman allegedly told the dispatcher, "These a**holes always get away." Statements were also found on an old MySpace page belonging to Zimmerman where he disparaged Mexicans. In the end, the FBI concluded in July that Zimmerman was not motivated by racial bias or hatred when he shot Martin.

In March, Governor Scott responded to the killing, calling for the creation of a Task Force on Citizen Safety and Protection. According to the governor, the task force would "thoroughly review Florida's 'Stand Your Ground' law" and any other such rules or regulations that impact the safety of Florida citizens. Scott said he wanted to ensure that citizens are able to feel secure in public and private, while having "an open and honest discussion" on how to "avoid such tragedies in the future." The task force was set to convene and begin conducting hearings after the conclusion of the state's investigation into Martin's death.

STAND YOUR GROUND LAWS VERSUS CASTLE DOCTRINES

Zimmerman's claim that he was acting in self-defense raises larger questions about Florida's SYG law. In 2005, Florida became the first state to expand the right of a person to use deadly force for self-defense without a requirement to retreat if possible. In the Florida law, deadly force can be justified if a person is threatened in the home or "any other place where he or she has a right to be." When self-defense is invoked in Florida murder cases, it is up to the prosecution to disprove the claim. Additionally, anyone claiming that they shot someone in self-defense cannot be sued. Since the law went into effect, the number of those claiming self-defense has increased. The law at times is used by gang members, drug dealers, and in cases of road rage and bar fights. Coupled with Florida's wide-ranging gun rights laws, it has put a strain on the legal system. In most instances, because the victim cannot testify, the gun user's version of the story is accepted as truth in court, meaning that prosecutors sometimes have no choice but to drop the case.

More than twenty SYG laws exist in the United States, with most enacted in recent years. Eight states, all in the South, use the phrase "Stand Your Ground," but the law is known in some other areas as "Shoot First" or "Make My Day." The law is supported by the National Rifle Association (NRA), which, along with other supporters, says that the good guys need to be armed if the bad guys will be and that the law is useful in domestic abuse situations in which one person may not have the option to flee. Law enforcement stands in opposition, claiming that the law encourages vigilante justice. Overall homicide rates in Florida and sixteen other states that passed SYG laws after 2005 stayed flat between 2000 and 2010, while justifiable homicide nearly doubled during that same time frame.

An alternative to SYG is commonly referred to as the Castle Doctrine and exists in almost every state. Under this law, you have the right to use deadly force to protect yourself in your home, but in many states you must first make an attempt to retreat if threatened with a gun or knife. Those who have the possibility of escape but kill someone instead can be prosecuted in some states following the Castle Doctrine.

According to a June 2012 study by Texas A&M University researchers, murder and manslaughter rates increased 8 percent, or 600 homicides per year, in states with SYG laws. This could be because more people use lethal force in self-defense or because situations escalate into violence more often. "Regardless," researchers wrote, "the results indicate that a primary consequence of strengthening self-defense law is increased homicide." Contradicting the arguments of supporters who claim that SYG and Castle Doctrine laws deter crime, the researchers found "no evidence of deterrence effects on burglary, robbery, or aggravated assault. . . . In contrast, we find significant evidence that the laws increase homicides. Suggestive but inconclusive evidence indicates that castle doctrine laws increase the narrowly defined category of justifiable homicides by private citizens by 17 to 50 percent."

RACIAL BIAS IN STAND YOUR GROUND?

A report by John Roman, a senior fellow at the Urban Institute's Justice Policy Center, found that the killing of African Americans by whites is more likely to be considered justified in court than the killing of whites by African Americans. His research found that in non-SYG states, white people are 250 percent more likely to be justified in killing an African American than another white person, but in SYG states, that number increases to 354 percent.

The U.S. Commission on Civil Rights opened an investigation into racial bias concerns pertaining to SYG laws. The lead researcher on the study expects it to take at least one year. In a press release on the scope of the investigation, the commission said "the most divisive and inflammatory of those questions is whether racial bias skews our justice system through 'Stand Your Ground' (SYG) laws that shield those who claim self defense." The commission will look at state investigations and charges in self-defense homicide cases since 2000, including the race of the victims and perpetrators, procedures and investigations, and public allegations of bias in the law. Florida will be one state of focus to determine whether such racial bias exists.

—Heather Kerrigan

Following is a statement by Florida Governor Rick Scott on March 22, 2012, announcing the creation of a task force to investigate the Trayvon Martin shooting.

Gov. Scott Creates Trayvon Martin
DOCUMENT *Task Force*

March 22, 2012

Tallahassee, Fla.—Governor Rick Scott and Attorney General Pam Bondi today worked together to appoint Angela B. Corey (of the 4th Judicial Circuit) as the newly Assigned State Attorney in the investigation into the death of Trayvon Martin. The Governor and Attorney General reached out to State Attorney Norman Wolfinger today. After the conversation, Wolfinger decided to step down from this investigation and turn it over to another state attorney. The Governor has also announced the formation of a task force which will convene following the conclusion of the investigation by State Attorney Corey. The Governor and General Bondi have full faith in the Florida Department of Law Enforcement, the U.S. Department of Justice and State Attorney Corey that a full and thorough investigation will be conducted.

See below a statement from Governor Scott regarding the formation of the task force, and attached the Executive Order appointing Angela B. Corey as the Assigned State

Attorney and a letter from State Attorney Norman Wolfinger requesting the assignment of another state attorney to the investigation.

STATEMENT FROM FLORIDA GOVERNOR RICK SCOTT REGARDING THE CREATION OF A TASK FORCE ON CITIZEN SAFETY AND PROTECTION

"As law enforcement investigates the death of Trayvon Martin, Floridians and others around the country have rightly recognized this as a terrible tragedy. Like all Floridians, I believe we must take steps to ensure tragedies like this are avoided. After listening to many concerned citizens in recent days, I will call for a Task Force on Citizen Safety and Protection to investigate how to make sure a tragedy such as this does not occur in the future, while at the same time, protecting the fundamental rights of all of our citizens— especially the right to feel protected and safe in our state.

"To this end, I have asked Lieutenant Governor Jennifer Carroll to lead the Task Force, conduct public hearings, take testimony and recommend actions—legislative and other- wise—to both protect our citizens and safeguard our rights. Reverend R. B. Holmes, Jr., the pastor of the Bethel Missionary Baptist Church in Tallahassee, has agreed to be the vice-chair of the Task Force. I have also reached out to Attorney General Pam Bondi, Speaker Dean Cannon, President Mike Haridopolos and incoming presiding officers Don Gaetz and Will Weatherford, who all agree that a Task Force needs to be assembled. They will be recommending individuals for me to appoint to the Task Force, which will thor- oughly review Florida's "Stand Your Ground" law and any other laws, rules, regulations or programs that relate to public safety and citizen protection.

"It is my intention to have the Task Force on Citizen Safety and Protection convene immediately after the investigation into the death of Trayvon Martin by the newly Assigned State Attorney Angela B. Corey (of the 4th Judicial Circuit) formally ends. At that time they can define their mission and scope as well as set a timetable for a report, with recom- mendations to be delivered to my office and to the Florida Legislature. The Task Force will hold public hearings, take testimony, solicit ideas and review all matters related to the rights of all Floridians to feel safe and secure in our state. As we exercise our right to be free and secure both in public and in the privacy of our own homes it is important that we have an open and honest discussion on these issues so that we might help avoid such trag- edies in the future."

SOURCE: Office of the Governor of Florida. News Releases. "Governor Rick Scott Announces New State Attorney and Task Force in Response to Trayvon Martin Incident." March 22, 2012. http://www .flgov.com/2012/03/22/governor-rick-scott-announces-new-state-attorney-and-task-force-in-response- to-trayvon-martin-incident.

OTHER HISTORIC DOCUMENTS OF INTEREST

FROM THIS VOLUME

FROM PREVIOUS *HISTORIC DOCUMENTS*

April

Supreme Court Rules on Jail Strip Searches

APRIL 2, 2012

In *Florence v. Board of Chosen Freeholders of the County of Burlington,* one of the prominent Fourth Amendment cases of the term, a divided Supreme Court upheld prison strip searches for new inmates introduced into the general jail population. The majority refused to make an exception even for those charged with minor offenses whose ultimate conviction would not lead to incarceration. In so doing, the Court emphasized that jails are dangerous places that depend on the expertise of correctional officials to maintain order and safety. Admitting more than 13 million inmates a year, jails have, the Court found, a significant interest in conducting thorough searches as part of a standard intake process to protect against the dangers of introducing lice or infectious diseases into the prison population and to search for evidence of gang affiliation or weapons and contraband. *Florence* presented a classic balancing case, weighing the prison authorities' needs for security against the privacy concerns of the individual. In finding that, in this case, security outweighs privacy, the Court split along traditional ideological lines with Justice Anthony Kennedy delivering the opinion of the Court, joined by the more conservative members of the Court: Chief Justice John Roberts Jr. and Justices Antonin Scalia, Clarence Thomas, and Samuel Alito Jr.

FLORENCE ARREST

In 2005, Albert Florence was in his car with his pregnant wife and his four-year-old son, who was in the backseat. They were going to dinner at his mother-in-law's house when they were pulled over by a state trooper. In interviews, Florence has said that he believed he was targeted because he was a black man in an expensive car. The officer discovered a two-year-old outstanding bench warrant against Florence for failure to pay a fine. In fact, Florence had paid the balance of the fine less than a week after the warrant was issued, but, for some unexplained reason, the warrant remained in a statewide computer database. Florence had unsuccessfully tried to correct this issue and carried proof that he had paid his fine in the glove compartment of his car. Nevertheless, the officer handcuffed him and arrested him in front of his distraught family.

He was taken to Burlington County Detention Center where, as part of the intake procedures, he was stripped naked and showered with a delousing agent. Officials conducted a close visual inspection of him while he was naked, looking for body markings, wounds, and contraband. Without physically touching him, the prison officials inspected his mouth, nose, ears, and genitals to see if he was hiding anything. Florence was instructed to open his mouth, lift his tongue, hold out his arms, turn around, and lift his genitals. After six days, he was moved to Essex County Correctional Facility, the largest county jail in New Jersey. It admits 25,000 inmates a year and houses roughly 1,000 gang members at any given time. Here, Florence was again stripped naked and closely inspected by officials who, he said, made him squat and cough in front of others. The next day, Florence was finally brought before a judge, who released him and dropped all charges against him.

LEGAL BACKGROUND

Florence brought a suit against the government entities operating the jails for violations of his Fourth Amendment right to be free of unreasonable searches and seizures. He argued that people arrested for minor nonviolent offenses should not be required to endure humiliating close inspections of private areas of the body unless there is reason to suspect the particular inmate is concealing weapons, drugs, or other contraband. He won in the district court, which concluded that jails cannot strip search those arrested for nonindictable offenses without some reasonable suspicion that the inmate is hiding contraband. This was reversed by the Third Circuit Court of Appeals, which found that the strip searches at issue struck a reasonable balance between inmate privacy and the security needs of the jail. Florence appealed his case to the U.S. Supreme Court.

HIGH COURT RULES

This case does not address whether it was proper for the police to arrest and take to jail someone who had committed a minor offense that could not possibly result in jail time. That issue was resolved in 2001 in the case *Atwater v. Lago Vista*. In *Atwater*, the police arrested and took to jail a woman after noticing that she and her children were not wearing seat belts. The Court rejected her argument that the Fourth Amendment prohibited her incarceration without a warrant when the offense could not possibly result in jail time and there was no compelling need for immediate detention. Such a rule, the Court held, would require too many sensitive, case-by-case determinations by arresting officers to be practicable. So, after *Atwater*, anyone the police believe they have seen commit a criminal offense can be arrested and taken to jail, even if it is for a traffic offense, expired license, other misdemeanor, or, as in the *Florence* case, failure to pay a fine. Thus, Florence could not challenge his incarceration in this instance but only argue for special restrictions on the type of searches performed on such minor offenders once they are taken to jail.

Writing for the majority in *Florence v. Board of Chosen Freeholders of the County of Burlington*, Justice Kennedy went to great pains to emphasize the significant interest correctional officers have in conducting a thorough search as part of an intake process. "The danger of introducing lice or contagious infections," he wrote, "is well documented." Injuries or illness requiring medical attention may be difficult to identify until detainees remove their clothes for visual inspection. Escalating problems with gang members in prison provide a reasonable basis to justify a visual inspection for tattoos and other marks of gang affiliation during the intake process. Furthermore, the dangers posed by concealed contraband are very serious. Justice Kennedy cited evidence that correctional officers "have had to confront arrestees concealing knives, scissors, razor blades, glass shards, and other prohibited items on their person, including in their body cavities." Even everyday items that may seem innocuous, such as money, cigarettes, lighters, matches, cell phones, pills, gum, hair pins, or pens, can, he wrote, "undermine security if introduced into a detention facility." According to the Department of Justice, every year more than 10,000 assaults on correctional staff are committed by inmates, and many more among themselves. For all these reasons, the Court has repeatedly held that much deference must be given to those running jails unless there is "substantial evidence" that demonstrates their response to a situation is exaggerated.

The majority of the Court rejected Florence's argument that detainees arrested for minor offenses not involving any weapons or drugs should be exempted from the strip search unless there is a particular reason to suspect that they are hiding contraband. Citing such notorious criminals as Oklahoma City bomber Timothy McVeigh and serial killer Joel Rifkin, who were both finally stopped by state troopers for the minor offense of driving without a license, Justice Kennedy wrote that "people detained for minor offenses can turn out to be the most devious and dangerous criminals." Requiring correctional officials to treat new inmates, who are being introduced into the general population, differently, based on the underlying offense that has brought them to jail in the first place, would be, the Court held, unworkable. "The seriousness of an offense is a poor predictor of who has contraband," Justice Kennedy wrote, concluding that "it would be difficult in practice to determine whether individual detainees fall within the proposed exemption."

Interestingly, Justice Kennedy added a Part IV to his opinion that stressed the limits of its application. This section made it clear that the Court was not ruling on whether such invasive searches would be permissible if a detainee were not going to be introduced into the general jail population. "There also may," he wrote, "be legitimate concerns about the invasiveness of searches that involve the touching of detainees." Chief Justice Roberts and Justice Alito each wrote separate, concurring opinions, emphasizing the importance of this caveat to their willingness to sign on to the majority opinion. Justice Alito wrote, "It is important to note, however, that the Court does not hold that it is *always* reasonable to conduct a full strip search of an arrestee whose detention has not been reviewed by a judicial officer and who could be held in available facilities apart from the general population." In contrast, a footnote on the opinion's first page states that "Justice Thomas joins all but Part IV of this opinion." Justice Thomas did not write a separate opinion to explain this vote, but the implication is that he would not admit to any limits in any situations on the power of correctional officers to determine what procedures are required to maintain security.

The four more liberal justices on the Court signed on to a dissenting opinion written by Justice Stephen Breyer, who wrote, "In my view, such a search of an individual arrested for a minor offense that does not involve drugs or violence—say a traffic offense, a regulatory offense, an essentially civil matter, or any other such misdemeanor—is an 'unreasonable search' forbidden by the Fourth Amendment, unless prison authorities have reasonable suspicion to believe that the individual possesses drugs or other contraband."

IMPACT OF THE RULING

Prior to the September 11, 2001, terror attacks, lower courts generally prohibited routine strip searches for minor offenses, but this decision follows the trend since the attacks of giving broader discretion to prison officials to maintain security. The *Florence* holding settles a conflict among appellate courts, overturning the rulings of seven federal appeals courts that had required a "reasonable suspicion" before conducting strip searches on those arrested for only minor infractions. The ruling, however, does not apply in at least ten states that have passed laws prohibiting suspicionless strip searches for minor or traffic offenses, including Colorado, Florida, Illinois, Iowa, Kansas, Kentucky, Michigan, Missouri, Tennessee, and Washington. Similarly, the Federal Bureau of Prisons does not subject those arrested for misdemeanor or civil contempt offenses to visual body-cavity searches without their consent or reasonable suspicion; rather, it segregates them from the general population.

Lawyers on both sides of the case called this a narrow ruling, particularly because of the separate concurring opinions by Justices Roberts and Alito. "It is important for me that the court does not foreclose the possibility of an exception to the rule it announces," Justice Roberts wrote.

—Melissa Feinberg

The following are excerpts from the U.S. Supreme Court ruling in Florence v. Board of Chosen Freeholders of the County of Burlington, *in which the Court ruled 5–4 that strip searches of those in the general jail population do not require reasonable suspicion.*

Florence v. Board of Chosen Freeholders of the County of Burlington

April 2, 2012

No. 10–945

Albert W. Florence, Petitioner

v.

Board of Chosen Freeholders of the County of Burlington et al.

On writ of certiorari to the United States Court of Appeals for the Third Circuit

[April 2, 2012]

[Footnotes and most citations have been omitted.]

JUSTICE KENNEDY delivered the opinion of the Court, except as to Part IV.*

Correctional officials have a legitimate interest, indeed a responsibility, to ensure that jails are not made less secure by reason of what new detainees may carry in on their bodies. Facility personnel, other inmates, and the new detainee himself or herself may be in danger if these threats are introduced into the jail population. This case presents the question of what rules, or limitations, the Constitution imposes on searches of arrested persons who are to be held in jail while their cases are being processed. The term "jail" is used here in a broad sense to include prisons and other detention facilities. The specific measures being challenged will be described in more detail; but, in broad terms, the controversy concerns whether every detainee who will be admitted to the general population may be required to undergo a close visual inspection while undressed.

The case turns in part on the extent to which this Court has sufficient expertise and information in the record to mandate, under the Constitution, the specific restrictions and limitations sought by those who challenge the visual search procedures at issue. In addressing this type of constitutional claim courts must defer to the judgment of correctional officials unless the record contains substantial evidence showing their policies are an unnecessary or unjustified response to problems of jail security. That necessary showing has not been made in this case.

[Section I has been omitted and contains background information on the case.]

II

The difficulties of operating a detention center must not be underestimated by the courts. Jails (in the stricter sense of the term, excluding prison facilities) admit more than 13 million inmates a year. The largest facilities process hundreds of people every day; smaller jails may be crowded on weekend nights, after a large police operation, or because of detainees arriving from other jurisdictions. Maintaining safety and order at these institutions requires the expertise of correctional officials, who must have substantial discretion to devise reasonable solutions to the problems they face. The Court has confirmed the importance of deference to correctional officials and explained that a regulation impinging on an inmate's constitutional rights must be upheld "if it is reasonably related to legitimate penological interests."

[Additional discussion of case precedent has been omitted.]

III

The question here is whether undoubted security imperatives involved in jail supervision override the assertion that some detainees must be exempt from the more invasive search procedures at issue absent reasonable suspicion of a concealed weapon or other contraband. The Court has held that deference must be given to the officials in charge of the jail unless there is "substantial evidence" demonstrating their response to the situation is exaggerated. Petitioner has not met this standard, and the record provides full justifications for the procedures used.

A

Correctional officials have a significant interest in conducting a thorough search as a standard part of the intake process. The admission of inmates creates numerous risks for facility staff, for the existing detainee population, and for a new detainee himself or herself. The danger of introducing lice or contagious infections, for example, is well documented.

The Federal Bureau of Prisons recommends that staff screen new detainees for these conditions. Persons just arrested may have wounds or other injuries requiring immediate medical attention. It may be difficult to identify and treat these problems until detainees remove their clothes for a visual inspection.

Jails and prisons also face grave threats posed by the increasing number of gang members who go through the intake process. "Gang rivalries spawn a climate of tension, violence, and coercion." The groups recruit new members by force, engage in assaults against staff, and give other inmates a reason to arm themselves. Fights among feuding gangs can be deadly, and the officers who must maintain order are put in harm's way. These considerations provide a reasonable basis to justify a visual inspection for certain tattoos and other signs of gang affiliation as part of the intake process. The identification and isolation of gang members before they are admitted protects everyone in the facility.

Detecting contraband concealed by new detainees, furthermore, is a most serious responsibility. Weapons, drugs, and alcohol all disrupt the safe operation of a jail.

Correctional officers have had to confront arrestees concealing knives, scissors, razor blades, glass shards, and other prohibited items on their person, including in their body cavities. They have also found crack, heroin, and marijuana. The use of drugs can embolden inmates in aggression toward officers or each other; and, even apart from their use, the trade in these substances can lead to violent confrontations.

There are many other kinds of contraband. The textbook definition of the term covers any unauthorized item. Everyday items can undermine security if introduced into a detention facility:

> "Lighters and matches are fire and arson risks or potential weapons. Cell phones are used to orchestrate violence and criminality both within and without jailhouse walls. Pills and medications enhance suicide risks. Chewing gum can block locking devices; hairpins can open handcuffs; wigs can conceal drugs and weapons."

Something as simple as an overlooked pen can pose a significant danger. Inmates commit more than 10,000 assaults on correctional staff every year and many more among themselves.

Contraband creates additional problems because scarce items, including currency, have value in a jail's culture and underground economy. Correctional officials inform us "[t]he competition . . . for such goods begets violence, extortion, and disorder." Gangs exacerbate the problem. They "orchestrate thefts, commit assaults, and approach inmates in packs to take the contraband from the weak." This puts the entire facility, including detainees being held for a brief term for a minor offense, at risk. Gangs do coerce inmates who have access to the outside world, such as people serving their time on the weekends, to sneak things into the jail. These inmates, who might be thought to pose the least risk, have been caught smuggling prohibited items into jail. Concealing contraband often takes little time and effort. It might be done as an officer approaches a suspect's car or during a brief commotion in a group holding cell. Something small might be tucked or taped under an armpit, behind an ear, between the buttocks, in the instep of a foot, or inside the mouth or some other body cavity.

It is not surprising that correctional officials have sought to perform thorough searches at intake for disease, gang affiliation, and contraband. Jails are often crowded, unsanitary, and dangerous places. There is a substantial interest in preventing any new inmate, either of his own will or as a result of coercion, from putting all who live or work at these institutions at even greater risk when he is admitted to the general population.

B

Petitioner acknowledges that correctional officials must be allowed to conduct an effective search during the intake process and that this will require at least some detainees to lift their genitals or cough in a squatting position. These procedures, similar to the ones upheld in *Bell*, are designed to uncover contraband that can go undetected by a patdown, metal detector, and other less invasive searches. Petitioner maintains there is little benefit to conducting these more invasive steps on a new detainee who has not been arrested for a serious crime or for any offense involving a weapon or drugs. In his view these detainees should be exempt from this process unless they give officers a particular reason to suspect them of hiding contraband. It is reasonable, however, for correctional officials to conclude this standard would be unworkable. The record provides evidence that the seriousness of an offense is a poor predictor of who has contraband and that it would be difficult in practice to determine whether individual detainees fall within the proposed exemption.

1

People detained for minor offenses can turn out to be the most devious and dangerous criminals. Hours after the Oklahoma City bombing, Timothy McVeigh was stopped by a state trooper who noticed he was driving without a license plate. Police stopped serial killer

Joel Rifkin for the same reason. One of the terrorists involved in the September 11 attacks was stopped and ticketed for speeding just two days before hijacking Flight 93. Reasonable correctional officials could conclude these uncertainties mean they must conduct the same thorough search of everyone who will be admitted to their facilities.

Experience shows that people arrested for minor offenses have tried to smuggle prohibited items into jail, sometimes by using their rectal cavities or genitals for the concealment. They may have some of the same incentives as a serious criminal to hide contraband. A detainee might risk carrying cash, cigarettes, or a penknife to survive in jail. Others may make a quick decision to hide unlawful substances to avoid getting in more trouble at the time of their arrest. . . .

2

It also may be difficult, as a practical matter, to classify inmates by their current and prior offenses before the intake search. Jails can be even more dangerous than prisons because officials there know so little about the people they admit at the outset.

An arrestee may be carrying a false ID or lie about his identity. The officers who conduct an initial search often do not have access to criminal history records. And those records can be inaccurate or incomplete. Petitioner's rap sheet is an example. It did not reflect his previous arrest for possession of a deadly weapon. In the absence of reliable information it would be illogical to require officers to assume the arrestees in front of them do not pose a risk of smuggling something into the facility.

The laborious administration of prisons would become less effective, and likely less fair and evenhanded, were the practical problems inevitable from the rules suggested by petitioner to be imposed as a constitutional mandate. . . .

[Discussion of principles applied from earlier cases have been omitted.]

IV

This case does not require the Court to rule on the types of searches that would be reasonable in instances where, for example, a detainee will be held without assignment to the general jail population and without substantial contact with other detainees. This describes the circumstances in *Atwater*. The accommodations provided in these situations may diminish the need to conduct some aspects of the searches at issue. The circumstances before the Court, however, do not present the opportunity to consider a narrow exception of the sort JUSTICE ALITO describes, *post*, at 2–3 (concurring opinion), which might restrict whether an arrestee whose detention has not yet been reviewed by a magistrate or other judicial officer, and who can be held in available facilities removed from the general population, may be subjected to the types of searches at issue here.

Petitioner's *amici* raise concerns about instances of officers engaging in intentional humiliation and other abusive practices. There also may be legitimate concerns about the invasiveness of searches that involve the touching of detainees. These issues are not implicated on the facts of this case, however, and it is unnecessary to consider them here.

V

Even assuming all the facts in favor of petitioner, the search procedures at the Burlington County Detention Center and the Essex County Correctional Facility struck a reasonable balance between inmate privacy and the needs of the institutions. The Fourth and Fourteenth Amendments do not require adoption of the framework of rules petitioner proposes.

The judgment of the Court of Appeals for the Third Circuit is affirmed.

It is so ordered.

CHIEF JUSTICE ROBERTS, concurring.

I join the opinion of the Court. As with JUSTICE ALITO, however, it is important for me that the Court does not foreclose the possibility of an exception to the rule it announces. JUSTICE KENNEDY explains that the circumstances before it do not afford an opportunity to consider that possibility. Those circumstances include the facts that Florence was detained not for a minor traffic offense but instead pursuant to a warrant for his arrest, and that there was apparently no alternative, if Florence were to be detained, to holding him in the general jail population.

Factual nuances have not played a significant role as this case has been presented to the Court. Both courts below regarded acknowledged factual disputes as "immaterial" to their conflicting dispositions, and before this Court Florence challenged suspicionless strip searches "no matter what the circumstances."

The Court makes a persuasive case for the general applicability of the rule it announces. The Court is nonetheless wise to leave open the possibility of exceptions, to ensure that we "not embarrass the future."

JUSTICE ALITO, concurring.

[Justice Alito's discussion of the Court's findings has been omitted.]

The Court does not address whether it is always reasonable, without regard to the offense or the reason for detention, to strip search an arrestee before the arrestee's detention has been reviewed by a judicial officer. The lead opinion explicitly reserves judgment on that question. In light of that limitation, I join the opinion of the Court in full.

* JUSTICE THOMAS joins all but Part IV of this opinion.

[The dissenting opinion of Justices Breyer, Ginsburg, Sotomayor, and Kagan has been omitted.]

SOURCE: U.S. Supreme Court. *Florence v. Board of Chosen Freeholders of the County of Burlington*, 566 U.S. __ (2012). http://www.supremecourt.gov/opinions/11pdf/10-945.pdf.

OTHER HISTORIC DOCUMENTS OF INTEREST

FROM PREVIOUS *HISTORIC DOCUMENTS*

North Korea Remarks on Satellite Launches

APRIL 13, APRIL 16, AND DECEMBER 12, 2012

North Korea's nuclear ambition over the past two decades has been a persistent source of international tension and anxiety. But the struggling nation has wavered between a strong desire to continue its drive to build nuclear weapons and to work with the international community to scale back its plans in return for economic and food aid and diplomatic assistance. With a new leader in place following the death of Kim Jong-il in December 2011, the international community was left to wonder whether his son, Kim Jong-un, would follow through on UN resolutions banning weapons testing by North Korea or continue the plans of his father, who had defied the international community year after year. In 2012, Kim made his plans clear through two provocative satellite launches that immediately drew ire from South Korea, the United States, Japan, and the United Nations and raised questions about whether the North was truly capable of reaching the United States with an intercontinental ballistic missile.

NORTH KOREA'S NUCLEAR AMBITION

The secretive Asian nation has long had a nuclear program, and in 1994, then-president Bill Clinton's administration considered strikes against the nation's nuclear facilities. But North Korea instead agreed that it would end its nuclear program. In 2002, officials in President George W. Bush's administration alleged that the agreement had been violated, and the communist state was declared a member of the "axis of evil." In response, North Korea barred nuclear inspectors from the country and formally ended its 1994 agreement. In 2005, North Korea agreed to enter six-party talks with China, Japan, Russia, the United States, and South Korea and end its nuclear program in exchange for economic assistance. The agreement was short lived. After conducting its first atomic test in 2006, North Korea's nuclear program remained relatively quiet—until it ignored international warnings and set off its second nuclear device in 2009. In late 2010, North Korea revealed a secret uranium enrichment plant, which led then–defense secretary Robert Gates to declare in January 2011 that North Korea would have the capability to reach the United States with an intercontinental ballistic missile within five years. That summer, after meeting with Russian leaders, Kim Jong-il agreed to again suspend the nuclear program and return to the six-party talks.

When Kim Jong-il died of a heart attack on December 17, 2011, world leaders hoped his son and successor, Kim Jong-un, might be more willing to continue the six-party nuclear talks and officially end the North's nuclear program. In the first month of his reign, the new Kim said he would be open to additional discussions and one month later agreed to end weapons tests and uranium enrichment while allowing international nuclear inspectors into the country. Kim's government also agreed to reenter the six-party talks and stop any long-range missile launches.

The United States, South Korea, and Japan all expressed doubt that North Korea would follow through on any of the agreements, and shortly after agreeing to reenter the six-party talks, Kim's government announced its plan to launch a satellite into orbit and also declared its intention to build a nuclear weapon that could reach the United States within the next few years. The United States and the United Nations called the planned satellite launch a clear attempt to cover up long-range missile testing.

FAILED ATTEMPT

In March, reports first came out of Japan indicating that North Korea was beginning to fuel its satellite for launch. Then Pyongyang's foreign ministry spokesperson said preparations for launch "have entered a full-fledged stage of action." The spokesperson also said, "The projected launch of the working satellite is a gift to be presented by the Korean people to the centenary of the birth of President Kim Il Sung." The Korean Central News Agency (KCNA), the government's official news arm, continued to contend that the satellite had nothing to do with weapons testing but was instead to be used to estimate crop yields and survey weather patterns. North Korea's government invited international observers from foreign media outlets to watch the launch as a further attempt to show its peaceful intention. In response to the preparations, Japan announced that it would ready surface-to-air missiles to strike anything threatening its airspace.

Prior to the launch, the United States, Russia, and Japan all urged North Korea not to follow through on its plans. "A launch is a serious act of provocation that would affect peace and stability in the region that includes our country," said Japanese Prime Minister Yoshihiko Noda. Speaking to the Group of Eight (G-8) meeting in New York, Secretary of State Hillary Rodham Clinton said, "Pyongyang has a clear choice: It can pursue peace and reap the benefits of closer ties with the international community, including the United States; or it can continue to face pressure and isolation." China's response was less direct. "We are very concerned about that issue," said China's UN Ambassador, Li Baodong, adding that China's desire is to "diffuse tension, not inflame it."

Despite its lofty goals, when the satellite was launched on April 13, marking the one-hundredth anniversary of the birth of the nation's founder, it splintered into pieces about one minute after lift-off, well short of entering orbit, and fell into the Yellow Sea. Even the powerfully controlled state-run media were forced to admit to citizens the failure of the satellite. The failure raised a host of questions for the international community, including whether Kim, perhaps embarrassed by the situation, would use another method to cement the North's credibility. International observers were also left wondering whether Kim wanted the launch to occur, especially in defiance of the North's closest ally, China, but was instead forced to follow through by the powerful advisers with which he surrounds himself. This, some experts said, could indicate a power struggle at the top of North Korea's government.

Despite the failure and condemnation from the international community, North Korea pressed on with its nuclear development. Satellite imagery released in May revealed that work on the nation's main nuclear reactor had restarted. In October 2012, the nation claimed that it had developed missiles that could reach the mainland of the United States. The announcement was largely viewed as a domestic attempt to paint the United States as a growing threat and make clear that Kim was bringing North Korea to the forefront of international affairs. "They wanted to introduce the Kim Jong-un era with a big celebratory bang. They wanted to make their people believe that they were now a powerful nation," said Kim Yong-hyun, a professor of North Korean studies at Dongguk University in Seoul, South Korea.

SECOND ATTEMPT SUCCEEDS

On December 12, 2012, North Korea launched its second satellite, attached to a long-range rocket. It successfully entered orbit, although scientists think its tumbling pattern means it is most likely nonfunctioning. In North Korea, however, state-run media celebrated Kim's success, using vehicles with loudspeakers driven through the nation's capital, announcing the news. "We are proud of the glorious success of our satellite technology," said a KCNA presenter. "This is a landmark achievement."

According to the North American Aerospace Defense Command (NORAD), the satellite followed its expected path, traveling south from the Korean peninsula. Japanese and South Korean emergency and military systems also confirmed the launch of what was thought to be a Taepodong 2 missile. North Koreans refer to the missile as an Unha-3, which translated means Galaxy-3, and it is the same type of missile used in failed satellite attempts in 2006, 2009, and April 2012. It is estimated that the missile can travel up to 3,400 miles, making it capable of hitting the United States.

INTERNATIONAL REACTION

After the failed April launch, the UN Security Council called it "a serious violation" of the 2009 resolution banning ballistic missile tests, but North Korea responded that it "never recognized" the UN resolution because it was "a product of sinister intentions of the hostile forces." Although the Security Council had announced that it would meet to discuss new sanctions or resolutions against North Korea, indications from China and Russia that they would veto any such action kept any formal UN reaction at bay. "We do not believe in new sanctions—they will not do anything in terms of resolving the situation," said Russian Foreign Minister Sergei Lavrov. "We are convinced it is necessary to respond to the challenges at hand exclusively through political and diplomatic means," he continued. Chinese Foreign Minister Yang Jiechi echoed Russian sentiment, calling for "restrained actions by the corresponding sides with the aim of preserving stability on the peninsula."

In April, the White House reiterated its desire to work with North Korea to reach an agreement on its nuclear program but said the nation needed to abide by earlier international agreements. "Despite the failure of its attempted missile launch, North Korea's provocative action threatens regional security, violates international law and contravenes its own recent commitments," said a White House statement. The United States also announced that it would halt a plan to send food aid to North Korea that it had agreed to in exchange for the suspension of its nuclear program.

The success of the December launch drew even stronger condemnation from the international community. One of the most surprising reactions came from the North's close ally, China, which said it "regrets" the launch. Hong Lei, Chinese Foreign Ministry spokesperson, said that if this was in fact an attempt at a space program, that right is "subject to limitations by relevant United Nations Security Council resolutions." This was the first time China had taken such a tough stance on North Korea's program. The North Korean government continued to stand by its assertions that the launch was a portion of its budding space program and not a covert missile launch banned by UN regulations.

"The successful launch of the satellite is a proud fruition of the Workers' Party of Korea's policy of attaching importance to . . . science and technology. It is also an event of great turn in developing the country's science, technology and economy by fully exercising the independent right to use space for peaceful purposes," KCNA reported after the launch.

The UN Security Council condemned the December launch and said it would consider how to further respond to the situation. U.S. Ambassador to the United Nations Susan Rice said that the Obama administration wanted "a clear and meaningful response." She continued, "Members of the council must now work in a concerted fashion to send North Korea a clear message that its violations of UN Security Council resolutions have consequences." Other Western diplomats joined the call for a stronger UN response, with possible sanctions including banning travel and freezing the assets of North Korean officials, more stringent cargo inspection, or adding more North Korean entities to a UN blacklist. However, any response from the Security Council will depend on what China and Russia will accept.

—Heather Kerrigan

Following is a statement from the Korean Central News Agency (KCNA) of the Democratic People's Republic of Korea (DPRK) on April 13, 2012, announcing the failure of its Earth observation satellite to enter orbit; a United Nations Security Council condemnation of the launch issued on April 16, 2012; and a document from KCNA on December 12, 2012, announcing a successful satellite launch.

DPRK Announces Satellite Failure

April 13, 2012

The DPRK launched its first application satellite Kwangmyongsong-3 at the Sohae Satellite Launching Station in Cholsan County, North Phyongan Province at 07:38:55 a.m. on Friday.

The earth observation satellite failed to enter its preset orbit.

Scientists, technicians and experts are now looking into the cause of the failure.

SOURCE: Korean Central News Agency of DPRK. "DPRK's Satellite Fails to Enter Its Orbit." April 13, 2012. http://www.kcna.co.jp/item/2012/201204/news13/20120413-41ee.html.

United Nations Condemns Satellite Launch

April 16, 2012

Strongly condemning the 13 April satellite launch by the Democratic People's Republic of North Korea, the Security Council this morning demanded that the country stop all ballistic missile activity and not conduct any nuclear tests, while also tightening the sanctions regime on the country.

"This satellite launch, as well as any launch that uses ballistic missile technology, even if characterized as a satellite launch or space launch vehicle, is a serious violation of Security Council resolutions 1718 (2006) and 1874 (2009)," the Council said through a statement read out by Susan Rice of the United States, which holds the April presidency.

Also as part of that response, the Council directed the relevant Committee to designate additional groups and items subjected to the arms and technology embargoes and other restrictions imposed in 2006 and strengthened in 2009, adding that if the Committee did not act within 15 days, the Council itself "will complete action" to adjust those and related measures within five days.

Deploring that the launch had caused grave security concerns in the region, the Council also demanded that the country immediately abandon all nuclear weapons, related programmes and other provocations and fully comply with its obligations under the above-cited resolutions.

In a related provision, the Council expressed its determination to take action accordingly in the event of a further launch or nuclear test by that country.

The meeting began at 10:11 a.m. and ended at 10:15 a.m.

Presidential Statement

The full text of the statement contained in document S/PRST/2012/13 reads as follows:

"The Security Council strongly condemns the 13 April 2012 (local time) launch by the Democratic People's Republic of Korea (DPRK).

"The Security Council underscores that this satellite launch, as well as any launch that uses ballistic missile technology, even if characterized as a satellite launch or space launch vehicle, is a serious violation of Security Council resolutions 1718 (2006) and 1874 (2009).

"The Security Council deplores that such a launch has caused grave security concerns in the region.

"The Security Council demands that the DPRK not proceed with any further launches using ballistic missile technology and comply with resolutions 1718 (2006) and 1874 (2009) by suspending all activities related to its ballistic missile programme and in this context re-establish its pre-existing commitments to a moratorium on missile launches.

"The Security Council agrees to adjust the measures imposed by paragraph 8 of resolution 1718 (2006), as modified by resolution 1874 (2009). The Security Council directs the Committee established pursuant to resolution 1718 (2006) to undertake the following tasks and to report to the Security Council within 15 days:

a) Designate additional entities and items;
b) Update the information contained on the Committee's list of individuals, entities, and items (S/2009/205 and INFCIRC/254/Rev.9/Part.1), and update on an annual basis thereafter;
c) Update the Committee's annual work plan.

"The Security Council further agrees that, if the Committee has not acted pursuant to the paragraph above within 15 days, then the Security Council will complete action to adjust these measures within an additional five days.

"The Security Council demands that the DPRK immediately comply fully with its obligations under Security Council resolutions 1718 (2006) and 1874 (2009), including that it: abandon all nuclear weapons and existing nuclear programmes in a complete, verifiable and irreversible manner; immediately cease all related activities; and not conduct any further launches that use ballistic missile technology, nuclear tests or any further provocation.

"The Security Council calls upon all Member States to implement fully their obligations pursuant to resolutions 1718 (2006) and 1874 (2009).

"The Security Council expresses its determination to take action accordingly in the event of a further DPRK launch or nuclear test."

SOURCE: United Nations Security Council. Department of Public Information. "Security Council Condemns Democratic People's Republic of Korea's Satellite Launch as Breach of Resolutions Barring Country's Use of Ballistic Missile Technology." April 16, 2012. http://www.un.org/News/Press/docs/2012/sc10610.doc.htm.

DOCUMENT *DPRK on Successful Satellite Launch*

December 12, 2012

Scientists and technicians of the DPRK successfully launched the second version of satellite Kwangmyongsong-3 into its orbit by carrier rocket Unha-3, true to the last instructions of leader Kim Jong Il.

Carrier rocket Unha-3 with the second version of satellite Kwangmyongsong-3 atop blasted off from the Sohae Space Center in Cholsan County, North Phyongan Province at 09:49:46 on December 12, Juche 101(2012). The satellite entered its preset orbit at 09:59:13, 9 minutes and 27 seconds after the lift-off.

The satellite is going round the polar orbit at 499.7 km perigee altitude and 584.18 km apogee altitude at the angle of inclination of 97.4 degrees. Its cycle is 95 minutes and 29 seconds.

The scientific and technological satellite is fitted with survey and communications devices essential for the observation of the earth.

The successful launch of the satellite is a proud fruition of the Workers' Party of Korea's policy of attaching importance to the science and technology. It is also an event of great turn in developing the country's science, technology and economy by fully exercising the independent right to use space for peaceful purposes.

At a time when great yearnings and reverence for Kim Jong Il pervade the whole country, its scientists and technicians brilliantly carried out his behests to launch a scientific and technological satellite in 2012, the year marking the 100th birth anniversary of President Kim Il Sung.

SOURCE: Korean Central News Agency of DPRK. "KCNA Releases Report on Satellite Launch." December 12, 2012. http://www.kcna.co.jp/item/2012/201212/news12/20121212-09ee.html.

OTHER HISTORIC DOCUMENTS OF INTEREST

FROM PREVIOUS *HISTORIC DOCUMENTS*

Secret Service Responds to Sexual Misconduct in Colombia

APRIL 14 AND MAY 23, 2012

On April 11, 2012, in Cartagena, Colombia, a dozen U.S. Secret Service agents enjoyed a night of revelry that included bringing several prostitutes back to their hotel rooms. A number of military personnel also took part in the evening's indiscretions. The government employees had traveled to the Caribbean resort town in advance of President Barack Obama's trip there for the Sixth Summit of the Americas on April 14 and 15. News of the agents' misconduct broke in the international press on the day the president arrived in Colombia. Overshadowing the trade talks among the hemisphere's heads of state, the incident became the most well-publicized scandal the Secret Service had ever faced. As multiple investigations unfolded, questions were left hanging about the internal culture of one of the nation's elite law enforcement agencies.

Quarrel Attracts Attention

As part of the Secret Service's protective mission, agents routinely travel overseas several days ahead of presidential trips in order to verify routes and venues, identify potential threats and emergency options, and coordinate security in partnership with the host country and its security organizations. The particular group of personnel sent to Cartagena included special agents and officers in the Uniformed Division, the part of the Secret Service concerned with executive protection. However, none of these men had been assigned to the elite Presidential Protective Division, and, according to testimony Secret Service Director Mark Sullivan gave before the Senate on May 23, none had access to the top-secret security details of the president's visit.

The April 11 incident began at a Cartagena nightclub where the Secret Service employees and members of the U.S. armed forces were dancing and drinking. Accounts of the number of women the American men picked up range from thirteen to twenty-one. Not all the women were in the sex trade. However, prostitution is legal in certain "tolerance zones" within Colombian cities, and the establishment in question, known as the Pley Club, is a brothel.

Dania Londoño Suarez, one of the escorts who was there that night, claims that after dancing with Secret Service Agent Arthur Huntington, he agreed to her fee of $800 for sexual services, and they subsequently left the club together for his room at the Hotel Caribe. Like the other women who came to the hotel, she left her ID with the front desk. At 6:30 the following morning, the pair was awakened by a call informing them that Suarez had to leave, in accordance with the hotel's policy regarding nonpaying guests. When Suarez demanded her pay, Huntington refused, claiming to have been drunk at the time, and offered her a much smaller amount, on the order of $50. Suarez subsequently knocked on a neighboring door, where a friend of hers had spent the night with a fellow agent—not as a business transaction, according to an account Suarez later gave the press. She sought help from a local police officer inside the hotel, who sympathized with her situation; then Suarez proclaimed she would go in search of an English-speaking officer. The hotel manager was alerted and came to Huntington's door, but Huntington refused to open it. His fellow Secret Service agents, eager to keep the matter quiet, cobbled together approximately $250, which Suarez accepted.

The involvement of hotel staff and the police led to a call to the U.S. Embassy in Bogotá. Secret Service administrators were then alerted. Paula Reid, head of the agency's Miami office in charge of Latin American operations, was in Cartagena at the time. She immediately began investigating the matter and swiftly ordered all twelve agents, including supervisors David Chaney and Greg Stokes, to leave the country. All the officers were placed on administrative leave, their equipment confiscated, and their security clearances revoked. All the agents were replaced in Cartagena before President Obama arrived in the country on April 13. That day, the *Washington Post* became the first media outlet to report the news. Ronald Kessler, a former *Post* reporter and author of an investigative book about the Secret Service, was instrumental in breaking the story, which he called "the biggest scandal in Secret Service history."

Diplomatic Embarrassment

With world media reporting the salacious details of the event and lawmakers in Washington asking pointed questions, the scandal threatened to overwhelm the sensitive trade discussions taking place among the leaders at the Organization of American States gathering. The White House refused to comment on the matter until the summit concluded. A statement from Secret Service Assistant Director Paul S. Morrissey admitted that eleven Secret Service personnel had been replaced in Cartagena (a twelfth participant in the evening's improprieties was later identified) and that the agency's Office of Professional Responsibility would conduct a thorough investigation. "These actions," Morrissey said, "have had no impact on the Secret Service's ability to execute a comprehensive security plan for the President's visit to Cartagena." All subsequent press reports concurred that the agents' misconduct had in no way impaired or threatened the president's security.

Nevertheless, the shocking news appeared symptomatic of the weakness in the diplomatic position of President Obama and the U.S. delegation in Cartagena. Latin American nations have grown increasingly less dependent on the U.S. economy in recent years. Much of the region is asserting its political independence from Uncle Sam as well, with many states now led by democratically elected leftist governments sharply critical of U.S. foreign policy. Bolivia's president, Evo Morales, told Reuters he saw evidence of "a rebellion of Latin American countries against the United States" in Cartagena. The summit, focused primarily on trade issues, ended on a discordant note without a joint declaration. The United States and Canada were alone in opposition to a resolution demanding that Cuba be invited to future meetings. Several nations also publicly criticized U.S. drug policies, arguing that the "drug war" has failed to reduce the violence related to drug trafficking and a new paradigm is needed.

As the summit concluded on April 15, President Obama, in a joint news conference with Colombian President Juan Manuel Santos, broke his silence on the Secret Service misconduct. The president said he would await the results of the Secret Service investigation before drawing conclusions. "I expect that investigation to be thorough and I expect it to be rigorous. If it turns out that some of the allegations that have been made in the press are confirmed, then of course I'll be angry," he added. By April 16, military officials had revealed that ten uniformed personnel, rather than five as originally reported, were accused of involvement. The U.S. Southern Command said the armed forces would conduct a separate investigation and would deliver appropriate punishments, according to the Uniform Code of Military Justice.

MULTIPLE INVESTIGATIONS

The investigation carried out by the Secret Service included interviews with over 200 people, including several of the women involved. All the agents alleged of misconduct underwent a drug test and a polygraph exam. Both houses of Congress began investigations as well. Rep. Peter King, R-N.Y., chair of the House Committee on Homeland Security, concluded that the Secret Service personnel were not likely to face criminal charges but may have violated the elite agency's code of conduct. Rep. Darrell Issa, R-Calif., chair of the House Committee on Oversight and Government Reform, and that committee's ranking Democrat, Rep. Elijah Cummings of Maryland, issued a letter to Secret Service Director Sullivan, demanding details of the incident and of any prior disciplinary actions taken against the agents involved. The events in Cartagena, their letter said, "raised questions about the agency's culture."

The involvement of two supervisors, each with nearly twenty years of employment in the Secret Service, appeared to suggest that the officers had felt minimal concern over the consequences of their actions. In public hearings and press interviews, several members of Congress suggested the misbehavior was probably not an isolated occurrence. Director Sullivan's public testimony before the Senate Homeland Security and Governmental Affairs Committee on May 23 led to heated exchanges on this point. Sullivan issued the agency's first public apology for the wrongdoing but insisted that what happened in Cartagena was an aberration from the behavioral standards set by the thousands of Secret Service personnel on assignment around the world. The senators, armed with evidence of prior allegations against the agency's employees, begged to differ. Sen. Susan Collins, R-Maine, the panel's senior Republican, told the Associated Press, "[Sullivan] kept saying over and over again that he basically does think this was an isolated incident and I don't think he has any basis for that conclusion."

As a result of the widely publicized improprieties, in late April the Secret Service issued new rules of personal conduct for all employees. The reforms included a mandatory class in ethics. Agents were explicitly prohibited from patronizing "non-reputable establishments" overseas, such as strip clubs, and from receiving visits from any foreign nationals in their hotel rooms. Consumption of alcohol was now banned both while on duty and ten hours before coming on assignment.

Eight of the twelve Secret Service agents implicated, including Arthur Huntington, lost their jobs; three were cleared of serious wrongdoing, and the remaining man was retained but stripped of his security clearance. One of the two supervisors was terminated, while the other was permitted to retire. The woman at the center of the imbroglio, Dania Londoño Suarez, discovered only after the story appeared in the news media that the man with whom she had argued was a Secret Service man. Photos of Suarez soon appeared in the press, and she fled Colombia, eluding investigators for several weeks before volunteering to be interviewed at the U.S. Embassy in Madrid. In press interviews on May 4, Suarez had harsh words for the man she had been with on the night of April 11. "There wouldn't have been a problem if he had paid me money," she said.

—Roger K. Smith

Following is a statement from the U.S. Secret Service, released on April 14, 2012, pertaining to the allegations of misconduct against Secret Service personnel in Colombia; and the text of the written testimony by Secret Service Director Mark Sullivan before the Senate Committee on Homeland Security and Governmental Affairs on May 23, 2012.

Secret Service Response to Colombia Incident

April 14, 2012

The following is a statement from Assistant Director Paul S. Morrissey, U.S. Secret Service Office of Government and Public Affairs:

"On Thursday, April 12, 2012, allegations of misconduct were made against 11 Secret Service personnel in Cartagena, Colombia, in advance of the President's trip. These personnel were comprised of both special agents and Uniformed Division officers, none of whom are assigned to the Presidential Protective Division.

The nature of the allegations, coupled with a zero tolerance policy on personal misconduct, resulted in the Secret Service taking the decisive action to relieve these individuals of their assignment, return them to their place of duty and replace them with additional Secret Service personnel. These actions have had no impact on the Secret Service's ability to execute a comprehensive security plan for the President's visit to Cartagena.

This matter was turned over to our Office of Professional Responsibility, which serves as the agency's internal affairs component. The personnel involved were brought to Secret Service Headquarters in Washington, D.C., for interviews today. These interviews have been completed. As a result, all 11 employees have been placed on administrative leave. This is standard procedure and allows us the opportunity to conduct a full, thorough and fair investigation into the allegations.

This matter is now in a personnel action phase which prohibits any comment per Secret Service policy.

The Secret Service demands more from its employees and these expectations are met and exceeded every day by the vast majority of our workforce. This incident is not reflective of the behavior of our personnel as they travel every day throughout the country and the world performing their duties in a dedicated, professional manner.

We regret any distraction from the Summit of the Americas this situation has caused."

SOURCE: U.S. Department of Homeland Security. United States Secret Service. "Statement by Assistant Director Paul S. Morrissey." April 14, 2012. http://www.secretservice.gov/press/GPA04-12_Statement.pdf.

Secret Service Director Testifies Before Congress

May 23, 2012

INTRODUCTION

Good morning, Chairman Lieberman, Ranking Member Collins and distinguished members of the Committee. Thank you for the opportunity to appear before you today to discuss the facts of the misconduct that occurred in Cartagena, Colombia, the immediate actions taken, the results of our internal investigation and the corrective actions that have been implemented.

The Secret Service is an organization that maintains deep pride in the work it does on behalf of this nation. Throughout our long and proud 147 year history, the Secret Service has demanded service with honor and distinction by its officers, agents and administrative staff. All must adhere to the highest standards of professionalism, ethics and recognize that our agency's capacity to carry out our mission depends on the character and judgment of all of our employees.

The Secret Service has five core values: justice, duty, courage, honesty and loyalty. The overwhelming majority of the men and women who serve in this agency exemplify these values. On a daily basis, they are prepared to lay down their lives to protect others in service to their country. It is precisely because of these long standing core values that the men and women of this agency are held to higher standard. This standard is one that our colleagues in the law enforcement community and the American people have come to expect. Clearly, the misconduct that took place on April 11, 2012, in Cartagena, Colombia is not representative of these values or of the high ethical standards we demand from our almost 7,000 employees.

SYNOPSIS OF INVESTIGATION

From the beginning of this incident, I have continually briefed Members of this Committee and other Congressional committees and Members on the facts in this matter in an effort to be as transparent as possible. The information provided in this testimony provides an overview of the findings to date and we will continue to keep you informed as our review continues.

Immediately upon learning of the allegations of misconduct in Colombia, I instructed Secret Service supervisory personnel in Cartagena to initiate a review of the hotel records and conduct preliminary interviews of any employees alleged to be involved in misconduct. Preliminary findings indicated twelve Secret Service employees were allegedly involved in misconduct. Subsequent information obtained ultimately cleared one of those individuals of any misconduct and that individual remained in Cartagena.

Once the initial interviews had taken place, I ordered that all individuals alleged to have been involved in misconduct immediately return to the United States on Friday, April 13, 2012, and report to the Office of Professional Responsibility (RES) on Saturday,

April 14, 2012, to be interviewed. Subsequent to the interviews conducted by RES, all the employees alleged to have been involved with misconduct were placed on administrative leave, their security clearances were suspended, and all Secret Service issued equipment was surrendered.

The immediate removal of these individuals from Cartagena allowed sufficient time for the Secret Service to make necessary adjustments to the security plan.

Working with the Assistant Director of our Office of Protective Operations (OPO), the Assistant Director of our Office of Investigations (INV) and senior supervisory personnel in Cartagena, we ensured the logistical staffing changes had no negative impact on the overall operational security plan for the Summit of Americas, scheduled to begin Friday evening, April 13, 2012, and end on Sunday, April 15, 2012.

I received a comprehensive briefing from the senior supervisory personnel in Cartagena, AD INV and AD OPO concerning the additional personnel that would be brought into Cartagena to replace those individuals who had returned to the United States and other logistical alterations that had been made. After receiving the security operation briefing, I was confident that the staffing changes would not impact our protective mission. The security plan was extremely thorough and comprehensive, and no aspect of the security plan was compromised due to the misconduct. From Friday, April 13 to Sunday, April 15, no negative security related incidents occurred during the Summit of Americas.

By Friday, May 4, 2012 we had interviewed over 220 individuals in three weeks. During the course of this investigation, it was confirmed that Secret Service personnel were scheduled to receive their protective briefing on Thursday, April 12, 2012, concerning their upcoming assignments. Thus, at the time the misconduct occurred, none of the individuals involved in misconduct had received any specific protective information, sensitive security documents, firearms, radios or other security related equipment in their hotel rooms.

Additionally, during the course of our internal investigation we had one individual self report an incident, unrelated to the misconduct that occurred at the El Caribe hotel on Wednesday night April 11, 2012. This individual has been placed on administrative leave pending a full investigation into that matter.

We recognized the potential compromise related to the type of behavior engaged in by these employees in Cartagena. We reached out to the intelligence community as well to cast as wide a net as possible in determining if there was any type of breach in operational security as a result of the incident. No adverse information was found as a result of these inquiries.

There were approximately 200 Secret Service personnel in Cartagena, Colombia when the misconduct occurred. Ultimately, nine were found to have been involved in serious misconduct and three individuals were ultimately cleared of the most serious allegations.

In the midst of our internal investigation, allegations were made that similar misconduct may have occurred in other foreign countries on previous protective assignments. Specifically, allegations were made that Secret Service personnel had been involved in misconduct in San Salvador, El Salvador in March 2011. Although, no case of similar misconduct had been reported to our RES, I directed Secret Service Inspectors to travel to San Salvador, El Salvador to conduct a thorough investigation of the allegations made. After several days in San Salvador and conducting 28 interviews with hotel managers and employees, individuals from the U.S. Department of State, other government agencies and contract employees assigned to assist the Secret Service with the visit, no evidence was found to substantiate the allegations.

During our investigation in San Salvador several hotel managers and employees were interviewed, along with individuals from the U.S. Department of State and other government agencies. During those interviews, none of the 28 people interviewed had any personal knowledge, records or any other information to indicate that Secret Service personnel had been involved in misconduct while in San Salvador, El Salvador in March of 2011.

Additionally, while Secret Service Inspectors were in San Salvador they interviewed the owner of a business where purportedly Secret Service personnel had been involved in misconduct. The owner of the business provided a sworn written statement that he had no knowledge or any other information that any Secret Service personnel had been to his business or information about misconduct by Secret Service personnel. This individual informed Secret Service Inspectors that at no time had he told anyone that Secret Service personnel had ever been to his place of business.

I can assure this Committee that the Secret Service is committed to investigate any allegation of misconduct where witnesses are willing to come forward with facts, provide information, be interviewed and assist Secret Service Inspectors. If anyone has personal knowledge concerning misconduct by a Secret Service employee, I request that they contact our RES office directly or the Department of Homeland Security—Office of Inspector General (DHS-OIG).

From the onset of our internal investigation the Secret Service has been cooperating fully with the DHS-OIG. During the course of our investigation the Secret Service met with and provided numerous briefings and documents to the DHS-OIG concerning all investigative developments. The Secret Service is committed to fully cooperating with the DHS-OIG investigation and assisting in any way possible.

Standards of Conduct/Ethics Training

The Secret Service regularly provides ethics and standards of conduct training to our employees throughout their careers. Below is a list of training courses and programs where this information is covered.

- Orientation for all new employees
- Special Agent Recruit Training Course
- Uniformed Division Officer Recruit Training Course
- Seminar for First Line Supervisors
- Emerging Leaders Seminar
- Seminar for Mid-Level Managers
- Emerging Executives Seminar
- Ethics in Law Enforcement
- Elicitation Briefing

This training is reinforced yearly with each Secret Service employee certifying on a Secret Service form (SSF) 3218 ("Annual Employee Certification"), that they have read and reviewed agency policies, to include the Secret Service's "Standards of Conduct."

Corrective Actions: Enhanced Codes of Conduct/New Policies

While the overwhelming majority of the men and women who serve in this agency exemplify the highest standards of professionalism and integrity, we wanted to ensure that the type of misconduct that occurred in Cart[a]gena, Colombia is not repeated. Therefore, on April 27, 2012, several codes of conduct were enhanced, along with a few new policies.

- All laws of the United States shall apply to Secret Service personnel while abroad.
- Standards of conduct briefings will be conducted for all protective visits, events and NSSEs, as well as prior to Secret Service personnel traveling aboard military aircraft prior to departure for a foreign country.
- The U.S. Department of State Regional Security Officer will work with the Secret Service advanced team to provide intensified country-specific briefings immediately upon arrival in a foreign country. The briefings will update personnel on safety issues, off-limit zones and off-limit establishments for Secret Service personnel, and any country-specific rules imposed by the Ambassador.
- Foreign nationals, excluding hotel staff and official law enforcement counterparts, are prohibited from all Secret Service personnel hotel rooms.
- Patronization of non-reputable establishments is prohibited.
- Alcohol may only be consumed in moderate amounts while off-duty on a TDY assignment and alcohol use is prohibited within 10 hours of reporting for duty.
- Alcohol may not be consumed at the protectee hotel once the protective visit has begun.

The following measures related to foreign car plane staffing:

- Car planes will now be staffed with two GS-15 supervisors—one from the Office of Professional Responsibility and one from the field.
- The car plane supervisors will be responsible for briefing the standards of conduct expectations prior to departure to the destination country, as well as for enforcing these standards while in the foreign country.
- All personnel traveling will have to have completed relevant on-line ethics training in order to be eligible for protective travel.
- The Security Clearance Division will intensify country-specific briefings covering all pertinent topics prior to departure for the destination country.

PROFESSIONALISM REINFORCEMENT WORKING GROUP

In April 2012, I established the Professionalism Reinforcement Working Group (PRWG). The PRWG will conduct a comprehensive review of the Secret Service's professional standards of conduct. This process will include evaluation of policy related to employment standards and background investigation; patterns of discipline related to misconduct; ethics training; and all law, policies, procedures and practices related to the same. Director John Berry of the Office of Personnel Management and Director Connie Patrick of the Federal Law Enforcement Training Center will Co-Chair the PRWG.

The PRWG will:

1. Collect and analyze comprehensive information across broad categories related to organizational performance and accountability;

2. Benchmark against best practices; and

3. Prepare an action plan with recommendations for reinforcing professional conduct.

To assist the working group in completing its review, Secret Service personnel will serve as subject matter experts and will represent a cross section of the agency.

I am confident that this review will provide the Secret Service with an objective perspective on our practices, highlighting both areas in which we excel and identify areas in which we can continue to improve.

Work Ethic of the Secret Service

Over the past few weeks there have been questions about the culture of the Secret Service. Through the finite lens of the misconduct that occurred on April 11, 2012, I can understand how that question could be asked, but if you examine what the men and women of the Secret Service accomplish every day—I would submit to you that the officers, agents and administrative, professional and technical staff of the Secret Service are among the most dedicated, hardest working, self-sacrificing employees within the federal government. They spend countless days, and at times, weeks, away from their families, routinely working multiple shifts each day and frequently transitioning between their protective and investigatory responsibilities.

I'd like to take this opportunity to tell you about some of the Secret Service's significant accomplishments this year and give you some examples of the hard work of our Secret Service Special Agents and Uniformed Division Officers.

Protection

Although we are only half way through the fiscal year, the Secret Service has worked diligently on multiple trips and events. Thus far in FY 2012, the Secret Service has successfully developed and executed security plans for 3,174 domestic protective trips and 236 foreign protective trips. Over the past five years, the Secret Service has conducted over 33,728 domestic protective trips and 2,414 foreign protective trips. These protective missions are successfully accomplished because of the dedication, hard work and sacrifices of the men and women of the Secret Service.

This past November, we successfully developed and executed our security plan for the Asian Pacific Economic Cooperation conference (APEC) in Honolulu, Hawaii. As this event had been designated as a National Special Security Event, the Secret Service was the lead federal agency responsible for the security planning of this event. During the APEC, we were responsible for the safety and security of thirty-six protectees. Throughout this event, no security issues arose.

Later that same month, the Secret Service began protection for its first Presidential Candidate of the 2012 Presidential Campaign. Since November 2011, the Secret Service has provided protection to four Presidential Candidates. We were well-prepared to initiate the protection, as we had campaign details trained and assembled.

This past weekend, the Secret Service successfully provided security for two significant events with heads of state attending from more than forty countries at the G8 Summit at Camp David in Maryland and the North Atlantic Treaty Organization (NATO) Summit in Chicago, Illinois. In partnership with the local police departments from Chicago and the National Capital Region, and our other law enforcement partners, the Secret Service established a comprehensive security plan to keep the President, visiting heads of state and the public safe.

As I appear before you today, planning for the upcoming Democratic National Convention and Republican National Convention has been well underway for the past ten months. Each of these events has been designated as an NSSE. The Secret Service coordinators for these events have established an Executive Steering Committee with their respective law enforcement partners and emergency medical partners.

Additionally, security plans are now being developed for the upcoming Presidential Debates and Vice-Presidential Debate this fall. Lastly, planning for the 57th Presidential Inauguration has also begun with our law enforcement partners in the metropolitan Washington, D.C. area.

INVESTIGATIONS

Over the past five years, the Secret Service has investigated over 17,000 protective intelligence threat cases around the world.

In the investigative arena, the Secret Service keeps American citizens safe from a variety of financial fraud schemes. Thus far in FY 2012, we have arrested over 3,000 for identity theft, mortgage fraud, [and] cyber crimes and 1,500 for the manufacturing and passing of counterfeit currency. From FY 2007 to the present, we have arrested over 30,000 criminals for various financial and cyber crimes.

In FY 2011 investigations of financial crimes prevented $5.6 billion in potential losses and cyber crime investigations prevented an additional $1.6 billion in potential losses. Domestically in FY 2011 $7.5 million dollars of counterfeit U.S. currency was seized before entering public circulation; abroad, $63.6 million was seized.

CAREER DEMANDS OF A SECRET SERVICE AGENT

Another significant challenge that specifically affects the special agent population of the Secret Service is the requirement to geographically relocate several times during their career.

Agents begin their career assigned to a field office conducting criminal investigations and working temporary protective assignments. After approximately six to eight years, the agent will likely be required to transfer to the Washington, D.C. area for a permanent protective assignment on the Presidential Protective Division (PPD) or the Vice-Presidential Protective Division (VPPD). Some agents are transferred to a Former President's Protective Detail in other geographic locations to fulfill their protective assignment requirement.

Agents serve on a permanent protective detail for approximately four to five years. During this assignment, agents live their lives week to week, depending on the schedule of their protectee.

Additionally, agents rotate shifts every two weeks—from day shift, to afternoons to the midnight shift. In addition to the rotating schedules, there is a constant requirement for personnel to travel on an "advance team" several days or weeks in advance for an upcoming protective trip or for the actual trip itself.

The constant travel and shift work associated with our protective mission, the long hours conducting surveillance, and the dangers associated with executing a search warrant and working undercover are daily challenges that law enforcement officers and special agents face.

Conclusion

Whether it is in conjunction with our investigative mission or our protective mission, the men and women of the Secret Service work tirelessly everyday to protect the citizens of this country from financial frauds and to ensure the safety of our nation's leaders. Clearly, the misconduct that took place on April 11, 2012 in Cartagena, Colombia is not representative of our core values or the high ethical standards we demand. Although this misconduct was an aberration, the Secret Service is committed to learning from this incident and has taken the necessary corrective measures to ensure that it will never occur again.

Thank you for the opportunity to testify before this Committee and I would be glad to address any additional questions you may have.

SOURCE: U.S. Department of Homeland Security. "Written Testimony of U.S. Secret Service Director Mark Sullivan for a Senate Committee on Homeland Security and Governmental Affairs Hearing Titled 'Secret Service on the Line: Restoring Trust and Confidence.'" May 23, 2012. http://www.dhs.gov/news/2012/05/23/written-testimony-us-secret-service-senate-committee-homeland-security-and.

International Organizations Respond to Coup in Guinea-Bissau

APRIL 21 AND 24, 2012

Guinea-Bissau, a chronically unstable country, has suffered four coups since its independence from Portugal in 1974, in addition to multiple attempted coups and military mutinies. No head of government has completed a full term in office. Political instability has facilitated the development of a "narco-state," illustrating a trend seen in other volatile West African countries with isolated Atlantic islands, which are ideal for discreet transshipment of narcotics. Members of the government and the military collude in providing a hub for drug traffickers, particularly cocaine runners from Latin America seeking access to the European market. Official corruption has led to poor social and economic conditions in the country. Governments perceived as hostile to military interests face probable intervention by elite officers, as in the case of the April 2012 coup. The coup, which attracted international opprobrium, was staged after the sitting prime minister, Carlos Gomes Jr., won 49 percent of votes in the first round of presidential elections on March 18 that year. The prime minister was viewed by the military as a threat to its interests. Consequently, a "military command" headed by Armed Forces Chief of Staff General António Indjai arrested both the prime minister and the interim head of government, Raimundo Pereira, on April 12, installing a transitional government on May 16.

The United Nations Secretary General "condemn[ed] [the coup] in strongest possible terms," while the African Union (AU) rejected the subsequent "protocol on the establishment and management of the constitutional and democratic order." The protocol created the so-called Transitional National Council. It was signed on April 18, 2012, between the military command and political parties of the minority parliamentary opposition. The AU characterized the protocol as "a vain and unacceptable attempt to legitimize the coup d'état." Meanwhile, the UN Security Council and the AU determined to "remain actively seized of the matter," indicating their view of the situation as serious and their desire to see its resolution.

Nevertheless, the AU also upheld the principle of subsidiarity, or delegation, and thus supported the actions taken by the Economic Community of West African States (ECOWAS) to address the crisis. This principle was upheld throughout the developments that followed the coup, in which ECOWAS was the most prominent regional actor and mediator. The organization facilitated both Guinea-Bissau's fraught political transition and lobbied for the gradual restoration of the country's institutional relationships. The ECOWAS stabilization mission, which operated in Guinea-Bissau from May 2012, was endorsed by the AU.

BUILDUP TO A COUP

The ECOWAS mission aimed to support the restoration of representative government in Guinea-Bissau. Despite electoral trappings, however, the military traditionally has influenced politics since independence, due to its popular legitimacy as a major force in the fight for independence from Portugal. No subsequent democratic government has implemented substantial reforms to curb military power. Political stability in recent years had been secured only by the ailing president, Malam Bacai Sanha, a liberation icon and experienced member of the African Party for the Independence of Guinea and Cape Verde (PAIGC), who died in December 2011. President Sanha succeeded his PAIGC colleague, João Bernardo "Nino" Vieira, who was assassinated in office in January 2009.

During his tenure, President Sanha weathered multiple challenges, including an attempted coup in April 2010. Nevertheless, the president appointed the coup leader, Indjai, as head of the armed forces in June that year, breaking with international opinion. Indjai had previously served as deputy chief of the armed forces. The president later named José Américo Bubo Na Tchuto, an alleged drug trafficker suspected to be the mastermind of multiple coup attempts, as head of the navy in October 2010. Rear Admiral Bubo Na Tchuto subsequently spearheaded another coup attempt in December 2011, as President Sanha was on his deathbed.

The failed coup in December 2011 was supported by soldiers demanding increased pay and resulted in fighting between military branches. Hopes for higher pay had been raised by proposals for security sector reforms. These reforms included reduced troop numbers and improved benefits. The security proposals were backed by international funding provided by the Community of Portuguese Speaking Countries (CPLP), the UN, Angola, and Brazil. After the attempted coup, Rear Admiral Bubo Na Tchuto was arrested in January 2012, suggesting that the military might finally be brought under civilian control.

APRIL 2012 COUP

Following President Sanha's death in December 2011, Pereira of the PAIGC took the helm of an interim government. The military regarded the probable election of Carlos Gomes Jr., the incumbent PAIGC prime minister, with trepidation. Gomes had criticized the role of the military in society and had pledged to limit its clout upon taking office. The prime minister was also supported by the country's erstwhile colonial ruler, Portugal. Following his strong showing against rival Kumba Yala of the Party for Social Renewal (PRS) in an initial round of elections in March 18, 2012, he was expected to win a runoff scheduled for April 22. Yala, who was himself ousted from the presidency in September 2003, threatened not to participate in the second round of voting, citing alleged fraud in the initial vote. The military responded by staging a coup in which it arrested both Gomes and Pereira on April 12. The interim president and would-be president were released into exile on April 27. They were initially flown to Côte d'Ivoire, where they were received by the Ivorian government, fulfilling the terms of a postcoup agreement brokered by ECOWAS.

The new military command led by Armed Forces Chief of Staff General Indjai justified the coup by claiming that Gomes planned to reduce the size of the military. Coup leaders were also critical of his support for cooperation with Angola, which was presented as a threat to national sovereignty. They also claimed that 200 Angolan troops present in the country were a de facto personal protection unit for Gomes and that Angola was "conspiring against the army."

A new interim government was formed on April 16. This government was led by a former speaker of the parliament and erstwhile presidential candidate, Manuel Serifo Nhamadjo, who in turn appointed Rui Duarte Barros, an economist and an ally of Yala, to lead a transitional government, which then took office on May 16. The ECOWAS stabilization mission arrived in the country that same day.

Negotiations for a transitional government did not include the PAIGC, which led to disagreements over power sharing that delayed the opening of the legislature. The country was also suspended from the AU. Meanwhile, donor aid from the African Development Bank and the World Bank was withdrawn, exerting further pressure on Guinea-Bissau's fragile economy. The United Nations imposed travel sanctions on the coup leaders on May 18. Many external bodies, including the European Union, withheld recognition of the transitional government, notwithstanding its plans to hold fresh elections sometime in 2013.

AFTERMATH

The transitional government faced challenges to its own rule. On October 21, 2012, Captain Pansao Ntchama, a supporter of the outgoing regime, led a strike on the barracks of the army elite in a bid to restore the previous order. He was arrested on October 27. The new leaders believed that Prime Minister Gomes, who had expressed his desire to return to the government, was behind the attack. The government of Guinea-Bissau accordingly sent an extradition request to Portugal, where Gomes was in exile at the time of the attempted countercoup.

The United Nations remained "seriously concerned" by the continued suspension of constitutional order in December 2012. ECOWAS urged the AU to recognize Guinea-Bissau's transitional government in November of that year. ECOWAS helped establish the interim government and held that cooperation with the de facto authorities could facilitate a faster return to democratic norms. In that vein, ECOWAS condemned the failed countercoup of targeting an air force base outside the capital, Bissau, in October 2012 as an attempt to further destabilize the political situation, and it called on international partners to lift economic sanctions. The economic situation was seen as particularly urgent as the demand for cashews, the key export crop, fell in 2012, leaving many without a means of income in an already destabilized environment.

Economic pressure was expected to be sustained ahead of the next elections due in April 2013. A return to previous levels of foreign aid will depend on whether the elections are viewed as credible. In its meeting on January 18, 2013, the AU welcomed the reopening of the parliament in November 2012 as well as moves toward broader representativeness in the legislature ahead of elections. The PAIGC had previously rejected a legislative arrangement in which it would hold no leadership posts—despite winning the popular vote in the last elections. Upon PRS suggestions that parliament instead be succeeded by a consensual union that would solidify its grip on power, the PAIGC agreed to open the parliament, extending the mandate of its members until the next elections. The parliament was expected to affirm the legitimacy of the transitional government.

The AU also praised the work of ECOWAS in the country, which included financial support for military reform and the provision of a "Plan of Action" to counter money laundering and drug trafficking in West Africa. Additionally, the AU agreed to consider the ECOWAS request that Guinea-Bissau be reinstated as a union member in light of recent progress. This progress was expected to be described by the report of a joint UN, EU, CPLP, AU, and ECOWAS fact-finding mission, whose members visited the country from December 16 through December 21, 2012.

Although the next government was anticipated to garner wider international support, major structural reforms will be required, following the renewal of representative government. The military remains a powerful and disruptive force in society. Long-term political stability will depend upon the implementation of laws to curb military influence and hold officers, as well as political authorities, accountable to the rule of law.

—Anastazia Clouting

Following is the text of the reaction from the United Nations Security Council to the coup in Guinea-Bissau, delivered by U.S. Ambassador to the United Nations Susan Rice, on April 21, 2012; and the text of a decision adopted by the security council of the African Union on April 24, 2012, in response to the situation in Guinea-Bissau.

DOCUMENT *UN Security Council Responds to Coup*

April 21, 2012

[An introductory press release, detailing the Security Council meeting, has been omitted.]

Presidential Statement

"The Security Council recalls its Press Statement SC/10607 of 13 April 2012 and *reiterates* its strong condemnation of the military coup by the military leadership and political elements in Guinea-Bissau, thereby undermining the conclusion of the legitimate presidential electoral process.

"The Security Council rejects the unconstitutional establishment of a Transitional National Council by the military leadership and its supporters.

"The Security Council demands the immediate restoration of the constitutional order as well as the reinstatement of the legitimate Government of Guinea-Bissau. The Security Council further demands the immediate and unconditional release of the interim President Raimundo Pereira, Prime Minister Carlos Gomes Junior and all officials currently detained in order to enable the completion of the presidential and legislative elections. In this regard, the Council welcomes the decision of the African Union Peace and Security Council to suspend, with immediate effect, Guinea-Bissau from the African Union until the effective restoration of constitutional order.

"The Security Council underlines *the* need *to* ensure the safety and security of those detained and that those responsible for violent and illegal acts must be held accountable.

"The Security Council is deeply concerned by reports of violent repression of peaceful demonstrations, looting, restriction of freedom of movement, the arbitrary detention of civilians and demands their release. The Council calls on the military leadership to release information on the number of arrests and the names and whereabouts of those arrested and *further calls upon* the military to protect human rights including the rights to freedom of movement, peaceful assembly and expression.

"The Security Council *welcomes and supports* the active engagement and measures undertaken by the African Union, the Economic Community of West African States (ECOWAS) and the Community of Portuguese Speaking Countries (CPLP), and encourages the coordination of these efforts for the immediate restoration of the constitutional order in Guinea-Bissau.

"The Security Council urges Guinea-Bissau's partners to further strengthen these efforts and *requests* the Secretary-General to support these endeavours, namely through his Special Representatives.

"The Council stands ready to *consider* possible further measures, including targeted sanctions against the perpetrators and supporters of the military coup, should the situation remain unresolved.

"The Security Council takes note of the African Union's decision to initiate consultations with ECOWAS, the CPLP, the United Nations and other partners on possible additional means necessary for the stabilization of the country, in consultation with the legitimate Government of Guinea-Bissau.

"The Security Council requests the Secretary-General to keep it informed on developments in Guinea-Bissau and to submit a report by 30 April 2012, concerning the reestablishment of the constitutional order in Guinea-Bissau.

"The Security Council *stresses* that the recurrence of illegal interference of the military in politics contributes to the persistence of instability and a culture of impunity, and hampers efforts towards consolidation of the rule of law, implementation of security sector reform, promotion of development and entrenchment of a democratic culture. In this regard, the Council welcomes the efforts of the Peacebuilding Commission Country Specific Configuration and of the Angolan bilateral Mission (MISSANG) in pursuit of peace and stability in the country.

"The members of the Security Council *emphasize* the need to uphold and respect the sovereignty, unity and territorial integrity of Guinea-Bissau.

"The Security Council will remain actively seized of the matter."

SOURCE: United Nations Security Council. Department of Public Information. "Security Council Presidential Statement Reiterates Condemnation of Military Coup in Guinea-Bissau, Demands Immediate Reinstatement of Legitimate Government." April 21, 2012. http://www.un.org/News/Press/docs/2012/sc10617.doc.htm.

African Union Adopts Resolution in Response to Guinea-Bissau Coup

April 24, 2012

The Peace and Security Council of the African Union (AU), at its 319th meeting held at ministerial level, on 24 April 2012, adopted the following decision on the situation in Guinea-Bissau:

Council,

1. **Takes note** of the paragraphs on Guinea-Bissau, as contained in the report of the Chairperson of the Commission on the situation in Guinea-Bissau, Mali and the situation

between Sudan and South Sudan [PSC/MIN/3 (CCCXIV)]. Council **also takes note** of the statements made by Côte d'Ivoire, in its capacity as the Chair of the Economic Community of West African States (ECOWAS), the ECOWAS Commission and Angola, in its capacity as the Chair of the Community of Portuguese Speaking Countries (CPLP), as well as by other AU bilateral and multilateral partners;

2. **Reaffirms** the provisions on unconstitutional changes of Government contained in the AU Constitutive Act, the Protocol Relating to the Establishment of the Peace and Security Council and Chapter VIII of the African Charter on Democracy, Elections and Governance, as well as the ECOWAS Protocol on Democracy and Good Governance Supplementary to the Protocol relating to the Mechanism for Conflict Prevention, Management, Resolution, Peacekeeping and Security;

3. **Endorses** the press statements issued by the Chairperson of the Commission on the situation in Guinea-Bissau on 13, 14 and 19 April 2012, and **commends** him for his efforts. Council **recalls and reaffirms** the terms of communiqué PSC/PR/COMM (CCCXVIII) adopted on the occasion of its 318th meeting held on 17 April 2012;

4. **Reaffirms** the principles of subsidiarity and, in this respect, **endorses** the decisions of ECOWAS, in particular the deployment of a stabilization mission, **welcomes** the commitment and dynamism of ECOWAS in dealing with the crisis in Guinea-Bissau, and **expresses its support** to the mediation conducted by the Republic of Guinea. Council **expresses appreciation** to the CPLP, for its principled position on the situation, to the UN Secretary-General and Security Council, **welcoming** the latter's statement to the press and presidential statement of 13 and 21 April 2012, respectively, as well as to the European Union (EU). Council **further welcomes** the position adopted by the OIF and its decision to suspend the participation of Guinea-Bissau in its activities until the restoration of constitutional order;

5. **Reiterates** its strong condemnation of the coup d'état perpetrated on 12 April 2012, with the specific intent to stop the electoral process underway, with the non-organization of the second round of the presidential election on 29 April 2012, and **totally rejects** "the Protocol on the establishment and management of the constitutional and democratic order," which created the so-called "Transitional National Council," signed on 18 April 2012, between the "Military Command" and political parties of the minority parliamentary opposition. Council **notes** that this "Protocol" is a vain and unacceptable attempt to legitimize the coup d'état;

6. **Reiterates** the concern of the AU about the recurrence of illegal and unacceptable interference of the army in the political life of Guinea-Bissau, which hinders all efforts to stabilize the country, fight against impunity and drug trafficking, and promote socio-economic development. Council **stresses** the duty of Africa, through the AU and ECOWAS, with the support of the UN, the CPLP and other members of the international community, to ensure that the coup d'état of 12 April 2012 fails and put an end to the destabilizing actions of the army in Guinea-Bissau;

7. **Reiterates** the demand for the restoration, without further delay, of constitutional order, and completion of the electoral process that began with the first round of the presidential election held on 18 March 2012, which was deemed to be credible, free and fair by all international observer missions, including those of the AU and ECOWAS. Council **also reiterates** its demand for the immediate and unconditional release of the Acting President of the Republic, Raimundo Pereira, Prime Minister Carlos Gomes Junior,

and other political personalities sequestrated by the military and respect for their dignity and physical integrity;

8. **Requests** the Commission, in view of the refusal of the coup perpetrators to respond positively to the calls from the AU, ECOWAS, the CPLP and the UN Security Council and other members of the international community, for the restoration of constitutional order, to compile and disseminate to all Member States, after appropriate consultations, the list of the members of the military junta and their military and civilian supporters, for application of the individual measures mentioned in paragraph 6 of communiqué PSC/PR/COMM (CCCXVIII). Council **calls on** all Member States to fully implement these sanctions. Council **further requests** the Commission to expedite, in consultation with ECOWAS, the finalization of its proposals on additional sanctions to be imposed on members of the junta and their military and civilian supporters;

9. **Requests** the UN Security Council, pursuant to the relevant paragraph of its presidential statement of 21 April 2012, to support these sanctions. Council **also urges** the European Union, the CPLP, OIF and OIC and other bilateral and multilateral partners to support the measures taken by ECOWAS and the AU;

10. **Requests** the Chairperson of the Commission to urgently convene, in the context of a Multilateral Consultation and Coordination Framework on the Stabilization of Guinea-Bissau, a meeting that will bring together all stakeholders, in particular ECOWAS, the CPLP, the United Nations and the EU, to develop a comprehensive strategy, with a view to facilitating a speedy and lasting solution. Council **stresses** that this strategy should have, as its priority objective, the restoration of constitutional order in Guinea-Bissau, as soon as possible, by using all appropriate means, and would notably cover the defense and security sector reform, the deployment of a stabilization mission to continue the work undertaken as part of the ECOWAS-CPLP Roadmap, the fight against drug trafficking and impunity, and other related aspects, including the development of the country. Council **expresses its intention** to consider this strategy as quickly as possible for endorsement, before submission to the UN Security Council and to other multilateral partners concerned so as to mobilize the necessary support and facilitate its effective implementation;

11. **Requests** the Chairperson of the Commission to transmit this decision to the UN Security Council and other AU partners and to keep it regularly informed of the progress made in its implementation;

12. **Decides** to remain actively seized of the matter.

SOURCE: African Union. "Communiqué." April 24, 2012. http://www.au.int/en/sites/default/files/psc%20 comm%20319%20guinée%20bissau%2024%2004%202012%20ENG.pdf.

OTHER HISTORIC DOCUMENTS OF INTEREST

FROM PREVIOUS *HISTORIC DOCUMENTS*

Medicare Trustees Assess Program's Financial Challenges

APRIL 23, 2012

Every year, the board of trustees for Medicare publishes a report detailing the financial status, including future projections, of the nation's health care program for the elderly. The letter released on April 23, 2012, revealed that Medicare's trust fund for hospital coverage was operating at a severe deficit and forecast that the program will become insolvent in the year 2024. An accounting adjustment in this year's calculations caused the trustees to increase Medicare's projected long-term deficit by over 70 percent. With escalating health costs, the trustees estimated that Medicare's cost will increase from 3.7 percent to 6.7 percent of the nation's gross domestic product (GDP) over the next seventy-five years. Darkening the picture further, political leaders in both parties agreed that certain cost savings assumed in these figures may not be realistic or achievable. The trustees' report serves as an official warning to lawmakers that they must take legislative action to ensure that this crucial component of the nation's social safety net retains an adequate long-term fiscal base.

THE MECHANICS OF MEDICARE

Medicare, created in 1965 through an amendment of the Social Security Act, provides guaranteed health care coverage to more than 49 million people above age sixty-five or who have disabilities. Financially, the program is administered through two separate trust funds. The Hospital Insurance Trust Fund (HI), which covers hospital care and related costs, receives revenue from the Medicare payroll tax, paid by employers and workers at the same rate, currently 1.45 percent of wages. The Supplemental Medical Insurance Trust Fund (SMI), which pays for outpatient and physician costs (under Medicare Part B) and the optional prescription drug plan (Part D), receives the majority of its funding from the federal government's general revenues and the remainder mostly from beneficiary premiums. In 2011, according to the Center for Budget and Policy Priorities (CBPP), Medicare alone composed 13.5 percent of the federal budget. Structured as a single-payer program, Medicare's low administrative expenses make the program more cost effective than the private insurance market in covering the elderly population.

A single set of public officials serve as the trustees for Medicare and Social Security. This board always includes three cabinet members: the secretaries of the Treasury (Timothy Geithner), Labor (Hilda Solis), and Health and Human Services (Kathleen Sebelius). The Commissioner of Social Security and two presidential appointees fill the remaining positions. The board's annual reports, issued simultaneously for Medicare and Social Security, project the future revenues and expenses of these programs, based on current law and policy frameworks. Since they began issuing these reports in 1970, the trustees have projected the insolvency of the HI fund at dates ranging from four to twenty-eight years in the future. Since 2008, the HI fund has paid out more in benefits than it has earned in revenues, a trend the trustees say will continue indefinitely.

Because of the size and importance of Medicare and the perceived precariousness of its financial position, the prospect of cutting benefits or reducing the program's scope is a perennial theme of budget negotiations in Washington. In the partisan battle over raising the debt ceiling in the summer of 2011, conservative Republicans in Congress refused to consider raising taxes, while Democrats, such as House Majority Leader Nancy Pelosi of California, vowed to oppose cuts to Medicare, Medicaid, and Social Security. The deal the parties struck to allow the debt ceiling to rise, known as the Budget Control Act of 2011, and the subsequent failure of the congressional "super committee" to craft a bipartisan debt reduction plan, triggered a 2 percent, across-the-board cut to Medicare that was scheduled to become effective at the start of 2013.

Projections and Complications

The date by which the trustees project the HI trust fund would exhaust its assets under current policies, the year 2024, is unchanged from the prior year's report. The trustees point out that this means the time remaining to head off Medicare insolvency is now one year shorter. If no policy changes were put in place, the fund would henceforth be able to cover only 87 percent of covered benefits. The trustees adjusted their actuarial projection of Medicare's long-term costs and deficits upward, using higher projections of future health care costs, a methodological change recommended by Medicare's Technical Review Panel. The new calculations put the HI deficit, or unfunded liability, at 1.35 percent of taxable payroll by the year 2086, a major increase over last year's long-term estimate of 0.79 percent of total payroll tax revenues. In the near term, these increases would be virtually offset by the 2 percent reduction in Medicare outlays under the Budget Control Act.

Presently, Medicare's overall costs are lower than those of Social Security, but the trustees predict that Medicare will become the more expensive of the two entitlements in coming decades. The baby boom generation is beginning to reach retirement age: By the year 2030, Medicare beneficiaries may number 80 million, nearly double the current enrollment level. The population below retirement age—that is, the nation's labor force, from whom payroll tax revenues are derived—is projected to grow more slowly. The largest driver of Medicare costs, of course, is health care expenses, which by all accounts are expected to rise more steeply than the tax base and the GDP for the foreseeable future.

The SMI trust fund, unlike the HI fund, is ensured adequate funding by law out of the government's general fund. Its costs are also slated to rise, from current levels of 2 percent of GDP to roughly 3.4 percent of GDP by 2035 and 4 percent of GDP by 2086. The trustees point out that these trends, if not addressed by policy reforms, will place increasingly severe pressures on the federal budget.

In addition, several factors holding down the cost estimates in the trustees' report could fail to pan out or provide, in practice, the savings promised on paper. For example, future rounds of debt reduction negotiations in Congress could supersede or nullify the 2 percent Medicare cut slated for January 2013. Similarly, the trustees assumed that a 31 percent reduction in Medicare payments to physicians, to be implemented in 2013 under current mandates, would remain in place despite the fact that Congress has postponed similarly steep reimbursement reductions on several prior occasions and would undoubtedly face strong pressure from the medical lobby to do so again.

Partisan Debate

Last, the report notes that the Patient Protection and Affordable Care Act (ACA), the landmark health reform law championed by President Barack Obama, contains cost-saving provisions that appear to significantly lower Medicare's projected deficits in the near and distant future. Health and Human Services Secretary Sebelius, at a press conference on April 23, said the trustees' report "confirms that Medicare is in a much stronger position than it was a few years ago without the Affordable Care Act." Absent the ACA reforms, she said, the researchers would have predicted Medicare to reach insolvency as early as 2016. However, the trustees forcefully state that realizing some of the cost savings envisioned in the Affordable Care Act, on a sustainable basis, "will require unprecedented efficiency-enhancing innovations in health care payment and delivery systems that are by no means certain." At the time the trustees' report was released, the ACA itself was facing a challenge to its constitutionality in the United States Supreme Court. On June 28, the Court upheld the law in a surprising 5–4 decision, penned by Chief Justice John Roberts.

Reaction to the annual update on the health of Medicare broke, predictably, along party lines. For Democrats and Obama administration officials, such as Sebelius, the most noteworthy aspect of the report appeared to be the contribution the ACA had made toward extending the social insurance program's life span. Republicans in Congress and conservative policy groups zeroed in on the questionable assumptions underpinning the report's projections; they also questioned a separate statement by Rick Foster, Medicare's chief actuary, who argued that the program's financial outlook could in reality prove far more dire than the picture painted by the trustees' figures. Republicans contended that the cuts in provider reimbursements under the ACA would inevitably force doctors to stop accepting Medicare patients, threatening beneficiary access to care. Commentators with policy groups, such as AARP and the CBPP asserted that public policy should focus on slowing the growth of medical costs across the entire national health care system rather than on the more narrow issue of Medicare's challenges.

Medicare loomed large as an issue in the 2012 presidential campaign. On numerous occasions, including several debates, Republican challenger and former Massachusetts governor Mitt Romney accused President Obama of weakening Medicare, citing $716 billion in spending cuts to the program under the ACA. Media outlets found Romney's criticism only partially accurate: While the dollar figure did come from a Congressional Budget Office report about the impact of health care reform, the reductions in future reimbursements to insurance companies and hospitals were designed to contribute toward Medicare's financial viability. For their part, President Obama and Vice President Joe Biden attacked Romney and his running mate, Rep. Paul Ryan of Wisconsin, over their plan to cap Medicare subsidies at a fixed amount. The Democrats accused their opponents of trying to turn Medicare into a voucher program, suggesting that such a plan, if enacted, could cost seniors thousands of dollars in annual medical outlays. The Democrats appeared to benefit from their focus on Medicare as a campaign issue, in both the presidential and congressional races. Rep. Pelosi joked that "the three most important issues in the campaign, in alphabetical order, have been Medicare, Medicare, and Medicare."

On January 1, 2013, in a deal to stave off the so-called fiscal cliff, Congress passed legislation that delayed for two months the scheduled sequestration from the Budget Control Act of 2011, including the 2 percent cut to the Medicare budget, and forestalled for one year the required 31 percent reduction in Medicare payments to physicians.

—Roger K. Smith

The following are excerpts from the summary of the 2012 annual reports on the status of Social Security and Medicare, released by the Social Security and Medicare Board of Trustees on April 23, 2012.

2012 Report on Medicare

April 23, 2012

A Message to the Public:

Each year the Trustees of the Social Security and Medicare trust funds report on the current and projected financial status of the two programs. This message summarizes our 2012 Annual Reports.

The long-run actuarial deficits of the Social Security and Medicare programs worsened in 2012, though in each case for different reasons. The actuarial deficit in the Medicare Hospital Insurance program increased primarily because the Trustees incorporated recommendations of the 2010–11 Medicare Technical Panel that long-run health cost growth rate assumptions be somewhat increased. The actuarial deficit in Social Security increased largely because of the incorporation of updated economic data and assumptions. Both Medicare and Social Security cannot sustain projected long-run program costs under currently scheduled financing, and legislative modifications are necessary to avoid disruptive consequences for beneficiaries and taxpayers.

Lawmakers should not delay addressing the long-run financial challenges facing Social Security and Medicare. If they take action sooner rather than later, more options and more time will be available to phase in changes so that the public has adequate time to prepare. Earlier action will also help elected officials minimize adverse impacts on vulnerable populations, including lower-income workers and people already dependent on program benefits.

Social Security and Medicare are the two largest federal programs, accounting for 36 percent of federal expenditures in fiscal year 2011. Both programs will experience cost growth substantially in excess of GDP growth in the coming decades due to aging of the population and, in the case of Medicare, growth in expenditures per beneficiary exceeding growth in per capita GDP. Through the mid-2030s, population aging caused by the large baby-boom generation entering retirement and lower-birth-rate generations entering employment will be the largest single factor causing costs to grow more rapidly than GDP. Thereafter, the primary factors will be population aging caused by increasing longevity and health care cost growth somewhat more rapid than GDP growth.

[The section on the status of the Social Security program has been omitted.]

MEDICARE

The Medicare HI Trust Fund faces depletion earlier than the combined Social Security Trust Funds, though not as soon as the Disability Insurance Trust Fund when separately considered. The projected HI Trust Fund's long-term actuarial imbalance is smaller than that of the combined Social Security Trust Funds under the assumptions employed in this report.

The Trustees project that Medicare costs (including both HI and SMI expenditures) will grow substantially from approximately 3.7 percent of GDP in 2011 to 5.7 percent of GDP by 2035, and will increase gradually thereafter to about 6.7 percent of GDP by 2086.

The projected 75-year actuarial deficit in the HI Trust Fund is 1.35 percent of taxable payroll, up from 0.79 percent projected in last year's report. The HI fund again fails the test of short-range financial adequacy, as projected assets are already below one year's projected expenditures and are expected to continue declining. The fund also continues to fail the long-range test of close actuarial balance. The Trustees project that the HI Trust Fund will pay out more in hospital benefits and other expenditures than it receives in income in all future years, as it has since 2008. The projected date of HI Trust Fund exhaustion is 2024, the same date projected in last year's report, at which time dedicated revenues would be sufficient to pay 87 percent of HI costs. The Trustees project that the share of HI expenditures that can be financed with HI dedicated revenues will decline slowly to 67 percent in 2045, and then rise slowly until it reaches 69 percent in 2086. The HI 75-year actuarial imbalance amounts to 36 percent of tax receipts or 26 percent of program cost.

The worsening of HI long-term finances is principally due to the adoption of short-range assumptions and long-range cost projection methods recommended by the 2010–11 Medicare Technical Review Panel. Use of those methods increases the projected long-range annual growth rate for Medicare's costs by 0.3 percentage points. The new assumptions increased projected short-range costs, but those increases are about offset, temporarily, by a roughly 2 percent reduction in 2013–21 Medicare outlays required by the Budget Control Act of 2011.

The Trustees project that Part B of Supplementary Medical Insurance (SMI), which pays doctors' bills and other outpatient expenses, and Part D, which provides access to prescription drug coverage, will remain adequately financed into the indefinite future because current law automatically provides financing each year to meet the next year's expected costs. However, the aging population and rising health care costs cause SMI projected costs to grow rapidly from 2.0 percent of GDP in 2011 to approximately 3.4 percent of GDP in 2035, and then more slowly to 4.0 percent of GDP by 2086. General revenues will finance roughly three quarters of these costs, and premiums paid by beneficiaries almost all of the remaining quarter. SMI also receives a small amount of financing from special payments by States and from fees on manufacturers and importers of brand-name prescription drugs.

Projected Medicare costs over 75 years are substantially lower than they otherwise would be because of provisions in the Patient Protection and Affordable Care Act, as amended by the Health Care and Education Reconciliation Act of 2010 (the "Affordable Care Act" or ACA). Most of the ACA-related cost saving is attributable to a reduction in the annual payment updates for most Medicare services (other than physicians' services and drugs) by total economy multifactor productivity growth, which the Trustees project will average 1.1 percent per year. The report notes that sustaining these payment reductions indefinitely will require unprecedented efficiency-enhancing innovations in health care payment and delivery systems that are by no means certain. In addition, the Trustees assume an almost 31-percent reduction in Medicare payment rates for physician services will be implemented in 2013 as required by current law, which is also highly uncertain.

The drawdown of Social Security and HI trust fund reserves and the general revenue transfers into SMI will result in mounting pressure on the Federal budget. In fact, pressure is already evident. For the sixth consecutive year, the Social Security Act requires that the Trustees issue a "Medicare funding warning" because projected non-dedicated sources of revenues—primarily general revenues—are expected to continue to account for more than 45 percent of Medicare's outlays, a threshold breached for the first time in fiscal year 2010.

CONCLUSION

Lawmakers should address the financial challenges facing Social Security and Medicare as soon as possible. Taking action sooner rather than later will leave more options and more time available to phase in changes so that the public has adequate time to prepare.

[The names of the trustees, as well as the expanded summary of the report and accompanying charts and graphs, have been omitted.]

SOURCE: Social Security Administration. "A Summary of the 2012 Annual Reports." April 23, 2012. http://www.ssa.gov/oact/trsum/index.html.

OTHER HISTORIC DOCUMENTS OF INTEREST

FROM THIS VOLUME

- President Obama and Former Gov. Romney Meet in Second Presidential Debate, p. 482
- President Obama Remarks on 2012 Reelection Victory, p. 531
- Supreme Court Rules on Affordable Care Act, p. 292

FROM PREVIOUS *HISTORIC DOCUMENTS*

- Federal Deficit Reduction Committee Folds Without Conclusion, *2011*, p. 618
- President Obama Remarks on the Debt Ceiling and Credit Downgrade, *2011*, p. 423
- U.S. Comptroller General on the Nation's Long-Term Deficit, *2007*, p. 728
- Comptroller General on Budget Issues Facing the Government, *2005*, p. 121
- GAO on Withholding Medicare Cost Estimates From Congress, *2004*, p. 577
- President Bush on Signing Medicare Reform Law, *2003*, p. 1119
- Harvard Report on Medicare Reform, *1986*, p. 273

International Court Convicts Charles Taylor of War Crimes

APRIL 26 AND MAY 30, 2012

On April 26, 2012, Charles Taylor, the former president of Liberia, became the first head of state to be convicted of war crimes by an international court since World War II. Taylor was the last person tried and sentenced by the Special Court for Sierra Leone, a UN-backed tribunal set up in 2002 to bring to justice perpetrators of crimes against humanity committed in the Sierra Leone region since 1996. The court found him guilty on eleven counts, including enslavement, unlawful killing, pillage, sexual violence, and use of child soldiers. Taylor was sentenced to fifty years in a British jail; however, in January 2013, Taylor's lawyers appealed the ruling.

FEARED WARLORD

Taylor received much of his education in the United States, attending Chamberlayne Junior College in Newton, Massachusetts, and Bentley College in Waltham, Massachusetts. While studying for his economics degree, Taylor became involved with the Union of Liberian Associations (ULA) and eventually became the group's U.S. chairperson. When then–Liberian president William Tolbert came to the United States in 1979, Taylor and the ULA demonstrated outside of the Liberian mission in New York City. Tolbert noticed Taylor and invited him to a debate, during which Taylor performed much better than the president and said he would take over the Liberian mission. For his comments, Taylor was arrested, but Tolbert did not press charges and instead asked Taylor to return to Liberia, which he did in 1980.

Tolbert was murdered during a military coup the year Taylor returned. The new leader, Samuel Doe, gave Taylor a position in his government as head of the General Services Agency. Taylor had the power to make purchasing decisions within Liberia; however, he was ousted from this position in 1983 after being accused of embezzlement. Following his ousting, Taylor returned to the United States, where he was arrested while a court determined whether to extradite him to Liberia. Taylor escaped in 1985 from the jail in Boston where he was being held, and his whereabouts were largely unknown until he returned to Liberia in 1989.

Upon his return, Taylor formed and led the National Patriotic Front of Liberia with the aim of toppling the government. "The best Doe is a dead Doe," Taylor was reported to have said. As a warlord participating in the First Liberian Civil War, Taylor oversaw forces that raped women, pillaged villages, and conscripted child soldiers as young as eight who were allegedly brainwashed and given drugs to desensitize them to killing. Thousands were killed by Taylor's forces, whose signature was cutting off the limbs of victims both dead and alive.

In July 1990, Taylor's forces entered the capital city of Monrovia to topple the Doe government. During the effort, Taylor's forces divided into two parts—he led one, and

Prince Johnson, formerly Taylor's right-hand man, another. In September, Doe was ousted by the Taylor-Johnson coup, and it was Johnson's portion of the group that captured and killed Doe as he tried to flee Liberia. From 1990 through 1995, a war ensued between Taylor and Johnson's forces.

Following a peace agreement in 1995 to end the civil war, Taylor was elected president of Liberia in 1997 with more than 75 percent of the vote. International election observers determined that the vote was properly held and that Taylor had been fairly elected to the position. As president, Taylor was accused of supporting rebels in Sierra Leone who were fighting a civil war and killing innocent civilians. Opposition inside Liberia to Taylor's government led to the Second Liberian Civil War, which took place from 1999 to 2003, at which point Taylor resigned and went into exile in Nigeria. While in exile, Taylor was arrested in 2006 for aiding the Sierra Leone rebels and brought to Sierra Leone before being sent to The Hague for his war crimes trial.

FIVE-YEAR TRIAL

In 2007, the UN-backed Special Court for Sierra Leone based in The Hague, the Netherlands, charged Taylor with overseeing sexual slavery, rape, murder, sponsoring a ruthless rebel group, and attempting to seize diamond-mining land in Sierra Leone. Taylor was the first African head of state to face war crimes charges before an international court.

The prosecution in the case faced an uphill battle, linking Taylor to the charges. There were no documents that could show that he gave orders to carry out any of the heinous acts he was accused of committing, nor was their any proof that Taylor was at the scene of any of the crimes. Additionally, Liberia's official army, which was under Taylor's control during his time as president, did not carry out the acts. Prosecutors had to rely on intercepted radio and telephone conversations between Taylor's presidential mansion and the rebels in Sierra Leone. Radio operators and Taylor's inner circle, including bodyguards, were brought in to testify.

Much of the testimony against Taylor revolved around his wealth—most of which the prosecution contended is hidden—and large quantities of diamonds, which the prosecution alleged Taylor received as payment for supplying arms to rebels. It is estimated that Taylor's hidden wealth could run anywhere from $280 million to $3 billion, made up of money from diamond and timber trades, Liberia's merchant shipping, government tax coffers, and other sources. Taylor's closest allies during his time as president testified to seeing arms leave Liberia and being quickly replaced by raw diamonds. Model Naomi Campbell was summoned to testify before the court at one point because she was suspected of receiving diamonds from Taylor.

Taylor took the stand in 2009 and spent eighty-one days of the trial testifying in his defense. He denied all of the charges against him and claimed that he had tried to bring peace to Sierra Leone and Liberia. He also denied that he ever owned diamonds or received them as payment and claimed his wealth to be $0. Instead, Taylor said that any money that came into the country was used to buy weapons on the black market to help defend Liberia against insurgents within the country and in Sierra Leone. At the time Taylor made the weapons purchases, the United Nations had imposed a weapons embargo on Liberia to stop Taylor's attacks against Sierra Leone and within Liberia. "The country is at war. This is our remedy," he said during the trial.

The prosecution took issue with leeway given to Taylor during the trial—during his seven months on the stand, he gave his political views, spoke about his life, and digressed into a variety of other topics without ever being cut off. He told the court that he was aware of the atrocities but that he would "never, ever" have permitted them.

CONVICTION AND SENTENCING

On April 26, after a year of deliberations, Taylor was convicted by the special court on eleven counts, including acts of terrorism, unlawful killings, sexual violence including rape and sexual slavery, physical violence, use of child soldiers, enslavement, and pillage. In its ruling, the court found that Taylor had given "sustained and significant" support to the rebel Revolutionary United Front in Sierra Leone, selling diamonds to purchase weapons to give to the rebels, who Taylor knew were committing heinous crimes.

Although Taylor was convicted of war crimes and crimes against humanity, the three-judge panel ultimately decided in their 2,500-page judgment that there was no solid proof that Taylor had any direct command over the eleven counts. "The trial chamber finds the accused cannot be held responsible for ordering the crimes," said Judge Richard Lussick.

Taylor was sentenced to fifty years in prison on May 30, thirty years less than the sentence for which the prosecution had hoped. During the sentencing hearing, Judge Lussick said Taylor was guilty of "aiding and abetting, as well as planning, some of the most heinous and brutal crimes recorded in human history." He continued, "Leadership must be carried out by example, by the prosecution of crimes, not the commission of crimes." An earlier agreement meant Taylor would serve his sentence, which at age sixty-four will likely be the remainder of his life, in Great Britain. The Netherlands agreed to host the trial only if another country would jail Taylor. However, there is not yet an indication of when Taylor will actually begin serving his sentence because his defense appealed the conviction and sentence in January 2013, meaning Taylor will remain in The Hague until the outcome of the appeals process.

REACTION AND IMPACT

The prosecution hailed the conviction and sentencing, but it noted that it might consider an appeal to increase the level of responsibility attributed to Taylor in the charges, which it did in January 2013. "The sentence today does not replace amputated limbs; it does not bring back those who were murdered," said chief prosecutor Brenda Hollis. "It does not heal the wounds of those who were raped or forced to become sexual slaves," she continued.

Morris Anya, one of Taylor's defense lawyers, promised to file an appeal. "The sentence is clearly excessive, clearly disproportionate to his circumstances, his age and his health, and does not take into account the fact that he stepped down from office voluntarily," said Anya. The defense further claimed that those who testified gave false accounts to the court. Chief defense lawyer Courtenay Griffiths said Taylor was the legitimate ruler of Liberia, elected fairly by the people, who supported a rebel movement in Sierra Leone but who could not be held accountable for the actions of the rebel movement, just as nations like the United States are not held responsible for supporting rebel action in countries like Afghanistan. "If such behavior is being deemed illegal, then I'd like to see it deemed illegal across the board," Griffiths said.

With the conclusion of the Taylor trial, the special court had achieved its mandate and shut down. Critics of the court say it is possible, because of the limited jurisdiction and scope awarded to the body, that many supposed war criminals might have escaped prosecution. Sierra Leone has indicated an unwillingness to open its own trials, and it is therefore unlikely that some Taylor associates, or others thought to have committed atrocities during the civil war, will be brought to justice.

—Heather Kerrigan

Following are two press releases issued by the International Criminal Court's Special Court for Sierra Leone. The first, from April 26, 2012, announces a guilty verdict in the trial of Charles Taylor and details the counts on which he was convicted; and the second, from May 30, 2012, announces his fifty-year sentence.

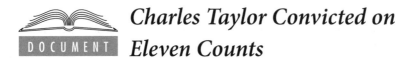

DOCUMENT

Charles Taylor Convicted on Eleven Counts

April 26, 2012

Charles Ghankay Taylor, the former President of Liberia, was convicted today on all counts of an 11-count indictment which alleged that he was responsible for crimes committed by rebel forces during Sierra Leone's decade-long civil war. The Special Court's Trial Chamber II found unanimously that Mr. Taylor aided and abetted RUF and AFRC rebels in the commission of war crimes and crimes against humanity in Sierra Leone.

Mr. Taylor was convicted on Count 1 for acts of terrorism (a war crime), on Count 2 for murder (a crime against humanity), on Count 3 for murder (a war crime), on Count 4 for rape (a crime against humanity), on Count 5 for sexual slavery (a crime against humanity), on Count 6 for outrages upon personal dignity (a war crime), on Count 7 for cruel treatment (a war crime), on Count 8 for inhumane acts, including mutilations and amputations, (a crime against humanity), on Count 9 for the recruitment, enlistment and use of child soldiers, on Count 10 for enslavement (a crime against humanity), and on Count 11 for pillage (a war crime).

The Prosecution had not alleged that Mr. Taylor had committed these crimes in person, but that he participated from Liberia in the commission of crimes by AFRC and RUF rebels and, under Articles 6.1 and 6.3 of the Special Court Statute, was individually responsible for them. The Chamber found that he had aided and abetted the rebels by providing them with arms and ammunition, military personnel, operational support and moral support, making him individually responsible for their crimes.

Charles Taylor is the first head of state to be indicted, tried and convicted by an international tribunal.

The Chamber has scheduled a sentencing hearing for Wednesday, 16 May 2012, and the sentencing judgement will be delivered on Wednesday, 30 May 2012. Under the Special Court Rules, sentences must be given in a specified term of years. The Special Court may not impose a life sentence or the death penalty.

Mr. Taylor was ordered remanded in custody until the 16 May hearing.

At the Special Court, both Prosecution and Defence may appeal. A notice of appeal must be filed within 14 days of the full judgement and sentence.

The Special Court for Sierra Leone is the first "hybrid" tribunal, created by an agreement between the United Nations and the Government of Sierra Leone, and is the first modern court to have its seat in the country where the crimes took place. It is the first court to convict former rebel and militia leaders for the use of child soldiers, for forced marriage as a crime against humanity, and for attacks directed at United Nations peacekeepers.

With today's judgement, the Special Court has reached a major milestone, and is on course towards being the first modern international criminal tribunal to complete its mandate.

SOURCE: Special Court for Sierra Leone. Outreach and Public Affairs Office. "Charles Taylor Convicted on All 11 Counts; Sentencing Scheduled for 30 May." April 26, 2012. http://www.sc-sl.org/LinkClick.asp x?fileticket=by3HPDDiFTM%3d&tabid=232.

Charles Taylor Sentenced to Fifty Years in Prison

DOCUMENT

May 30, 2012

The Judges of Trial Chamber II today sentenced convicted former Liberian President Charles Ghankay Taylor to a term of 50 years in prison for planning and for aiding and abetting crimes committed by rebel forces in Sierra Leone during the country's decade-long civil war.

The Trial Chamber, comprised of Justice Richard Lussick of Samoa (Presiding), Justice Teresa Doherty of Northern Ireland, and Justice [Julia] Sebutinde of Uganda, unanimously imposed the single global sentence for all 11 counts of the crimes for which Mr. Taylor was convicted. These included acts of terrorism, murder, rape, sexual slavery, outrages upon personal dignity, cruel treatment, other inhumane acts, conscripting or enlisting of child soldiers, enslavement and pillage.

Justice Lussick, who read out the judgement in court, said the Trial Chamber found that Mr. Taylor's abuse of his position as President of Liberia to aid and abet the commission of crimes in Sierra Leone, and the abuse of his position as a member of the ECOWAS Committee of Five (later Six), which was "part of the process relied on by the international community to bring peace to Sierra Leone," was "an aggravating factor of great weight."

The Judges also cited the extra-territoriality of Mr. Taylor's acts, and his exploitation of the Sierra Leone conflict for financial gain, as aggravating factors considered in the sentencing.

The Judges took into account the report of Mr. Taylor's good conduct in detention, but otherwise rejected a number of mitigating factors proposed by the Defence.

While the jurisprudence of the Special Court and other tribunals "holds that aiding and abetting as a mode of liability generally warrants a lesser sentence than that imposed for more direct forms of participation," Justice Lussick said that Mr. Taylor's leadership role "puts him in a class of his own."

"The Trial Chamber wishes to underscore the gravity it attaches to Mr. Taylor's betrayal of the public trust," Justice Lussick said. "In the Trial Chamber's view, this betrayal outweighs the distinctions that might otherwise pertain to the modes of liability discussed above."

The parties, if they intend to appeal, must submit written notice to the Appeals Chamber within 14 days of today's sentencing judgement, setting forth the grounds of their appeal.

SOURCE: Special Court for Sierra Leone. Outreach and Public Affairs Office. "Charles Taylor Sentenced to 50 Years in Prison." May 30, 2012. http://www.sc-sl.org/LinkClick.aspx?fileticket=wMFT32KRyiY%3d&tabid=232.

OTHER HISTORIC DOCUMENTS OF INTEREST

FROM PREVIOUS *HISTORIC DOCUMENTS*

May

Pro-Democracy Leader Aung San Suu Kyi Wins Seat in Burmese Parliament

MAY 1, 2012

On April 1, 2012, Burma (Myanmar) held by-elections for parliamentary seats vacated after members were promoted to ministerial roles. The National League for Democracy (NLD), led by Aung San Suu Kyi, the country's de facto pro-democracy leader, achieved an overwhelming victory against the ruling military-backed Union Solidarity and Development Party (USDP), winning forty-three of the forty-five seats. After nearly twenty years of on-and-off house arrest, Suu Kyi, a Nobel laureate, was able to seek a seat in parliament. Although international observers noted some voting irregularities, the by-election proved to be relatively free and fair. However, the government faces significant challenges in terms of balancing the demands of the pro-democracy movement and political reforms with the agenda of the hard-line military leadership, which is loath to see its power eroded.

Burma's Leadership Seeks Reform

A military junta took power in Burma in a coup d'état on March 2, 1962. By 1988, public dissatisfaction over the government's economic management and political status quo resulted in widespread pro-democracy protests, known as the 8888 Uprising. Security forces killed thousands of protesters, and the uprising spurred another military coup d'état. Ongoing demonstrations by pro-democracy protesters resulted in the government imposing martial law in 1989. The country's military leadership determined that elections would be held, and in May 1990, Burma's first free elections in thirty years took place. The opposition NLD, led by Suu Kyi, won 392 out of the 492 seats in the legislature. However, the military junta refused to recognize the results of the election and Suu Kyi was placed under house arrest. She remained under house arrest for the majority of the next twenty years, until her release in November 2010.

In November 2010, Burma held parliamentary elections for the first time in two decades. The country's parliament was established through a constitutional referendum passed in May 2008. The polls, which were marred by voting irregularities, resulted in the military-aligned political party, the USDP, securing the majority of contested seats (an additional 25 percent of seats were reserved for the military). Although the opposition parties did pick up a small number of seats, the military's cement-like grip on power remained in place. Suu Kyi was banned by law from running in the election, and as a result, the NLD boycotted the vote.

Shortly after the elections, the NLD announced that it would reenter the political fold and contest parliamentary by-elections. As a result of the appointment of ministers, forty-eight parliamentary seats were left open. With regard to running for parliament, Suu Kyi stated, "If I think I should take part in the election, I will. Some people are worried that taking part could harm my dignity. Frankly, if you do politics, you should not be thinking about your dignity. . . . I stand for the re-registration of the NLD party. I would like to work effectively toward amending the constitution. So we have to do what we need to do." On January 18, 2012, she formally registered to contest the election for a seat in the Pyithu Hluttaw, the People's Assembly, or lower house of parliament, in Kawhmu Township. The seat was vacated by Soe Tint after he was appointed as the Deputy Minister for Construction. Suu Kyi faced Soe Min, a former army physician and member of the USDP.

Relatively Quiet Campaign Process

The NLD and Suu Kyi campaigned on a platform calling for reforms, including the repeal of legislation that it said curbs human rights, as well as changes to the country's constitution that would limit the power of the military. Moreover, the party called for an end to ethnic conflict. Suu Kyi also specifically called for increased government spending on education and health care.

The NLD was able to carry out its campaign activities with relatively little interference from the government. However, there were notable exceptions. The NLD's spokesperson, Nyan Win, publicly complained that it was facing obstacles in obtaining the needed permissions to utilize public facilities for its campaign events. In response, the Union Electoral Commission (UEC) quickly did away with all election restrictions. This was an encouraging sign of the Electoral Commission's desire to ensure that public and international perceptions of the election were positive, especially after Burma's president, U Thein Sein, had promised a free and fair process.

NLD Wins Overwhelming Victory

Elections were held on April 1, 2012. The NLD won a landslide victory, capturing forty-three of the forty-five contested seats. The ruling USDP won just one seat in a constituency where the NLD candidate was disqualified from running because of a technicality. The other seat was won by a Shan Nationalities Democratic Party candidate in Shan state, reflecting strong community support. According to the UEC, the NLD won all thirty-seven of the contested seats in the 440-member Pyithu Hluttaw, as well as four of the six contested seats in the 224-member Amyotha Hluttaw, the House of Nationalities, or upper house of parliament. In addition, the party won two of the vacant regional assembly seats. Voter turnout was reportedly high throughout the country, and the NLD candidates secured victories with strong majorities across the board. This was true even in Naypyidaw, the new capital, where NLD candidates won all four constituencies. The NLD walked away from the election with forty-four seats in total, forty-three secured in the by-elections and one gained from the defection of a member of the upper house from another party to the NLD.

Meanwhile, Suu Kyi easily won the election in Kawhmu Township. The by-election was the first time that voters had been able to vote for the de facto leader of the democracy movement. In both the national elections of 1990 and 2010, Suu Kyi was under house arrest and unable to run for office.

The voting process went relatively smoothly compared with previous elections, which were marred by accusations of vote rigging and other irregularities. Indeed, opposition groups claimed that in the 2010 elections, a large number of advance votes were cast in support of the USDP. The UEC indicated that it would investigate all irregularities in the 2012 polls. Moreover, the government allowed a small number of international observers to monitor the elections. Although there were some irregularities, including intimidation of NDC supporters, ballot tampering, and manipulation of voter lists—all of which helped to secure support for the military-backed USDP—overall the elections were seen as relatively free and fair.

Balance of Power Unchanged

Despite the significant gains made by the NDP, the country's political status quo remained relatively unchanged. After the election, the ruling USDP still held over half of the elected seats in both the upper and lower houses of parliament. Under the constitution, a further 25 percent of seats are set aside for military appointees, ensuring that the military and its supporters have the power to veto any proposed changes to the constitution.

Although the balance of power remains firmly with the military, the by-elections were significant in that the USDP both allowed the NDP to participate and to do so on a relatively level playing field. This suggests that the country's leadership was eager to bolster the legitimacy of the political reform process in an effort to see international sanctions, imposed on Burma, removed. The results of the by-elections were also symbolic in that more than twenty years after the NDP won its landslide victory in the 1990 elections, Suu Kyi finally took her place in parliament. With the leader of the pro-democracy movement now a member of parliament, many observers and supports alike expect that she will help to galvanize support for the movement, in part by working with other small pro-democracy parties that already hold seats in parliament.

On May 2, 2012, Suu Kyi and other newly elected members of parliament were sworn into office. The swearing-in ceremony had proved to be contentious, as the oath in part states that members of parliament will "safeguard" the constitution. For opposition party members keen to see some of the articles of the constitution removed or changed, this proved to be a sticking point. Nevertheless, the new members all swore the oath as is and began their terms in office.

Meanwhile, the president, Thein Sein, publicly declared the elections a success. But the NLD's overwhelming victory at the polls was an embarrassment to the ruling party and raised concerns about the upcoming 2015 general election. The NLD's widespread support in the by-elections foreshadows a victory in 2015, which could see the USDP lose most of its seats in parliament, barring the 25 percent set aside for military appointees. The president must now try to find a balance between managing hard-liners within the government and military who fear a loss of power and continuing on the path of political reform. In late March, the commander in chief of the armed forces, Vice Senior General Min Aung Hlaing, who is the second-highest-ranking military officer in the country, stated that it was the military's "main duty" to "protect and maintain" the constitution. His comments suggested that the military will not support changes to the constitution that could erode its power.

During the campaign for her parliamentary seat, Suu Kyi made clear that her party would seek changes to the 2008 constitution, which observers assumed included the role of the military in the government. The contrast in viewpoints between the leader of the country's strengthening democracy movement and Burma's powerful military serve to highlight the president's challenge in pleasing both the opposition and the regime's incumbent leadership. In a visit to the United States in late 2012, Suu Kyi voiced her hopes for a transition to democracy in Burma, saying, "We wish to learn from everybody who has achieved a transition to democracy, and also . . . our great strong point is that, because we are so far behind everybody else, we can also learn which mistakes we should avoid."

—Hilary Ewing

Following is the text of a press conference held on May 1, 2012, by Aung San Suu Kyi and UN Secretary-General Ban Ki-moon, on Burma's changing political landscape and the challenges ahead.

UN Secretary-General and Aung San Suu Kyi Discuss Challenges and Changes in Burma

May 1, 2012

DASSK [Daw Aung San Suu Kyi]: I would like to introduce the Secretary-General to you. I just want to say that it has been a great pleasure to be able to welcome him to my home. I can't say to Burma, because this is not the first time he has been to Burma. He has been welcomed to Burma before, but this is the first time that I have been able to welcome him to my home, and it has been a great pleasure to meet him and to meet Mrs. Ban.

The Secretary-General has very kindly agreed to take a few questions from the press, but I understand that the time is running out. He probably has another appointment, so if we could keep the questions to two or three, after the Secretary-General has made a few opening remarks.

SG [Secretary-General Ban Ki-moon]: Thank you, Daw Aung San Suu Kyi. Good morning, ladies and gentlemen. *Minglapa*. It is a great honour for me to finally have a face-to-face meeting with Daw Aung San Suu Kyi. It is not for lack of my trying, but simply it didn't happen and they didn't allow [it]. Only at the third time, I am meeting her, and we had a very constructive exchange of views on all spectrums of the issues which the Myanmar Government and the Myanmar people will work together [on] with the international community, including the United Nations.

In fact, this is the first time we have been in constant contact through telephone or correspondence or through my special advisers, particularly Vijay Nambiar.

What I saw of her has been confirmed this morning. She is really a strong and dedicated leader of this country for democracy and development and human rights for all. I, like everybody in the world, fully admire her leadership and commitment, during the last two or three decades for peace and development and human rights for this country, for this region, and for the world. She has been a symbol of our hope for human rights for all, all around the world.

I congratulated her on her election as a parliamentarian, and I also commended her decision of yesterday to take the oath and become a parliamentarian. I know that it must have been a very difficult decision. Politicians sometimes will continue to have differences on some issues, but a real leader demonstrates flexibility for the greater cause of people and country. This is what she has done yesterday, and I really admire and respect her decision. I am sure that she will play a very constructive and active role as a parliamentarian for the betterment and well-being of this great country.

In the course of my meetings with President Thein Sein and Daw Aung San Suu Kyi and other leaders of this Government, I have always emphasized the importance of flexibility and wisdom and compromise when they discussed all different ideas and options and policies, regardless of what party one represents. The politicians and political leadership—they have to look to the people, be accountable to the people, and always work together for the prosperity and long-term interest of their people.

President Thein Sein and Daw Aung San Suu Kyi have [come] far. I am sure of that. I am convinced that they will continue to make progress, further still. This is what I expect.

The Myanmar people and Government have embarked on a path of reform, democratization, and fuller participatory democracy. They deserve our support. They deserve the support of the whole international community. The United Nations will continue to stand by the people in every step and in any way we can. This is my pledge.

The process may be difficult. There are still challenges, but this process should be irreversible. There is no turning back. We will have to support their efforts for fuller participatory democracy, development and human rights. That is my pledge as Secretary-General of the United Nations—to work with her and to work with President Thein Sein and the Myanmar people for this purpose.

And finally, I have invited her to visit the United Nations at a time convenient for her, and to the United Nations, and I received a very positive answer from her, and I am looking forward to continuing our good offices role for peace and development and human rights of Myanmar.

Thank you very much.

* * *

Q: When can you expect to visit the United Nations?

SG: Please ask Daw Aung San Suu Kyi.

DASSK: I didn't give a definite date. I would like to go to the United Nations and I will make every effort to do so, but I can't say when I shall be going.

SG: We will continue to discuss [this], yes.

Q: What can other Asian countries learn from Myanmar's democracy process?

SG: Yesterday, I have conveyed my message through a parliamentary address. This is quite difficult. The decisions political leaders will make over a few months or over a few years will shape the future of this country for the coming many generations, therefore you are going through a very important period. It means courage and leadership and perseverance and wisdom, flexibility and compromise. While moving toward democratization, you need to have reconciliation among all the people of Myanmar. That will be very important. The United Nations will try to help this process of reconciliation in any way we can through a peacebuilding process.

Q: On aid, what sort of role would you like for the UN to play? Also, there seems to be quite a rush of private foreign companies coming in, but is there anything that they should be careful about?

DASSK: It's difficult to answer this question in a few short sentences, but I've always said that what is important is that whatever aid comes to Burma—whether development aid or humanitarian aid—should come in such a way that it empowers the people and decreases their dependency on the government. That is the only way in which we can ensure that the democratic process in Burma will go along the right path. And I think the Secretary-General understands my concerns.

SG: About your second part, there is a high expectation of the international community. As we have seen recently, there is a stream of world leaders coming to Myanmar to discuss and help the future of Myanmar. At the same time, it is important that Myanmar's people would have an opportunity to develop their own country. That is why I am going to launch the UN Global Compact's Myanmar network right after this meeting. This is an initiative of the United Nations where 7,000 world-class business leaders are discussing among themselves how they can promote and help each other—good trade, good business opportunities among themselves for the world economy. I hope that Myanmar's local business entrepreneurs will have the opportunity to fully utilize and interact with international business leaders to widen and deepen their business opportunities for direct foreign investment, as well as job creation. Through this interaction, they can strengthen their capacity in terms of good business management and accountability and transparency and even human rights, labour rules. All of these are good principles which the UN Global Compact tries to promote. I hope that this will be a good opportunity for them to mutually benefit for economic development.

Q: (inaudible)

DASSK: We have always believed in flexibility in the political process, not just as now that we are going to be members of Parliament, but we have always believed and have been flexible throughout the years of our struggle because that is the only way in which we can achieve our goal without violence. So I do not think flexibility is going to be a new concept for us, newly-acquired because we are going into the national assembly. It has been part of the political equipment with which we have been working for the last 23-odd years.

SOURCE: United Nations Information Center Yangon. "Joint Press Encounter by Secretary-General Ban Ki-moon and Daw Aung San Suu Kyi—Yangon, Myanmar, 1 May 2012." May 1, 2012. http://www.un.org/sg/offthecuff/index.asp?nid=2325.

OTHER HISTORIC DOCUMENTS OF INTEREST

FROM PREVIOUS *HISTORIC DOCUMENTS*

U.S. and China Officials
on Chinese Dissident

MAY 2 AND 3, 2012

In the spring of 2012, a human rights case surrounding a well-known Chinese dissident challenged diplomatic relations between the United States and China. Lawyer and advocate Chen Guangcheng escaped from house arrest and traveled to the U.S. Embassy in Beijing, requesting medical treatment and an investigation into his alleged mistreatment at the hands of local officials. His appeal occurred as U.S. officials sought greater collaboration from China on several matters of international concern, raising the stakes for negotiations between the two countries on how best to handle Chen's requests.

An Advocate for China's Disabled and Families

Born the son of a peasant family, Chen grew up in the village of Dongshigu in Shandong Province, approximately 300 miles from Beijing. Blinded by a severe fever at an early age and a self-taught lawyer, Chen became known as an advocate for the disabled and the poor. His legal career began in 1996, when Chen went to Beijing to protest taxes levied against his family. Under Chinese law, the disabled are exempt from taxation and fees. Following his success in that case, Chen began petitioning for others with disabilities and also defended farmers against illegal land seizures.

Chen's most notable case occurred in 2005, when he represented thousands of women from the city of Linyi who alleged that local government officials had forced them to have late-term abortions or be sterilized in order to ensure compliance with China's population control policies, which allow only one child per family. The Linyi women also accused officials of detaining and abusing relatives of those who attempted to avoid the policy's enforcement. Such actions are against Chinese law, which says the government may levy fines only against families who exceed birth quotas. The class-action lawsuit drew international attention, and China's National Population and Family Planning Commission launched an investigation into the allegations in August 2005. The following month, the commission announced that it had found evidence of abuses in Linyi and that it had fired and detained several local officials.

Chen on Trial

The lawsuit angered Linyi officials, who sought Chen out in September 2005 while he was in Beijing. Chen told Radio Free Asia that when the Linyi officials found him, they forcibly dragged him to a car, beat him, then took him to a hotel for questioning. Officials later drove him back to Dongshigu, where they confined him to his house and, at times, in a government-run hotel. Communist Party sources also said Linyi officials distributed a report throughout Beijing that claimed Chen was a tool of "foreign anti-China forces" and had received funding from international sources for his activist work for the disabled, a move that made it politically risky for others to intervene on his behalf.

Chen was formally arrested in June 2006 on charges of destroying property and assembling a crowd to disrupt traffic, though he was under house arrest at the time these incidents allegedly occurred. Chen's lawyers decried his August 2006 trial as a "sham." Local police had reportedly allowed the lawyers to meet with Chen in June but prevented them from discussing his defense. Chen's lawyers were also arrested shortly before his trial, and local authorities appointed a public defender. The trial occurred behind closed doors and lasted only two hours before the court convicted Chen of both charges and sentenced him to fifty-one months in prison.

When Chen was released from prison in September 2010, he was once again confined to his house in Dongshigu though there were no outstanding legal charges against him. His wife, and for some time his young daughter, were also confined with him. Plainclothes security officers guarded the house and installed surveillance cameras and floodlights on the grounds. Supporters who attempted to visit Chen were often violently forced away; security guards hit them with sticks and threw rocks, and in some cases, visitors were beaten, robbed, and left in remote locations.

An Escape Causes Diplomatic Turmoil

Then on the evening of April 22, 2012, Chen escaped, purportedly with the help of an underground network of human rights activists. Chen managed to climb over the wall surrounding his house, breaking his foot in the process, and met family friend He Peirong outside of the village. The two drove to Beijing, where Chen requested help and medical treatment from the U.S. Embassy. American officials allowed him into the embassy on humanitarian grounds on April 26, but only for a temporary stay. They initially did not confirm his presence at the embassy, but on April 27, Assistant Secretary of State for East Asia and Pacific Affairs Kurt Campbell informed the Chinese ambassador in Washington, D.C., of Chen's location.

That same day, a video appeared on YouTube of Chen describing his house arrest and the abuse he and his family had purportedly been subjected to, and appealing to Prime Minister Wen Jiabao to intervene. Chen said his daughter was followed to school and that their guards had kicked his wife for hours. In one instance in 2011, Chen and his wife were severely beaten after a video that they had recorded and smuggled out of their house was posted online.

Meanwhile, U.S. medical personnel administered treatment for Chen but expressed concern that he might have colon cancer in addition to his broken foot and should be transferred to a hospital. During a press conference several days after Chen's arrival at the embassy, State Department officials noted that Chen repeatedly said he wanted to stay in China but that he wanted to be reunited with his family and moved to a safer location. He also told U.S. officials that he wanted the Chinese government's help in addressing his concerns about the mistreatment he and his family had endured at the hands of local officials in his home province.

Chen's escape occurred at an inopportune time for U.S. and Chinese officials. Secretary of State Hillary Rodham Clinton and Treasury Secretary Timothy Geithner were scheduled to arrive in China for the two countries' annual Strategic and Economic Dialogue, beginning on May 3. U.S. officials were hoping to gain increased cooperation from China on diplomatic efforts to pressure Iran and North Korea to suspend their nuclear programs and to achieve a ceasefire in Syria, as well as commitments on several economic issues of concern. Human rights issues had long been a point of contention between the two countries, but Secretary Clinton had been clear in the past that U.S. diplomacy with China would not be held captive by human rights cases.

Given these sensitivities, U.S. officials sought an agreement with the Chinese government that would help to ensure Chen's safety but would not jeopardize the countries' diplomatic relationship. According to a State Department briefing on May 2, Chinese authorities ultimately agreed that once Chen left the hospital, he and his family would be relocated to one of seven cities of their choosing, where Chen could also attend a university to study law. Additionally, Chinese authorities promised to investigate purported actions by local province authorities against Chen and his family, that Chen would be treated humanely while he remained in the country, and that U.S. doctors and visitors would have access to him. One senior State Department official affirmed that the United States would "look to confirm at regular intervals that the commitments he has received are carried out."

That same day, Chen left the U.S. Embassy and went to Chaoyang Hospital in Beijing. Officials believed they had arrived at a satisfactory arrangement and were surprised when Chen's lawyer suddenly said that Chen had "changed his mind" and, because he no longer felt secure in China, wanted to leave the country, preferably to go to the United States. In interviews with journalists, Chen said he wanted to leave China because "guaranteeing citizens' rights in China is empty talk" and that "my safety and my family's safety are not guaranteed even now."

Some speculated that Chen may have panicked during his first evening in the hospital. Chinese authorities had reportedly cordoned off his hospital room, denied visitors, and limited his phone calls, including preventing contact with extended family members. Others believed the change of heart may have been sparked by conversations with his wife. Chen told reporters his wife said she and their children had been threatened by the security guards at their home in his absence. And in an interview with the *New York Times,* Chen said he had felt some pressure to leave the U.S. Embassy after hearing that Chinese officials allegedly threatened to beat his wife if he stayed under U.S. protection. For their part, U.S. officials denied they had told Chen of any such threats and insisted they had not coerced Chen into leaving the embassy.

Chen's decision angered the Chinese government, which placed the blame squarely on the United States. "The U.S. move is an interference in China's internal affairs, which is completely unacceptable to China," said Foreign Ministry spokesperson Liu Weimin in a statement. "China demands the U.S. to apologize for that, carry out a thorough investigation into the incident, deal with those responsible, and promise not to let similar incidents happen again." Human rights groups and Republicans in the United States were also quick to criticize the Obama administration for rushing to an ill-conceived resolution in an effort not to disrupt the Strategic and Economic Dialogue.

On May 3, Chen appealed directly to the U.S. Congress, calling in to a congressional hearing to request help in leaving China. U.S. officials scrambled to devise a second plan, but they noted it was difficult to determine the best course of action for Chen because the Chinese would not allow them to speak to him in person. Meanwhile, Chinese authorities further restricted the number of friends and supporters able to visit Chen.

Then on May 4, the United States and China reached an agreement that would allow Chen to travel to the United States with his family to attend a university but not to seek asylum. Chen had been offered a fellowship at New York University to study law. State Department officials said they expected Chinese officials to "expeditiously process his applications" for necessary travel documents and promised to hasten Chen's visa request as well.

LINGERING CONCERNS

Though the new deal appeared to appease all sides, Chen remained concerned about his other family members and his supporters. On May 15, Chen participated by phone in a U.S. congressional hearing before the House Subcommittee on Africa, Global Health, Global Human Rights, and International Organizations. Chen described an incident in which authorities broke into his brother's house and beat those they found. When his nephew attempted to defend himself with a kitchen knife, he was arrested and put in a detention center on what Chen claimed were "trumped up" charges. Subcommittee Chair Rep. Christopher Smith, R-N.J., also noted that Congress had received reports that Chinese authorities, for the purpose of interrogations, had broken into the homes of other family members and rounded up those who had assisted Chen in his escape. The woman who drove him to Beijing, for example, had been detained on April 27 and held for a week of questioning.

LIFE IN THE UNITED STATES

Chen arrived in New York City on May 19 with his wife and two children and moved into a faculty apartment in Manhattan, furnished by the university. He began taking English classes and law classes in June. Chen largely kept out of the spotlight, turning down invitations to appear on television news programs and requests from Hollywood producers, but he announced plans to publish his memoirs in 2013. In his free time, he began to participate in campaigns for disabled rights in New York. Chen remained critical of the Chinese government, and he expressed anger that it had not begun its promised investigation of his treatment by local officials. But, he told the *Washington Post,* he still hopes to return to China once he completes his studies, believing that the country is changing and that democracy and the rule of law will ultimately prevail.

—Linda Fecteau

Following is a statement by a Chinese foreign ministry spokesperson on May 2, 2012, regarding Chen Guangcheng's entrance into the U.S. Embassy in Beijing, China; the edited text of a briefing with U.S. State Department officials on May 2, 2012, on Chen's stay and exit from the U.S. Embassy and the edited text of a statement by U.S. Ambassador to China Gary Locke, on May 3, 2012, on the options presented to Chen.

Chinese Foreign Ministry Remarks on Dissident Chen Guangcheng

May 2, 2012

Q: On Chen Guangcheng's entering the US Embassy in China, does China believe the US interferes in China's internal affairs? Does China demand an apology from the US?

A: According to our knowledge, Chen Guangcheng, a native of Yinan county, Shandong Province, entered the US Embassy in China in late April, and left of his own volition after a six-day stay. It should be pointed out that the US Embassy in China took Chen

Guangcheng, a Chinese citizen, into the Embassy via abnormal means, with which China expresses strong dissatisfaction. The US move is an interference in China's internal affairs, which is completely unacceptable to China. The US Embassy in China has the obligation to abide by relevant international laws and Chinese laws, and should not engage in activities irrelevant to its duties.

China demands the US to apologize for that, carry out a thorough investigation into the incident, deal with those responsible, and promise not to let similar incidents happen again. China noted that the US has expressed the importance it attaches to China's demands and concerns, and promised to take necessary measures to prevent similar incidents. The US side should reflect upon its policies and actions, and take concrete actions to maintain the larger interests of China-US relations.

China emphasizes that China is a country under the rule of law, and every citizen's legitimate rights and interests are protected by the Constitution and laws. Meanwhile, every citizen has the obligation to abide by the Constitution and laws.

SOURCE: Ministry of Foreign Affairs of the People's Republic of China. "Foreign Ministry Spokesperson Liu Weimin's Remarks on Chen Guangcheng's Entering the US Embassy in China." May 2, 2012. http://www.fmprc.gov.cn/eng/xwfw/s2510/2535/t928382.htm.

U.S. State Department Briefing on Chen Guangcheng

DOCUMENT

May 2, 2012

MODERATOR: Thank you all for being here. This will be a briefing on background to discuss the events of the last few days with regard to Chen Guangcheng. We have with us two senior State Department officials. For your records, the first is [Senior State Department Official One], the second is [Senior State Department Official Two], both of whom are intimately involved in all of this.

[Senior State Department Official One] will have a statement, and then we'll take about three or four questions from the room. People on the phone will be able to hear, but they will not be able to ask questions. . . .

SENIOR STATE DEPARTMENT OFFICIAL ONE: Okay. Good afternoon, everyone. Sorry to keep you all waiting here a little bit. I'll have a statement, and then again as [Moderator] said, I think we'd be pleased to take some questions subsequently.

Chen Guangcheng, who I think of you all know, entered the United States Embassy in Beijing under exceptional circumstances on April 26, 2012, requesting medical treatment from the Embassy. In part because of his visual disability, he was injured while traveling to Beijing from his home village of Donshigu in Shandong province. That's a couple hundred miles away. On humanitarian grounds, we assisted Mr. Chen in entering our facilities and allowed him to remain on a temporary basis. U.S. medical personnel conducted a series of medical tests and administered appropriate treatment while he was there.

Throughout his stay at the Embassy, U.S. officials consulted regularly with Mr. Chen to discuss his wishes. Mr. Chen made clear from the beginning that he wanted to remain in China and that he wanted his stay in the United States Embassy to be temporary. He indicated that he placed priority on reunification with his family and that he sought relocation to a safe environment elsewhere in China from the province that he's been living in. He expressed his desire for assistance from the central government in addressing his concerns and grievances, primarily relating to his reported mistreatment and that of his family at the hands of local officials.

Mr. Chen decided to depart the Embassy today and traveled to a hospital in Beijing. He did so on the basis of a number of understandings. China acknowledged that Mr. Chen will be treated humanely while he remains in China. During his stay at the hospital over the coming days, U.S. doctors and other visitors, including those from the U.S. Embassy, will have access to him. He has been reunited with his family, his wife and two children, at the hospital, and they will remain together with him as a family. He had not seen his son in a few years, and his wife had not seen him either, so this was a family reunification after a long and difficult separation.

When he leaves the hospital, the Chinese authorities have stated that Mr. Chen and his family will be relocated to a safe environment so that he may attend a university to pursue a course of study. I think many of you know that he is a self-taught lawyer, but he has long sought the opportunity to study in university. He will have several university options from which to choose. We understand that there are no remaining legal issues directed at Mr. Chen and that he will be treated like any other student in China. Chinese officials have further stated that they will investigate reported extralegal activities committed by local Shandong authorities against Mr. Chen and his family.

The United States will take a continuing interest in the well-being of Mr. Chen and his family, including seeking periodic welfare visits and raising his case with the appropriate authorities. We will look to confirm at regular intervals that the commitments he has received are carried out. We have conveyed to the Chinese Government the concerns he's expressed about friends who helped him travel to Beijing and have urged authorities to take no retribution against them.

We have worked together. We have sought to resolve this case in a manner consistent with American values and our commitment to human rights and in the context of a cooperative U.S.-China partnership.

Thank you. . . .

SENIOR STATE DEPARTMENT OFFICIAL TWO: I want to pick up on the last statement made, which is that we've sought to resolve the case in a manner consistent with American values, our commitment to human rights, and in the context of a cooperative U.S.-China partnership. We were true to our values. We respected Mr. Chen's freewill, both his desire to depart the Embassy, which he did with his own—of his own freewill, and most fundamentally his consistently stated desire to stay and work in his own country and to continue his work.

In the process, we think we have helped to secure for him a better future, the reunification of his family after years apart, a relocation to a better place, and new educational opportunities. We think we were also true to our human rights policy, which is one in which individuals within their own societies are given an opportunity to engage, not to remain in isolation. And we think we were true to our broader foreign policy strategy, which is to recognize that our relationships with other countries are not zero-sum, that they could work together with us to achieve a common outcome. We exercised intensive diplomacy, the use of partnerships with private entities, commitment to international law, all to bring about this outcome.

MODERATOR: Good. Let's take three or four questions. Let's start with Michele.

QUESTION: The Chinese are asking for an apology for accepting him. What—have you offered any sort of apology?

SENIOR STATE DEPARTMENT OFFICIAL ONE: Let me just answer it this way if I can. This was an extraordinary case involving exceptional circumstances, and we do not anticipate that it will be repeated. Recognizing the exceptional circumstances under which Mr. Chen entered the U.S. Embassy, we intend to work closely inside the U.S. Government to fully ensure that our policies are consistent and—with our values. And that's about all I'll say on that one.

[The following five pages have been omitted. They contain additional questions about a U.S. apology, Secretary Clinton's role in the negotiations, as well as comments about Chen's history, personality, and medical condition.]

SOURCE: U.S. Department of State. "Background Briefing With Senior State Department Officials on Chen Guangcheng." May 2, 2012. http://www.state.gov/p/eap/rls/rm/2012/05/182850.htm.

U.S. Ambassador Locke Addresses Options Offered to Chen Guangcheng

May 3, 2012

MS. [Victoria] NULAND: All right, everybody. We are sorry to keep you waiting this morning. I am delighted to have with us Ambassador Locke. He is going to speak to you on the record briefly about his experiences with Chen Guangcheng leading—while he was in the Embassy and leading up to his decision to depart. . . .

AMBASSADOR LOCKE: . . . Let me just say that I and the Embassy have long had interest in Mr. Chen Guangcheng, and of course, the U.S. Government has long had an interest, and we've mentioned him in so many of our human rights statements, and have advocated for his humane treatment ever since for many, many years.

Last week, under most unusual extraordinary circumstances, he contacted us, we went out and met with him, and given the fact that he has a—he's blind, he was injured, we took the extraordinary step in a very unusual situation, exceptional situation, to bring him into the Embassy. I have spent sometimes five hours during the day with him almost every day, two to three, three-plus hours talking with him—so have other Embassy people—trying to determine what it is that he want[s].

He made it very, very clear from the very, very beginning that he wanted to stay in China, that he wanted to be part of the struggle to improve the human rights within China, and to gain greater liberty and democracy for the people of China. We asked him, did you want to go to the United States, and he said no; maybe someday to study, but his immediate goal was to stay in China and to help with the cause.

We spent a lot of time determining what it is that he want[s]. First and foremost, he did not want to go back to the village and be in Shangdong Province, and he outlined all the mistreatment that he and his family had received there. And he talked about his dreams of wanting to study law and to pursue his studies. He wanted a safe future for his family. And he also was, of course, concerned about those who had helped him during his escape and his travel to Beijing. So we had numerous meetings with the Chinese Government, and I was involved in every single one of those meetings. Sometimes those were—some of those meetings were three times a day trying to present proposals that—to the Chinese Government that met his objectives, and we were constantly trying to determine what those objectives might be and how we could accomplish those objectives.

We consulted with him regularly, and one thing that he really expressed an interest in was wanting to study, pursue the study of law. So we came up with a proposal. Some of it was then—we negotiated with the Chinese on it and it was changed. And we finally had a proposal that met with his agreement. I can tell you that he knew the stark choices in front of him. He knew that—and was very aware that he might have to spend many, many years in the Embassy, and that—but he was prepared to do that unless the terms of an agreement with the Chinese Government was not acceptable to him. He also was fully aware of the plight of his family if he stayed in the Embassy.

At one point on Tuesday, we presented a proposal to him, and he said it was unacceptable—unacceptable—and that he would stay in the Embassy. From then on, we started focusing on what that would mean in terms of procedures with the Embassy, and we left him alone. Later that night, a person went back in to deliver food and asked him if he was still comfortable with that decision, and he said he was, and we respected that. That night, however, we were able to meet with the Chinese Government, because he constantly said he needed some first steps by the Chinese Government as a demonstration of good faith, that they were always asking him to leave the Embassy before they would implement new procedures or part of the agreement, and he wanted a first step by the Chinese Government. And he said why can't they bring his family up to Beijing. And so we approached the Chinese Government on that, and they said yes.

And the agreement was that if you brought—if the family were brought to the hospital, that he would then be able to talk with his wife, and that would enable him to make the very final decision on whether or not he would leave the Embassy. So while the Chinese Government had agreed to his request to have the family come to Beijing, it was not necessarily in his mind, and we stated it—did not mean that he would definitely leave the Embassy until he had a chance to talk with his wife over the phone, and then he would make his final decision.

He spoke with his wife over the phone, two conversations with his wife over the phone. . . . And then we asked him what did he want to do, did he want to leave, was he ready to leave. And we waited several minutes and then suddenly he jumped up, very excited, very eager, and said, "Let's go," in front of many, many witnesses. We then proceeded to take him down to the van with the doctors, translators, and many other personnel. Before he went into the van, I asked him again, "Is this what you want to do? Are you ready to leave the Embassy?" And he said yes. We then gave him a phone and he talked with Secretary Clinton. He called his lawyer. He wanted to reach out to a member of the press. And we made that—and facilitated, made all those connections for him.

We stayed with him in the hospital. Of many, many people, I was there for probably an hour and a half after he entered the hospital, met with the family, met with the children. The doctors were there for many, many hours. And so at all points, we were intent on carrying out his wishes and ensuring that we could put together something that met his needs.

Number one, relocation to another part of China, and the Chinese Government gave him seven different universities and places that he could choose from. Number two, that he would receive a college education paid for by the Chinese Government with living expenses and housing for him and his entire family at one of seven institutions of his choosing. Number three, that while he was in the hospital for medical treatment, that the Chinese Government would listen to his complaints of abuse and conduct a full investigation, and [four], that he would be given all the rights and privileges of any student at any university, which included the opportunity to apply for a different university down the road.

And so I can tell you unequivocally that he was never pressured to leave, he was excited and eager about leaving when he made his decision, announced it. He simply— while he was sitting there, we waited for him to make his decision. He also fully knew of what would be—of what staying in the Embassy would entail if he decided not to leave. And he was fully aware of and talked about what might happen to his family if he stayed in the Embassy and they stayed in the village in Shangdong Province.

QUESTION: Toria, he said he made an offer on Tuesday night? I just wanted to clarify. You said you made an offer on Tuesday night and he said it was not acceptable. Was that an offer for asylum?

AMBASSADOR LOCKE: No. He never asked for asylum.

QUESTION: Okay.

[The following two pages have been omitted. They contain questions about U.S. efforts to arrive at a second agreement with Chinese officials on Chen's future.]

QUESTION: I just want to clarify, what was wrong with the initial deal that he was given on Tuesday? And given that you had trust in this deal, what is your understanding of why he changed his mind? I mean, is it—if the central authorities were giving their word that they were going to do this for him, why should he have freaked out and changed his mind?

AMBASSADOR LOCKE: On Tuesday when we presented the latest offer and response by the Chinese Government to all of our proposals, we were constantly giving—presenting proposals that talked especially about education—which institutions, where, and the like. On Tuesday afternoon, we presented the latest proposal or response by the Chinese Government. He said that that was unacceptable, and he said he, in fact, needed to speak to Premier Wen Jiabao. . . .

And later on that evening, after we checked on him again and he said he was still comfortable with his decision to stay at the Embassy, he indicated that why can't the Chinese Government take a first step as a sign of good faith; they're asking me to leave the—or proposing that I leave the Embassy and all these other benefits would follow; why can't they do something first like bring my family here.

So we went back to the Chinese Government and said he needs some assurance; you're asking him to take a leap of faith and he wants the Chinese Government to take a first step. And so it was agreed by the Chinese Government that they would put the family on the fast train, the high-speed train, bring them up to the hospital. And that night, Tuesday night, after we informed him that the Chinese Government was willing to do that, but before they did that, we needed to find out that if they—in fact, they did that, and if in fact he was able to talk to his wife, would in—was he inclined to leave the Embassy.

The Chinese Government did not want to go to the effort of bringing the family up if it was still not acceptable. And he said it was, provided he still had the opportunity to talk to his wife at the—when she was at the hospital before he made his final, final decision.

[The following page has been omitted. It contains questions about Chen's wife.]

Source: U.S. Department of State. "United States Ambassador to China Gary Locke Briefs the Press." May 3, 2012. http://www.state.gov/p/eap/rls/rm/2012/05/189214.htm.

Other Historic Documents of Interest

From this volume

- China and Japan Dispute Island Territory, p. 446
- China Unveils New Leadership, p. 544
- Wife of Chinese Politician Sentenced to Death With Reprieve for Murder, p. 387

From previous *Historic Documents*

- Senate Passes Currency Misalignment Act, *2011,* p. 527
- Chinese Dissident Awarded Nobel Peace Prize, *2010,* p. 498
- President Obama Visits East Asia, *2009,* p. 543
- State Department on Human Rights in China, *1996,* p. 133

French President Hollande Delivers Inaugural Address

MAY 15, 2012

On May 15, 2012, Europe's second-largest economy, France, inaugurated a socialist as its president for only the second time since the Fifth French Republic was established in 1958. François Hollande, a modest, low-key party leader who prior to winning the presidential contest had never held a position in national government, defeated the incumbent, Nicolas Sarkozy. His victory owed at least as much to Sarkozy's unpopularity and the precarious state of the French economy as it did to Hollande's own policy blueprint or personal appeal to the electorate. The change of leaders in France altered the political balance in Europe significantly, causing more emphasis to be placed on policies promoting economic growth and job creation, as opposed to focusing only on debt reduction. Hollande's election was also a measure of the growing public repudiation of the austerity policies that his predecessor, Sarkozy, had championed.

Long and Colorful Campaign

The presidential campaign was long and comprised numerous stages. Hollande's path to victory began in a New York hotel in May 2011, owing to a sexual encounter between a Guinean chambermaid and the man who tipped her—the man who was to become the Socialist Party's presidential nominee, Dominique Strauss-Kahn, then managing director of the International Monetary Fund (IMF). The scandal created by the maid's accusations of sexual assault scuppered Strauss-Kahn's presidential bid, even though the criminal charges brought against him by the New York prosecutors were later dropped as doubts surfaced about the accuser's credibility.

Having been hurt by party infighting in previous elections, the Socialist Party decided to change the way it selected its candidate. To boost citizens' participation in the process, it opted for U.S.-style primaries in which anyone who professed a left-leaning political allegiance could vote. The initiative generated strong grassroots interest and more than a million people turned out to vote in the first round on October 9, 2011. Hollande and Socialist Party leader Martine Aubry emerged as the two front-runners from the field of candidates, with each winning just over a quarter of the votes cast. The losing candidates included Ségolène Royal, the woman with whom Hollande had four children over the course of their three-decade-long relationship before the two announced their separation in 2007. Royal had been the Socialist Party candidate in the 2007 presidential elections, which she lost to Sarkozy. In the Hollande-Aubry runoff ballot on October 16, Hollande scored a convincing win, taking almost 57 percent of the vote compared to Aubry's 43 percent.

Meanwhile, President Sarkozy, who was running for a second term, was struggling in the polls. The financial crisis of 2008 and subsequent global economic recession had impacted France very negatively. By early 2012, unemployment was around 10 percent,

Sarkozy's government was running a fiscal deficit of 5 percent of gross domestic product (GDP), and France's credit rating had been downgraded by one of the main rating agencies, Standard & Poor's. In addition, Sarkozy's bombastic style and penchant for glitz, glamor, and personal drama were viewed with distaste by much of the French public. In a bid to bolster his ratings, Sarkozy embraced populist policies and rhetoric, railing against immigrants, advocating stronger powers for the police, and calling for the European Union (EU) to reintroduce border controls between EU countries as an emergency measure to curb immigration.

Other candidates in the presidential race included the centrist François Bayrou, Norwegian-born ecologist Eva Joly, militant Socialist Jean-Luc Mélenchon, and far-right National Front nominee Marine Le Pen. In the first round of voting on April 22, 2012, Hollande emerged in first place, with 29 percent of the vote, while Sarkozy trailed him in second place, with 27 percent. The biggest shock of the night, however, was the strong showing of Le Pen, who came in third place, with 18 percent—the highest share the National Front had ever received in a presidential ballot. Le Pen's father, Jean-Marie, had won 17 percent in the 2002 presidential election. His score had caused an even bigger upset at the time because he also took second place and thus qualified for the second-round runoff against incumbent Jacques Chirac, who easily defeated him. Marine Le Pen achieved her electoral success by espousing a similar cocktail of policies as her father, including hostility to immigrants, Muslims, the EU, and globalization, all the while supporting more government spending on employment and pensions.

In the two weeks between the first and second rounds, Sarkozy made a rightward lurch in a bid to win over enough of Le Pen's supporters to return him to the presidency. Hollande steered away from populist rhetoric and sought to portray himself instead as "Mr. Normal," a principled politician who could be trusted to steer the country sensibly toward calmer waters. His policy platform included a pledge to raise taxes on France's wealthiest citizens by imposing a 75 percent tax rate on income above $1.3 million and the introduction of a tax on financial transactions. Under his fiscal plan, France would aim to eliminate its public deficit by 2017, whereas Sarkozy's plan provided for a balanced budget by 2016.

On May 2, Hollande and Sarkozy held their only debate in which Europe's debt crisis featured prominently. Hollande spoke in favor of creating Eurobonds—debt obligations that could be issued by one country in the seventeen-member eurozone and would be guaranteed by the sixteen other countries that use the euro as their currency. By contrast, Sarkozy was strongly opposed to Eurobonds. Throughout the campaign Sarkozy was accused of being too close and too subservient to German Chancellor Angela Merkel, who was spearheading the move to force Europe's governments to slash public spending in order to reduce deficit and debt levels. The Merkel-Sarkozy partnership was dubbed "Merkozy" by the media, who also noted how Germany, with its bigger and faster-growing economy, was the dominant partner in the relationship. Hollande argued that France and Europe had too onesidedly embraced Merkozy-style austerity to the detriment of economic growth. His argument struck a chord with French voters, who chose Hollande over Sarkozy, albeit by a relatively narrow margin of 51.6 percent to 48.4 percent. The socialists followed up their triumph in June by winning a convincing victory in France's parliamentary elections, which further consolidated Hollande's power base.

MODESTY, PRUDENCE ADVOCATED AT INAUGURATION

The inauguration of the Fifth Republic's seventh president was a more modest affair than that of Sarkozy in 2007, in tune with the more somber economic times. Whereas Sarkozy's inauguration was a lavish occasion in which his wife and children were center-stage,

Hollande invited fewer personal guests and his four children were absent, although his current partner, journalist Valérie Trierweiler, did attend. The day was marred by bad weather, and a torrential downpour caused the new president to be soaked to the skin. Later that afternoon, the presidential plane was struck by lightning and forced to turn back when it was flying Hollande to Berlin to meet Chancellor Merkel. Hollande boarded a second plane and the meeting went ahead as scheduled.

In his inauguration speech, Hollande said, "The mandate I received from the French people on 6 May is to put France back on her feet, in a fair way." The new president reaffirmed his commitment to upholding the secular nature of the French state, which requires a strict separation to be maintained between church and state. On economic policy, he sought to draw a sharp distinction between his values and those of his predecessor, saying, "It's time to put production back above speculation, future investment above present satisfaction, sustainable employment above immediate profit." He promised to push the European Union to adopt a new compact to promote jobs and growth to complement the Fiscal Treaty that twenty-five of the twenty-seven EU countries had signed in March 2012. The Fiscal Treaty strengthened EU-level controls over national budgets, providing for automatic fines to be imposed on countries that exceeded the agreed public spending limits. Hollande also made two symbolic gestures that were revealing of his values: He laid wreaths to Jean Ferry, architect of France's secular public education system, and to Marie Curie, the Polish-born Nobel Prize–winning scientist.

Pivoting Away From Austerity

Hollande's election immediately altered the tenor of the discourse surrounding Europe's debt crisis. Whereas austerity had been the buzzword for the previous couple of years, jobs and growth became the new mantra. Just days after his inauguration, this mood shift was evident when he attended the Group of Eight (G8) world leaders' summit at the U.S. president's retreat in Camp David, Maryland, on May 18 to 19. "There's now an emerging consensus that more must be done to promote growth and job creation," said U.S. President Barack Obama, following a bilateral meeting with Hollande. On June 29, EU leaders reached an agreement on a new "compact for growth and jobs" through which they planned to leverage up to $156 billion through the European Investment Bank to help the most troubled EU economies back on their feet. On September 6, 2012, the European Central Bank (ECB) unveiled a new plan to support indebted countries by buying back their sovereign bonds from secondary markets.

The move was welcomed by Hollande, as it was by most European leaders, one notable exception being the German central bank—the Bundesbank—which argued that it undermined the credibility of political leaders to resolve the debt crisis. The Bundesbank has grown increasingly hostile to the ECB's interventions to help indebted countries, alleging they encourage governments to be fiscally irresponsible. On domestic policy, Hollande immediately reversed Sarkozy's plan to increase the retirement age from sixty to sixty-two years for workers who entered employment at age eighteen.

By the end of 2012, however, Hollande's popularity had plummeted as the outlook for the French economy remained bleak. The new president was attracting growing criticism both on matters of style—he was accused of being weak and indecisive—and substance, with detractors alleging that his policies were doing nothing to restore growth and competitiveness to the country. For example, his planned 75 percent tax rate on the top income bracket was being slammed for driving France's wealthiest entrepreneurs into exile to countries with lower tax rates, such as the United Kingdom and Switzerland. Doubts were being expressed too about his willingness and ability to push through the kind of structural reforms to France's rigidly regulated labor and product markets—similar to the reforms that Germany made in the early 2000s and that have given Germany a competitive edge over its neighbor ever since.

In the foreign policy domain, Hollande differed from Sarkozy too, although perhaps not quite as much as some had predicted before his election. For example, with Iran, many had thought that Hollande would be less hawkish than Sarkozy, who had led Western countries' efforts to tighten sanctions against the Iranian leadership to dissuade them from developing nuclear weapons. However, while Hollande employed less-combative rhetoric, he endorsed the extremely tough economic sanctions against Iran that Sarkozy and his EU partners had crafted together with the blessing of the United States. On Afghanistan, Hollande reaffirmed his campaign pledge to bring French combat troops home by the end of 2012, some eighteen months before the North Atlantic Treaty Organization (NATO) mission was due to complete the handover of the country's national security to the Afghans. At the same time, he stressed that France would continue to support the international effort to aid Afghanistan by providing some noncombat troops.

—Brian Beary

Following is the text of the inauguration speech delivered by François Hollande, president of France, on May 15, 2012.

DOCUMENT   *President Hollande's Inaugural Address*

May 15, 2012

On this day of my investiture into the highest office of the state, I send the French people a message of confidence.

We are a great country which, through its history, has always been able to brave the ordeals and take up the challenges facing it. Every time, it succeeded in doing so by remaining what it is. Always through high-mindedness and openness. Never through self-abasement or by self-absorption.

The mandate I received from the French people on 6 May is to put France back on her feet, in a fair way. Open up a new way in Europe. Contribute to world peace and the protection of the planet.

I appreciate the fact that we are under great pressure: massive debt, weak growth, high unemployment, damaged competitiveness and a Europe struggling to overcome the crisis.

But I say this right here: there's no inevitability, if a common desire motivates us, a clear direction is set and we fully mobilize our strengths and assets. These are significant: the productiveness of our workforce, the excellence of our researchers, the dynamism of our entrepreneurs, the work of our farmers, the quality of our public services, the global influence of our culture and language, without forgetting our demographic vitality and the eagerness of our young people.

The first condition for new-found confidence is the nation's unity. Our differences mustn't become divisions, or our diversity discord. The country needs calm, reconciliation and to come together. It's the President of the Republic's role to help bring this about.

To enable all French people, without exception, to live by the same values, those of the Republic. This is my pressing duty. Whatever our age, whatever our firm beliefs, wherever we live—in mainland France or in overseas France, in our towns and cities or in our rural areas, we are France. Not one France set against another, but a reunited France with the same community of destiny.

And I'll reaffirm on every occasion our inviolable principles of laïcité [secularism],* just as I will fight racism, anti-Semitism and all forms of discrimination.

Confidence is also about setting the example.

As President of the Republic, I shall fully shoulder the exceptional responsibilities of this high office. I shall set the priorities, but I shall not decide everything or on behalf of everyone. In accordance with the constitution, the government will determine and conduct the nation's policy. The rights of parliament will be respected. The judiciary will have every guarantee of independence. State power will be exercised with dignity but simplicity. With great ambition for the country. And scrupulous sobriety of conduct. The state will be impartial, because it is the property of all French people and does not belong to those who have been given responsibility for it. The rules on the appointment of public officials will be strict. And loyalty, competence and a sense of the general interest will be the sole criteria in determining my choice of the state's most senior servants. France has the good fortune to have an excellent civil service. I want to express to it my gratitude and my expectations of it and each of its members. Confidence lies in democracy itself. I believe in local democracy and intend to revitalize it through a new act of decentralization that gives new freedom to develop our territories.

I believe in social democracy, and new areas of negotiation will be opened up to the two sides of industry, whom I shall respect—both the employees' representatives and professional organizations. I believe in citizens' democracy, that of voluntary organizations and civic engagement, which will be supported for the millions of volunteers who dedicate themselves to it.

Confidence depends on the justice of decisions. Justice in the very concept of wealth creation. It's time to put production back above speculation, future investment above present satisfaction, sustainable employment above immediate profit. It's time to embark on a transition on energy and the environment. It's time to push back a new frontier for technological development and innovation. But justice, too, in the way the essential effort is distributed. There cannot be sacrifices for ever more people and privileges for ever fewer. This will be the thrust of the reforms the government will carry out, with a concern to reward merit, work and initiative and to discourage exorbitant income and remuneration.

Justice will be the criterion on which each public decision will be taken.

Finally, the Republic must have confidence in young people. I shall put them back in their rightful place: first place. That's the basis of my commitment to the Republic's schools, because their mission is vital to our country's cohesion and the success of our economy. That's the desire that drives me to modernize professional training, support young people into work and fight job insecurity. That's also the admirable idea of civic service that I intend to revive.

Ladies and gentlemen,

Today many peoples—above all in Europe—are watching us expectantly.

To overcome the crisis that is hitting it, Europe needs projects. It needs solidarity. It needs growth. I shall propose to our partners a new pact combining the necessary reduction in public debt with the essential stimulation of the economy. And I shall express to them the need for our continent to protect, in such an unstable world, not only its values but also its interests, in the name of the reciprocity principle in trade.

France is a nation engaged in the world. Through her history, her culture, her values of humanism, universality and freedom, she holds a unique place in it. The Declaration of the Rights of Man and of the Citizen has reached every corner of the globe. We must be its guardians and stand alongside all those democratic forces in the world that swear by its principles. France will respect all peoples; she will be true everywhere to her destiny, which is to uphold the freedom of peoples, the honour of the oppressed, the dignity of women.

At this moment, when I bear responsibility for our country's destiny and for representing it in the world, I pay tribute to my predecessors—all those before me who have held the responsibility of leading the Republic: Charles de Gaulle, who put his prestige at the service of France's greatness and sovereignty, Georges Pompidou, who made the industrial imperative a national challenge, Valéry Giscard d'Estaing, who relaunched society's modernization, François Mitterrand, who did so much for freedoms and social progress, Jacques Chirac, who marked his commitment to the values of the Republic, and Nicolas Sarkozy, to whom I extend my best wishes for the new life that opens up before him.

Long live the Republic.

Long live France.

*Laïcité goes beyond the concept of secularism, embracing the strict neutrality of the state.

SOURCE: Embassy of France in Washington. "President François Hollande's Inauguration Speech." May 15, 2012. http://ambafrance-us.org/spip.php?article3469.

OTHER HISTORIC DOCUMENTS OF INTEREST

FROM THIS VOLUME

FROM PREVIOUS *HISTORIC DOCUMENTS*

U.S. Task Force Makes Recommendations Against Routine Prostate Cancer Screening

MAY 22, 2012

Prostate cancer is the most common type of cancer for men and the number two cancer killer after lung cancer. It was estimated that nearly 250,000 men would be diagnosed with prostate cancer in 2012. And although many men view a prostate cancer diagnosis as a death sentence, the tumor grows very slowly, and most doctors say that one is more likely to die with prostate cancer than from it. Even so, the National Cancer Institute estimated that approximately 28,170 men would die from prostate cancer in 2012.

Approximately 81 percent of those diagnosed each year find their cancer at a very early stage using a routine screening test known as the prostate-specific antigen, or PSA, test, and for younger men, doctors often choose biopsies and blood tests to monitor cancer growth. In older men, however, surgery is currently the preferred option. This year, studies and recommendations turned the tables on screenings and how prostate cancer is monitored and treated. The most controversial among them was the decision released in May by the U.S. Preventive Services Task Force (USPSTF), recommending against routine prostate cancer screening. Backlash against the decision was swift and raised concern in medical circles about the likelihood that men would forgo discussions with their doctors about whether prostate cancer screening might be right for them. The general finding of research released in 2012 was that many men might be better off not knowing that they have prostate cancer because of the risks associated with treatments that may not be necessary. "The more technology advances to detect asymptomatic disease, the more we learn that not all of it needs to be detected," said Dr. Michael LeFevre, co–vice chair of the USPSTF. Before, he said, "The assumption was that any cancer we found was the bad kind."

New Guidelines

In 2008, the USPSTF recommended that men over age seventy-five should not get a prostate cancer screening; however, it called the benefits for younger men "uncertain." In 2012, the USPSTF reversed its earlier recommendation, saying that it "recommends against PSA-based screening for prostate cancer" regardless of the person's age, as long as he is overall healthy. This recommendation does not apply to men who currently have cancer because the USPSTF did not examine this group in its research.

The USPSTF, an independent body that advises the government on health matters, reached its conclusion because the PSA test can be unreliable. The data reviewed by the task force indicate that the test prevents very few deaths—at most 1 in 1,000—and can lead to false positives. These false positives, or even accurate positive diagnoses of prostate cancer, can cause men to choose radical treatments. According to their data, the USPSTF reports that of

1,000 men screened for the disease, the treatment path chosen afterward leaves 1 man with a blood clot, 2 with heart attacks, and as many as 40 with impotence or urinary incontinence.

The task force, however, did recognize the importance of finding a way to more accurately detect and treat prostate cancer. "There is a critical need for a better test—one that leads to early detection of cancers that threaten men's health, but minimizes unnecessary, risky tests and treatments that do not lead to longer or more healthful lives," said Dr. Virginia Moyer, the USPSTF chair. Moyer added that she would like to see additional research done on reducing the number of false positives produced by the PSA test as well as a better method for distinguishing between men with slow-progressing versus rapidly progressing lethal prostate cancer.

The USPSTF's recommendation experienced a backlash similar to that in 2009 when it recommended against routine mammograms for women younger than fifty. "It is inappropriate and irresponsible to issue a blanket statement against PSA testing, particularly for at-risk populations, such as African American men. Men who are in good health and have more than a 10–15 year life expectancy should have the choice to be tested and not discouraged from doing so. There is strong evidence that PSA testing saves lives. . . . Rather than instruct primary care physicians to discourage men from having a PSA test, the Task Force should instead focus on how best to educate primary care physicians regarding targeted screening and how to counsel patients about their prostate cancer risk," said American Urological Association President Sushil Lacy of the 2012 recommendations. Dr. Ian Thompson, chair of the prostate cancer panel at the American Urological Association, said it would be better if the USPSTF had recommended testing on an individual basis, based on risk factors. According to Thompson, since the test has been in use, prostate cancer deaths have been reduced by nearly half, and many advances have been made in treating tumors early with lower-risk strategies that become unavailable once the tumor reaches later stages. A study released in the journal *Cancer* concluded that the test causes 17,000 fewer cases of deadly forms of prostate cancer and that without a routine test, the rate of metastatic prostate cancer increases threefold.

The USPSTF, as well as the American Cancer Society, however, contends that previous studies have not truly evaluated the survival benefits associated with the test because most have looked at a five-year survival rate. Men who got the test were more likely to survive the five-year period after being diagnosed than those who were not tested, but there was no indication that the test itself helped extend a person's life. "They were finding the cancer earlier, so the time from diagnosis to death was longer, but the patient wasn't actually living longer," said Dr. Otis Brawley, chief medical officer at the American Cancer Society. "So these men were living a longer proportion of their lives knowing they have cancer, but they weren't dying at a later date."

Some medical experts have expressed concern that, because general practitioners often rely on USPSTF guidelines to determine what to talk about with and test their patients for, it may now be up to the patient to discuss prostate cancer risk and testing with their doctors. The USPSTF said that men who elect to are still able to get a PSA test, and it can still be offered by doctors to their patients as long as the risks and benefits are discussed. Many medical experts advise that once men reach their fifties, they begin talking about their prostate cancer risk factors with their doctors.

WATCHFUL WAITING

Approximately 90 percent of men who receive a prostate cancer diagnosis opt for surgery to remove the tumor, invasive biopsies, or other treatments. Approximately 100,000 to

120,000 men choose to have their prostate removed each year, and more than 1,000 men die from complications related to treatment. However, according to a study published in the *New England Journal of Medicine* in July 2012, men in the early stages of the disease will live just as long, and avoid some of the risks associated with surgery including impotence and incontinence, if they adopt a "watchful waiting" approach instead.

In the largest trial on this topic to date, the Prostate Cancer Intervention Versus Observation Trial (PIVOT) watched 731 men in the early stages of the disease. The men in the trial were randomly assigned to one of two groups—those who received surgery to remove the tumor and those who followed a watchful waiting approach until the disease showed progression. After the median follow-up of ten years, approximately half of the men in the study died, most of them from reasons other than prostate cancer. The researchers concluded that there was no statistical significance in the number of men who died in each of the two groups. Only fifty-two men in the study died from prostate cancer during the trial period. "Men have a strong belief that if they are diagnosed with cancer, they will die from the cancer if it's left untreated, and they believe that treatment will cure them," said lead study author Dr. Timothy J. Wilt. "This study adds to growing evidence that observation can be a wise and preferred treatment option for the vast majority of men. It allows them to live a similar length of life and avoid death from prostate cancer and avoid the harms of treatment," he continued.

The study was not an overall recommendation against surgery. Within the trial group, researchers watched a subgroup of men that had high-risk cancers, and those undergoing surgery saw 13 percent fewer deaths than the group that was assigned to watchful waiting. Researchers also caution that they looked only at men in early stages of the disease and only older patients.

BENEFITS OF ASPIRIN

In August, the results of a study on the impact of aspirin on prostate cancer were published in the *Journal of Clinical Oncology*. Researchers looked at nearly 6,000 men with prostate cancer who had received surgery or radiotherapy as treatment. The researchers, who chose the men from the national database Cancer of the Prostate Strategic Urologic Research Endeavor known as CaPSURE, found slightly more than one third were taking anticoagulants, and most of those were taking aspirin, an anti-inflammatory drug. According to the study, the men who regularly took aspirin were less than half as likely to die as those who did not take aspirin over a ten-year period. In total, 8 percent of those who did not take aspirin died during the ten-year period, while only 3 percent of those taking aspirin did. Additionally, those taking aspirin regularly had a lower percentage of cancer recurrence as well as a lower likelihood of the cancer spreading into the bones. "The results from this study suggest that aspirin prevents the growth of tumor cells in prostate cancer, especially in high-risk prostate cancer, for which we do not have a very good treatment currently," said Dr. Kevin Choe, an author of the study. "But we need to better understand the optimal use of aspirin before routinely recommending it to all prostate cancer patients," he said.

A similar study was conducted in 2012 at the Fox Chase Cancer Center in Pennsylvania, where 2,051 men were followed for eighteen months. Those not taking aspirin were twice as likely to have their cancer recur within the study period. According to the American Cancer Society's Dr. Brawley, "Inflammation may not cause a cancer, but it may promote cancer—it may be the fertilizer that makes it grow."

ADDITIONAL STUDIES

A number of other studies on prostate cancer were released in 2012. One, published in the *American Journal of Epidemiology,* said that men working the night shift had a nearly three times greater risk of developing prostate cancer. Other studies concluded that some risky behaviors, like eating pan-fried meat on a weekly basis, could increase prostate cancer risk. Research also linked high blood pressure with the increased risk of dying from prostate cancer and identified a possible genetic signature—or the way genes switch on and off—that could help indicate which prostate cancer patients are least likely to survive. Another study conducted by scientists at the Fred Hutchinson Cancer Research Center found that circumcision lowers a risk of developing prostate cancer, while the American Association for Cancer Research found drinking green tea could help reduce inflammation in those men who will undergo prostate-removal surgery.

—Heather Kerrigan

> *Following is the edited text of the recommendation of the U.S. Preventive Services Task Force, released on May 22, 2012, advising against prostate cancer screening in most cases.*

USPSTF Recommendation Against Prostate Cancer Screening

May 22, 2012

[All footnotes and tables, and references to them, have been omitted.]

SUMMARY OF RECOMMENDATION AND EVIDENCE

The U.S. Preventive Services Task Force (USPSTF) recommends against prostate-specific antigen (PSA)–based screening for prostate cancer.

Rationale

Importance

Prostate cancer is the most commonly diagnosed non-skin cancer in men in the United States, with a lifetime risk for diagnosis currently estimated at 15.9%. Most cases of prostate cancer have a good prognosis, even without treatment, but some are aggressive; the lifetime risk of dying of prostate cancer is 2.8%. Prostate cancer is rare before age 50 years and very few men die of prostate cancer before age 60 years. Seventy percent of deaths due to prostate cancer occur after age 75 years.

Detection

Contemporary recommendations for prostate cancer screening all incorporate the measurement of serum PSA levels; other methods of detection, such as digital rectal examination or ultrasonography, may be included. There is convincing evidence that PSA-based screening programs result in the detection of many cases of asymptomatic prostate cancer. There is also convincing evidence that a substantial percentage of men who have asymptomatic cancer detected by PSA screening have a tumor that either will not progress or will progress so slowly that it would have remained asymptomatic for the man's lifetime. The terms "overdiagnosis" or "pseudo-disease" are used to describe both situations. The rate of overdiagnosis of prostate cancer increases as the number of men subjected to biopsy increases. The number of cancer cases that could be detected in a screened population is large; a single study in which men eligible for PSA screening had biopsy regardless of PSA level detected cancer in nearly 25% of men. The rate of overdiagnosis also depends on life expectancy at the time of diagnosis. A cancer diagnosis in men with shorter life expectancies because of chronic diseases or age is much more likely to be overdiagnosis. The precise magnitude of overdiagnosis associated with any screening and treatment program is difficult to determine, but estimates from the 2 largest trials suggest overdiagnosis rates of 17% to 50% for prostate cancer screening.

Benefits of Detection and Early Treatment

The primary goal of prostate cancer screening is to reduce deaths due to prostate cancer and, thus, increase length of life. An additional important outcome would be a reduction in the development of symptomatic metastatic disease. Reduction in prostate cancer mortality was the primary outcome used in available randomized, controlled trials of prostate cancer screening. Although 1 screening trial reported on the presence of metastatic disease at the time of prostate cancer diagnosis, no study reported on the effect of screening on the development of subsequent metastatic disease, making it difficult to assess the effect of lead-time bias on the reported rates.

Men with screen-detected cancer can potentially fall into 1 of 3 categories: those whose cancer will result in death despite early diagnosis and treatment, those who will have good outcomes in the absence of screening, and those for whom early diagnosis and treatment improves survival. Only randomized trials of screening allow an accurate estimate of the number of men who fall into the latter category. There is convincing evidence that the number of men who avoid dying of prostate cancer because of screening after 10 to 14 years is, at best, very small. Two major trials of PSA screening were considered by the USPSTF: the U.S. PLCO (Prostate, Lung, Colorectal, and Ovarian) Cancer Screening Trial and the ERSPC (European Randomized Study of Screening for Prostate Cancer). The U.S. trial did not demonstrate any prostate cancer mortality reduction. The European trial found a reduction in prostate cancer deaths of approximately 1 death per 1000 men screened in a subgroup of men aged 55 to 69 years. This result was heavily influenced by the results of 2 countries; 5 of the 7 countries reporting results did not find a statistically significant reduction. All-cause mortality in the European trial was nearly identical in the screened and nonscreened groups.

There is adequate evidence that the benefit of PSA screening and early treatment ranges from 0 to 1 prostate cancer deaths avoided per 1000 men screened.

Harms of Detection and Early Treatment

Harms Related to Screening and Diagnostic Procedures

Convincing evidence demonstrates that the PSA test often produces false-positive results (approximately 80% of positive PSA test results are false-positive when cutoffs between 2.5 and 4.0 µg/L are used). There is adequate evidence that false-positive PSA test results are associated with negative psychological effects, including persistent worry about prostate cancer. Men who have a false-positive test result are more likely to have additional testing, including 1 or more biopsies, in the following year than those who have a negative test result. Over 10 years, approximately 15% to 20% of men will have a PSA test result that triggers a biopsy, depending on the PSA threshold and testing interval used. New evidence from a randomized trial of treatment of screen-detected cancer indicates that roughly one third of men who have prostate biopsy experience pain, fever, bleeding, infection, transient urinary difficulties, or other issues requiring clinician follow-up that the men consider a "moderate or major problem"; approximately 1% require hospitalization.

The USPSTF considered the magnitude of these harms associated with screening and diagnostic procedures to be at least small.

Harms Related to Treatment of Screen-Detected Cancer

Adequate evidence shows that nearly 90% of men with PSA-detected prostate cancer in the United States have early treatment with surgery, radiation, or androgen deprivation therapy. Adequate evidence shows that up to 5 in 1000 men will die within 1 month of prostate cancer surgery and between 10 and 70 men will have serious complications but survive. Radiotherapy and surgery result in long-term adverse effects, including urinary incontinence and erectile dysfunction in at least 200 to 300 of 1000 men treated with these therapies. Radiotherapy is also associated with bowel dysfunction.

Some clinicians have used androgen deprivation therapy as primary therapy for early-stage prostate cancer, particularly in older men, although this is not a U.S. Food and Drug Administration (FDA)–approved indication and it has not been shown to improve survival in localized prostate cancer. Adequate evidence shows that androgen deprivation therapy for localized prostate cancer is associated with erectile dysfunction (in approximately 400 of 1000 men treated), as well as gynecomastia and hot flashes.

There is convincing evidence that PSA-based screening leads to substantial overdiagnosis of prostate tumors. The amount of overdiagnosis of prostate cancer is of important concern because a man with cancer that would remain asymptomatic for the remainder of his life cannot benefit from screening or treatment. There is a high propensity for physicians and patients to elect to treat most cases of screen-detected cancer, given our current inability to distinguish tumors that will remain indolent from those destined to be lethal. Thus, many men are being subjected to the harms of treatment of prostate cancer that will never become symptomatic. Even for men whose screen-detected cancer would otherwise have been later identified without screening, most experience the same outcome and are, therefore, subjected to the harms of treatment for a much longer period of time. There is convincing evidence that PSA-based screening for prostate cancer results in considerable overtreatment and its associated harms.

The USPSTF considered the magnitude of these treatment-associated harms to be at least moderate.

USPSTF Assessment

Although the precise, long-term effect of PSA screening on prostate cancer–specific mortality remains uncertain, existing studies adequately demonstrate that the reduction in prostate cancer mortality after 10 to 14 years is, at most, very small, even for men in what seems to be the optimal age range of 55 to 69 years. There is no apparent reduction in all-cause mortality. In contrast, the harms associated with the diagnosis and treatment of screen-detected cancer are common, occur early, often persist, and include a small but real risk for premature death. Many more men in a screened population will experience the harms of screening and treatment of screen-detected disease than will experience the benefit. The inevitability of overdiagnosis and overtreatment of prostate cancer as a result of screening means that many men will experience the adverse effects of diagnosis and treatment of a disease that would have remained asymptomatic throughout their lives. Assessing the balance of benefits and harms requires weighing a moderate to high probability of early and persistent harm from treatment against the very low probability of preventing a death from prostate cancer in the long term.

The USPSTF concludes that there is moderate certainty that the benefits of PSA-based screening for prostate cancer do not outweigh the harms.

Clinical Considerations

Although the USPSTF discourages the use of screening tests for which the benefits do not outweigh the harms in the target population, it recognizes the common use of PSA screening in practice today and understands that some men will continue to request screening and some physicians will continue to offer it. The decision to initiate or continue PSA screening should reflect an explicit understanding of the possible benefits and harms and respect patients' preferences. Physicians should not offer or order PSA screening unless they are prepared to engage in shared decision making that enables an informed choice by patients. Similarly, patients requesting PSA screening should be provided with the opportunity to make informed choices to be screened that reflect their values about specific benefits and harms. Community- and employer-based screening should be discontinued.

The treatment of some cases of clinically localized prostate cancer can change the natural history of the disease and may reduce morbidity and mortality in a small percentage of men, although the prognosis for clinically localized cancer is generally good regardless of the method of detection, even in the absence of treatment. The primary goal of PSA-based screening is to find men for whom treatment would reduce morbidity and mortality. Studies demonstrate that the number of men who experience this benefit is, at most, very small, and PSA-based screening as currently implemented in the United States produces more harms than benefits in the screened population. It is not known whether an alternative approach to screening and management of screen-detected disease could achieve the same or greater benefits while reducing the harms. Focusing screening on men at increased risk for prostate cancer mortality may improve the balance of benefits and harms, but existing studies do not allow conclusions about a greater absolute or relative benefit from screening in these populations. Lengthening the interval between screening tests may reduce harms without affecting cancer mortality; the only screening trial that demonstrated a prostate cancer–specific mortality benefit generally used a 2- to 4-year screening interval. Other potential ways to reduce diagnostic- and treatment-related harms include increasing the PSA threshold used to trigger the decision for biopsy or need for treatment, or reducing the number of men having active treatment at the time of diagnosis through watchful waiting or active surveillance. Periodic digital rectal examinations could also be an alternative strategy worthy of further study. In the only randomized trial demonstrating a mortality reduction from radical prostatectomy for clinically localized cancer, a high percentage of men had palpable cancer. All of these approaches require additional research to better elucidate their merits and pitfalls and more clearly define an approach to the diagnosis and management of prostate cancer that optimizes the benefits while minimizing the harms.

Patient Population Under Consideration

This recommendation applies to men in the general U.S. population. Older age is the strongest risk factor for the development of prostate cancer. However, neither screening nor treatment trials show benefit in men older than 70 years. Across age ranges, black men and men with a family history of prostate cancer have an increased risk of developing and dying of prostate cancer. Black men are approximately twice as likely to die of prostate cancer than other men in the United States, and the reason for this disparity is unknown. Black men represented a small minority of participants in the randomized clinical trials of screening (4% of enrolled men in the PLCO trial were non-Hispanic black; although the ERSPC and other trials did not report the specific racial demographic characteristics of participants, they likely were predominately white).Thus, no firm conclusions can be made about the balance of benefits and harms of PSA-based screening in this population. However, it is problematic to selectively recommend PSA-based screening for black men in the absence of data that support a more favorable balance of risks and benefits. . . .

Screening Tests

Prostate-specific antigen–based screening in men aged 50 to 74 years has been evaluated in 5 unique randomized, controlled trials of single or interval PSA testing with various PSA cutoffs and screening intervals, along with other screening methods, such as digital rectal examination or transrectal ultrasonography. Screening tests or programs that do not incorporate PSA testing, including digital rectal examination alone, have not been adequately evaluated in controlled studies.

The PLCO trial found a nonstatistically significant increase in prostate cancer mortality in the annual screening group at 11.5 and 13 years, with results consistently favoring the usual care group.

A prespecified subgroup analysis of men aged 55 to 69 years in the ERSPC trial demonstrated a prostate cancer mortality rate ratio (RR) of 0.80 (95% CI, 0.65 to 0.98) in screened men after a median follow-up of 9 years, with similar findings at 11 years (RR, 0.79 [CI, 0.68 to 0.91]). Of the 7 centers included in the ERSPC analysis, only 2 countries (Sweden and the Netherlands) reported statistically significant reductions in prostate cancer mortality after 11 years (5 did not), and these results seem to drive the overall benefit found in this trial. No study reported any factors, including patient age, adherence to site or study protocol, length of follow-up, PSA thresholds, or intervals between tests, that could clearly explain why mortality reductions were larger in Sweden or the Netherlands than in other European countries or the United States (PLCO trial). Combining the results through meta-analysis may be inappropriate due to clinical and methodological differences across trials.

No study found a difference in overall or all-cause mortality. This probably reflects the high rates of competing mortality in this age group, because these men are more likely to die of prostate cancer, as well as the limited power of prostate cancer screening trials to detect differences in all-cause mortality, should they exist. Even in the "core" age group of 55 to 69 years in the ERSPC trial, only 462 of 17,256 deaths were due to prostate cancer. The all-cause mortality RR was 1.00 (CI, 0.98 to 1.02) in all men randomly assigned to screening versus no screening. Results were similar in men aged 55 to 69 years. The absence of any trend toward a reduction in all-cause mortality is particularly important in the context of the difficulty of attributing death to a specific cause in this age group.

Treatment

Primary management strategies for PSA-detected prostate cancer include watchful waiting (observation and physical examination, with palliative treatment of symptoms), active surveillance (periodic monitoring with PSA tests, physical examinations, and repeated prostate biopsy) with conversion to potentially curative treatment at the sign of disease progression or worsening prognosis, and surgery or radiation therapy. There is no consensus about the optimal treatment of localized disease. From 1986 through 2005, PSA-based screening likely resulted in approximately 1 million additional U.S. men being treated with surgery, radiation therapy, or both compared with the time before the test was introduced.

At the time of the USPSTF's commissioned evidence review, only 1 recent randomized, controlled trial of surgical treatment versus observation for clinically localized prostate cancer was available. In the Scandinavian Prostate Cancer Group Study 4 trial, surgical management of localized, primarily clinically-detected prostate cancer was associated with an approximate 6% absolute reduction in prostate cancer and all-cause mortality at 12 to 15 years of follow-up; benefit seemed to be limited to men younger than 65 years. Subsequently, preliminary results were reported from another randomized trial that compared external beam radiotherapy (EBRT) with watchful waiting in 214 men with localized prostate cancer detected before initiation of PSA screening. At 20 years, survival did not differ between men randomly assigned to watchful waiting or EBRT (31% vs. 35%; $P = 0.26$). Prostate cancer mortality at 15 years was high in each group but did not differ between groups (23% vs. 19%; $P = 0.51$). External beam radiotherapy did reduce distant progression and recurrence-free survival. In men with localized prostate cancer detected in the early PSA screening era, preliminary findings from PIVOT show that, after 12 years, intention to treat with radical prostatectomy did not reduce disease-specific or all-cause mortality compared with observation; absolute differences were less than 3% and not statistically different. An ongoing trial in the United Kingdom (ProtecT [Prostate Testing for Cancer and Treatment]) comparing radical prostatectomy with EBRT or active surveillance has enrolled nearly 2000 men with PSA-detected prostate cancer. Results are expected in 2015.

Up to 0.5% of men will die within 30 days of having radical prostatectomy, and 3% to 7% will have serious surgical complications. Compared with men who choose watchful waiting, an additional 20% to 30% or more of men treated with radical prostatectomy will experience erectile dysfunction, urinary incontinence, or both after 1 to 10 years. Radiation therapy is also associated with increases in erectile, bowel, and bladder dysfunction.

[The section titled Other Considerations has been omitted. It contains information on research gaps, public comments received on a draft version of the recommendations, and response to those comments.]

SOURCE: U.S. Preventive Services Task Force. "Screening for Prostate Cancer. U.S. Preventive Services Task Force Recommendation Statement." May 22, 2012. http://www.uspreventiveservicestaskforce.org/prostatecancerscreening/prostatefinalrs.htm#summary.

OTHER HISTORIC DOCUMENTS OF INTEREST

FROM PREVIOUS *HISTORIC DOCUMENTS*

WikiLeaks Founder Denied Stay of Extradition

MAY 30, 2012

The nearly two-year legal effort to extradite WikiLeaks founder Julian Assange from the United Kingdom to Sweden for questioning related to sexual assault allegations came to a conclusion in the spring of 2012. The Supreme Court of the United Kingdom denied Assange's final appeal in the case in May, but Assange requested and received asylum from the Ecuadorian government in a last-ditch effort to avoid extradition. However, negotiations between Ecuador and the United Kingdom to arrange for Assange's safe departure have stalled, and Assange remains a temporary resident of the Ecuadorian Embassy in London.

A CONTROVERSIAL LEADER

An Australian citizen with a background in computer security, Assange gained worldwide fame as the founder of WikiLeaks, which describes itself as a "non-profit media organization dedicated to bringing important news and information to the public" that provides a "universal way for the revealing of suppressed and censored injustices." WikiLeaks maintains a website on which it publishes information submitted, or leaked, by anonymous sources to the organization's volunteer journalists. Such information is typically sensitive or classified material.

Under Assange's leadership, WikiLeaks published a series of reports on U.S. defense and diplomatic activities, making public the U.S. operations manual for the Guantánamo Bay Detention Center, the confidential Rules of Engagement for the War in Iraq, and a video of U.S. service members shooting Iraqi civilians from a helicopter. In 2010, WikiLeaks released more than 700,000 confidential U.S. documents, including internal records of the country's military action in Iraq and Afghanistan, as well as more than 250,000 diplomatic cables collected from approximately 250 U.S. embassies around the world. This last report not only created an embarrassment for the United States; State Department officials also warned the leak could have a real impact on the country's national security, including by potentially compromising some sources and intelligence officers. Following the leak, U.S. officials announced they were exploring possibilities for filing criminal charges against Assange.

A LEGAL PURSUIT

As the United States considered its legal options, prosecutors in Sweden also prepared a case against Assange. On August 20, 2010, Swedish prosecutors issued an arrest warrant for Assange, following allegations by two female WikiLeaks volunteers that he raped or sexually molested them. Assange decried the charges as a smear campaign and denied wrongdoing, though he did admit to having unprotected but consensual encounters with two women during a visit to Sweden in August. A preliminary investigation concluded there was no case against him with regard to the alleged rape, and prosecutors rescinded the warrant, though the molestation allegation remained. Assange left Sweden shortly after being questioned in the case and reportedly went into hiding in the United Kingdom. Assange's attorneys questioned the motivation behind the warrant and suggested that

American officials might be pressuring Sweden to arrest him so that he could be extradited to the United States for questioning and a possible trial.

Then in September 2010, Swedish prosecutors announced they were reopening the rape case against Assange after the complainants appealed the prosecutors' earlier decision to rescind the warrant. On November 18, Swedish courts approved the prosecutors' request to issue warrants to question Assange, and on November 20, the Stockholm Criminal Court issued an international arrest warrant. Ten days later, Interpol added Assange to its worldwide wanted list.

The following month, on December 2, the Swedish Prosecution Authority also issued a European Arrest Warrant, which allows for fast-tracked extradition between European Union (EU) member states. Assange turned himself in at a London police station on December 7 and was promptly arrested. While initially denied bail before the City of Westminster Magistrates' Court, Assange was released on conditional bail on December 16 after several of his supporters made arrangements to pay his bail and provide a location outside of London for his house arrest.

Legal proceedings against Assange continued through 2011. In February, Assange appeared before London's Belmarsh Magistrates' Court, which ruled in favor of his extradition to Sweden. Assange appealed the decision to the British High Court, which heard his case in July. On November 2, the High Court ruled against Assange; however, it later granted him permission to appeal its decision to the Supreme Court of the United Kingdom on a legal technicality. Under a European Council framework decision reached in 2002 and the Extradition Act of 2003, European Arrest Warrants must be issued by a "judicial authority." Assange and his lawyer, Dinah Rose, claimed that the Swedish prosecutor who issued the warrant for his arrest, Marianne Ny, did not qualify as such an authority. They argued that a judicial authority "must be a person who is competent to exercise judicial authority and that such competence requires impartiality and independence of both the executive and the parties" and that since Ny was a party in the criminal proceeding against Assange, she could not be considered objective and did not qualify as a judicial authority. Ny's lawyers argued in turn that judicial authority has a broader meaning that describes "any person or body authorised to play a part in the judicial process." In Britain, for example, only judges can order a European Arrest Warrant, but it is standard practice in Sweden to issue warrants by public prosecutor.

The Final Decision

On February 1 and 2, 2012, the Supreme Court of the United Kingdom heard Assange's appeal, which it denied in a 5–2 decision on May 30. In a formal press statement, the Court said, "By a majority the court has concluded that the Swedish public prosecutor was a 'judicial authority' within the meaning of both the framework decision and the Extradition Act." The Court ruled that under the Treaty on European Union, framework decisions bind member states only to the intended result of a decision, but they allow national authorities to determine what method they will use to achieve that result. The Court concluded that the framework decision applying to European Arrest Warrants was not intended to restrict the meaning of a judicial authority to a judge, noting that an earlier draft of the decision included a statement expressly identifying prosecutors as judicial authorities. They further acknowledged that eleven member states had designated public prosecutors as judicial authorities who could issue European Arrest Warrants, and that subsequent reviews of such practices had found no cause for concern.

In an unusual move, the Court granted Assange's lawyers two weeks to submit an application to reopen the case, as well as a stay of extradition for Assange while the application was prepared. Rose had pointed out that the justices' decision suggested they had based their ruling on a point of law in the Vienna Convention on the Law of Treaties that had not been argued on by either side in court, and which the Court had not told either side it would be taking into account. The Court ultimately found that Rose had indeed been given an opportunity to challenge the applicability of the Vienna Convention to Assange's case, and dismissed Assange's application on June 14. Assange could have made a final appeal to the European Court of Human Rights, but he did not, removing the last legal barrier to his extradition to Sweden.

Asylum Sought, Granted

On June 19, Assange appeared at the Ecuadorian Embassy in London, requesting political asylum. He and his legal team said they believed it very likely that if he were sent to Sweden, he would ultimately be extradited to the United States, where he would be prosecuted in an unfair trial and would face life in jail or the death penalty. Assange claimed Ecuadorian President Rafael Correa had invited him to seek asylum in that country during an interview for Assange's television show on Russia Today that had been filmed earlier in the year.

Scotland Yard said that by leaving his house arrest, Assange had broken the terms of his bail and could be subject to arrest, but only if he left the embassy. Britain's Foreign Office had confirmed that the embassy was diplomatic territory and therefore beyond the reach of police. Under these circumstances, many questioned whether Assange would even be able to travel to Ecuador if he received asylum, noting that the Ecuadorians could make Assange a diplomat accredited to the Court of St. James by the Foreign Office in order for him to evade arrest but that any such attempt would be rebuffed by UK officials. Alternatively, Assange could be given an Ecuadorian diplomatic passport, but that could also make him an Ecuadorian national, in which case, he would not be able to seek asylum in his own country's embassy. British Foreign Secretary William Hague affirmed during a press conference on the matter that Britain would not grant Assange safe passage out of the country and that the country was legally bound to extradite him to Sweden.

Ecuador considered Assange's request for nearly two months. In a statement, Ecuadorian Ambassador Anna Alban emphasized Ecuador's "long and well-established tradition of supporting human rights" but added it was "not the intention of the Ecuadorian government to interfere with the processes of either the UK or Swedish governments." The two countries held a series of negotiations over the course of those two months, with Secretary Hague describing "seven formal discussions as well as many other conversations." British officials at one point threatened to force their way into the embassy to arrest Assange under an obscure law that would enable them to temporarily suspend the embassy's immunity and send in police.

On August 16, Ecuadorian Foreign Minister Ricardo Patiño announced that "faithful to its tradition of protecting those who seek refuge in its territory or in its diplomatic missions," Ecuador had "decided to grant diplomatic asylum to Julian Assange." Patiño said the government made its decision after British, Swedish, and U.S. authorities refused to guarantee that if Assange were extradited to Sweden, he would not be sent to the United States to face other charges. He also said Ecuadorian officials thought there "could be political persecution" and that Assange would not get a fair trial in the United States.

Swedish officials reacted angrily to the news. "Our firm legal and constitutional system guarantees the rights of each and everyone," said Swedish Foreign Minister Carl Bildt. "We firmly reject any accusations to the contrary." A foreign ministry spokesperson, Anders Jorle, said Sweden's legal system had been impugned by the decision and that the Ecuadorian ambassador had been summoned.

Assange at an Impasse

With the British threatening his arrest and between twenty and thirty Scotland Yard officers standing guard outside, Assange had little choice but to remain at the Ecuadorian Embassy. He reportedly slept on an air mattress in a small office that had been converted into a bedroom, had at least one cell phone, and had access to a computer with a broadband connection, enabling him to continue overseeing WikiLeaks.

Although WikiLeaks had shrunk significantly during Assange's nearly two-year legal battle in Britain, losing some of its best computer programmers and Assange loyalists, he continued to be active and outspoken. On August 19, Assange spoke from the balcony of the Ecuadorian Embassy, calling on the United States and President Barack Obama to end the "witch hunt against WikiLeaks" and promise not to prosecute the organization's staff or supporters. In October, publishing company OR Books announced it had acquired the rights to *Cypherpunks*, a book authored by Assange, Jacob Appelbaum, Jérémie Zimmermann, and Andy Müller-Maguhn about freedom and the Internet. Assange said the book, which went on sale in November, was meant as a response to long-standing worries about government control of the Internet. Then on December 20, Assange once again addressed supporters from the embassy balcony, assuring them he would press on with releasing more than a million new documents obtained from whistle-blowers and hackers by WikiLeaks.

Assange is likely to continue living inside the embassy until Ecuador and Britain reach a formal agreement that enables him to leave the embassy and country without being subject to arrest.

—Linda Fecteau

Following is the edited text of the judgment released on May 30, 2012, by the Supreme Court of the United Kingdom, denying WikiLeaks founder Julian Assange a stay of extradition.

British Court Issues Ruling on Assange Extradition

DOCUMENT

May 30, 2012

Easter Term
[2012] UKSC 22
On appeal from: [2011] EWHC Admin 2849

JUDGMENT
Assange (Appellant) v The Swedish Prosecution
Authority (Respondent)

before

Lord Phillips, President
Lord Walker
Lady Hale
Lord Brown

Lord Mance
Lord Kerr
Lord Dyson

JUDGMENT GIVEN ON

30 May 2012

Heard on 1 and 2 February 2012

Appellant	*Respondent*
Dinah Rose QC	Clare Montgomery QC
Mark Summers	Aaron Watkins
Helen Law	Hannah Pye
(Instructed by	(Instructed by Special
Birnberg Peirce and	Crime Division, Crown
Partners)	Prosecution Service)

Interveners (Mr	*Intervener (Lord*
Gerard Batten MEP	*Advocate)*
and Mr Vladimir	
Bukovsky)	
Paul Diamond	P Jonathan Brodie QC

(Instructed by	(Instructed by The
Chambers of Paul	Appeals Unit, Crown
Diamond)	Office)

LORD PHILLIPS

Introduction

1. On 2 December 2010 the Swedish Prosecution Authority ("the Prosecutor"), who is the respondent to this appeal, issued a European Arrest Warrant ("EAW") signed by Marianne Ny, a prosecutor, requesting the arrest and surrender of Mr Assange, the appellant. Mr Assange was, at the time, in England, as he still is. The offences of which he is accused and in respect of which his surrender is sought are alleged to have been committed in Stockholm against two women in August 2010. They include "sexual molestation" and, in one case, rape. At the extradition hearing before the Senior District Judge, and subsequently on appeal to the Divisional Court, he unsuccessfully challenged the validity of the EAW on a number of grounds. This appeal relates to only one of these. Section 2(2) in Part 1 of the Extradition Act 2003 ("the 2003 Act") requires an EAW to be issued by a "judicial authority." Mr Assange contends that the Prosecutor does not fall within the meaning of that phrase and that, accordingly, the EAW is invalid. This point of law is of general importance, for in the case of quite a number of Member States EAWs are issued by public prosecutors. Its resolution does not turn on the facts

of Mr Assange's case. I shall, accordingly, say no more about them at this stage, although I shall revert briefly to them towards the end of this judgment.

2. . . . As can be seen, the phrase "judicial authority" is used in a number of places in the Framework Decision. In particular it is used in article 6, which provides:

"1. The issuing judicial authority shall be the judicial authority of the issuing Member State which is competent to issue a European arrest warrant by virtue of the law of that State." . . .

The issue

4. Miss Rose contends that a "judicial authority" must be a person who is competent to exercise judicial authority and that such competence requires impartiality and independence of both the executive and the parties. As, in Sweden, the Prosecutor is and will remain a party in the criminal process against Mr Assange, she cannot qualify as a "judicial authority." In effect, Miss Rose's submission is that a "judicial authority" must be some kind of court or judge.

5. Miss Clare Montgomery QC for the Prosecutor contends that the phrase "judicial authority," in the context of the Framework Decision, and other European instruments, bears a broad and autonomous meaning. It describes any person or body authorised to play a part in the judicial process. The term embraces a variety of bodies, some of which have the qualities of impartiality and independence on which Miss Rose relies, and some of which do not. In some parts of the Framework Decision the term "judicial authority" describes one type, in other parts another. A prosecutor properly falls within the description "judicial authority" and is capable of being the judicial authority competent to issue an EAW under article 6 if the law of the State so provides. Judicial authority must be given the same meaning in the 2003 Act as it bears in the Framework Decision.

[The following page has been omitted. It explains the approach in interpreting Part 1 of the 2003 Act.]

8. Article 34.2(b) of the EU Treaty provides:

"Framework decisions shall be binding upon the Member States as to the result to be achieved but shall leave to the national authorities the choice of form and methods. They shall not entail direct effect."

In *Pupino* the European Court of Justice held at para 43:

"When applying the national law, the national court that is called on to interpret it must do so as far as possible in the light of the wording and purpose of the framework decision in order to attain the result which it pursues and thus comply with article 34.2(b) EU."

[The following two pages have been omitted. They further discuss the approach and examine parliamentary material.]

The meaning of "judicial authority" in the Framework Decision

14. It is necessary at the outset to decide how the task of interpreting the Framework Decision should be approached. *Craies on Legislation*, 9th ed (2008), remarks at

para 31.1.21 that the text of much European legislation is arrived at more through a process of political compromise, so that individual words may be chosen less for their legal certainty than for their political acceptability. That comment may be particularly pertinent in the present context in that, as we shall see, an earlier draft of the Framework Decision left no doubt as to the meaning of "judicial authority" but a subsequent draft expunged the definition that made this clear. . . .

The natural meaning

16. As we are here concerned with the meaning of only two words, I propose at the outset to consider the natural meaning of those words. It is necessary to do this in respect of both the English words "judicial authority" and the equivalent words in the French text. Those words are "autorité judiciaire." In the final version of the Framework Decision the same weight has to be applied to the English and the French versions. It is, however, a fact that the French draft was prepared before the English and that, in draft, in the event of conflict, the meaning of the English version had to give way to the meaning of the French. The critical phrase does not bear the same range of meanings in the English language as in the French and, as I shall show, the different contexts in which the phrase is used more happily accommodate the French rather than the English meanings.

17. The first series of meanings of "judicial" given in the Oxford English Dictionary is:

"Of or belonging to judgment in a court of law, or to a judge in relation to this function; pertaining to the administration of justice; proper to a court of law or a legal tribunal; resulting from or fixed by a judgment in court."

In the context of "a judicial authority" the more appropriate meanings are: "having the function of judgment; invested with authority to judge causes"; a public prosecutor would not happily fall within this meaning.

18. "Judiciaire" is capable of bearing a wide or a narrow meaning. . . . A computer dictionary search discloses a number of examples of its use in the "sens vague," for instance "affaire judiciaire/legal case; aide judiciaire/legal aid; annonce judiciaire/legal notice; poursuite judiciaire/legal proceedings" and last but not least, "autorité judiciaire/legal authority."

19. Having regard to the range of meanings that "autorité judiciaire" is capable of embracing, it is no cause for surprise that the phrase often receives some additional definition. . . . Miss Rose in her written case referred to a further example, in the English version, in the definition of an "issuing authority" in respect of a European Evidence Warrant under article 2(c) of the relevant Framework Decision (2008/978/JHA), namely :

" . . . (i) a judge, a court, an investigating magistrate, a public prosecutor; or (ii) any *other* judicial authority as defined by the issuing State and, in the specific case, acting in its capacity as an investigating authority in criminal proceedings . . ." (my emphasis) . . .

The purpose of the Framework Decision

25. Thus the Framework Decision did not set out to build a new extradition structure from top to bottom, but rather to remove from it the diplomatic or political procedures that were encumbering it. The objective was that the extradition process should involve direct co-operation between those authorities responsible on the ground for what I have described as the antecedent process and those authorities responsible on the ground for the execution process. It is important for the purposes of this appeal, to consider the manner in which extradition used to work under the 1957 Convention and, in particular, to identify those who, under the operation of that Convention, were responsible for the antecedent process.

[The following three-and-a-half pages have been omitted. They discuss the 1957 Convention in greater detail.]

Public prosecutors

36. As the issue on this appeal is whether a public prosecutor constitutes a "judicial authority" under Part 1 of the 2003 Act, it is appropriate to consider the nature of that office. Public prosecutors as their name suggests are public bodies that carry out functions relating to the prosecution of criminal offenders. On 8 December 2009 the Consultative Council of European Judges and the Consultative Council of European Prosecutors published for the attention of the Committee of Ministers a joint Opinion (2009) that consisted of a Declaration, called the Bordeaux Declaration together with an Explanatory Note. This comments at para 6 on the diversity of national legal systems, contrasting the common law systems with the Continental law systems. Under the latter the prosecutors may or may not be part of the "judicial corps." Equally the public prosecutor's autonomy from the executive may be complete or limited. Para 23 of the Note observes:

> "The function of judging implies the responsibility for making binding decisions for the persons concerned and for deciding litigation on the basis of the law. Both are the prerogative of the judge, a judicial authority independent from the other state powers. This is, in general, not the mission of public prosecutors, who are responsible for bringing or continuing criminal proceedings."

37. A recurrent theme of both the Declaration and the Note is the importance of the independence of the public prosecutors in the performance of their duties. Para 3 of the Declaration states that judges and public prosecutors must both enjoy independence in respect of their functions and also be and appear to be independent of each other. Para 6 states:

> "The enforcement of the law and, where applicable, the discretionary powers by the prosecution at the pre-trial stage require that the status of public prosecutors be guaranteed by law, at the highest possible level, in a manner similar to that of judges. They shall be independent and autonomous in their decision-making and carry out their functions fairly, objectively and impartially."

The Note comments at paras 33 and 34 that public prosecutors must act at all times honestly, objectively and impartially. Judges and public prosecutors have, at all times, to respect the integrity of suspects. The independence of the judge and the prosecutor is inseparable from the rule of law.

38. Later the Note deals with the roles and functions of judges and public prosecutors in the "pre-criminal" procedures:

> "48 At the pre-trial stage the judge independently or sometimes together with the prosecutor, supervises the legality of the investigative actions, especially when they affect fundamental rights (decisions on arrest, custody, seizure, implementation of special investigative techniques, etc)."

Both the function and the independence of the prosecutor must be borne in mind when considering whether, under the Framework Decision, the term "judicial authority" can sensibly embrace a public prosecutor.

[The following five pages have been omitted. They discuss explicit definitions of "judicial authority" included in previous drafts of the framework decision, and the current language of the decision.]

55. Had the final Framework Decision followed the September draft, the issue that has led to this appeal could never have arisen. Article 3 expressly provided that the "issuing judicial authority" might be a public prosecutor. Elsewhere the "judicial authority" might or might not be a public prosecutor depending upon the function being performed. The September draft was, however, amended in a manner that obfuscated the position. The relevant changes appear to have been made in the course of discussion in the Council of Ministers. On 6 December the Presidency noted that fourteen delegations agreed on the new draft ("the December draft"), noting parliamentary scrutiny reservations from, inter alia, the United Kingdom. The December draft formed the basis of the final Framework Decision approved by the Council. I turn to consider the manner in which the Framework Decision differs from the September draft. . . .

57. Most significantly, for present purposes, the definitions of issuing judicial authority and executing judicial authority in the final version no longer define these as being a judge or public prosecutor. The new definitions, now in article 6, are as follows:

> "1. The issuing judicial authority shall be the judicial authority of the issuing Member State which is competent to issue a European arrest warrant by virtue of the law of that State.
>
> 2. The executing judicial authority shall be the judicial authority of the executing Member State which is competent to execute the European arrest warrant by virtue of the law of that State.
>
> 3. Each Member State shall inform the General Secretariat of the Council of the competent judicial authority under its law."

[The following page has been omitted. It further discusses the definition of "judicial authority."]

The critical question

60. The critical question is whether the changes made to the draft Framework Decision between September and December altered the meaning of "judicial authority" so as to exclude a public prosecutor from its ambit. There would seem to be two possible reasons for removing the precise definition of "judicial authority" that had been included in article 3 of the September draft. The first was to restrict the meaning by excluding from its ambit the public prosecutor. The second was to broaden the meaning so that it was not restricted to a judge or a public prosecutor. For a number of reasons I have reached the firm conclusion that the second explanation is the more probable.

61. *In the first place,* had the intention been to restrict the power to issue an EAW or to participate in its execution to a judge, I would expect this to have been expressly stated. The change would have been radical, and would have prevented public prosecutors from performing functions that they had been performing in relation to the issue of provisional arrest warrants since 1957.

62. *In the second place* it is hard to see why the majority of Member States would have wished to restrict the ambit of the issuing judicial authority in this way. The significant safeguard against the improper or inappropriate issue of an EAW lay in the antecedent process which formed the basis of the EAW. If there had been concern to ensure the involvement of a judge in relation to the issue of an EAW, the obvious focus should have been on this process. The function of the issuing authority was of less significance. That fact is underlined by the only case outside the United Kingdom to which we have been referred where a challenge was made to the issue of an EAW by a public prosecutor. In *Piaggio* (*Germany*) (14 February 2007, Court of Cassation Sez 6 (Italy)) the appellant challenged the issue by the Hamburg Public Prosecutor's Office of an EAW on the ground that it should have been issued and signed by a judge. The Court rejected this contention for the following reasons:

> "The claim alleging breach of article 1(3) of Law no 69 of 2005 on the ground that the EAW was not signed by a judge is completely unfounded. . . .
>
> Moreover, article 6 of the framework decision leaves to the individual Member State the task of determining the judicial authority responsible for issuing (or executing) a European Arrest Warrant, and the Italian implementing law, with regard to the active extradition procedure, provides for certain cases in which the Public Prosecutor's office is to be responsible for issuing the EAW (article 28 of Law no 69/2005)." . . .

[The following page has been omitted. It discusses findings of a report on Italy's EAW procedures.]

65. *In the third place* I find it likely that the removal of the definition of judicial authority as being a "judge or public prosecutor" was not because Member States wished to narrow its meaning to a judge, but because they were not content that its meaning should be restricted to a judge or a public prosecutor. Member States had existing procedures for initiating an extradition request and for requesting provisional arrest in another Member State which involved their domestic arrest

procedures. They also had existing procedures for giving effect to extradition requests. The authorities involved in these procedures were not restricted to judges and prosecutors. It seems to me likely that the removal of a precise definition of judicial authority was intended to leave the phrase bearing its "sens vague" so as to accommodate a wider range of authorities. . . .

Implementation of the Framework Decision by the Member States

68. Had the omission of the definition of "judicial authority" in the final version of the Framework Decision reflected an intention on the part of the Member States that negotiated it that only a judge or court could act as an issuing or executing authority, I would have expected the Member States to have implemented that intention when giving effect to the Framework Decision. I would equally have expected Reports published by the Commission and the Experts' Evaluation Reports for the Council to have commented critically on any failure by a Member State to appoint a court or judge as the issuing and executing judicial authority. This was far from the case. 11 Member States designated a prosecutor as the issuing judicial authority in relation to fugitives sought for prosecution and 10, not in every case the same, designated a prosecutor as the issuing judicial authority in respect of fugitives who had been sentenced. 10 Member States designated a prosecutor as the executing judicial authority. Some of these had designated a judge or court as the issuing judicial authority. A handful of Member States had designated the Ministry of Justice as the issuing or executing judicial authority.

[The following seven pages have been omitted. They include further discussion of the framework decision's implementation, the 2003 Act, the facts of Assange's case, and consideration of proportionality in the EAW process.]

91. For the reasons that I have given I would dismiss this appeal.

[The remaining eighty-five pages have been omitted. They include opinions from the other justices and several attachments.]

SOURCE: The Supreme Court of the United Kingdom. *Assange (Appellant) v The Swedish Prosecution Authority (Respondent),* [2012] UKSC 22. May 30, 2012. http://www.supremecourt.gov.uk/decided-cases/docs/UKSC_2011_0264_Judgment.pdf.

OTHER HISTORIC DOCUMENTS OF INTEREST

FROM PREVIOUS *HISTORIC DOCUMENTS*

June

May U.S. Jobs Report Released

JUNE 1, 2012

The U.S. economic recovery continued at a slow but steady clip in 2012, despite a disappointing jobs report released by the federal government on June 1 showing unemployment rising to 8.2 percent in May. In a presidential election year, both the incumbent president, Barack Obama, and his challenger, former Massachusetts governor Mitt Romney, used the report to bolster campaign talking points. The former said the report proved that current economic policy was working as planned, as evidenced by the 69,000 jobs created in May, while the latter used it as proof that the current administration was failing at its promise to rebuild the middle class. Although unemployment eventually fell to 7.7 percent in November, economists and politicians alike looked for a place to lay the blame of a slow economic recovery, and they found problems, ranging from a contracting European market to the inability of Congress to agree on tax cuts and job legislation.

DISAPPOINTING JOBS REPORT

After strong job growth from January through March 2012, when an average of 226,000 jobs were created per month, the May report from the Bureau of Labor Statistics (BLS), released on June 1, showed only 69,000 nonfarm jobs created. "It was really shockingly low," said Bill Dunkelberg, the chief economist for the National Federation of Independent Business. This was the smallest number of jobs created during the past year and brought the unemployment rate from 8.1 percent to 8.2 percent, the first increase in eleven months. The number of long-term unemployed also rose from 5.1 million to 5.4 million, while the underemployment rate, often considered a better measure of the health of the job market because it counts those who could not find work as well as those who found only part-time positions, rose to 14.8 percent.

According to the May report, the bulk of the job creation problem came from construction companies, which cut 28,000 jobs—the largest number reported in two years. Ellen Zentner, an economist at Nomura Securities, attributed this decline to a warm winter across the United States. Typically, construction hiring occurs in the spring, but this year, this sector did the bulk of its hiring in December 2011 and January 2012 and then cut back.

Given the weak performance, economists estimated that the economy may not be strong enough to sustain the growth seen at the beginning of the year, especially given the gross domestic product's (GDP) low annualized growth rate as compared to late 2011. The BLS report echoed that concern, adjusting the job growth numbers downward for March and April, meaning there were 49,000 fewer jobs created than originally thought. Falling global demand for American products was also considered an obstacle to continued growth. In 2011 and early 2012, economic growth was largely driven by manufacturing, and as Europe and China faced their own financial crises, demand was not keeping up with production. "The reason why it was never going to build momentum going forward was simply because the rest of the world was slowing down," said Steve Blitz, chief economist at ITG Investment Research.

PLACING BLAME

The slowdown in job growth was blamed on a number of factors, including Europe's economic crisis and China's economic contraction. Perhaps most significant, however, was Washington's inability to reach a compromise on job legislation or tax cuts. Bush-era payroll tax cuts that were temporarily extended in early 2012 were set to expire at the end of the year. With uncertainty growing as to whether an agreement could be reached, companies became less likely to hire, uncertain about what their future tax liability would be. "Whenever uncertainty abounds, it's hard to open the floodgates on hiring," said Zentner. "It's hard for an employer to hire somebody when you don't know what the tax rates are going to be in six months," said Wells Fargo chief economist John Silva.

The May jobs report was another talking point for the White House and Republicans in Congress to use to argue for new job creation legislation. Speaker of the House John Boehner, R-Ohio, called the report indicative of "Obama's failed policies [that] have made high unemployment and a weak economy the sad new normal for families and small businesses." He reminded the American public that the House of Representatives had passed upward of thirty jobs bills to do things ranging from approving the Keystone XL pipeline to repealing Obamacare. But, Boehner said, Senate Democrats were blocking passage of the bills, holding Americans hostage in a political game.

The White House retorted that it too had proposed job creation legislation but that it was Republicans in the House who were being stopped by their most conservative Tea Party members, who refused to expand the scope of government's ability to create jobs. "In the American Jobs Act and in the State of the Union Address, the President put forward a number of proposals to create jobs and strengthen the economy, including proposals that would put teachers back in the classroom and cops on the beat, and put our nation's construction workers back on the job rebuilding our nation's infrastructure," said Alan Krueger, chair of the White House Council of Economic Advisers. But regardless of which path Congress ultimately follows, Krueger said, "Problems in the job market were long in the making and will not be solved overnight."

ECONOMIC IMPACT ON THE PRESIDENTIAL CAMPAIGN

According to a March Gallup poll, chief on the minds of voters heading into the 2012 election season was the economy. Seventy-one percent of those surveyed reported that they worry "a great deal" about the economy, the same percentage seen in 2011, but still the highest level ever recorded by the organization since 2001, when it began collecting these data.

Given the concern of the American electorate, Romney made the economy and jobs a central part of his campaign. After the May jobs report, Republicans seized the opportunity to attack the president's economic record and paint their candidate as the best choice. "Today's extremely troubling jobs report proves yet again that President Obama's policies simply are not working and that he has failed to live up to the promise of his presidency," said Republican National Committee (RNC) Chair Reince Priebus. Romney called the report "devastating news for American workers and American families" and a "harsh indictment of the president's handling of the economy."

Throughout the election season, media outlets closely watched and analyzed jobs data coming from the Labor Department, using these as a predictor of which candidate might fare better in November. Historically speaking, Obama was facing a difficult fight: No president since the Great Depression had ever sought reelection with unemployment as high as 8.2 percent. And in past presidential campaigns, the incumbent has lost if the unemployment rate was climbing, so the Obama campaign chose to focus on the positives of the lackluster May jobs report, pointing to the twenty-seventh straight month of job growth.

In their debates, the two candidates sparred over who would succeed at job creation moving forward, with each candidate arguing that he was better for middle-class Americans than his opponent. Romney attacked the president's record on jobs and the nation's unemployment rate, saying, "There's no question in my mind if the president is re-elected, you'll continue to see a middle-class squeeze." Echoing a longtime promise of the president to hire more teachers, Romney noted that the $90 billion spent by the Obama administration on developing alternative energy could have gone toward hiring those teachers to help lower the unemployment rate. Obama defended his record, noting that the economy was continuing to recover and that he had inherited a crisis, not created one. Obama's strongest attack on Romney was for the Republican candidate's unwillingness to talk specifically about the economic plans he would use to continue the recovery. "At some point, the American people have to ask themselves if the reason that Governor Romney is keeping all these plans secret is because they're too good," Obama quipped.

Less than two weeks before the November general election, the Department of Commerce released data on the third quarter growth of the economy, up 2 percent compared with only 1.3 percent in the second quarter and better than expected (the growth rate was later adjusted to 2.7 percent). Exports were down by 1.6 percent, compared to an increase of 5.3 percent in the second quarter, the first time they had fallen since the first quarter of 2009, and business investment also fell, a sign that business owners were taking action in case no agreement was reached on tax cuts. Despite a better-than-expected report, Romney called it "discouraging" and said "slow economic growth means slow job growth and declining take-home pay." But the president's campaign got a boost from the report because consumer spending, a key economic indicator, was up an annual rate of 2 percent, and residential investment was rising as well, standing at 14.4 percent compared with 8.5 percent in the second quarter.

NOVEMBER UPTICK

The job market rebounded in November, bringing unemployment to its lowest level in nearly four years, or 7.7 percent, continuing a downward trend that began midyear and continued into December. At its current rate of decline, according to Dean Maki, the chief U.S. economist at Barclays Capital, the unemployment rate would reach 7.1 percent by December 2013. Employers added 146,000 jobs in November, in line with the average 151,000 per month created earlier in the year. The report was a surprise to economists who estimated the creation of only 86,000 jobs, largely because of an anticipated impact from Hurricane Sandy that did not come to fruition.

The decreasing unemployment rate was good news for states across the country. In November forty-five states and the District of Columbia experienced a decline in the jobless rate, and no state saw an increase in unemployment, marking the first time this had occurred since 2007. Nevada led the nation with 10.8 percent unemployment, down from around 15 percent at the height of the recession, while North Dakota had the lowest rate at 3.1 percent.

Not everyone saw the decline in the unemployment rate as entirely positive—economists said it was more due to a smaller labor force than a large number of jobs created, as well as the addition of 53,000 seasonal retail jobs. Construction experienced another decline in November, losing 20,000 jobs, and manufacturing lost 7,000 jobs partly because of the decrease in demand from overseas.

The ongoing fight in Congress to reach an agreement on tax cuts largely overshadowed the strong November jobs report. Economists expressed concern that an inability to extend tax cuts could force another economic contraction. Although Republicans and Democrats reached an agreement in early January 2013, on January 30, the Commerce Department reported that for the first time since the recession, the economy shrank in the fourth quarter of 2012.

—Heather Kerrigan

Following is a portion of the text of the May 2012 jobs report released by the Department of Labor on June 1, 2012; a statement from Speaker of the House John Boehner, R-Ohio, on June 1, 2012, responding to the May jobs report released by the Bureau of Labor Statistics; and a statement by Alan Krueger, chair of the White House Council of Economic Advisers, on June 1, 2012, regarding the May jobs report.

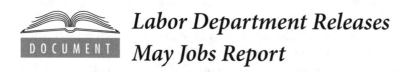

Labor Department Releases
May Jobs Report

June 1, 2012

[All charts, graphs, footnotes, and references to them have been omitted.]

THE EMPLOYMENT SITUATION—MAY 2012

Nonfarm payroll employment changed little in May (+69,000), and the unemployment rate was essentially unchanged at 8.2 percent, the U.S. Bureau of Labor Statistics reported today.

Employment increased in health care, transportation and warehousing, and wholesale trade but declined in construction. Employment was little changed in most other major industries.

Household Survey Data

Both the **number of unemployed persons** (12.7 million) and the **unemployment rate** (8.2 percent) changed little in May.

Among **the major worker groups**, the unemployment rates for adult men (7.8 percent) and Hispanics (11.0 percent) edged up in May, while the rates for adult women (7.4 percent), teenagers (24.6 percent), whites (7.4 percent), and blacks (13.6 percent) showed little or no change. The jobless rate for Asians was 5.2 percent in May (not seasonally adjusted), down from 7.0 percent a year earlier.

The number of **long-term unemployed** (those jobless for 27 weeks and over) rose from 5.1 to 5.4 million in May. These individuals accounted for 42.8 percent of the unemployed.

The **civilian labor force** participation rate increased in May by 0.2 percentage point to 63.8 percent, offsetting a decline of the same amount in April. The **employment-population ratio** edged up to 58.6 percent in May.

The number of persons employed **part time for economic reasons** (sometimes referred to as involuntary part-time workers) edged up to 8.1 million over the month. These individuals were working part time because their hours had been cut back or because they were unable to find a full-time job.

In May, 2.4 million persons were **marginally attached to the labor force**, up from 2.2 million a year earlier. (The data are not seasonally adjusted.) These individuals were not in the labor force, wanted and were available for work, and had looked for a job sometime in the prior 12 months. They were not counted as unemployed because they had not searched for work in the 4 weeks preceding the survey.

Among the marginally attached, there were 830,000 **discouraged workers** in May, about the same as a year earlier. (The data are not seasonally adjusted.) Discouraged workers are persons not currently looking for work because they believe no jobs are available for them. The remaining 1.6 million persons marginally attached to the labor force in May had not searched for work in the 4 weeks preceding the survey for reasons such as school attendance or family responsibilities.

Establishment Survey Data

Total **nonfarm payroll employment** changed little in May (+69,000), following a similar change in April (+77,000). In comparison, the average monthly gain was 226,000 in the first quarter of the year. In May, employment rose in health care, transportation and warehousing, and wholesale trade, while construction lost jobs.

Health care employment continued to increase in May (+33,000). Within the industry, employment in ambulatory health care services, which includes offices of physicians and outpatient care centers, rose by 23,000 over the month. Over the year, health care employment has risen by 340,000.

Transportation and warehousing added 36,000 jobs over the month. Employment gains in transit and ground passenger transportation (+20,000) and in couriers and messengers (+5,000) followed job losses in those industries in April. Employment in both industries has shown little net change over the year. In May, truck transportation added 7,000 jobs.

Employment in **wholesale trade** rose by 16,000 over the month. Since reaching an employment low in May 2010, this industry has added 184,000 jobs.

Manufacturing employment continued to trend up in May (+12,000) following a similar change in April (+9,000). Job gains averaged 41,000 per month in the first quarter of this year. In May, employment rose in fabricated metal products (+6,000) and in primary metals (+4,000). Since its most recent low in January 2010, manufacturing employment has increased by 495,000.

Construction employment declined by 28,000 in May, with job losses occurring in specialty trade contractors (-18,000) and in heavy and civil engineering construction (-11,000). Since reaching a low in January 2011, employment in construction has shown little change on net.

Employment in **professional and business services** was essentially unchanged in May. Since the most recent low point in September 2009, employment in this industry has grown by 1.4 million. In May, job losses in accounting and bookkeeping services (-14,000) and in services to buildings and dwellings (-14,000) were offset by small gains elsewhere in the industry.

Employment in other major industries, including **mining and logging, retail trade, information, financial activities, leisure and hospitality,** and **government,** changed little in May.

The **average workweek for all employees** on private nonfarm payrolls edged down by 0.1 hour to 34.4 hours in May. The manufacturing workweek declined by 0.3 hour to 40.5 hours, and factory overtime declined by 0.1 hour to 3.2 hours. The average workweek for **production and nonsupervisory employees** on private nonfarm payrolls was unchanged at 33.7 hours.

In May, average **hourly earnings for all employees** on private nonfarm payrolls edged up by 2 cents to $23.41. Over the past 12 months, average hourly earnings have increased by 1.7 percent. In May, average hourly earnings of private-sector **production and nonsupervisory employees** edged down by 1 cent to $19.70.

The change in total nonfarm payroll employment for March was revised from +154,000 to +143,000, and the change for April was revised from +115,000 to +77,000.

[The remaining tables, a correction on women's employment data, frequently asked questions, and a technical note have been omitted.]

Source: U.S. Department of Labor. Bureau of Labor Statistics. "The Employment Situation—May 2012." June 1, 2012. http://www.bls.gov/news.release/archives/empsit_06012012.pdf.

Speaker Boehner Responds to May Jobs Report

June 1, 2012

House Speaker John Boehner (R-OH) released the following statement today regarding the Department of Labor's unemployment report for May 2012:

"President Obama's failed policies have made high unemployment and a weak economy the sad new normal for families and small businesses. For three years the unemployment rate has remained far above what the administration predicted with the 'stimulus' spending binge. Half of recent college graduates are out of work or underemployed, and for those lucky enough to have a job, prices for everything from gas to groceries have risen faster than paychecks.

"But the American people don't have to accept the president's new normal of fewer jobs and higher prices. Republicans have a Plan for America's Job Creators designed to remove the government barriers holding back economic growth and hurting job creation. The House has passed more than 30 jobs bills to expand energy production and approve popular projects like Keystone XL, eliminate excessive federal red tape, repeal laws like ObamaCare that are making it harder for small businesses to hire new workers, and more.

"While Senate Democrats are blocking these and other important jobs bills, and President Obama is occupied campaigning, the House will continue to focus on liberating job creators and building a stronger economy for all Americans. In the weeks ahead, we will vote to repeal ObamaCare's medical device tax, impose a moratorium on new federal regulations, and stop the tax hike on small businesses that is scheduled to hit on January 1, 2013. The American people are still asking, 'where are the jobs?' Republicans are listening. It's time for President Obama and Senate Democrats to stop playing games and start listening too."

SOURCE: Office of Speaker of the House John Boehner. "Speaker Boehner Statement on May Unemployment Report." June 1, 2012. http://www.speaker.gov/press-release/speaker-boehner-statement-may-unemployment-report.

White House Economic Advisers on May Jobs Numbers

June 1, 2012

Problems in the job market were long in the making and will not be solved overnight. The economy lost jobs for 25 straight months beginning in February 2008, and over 8 million jobs were lost as a result of the Great Recession. We are still fighting back from the worst economic crisis since the Great Depression.

Today we learned that the economy has added private sector jobs for 27 straight months, for a total of 4.3 million payroll jobs over that period. The economy is growing but it is not growing fast enough. BLS's establishment survey shows that private businesses added 82,000 jobs last month, and overall non-farm payroll employment rose by 69,000. The unemployment rate ticked up from 8.1 percent in April to 8.2 percent in May, according to BLS's household survey. However, the labor force participation rate increased 0.2 percentage point to 63.8 percent, and employment rose by 422,000 according to the household survey.

There is much more work that remains to be done to repair the damage caused by the financial crisis and deep recession that began at the end of 2007. Just like last year at this time, our economy is facing serious headwinds, including the crisis in Europe and a spike in gas prices that hit American families' finances over the past months. It is critical that we continue the President's economic policies that are helping us dig our way out of the deep hole that was caused by the severe recession.

In the American Jobs Act and in the State of the Union Address, the President put forward a number of proposals to create jobs and strengthen the economy, including proposals that would put teachers back in the classroom and cops on the beat, and put our nation's construction workers back on the job rebuilding our nation's infrastructure. The President has also proposed a "To-Do List" of actions that Congress should take to create jobs and help restore middle-class security. This includes eliminating tax incentives to ship jobs overseas, cutting red tape so responsible homeowners can refinance, giving small businesses that increase employment or wages a 10 percent income tax credit, investing in affordable clean energy, and helping returning veterans find work. The President is in Minneapolis today to announce a new executive action that will establish private sector partnerships to help military service members acquire recognized occupational credentials—as welders, as machinists, and ultimately in a broader range of occupations. These partnerships will help service members find private sector jobs once they leave the military, and they will help firms in manufacturing and other industries that need workers to fill their vacant positions.

Manufacturing employment continues to expand and manufacturers added 12,000 jobs in May. After losing millions of good manufacturing jobs in the years before and during the recession, the economy has added 495,000 manufacturing jobs since January 2010—the strongest growth for any 28-month period since April 1995. To continue the revival in manufacturing jobs and output, the President has proposed tax incentives for manufacturers, enhanced training for the workforce, and measures to create manufacturing hubs and encourage the growing trend of insourcing.

Other sectors with net job increases included education and health services (+46,000), transportation and warehousing (+35,600), wholesale trade (+15,900), and temporary help services (+9,200). Construction lost 28,000 jobs, accounting services lost 14,000 jobs, government lost 13,000 jobs, and leisure and hospitality lost 9,000 jobs. State and local governments shed 8,000 jobs, mostly in education.

As the Administration stresses every month, the monthly employment and unemployment figures can be volatile, and employment estimates can be subject to substantial revision. Therefore, it is important not to read too much into any one monthly report and it is helpful to consider each report in the context of other data that are becoming available.

[A corresponding graphic has been omitted.]

Source: The White House. Council of Economic Advisers. "The Employment Situation in May." June 1, 2012. http://www.whitehouse.gov/blog/2012/06/01/employment-situation-may.

OTHER HISTORIC DOCUMENTS OF INTEREST

FROM THIS VOLUME

- European Leaders Agree to New Greek Bailout, p. 113
- President Obama and Former Gov. Romney Meet in Second Presidential Debate, p. 482
- President Obama Remarks on 2012 Reelection Victory, p. 531

FROM PREVIOUS *HISTORIC DOCUMENTS*

Wisconsin Governor Survives Recall Election

JUNE 5, 2012

In February 2011, newly elected Wisconsin Governor Scott Walker, a Republican, proposed a budget repair bill intended to close a $137 million budget gap. The bill restricted the collective bargaining rights of the state's public employees, drawing thousands of union members and their supporters from across the country to the state capitol in Madison, where protests continued for weeks. Despite strong labor opposition, the bill was signed into law, and opponents took their fight to the ballot box. In 2011, six Republicans and three Democrats faced recall elections, and in 2012, Governor Walker faced his own recall. With millions of dollars more in support than his Democratic opponent, Milwaukee Mayor Tom Barrett, Walker easily held onto his seat, making him the first governor in the nation to survive a recall election. The election dealt a blow to labor unions across the country and emboldened public officials eager to amend the bargaining rights of their employees.

Budget Repair Bill Sparks First Set of Recalls

Wisconsin was the first state in the nation to extend collective bargaining rights to public sector employees, so it was unsurprising that Walker's budget repair drew such strong reaction. The Wisconsin governor unabashedly made his opinion of the state's public unions clear from his election in late 2010: They serve little purpose given the strong public service laws that exist today. "I get why unions make sense in the private sector," the governor said, "but at the public level, it's the government, it's the people, who are the ones who are the employers." Walker argued that the state would need to lay off up to 6,000 of its 175,000 workers without passage of a partial-year budget bill. In the bill, the governor and Republican legislators proposed ending collective bargaining rights for anything other than salaries and called for additional pension and health care contributions from state employees. The bill was expected to cost employees 8 percent of their salaries each year.

Unions, even those representing those unaffected by the bill such as public safety workers, quickly came out against the budget repair bill, saying that because it prohibited unions from collecting dues from state employees who are eligible but opt not to participate in a union, the governor was only impacting union coffers and the bill would have little impact on the state's budget gap. Labor supporters called the measure a clear attempt to bust unions. With Republicans holding a majority of seats in the state legislature, the bill looked almost certain to pass.

While tens of thousands of protesters gathered in Madison, Wisconsin, fourteen Democratic state senators fled to Illinois to prevent Republicans from having a quorum to hold a vote on the budget bill. As the standoff wore on, and protesters camped inside the

capitol building, the governor issued threats to the fourteen senators, including withholding pay and fining them for each day outside of the state. Republicans had only one option
to bring the bill to a vote: Remove all spending provisions and vote only on the collective
bargaining portions. This required no quorum and, therefore, no Democratic presence.
The state senate and assembly quickly passed the stripped-down version of the bill, and
Governor Walker signed it on March 11.

Lawsuits against the bill were immediately filed, and the new law ended up at the state
supreme court, where it was reinstated after being halted by a county circuit judge. While
the case made its way through the state's courts, opponents circulated recall petitions
against eight Democratic and eight Republican lawmakers. Only nine petitions were successful in garnering enough signatures to appear on the ballot in 2011, and of those,
Democrats gained only two seats, leaving the assembly and senate firmly in Republican
hands.

Undeterred by the losses, opponents began gathering signatures for a recall attempt
against Governor Walker. By January 2012, more than 900,000 signatures were collected—
enough to force a recall. The signatures were validated and a recall was ordered on March
30. The primary was set for May 8, with the general election taking place on June 5.

Campaign and Election

With the election date set, Walker's campaign kicked into high gear. A state law allows
recalled governors the opportunity to raise unlimited funds for a set period of time to
defend the seat, which the governor used to his advantage, raising more than $30 million
in his recall bid.

Walker's opponent in the recall election was Milwaukee Mayor Tom Barrett—the two
had previously faced off in the 2010 gubernatorial election, which Walker won 52 percent
to 47 percent. "We need to bring our state back," Barrett wrote to his supporters in an
e-mail announcing his candidacy. "Wisconsin needs a governor who is focused on jobs,
not ideology; a leader committed to bringing our state together and healing political
wounds, not pitting people against each other and catering to the special interests."

During the brief campaign season, Barrett and Walker sparred over the economy,
jobs, collective bargaining rights, and a criminal investigation into former Walker aides.
Noting his belief that Governor Walker had cut funds for education, women's health, and
public employees, Barrett said the governor's plans were "working for the wealthiest people in the state but they're not working for the middle class." In one of two debates the
candidates held, Barrett told viewers that Walker intended to make Wisconsin "the Tea
Party capital of the country" by continuing to shrink the size of state government to the
detriment of Wisconsin's citizens.

Walker painted himself as the stronger of the two candidates, who was willing to face
tough challenges and stand up to special interests. In their last debate, this posturing led
the two candidates to argue about collective bargaining. Barrett said Walker wanted "to pit
people against each other" while Walker stood by his law, stating, "We drew a line in the
sand and said we're going to put the power back in the hands of taxpayers." He continued,
"Our reforms are working. That's why our opponents don't talk about them anymore. . . . We're moving in the right direction."

On the economic front, Walker heavily criticized tax increases in the city of Milwaukee
that occurred during Barrett's term. But the biggest point of contention between the two
candidates was the number of jobs created, or lost, since Walker came to office. Relying on

state data only recently reviewed by the U.S. Bureau of Labor Statistics (BLS), Walker said 23,300 jobs were created in Wisconsin in 2011. Prior to Walker's pronouncement, official data from BLS showed a loss of 33,900 jobs, the worst in the country in 2011. "I know this undermines your ads of the past two months, but the facts are the facts," Walker told Barrett, calling the data previously released by BLS unreliable. Barrett argued that regardless of which facts were correct, Walker was well off track to meet his 2010 campaign promise of bringing 250,000 new jobs to Wisconsin by the end of 2014.

Even after the hard-fought campaign on the part of labor unions, exit-polling data showed a voter base unaffected by union politics. According to CNN, 52 percent of Wisconsin voters supported collective bargaining reform. And that percentage nearly matched the election results—ultimately, on June 6, Wisconsin voters kept their governor by a margin of more than 53 percent to 46 percent. In his concession speech, Barrett urged Republicans and Democrats in the state to "work together" and "listen to each other," which drew boos from the crowd gathered to see him. Celebrating his victory, Walker said, "Tonight, we tell Wisconsin, we tell our country and we tell people all across the globe that voters really do want leaders who stand up and make the tough decisions." Walker's lieutenant governor and the state senate's majority leader survived their own recall elections on June 6.

NATIONWIDE IMPACT

Collective bargaining rights for public employees are a contentious issue across the country. Five states ban collective bargaining by any public employee, while a range of other states impose specific restrictions on bargaining rights. Private sector workers are quick to criticize public employee unions because benefits are often not as lucrative in the private sector, while many public sector employees enjoy fully funded pensions and more robust health care benefits in retirement. With only 7 percent of private sector workers in unions, as compared to nearly 37 percent of their public sector counterparts, it can be difficult to find sympathy when arguing against reductions in benefits paid for by taxpayers.

Walker's 2011 budget bill sparked other collective bargaining restrictions in Idaho, Indiana, Michigan, Nebraska, Nevada, New Hampshire, Ohio, Oklahoma, and Tennessee, some of which were rejected by voters, but all of which were less stringent than Wisconsin's. However, it was Walker's ability to retain his seat in the recall election that political analysts pointed to as indicative of the growing problem for unions. "This is a watershed moment, a historic moment," said Gary Chaison, a professor of labor relations at Clark University in Massachusetts. "[Unions] gambled heavily and they lost heavily. It's really a problem for them." The sentiment was reflected in CNN's exit polling from the Wisconsin recall, which found that 37 percent of voters said they had a union member in their household but ultimately voted for Governor Walker.

Nationwide interest in the election was clear—Walker raised more than half of his campaign funds from out-of-state donors, including nearly $9 million from the Republican Governors Association. "[Republicans] wanted to make sure that the Wisconsin election would be a favorable agenda for them," said Mike McCabe, executive director of the Wisconsin Democracy Campaign, a group that tracks campaign spending. Barrett faced greater difficulty raising capital, even in spite of the *Citizens United* ruling, which arguably gives labor unions a greater impact on campaigns and was outspent seven-to-one on television advertising, according to the *Washington Post*. In total, the candidates and other outside groups spent more than $80 million on the race. Between the 2011 and 2012 recalls, the Wisconsin Democracy Campaign estimates that between $125 million and

$130 million was spent. Democrats argued that this gave Walker an unfair advantage. Because of the funds, Walker was able to "muddy the waters when it came to his jobs record, his involvement in a criminal corruption probe and his massive cuts to health care and education," said Graeme Zielinski, Wisconsin's Democratic Party spokesperson.

Republicans used Walker's win as a rallying cry. "Voters are ready for political leaders who are willing to follow Governor Walker's lead and take on the toughest issues; governing with a greater focus on the next generation than the next election," said Governor Bob McDonnell of Virginia, chair of the Republican Governors Association. "[Walker's] executive leadership contrasts sharply with the absence of leadership in the White House," McDonnell said. On the presidential campaign trail, Republican candidate Mitt Romney said the result would "echo beyond the borders of Wisconsin" and was proof that "citizens and taxpayers can fight back—and prevail—against the runaway government costs imposed by labor bosses."

Democrats said that despite the loss, the close race coupled with the number of signatures received for the recall should serve as a wake-up call for Republicans. "Republican governors across the country are on notice: the people of their states will not tolerate partisan overreach," said Democratic Governors Association Chair Martin O'Malley of Maryland. President Barack Obama's campaign attempted to downplay the outcome of the Wisconsin race, while leaning on exit polling that showed 18 percent of Walker supporters also supported the president, who they said would be better than his challenger for the middle class. "Even among the electorate that voted in Wisconsin," said Obama press secretary Jay Carney, "voters substantially approved of the president's positions when it comes to who they felt had the best vision for protecting and securing the middle class."

—Heather Kerrigan

Following is a press release from the Democratic Governors Association on June 5, 2012, responding to the recall election results in Wisconsin; and a statement from the Republican Governors Association also on June 5, 2012, congratulating Governor Scott Walker on his victory.

 **DOCUMENT**

Democratic Governors Respond to Wisconsin Recall Results

June 5, 2012

Governor Martin O'Malley, chair of the Democratic Governors Association, released the following statement tonight on the results of the Wisconsin recall election:

"Tonight, we fell just short of an historic upset. Despite our side getting outspent ten to one by Governor Walker and his extreme right-wing allies, Democrats worked together and were incredibly united behind the people of Wisconsin—allowing us to make the race close and keep it neck-and-neck. While the recall has always been led by the people of Wisconsin first and foremost, the Democratic Governors Association is proud to have worked with our allies at Greater Wisconsin, We Are Wisconsin, and labor to fully fund an aggressive operation on the air and the ground.

"We know that the battle in Wisconsin is part of an ongoing fight to restore states' economies and create jobs across the country. Since Ohioans rejected Ohio Governor Kasich's assault on workers late last year and Wisconsinites submitted over a million signatures in support of a recall and brought the fight to Scott Walker's doorstep tonight, Republican governors across the country are on notice: the people of their states will not tolerate partisan overreach. We look forward to continuing to support and elect Democratic governors who will work to create jobs, expand opportunity, and move our country forward."

SOURCE: Democratic Governors Association. "Wisconsin Recall Election." June 5, 2012. http://democraticgovernors.org/statement-from-dga-chair-governor-martin-omalley-on-wisconsin-recall-election.

Republican Governors Congratulate Gov. Walker

June 5, 2012

Republican Governors Association Chairman Bob McDonnell congratulated Governor Scott Walker on his historic victory tonight in Wisconsin. The RGA spent close to $9 million in Wisconsin, including airing eight television ads and investing in an unprecedented ground game:

"Tonight, Wisconsin voters rewarded political courage. Upon taking office, Governor Walker fearlessly took on the staunch defenders of the status quo and tackled unsustainable entitlements and long-term fiscal liabilities. Governor Walker closed a $3.6 billion deficit without raising taxes; he ushered in the first property tax decrease in a dozen years; he strengthened schools; and he turned around the state's economy. His actions have made Wisconsin stronger today, and tomorrow. And they have improved the lives of the citizens of Wisconsin.

Voters are ready for political leaders who are willing to follow Governor Walker's lead and take on the toughest issues; governing with a greater focus on the next generation than the next election. That's exactly what Governor Walker has done, and his executive leadership contrasts sharply with the absence of leadership in the White House.

While Governor Walker has reined in the state's debt, dramatically improved the state's fiscal outlook and helped the private sector create more than 30,000 new jobs, President Obama has added more than $4.7 trillion to the national debt and proposed more than $1 trillion in higher taxes, and the unemployment rate has exceeded 8 percent for 40 consecutive months.

Governor Walker is proof that voters recognize that the status quo is unacceptable and unsustainable. He has shown there is a better way; a way that leads to prosperity and job creation. Tonight, the voters of Wisconsin have approved of that positive path forward."

SOURCE: Republican Governors Association. "RGA Congratulates Governor Scott Walker." June 5, 2012. http://www.rga.org/homepage/rga-congratulates-governor-scott-walker.

OTHER HISTORIC DOCUMENTS OF INTEREST

FROM PREVIOUS *HISTORIC DOCUMENTS*

Secretary of Homeland Security Amends Immigration Policy

JUNE 15, 2012

Immigration policy has long been a charged issue in the United States, with policymakers struggling to balance economic and social concerns with reasonable regulations on the influx of immigrants. The presence of illegal immigrants in the country has been and continues to be a particularly troubling concern for many. Recent efforts to pass and implement comprehensive immigration reform, thereby reducing the number of undocumented immigrants, have been ongoing since at least 2001. Failure to develop national policies led many states to pass their own laws, including a controversial Arizona law that was mostly overturned in June 2012 by the U.S. Supreme Court. That same month, President Barack Obama issued an executive order offering temporary legal protection to young immigrants who had been brought to the country illegally as children by their parents, and who met several criteria. The move underscored the president's immigration policy objectives, which included focusing resources on deporting undocumented immigrants who were a danger to national security or public safety while providing a path to legalization for those who were already in the country and posed no such threat. The order was admittedly a "stopgap" measure until Congress could pass immigration reform legislation, and, while praised by Democrats and immigrant advocacy groups, it was assailed by Republicans.

ILLEGAL IMMIGRANTS IN THE UNITED STATES

According to the Pew Hispanic Center, approximately 11.5 million illegal immigrants were living in the United States in 2011, compared to roughly 11.1 million in 2009. As the number of illegal immigrants grew, along with the country's unemployment rate, calls for national, comprehensive immigration reform increased.

The last significant effort to pass immigration reform had occurred in 2007 under then-president George W. Bush. The Secure Borders, Economic Opportunity and Immigration Reform Act combined various elements of three previously failed immigration bills and sought to provide a path to citizenship for illegal immigrants, while also increasing security along the Mexican border. Yet the bill failed to garner enough votes in the Senate, with opponents claiming it would essentially be an amnesty program for those who had broken the law. Prior to the 2007 effort, some in Congress introduced proposals aimed at illegal immigrants who had been brought to the United States at a young age by their parents. In 2001, Sen. Orrin Hatch, R-Utah, introduced the Development, Relief, and Education for Alien Minors (DREAM) Act, which would have allowed these youths to remain in the United States if they met a number of requirements. This first DREAM Act was never voted on, but variations of the bill were introduced periodically over the next several sessions of Congress. In 2010, Sen. Dick Durbin, D-Ill., introduced a new version of the DREAM Act that included a two-year college enrollment or military service require-ment that must be met before an illegal immigrant could become a permanent U.S. resident. The bill passed in the House in 2010 but failed to get the sixty votes it needed in the Senate to end a Republican filibuster. Meanwhile, states increasingly sought to form their own immigration policies in the absence of national reform. In 2008, for example, state legislatures adopted 206 laws related to immigration, the vast majority of which were designed to curb illegal immigration. Others passed laws to help immigrants assimilate, and by November 2012, twelve states had passed their own version of the DREAM Act.

Interestingly, the Pew Hispanic Center released a report in April 2012, indicating that the net migration flow from Mexico to the United States had stopped and may even have reversed. The report indicated the downward trend began in 2007, when the number of illegal Mexican immigrants in the United States reached a peak of nearly 7 million. By 2011, that number had decreased to 6.1 million. The report pointed to factors such as weakened U.S. job and construction markets, heightened border enforcement, a rise in deportations, the growing danger inherent in illegal border crossings, a long-term decline in Mexico's birth rates, and broader economic conditions in Mexico as reasons for the trend. In contrast, the U.S. immigrant population from all countries continued to grow, numbering 39.6 million in 2011.

IMMIGRATION UNDER PRESIDENT OBAMA

As a candidate for president in 2008, Obama promised to revive efforts to achieve compre-hensive immigration reform, but by 2012, he had not succeeded and faced pressure from a number of Democrats and leaders within the Latino community to do more on the issue. They cautioned that the president was losing support among Latino voters, in part because of his strict enforcement of existing immigration laws. As of July 2012, President Obama had deported 1.4 million illegal immigrants since taking office—the most by any presi-dent since the 1950s. Furthermore, a Pew Research Center survey found that 91 percent of Latinos supported the DREAM Act.

On June 15, President Obama responded by issuing an executive order that some described as "DREAM Act lite." The order implemented a program called "Consideration of Deferred Action for Childhood Arrivals," which temporarily decriminalized the status of those children of undocumented or illegal immigrants who were raised in the United States, and delayed the threat of deportation, in hopes that Congress would ultimately pass like-minded legislation. Under the program, the Department of Homeland Security—including U.S. Customs and Border Protection, U.S. Immigration and Customs Enforcement, and U.S. Citizenship and Immigration Services—was instructed to exercise "prosecutorial discretion" in enforcing immigration laws against young people who came to the United States as children. If an individual arrived in the United States when he or she was less than sixteen years old and was currently younger than thirty-one; had con-tinuously lived in the United States for at least five years; was in school, had graduated high school or obtained a GED, or was an honorably discharged U.S. veteran; and had no criminal record and was not perceived as a threat to national security, the Department of Homeland Security would defer any enforcement actions against that individual for a period of two years. Immigrants would need to apply for deferred action every two years, and officials would consider each application on a case-by-case basis. Secretary of Homeland Security Janet Napolitano provided further detail on how the program should be implemented in a memo to the department's various components. She noted that the memo, and by extension the president's order, did not provide any "substantive right, immigration status or pathway to citizenship" because only Congress can do that, but that the executive branch does have the power "to set forth policy for the exercise of discretion within the framework of the existing law."

President Obama acknowledged these realities in announcing his executive order. "This is not amnesty. This is not immunity. This is not a path to citizenship," he said. "It's not a permanent fix. This is a temporary, stopgap measure that lets us focus our resources wisely while giving a degree of relief and hope to . . . patriotic young people." He called on Congress to pass the DREAM Act, and added that the young people his executive order would impact "are Americans in their hearts, in their minds, in every single way but one: on paper." The president also noted that the program would help the Department of Homeland Security more effectively focus its resources on identifying and deporting illegal immigrants with criminal backgrounds, a key component of his immigration policies.

Perhaps the most significant change President Obama's order wrought was enabling young immigrants who received deferred action to apply for work permits. Supporters of the move argued it would provide U.S. employers with a new source of educated, qualified workers who had previously been in the "shadows" of the economy. Many of those eligible for the program were at the time limited to jobs that did not require proof of citizenship or a work permit—namely, service jobs that paid cash in either wages or tips. Some also believed the work permits would give them a greater chance of eventually attending college, as new job opportunities would help them pay for classes in the absence of federal loans and tuition assistance. The program further enabled young immigrants to obtain driver's licenses and other documentation, such as Social Security numbers, though it provided no guarantee that states would be willing to give them.

Republicans reacted angrily to the announcement, claiming it was a politically motivated move in an election year that was aimed at gaining support from crucial Hispanic voting blocs in several swing states. "The fact that the president would use children as an election-year ploy is offensive," said Sen. Hatch. Others argued that the president had overstepped his authority and had perhaps even violated the law. "The president's action is an affront to the process of representative government by circumventing Congress and with a directive he may not have the authority to execute," said Sen. Charles Grassley, R-Iowa. Rep. Steven King, R-Iowa, threatened to sue the White House to stop the measure. Still others said the president was taking jobs away from Americans: a particularly ill-timed move given the high unemployment rate. Some states later acted to oppose the program as well. On August 15, Arizona Governor Jan Brewer issued an executive order directing state agencies to deny benefits, including driver's licenses, to deferred action recipients, claiming that providing such benefits would have "significant and lasting impacts" on the state's budget. Two days later, Nebraska Governor Dave Heineman said his state would continue to deny driver's licenses, welfare benefits, and other public benefits to illegal immigrants, even if they had deferred status. Conversely, Democrats welcomed the announcement, as did Latino and immigrant groups. "People are just breaking down and crying for joy when they find out what the president did," said Lorella Praeli, a leader of the immigrant student coalition United We Dream Network. Sen. Durbin said the program would "give these young immigrants their chance to come out of the shadows and be part of the only country they've ever called home."

The Department of Homeland Security and its various offices were given sixty days to implement the new process outlined by the president, giving them time to establish the necessary procedures. Some did question whether it would be safe for immigrants to identify themselves through the program, as the president's order would be in effect for only two years and would need to be renewed in 2014 unless Congress took similar legislative action. If Congress did not act and the next president did not renew the order, immigrants worried that the government might use their voluntarily submitted information to try to deport them.

DREAMers Turn Out

On August 3, the Department of Homeland Security announced the final details of the deferred status application process. Officials said U.S. Citizenship and Immigration Services expected to make all forms available for potential applicants and would immediately begin processing applications on August 15. Applicants would need to submit a completed deferred action request form with an application for a work permit, along with a $465 fee. They must also provide officials with biometrics and undergo a background check. Department officials cautioned applicants to be wary of scams in which "unauthorized practitioners of immigration law" might charge them an additional fee to submit the forms on their behalf.

Many expected there would be a significant response from immigrants. The Pew Hispanic Center estimated as many as 950,000 could qualify for the program, and the number could rise to 1.7 million in the future, once youths aged less than fifteen and school dropouts who re-enrolled became qualified. On August 15, immigration lawyers' offices and help centers opened to long lines of people seeking help in filling out the necessary forms, stretching the capacity of immigration advocacy groups to provide assistance. By the week of September 11, more than 72,000 people had applied for deferred action, and the government had granted its first approvals.

—Linda Fecteau

Following is the text of a June 15, 2012, memorandum from Secretary of Homeland Security Janet Napolitano, outlining the criteria to be used when determining whether individuals brought to the United States as children should be allowed to remain in the United States.

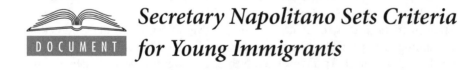

DOCUMENT

Secretary Napolitano Sets Criteria for Young Immigrants

June 15, 2012

Secretary

U.S. Department of Homeland Security

Washington, DC 20528

June 15, 2012

MEMORANDUM FOR:

David V. Aguilar
Acting Commissioner, U.S. Customs and Border Protection

Alejandro Mayorkas
Director, U.S. Citizenship and Immigration Services

John Morton
Director, U.S. Immigration and Customs Enforcement

FROM:

Janet Napolitano
Secretary of Homeland Security

SUBJECT: Exercising Prosecutorial Discretion with Respect to Individuals Who Came to the United States as Children

By this memorandum, I am setting forth how, in the exercise of our prosecutorial discretion, the Department of Homeland Security (DHS) should enforce the Nation's immigration laws against certain young people who were brought to this country as children and know only this country as home. As a general matter, these individuals lacked the intent to violate the law and our ongoing review of pending removal cases is already offering administrative closure to many of them. However, additional measures are necessary to ensure that our enforcement resources are not expended on these low priority cases but are instead appropriately focused on people who meet our enforcement priorities.

The following criteria should be satisfied before an individual is considered for an exercise of prosecutorial discretion pursuant to this memorandum:

- came to the United States under the age of sixteen;
- has continuously resided in the United States for a least five years preceding the date of this memorandum and is present in the United States on the date of this memorandum;
- is currently in school, has graduated from high school, has obtained a general education development certificate, or is an honorably discharged veteran of the Coast Guard or Armed Forces of the United States;
- has not been convicted of a felony offense, a significant misdemeanor offense, multiple misdemeanor offenses, or otherwise poses a threat to national security or public safety; and
- is not above the age of thirty.

Our Nation' s immigration laws must be enforced in a strong and sensible manner. They are not designed to be blindly enforced without consideration given to the individual circumstances of each case. Nor are they designed to remove productive young people to countries where they may not have lived or even speak the language. Indeed, many of these young people have already contributed to our country in significant ways. Prosecutorial discretion, which is used in so many other areas, is especially justified here.

As part of this exercise of prosecutorial discretion, the above criteria are to be considered whether or not an individual is already in removal proceedings or subject to a final order of removal. No individual should receive deferred action under this memorandum unless they first pass a background check and requests for relief pursuant to this memorandum are to be decided on a case by case basis. DHS cannot provide any assurance that relief will be granted in all cases.

1. With respect to individuals who are encountered by U.S. Immigration and Customs Enforcement (ICE), U.S. Customs and Border Protection (CBP), or U.S. Citizenship and Immigration Services (USCIS):

- With respect to individuals who meet the above criteria, ICE and CBP should immediately exercise their discretion, on an individual basis, in order to prevent low priority individuals from being placed into removal proceedings or removed from the United States.
- USCIS is instructed to implement this memorandum consistent with its existing guidance regarding the issuance of notices to appear.

2. With respect to individuals who are *in* removal proceedings but not yet subject to a final order of removal, and who meet the above criteria:

- ICE should exercise prosecutorial discretion, on an individual basis, for individuals who meet the above criteria by deferring action for a period of two years, subject to renewal, in order to prevent low priority individuals from being removed from the United States.
- ICE is instructed to use its Office of the Public Advocate to permit individuals who believe they meet the above criteria to identify themselves through a clear and efficient process.
- ICE is directed to begin implementing this process within 60 days of the date of this memorandum.
- ICE is also instructed to immediately begin the process of deferring action against individuals who meet the above criteria whose cases have already been identified through the ongoing review of pending cases before the Executive Office for Immigration Review.

3. With respect to the individuals who are *not* currently in removal proceedings and meet the above criteria, and pass a background check:

- USCIS should establish a clear and efficient process for exercising prosecutorial discretion, on an individual basis, by deferring action against individuals who meet the above criteria and are at least 15 years old, for a period of two years, subject to renewal, in order to prevent low priority individuals from being placed into removal proceedings or removed from the United States.
- The USCIS process shall also be available to individuals subject to a final order of removal regardless of their age.
- USCIS is directed to begin implementing this process within 60 days of the date of this memorandum.

For individuals who are granted deferred action by either ICE or USCIS, USCIS shall accept applications to determine whether these individuals qualify for work authorization during this period of deferred action.

This memorandum confers no substantive right, immigration status or pathway to citizenship. Only the Congress, acting through its legislative authority, can confer these rights. It remains for the executive branch, however, to set forth policy for the exercise of discretion within the framework of the existing law. I have done so here.

Janet Napolitano

Source: U.S. Department of Homeland Security. "Exercising Prosecutorial Discretion with Respect to Individuals Who Came to the United States as Children." June 15, 2012. http://www.dhs.gov/xlibrary/assets/s1-exercising-prosecutorial-discretion-individuals-who-came-to-us-as-children.pdf.

OTHER HISTORIC DOCUMENTS OF INTEREST

FROM THIS VOLUME

FROM PREVIOUS *HISTORIC DOCUMENTS*

Supreme Court Rules on
Indecency in Broadcasting

JUNE 21, 2012

In *FCC v. Fox Television Stations, Inc.*, the U.S. Supreme Court reviewed penalties that the Federal Communications Commission (FCC), the government agency that regulates radio and television stations, imposed on two television networks for broadcasting fleeting curse words and momentary nudity. The case presented the Court with the opportunity to review the FCC's ability to curb indecency for the first time since 1978, when it found comedian George Carlin's monologue, "Seven Dirty Words," to be indecent and upheld the FCC penalty applied to the radio station that aired it against a First Amendment challenge. The world of media has changed dramatically since 1978. The cable and satellite television industries have grown as well as the Internet, all of which are free of any government regulation of indecent content. Many anticipated that the Court's opinion in this case would take on the issue of whether these changes have undercut the constitutional rationale for the FCC's regulation of television and radio. The Supreme Court, however, in an opinion by Justice Anthony Kennedy, found a way to resolve the issues before it without addressing the broad underlying First Amendment question. Instead, the Court ruled that the FCC had failed to give the networks adequate notice about what would be considered indecent under their regulations. The FCC had publicized a changed enforcement policy about what it considers "indecent" only after it had challenged the broadcasts at issue in this case. For that reason, the FCC failed to give Fox and ABC fair notice in advance of their broadcasts that they would violate the indecency standards. The Court overturned the FCC fines and sanctions against the networks.

BROADCASTS THAT LED TO FCC COMPLAINTS

The case *FCC v. Fox Television Stations, Inc.*, consolidated two separate appellate court cases, one against Fox Television Stations, Inc., for incidents arising in two award show broadcasts and the second involving ABC, Inc., for brief nudity in a broadcast of an episode of the television show *NYPD Blue*. Because of the way the Supreme Court ruled, an understanding of the chronology of events is necessary to understanding the holding.

According to federal law, "Whoever utters any obscene, indecent or profane language . . . shall be fined . . . or imprisoned not more than two years, or both." The FCC has been instructed by Congress to enforce this law between the hours of 6 a.m. and 10 p.m., when it is considered most likely that children will be in the audience. In 1978, the FCC determined that a 2 p.m. radio broadcast of Carlin's "Filthy Words" monologue was indecent. The Supreme Court ruled that this was not impermissible censorship in a case called *FCC v. Pacifica*. The "uniquely pervasive presence of broadcast media in the lives of all Americans," at a time that is "uniquely accessible to children, even those too young to read," the Court wrote, led it to the conclusion that broadcasting receives only limited First

Amendment protection. The Court upheld the FCC's penalty in this case but noted that it was not deciding whether "an occasional expletive . . . would justify any sanction." In the following decades, the FCC brought very few indecency cases, and in 2001 it released a policy statement to provide guidance to the industry. In this statement, it found that "whether the material dwells on or repeats at length descriptions of sexual or excretory organs or activities" was a factor in determining indecency. Examples given clarified that a "fleeting and isolated utterance" or a "brief moment of indecency" would not be actionable.

The three incidents challenged in *FCC v. Fox Television Stations, Inc.*, all occurred from 2002 to 2003. At the 2002 Billboard Music Awards, broadcast by Fox Television Stations, the singer Cher accepted an award saying, in an unscripted speech: "I've also had my critics for the last 40 years saying that I was on my way out every year. Right. So f*** 'em." Again, at the 2003 Fox broadcast of the Billboard Music Awards, Nicole Ritchie and Paris Hilton were presenting an award. In an unscripted remark, Ritchie joked: "Have you ever tried to get cow s*** out of a Prada purse? It's not so f***ing simple." Also that year, on February 25, 2003, ABC broadcast an episode of the television show *NYPD Blue* in which it showed the nude buttocks of an adult female character for approximately seven seconds and a momentary view of the side of her breast.

While the FCC was reviewing viewer complaints about these broadcasts, Janet Jackson, performing during the half-time show of the February 2004 Super Bowl, had a "wardrobe malfunction" and exposed her breast for nine-sixteenths of a second before an audience of 90 million people. The incident ignited massive public outcry and congressional inquiries, leading the FCC to fine CBS $550,000, although the fine was later overturned by a court of appeals. Organizations, concerned that broadcast television would become more like the coarser cable networks, became much more active at this time. One such group, the Parents Television Council, added a complaint button on its website that allowed a viewer to file an FCC complaint with a single click. While the FCC had received only 100 viewer complaints about indecent content during 2000, it received 1.4 million in the six months following the incident with Jackson.

In March 2004, the FCC reversed earlier rulings on "fleeting expletives," to announce a new policy. The commission held that "the mere fact that specific words or phrases are not sustained or repeated does not mandate a finding that material that is otherwise patently offensive to the broadcast medium is not indecent." In 2006, the FCC, under a new chair, applied this new policy to thousands of pending complaints, including the ones against Fox arising from the Billboard Music Awards. Fox appealed the order against it to the United States Court of Appeals for the Second Circuit, which ruled in its favor. The court found that the order was arbitrary and capricious because the FCC had taken a "180-degree turn regarding its treatment of 'fleeting expletives' without providing a reasoned explanation justifying the about-face." The FCC appealed this finding to the U.S. Supreme Court, which, in a 5–4 decision, overturned the Second Circuit, holding that the change in policy was rational and not "arbitrary and capricious." The Supreme Court sent the case back down to the Second Circuit Court of Appeals to resolve Fox's First Amendment and Fifth Amendment challenges to the FCC action.

The Second Circuit, reviewing the Fox broadcast a second time, held that the FCC's indecency policy was unconstitutionally vague and invalidated it in its entirety. It is that ruling that was appealed again to the Supreme Court as *FCC v. Fox Television Stations, Inc.*

On appeal to the Supreme Court, the case against Fox was consolidated with the FCC's case against ABC. In 2008, the FCC had issued an order against ABC, finding that the brief display of a woman's nude buttocks was actionably indecent. It imposed a fine of

$27,500 on each of the forty-five ABC-affiliated stations that had aired the indecent episode. The court of appeals reviewing this penalty found that it was bound by its earlier decision in the Fox case and overturned the order. The FCC appealed it together with its appeal of the Fox ruling.

NETWORKS LACKED FAIR NOTICE

All the justices with the exception of Justice Sonia Sotomayor, who recused herself because she had been involved with the case before joining the Supreme Court, joined Justice Kennedy's opinion. Kennedy's opinion did not address whether the FCC's indecency regulations violated the First Amendment, as the networks argued in their briefs. Instead, the Court ruled that the commission's standards regarding momentary nudity and fleeting expletives had failed to provide the constitutionally required fair notice to the networks and therefore, as applied to the broadcasts at issue, were vague and must be set aside.

Justice Kennedy explained that it is "a fundamental principle in our legal system, that laws "must give fair notice of conduct that is forbidden or required." The Due Process Clause of the Fifth Amendment is violated when a regulation is so vague that it "fails to provide a person of ordinary intelligence fair notice of what is prohibited, or is so standardless that it authorizes or encourages seriously discriminatory enforcement." This is particularly important when speech is involved, because any ambiguity may put an impermissible chill on protected speech.

The Court had little trouble concluding that the parties to this case did not have fair notice of what was forbidden. The Court focused on the FCC's announcement of an abrupt change of course regarding fleeting utterances—that occurred after Fox's challenged broadcasts—as well as prior rulings by the FCC regarding nudity that had deemed, for example, that thirty seconds of nude buttocks were "very brief" and not actionably indecent. In light of the history of FCC enforcement, Justice Kennedy found it "apparent that the Commission policy in place at the time of the broadcasts gave no notice to Fox or ABC that a fleeting expletive or a brief shot of nudity could be actionably indecent; yet Fox and ABC were found to be in violation." He therefore concluded that the FCC orders against both networks had to be set aside. Unlike the Second Circuit, which had found the whole policy to be unconstitutionally vague, the Supreme Court justices ruled that, as applied to these defendants, it violated the constitutional requirements of fair notice.

FEW CLUES ON HOW THE COURT WILL VIEW FUTURE FCC INDECENCY REGULATION

The Court, having resolved the case before it on vagueness grounds, declined to address the First Amendment implications of the FCC's indecency standards, finding it unnecessary to reconsider its 1978 ruling in *FCC v. Pacifica*. Only one justice, Ruth Bader Ginsburg, appeared ready to tackle the bigger issue of whether it still makes sense for the government to censor indecency in broadcast television and radio. Agreeing with the result in this case, she wrote separately to indicate that she disagreed with the Court's First Amendment decision in *FCC v. Pacifica* and thinks that "time, technological advances, and the Commission's untenable rulings" make the time right to reconsider it.

Justice Kennedy's majority opinion did not take a direct stance on this issue but did suggest to the FCC that it was "free to modify its current indecency policy in light of its determination of the public interest and applicable legal requirements." At the same time, he emphasized, his opinion "leaves the courts free to review the current policy or any modified policy in light of its content and application." This almost guarantees that there will be future litigation, presenting the Court with another opportunity to review the First Amendment implications of the FCC's indecency rulings.

—Melissa Feinberg

Following are excerpts from the U.S. Supreme Court ruling in FCC v. Fox Television Stations, Inc., *in which the Court ruled unanimously to overturn the fines imposed on television networks ABC and Fox because the FCC had failed to give the networks adequate notice about what would be considered indecent under its regulations.*

DOCUMENT   *FCC v. Fox Television Stations, Inc.*

June 21, 2012

No. 10–1293

| Federal Communications Commission, et al., Petitioners | On writ of certiorari to the United States Court of Appeals for the Second Circuit |

v.

Fox Television Stations, Inc., et al.

Federal Communications Commission, et al., Petitioners

v.

ABC, Inc., et al.

[June 21, 2012]

[Footnotes and most citations have been omitted.]

JUSTICE KENNEDY delivered the opinion of the Court.

In *FCC* v. *Fox Television Stations, Inc.*, the Court held that the Federal Communication Commission's decision to modify its indecency enforcement regime to regulate so-called fleeting expletives was neither arbitrary nor capricious. The Court then declined to address the constitutionality of the policy, however, because the United States Court of Appeals for the Second Circuit had yet to do so. On remand, the Court of Appeals found the policy was vague and, as a result, unconstitutional. The case now returns to this Court for decision upon the constitutional question.

[Section I, containing a discussion of the background of the case, has been omitted.]

II

A fundamental principle in our legal system is that laws which regulate persons or entities must give fair notice of conduct that is forbidden or required. This requirement of clarity in regulation is essential to the protections provided by the Due Process Clause of the Fifth Amendment. It requires the invalidation of laws that are impermissibly vague. A conviction or punishment fails to comply with due process if the statute or regulation under which it is obtained "fails to provide a person of ordinary intelligence fair notice of what is prohibited, or is so standardless that it authorizes or encourages seriously discriminatory enforcement." As this Court has explained, a regulation is not vague because it may at times be difficult to prove an incriminating fact but rather because it is unclear as to what fact must be proved.

Even when speech is not at issue, the void for vagueness doctrine addresses at least two connected but discrete due process concerns: first, that regulated parties should know what is required of them so they may act accordingly; second, precision and guidance are necessary so that those enforcing the law do not act in an arbitrary or discriminatory way. When speech is involved, rigorous adherence to those requirements is necessary to ensure that ambiguity does not chill protected speech.

These concerns are implicated here because, at the outset, the broadcasters claim they did not have, and do not have, sufficient notice of what is proscribed. And leaving aside any concerns about facial invalidity, they contend that the lengthy procedural history set forth above shows that the broadcasters did not have fair notice of what was forbidden. Under the 2001 Guidelines in force when the broadcasts occurred, a key was "'whether the material dwell[ed] on or repeat[ed] at length'" the offending description or depiction. In the 2004 *Golden Globes* Order, issued after the broadcasts, the Commission changed course and held that fleeting expletives could be a statutory violation. In the challenged orders now under review the Commission applied the new principle promulgated in the *Golden Globes* Order and determined fleeting expletives and a brief moment of indecency were actionably indecent. This regulatory history, however, makes it apparent that the Commission policy in place at the time of the broadcasts gave no notice to Fox or ABC that a fleeting expletive or a brief shot of nudity could be actionably indecent; yet Fox and ABC were found to be in violation. The Commission's lack of notice to Fox and ABC that its interpretation had changed so the fleeting moments of indecency contained in their broadcasts were a violation of §1464 as interpreted and enforced by the agency "fail[ed] to provide a person of ordinary intelligence fair notice of what is prohibited." This would be true with respect to a regulatory change this abrupt on any subject, but it is surely the case when applied to the regulations in question, regulations that touch upon "sensitive areas of basic First Amendment freedoms."

The Government raises two arguments in response, but neither is persuasive. As for the two fleeting expletives, the Government concedes that "Fox did not have reasonable notice at the time of the broadcasts that the Commission would consider non-repeated expletives indecent." The Government argues, nonetheless, that Fox "cannot establish unconstitutional vagueness on that basis . . . because the Commission did not impose a sanction where Fox lacked such notice." As the Court observed when the case was here three Terms ago, it is true that the Commission declined to impose any forfeiture on Fox, and in its order the Commission claimed that it would not consider the indecent broadcasts either when considering whether to renew stations' licenses or "in any other context." This "policy of forbearance," as the Government calls it, does not suffice to make the issue moot. Though the Commission claims it will not consider the prior indecent broadcasts "in any context," it has the statutory power to take into account "any history of prior offenses" when setting the level of a forfeiture penalty. Just as in the First Amendment context, the due process protection against vague regulations "does not leave [regulated parties] . . . at the mercy of *noblesse oblige.*" Given that the Commission found it was "not inequitable to hold Fox responsible for [the 2003 broadcast]," and that it has the statutory authority to use its finding to increase any future penalties, the Government's assurance it will elect not to do so is insufficient to remedy the constitutional violation.

In addition, when combined with the legal consequence described above, reputational injury provides further reason for granting relief to Fox. As respondent CBS points out, findings of wrongdoing can result in harm to a broadcaster's "reputation with viewers and advertisers." This observation is hardly surprising given that the challenged orders, which are contained in the permanent Commission record, describe in strongly disapproving terms the indecent material broadcast by Fox, and Fox's efforts to protect children from being exposed to it. Commission sanctions on broadcasters for indecent material are widely publicized. The challenged orders could have an adverse impact on Fox's reputation that audiences and advertisers alike are entitled to take into account.

With respect to ABC, the Government with good reason does not argue no sanction was imposed. The fine against ABC and its network affiliates for the seven seconds of nudity was nearly $1.24 million. The Government argues instead that ABC had notice that the scene in NYPD Blue would be considered indecent in light of a 1960 decision where the Commission declared that the "televising of nudes might well raise a serious question of programming contrary to 18 U. S. C. §1464." This argument does not prevail. An isolated and ambiguous statement from a 1960 Commission decision does not suffice for the fair notice required when the Government intends to impose over a $1 million fine for allegedly impermissible speech. The Commission, furthermore, had released decisions before sanctioning ABC that declined to find isolated and brief moments of nudity actionably indecent. This is not to say, of course, that a graphic scene from Schindler's List involving nude concentration camp prisoners is the same as the shower scene from NYPD Blue. It does show, however, that the Government can point to nothing that would have given ABC affirmative notice that its broadcast would be considered actionably indecent. It is likewise not sufficient for the Commission to assert, as it did in its order, that though "the depiction [of nudity] here is not as lengthy or repeated" as in some cases, the shower scene nonetheless "does contain more shots or lengthier depictions of nudity" than in other broadcasts found not indecent. This broad language fails to demonstrate that ABC had fair notice that its broadcast could be found indecent. In fact, a Commission ruling prior to the airing of the NYPD Blue episode had deemed 30 seconds of nude buttocks "very brief" and not actionably indecent in the context of the broadcast. In light of this record of agency decisions, and the absence of any notice in the 2001 Guidance that seven seconds of nude buttocks would be found indecent, ABC lacked constitutionally sufficient notice prior to being sanctioned.

The Commission failed to give Fox or ABC fair notice prior to the broadcasts in question that fleeting expletives and momentary nudity could be found actionably indecent. Therefore, the Commission's standards as applied to these broadcasts were vague, and the Commission's orders must be set aside.

III

It is necessary to make three observations about the scope of this decision. First, because the Court resolves these cases on fair notice grounds under the Due Process Clause, it need not address the First Amendment implications of the Commission's indecency policy. It is argued that this Court's ruling in *Pacifica* (and the less rigorous standard of scrutiny it provided for the regulation of broadcasters) should be overruled because the rationale of that case has been overtaken by technological change and the wide availability of multiple other choices for listeners and viewers. The Government for its part maintains that when it licenses a conventional broadcast spectrum the public may assume that the Government has its own interest in setting certain standards. These arguments need not be addressed here. In light of the Court's holding that the Commission's policy failed to provide fair notice it is unnecessary to reconsider *Pacifica* at this time.

This leads to a second observation. Here, the Court rules that Fox and ABC lacked notice at the time of their broadcasts that the material they were broadcasting could be found actionably indecent under then-existing policies. Given this disposition, it is unnecessary for the Court to address the constitutionality of the current indecency policy as expressed in the *Golden Globes* Order and subsequent adjudications. The Court adheres to its normal practice of declining to decide cases not before it.

Third, this opinion leaves the Commission free to modify its current indecency policy in light of its determination of the public interest and applicable legal requirements. And it leaves the courts free to review the current policy or any modified policy in light of its content and application.

* * *

The judgments of the United States Court of Appeals for the Second Circuit are vacated, and the cases are remanded for further proceedings consistent with the principles set forth in this opinion.

It is so ordered.

JUSTICE SOTOMAYOR took no part in the consideration or decision of these cases.

JUSTICE GINSBURG, concurring in the judgment.

In my view, the Court's decision in *FCC v. Pacifica Foundation* was wrong when it issued. Time, technological advances, and the Commission's untenable rulings in the cases now before the Court show why *Pacifica* bears reconsideration. (THOMAS, J., concurring).

Source: U.S. Supreme Court. *FCC v. Fox Television Stations, Inc.,* 567 U.S. __ (2012). http://www.supreme court.gov/opinions/11pdf/10–1293f3e5.pdf.

Other Historic Documents of Interest

From previous *Historic Documents*

- ■ Court on "Indecent" Broadcasts, *1978,* p. 515

New Egyptian President Delivers Victory Speech

JUNE 24, 2012

Egypt's February 2011 revolution that toppled longtime leader Hosni Mubarak ushered in an era of instability for the Arab world's most populous country. Protesters without a well-defined political agenda or cohesive leadership structure watched as power was initially handed over to the Egyptian military, which was expected to be the savior of the people and institute democratic reform. But soon, Egyptians were finding their fate similar to that under Mubarak's rule—the military cracked down on opposition and issued decrees that made it clear that it did not intend to hand over power to a new, democratically elected president, as it had initially promised.

In 2012, however, elections went forward to choose a president, with Mohamed Morsi winning the election. As the newly inaugurated leader, and first Islamist head of state in an Arab nation, Morsi faced wide-ranging challenges from a faltering economy to ensuring political stability and bringing together supporters of the military and Mubarak, young secular activists, and his own party, the Muslim Brotherhood. Morsi succeeded in weakening the role of the military in executive and legislative affairs and awarded himself the power to influence the drafting and ratification of the nation's new constitution.

ARAB SPRING TOPPLES LEADER

Mubarak took the reins in Egypt, following the assassination of Anwar el-Sadat in 1981. Mubarak kept his dissenters quiet by governing under an emergency law, giving his regime the power to arrest without reason, detain prisoners without charges or trials, and stop any form of assembly. Although increasingly unpopular, for many years, Mubarak's rule was largely uncontested because there was little cohesive, legitimate opposition among the Egyptian people. While the Muslim Brotherhood at the time stood as a unified opposition party, it was banned by Mubarak from political participation.

But after Tunisians overthrew their own autocratic ruler, Zine al-Abidine Ben Ali, in early 2011, Egyptians took that as a cue to make changes in their own country. Protesters took to the streets beginning on January 25, demonstrating mainly in Cairo's Tahrir Square, calling for greater democratic freedom and accountability for government leaders. Young, secular activists joined members of the Muslim Brotherhood, calling for Mubarak to resign, which he did after eighteen days of protest on February 11, 2011, having lost the support of his military and no longer able to withstand the continued opposition.

MILITARY TAKES CONTROL

In resigning, Mubarak handed control to the Supreme Council of the Armed Forces (SCAF). The military did little to open up the government, as had initially been the hope of many protesters, sparking fears that little freedom would come from the revolution. After taking control, the military kept Mubarak's emergency laws in place to stop any remaining demonstrations. Although it first announced that it would not hand over power until after parliamentary and presidential elections in 2012, the SCAF reversed its decision in October 2011, stating that it would give the president and parliament a subordinate role in the government and would appoint a prime minister and cabinet itself. However, the SCAF allowed parliamentary elections to move forward as planned, which put members of the Muslim Brotherhood in a majority of the seats, but the October 2011 decree allowed the military to retain a large portion of government control.

NEW PRESIDENT FACES MANY CHALLENGES

Initially, the Brotherhood, the largest political force in Egypt, had promised not to seek the presidency, but in March it put forward a candidate who was subsequently denied the opportunity to run because of a criminal conviction during Mubarak's reign. Instead, the Brotherhood turned to Morsi, a conservative, American-educated Islamist who supports a strict Islamic vision. Following the first round of voting in May 2012, Morsi came out on top with Mubarak's last prime minister, Ahmed Shafik, in a field of thirteen candidates.

Shortly before the June runoff election between Morsi and Shafik, the SCAF dissolved parliament, giving itself control of all legislative activities and further limiting the power of the presidency. The SCAF based its decision on a court ruling that found the governing law under which the parliament was elected was partly unconstitutional. The presidential election went ahead as planned, and when the polls closed on June 17, Morsi declared victory. However, it was not until a week later when the Supreme Presidential Electoral Commission declared him the victor with nearly 52 percent of the vote to Shafik's 48 percent. In Tahrir Square, hub of the 2011 revolution, crowds cheered. "For the first time in history, we have our own president, elected by us. The power of the people is now in the hands of the president," said Abdul Mawgoud Dardery, a member of parliament from the Muslim Brotherhood Freedom and Justice Party.

In his first victory speech on June 18, Morsi said the new era ushered in by the election would be one of "stability, love and brotherhood for the Egyptian civil, national, democratic, constitutional and modern state." He continued, "We are all brothers of this nation, we own it together, and we are equal in rights and duties." He urged Egyptians from all religions and parties to begin working together because "national unity is the only way to get Egypt out of this difficult crisis." During his official victory speech on June 24, Morsi promised to show the world an Egyptian renaissance. He said he would "establish balanced relations with the world"; send a "message of peace" in international relations; and "maintain Egypt's national security." Morsi said he would "exert all efforts to deliver on my pledges. Egypt will be for all its sons. We are all equal in rights and duties."

With the presidency, although largely a figurehead position under SCAF decree, secured, Morsi faced many challenges, including boosting a floundering economy. Gross domestic product (GDP) increased less than 2 percent in 2011, down from around 7 percent in 2009, and unemployment increased from 9 percent in 2011 to 12 percent in 2012. Because of the uncertainty and instability throughout 2011 and 2012, foreign investment was almost nonexistent, and tourism, a pillar of the Egyptian economy, also fell in light of the revolution.

Perhaps a bigger challenge in the near term was how Morsi would bring about some form of political stability, especially as the nation drafted and ratified a new constitution.

Morsi showed his intent to circumvent the military on July 8, when he ordered parliament back into session. Later that month, Morsi named his own prime minister, Hesham Qandil, head of the Ministry of Water Resources and Irrigation under the SCAF interim cabinet. Regardless, the SCAF remained firm in its decision to retain military, legislative, and budgetary decisions until the new constitution was ratified. But in early August, Morsi forced the resignation of the army chief of staff, defense minister, and other senior military officials. He subsequently repealed the SCAF decree that took power away from the presidency, giving himself far-reaching executive and legislative power. According to the SCAF, the resignations took place only after consultations with Morsi and his top officials. Morsi said he did not want to embarrass military leaders but simply was acting for the good of the Egyptian people. "Today, this nation returns—this people return—with its blessed revolution," Morsi said, following the resignations.

In forming his government and solidifying his rule, Morsi also faced challenges from his secular opponents, many of whom fear that giving the Brotherhood so much power could lead to Egypt becoming an Islamic state. Morsi attempted to calm those fears, first by stepping down from the Brotherhood and its affiliated political party. He also met with the Coptic pope and has not taken positions on any social issues, which his dissenters view as biding his time until he has enough power to enforce Islamic social code on the Egyptian population.

MUBARAK SENTENCED

In May 2011, it was announced that Mubarak would stand trial in Egypt for the killing of at least 800 unarmed demonstrators during the January to February 2011 revolution. Mubarak's crimes were listed as "intentional murder, attempted killing of some demonstrators . . . , misuse of influence and deliberately wasting public funds and unlawfully making private financial gains and profits." Mubarak, who sought medical treatment in a Red Sea resort following his ouster, was wheeled into the courtroom on a hospital bed when his trial began in August 2011.

On June 2, 2012, after ten months of trial proceedings, the court found Mubarak guilty of accessory to murder and complacency in not stopping his security forces from killing unarmed demonstrators. Judge Ahmed Rifaat, in a statement before issuing the ruling, described Mubarak's reign as "a darkened nightmare" that was brought to an end only by those who "peacefully demanded democracy from rulers who held tight grip on power." Rifaat said in his ruling that the prosecution failed to "prove that main defendants committed" the killings but that there was enough evidence to conclude that they were responsible for failing to stop the acts.

Mubarak was sentenced to life in prison, a judgment met with anger from many Egyptians who thought the former ruler should receive the death penalty. Six senior interior ministry officials tried alongside Mubarak were acquitted, while former interior minister Habib al Adli was found guilty of accessory to murder. Mubarak's two sons were also acquitted on charges of corruption.

It is unknown when Mubarak will begin serving his sentence, as the ruling is likely to be appealed. Critics of the trial said that investigations into wrongdoing by Mubarak were sloppy and that relatively little evidence was presented against the former ruler on the charge of killing protesters, which may lead to an acquittal upon appeal. The Muslim Brotherhood called the verdict an attempt to "cover up crimes, waste the blood of the martyrs and impede the establishment of truth and justice." Opponents also said that the ruling would embolden the SCAF by making it clear that it was free to do as it pleased without risking prosecution.

—Heather Kerrigan

Following is the text of the victory speech delivered by Egyptian President Mohamed Morsi on June 24, 2012.

President Morsi Delivers Victory Speech

June 24, 2012

In the name of Allah Most Gracious and Compassionate

The Great Egyptian people, who are celebrating today the gala of democracy. I thank God for having lived this historic moment in which a new bright page of Egypt's history was written by the hands of Egyptians and their sacrifices and will.

I would not have stood before you today as an elected president through the free will of the Egyptians in the first presidential elections after [the] January revolution but through the providence of God and the sacrifices of the great martyrs of the revolution.

I thank all those who lost a dear next of kin and sacrificed for the sake of Egypt. I pray for the souls of the martyrs and the injured who nourished with their blood the tree of freedom and paved the way for us to live this moment. All appreciation and thanks to the families of the martyrs who endured the loss of their sons and paid that price for freedom. I renew my pledge that this clean blood will not go in vain.

All salute to the great people of Egypt and its Army men; the best soldiers on earth. I salute the Armed Forces with all its members. I appreciate their role and assert that I am keen on maintaining this great institution which we all respect and appreciate. I also salute the policemen.

All the honorable policemen deserve a heartfelt salute for the major role they are undertaking in maintaining the safety and security of the homeland.

I salute the men of the judiciary who supervised the elections. I also salute those who did not supervise the elections. The judiciary are the third authority that should remain sublime and high and separate from the executive authority. This will be my responsibility in the future, to keep the judges independent from the executive and legislative authorities.

I tell all the Egyptian people on this landmark day that today I became president thanks to your will and choice.

I became president thanks to you and I will be president to all Egyptians standing at the same distance from you all with no discrimination among Egyptians but through how much each of them would contribute to their homeland and how far they would respect the law and constitution.

Egypt has dazzled the world with its revolution and the sacrifices of its youths. It has also fascinated the world with the queues of voters at polling stations and their keenness on participating in the elections during the polls on the constitutional declaration in March 2011, the legislative elections at the end of 2011 or the Shura Council in 2012 and the presidential elections in its two rounds which ended on June 17, and which we celebrate its results today.

Egypt is now in need to unify ranks and pool all efforts together so that that great people would reap the fruits of their sacrifices represented in living in dignity, social justice and freedom. These were the major and basic principles of the revolution in all Egyptian squares on January 25, 2011. The revolutionaries will remain calling for realizing these goals until they are fulfilled.

The Egyptian people have been patient for so long and suffered a great deal from diseases, hunger, oppression and marginalizing along with falsifying their public will in elections. We have been looking at other world countries and wonder when the Egyptian people would become the source of all authorities. Today you are the source of authorities with the world watching this great epic in Egypt that will pilot us to a better future.

With the help of God I have become your president. I promise to exert all efforts to deliver on my pledges. Egypt will be for all its sons. We are all equal in rights and duties. As for me, I have no rights but only have duties. So I ask you to help me in as long as I observed justice in my job. If not and if I would not be fair with you do not obey my instructions.

I urge you all the great Egyptian people at this historic moment to consolidate our national unity. We are all Egyptians even if we have different views. We are all patriotic even if we belong to different parties and trends. We are loyal to the revolution and to the blood of the martyrs. There is no room for confrontations or mistrust.

National unity is the only way so that Egypt would get out of this difficult phase and forge ahead towards a comprehensive national project for development through which all our potentials are harnessed. These potentials have been squandered and misused. But now we are seeking to attain the national interests of every body.

I urge you all to start our comprehensive project for development with the hands of the Egyptians. All Egyptians; Muslims and Copts, are advocates of civilization and construction. We will remain so and stand up to seditions and plots that are seeking to undermine our national unity and social fabric.

I am keen, with your help, to fascinate the world with the Egyptian renaissance that attains dignity, stability and decent living to everybody. I am determined, with your help, to build the new Egypt as a modern State of constitution.

I will work hard, with your assistance, to maintain Egypt's national security in all its Arab, African, regional and international dimensions. We will uphold all international treaties and agreements. We are driving home to the world a message of peace. I will abide by all Egyptian agreements and commitments with the whole world. We will work so that the system of Egyptian values and its civilizational identity be an addition to the humanitarian values especially in the fields of freedoms and respect of human rights along with maintaining the rights of women and children and eliminating all forms of discrimination.

I will work to establish balanced relations with the world countries and big powers on the basis of mutual respect and reciprocal interests among all parties concerned. We will not allow ourselves to interfere in the internal affairs of other countries and at the same time will not allow others to interfere in our own affairs. We will maintain our national sovereignty and the borders of the State of Egypt. Everybody should realize that the Egyptian decision emanates from the will of its sons and that Egypt is a peace advocate to the whole world at a time when it is able, with its Armed Forces and people to defend itself and deter any aggression on its territories or on any of its sons wherever he is in the world.

The great Egyptian people, I am well aware of the challenges of the current situation. But I am confident that with the help of God and your assistance we will be able to overcome this hard phase so that Egypt would become strong and [a] major country in the world.

While we are celebrating that gala of democracy after the elections, I renew my pledge not to betray you and to keep your interests always in my mind.

Repeat with me that with our will, unity and love we will be able to carve out a better future for all of us.

May God's peace and blessings be upon you all.

SOURCE: Egyptian State Information Service. "Statement by President Mohammed Morsi After Winning the Post of the President." June 24, 2012. http://www.sis.gov.eg/En/Story.aspx?sid=62577.

OTHER HISTORIC DOCUMENTS OF INTEREST

FROM THIS VOLUME

- Egypt Announces Presidential Decree, Acceptance of Draft Constitution, p. 567

FROM PREVIOUS *HISTORIC DOCUMENTS*

- Arab Spring: International Response to Mubarak's Resignation (Egypt), *2011,* p. 95

Supreme Court Rules on Arizona Immigration Law

On June 25, 2012, the U.S. Supreme Court, in a split decision, overturned some provisions of Arizona's controversial anti-illegal immigration law but left standing, at least for now, the law's centerpiece. The Court's decision in *Arizona v. United States* strongly asserted the primacy of the federal government's authority over the subject of immigration and the status of aliens. While acknowledging that Arizona has legitimate concerns regarding illegal immigration to its state, the majority of the Court held that three key provisions of the Arizona law, known as Senate Bill (SB) 1070, impermissibly conflict with federal immigration law and are, therefore, preempted. The Court unanimously upheld part of the Arizona law known to its critics as the "show me your papers" provision, which requires police to verify the immigration status of those they stop, detain, or arrest on some other legitimate basis if they have a reasonable suspicion they are undocumented aliens. While critics said this provision would be a recipe for racial profiling, the Court wrote that it was premature to make that judgment given that the law had been challenged before it had ever taken effect, so there was no record showing that its enforcement would similarly create conflicts with federal law.

ARIZONA'S IMMIGRATION LAW

On April 23, 2010, Arizona Governor Jan Brewer signed into law the Support Our Law Enforcement and Safe Neighborhoods Act, more commonly referred to as SB 1070. Supporters and critics alike called it the nation's toughest bill on illegal immigration in generations. The stated purpose of the law was to "discourage and deter the unlawful entry and presence of aliens and economic activity by persons unlawfully present in the United States," and it explicitly established a statewide policy of "attrition through enforcement." The law created new state offenses for being present in Arizona without legal immigration status and gave police new arrest authority and investigative duties with respect to certain aliens.

Anger over this new law fueled protests in Arizona and cities around the nation and brought the divisive issue of immigration to the presidential race. Before it was even signed, President Barack Obama criticized the law as threatening "to undermine basic notions of fairness that we cherish as Americans, as well as the trust between police and our communities that is so crucial to keeping us safe." The foreign ministry of Mexico released a statement that it was worried about the impact of the law on the rights of its citizens and its relations with Arizona. Within weeks, hundreds of thousands of protesters joined marches and rallies in more than seventy cities across the country, calling for a national overhaul of the nation's immigration law and a repeal of the law in Arizona. News coverage showed marchers in "Boycott Arizona" T-shirts and carrying banners reading "Overturn Arizona Apartheid." Most polling, however, showed the law to be broadly popular both in Arizona and the nation as a whole.

Supporters of Arizona's law said that the state was acting only because the federal government had failed to enforce immigration laws, and events such as the killing of a rancher in southern Arizona by a suspected smuggler were fueling fears of rising crime caused by illegal aliens. Critics, such as Mayor Antonio Villaraigosa of Los Angeles, told crowds: "Let me be clear about those laws that make suspects out of people based on the color of their skin; they have no place in our great country."

In a highly unusual step, the Obama administration sued Arizona to block the implementation of SB 1070. Typically, the Department of Justice will file a brief or intervene in a lawsuit filed by others against states, but only very rarely does the federal government sue a state directly. Just hours before the law was to take effect, United States District Court Judge Susan Bolton granted the Department of Justice's motion for a temporary injunction against the most contentious provisions of the Arizona law, ruling that these sections were preempted by the federal government's authority to determine immigration law. The Ninth Circuit Court of Appeals also ruled against Arizona, blocking the law from going into effect. Governor Brewer of Arizona appealed the ruling directly to the U.S. Supreme Court.

EMPHASIS ON FEDERAL PRIMACY

At issue before the Supreme Court was whether four challenged provisions of the state law were impermissibly "in conflict or at cross-purposes" with the national immigration framework and, therefore, "preempted" by the federal law. As the Court explained, in an opinion written by Justice Anthony Kennedy, the Supremacy Clause of Article VI, section 2, of the Constitution provides that federal law "shall be the supreme law of the land; and the judges in every state shall be bound thereby." States are precluded from regulating activity in any field that Congress, acting within its proper authority, determines it should regulate exclusively. The Court noted that there are three ways a state law can be preempted by a federal law: (1) the statute expressly contains a preemption provision (express preemption), (2) Congress intended to wholly occupy the regulatory field (field preemption), or (3) state or local action conflicts with or otherwise frustrates the purpose of the federal scheme (conflict preemption).

Against this background, Justice Kennedy emphasized that the federal government has "broad, undoubted power over the subject of immigration and the status of aliens." This power comes from Article 1 of the Constitution, which gives the federal government power to "establish an uniform Rule of Naturalization," as well as the "sovereign power to control and conduct foreign relations." The federal scheme to govern immigration and alien status is, Justice Kennedy describes, "pervasive," "extensive and complex", and provides for "broad discretion exercised by immigration officials," including with respect to aliens who may be deported for being present in the country in violation of federal immigration law. This discretion is important, as some decisions "involve policy choices that bear on this Nation's international relations" and must be consistent with U.S. foreign policy.

Turning to the four challenged provisions of SB 1070, the Court found that the first three were preempted by federal law. These included provisions (1) making failure to comply with federal alien-registration requirements a state misdemeanor, (2) making it a state crime for an alien to seek or engage in work in the state, and (3) authorizing state police to arrest aliens on the basis of possible removability from the United States. For various reasons, Justice Kennedy's majority opinion found all of these provisions to interfere impermissibly with a careful balance struck by Congress and to create obstacles to the full purposes of the immigration system Congress created.

The fourth challenged provision of SB 1070 was unanimously upheld by the Court. It requires Arizona police to "determine the immigration status" of any person they stop, detain, or arrest on some other legitimate basis if "reasonable suspicion exists that the person is an alien and is unlawfully present in the United States." The Court found that the federal scheme left room for a policy requiring state officials to contact the federal immigration officials as a routine matter. Emphasizing the need for caution when the federal government brings suit against a sovereign state to challenge a provision even before the law has gone into effect—when there is still basic uncertainty about how the law will be interpreted and enforced—the Court declined to interpret it in a way that creates a conflict with federal law. The opinion emphasized, however, that it is not foreclosing other challenges once the law has been applied.

Chief Justice John Roberts and Justices Ruth Bader Ginsburg, Stephen Breyer, and Sonia Sotomayor joined Justice Kennedy's opinion. Justice Elena Kagan recused herself, presumably because she had worked on the case in her previous position as solicitor general. Justices Antonin Scalia, Clarence Thomas, and Samuel Alito each wrote a separate dissent from the opinion. Justice Scalia took the unusual step of summarizing his dissent in a statement from the bench, indicating his deep disagreement. He argued that, as a sovereign state, "Arizona has the inherent power to exclude persons from its territory." In this case, he wrote, "Arizona has moved to protect its sovereignty—not in contradiction of federal law, but in complete compliance with it." He concludes, "If securing its territory in this fashion is not within the power of Arizona, we should cease referring to it as a sovereign state."

More unusual still than reading from a dissent, Justice Scalia criticized a recently articulated Obama administration policy on deportation, modeled on the DREAM (Development, Relief, and Education for Alien Minors) Act that was outside of the record of the case before the Court. The new enforcement policy would let immigrants who came to the United States as children avoid deportation if they are younger than thirty, have no criminal record, and meet other conditions. "To say, as the Court does," Justice Scalia writes, "that Arizona *contradicts federal law* by enforcing applications of the Immigration Act that the President declines to enforce boggles the mind."

Reaction to the Ruling

Arizona v. United States made it clear that the courts will allow a much more limited role for independent state action in the field of immigration enforcement than originally thought. States such as Alabama, Georgia, Indiana, South Carolina, and Utah, which had passed tough laws to stem illegal immigration that were patterned on the Arizona law, will no doubt face challenges. Lower courts will have to try to apply the holding of this case when addressing issues that were not specifically faced by the Supreme Court, such as state laws requiring schools to determine the immigration status of enrolling students or laws penalizing aliens for applying for driver's licenses. An Eleventh Circuit Court of Appeals case decided after *Arizona v. United States* struck down portions of both an Alabama and a Georgia law that imposed penalties for alien smuggling, holding that they were preempted by federal immigration law.

The political reaction to the case was immediate and profound. Stating that he was pleased with the decision, President Obama called for Congress to act on comprehensive immigration reform, since "a patchwork of state laws is not a solution to our broken immigration system." Republican presidential candidate Mitt Romney's spokesperson said, "The governor supports the states' rights to craft immigration laws when the federal government has failed to do so." Many report that reaction to the Arizona law and the Court decision were part of what fueled a record turnout of Latino voters in the 2012 presidential election, of which 71 percent voted for President Obama.

—Melissa Feinberg

The following are excerpts from the U.S. Supreme Court ruling in Arizona v. United States, *in which the Court ruled 5–3 that portions of Arizona's controversial immigration law, including the "show me your papers" provision, could remain intact, while other portions are preempted by federal immigration law.*

DOCUMENT   *Arizona v. United States*

June 25, 2012

No. 11–182

Arizona, et al., Petitioners

v.

United States

On writ of certiorari
to the United States
Court of Appeals for
the Ninth Circuit

[June 25, 2012]

[Footnotes and most citations have been omitted.]

JUSTICE KENNEDY delivered the opinion of the Court.

To address pressing issues related to the large number of aliens within its borders who do not have a lawful right to be in this country, the State of Arizona in 2010 enacted a statute called the Support Our Law Enforcement and Safe Neighborhoods Act. The law is often referred to as S. B. 1070, the version introduced in the state senate. Its stated purpose is to "discourage and deter the unlawful entry and presence of aliens and economic activity by persons unlawfully present in the United States." The law's provisions establish an official state policy of "attrition through enforcement." The question before the Court is whether federal law preempts and renders invalid four separate provisions of the state law.

[Section I, containing background on the case, has been omitted.]

II

A

The Government of the United States has broad, undoubted power over the subject of immigration and the status of aliens. This authority rests, in part, on the National Government's constitutional power to "establish an uniform Rule of Naturalization," and its inherent power as sovereign to control and conduct relations with foreign nations.

The federal power to determine immigration policy is well settled. Immigration policy can affect trade, investment, tourism, and diplomatic relations for the entire Nation, as well as the perceptions and expectations of aliens in this country who seek the full protection of its laws. Perceived mistreatment of aliens in the United States may lead to harmful reciprocal treatment of American citizens abroad.

It is fundamental that foreign countries concerned about the status, safety, and security of their nationals in the United States must be able to confer and communicate on this subject with one national sovereign, not the 50 separate States. This Court has reaffirmed that "[o]ne of the most important and delicate of all international relationships . . . has to do with the protection of the just rights of a country's own nationals when those nationals are in another country."

Federal governance of immigration and alien status is extensive and complex. Congress has specified categories of aliens who may not be admitted to the United States. Unlawful entry and unlawful reentry into the country are federal offenses. Once here, aliens are required to register with the Federal Government and to carry proof of status on their person. Failure to do so is a federal misdemeanor. Federal law also authorizes States to deny noncitizens a range of public benefits; and it imposes sanctions on employers who hire unauthorized workers.

Congress has specified which aliens may be removed from the United States and the procedures for doing so. Aliens may be removed if they were inadmissible at the time of entry, have been convicted of certain crimes, or meet other criteria set by federal law. Removal is a civil, not criminal, matter. A principal feature of the removal system is the broad discretion exercised by immigration officials. Federal officials, as an initial matter, must decide whether it makes sense to pursue removal at all. If removal proceedings commence, aliens may seek asylum and other discretionary relief allowing them to remain in the country or at least to leave without formal removal.

Discretion in the enforcement of immigration law embraces immediate human concerns. Unauthorized workers trying to support their families, for example, likely pose less danger than alien smugglers or aliens who commit a serious crime. The equities of an individual case may turn on many factors, including whether the alien has children born in the United States, long ties to the community, or a record of distinguished military service. Some discretionary decisions involve policy choices that bear on this Nation's international relations. Returning an alien to his own country may be deemed inappropriate even where he has committed a removable offense or fails to meet the criteria for admission. The foreign state may be mired in civil war, complicit in political persecution, or enduring conditions that create a real risk that the alien or his family will be harmed upon return. The dynamic nature of relations with other countries requires the Executive Branch to ensure that enforcement policies are consistent with this Nation's foreign policy with respect to these and other realities. . . .

B

The pervasiveness of federal regulation does not diminish the importance of immigration policy to the States. Arizona bears many of the consequences of unlawful immigration. Hundreds of thousands of deportable aliens are apprehended in Arizona each year. . . .

. . . The issue is whether, under preemption principles, federal law permits Arizona to implement the state-law provisions in dispute.

III

Federalism, central to the constitutional design, adopts the principle that both the National and State Governments have elements of sovereignty the other is bound to respect. From the existence of two sovereigns follows the possibility that laws can be in conflict or at cross-purposes. The Supremacy Clause provides a clear rule that federal law "shall be the supreme Law of the Land; and the Judges in every State shall be bound thereby, any Thing in the Constitution or Laws of any State to the Contrary notwithstanding." Under this principle, Congress has the power to preempt state law. There is no doubt that Congress may withdraw specified powers from the States by enacting a statute containing an express preemption provision.

State law must also give way to federal law in at least two other circumstances. First, the States are precluded from regulating conduct in a field that Congress, acting within its proper authority, has determined must be regulated by its exclusive governance. The intent to displace state law altogether can be inferred from a framework of regulation "so pervasive . . . that Congress left no room for the States to supplement it" or where there is a "federal interest . . . so dominant that the federal system will be assumed to preclude enforcement of state laws on the same subject."

Second, state laws are preempted when they conflict with federal law. *Crosby, supra,* at 372. This includes cases where "compliance with both federal and state regulations is a physical impossibility," and those instances where the challenged state law "stands as an obstacle to the accomplishment and execution of the full purposes and objectives of Congress." In preemption analysis, courts should assume that "the historic police powers of the States" are not superseded "unless that was the clear and manifest purpose of Congress."

The four challenged provisions of the state law each must be examined under these preemption principles.

IV

A

SECTION 3

Section 3 of S. B. 1070 creates a new state misdemeanor. It forbids the "willful failure to complete or carry an alien registration document . . . in violation of 8 United States Code section 1304(e) or 1306(a)." In effect, §3 adds a state-law penalty for conduct proscribed by federal law. The United States contends that this state enforcement mechanism intrudes on the field of alien registration, a field in which Congress has left no room for States to regulate. . . .

The framework enacted by Congress leads to the conclusion here, as it did in *Hines,* that the Federal Government has occupied the field of alien registration. The federal statutory directives provide a full set of standards governing alien registration, including the punishment for noncompliance. It was designed as a "'harmonious whole.'" Where Congress occupies an entire field, as it has in the field of alien registration, even complementary state regulation is impermissible. Field preemption reflects a congressional decision to foreclose any state regulation in the area, even if it is parallel to federal standards.

Federal law makes a single sovereign responsible for maintaining a comprehensive and unified system to keep track of aliens within the Nation's borders. If §3 of the Arizona statute were valid, every State could give itself independent authority to prosecute federal registration violations, "diminish[ing] the [Federal Government]'s control over enforcement" and "detract[ing] from the 'integrated scheme of regulation' created by Congress." . . .

. . . [T]he Court now concludes that, with respect to the subject of alien registration, Congress intended to preclude States from "complement[ing] the federal law, or enforc[ing] additional or auxiliary regulations." Section 3 is preempted by federal law.

B

Section 5(C)

Unlike §3, which replicates federal statutory requirements, §5(C) enacts a state criminal prohibition where no federal counterpart exists. The provision makes it a state misdemeanor for "an unauthorized alien to knowingly apply for work, solicit work in a public place or perform work as an employee or independent contractor" in Arizona. Violations can be punished by a $2,500 fine and incarceration for up to six months. The United States contends that the provision upsets the balance struck by the Immigration Reform and Control Act of 1986 (IRCA) and must be preempted as an obstacle to the federal plan of regulation and control.

[A discussion of conflicts in state and federal immigration law has been omitted.]

The ordinary principles of preemption include the well-settled proposition that a state law is preempted where it "stands as an obstacle to the accomplishment and execution of the full purposes and objectives of Congress." Under §5(C) of S. B. 1070, Arizona law would interfere with the careful balance struck by Congress with respect to unauthorized employment of aliens. Although §5(C) attempts to achieve one of the same goals as federal law—the deterrence of unlawful employment—it involves a conflict in the method of enforcement. The Court has recognized that a "[c]onflict in technique can be fully as disruptive to the system Congress enacted as conflict in overt policy." The correct instruction to draw from the text, structure, and history of IRCA is that Congress decided it would be inappropriate to impose criminal penalties on aliens who seek or engage in unauthorized employment. It follows that a state law to the contrary is an obstacle to the regulatory system Congress chose. Section 5(C) is preempted by federal law.

C

Section 6

Section 6 of S. B. 1070 provides that a state officer, "without a warrant, may arrest a person if the officer has probable cause to believe . . . [the person] has committed any public offense that makes [him] removable from the United States."

[Information on how Section 6 interferes with federal law has been omitted.]

Congress has put in place a system in which state officers may not make warrantless arrests of aliens based on possible removability except in specific, limited circumstances.

By nonetheless authorizing state and local officers to engage in these enforcement activities as a general matter, §6 creates an obstacle to the full purposes and objectives of Congress. Section 6 is preempted by federal law.

D

Section 2(B)

Section 2(B) of S. B. 1070 requires state officers to make a "reasonable attempt . . . to determine the immigration status" of any person they stop, detain, or arrest on some other legitimate basis if "reasonable suspicion exists that the person is an alien and is unlawfully present in the United States." The law also provides that "[a]ny person who is arrested shall have the person's immigration status determined before the person is released." The accepted way to perform these status checks is to contact ICE, which maintains a database of immigration records.

[Section I and the majority of Section II, containing additional discussion on Section 2(B), have been omitted.]

The nature and timing of this case counsel caution in evaluating the validity of §2(B). The Federal Government has brought suit against a sovereign State to challenge the provision even before the law has gone into effect. There is a basic uncertainty about what the law means and how it will be enforced. At this stage, without the benefit of a definitive interpretation from the state courts, it would be inappropriate to assume §2(B) will be construed in a way that creates a conflict with federal law. As a result, the United States cannot prevail in its current challenge. This opinion does not foreclose other preemption and constitutional challenges to the law as interpreted and applied after it goes into effect.

V

Immigration policy shapes the destiny of the Nation. On May 24, 2012, at one of this Nation's most distinguished museums of history, a dozen immigrants stood before the tattered flag that inspired Francis Scott Key to write the National Anthem. There they took the oath to become American citizens. These naturalization ceremonies bring together men and women of different origins who now share a common destiny. They swear a common oath to renounce fidelity to foreign princes, to defend the Constitution, and to bear arms on behalf of the country when required by law. The history of the United States is in part made of the stories, talents, and lasting contributions of those who crossed oceans and deserts to come here.

The National Government has significant power to regulate immigration. With power comes responsibility, and the sound exercise of national power over immigration depends on the Nation's meeting its responsibility to base its laws on a political will informed by searching, thoughtful, rational civic discourse. Arizona may have understandable frustrations with the problems caused by illegal immigration while that process continues, but the State may not pursue policies that undermine federal law.

* * *

The United States has established that §§3, 5(C), and 60f S. B. 1070 are preempted. It was improper, however, to enjoin §2(B) before the state courts had an opportunity to construe it and without some showing that enforcement of the provision in fact conflicts with federal immigration law and its objectives.

The judgment of the Court of Appeals for the Ninth Circuit is affirmed in part and reversed in part. The case is remanded for further proceedings consistent with this opinion.

It is so ordered.

JUSTICE KAGAN took no part in the consideration or decision of this case.

JUSTICE SCALIA, concurring in part and dissenting in part.

The United States is an indivisible "Union of Sovereign States." Today's opinion, approving virtually all of the Ninth Circuit's injunction against enforcement of the four challenged provisions of Arizona's law, deprives States of what most would consider the defining characteristic of sovereignty: the power to exclude from the sovereign's territory people who have no right to be there. Neither the Constitution itself nor even any law passed by Congress supports this result. I dissent.

[A majority of the remaining text, which includes Scalia's reasoning for his concurrence and dissent, has been omitted.]

As is often the case, discussion of the dry legalities that are the proper object of our attention suppresses the very human realities that gave rise to the suit. Arizona bears the brunt of the country's illegal immigration problem. Its citizens feel themselves under siege by large numbers of illegal immigrants who invade their property, strain their social services, and even place their lives in jeopardy. Federal officials have been unable to remedy the problem, and indeed have recently shown that they are unwilling to do so. Thousands of Arizona's estimated 400,000 illegal immigrants—including not just children but men and women under 30—are now assured immunity from enforcement, and will be able to compete openly with Arizona citizens for employment.

Arizona has moved to protect its sovereignty—not in contradiction of federal law, but in complete compliance with it. The laws under challenge here do not extend or revise federal immigration restrictions, but merely enforce those restrictions more effectively. If securing its territory in this fashion is not within the power of Arizona, we should cease referring to it as a sovereign State. I dissent.

[Justices Thomas's and Alito's dissents, in which they concur in part and dissent in part, have been omitted.]

Source: U.S. Supreme Court. *Arizona v. United States,* 567 U.S. __ (2012). http://www.supremecourt.gov/opinions/11pdf/11-182b5e1.pdf.

OTHER HISTORIC DOCUMENTS OF INTEREST

FROM THIS VOLUME

FROM PREVIOUS *HISTORIC DOCUMENTS*

Supreme Court Rules on Life Without Parole for Juvenile Killers

JUNE 25, 2012

In *Miller v. Alabama,* the U.S. Supreme Court reviewed the convictions of two fourteen-year-old offenders who had been convicted of murder. In each case, the presiding judge had no discretion but was required by a mandatory sentencing guideline to sentence the convicted juvenile to life without the possibility of parole. Justice Elena Kagan wrote for the Court in a 5–4 decision, joined by Justice Anthony Kennedy, who has been a leader on the Court in monitoring the sentences of juveniles, as well as Justices Ruth Bader Ginsburg, Stephen Breyer, and Sonia Sotomayor. Kagan wrote that mandating these juveniles to die in prison, without being given an opportunity to present mitigating evidence of youth and lack of maturity, violates the Eighth Amendment's prohibitions on "cruel and unusual punishments." The decision did not categorically bar all such sentences but instead required that the sentence must take into account the defendants' youthfulness, extending a line of recent cases which established that children are different from adults in constitutionally relevant ways that require different treatment at sentencing.

CONVICTED OF MURDER AT FOURTEEN

The case before the Court consolidated the appeals of two petitioners who had been involved in killings when they were fourteen years old. The first was Kuntrell Jackson. He and two other boys decided to rob a video store, and on the way there, he learned that one of the other boys was carrying a gun in his coat sleeve. Jackson decided to stay outside as the other boys entered the store. He went in later, in time to see the store clerk shot in the head. The three boys fled. In Arkansas the prosecutors have the discretion to charge fourteen-year-olds as adults when they have committed certain serious offenses, and here, the prosecutor charged Jackson as an adult with capital felony murder and aggravated robbery. After a jury later convicted Jackson, the judge, noting that "in view of [the] verdict, there's only one possible punishment," sentenced him to life imprisonment without parole.

The second petitioner, Evan Miller, had by the age of fourteen been in and out of foster care because his mother was an alcoholic and drug addict, and his stepfather abused him. He also regularly abused drugs and alcohol and had attempted suicide four times, the first time when he was six years old. After smoking marijuana with his mother's drug dealer, Miller and a friend tried to steal the drug dealer's wallet after he had passed out. When he awoke and attacked the boys, Miller repeatedly hit him with a nearby baseball bat. Miller and his friend then decided to cover up the evidence by lighting the victim's trailer on fire. The victim eventually died from his injuries and smoke inhalation. The district attorney charged Miller as an adult with murder in the course of arson, a charge that carries a mandatory minimum penalty of life without parole.

After the petitioners lost their appeals before the supreme court of Arkansas and the supreme court of Alabama, the U.S. Supreme Court granted appeals to hear their cases.

SUPREME COURT FINDS EIGHTH AMENDMENT VIOLATION

The Eighth Amendment to the Constitution prohibits cruel and unusual punishment and has been interpreted to guarantee "individuals the right not to be subjected to excessive sanctions." In her majority opinion in this case, Kagan, the newest justice on the court, found that mandatory sentences of life without parole violated this prohibition when applied to juveniles. In doing so, she relied on two separate lines of recent Supreme Court precedents reflecting a concern with proportionate punishment.

Justice Kagan described the first strand of precedents as adopting "categorical bans on sentencing practices based on mismatches between the culpability of a class of offenders and the severity of a penalty." Here, the Court has flatly banned the death penalty for the mentally handicapped and for those convicted of any crime other than murder. Recently, the Court has addressed several cases in this group that specifically involved juvenile offenders. In 2005, in *Roper v. Simmons,* the Court held that the Eighth Amendment bars capital punishment for children. Similarly, in 2010, in *Graham v. Florida,* the Court concluded that a sentence of life without the possibility of parole for a child who had committed a nonhomicide offense was categorically barred by the Eighth Amendment. These cases, Justice Kagan wrote, "establish that children are constitutionally different from adults for purposes of sentencing." She cited at length from these earlier cases, which described in detail the lack of maturity that leads to "recklessness, impulsivity, and heedless risk-taking." Their age also makes children more vulnerable to negative outside influences. Additionally, unlike adults, children's traits are less "well formed" and less likely to be "evidence of irretrievabl[e] deprav[ity]." These conclusions were based, Justice Kagan wrote, "not only on common sense—on what 'any parent knows'—but on science and social science as well." Brain science has continued to show fundamental differences between the minds of juveniles and adults, which supports treating them less severely than adults when it comes to sentencing.

Unlike in these earlier cases, however, the Court in the *Miller* case did not flatly bar a life-without-parole sentence for juvenile offenders in any circumstance. Instead, it focused on the mandatory nature of the sentence. Here, the Court looked to a second group of cases that do not involve juveniles but which have prohibited the mandatory imposition of the death penalty. These cases have held that the Eighth Amendment requires separate sentencing hearings to allow the jury to consider the specific character and record of the defendant and any possible mitigating evidence before they can sentence the defendant to death. Justice Kagan described this line of case law as requiring that judges and juries provide "individualized sentencing for defendants facing the most serious penalties."

Justice Kagan concluded, based on both these groups of precedents, that it is cruel and unusual punishment to have a mandatory sentence of life without the possibility of parole for homicide crimes committed by juveniles. The problem with such a mandatory sentence, Justice Kagan wrote, is that "it precludes consideration of [the juvenile's] chronological age and its hallmark features—among them, immaturity, impetuosity, and failure to appreciate risks and consequences." It also, she added, "prevents taking into account the family and home environment that surrounds him—and from which he cannot usually extricate himself—no matter how brutal or dysfunctional." Such mandatory punishment for a juvenile also disregards "the possibility of rehabilitation even when the circumstances most suggest it."

Justice Breyer agreed in full with the majority opinion but wrote separately, in a concurring opinion joined by Justice Sotomayor, to argue that the Eighth Amendment should, in any event, bar sentencing a minor, such as Jackson, to life without parole unless he personally killed or intended to kill the victim in the case.

There were three dissenting opinions in this case. Chief Justice John Roberts wrote one, joined by Justices Samuel Alito, Antonin Scalia, and Clarence Thomas, accusing the majority of confusing decency with leniency. Justice Thomas wrote a dissent, joined by Justice Scalia, and finally, Justice Alito wrote an opinion, joined by Justice Scalia. Reading his dissent from the bench, a rare move indicating deep disagreement, Justice Alito argued that the majority decision would require finding that "even a 17 ½-year-old who sets off a bomb in a crowded mall or guns down a dozen students and teachers is a 'child' and must be given a chance to persuade a judge to permit his release into society." He concluded that "nothing in the Constitution supports this arrogation of legislative authority."

IMPACT OF THE COURT'S DECISION

The holding in this case will require sentencing judges to hold a separate penalty phase after a juvenile is convicted of murder to determine whether to impose a sentence of life without parole. Bryan Stevenson, executive director of Equal Justice Initiative, the non-profit law firm that represented the defendants in this case, spoke after the win, saying that the "decision requires the lower courts to conduct new sentencing hearings where judges will have to consider children's individual character and life circumstances, including age, as well as the circumstances of the crime." State laws, such as those in Missouri, which allow only for the death penalty or life in prison without parole sentences for murder, will have to be rewritten for juveniles being tried as adults.

There will no doubt be litigation as to whether to apply the *Miller* holding retroactively. Currently, according to the National Conference of State Legislatures, there are about 2,500 inmates serving life sentences for crimes that they committed when they were juveniles. The vast majority of these are from states with the kind of mandatory sentencing system barred by this decision.

Beyond requiring that the sentence take into account how children are different, the opinion in the *Miller* case did not give trial court judges any specific guidelines or particular factors to balance against when holding these sentencing hearings. Justice Kagan did, however, put trial court judges on notice by stating that she thought "appropriate occasions for sentencing juveniles to this harshest possible penalty will be uncommon." While still a possible sentence, the Court now requires that the sentencing authority "take into account how children are different, and how those differences counsel against irrevocably sentencing them to a lifetime in prison."

—Melissa Feinberg

Following are excerpts from the U.S. Supreme Court ruling in Miller v. Alabama, *in which the Court ruled 5–4 that life sentences without the possibility of parole are unconstitutional for juvenile offenders.*

DOCUMENT *Miller v. Alabama*

June 25, 2012

Nos. 10–9646 and 10–9647

Evan Miller, Petitioner 10–9646

v.

Alabama

On write of certiorari
to the Court
of Criminal Appeals
of Alabama

Kuntrell Jackson, Petitioner 10–9647

v.

Ray Hobbs, Director, Arkansas
Department of Correction

On writ of certiorari
to the Supreme
Court of Arkansas

[June 25, 2012]

[Footnotes and most citations have been omitted.]

JUSTICE KAGAN delivered the opinion of the Court.

The two 14-year-old offenders in these cases were convicted of murder and sentenced to life imprisonment without the possibility of parole. In neither case did the sentencing authority have any discretion to impose a different punishment. State law mandated that each juvenile die in prison even if a judge or jury would have thought that his youth and its attendant characteristics, along with the nature of his crime, made a lesser sentence (for example, life *with* the possibility of parole) more appropriate. Such a scheme prevents those meting out punishment from considering a juvenile's "lessened culpability" and greater "capacity for change," and runs afoul of our cases' requirement of individualized sentencing for defendants facing the most serious penalties. We therefore hold that mandatory life without parole for those under the age of 18 at the time of their crimes violates the Eighth Amendment's prohibition on "cruel and unusual punishments."

[Section I, containing background on the cases, has been omitted.]

II

The Eighth Amendment's prohibition of cruel and unusual punishment "guarantees individuals the right not to be subjected to excessive sanctions." That right, we have explained, "flows from the basic 'precept of justice that punishment for crime should be graduated and proportioned'" to both the offender and the offense. As we noted the last time we considered life-without-parole sentences imposed on juveniles, "[t]he concept of proportionality is central to the Eighth Amendment." And we view that concept less through a historical prism than according to "'the evolving standards of decency that mark the progress of a maturing society.'"

The cases before us implicate two strands of precedent reflecting our concern with proportionate punishment. The first has adopted categorical bans on practices based on mismatches between the culpability of a class of offenders and the severity of a penalty. So, for example, we have held that imposing the death penalty for nonhomicide crimes against individuals, or imposing it on mentally retarded defendants, violates the Eighth Amendment. Several of the cases in this group have specially focused on juvenile offenders, because of their lesser culpability. Thus, *Roper* held that the Eighth Amendment bars capital punishment for children, and *Graham* concluded that the Amendment also prohibits a sentence of life without the possibility of parole for a child who committed a nonhomicide offense. *Graham* further likened life without parole for juveniles to the death penalty itself, thereby evoking a second line of our precedents. In those cases, we have prohibited mandatory imposition of capital punishment, requiring that sentencing authorities consider the characteristics of a defendant and the details of his offense before sentencing him to death. Here, the confluence of these two lines of precedent leads to the conclusion that mandatory life-without-parole sentences for juveniles violate the Eighth Amendment.

To start with the first set of cases: *Roper* and *Graham* establish that children are constitutionally different from adults for purposes of sentencing. Because juveniles have diminished culpability and greater prospects for reform, we explained, "they are less deserving of the most severe punishments." Those cases relied on three significant gaps between juveniles and adults. First, children have a " 'lack of maturity and an underdeveloped sense of responsibility,' " leading to recklessness, impulsivity, and heedless risk-taking. Second, children "are more vulnerable . . . to negative influences and outside pressures," including from their family and peers; they have limited "contro[l] over their own environment" and lack the ability to extricate themselves from horrific, crime-producing settings. And third, a child's character is not as "well formed" as an adult's; his traits are "less fixed" and his actions less likely to be "evidence of irretrievabl[e] deprav[ity]."

Our decisions rested not only on common sense—on what "any parent knows"—but on science and social science as well. In *Roper,* we cited studies showing that " '[o]nly a relatively small proportion of adolescents' " who engage in illegal activity " 'develop entrenched patterns of problem behavior.' " And in *Graham,* we noted that "developments in psychology and brain science continue to show fundamental differences between juvenile and adult minds"—for example, in "parts of the brain involved in behavior control. We reasoned that those findings—of transient rashness, proclivity for risk, and inability to assess consequences—both lessened a child's "moral culpability" and enhanced the prospect that, as the years go by and neurological development occurs, his " 'deficiencies will be reformed.' "

Roper and *Graham* emphasized that the distinctive attributes of youth diminish the penological justifications for imposing the harshest sentences on juvenile offenders, even when they commit terrible crimes. Because " '[t]he heart of the retribution rationale' " relates to an offender's blameworthiness, " 'the case for retribution is not as strong with a minor as with an adult.' " Nor can deterrence do the work in this context, because " 'the same characteristics that render juveniles less culpable than adults' "—their immaturity, recklessness, and impetuosity—make them less likely to consider potential punishment. Similarly, incapacitation could not support the life-without-parole sentence in *Graham*: Deciding that a "juvenile offender forever will be a danger to society" would require "mak[ing] a judgment that [he] is incorrigible"—but " 'incorrigibility is inconsistent with youth.' " And for the same reason, rehabilitation could not justify that sentence. Life without parole "forswears altogether the rehabilitative ideal." *Graham,* 560 U. S., at ___ (slip op., at 23). It reflects "an irrevocable judgment about [an offender's] value and place in society," at odds with a child's capacity for change. . . .

Most fundamentally, *Graham* insists that youth matters in determining the appropriateness of a lifetime of incarceration without the possibility of parole. In the circumstances there, juvenile status precluded a life-without-parole sentence, even though an adult could receive it for a similar crime. And in other contexts as well, the characteristics of youth, and the way they weaken rationales for punishment, can render a life-without-parole sentence disproportionate. "An offender's age," we made clear in *Graham,* "is relevant to the Eighth Amendment," and so "criminal procedure laws that fail to take defendants' youthfulness into account at all would be flawed." . . .

But the mandatory penalty schemes at issue here prevent the sentencer from taking account of these central considerations. By removing youth from the balance—by subjecting a juvenile to the same life-without-parole sentence applicable to an adult—these laws prohibit a sentencing authority from assessing whether the law's harshest term of imprisonment proportionately punishes a juvenile offender. That contravenes *Graham*'s (and also *Roper*'s) foundational principle: that imposition of a State's most severe penalties on juvenile offenders cannot proceed as though they were not children.

And *Graham* makes plain these mandatory schemes' defects in another way: by likening life-without-parole sentences imposed on juveniles to the death penalty itself. Life-without-parole terms, the Court wrote, "share some characteristics with death sentences that are shared by no other sentences." Imprisoning an offender until he dies alters the remainder of his life "by a forfeiture that is irrevocable." And this lengthiest possible incarceration is an "especially harsh punishment for a juvenile," because he will almost inevitably serve "more years and a greater percentage of his life in prison than an adult offender." The penalty when imposed on a teenager, as compared with an older person, is therefore "the same . . . in name only." . . . All of that suggested a distinctive set of legal rules: In part because we viewed this ultimate penalty for juveniles as akin to the death penalty, we treated it similarly to that most severe punishment. We imposed a categorical ban on the sentence's use, in a way unprecedented for a term of imprisonment. . . .

That correspondence—*Graham*'s "[t]reat[ment] [of] juvenile life sentences as analogous to capital punishment"—makes relevant here a second line of our precedents, demanding individualized sentencing when imposing the death penalty. In *Woodson,* we held that a statute mandating a death sentence for first-degree murder violated the Eighth Amendment. We thought the mandatory scheme flawed because it gave no significance to "the character and record of the individual offender or the circumstances" of the offense, and "exclud[ed] from consideration . . . the possibility of compassionate or mitigating factors." Subsequent decisions have elaborated on the requirement that capital defendants have an opportunity to advance, and the judge or jury a chance to assess, any mitigating factors, so that the death penalty is reserved only for the most culpable defendants committing the most serious offenses.

Of special pertinence here, we insisted in these rulings that a sentencer have the ability to consider the "mitigating qualities of youth." Everything we said in *Roper* and *Graham* about that stage of life also appears in these decisions. As we observed, "youth is more than a chronological fact." It is a time of immaturity, irresponsibility, "impetuousness[,] and recklessness." It is a moment and "condition of life when a person may be most susceptible to influence and to psychological damage." And its "signature qualities" are all "transient." *Eddings* is especially on point. There, a 16-year-old shot a police officer point-blank and killed him. We invalidated his death sentence because the judge did not consider evidence of his neglectful and violent family background (including his mother's drug abuse and his father's physical abuse) and his emotional disturbance. We found that evidence "particularly relevant"—more so than it would have been in the case of an adult offender. We held: "[J]ust as the chronological age of a minor is itself a relevant mitigating factor of great weight, so must the background and mental and emotional development of a youthful defendant be duly considered" in assessing his culpability.

In light of *Graham*'s reasoning, these decisions too show the flaws of imposing mandatory life-without-parole sentences on juvenile homicide offenders. Such mandatory penalties, by their nature, preclude a sentencer from taking account of an offender's age and the wealth of characteristics and circumstances attendant to it. Under these schemes, every juvenile will receive the same sentence as every other—the 17-year-old and the 14-year-old, the shooter and the accomplice, the child from a stable household and the child from a chaotic and abusive one. And still worse, each juvenile (including these two 14-year-olds) will receive the same sentence as the vast majority of adults committing similar homicide offenses—but really, as *Graham* noted, a *greater* sentence than those adults will serve. In meting out the death penalty, the elision of all these differences would be strictly forbidden. And once again, *Graham* indicates that a similar rule should apply when a juvenile confronts a sentence of life (and death) in prison.

So *Graham* and *Roper* and our individualized sentencing cases alike teach that in imposing a State's harshest penalties, a sentencer misses too much if he treats every child as an adult. To recap: Mandatory life without parole for a juvenile precludes consideration of his chronological age and its hallmark features—among them, immaturity, impetuosity, and failure to appreciate risks and consequences. It prevents taking into account the family and home environment that surrounds him—and from which he cannot usually extricate himself—no matter how brutal or dysfunctional. It neglects the circumstances of the homicide offense, including the extent of his participation in the conduct and the way familial and peer pressures may have affected him. Indeed, it ignores that he might have been charged and convicted of a lesser offense if not for incompetencies associated with youth—for example, his inability to deal with police officers or prosecutors (including on a plea agreement) or his incapacity to assist his own attorneys. And finally, this mandatory punishment disregards the possibility of rehabilitation even when the circumstances most suggest it.

Both cases before us illustrate the problem. Take Jackson's first. As noted earlier, Jackson did not fire the bullet that killed Laurie Troup; nor did the State argue that he intended her death. Jackson's conviction was instead based on an aiding-and-abetting theory; and the appellate court affirmed the verdict only because the jury could have believed that when Jackson entered the store, he warned Troup that "[w]e ain't playin,'" rather than told his friends that "I thought you all was playin.'" To be sure, Jackson learned on the way to the video store that his friend Shields was carrying a gun, but his age could well have affected his calculation of the risk that posed, as well as his willingness to walk away at that point. All these circumstances go to Jackson's culpability for the offense. And so too does Jackson's family background and immersion in violence: Both his mother and his grandmother had previously shot other individuals. At the least, a sentencer should look at such facts before depriving a 14-year-old of any prospect of release from prison.

That is true also in Miller's case. No one can doubt that he and Smith committed a vicious murder. But they did it when high on drugs and alcohol consumed with the adult victim. And if ever a pathological background might have contributed to a 14-year-old's commission of a crime, it is here. Miller's stepfather physically abused him; his alcoholic and drug-addicted mother neglected him; he had been in and out of foster care as a result; and he had tried to kill himself four times, the first when he should have been in kindergarten. Nonetheless, Miller's past criminal history was limited—two instances of truancy and one of "second-degree criminal mischief." That Miller deserved severe punishment for killing Cole Cannon is beyond question. But once again, a sentencer needed to examine all these circumstances before concluding that life without any possibility of parole was the appropriate penalty.

We therefore hold that the Eighth Amendment forbids a sentencing scheme that mandates life in prison without possibility of parole for juvenile offenders. By making youth (and all that accompanies it) irrelevant to imposition of that harshest prison sentence, such a scheme poses too great a risk of disproportionate punishment. Because that holding is sufficient to decide these cases, we do not consider Jackson's and Miller's alternative argument that the Eighth Amendment requires a categorical bar on life without parole for juveniles, or at least for those 14 and younger. But given all we have said in *Roper, Graham,* and this decision about children's diminished culpability and heightened capacity for change, we think appropriate occasions for sentencing juveniles to this harshest possible penalty will be uncommon. That is especially so because of the great difficulty we noted in *Roper* and *Graham* of distinguishing at this early age between "the juvenile offender whose crime reflects unfortunate yet transient immaturity, and the rare juvenile offender whose crime reflects irreparable corruption." Although we do not foreclose a sentencer's ability to make that judgment in homicide cases, we require it to take into account how children are different, and how those differences counsel against irrevocably sentencing them to a lifetime in prison.

[Section III, containing the arguments presented by Alabama and Arkansas, has been omitted.]

IV

Graham, Roper, and our individualized sentencing decisions make clear that a judge or jury must have the opportunity to consider mitigating circumstances before imposing the harshest possible penalty for juveniles. By requiring that all children convicted of homicide receive lifetime incarceration without possibility of parole, regardless of their age and age-related characteristics and the nature of their crimes, the mandatory sentencing schemes before us violate this principle of proportionality, and so the Eighth Amendment's ban on cruel and unusual punishment. We accordingly reverse the judgments of the Arkansas Supreme Court and Alabama Court of Criminal Appeals and remand the cases for further proceedings not inconsistent with this opinion.

It is so ordered.

[The concurring opinion of Justice Breyer, and the dissenting opinions of Justices Roberts, Thomas, and Alito, have been omitted.]

SOURCE: U.S. Supreme Court. *Miller v. Alabama,* 567 U.S. ___ (2012). http://www.supremecourt.gov/opinions/11pdf/10-9646g2i8.pdf.

OTHER HISTORIC DOCUMENTS OF INTEREST

FROM PREVIOUS *HISTORIC DOCUMENTS*

Supreme Court Rules on Affordable Care Act

JUNE 28, 2012

On June 28, 2012, the U.S. Supreme Court released its ruling in *National Federation of Independent Business v. Sebelius,* its most widely anticipated and closely watched decision in recent years. Before the Court in this case was the constitutionality of President Barack Obama's central legislative achievement—the Patient Protection and Affordable Care Act of 2010 (ACA), widely dubbed "Obamacare," a term initially used derisively by the law's detractors, but which eventually came to be embraced by President Obama himself. Specifically, the Court focused on whether the law's so-called individual mandate, a requirement that everyone purchase health insurance or pay a penalty, had been constitutionally enacted. Another issue concerned the constitutionality of the act's Medicaid expansion. With four justices arguing for striking down the entire act, and four justices willing to uphold it as a mandate, Chief Justice John Roberts cast the deciding vote to uphold the landmark health care reform act. While he agreed with the dissenters that the Commerce Clause of the Constitution does not give Congress the authority to enact the individual mandate, in what was somewhat of a surprise to those following the case, he upheld the law as a legitimate use of Congress's taxing power.

Legal Challenges to President Obama's Health Care Law

After a lengthy period of highly contentious debate, Congress passed the ACA along strictly partisan lines, and on March 23, 2010, President Obama signed the 2,700-page bill into law. Many described this overhaul of health care as the most significant since the 1965 passage of Medicare and Medicaid. The act aims to increase the number of Americans covered by health insurance and decrease the cost of health care. Specifically, it prohibits insurance companies from denying coverage to people with preexisting medical conditions and from setting dollar limits on health coverage payouts. It requires them to allow parents to keep children on their family policies until they are twenty-six and to cover preventive care at no additional cost. The ACA also requires states to expand the scope of their Medicaid programs, significantly increasing the number of people covered. Most states now cover only needy families with children and the disabled, but under the expansion, they would be required to provide coverage also to the poorest adults.

Starting in 2014, the law's individual mandate would take effect. This provision would require individuals to have health insurance, either through their employers or through a state-sponsored exchange, or else face a fine. Exemptions to this requirement were included for those with very low incomes, members of certain religious groups, or those for whom premiums would exceed 8 percent of family income. This mechanism was designed to bring in a large pool of new customers to insurance companies, helping to offset the cost of the expansion of health care coverage to tens of millions of lower-income Americans. Its supporters argue that it was economically critical to the success of the legislation and also necessary to prevent people from waiting until they need health care before purchasing insurance now that the law bans insurance companies from denying coverage for preexisting conditions.

The law ignited protests around the country and fueled the recently established conservative Tea Party movement. It was one of the dominant issues in the 2010 midterm elections with Republicans, who pledged to repeal it, gaining control of the House of Representatives. On the day the president signed the act, Florida and twelve other states filed legal challenges in federal courts, arguing that the health care law was beyond the scope of Congress's constitutional authority to enact. The lawsuit was later joined by thirteen additional states and by the National Federation of Independent Business. A district court found that the individual mandate exceeds Congress's power and struck down the entire act. On appeal, the Eleventh Circuit Court agreed but found that the mandate could be struck while retaining the rest of the act. Other courts of appeals were hearing challenges to the individual mandate, leading to conflicting rulings. The Sixth Circuit and the D.C. Circuit upheld the mandate as a valid exercise of Congress's commerce power. The Fourth Circuit ruled that the Anti-Injunction Act, a statute that prevents suits over taxes before those taxes have been paid, bars hearing the issue until the law is in effect.

In November 2011, the U.S. Supreme Court agreed to hear an appeal from the Eleventh Circuit Court of Appeals to resolve this split in the federal circuit courts. In March, the Court heard three days of oral arguments as attorneys debated whether the Anti-Injunction Act would require them to wait for the law to take effect before ruling; whether the individual mandate is constitutional; whether the individual mandate is severable from the rest of the act such that, if it is overturned, the rest of the act could still stand; and finally, whether the expansion of Medicaid is constitutional. Journalists and Court watchers parsed every word spoken as speculation about what the Court would do reached a fever pitch.

THE SUPREME COURT RULES

Much as the law ideologically split the nation, the legal challenge to the ACA split the justices of the Supreme Court. Four of the Court's justices, traditionally its most liberal, would uphold the law in its entirety: Justices Ruth Bader Ginsburg, Stephen Breyer, Sonia Sotomayor, and Elena Kagan. Four of the Court's most conservative members, Justices Anthony Kennedy, Antonin Scalia, Clarence Thomas, and Samuel Alito, would have ruled it "invalid in its entirety." Thus, Chief Justice Roberts held the decisive opinion, even though no other justice on the Court joined him in every aspect of his ruling. Implicitly acknowledging the political divisions on the Court and the political importance of the decision, Justice Roberts began his opinion by rejecting the notion that politics bore on the ruling. "We do not consider whether the Act embodies sound policies. That judgment is entrusted to the Nation's elected leaders," he wrote. The Court asked only, he continued, "whether Congress has the power under the Constitution to enact the challenged provisions." His opinion answered that question affirmatively, finding the authority in Congress's power to levy taxes.

In our federal system, the federal government is a government of "enumerated powers," meaning that its powers are limited to those specifically listed by the Constitution;

all other powers are retained by the states. In this case, lawyers for the government argued that Congress had the authority to pass the health care reform law under the Constitution's Commerce Clause, which empowers Congress "to regulate Commerce with foreign Nations, and among the several States." This power has been interpreted expansively by the Courts in the past and has served as the basis for a significant portion of laws passed, including environmental and civil rights laws. For these reasons, the Commerce Clause had been the focus of this litigation as the case worked its way through the federal courts.

In this case, however, Justice Roberts, agreeing in result with the four dissenters, held that the Commerce Clause is not broad enough to provide Congress with the authority to enact the individual mandate, which would, for the first time, require individuals to pay for a product that they do not want. Rather than regulating existing commercial activity, Justice Roberts wrote, this law "compels individuals to *become* active in commerce by purchasing a product on the ground that their failure to do so affects interstate commerce." Regulating individuals based on what they fail to do, he concluded, would expand the Commerce Clause beyond what was intended by the Framers of the Constitution, who "gave Congress the power to *regulate* commerce, not to *compel* it."

Another power given to Congress by the Constitution is the "power to lay and collect Taxes, Duties, Imposts and Excises." In his determination that the individual mandate is a tax permitted under this constitutional provision, Justice Roberts agreed with the four liberal justices who would uphold the law. Here, he noted that the individual mandate is codified in the tax code and enforced by the Internal Revenue Service (IRS), and it applies only to "taxpayers" to be paid upon the filing of regular income tax returns. He rejected the notion that it is a penalty rather than a tax, despite use of that word in the statute itself, because there are no other negative consequences for failure to purchase health insurance. People "may lawfully choose to pay in lieu of buying health insurance," and, he wrote, "if someone chooses to pay rather than obtain health insurance, they have fully complied with the law." While "the Federal government does not have the power to order people to buy health insurance," Justice Roberts concluded, "the federal government does have the power to impose a tax on those without health insurance." He emphasized again that "because the Constitution permits such a tax, it is not our role to forbid it, or to pass upon its wisdom or fairness."

Also at issue in the case was a provision of the ACA that sought to provide health care coverage to an additional 17 million of the poorest uninsured Americans by expanding Medicaid, the joint federal-state program that provides health care to poor and disabled people. By 2014, provisions of the ACA would require states to expand the coverage of their Medicaid programs dramatically to cover all individuals under the age of sixty-five with incomes below 133 percent of the federal poverty line. States could choose to participate in this expansion, and the federal government would pay all increased costs for the first few years and then 90 percent of the increase thereafter. However, if states chose not to participate, they would forgo all their current federal Medicaid funding. On this issue, seven justices agreed that coercing states into participating in the Medicaid expansion by threatening them with a loss of their existing payments exceeded Congress's constitutional authority. The Court agreed with the law's challengers that this threat violates the basic principle that "the Federal Government may not compel the States to enact or administer a federal regulatory program."

Congress had anticipated that the Affordable Care Act would provide most people with health coverage by subsidizing them to buy private insurance and that the very poor would get their health care through the expansion of Medicaid. The Supreme Court left in place the individual mandate, which would require Americans to purchase health insurance or pay a penalty. But, at the same time, it allowed states to opt out of the Medicaid expansion that was the law's method for covering up to 17 million of the nation's poorest people. This mixed decision leaves in doubt how the health care needs of those too poor to buy even discounted health insurance will be met if the half-dozen states which have expressed opposition to expanding Medicaid vote in 2013 to opt out of the expansion.

REACTIONS AND IMPLICATIONS

Because the case was decided during a presidential election year, the political impact of this victory for President Obama was immediate and crystallized the differences between the two candidates. "Whatever the politics," President Obama said, praising the decision from the White House, "today's decision was a victory for people all over this country whose lives are more secure because of this law." His opponent, former Massachusetts governor Mitt Romney, stated that "Obamacare was bad law yesterday; it's bad law today." And he vowed: "What the Court did not do in its last session, I will do on the first day if elected president of the United States, and that's to repeal Obamacare." Spokespeople for presidential candidate Romney revealed that his campaign raised more than $3.2 million in just hours after the decision was announced.

On a practical level, the Obama administration is continuing with the implementation of the ACA, which is scheduled to take full effect by 2014. Republican governors in states including Kansas, Nebraska, and South Carolina have expressed doubts as to whether they will expand their Medicaid programs, potentially leaving millions of poor people uncovered even after the completed implementation of the national health care law. State Representative Andrew J. Manuse of New Hampshire said of the expansion of Medicaid: "We can't afford it. It's as simple as that. Thank God the Supreme Court gave us an option."

The long-term legal impact of the Court's limited interpretation of Congress's powers under the Commerce Clause remains to be resolved, although it is the subject of much debate. Justice Roberts's opinion that Congress can regulate only commercial activity and not compel individuals to engage in such activity can be seen as creating a new limitation on the reach of the Commerce Clause. Yale law professor Akhil Reed Amar believes that the holding put more restrictions on federal power and that "going forward, there may even be laws on the books that have to be re-examined." This concern is shared by Lyle Denniston, reporter for SCOTUSblog, who wrote, "The rejection of the Commerce Clause . . . should be understood as a major blow to Congress' authority to pass social welfare laws." Others argued that the individual mandate was a unique requirement and may have little impact on future cases.

—Melissa Feinberg

The following are excerpts in the U.S. Supreme Court ruling in National Federation of Independent Business v. Sebelius, *in which the Court ruled 5–4 to uphold Congress's ability to enact most of President Barack Obama's Affordable Care Act.*

National Federation of Independent Business v. Sebelius

June 28, 2012

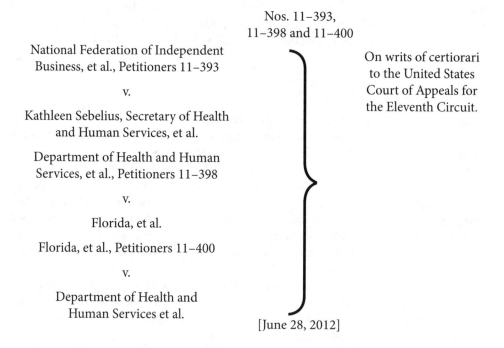

Nos. 11–393,
11–398 and 11–400

National Federation of Independent
Business, et al., Petitioners 11–393

v.

Kathleen Sebelius, Secretary of Health
and Human Services, et al.

Department of Health and Human
Services, et al., Petitioners 11–398

v.

Florida, et al.

Florida, et al., Petitioners 11–400

v.

Department of Health and
Human Services et al.

On writs of certiorari
to the United States
Court of Appeals for
the Eleventh Circuit.

[June 28, 2012]

[Footnotes and most citations have been omitted.]

CHIEF JUSTICE ROBERTS announced the judgment of the Court and delivered the opinion of the Court with respect to Parts I, II, and III-C, an opinion with respect to Part IV, in which JUSTICE BREYER and JUSTICE KAGAN join, and an opinion with respect to Parts III-A, III-B, and III-D.

Today we resolve constitutional challenges to two provisions of the Patient Protection and Affordable Care Act of 2010: the individual mandate, which requires individuals to purchase a health insurance policy providing a minimum level of coverage; and the Medicaid expansion, which gives funds to the States on the condition that they provide specified health care to all citizens whose income falls below a certain threshold. We do not consider whether the Act embodies sound policies. That judgment is entrusted to the Nation's elected leaders. We ask only whether Congress has the power under the Constitution to enact the challenged provisions.

[A discussion on the restrictions and powers of the federal government, and Sections I and II, detailing the background of the case and the Affordable Care Act's provisions, have been omitted.]

III

The Government advances two theories for the proposition that Congress had constitutional authority to enact the individual mandate. First, the Government argues that

Congress had the power to enact the mandate under the Commerce Clause. Under that theory, Congress may order individuals to buy health insurance because the failure to do so affects interstate commerce, and could undercut the Affordable Care Act's other reforms. Second, the Government argues that if the commerce power does not support the mandate, we should nonetheless uphold it as an exercise of Congress's power to tax. According to the Government, even if Congress lacks the power to direct individuals to buy insurance, the only effect of the individual mandate is to raise taxes on those who do not do so, and thus the law may be upheld as a tax.

A

[The government's contentions about the individual mandate have been omitted.]

1.

The Government contends that the individual mandate is within Congress's power because the failure to purchase insurance "has a substantial and deleterious effect on interstate commerce" by creating the cost-shifting problem. Brief for United States 34. The path of our Commerce Clause decisions has not always run smooth, but it is now well established that Congress has broad authority under the Clause. We have recognized, for example, that "[t]he power of Congress over interstate commerce is not confined to the regulation of commerce among the states," but extends to activities that "have a substantial effect on interstate commerce." Congress's power, moreover, is not limited to regulation of an activity that by itself substantially affects interstate commerce, but also extends to activities that do so only when aggregated with similar activities of others.

Given its expansive scope, it is no surprise that Congress has employed the commerce power in a wide variety of ways to address the pressing needs of the time. But Congress has never attempted to rely on that power to compel individuals not engaged in commerce to purchase an unwanted product. Legislative novelty is not necessarily fatal; there is a first time for everything. But sometimes "the most telling indication of [a] severe constitutional problem . . . is the lack of historical precedent" for Congress's action. At the very least, we should "pause to consider the implications of the Government's arguments" when confronted with such new conceptions of federal power.

The Constitution grants Congress the power to "*regulate* Commerce." The power to *regulate* commerce presupposes the existence of commercial activity to be regulated. If the power to "regulate" something included the power to create it, many of the provisions in the Constitution would be superfluous. For example, the Constitution gives Congress the power to "coin Money," in addition to the power to "regulate the Value thereof." And it gives Congress the power to "raise and support Armies" and to "provide and maintain a Navy," in addition to the power to "make Rules for the Government and Regulation of the land and naval Forces." If the power to regulate the armed forces or the value of money included the power to bring the subject of the regulation into existence, the specific grant of such powers would have been unnecessary. The language of the Constitution reflects the natural understanding that the power to regulate assumes there is already something to be regulated.

Our precedent also reflects this understanding. As expansive as our cases construing the scope of the commerce power have been, they all have one thing in common: They uniformly describe the power as reaching "activity." It is nearly impossible to avoid the word when quoting them.

The individual mandate, however, does not regulate existing commercial activity. It instead compels individuals to *become* active in commerce by purchasing a product, on the ground that their failure to do so affects interstate commerce. Construing the Commerce Clause to permit Congress to regulate individuals precisely *because* they are doing nothing would open a new and potentially vast domain to congressional authority. Every day individuals do not do an infinite number of things. In some cases they decide not to do something; in others they simply fail to do it. Allowing Congress to justify federal regulation by pointing to the effect of inaction on commerce would bring countless decisions an individual could *potentially* make within the scope of federal regulation, and—under the Government's theory—empower Congress to make those decisions for him. . . .

Indeed, the Government's logic would justify a mandatory purchase to solve almost any problem. To consider a different example in the health care market, many Americans do not eat a balanced diet. That group makes up a larger percentage of the total population than those without health insurance. The failure of that group to have a healthy diet increases health care costs, to a greater extent than the failure of the uninsured to purchase insurance. . . . Congress addressed the insurance problem by ordering everyone to buy insurance. Under the Government's theory, Congress could address the diet problem by ordering everyone to buy vegetables.

People, for reasons of their own, often fail to do things that would be good for them or good for society. Those failures—joined with the similar failures of others—can readily have a substantial effect on interstate commerce. Under the Government's logic, that authorizes Congress to use its commerce power to compel citizens to act as the Government would have them act.

That is not the country the Framers of our Constitution envisioned. James Madison explained that the Commerce Clause was "an addition which few oppose and from which no apprehensions are entertained." While Congress's authority under the Commerce Clause has of course expanded with the growth of the national economy, our cases have "always recognized that the power to regulate commerce, though broad indeed, has limits." The Government's theory would erode those limits, permitting Congress to reach beyond the natural extent of its authority, "everywhere extending the sphere of its activity and drawing all power into its impetuous vortex." Congress already enjoys vast power to regulate much of what we do. Accepting the Government's theory would give Congress the same license to regulate what we do not do, fundamentally changing the relation between the citizen and the Federal Government.

[Additional discussion on the individual mandate and the government's arguments in its favor has been omitted.]

Everyone will likely participate in the markets for food, clothing, transportation, shelter, or energy; that does not authorize Congress to direct them to purchase particular products in those or other markets today. The Commerce Clause is not a general license to regulate an individual from cradle to grave, simply because he will predictably engage in particular transactions. Any police power to regulate individuals as such, as opposed to their activities, remains vested in the States.

The Government argues that the individual mandate can be sustained as a sort of exception to this rule, because health insurance is a unique product. According to the Government, upholding the individual mandate would not justify mandatory purchases of items such as cars or broccoli because, as the Government puts it, "[h]ealth insurance is not purchased for its own sake like a car or broccoli; it is a means of financing health-care consumption and covering universal risks." But cars and broccoli are no more purchased for their "own sake" than health insurance. They are purchased to cover the need for transportation and food.

The Government says that health insurance and health care financing are "inherently integrated." But that does not mean the compelled purchase of the first is properly regarded as a regulation of the second. No matter how "inherently integrated" health insurance and health care consumption may be, they are not the same thing: They involve different transactions, entered into at different times, with different providers. And for most of those targeted by the mandate, significant health care needs will be years, or even decades, away. The proximity and degree of connection between the mandate and the subsequent commercial activity is too lacking to justify an exception of the sort urged by the Government. The individual mandate forces individuals into commerce precisely because they elected to refrain from commercial activity. Such a law cannot be sustained under a clause authorizing Congress to "regulate Commerce."

[Section 2, containing information on the government's argument that it has the power under the Necessary and Proper Clause to invoke the individual mandate, has been omitted.]

B

That is not the end of the matter. Because the Commerce Clause does not support the individual mandate, it is necessary to turn to the Government's second argument: that the mandate may be upheld as within Congress's enumerated power to "lay and collect Taxes."

[Additional information on the government's tax power argument has been omitted.]

C

The exaction the Affordable Care Act imposes on those without health insurance looks like a tax in many respects. The "[s]hared responsibility payment," as the statute entitles it, is paid into the Treasury by "taxpayer[s]" when they file their tax returns. It does not apply to individuals who do not pay federal income taxes because their household income is less than the filing threshold in the Internal Revenue Code. For taxpayers who do owe the payment, its amount is determined by such familiar factors as taxable income, number of dependents, and joint filing status. The requirement to pay is found in the Internal Revenue Code and enforced by the IRS, which—as we previously explained—must assess and collect it "in the same manner as taxes." This process yields the essential feature of any tax: it produces at least some revenue for the Government. Indeed, the payment is expected to raise about $4 billion per year by 2017.

[Early Supreme Court holdings have been omitted.]

The same analysis here suggests that the shared responsibility payment may for constitutional purposes be considered a tax, not a penalty: First, for most Americans the amount due will be far less than the price of insurance, and, by statute, it can never be more. It may often be a reasonable financial decision to make the payment rather than purchase insurance, unlike the "prohibitory" financial punishment in *Drexel Furniture*. Second, the individual mandate contains no scienter requirement. Third, the payment is collected solely by the IRS through the normal means of taxation—except that the Service is *not* allowed to use those means most suggestive of a punitive sanction, such as criminal prosecution. The reasons the Court in *Drexel Furniture* held that what was called a "tax" there was a penalty support the conclusion that what is called a "penalty" here may be viewed as a tax.

None of this is to say that the payment is not intended to affect individual conduct. Although the payment will raise considerable revenue, it is plainly designed to expand health insurance coverage. But taxes that seek to influence conduct are nothing new. . . . Today, federal and state taxes can compose more than half the retail price of cigarettes, not just to raise more money, but to encourage people to quit smoking. And we have upheld such obviously regulatory measures as taxes on selling marijuana and sawed-off shotguns. Indeed, "[e]very tax is in some measure regulatory. To some extent it interposes an economic impediment to the activity taxed as compared with others not taxed." That §5000A seeks to shape decisions about whether to buy health insurance does not mean that it cannot be a valid exercise of the taxing power.

In distinguishing penalties from taxes, this Court has explained that "if the concept of penalty means anything, it means punishment for an unlawful act or omission." While the individual mandate clearly aims to induce the purchase of health insurance, it need not be read to declare that failing to do so is unlawful. Neither the Act nor any other law attaches negative legal consequences to not buying health insurance, beyond requiring a payment to the IRS. The Government agrees with that reading, confirming that if someone chooses to pay rather than obtain health insurance, they have fully complied with the law.

Indeed, it is estimated that four million people each year will choose to pay the IRS rather than buy insurance. We would expect Congress to be troubled by that prospect if such conduct were unlawful. That Congress apparently regards such extensive failure to comply with the mandate as tolerable suggests that Congress did not think it was creating four million outlaws. It suggests instead that the shared responsibility payment merely imposes a tax citizens may lawfully choose to pay in lieu of buying health insurance.

[A discussion on congressional taxation power as it relates to the Affordable Care Act has been omitted.]

The Affordable Care Act's requirement that certain individuals pay a financial penalty for not obtaining health insurance may reasonably be characterized as a tax. Because the Constitution permits such a tax, it is not our role to forbid it, or to pass upon its wisdom or fairness.

[Section D, containing Justice Ginsburg's questions about the government's Commerce Clause argument and Section IV, containing a discussion of Medicaid, have been omitted.]

* * *

The Affordable Care Act is constitutional in part and unconstitutional in part. The individual mandate cannot be upheld as an exercise of Congress's power under the Commerce Clause. That Clause authorizes Congress to regulate interstate commerce, not to order individuals to engage in it. In this case, however, it is reasonable to construe what Congress has done as increasing taxes on those who have a certain amount of income, but choose to go without health insurance. Such legislation is within Congress's power to tax.

As for the Medicaid expansion, that portion of the Affordable Care Act violates the Constitution by threatening existing Medicaid funding. Congress has no authority to order the States to regulate according to its instructions. Congress may offer the States grants and require the States to comply with accompanying conditions, but the States must have a genuine choice whether to accept the offer. The States are given no such choice in this case. They must either accept a basic change in the nature of Medicaid, or risk losing all Medicaid funding. The remedy for that constitutional violation is to preclude the Federal Government from imposing such a sanction. That remedy does not require striking down other portions of the Affordable Care Act.

The Framers created a Federal Government of limited powers, and assigned to this Court the duty of enforcing those limits. The Court does so today. But the Court does not express any opinion on the wisdom of the Affordable Care Act. Under the Constitution, that judgment is reserved to the people.

The judgment of the Court of Appeals for the Eleventh Circuit is affirmed in part and reversed in part.

It is so ordered.

[The opinion of Justices Ginsburg, Sotomayor, Breyer, and Kagan, concurring in part and dissenting in part; the dissenting opinion of Justices Scalia, Kennedy, Thomas, and Alito; and a separate dissenting opinion of Justice Thomas have been omitted.]

Source: U.S. Supreme Court. *National Federation of Independent Business v. Sebelius*, 567 U.S. __ (2012). http://www.supremecourt.gov/opinions/11pdf/11-393c3a2.pdf.

Other Historic Documents of Interest

From previous *Historic Documents*

- Health Care Reform Signed into Law, *2010,* p. 84
- Congressional Debate on Health Care Reform, *2009,* p. 533
- President Obama Speaks to Congress on Health Care Reform, *2009,* p. 399

July

Justice Department Outlines Largest Health Care Fraud Settlement

JULY 2, 2012

On July 2, 2012, the Justice Department announced its largest health care fraud settlement to date after reaching an agreement with drug maker GlaxoSmithKline (GSK) over charges of deceptive marketing, off-label drug promotion, and physician kickbacks. The charges brought by the government against the company stemmed from a whistleblower lawsuit filed in Massachusetts in 2003 by four former employees of the company. In reaching its settlement, which covered a period from the 1990s through the early 2000s, the government brought to light the deceptive and aggressive sales tactics used by pharmaceutical companies to promote their drugs, including GSK's practice of paying its sales force based on the number of prescriptions each person could get a doctor to write. "At every level, we are determined to stop practices that jeopardize patients' health, harm taxpayers, and violate the public trust—and this historic action is a clear warning to any company that chooses to break the law," said Deputy Attorney General James Cole.

GLAXOSMITHKLINE PLEADS GUILTY

In 2009, Attorney General Eric Holder and Health and Human Services (HHS) Secretary Kathleen Sebelius announced the formation of a task force that would help "reduce and prevent Medicare and Medicaid financial fraud." That task force, known as the Health Care Fraud Prevention and Enforcement Action Team (HEAT), recovered $10.2 billion in its first three years of existence. According to the Justice Department, for every $1 it spends on investigations, HEAT brings in $15 in recovered funds. Recent recoveries have included a $1.6 billion settlement with Abbott Laboratories in May 2012 for improper marketing techniques of its antiseizure drug Depakote.

On July 2, the Justice Department announced that HEAT had helped the government reach another settlement, this time with British pharmaceutical giant GSK for $3 billion, to resolve civil and criminal complaints related to drug safety and fraudulent marketing. The settlement with GSK was the largest health care fraud settlement to date. "For a long time, our health care system had been a target for cheaters who thought they could make an easy profit at the expense of public safety, taxpayers, and the millions of Americans who depend on programs like Medicare and Medicaid," said Bill Corr, HHS deputy secretary. He continued, "Thanks to strong enforcement actions like those we have announced today, that equation is rapidly changing."

In the agreement, GSK pleaded guilty to three criminal charges and accepted responsibility for three civil allegations without admitting guilt. The company accepted the charges and apologized. "Whilst these originate in a different era for the company, they cannot and will not be ignored," said Andrew Witty, GSK's chief executive. "On behalf of GSK, I want to express our regret and reiterate that we have learned from the mistakes that were made." GSK officials said they had already been working to change many corporate policies since the terms of an initial agreement were announced in November 2011.

Although HEAT viewed the GSK settlement as a major victory, it is not without critics who say that fines levied by the task force are too small to deter wrongdoing. Eliot Spitzer, the former attorney general and governor of New York, who sued GSK in 2004, said, "What we're learning is that money doesn't deter corporate malfeasance." He continued, "The only thing that will work in my view is CEOs and officials being forced to resign and individual culpability being enforced." Patrick Burns, the spokesperson for Taxpayers Against Fraud, a whistle-blower advocacy group, agreed, noting that the $3 billion settlement represented a miniscule portion of GSK's profits from the drugs named in the deal. "A $3 billion settlement for half a dozen drugs over 10 years can be rationalized as the cost of doing business," he said, adding that prosecuting individuals or barring a pharmaceutical company from participating in federal health care programs might be the only way to stop wrongdoing.

CRIMINAL PLEA DEAL

GSK agreed to pay $1 billion and plead guilty on two criminal counts of misbranding its drugs Paxil and Wellbutrin, and one criminal count of failing to send the Food and Drug Administration (FDA) safety information about Avandia.

The Paxil settlement involved GSK's promotion of the drug from 1998 to 2003 for treatment of depression in children under age eighteen. The FDA had never approved the drug for this use. In an effort to encourage doctors to prescribe the drug for this off-label treatment, GSK published a medical journal article that incorrectly stated that a clinical trial had proven Paxil was useful in treating depression for this age group. The study actually found no such connection, nor did two additional studies conducted on the same drug. In addition to the article, GSK used paid speakers to promote the off-label use to doctors who received lavish meals, spa treatments, concert tickets, and other incentives. Today, Paxil packaging, along with that of other antidepressant drugs, is required to carry a warning label about an increase in the risk of suicidal behavior and thinking in those under age eighteen who use the drug.

GSK also tried to market its depression drug, Wellbutrin, for off-label purposes including weight loss, sexual dysfunction, substance addiction, and Attention Deficit Hyperactivity Disorder (ADHD). According to the federal government's allegations, "Glaxo sales representatives sometimes referred to Wellbutrin as 'the happy, horny, skinny pill' as a way to remind doctors of the unapproved uses." They used tactics similar to the off-brand promotion of Paxil, inviting doctors to retreats where speakers and sales representatives espoused the drug's benefits.

The final criminal count accepted by GSK related to its diabetes drug Avandia. The government alleged that from 2001 to 2007, GSK failed to provide updated safety data to the FDA relating to the drug's use. The FDA uses this information to determine the continuing safety of pharmaceuticals available to consumers. Some of the data GSK kept secret came from a study conducted after European officials raised concerns that the drug had a negative cardiovascular impact on its users. Avandia has since been banned from sale in Europe.

CIVIL SETTLEMENT

In addition to the actions GSK pleaded guilty to in the criminal case, it was also alleged to have promoted a number of other drugs for off-label uses, given kickbacks to doctors who prescribed certain drugs, made misleading and false statements about drug safety, and reported false best prices, which resulted in underpayment to the federal government's Medicaid Drug Rebate Program. GSK did not agree to plead guilty to these charges; however, it did accept liability to settle them.

Allegations against GSK for off-label promotion involve the diabetes drug Avandia, the antiepilepsy drug Lamictal, and Zofran, a drug approved to relieve nausea after surgery. According to the Justice Department, GSK promoted Avandia for use in patients suffering from mild asthma and for patients with chronic obstructive pulmonary disease. Lamictal was promoted for uses including pain management and neuropathic pain, and Zofran was touted as a treatment for morning sickness experienced by pregnant women. In addition, the Justice Department claimed, GSK paid kickbacks to doctors who prescribed these drugs as well as some of its other brands, including Imitrex, Lotronex, Flovent, and Valtrex. Because the drugs were being promoted for off-label uses, claims submitted by doctors and patients to federal health care programs, such as Medicaid, were false. GSK will pay $1 billion to settle the off-label promotion allegation.

The government further alleged that GSK used misleading information to promote its drug Avandia for treatment of cholesterol and cardiovascular problems. There is no well-founded evidence that Avandia has any positive impact on cholesterol, and its Avandia packaging includes a black box label warning of potential cardiovascular risks associated with the drug. To settle these allegations, GSK will pay $657 million.

The third and final allegation raised in the civil settlement by the Justice Department was false reporting of drug prices by GSK between 1994 and 2003. Drug companies often "bundle" drugs when they are sold to purchasers, resulting in a steep discount. Although GSK participated in the bundling practice, it failed to report a correct best price to HHS, ultimately resulting in overcharging some U.S. Public Health Service operations for some drugs and underpaying its rebates to the Medicaid program. A $300 million payout from GSK will settle this allegation, split between the federal government, states, and some Public Health Service organizations.

ADDITIONAL AGREEMENTS

In addition to agreeing to the civil and criminal charges, GSK signed onto a plan with HHS that will require it to make a number of changes to its business operations. Most important, the company will be responsible for implementing a new compensation plan for its sales representatives, who previously had been paid based on sales goals in a specific territory. The government said that these pay plans often led to sales people improperly influencing doctors to write additional prescriptions for GSK drugs. The new compensation plan will also change the way executives are paid and give GSK the opportunity to take back any bonuses or other performance pay incentives from company executives found to be involved in any instances of misconduct. GSK will also be required to follow a specific set of policies outlined by HHS when conducting research trials and publishing results. This agreement will remain in effect for five years.

—Heather Kerrigan

Following is a press release from the U.S. Department of Justice on July 2, 2012, outlining the details of a $3 billion settlement reached with GlaxoSmithKline.

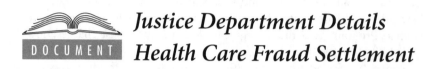

Justice Department Details Health Care Fraud Settlement

July 2, 2012

GLAXOSMITHKLINE TO PLEAD GUILTY AND PAY $3 BILLION TO RESOLVE FRAUD ALLEGATIONS AND FAILURE TO REPORT SAFETY DATA

LARGEST HEALTH CARE FRAUD SETTLEMENT IN U.S. HISTORY

Global health care giant GlaxoSmithKline LLC (GSK) agreed to plead guilty and to pay $3 billion to resolve its criminal and civil liability arising from the company's unlawful promotion of certain prescription drugs, its failure to report certain safety data, and its civil liability for alleged false price reporting practices, the Justice Department announced today. The resolution is the largest health care fraud settlement in U.S. history and the largest payment ever by a drug company.

GSK agreed to plead guilty to a three-count criminal indictment, including two counts of introducing misbranded drugs, Paxil and Wellbutrin, into interstate commerce and one count of failing to report safety data about the drug Avandia to the Food and Drug Administration (FDA). Under the terms of the plea agreement, GSK will pay a total of $1 billion, including a criminal fine of $956,814,400 and forfeiture in the amount of $43,185,600. The criminal plea agreement also includes certain nonmonetary compliance commitments and certifications by GSK's U.S. president and board of directors. GSK's guilty plea and sentence is not final until accepted by the U.S. District Court.

GSK will also pay $2 billion to resolve its civil liabilities with the federal government under the False Claims Act, as well as the states. The civil settlement resolves claims relating to Paxil, Wellbutrin and Avandia, as well as additional drugs, and also resolves pricing fraud allegations.

"Today's multi-billion dollar settlement is unprecedented in both size and scope. It underscores the Administration's firm commitment to protecting the American people and holding accountable those who commit health care fraud," said James M. Cole, Deputy Attorney General. "At every level, we are determined to stop practices that jeopardize patients' health, harm taxpayers, and violate the public trust—and this historic action is a clear warning to any company that chooses to break the law."

"Today's historic settlement is a major milestone in our efforts to stamp out health care fraud," said Bill Corr, Deputy Secretary of the Department of Health and Human

Services (HHS). "For a long time, our health care system had been a target for cheaters who thought they could make an easy profit at the expense of public safety, taxpayers, and the millions of Americans who depend on programs like Medicare and Medicaid. But thanks to strong enforcement actions like those we have announced today, that equation is rapidly changing."

This resolution marks the culmination of an extensive investigation by special agents from HHS-OIG, FDA and FBI, along with law enforcement partners across the federal government. Moving forward, GSK will be subject to stringent requirements under its corporate integrity agreement with HHS-OIG; this agreement is designed to increase accountability and transparency and prevent future fraud and abuse. Effective law enforcement partnerships and fraud prevention are hallmarks of the Health Care Fraud Prevention and Enforcement Action Team (HEAT) initiative, which fosters government collaboration to fight fraud.

CRIMINAL PLEA AGREEMENT

Under the provisions of the Food, Drug and Cosmetic Act, a company in its application to the FDA must specify each intended use of a drug. After the FDA approves the product as safe and effective for a specified use, a company's promotional activities must be limited to the intended uses that FDA approved. In fact, promotion by the manufacturer for other uses—known as "off-label uses"—renders the product "misbranded."

Paxil: In the criminal information, the government alleges that, from April 1998 to August 2003, GSK unlawfully promoted Paxil for treating depression in patients under age 18, even though the FDA has never approved it for pediatric use. The United States alleges that, among other things, GSK participated in preparing, publishing and distributing a misleading medical journal article that misreported that a clinical trial of Paxil demonstrated efficacy in the treatment of depression in patients under age 18, when the study failed to demonstrate efficacy. At the same time, the United States alleges, GSK did not make available data from two other studies in which Paxil also failed to demonstrate efficacy in treating depression in patients under 18. The United States further alleges that GSK sponsored dinner programs, lunch programs, spa programs and similar activities to promote the use of Paxil in children and adolescents. GSK paid a speaker to talk to an audience of doctors and paid for the meal or spa treatment for the doctors who attended. Since 2004, Paxil, like other antidepressants, included on its label a "black box warning" stating that antidepressants may increase the risk of suicidal thinking and behavior in short-term studies in patients under age 18. GSK agreed to plead guilty to misbranding Paxil in that its labeling was false and misleading regarding the use of Paxil for patients under 18.

Wellbutrin: The United States also alleges that, from January 1999 to December 2003, GSK promoted Wellbutrin, approved at that time only for Major Depressive Disorder, for weight loss, the treatment of sexual dysfunction, substance addictions and Attention Deficit Hyperactivity Disorder, among other off-label uses. The United States contends that GSK paid millions of dollars to doctors to speak at and attend meetings, sometimes at lavish resorts, at which the off-label uses of Wellbutrin were routinely promoted and also used sales representatives, sham advisory boards, and supposedly independentContinuingMedicalEducation(CME)programstopromoteWellbutrinforthese unapproved uses. GSK has agreed to plead guilty to misbranding Wellbutrin in that its labeling did not bear adequate directions for these off-label uses. For the Paxil and Wellbutrin misbranding offenses, GSK has agreed to pay a criminal fine and forfeiture of $757,387,200.

Avandia: The United States alleges that, between 2001 and 2007, GSK failed to include certain safety data about Avandia, a diabetes drug, in reports to the FDA that are meant to allow the FDA to determine if a drug continues to be safe for its approved indications and to spot drug safety trends. The missing information included data regarding certain post-marketing studies, as well as data regarding two studies undertaken in response to European regulators' concerns about the cardiovascular safety of Avandia. Since 2007, the FDA has added two black box warnings to the Avandia label to alert physicians about the potential increased risk of (1) congestive heart failure, and (2) myocardial infarction (heart attack). GSK has agreed to plead guilty to failing to report data to the FDA and has agreed to pay a criminal fine in the amount of $242,612,800 for its unlawful conduct concerning Avandia.

"This case demonstrates our continuing commitment to ensuring that the messages provided by drug manufacturers to physicians and patients are true and accurate and that decisions as to what drugs are prescribed to sick patients are based on best medical judgments, not false and misleading claims or improper financial inducements," said Carmen Ortiz, U.S. Attorney for the District of Massachusetts.

"Patients rely on their physicians to prescribe the drugs they need," said John Walsh, U.S. Attorney for Colorado. "The pharmaceutical industries' drive for profits can distort the information provided to physicians concerning drugs. This case will help to ensure that your physician will make prescribing decisions based on good science and not on misinformation, money or favors provided by the pharmaceutical industry."

Civil Settlement Agreement

As part of this global resolution, GSK has agreed to resolve its civil liability for the following alleged conduct: (1) promoting the drugs Paxil, Wellbutrin, Advair, Lamictal and Zofran for off-label, non-covered uses and paying kickbacks to physicians to prescribe those drugs as well as the drugs Imitrex, Lotronex, Flovent and Valtrex; (2) making false and misleading statements concerning the safety of Avandia; and (3) reporting false best prices and underpaying rebates owed under the Medicaid Drug Rebate Program.

Off-Label Promotion and Kickbacks: The civil settlement resolves claims set forth in a complaint filed by the United States alleging that, in addition to promoting the drugs Paxil and Wellbutrin for unapproved, non-covered uses, GSK also promoted its asthma drug, Advair, for first-line therapy for mild asthma patients even though it was not approved or medically appropriate under these circumstances. GSK also promoted Advair for chronic obstructive pulmonary disease with misleading claims as to the relevant treatment guidelines. The civil settlement also resolves allegations that GSK promoted Lamictal, an anti-epileptic medication, for off-label, non-covered psychiatric uses, neuropathic pain and pain management. It further resolves allegations that GSK promoted certain forms of Zofran, approved only for post-operative nausea, for the treatment of morning sickness in pregnant women. It also includes allegations that GSK paid kickbacks to health care professionals to induce them to promote and prescribe these drugs as well as the drugs Imitrex, Lotronex, Flovent and Valtrex. The United States alleges that this conduct caused false claims to be submitted to federal health care programs.

GSK has agreed to pay $1.043 billion relating to false claims arising from this alleged conduct. The federal share of this settlement is $832 million and the state share is $210 million.

This off-label civil settlement resolves four lawsuits pending in federal court in the District of Massachusetts under the *qui tam,* or whistleblower, provisions of the False Claims Act, which allow private citizens to bring civil actions on behalf of the United States and share in any recovery.

Avandia: In its civil settlement agreement, the United States alleges that GSK promoted Avandia to physicians and other health care providers with false and misleading representations about Avandia's safety profile, causing false claims to be submitted to federal health care programs. Specifically, the United States alleges that GSK stated that Avandia had a positive cholesterol profile despite having no well-controlled studies to support that message. The United States also alleges that the company sponsored programs suggesting cardiovascular benefits from Avandia therapy despite warnings on the FDA-approved label regarding cardiovascular risks. GSK has agreed to pay $657 million relating to false claims arising from misrepresentations about Avandia. The federal share of this settlement is $508 million and the state share is $149 million.

Price Reporting: GSK is also resolving allegations that, between 1994 and 2003, GSK and its corporate predecessors reported false drug prices, which resulted in GSK's underpaying rebates owed under the Medicaid Drug Rebate Program. By law, GSK was required to report the lowest, or "best" price that it charged its customers and to pay quarterly rebates to the states based on those reported prices. When drugs are sold to purchasers in contingent arrangements known as "bundles," the discounts offered for the bundled drugs must be reallocated across all products in the bundle proportionate to the dollar value of the units sold. The United States alleges that GSK had bundled sales arrangements that included steep discounts known as "nominal" pricing and yet failed to take such contingent arrangements into account when calculating and reporting its best prices to the Department of Health and Human Services. Had it done so, the effective prices on certain drugs would have been different, and, in some instances, triggered a new, lower best price than what GSK reported. As a result, GSK underpaid rebates due to Medicaid and overcharged certain Public Health Service entities for its drugs, the United States contends. GSK has agreed to pay $300 million to resolve these allegations, including $160,972,069 to the federal government, $118,792,931 to the states, and $20,235,000 to certain Public Health Service entities who paid inflated prices for the drugs at issue.

Except to the extent that GSK has agreed to plead guilty to the three-count criminal information, the claims settled by these agreements are allegations only, and there has been no determination of liability.

"This landmark settlement demonstrates the Department's commitment to protecting the American public against illegal conduct and fraud by pharmaceutical companies," said Stuart F. Delery, Acting Assistant Attorney General for the Justice Department's Civil Division. "Doctors need truthful, fair, balanced information when deciding whether the benefits of a drug outweigh its safety risks. By the same token, the FDA needs all necessary safety-related information to identify safety trends and to determine whether a drug is safe and effective. Unlawful promotion of drugs for unapproved uses and failing to report adverse drug experiences to the FDA can tip the balance of those important decisions, and the Justice Department will not tolerate attempts by those who seek to corrupt our health care system in this way."

Non-monetary Provisions and Corporate Integrity Agreement

In addition to the criminal and civil resolutions, GSK has executed a five-year Corporate Integrity Agreement (CIA) with the Department of Health and Human Services, Office of Inspector General (HHS-OIG). The plea agreement and CIA include novel provisions that require that GSK implement and/or maintain major changes to the way it does business, including changing the way its sales force is compensated to remove compensation based on sales goals for territories, one of the driving forces behind much of the conduct at issue in this matter. Under the CIA, GSK is required to change its executive compensation program to permit the company to recoup annual bonuses and long-term incentives from covered executives if they, or their subordinates, engage in significant misconduct. GSK may recoup monies from executives who are current employees and those who have left the company. Among other things, the CIA also requires GSK to implement and maintain transparency in its research practices and publication policies and to follow specified policies in its contracts with various health care payors.

"Our five-year integrity agreement with GlaxoSmithKline requires individual accountability of its board and executives," said Daniel R. Levinson, Inspector General of the U.S. Department of Health and Human Services. "For example, company executives may have to forfeit annual bonuses if they or their subordinates engage in significant misconduct, and sales agents are now being paid based on quality of service rather than sales targets."

"The FDA Office of Criminal Investigations will aggressively pursue pharmaceutical companies that choose to put profits before the public's health," said Deborah M. Autor, Esq., Deputy Commissioner for Global Regulatory Operations and Policy, U.S. Food and Drug Administration. "We will continue to work with the Justice Department and our law enforcement counterparts to target companies that disregard the protections of the drug approval process by promoting drugs for uses when they have not been proven to be safe and effective for those uses, and that fail to report required drug safety information to the FDA."

"The record settlement obtained by the multi-agency investigative team shows not only the importance of working with our partners, but also the importance of the public providing their knowledge of suspect schemes to the government," said Kevin Perkins, Acting Executive Assistant Director of the FBI's Criminal, Cyber, Response and Services Branch. "Together, we will continue to bring to justice those engaged in illegal schemes that threaten the safety of prescription drugs and other critical elements of our nation's healthcare system.""Federal employees deserve health care providers and suppliers, including drug manufacturers, that meet the highest standards of ethical and professional behavior," said Patrick E. McFarland, Inspector General of the U.S. Office of Personnel Management. "Today's settlement reminds the pharmaceutical industry that they must observe those standards and reflects the commitment of Federal law enforcement organizations to pursue improper and illegal conduct that places health care consumers at risk."

"Today's announcement illustrates the efforts of VA OIG and its law enforcement partners in ensuring the integrity of the medical care provided our nation's veterans by the Department of Veterans Affairs," said George J. Opfer, Inspector General of the Department of Veterans Affairs. "The monetary recoveries realized by VA in this settlement will directly benefit VA healthcare programs that provide for veterans' continued care."

"This settlement sends a clear message that taking advantage of federal health care programs has substantial consequences for those who try," said Rafael A. Medina, Special Agent in Charge of the Northeast Area Office of Inspector General for the U.S. Postal Service. "The U.S. Postal Service pays more than one billion dollars a year in workers' compensation benefits and our office is committed to pursuing those individuals or entities whose fraudulent acts continue to unfairly add to that cost."

A Multilateral Effort

The criminal case is being prosecuted by the U.S. Attorney's Office for the District of Massachusetts and the Civil Division's Consumer Protection Branch. The civil settlement was reached by the U.S. Attorney's Office for the District of Massachusetts, the U.S. Attorney's Office for the District of Colorado and the Civil Division's Commercial Litigation Branch. Assistance was provided by the HHS Office of Counsel to the Inspector General, Office of the General Counsel–CMS Division and FDA's Office of Chief Counsel as well as the National Association of Medicaid Fraud Control Units.

This matter was investigated by agents from the HHS-OIG; the FDA's Office of Criminal Investigations; the Defense Criminal Investigative Service of the Department of Defense; the Office of the Inspector General for the Office of Personnel Management; the Department of Veterans Affairs; the Department of Labor; TRICARE Program Integrity; the Office of Inspector General for the U.S. Postal Service and the FBI.

This resolution is part of the government's emphasis on combating health care fraud and another step for the Health Care Fraud Prevention and Enforcement Action Team (HEAT) initiative, which was announced in May 2009 by Attorney General Eric Holder and Kathleen Sebelius, Secretary of HHS. The partnership between the two departments has focused efforts to reduce and prevent Medicare and Medicaid financial fraud through enhanced cooperation. Over the last three years, the department has recovered a total of more than $10.2 billion in settlements, judgments, fines, restitution, and forfeiture in health care fraud matters pursued under the False Claims Act and the Food, Drug and Cosmetic Act.

SOURCE: U.S. Department of Justice. "GlaxoSmithKline to Plead Guilty and Pay $3 Billion to Resolve Fraud Allegations and Failure to Report Safety Data." July 2, 2012. http://www.justice.gov/opa/pr/2012/July/12-civ-842.html.

OTHER HISTORIC DOCUMENTS OF INTEREST

FROM PREVIOUS *HISTORIC DOCUMENTS*

Scientists Announce Possible Discovery of Universe Particle

JULY 4, 2012

On July 4, scientists at the European research organization known as the European Organization for Nuclear Research (CERN) made a long-awaited announcement that they had found a new particle that might be the sought-after Higgs boson, a particle thought to reveal how elements gained mass following the Big Bang and led to the creation of the universe as people know it today. Although media reports hailed the finding as a "breakthrough," scientists involved with the project were hesitant to use similar language, admitting that, while they believed they had found the elusive Higgs boson, years more study and research would be required to officially identify the new particle as such. But even if the new particle was an imposter, scientists said it would still unlock many mysteries physicists have been trying to solve for decades.

WHAT IS THE HIGGS BOSON?

Scientists believe that the universe was created more than 13 billion years ago following an event known as the Big Bang. Immediately following this violent event, extremely hot particles, including neutrons, electrons, photons and protons slowly began to cool. Some decayed, while others combined to form neutral atoms. Beginning in the 1930s, physicists began developing the standard model, which as of the 1970s is the currently accepted explanation of how fundamental particles, governed by four specific fundamental forces, are the building blocks of everything in the universe. Since the establishment of the standard model, scientists have struggled to figure out how particles that had had no mass suddenly gained mass following the Big Bang.

In the 1960s, physicist Peter Higgs, a University of Edinburgh theorist, worked with a team of scientists to fill this gap. Higgs and his team theorized that a particle exists that created an invisible electromagnetic force field throughout the universe that other particles passed through. The action of passing through this "wall" allowed particles to gain mass, making them free to create a variety of objects. The longer the interaction, the more mass a particle would gain, while those particles that never interacted with the force field would be left with no mass. Without this field, which resists changes in motion, particles would be unable to gain mass and would fly around faster than the speed of light, never creating the atoms that are the building blocks of life. The particles that joined together to create the field were dubbed the Higgs boson, after Peter Higgs.

CERN describes the Higgs boson as a crowded Hollywood party. When a big star arrives, the people closest to the door close in, and as that star tries to move through the room, he attracts additional people, while that first group goes back to where it was before the star arrived. As the star moves through the room, he gains momentum, and the crowd makes him harder to slow down. However, once he stops, it is difficult to get him moving again. This momentum created is a key indicator of mass known as inertia.

CERN SCIENTISTS REPORT NEW PARTICLE

Since the existence of the Higgs boson was proposed, scientists around the world have been searching for it. The most recent large-scale attempt occurred in Geneva, Switzerland, at the multinational research center, CERN. It was here that the Large Hadron Collider (LHC), a $10 billion particle accelerator, was built in 2010 to replace the Large Electron–Positron Collider that was shut down in 2000. The LHC allows physicists to shoot beams of subatomic particles, known as hadrons, made up of either protons or lead ions, at one another and see what happens when they collide. When two particles collide, they generally produce other particles. Scientists have used colliders around the world, including one in the United States that is now defunct, for a variety of research projects. According to the U.S. Department of Energy, particle research taking place at supercolliders have helped in the areas of food sterilization, cancer treatment simulation, shipping container scanning, nuclear weapons reliability testing, plastics curing, data mining, and a host of other practices.

Scientists at the LHC hoped that at some point a collision would result in the production of a Higgs boson. But identifying the particle would be difficult because they knew the Higgs boson would disintegrate into other particles in a millionth of a second after being produced by the collision. Adding to the complexity of the search, Higgs's theory gave no indication of how much the Higgs boson would weigh. All scientists knew was that the hallmark of a boson was the creation of two photons after a collision. Finding the Higgs boson would mean hoping that a trail of clues was left behind after photon creation.

Since the LHC came online, two groups of 3,000 scientists each, one named Atlas and the other Compact Muon Solenoid (CMS), worked separately to find the Higgs boson. Each team operated a separate detector inside of the supercollider and was responsible for identifying the subatomic particle debris that was left after particle collisions. In late 2011, each team of scientists separately discovered a portion of a particle that shared properties similar to what they expected of the Higgs boson. It was not until July 2012 that Atlas and CMS officially announced their findings, convinced that their experiments since the prior year had proved the new particle was not a fluke. "I think we have it," said Rolf-Dieter Heuer, the director general of CERN. The groups reported that their finding was "five sigma," the highest standard of discovery for physicists, which means there is less than a one in 3.5 million chance that the debris they detected was an error. Some combinations of data from CMS and Atlas showed a 4.9 sigma, or a one in 2 million chance of error, but Joe Incandela, a CMS team leader, said, "The results are preliminary, but the five-sigma signal . . . we're seeing is dramatic. This is indeed a new particle." A press release from CERN said that the finding meant "our knowledge of the fundamental structure of matter is about to take a major step forward."

If scientists have found the Higgs boson, not only would that verify the Standard Model, but it would also help scientists look into other unexplained issues such as what dark matter is and how its gravitational pull holds planets in place and why the universe is made up of matter rather than antimatter. "This could be the first in a ring of discoveries," said CERN's Guido Tonelli. "The discovery of a particle consistent with the Higgs boson opens the way to more detailed studies, requiring larger statistics, which will pin down the new particle's properties, and is likely to shed light on other mysteries of our universe," said Heuer.

MORE RESEARCH NECESSARY

Heuer and other scientists at CERN agreed that it was too early to say with absolute certainty that the new particle is the elusive Higgs boson. "What we have announced is the discovery of a new particle which is consistent with the Higgs boson," said Heuer. "We know there's a new particle, we know it is a boson. . . . But we don't know if we can say Higgs boson. It looks very much like the Higgs, but scientists are sometimes very careful and very cautious," he continued. "Only once we understand how it behaves, [will] we know if it's the Higgs boson or not. . . . If it's not, then it is maybe one of a family of Higgs bosons." So far, physicists working on the project have said that there are a number of possible imposters, but they have ruled out many of them in their experiments.

Scientists also agree that if the new particle is a Higgs imposter, that might be an even bigger breakthrough and a more exciting finding, which might bring science beyond the standard model. "It's something that may, in the end, be one of the biggest observations of any new phenomena in our field in the last 30 or 40 years," said Incandela. But, he cautioned, "The implications are very significant and it is precisely for this reason that we must be extremely diligent in all of our studies and cross-checks."

Scientists working with the Atlas and CMS teams hoped to complete many more experiments at the LHC before the end of 2012, in an effort to triple the data currently available on the Higgs-like particle. At the start of 2013, the LHC was scheduled to go offline for twenty months, allowing for necessary repairs and recharging to be completed. For that period, scientists will have to rely on any data collected in 2012, and the continuing study of the particle will take place without a supercollider. CMS scientists said that they had a lot of work ahead of them. "If this particle is indeed the SM [Standard Model] Higgs boson, its properties and implications for the standard model will be studied in detail. If it is not the SM Higgs boson, CMS will explore the nature of the new physics that it implies, which may include additional particles that are observable at the LHC," the CMS group said in a press release. "We're on the frontier now, on the edge of a new exploration," added Incandela. "This could be the only part of the story that's left, or we could open a whole new realm of discovery."

—Heather Kerrigan

Following is a press release from the European Organization for Nuclear Research's (CERN) Compact Muon Solenoid (CMS) experiment on July 4, 2012, announcing the discovery of a new particle that shares properties with the long-sought universe particle.

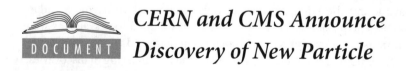

CERN and CMS Announce Discovery of New Particle

July 4, 2012

[All figures and footnotes, and parenthetical references to them, have been omitted.]

Summary

In a joint seminar today at CERN and the "ICHEP 2012" conference in Melbourne, researchers of the Compact Muon Solenoid (CMS) experiment at the Large Hadron Collider (LHC) presented their preliminary results on the search for the standard model (SM) Higgs boson in their data recorded up to June 2012.

CMS observes an excess of events at a mass of approximately 125 GeV with a statistical significance of five standard deviations (5 sigma) above background expectations. The probability of the background alone fluctuating up by this amount or more is about one in three million. The evidence is strongest in the two final states with the best mass resolution: first the two-photon final state and second the final state with two pairs of charged leptons (electrons or muons). We interpret this to be due to the production of a previously unobserved particle with a mass of around 125 GeV.

The CMS data also rule out the existence of the SM Higgs boson in the ranges 110–122.5 GeV and 127–600 GeV with 95% confidence level—lower masses were already excluded by CERN's LEP collider at the same confidence level.

Within the statistical and systematic uncertainties, results obtained in the various search channels are consistent with the expectations for the SM Higgs boson. However, more data are needed to establish whether this new particle has all the properties of the SM Higgs boson or whether some do not match, implying new physics beyond the standard model.

The LHC continues to deliver new data at an impressive rate. By the end of 2012, CMS hopes to have more than triple its total current data sample. These data will enable CMS to elucidate further the nature of this newly observed particle. They will also allow CMS to extend the reach of their many other searches for new physics.

CMS Search Strategy

CMS analysed the full data sample of proton-proton collisions collected in all of 2011 and in 2012, up until June 18. These data amount to up to 5.1 fb−1 of integrated luminosity, at a centre-of-mass energy of 7 TeV in 2011 and up to 5.3 fb−1 at 8 TeV in 2012.

The standard model predicts that the Higgs boson lasts for only a very short time before it breaks up, or "decays," into other well-known particles. CMS studied five main Higgs boson decay channels. Three channels result in pairs of bosonic particles ($\gamma\gamma$, ZZ or WW) and two channels result in pairs of fermionic particles (bb or $\tau\tau$), where γ denotes a photon, Z and W denote the force carriers of the weak interaction, b denotes a bottom quark, and τ denotes a tau lepton. The $\gamma\gamma$, ZZ and WW channels are equally sensitive in the search for a Higgs boson around 125 GeV and all are more sensitive than the bb and $\tau\tau$ channels.

The $\gamma\gamma$ and ZZ channels are especially important as they both allow the mass of the new particle to be measured with precision. In the $\gamma\gamma$ channel the mass is determined from the energies and directions of two high-energy photons measured by the CMS crystal electromagnetic calorimeter. In the ZZ channel the mass is determined from the decays of the two Zs to two pairs of electrons, or two pairs of muons, or a pair of electrons and a pair of muons. These are measured in the ECAL, inner tracking and muon detectors.

The WW channel is more complex. Each W is identified through its decay to an electron and a neutrino or a muon and a neutrino. The neutrinos pass through the CMS detectors undetected, so the SM Higgs boson in the WW channel would manifest itself as a broad excess in the mass distribution, rather than a narrow peak. The bb channel has large backgrounds from standard model processes, so the analysis searches for events in which a Higgs boson is produced in association with a W or Z, which then decays to electron(s) or muon(s). The ττ channel is measured by observing τ decays to electrons, muons and hadrons.

CMS Search Results

The CMS data sample should be sensitive enough to completely exclude the mass range 110–600 GeV at 95% confidence level, if the SM Higgs does not exist. In fact, the CMS data do rule out the existence of the SM Higgs boson in two broad mass ranges of 110–122.5 GeV and 127–600 GeV with 95% confidence level.

The range of 122.5–127 GeV cannot be excluded because we see an excess of events in three of the five channels analysed:

- **γγ channel**: the γγ mass distribution is shown in Figure 3. There is an excess of events above background with a significance of 4.1 sigma, at a mass near 125 GeV. The observation of the two-photon final state implies that the new particle is a boson, not a fermion, and that it cannot be a "spin 1" particle.
- **ZZ channel**: Figure 4 shows the mass distribution for the four leptons (two pairs of electrons, or two pairs of muons, or the pair of electrons and the pair of muons). Accounting also for the decay angle characteristics, it yields an excess of 3.2 sigma above background at a mass near 125 GeV.
- **WW channel**: a broad excess in the mass distribution of 1.5 sigma is observed.
- **bb and ττ channels**: no excess is observed.
- The statistical significance of the signal, from a combined fit to all five channels, is 4.9 sigma above background. A combined fit to just the two most sensitive and high-resolution channels (γγ and ZZ) yields a statistical significance of 5.0 sigma. The probability of the background alone fluctuating up by this amount or more is about one in three million.

The mass of the new particle is determined to be 125.3 ± 0.6 GeV, independent of any assumptions about the expected relative yields of the decay channels. The measured production rate (σDAT) of this new particle is consistent with the predicted rate (σSM) for the SM Higgs boson: σDAT/σSM = 0.80 ± 0.22.

Great care has also been taken to understand numerous details of the detector performance, the event selection, background determinations and other possible sources of systematic and statistical uncertainties. The 2011 analysis showed an excess of events at about 125 GeV. Therefore, to avoid a potential bias in the choice of selection criteria for the 2012 data that might artificially enhance this excess, the 2012 data analysis was performed "blind," meaning that the region of interest was not examined until after all the analysis criteria had been fully scrutinized and approved.

As a general cross-check, the analyses were performed by at least two independent teams. A number of other features reinforce confidence in the results:

- The excess is seen at around 125 GeV in both the 2011 data sample (7 TeV) and the 2012 data sample (8 TeV);
- The excess is seen at the same mass in both the high-resolution channels (γγ and ZZ);

- The excess seen in the WW is consistent with one that would arise from a particle at 125 GeV;
- The excess is seen in a range of final states involving photons, electrons, muons and hadrons.

The preliminary results presented today will be refined, with the aim of submitting them for publication towards the end of the summer.

Future Plans

The new particle observed at about 125 GeV is compatible, within the limited statistical accuracy, with being the SM Higgs boson. However, more data are required to measure its properties such as decay rates in the various channels ($\gamma\gamma$, ZZ, WW, bb and $\tau\tau$) and ultimately its spin and parity, and hence ascertain whether it is indeed the SM Higgs boson or the result of new physics beyond the standard model.

The LHC continues to perform extremely well. By the end of 2012, CMS expects to more than triple its total data sample, and hence to probe further the nature of this new particle. If this particle is indeed the SM Higgs boson, its properties and implications for the standard model will be studied in detail. If it is not the SM Higgs boson, CMS will explore the nature of the new physics that it implies, which may include additional particles that are observable at the LHC. In either case, searches will also continue for other new particles or forces that can be observed in future runs of the LHC at higher beam energies and intensities.

Source: European Organization for Nuclear Research. Compact Muon Solenoid Experiment. "Observation of a New Particle With a Mass of 125 GeV." July 4, 2012. https://cms-docdb.cern.ch/cgi-bin/PublicDocDB/RetrieveFile?docid=6116&filename=CMShiggs2012_EN.pdf.

European Central Bank
Cuts Rates to Record Low

JULY 5, 2012

The European Central Bank (ECB) reduced interest rates to their lowest-ever level on July 5, 2012, in a bid to shake the European economy out of its economic slump. The measure was designed to encourage banks to lend to one another more to stimulate the European Union's (EU) anemic economy, which registered zero growth in 2012. Reducing the rate on deposits to zero was viewed by analysts as a particularly significant step, meaning as it did that banks would receive nothing when they placed their money overnight with the ECB. The rate cut was one of a series of measures that the ECB took to prop up the EU's common currency, the euro. By the end of the year, these actions had helped stabilize the eurozone, although the situation remained delicately poised, especially in the most indebted nations of Cyprus, Greece, Ireland, Italy, Portugal, and Spain.

Interest rates on the main refinancing operations were reduced 25 basis points to 0.75 percent, on the marginal lending facility from 1.75 percent to 1.5 percent, and on the deposit facility from 0.25 percent to 0.00 percent. Mario Draghi, an Italian banker who became president of the Frankfurt-based ECB in November 2011, said that the decision had been unanimous. It came in response to bad economic news from Europe's largest economy, Germany, where a modest contraction was forecast. In the immediate aftermath of the rate cut, stocks rallied before falling, and the euro's value fell below $1.24. The cut followed hot on the heels of China and the United Kingdom's decision to lower rates. Banks were told that they would no longer get any return for parking funds of up to $1 trillion overnight in the ECB. Cited in a Bloomberg news article, James Nixon, chief European economist at the European bank Societe Generale SA, explained: "The benchmark rate doesn't really matter at the moment, but cutting the deposit rate all the way to zero takes the ECB into new territory."

MAJOR EXPANSION OF THE ECB'S ROLE

Taken in isolation, the rate cut would not be anything remarkable, following as it did similar moves in other major economies and in light of the underlying weakness of the EU's economy. But the action was a further example of the ECB's growing interventionism, in particular since the onset of a major credit crunch following the collapse of U.S. investment bank Lehman Brothers in 2008. Established in 1998, the ECB was entrusted with the task of overseeing the creation of the euro. This involved setting common interest rates for the eurozone and adopting monetary policies aimed at keeping inflation at around 2 percent. When the euro coins and notes were successfully introduced into circulation in 2002, the ECB's prominence continued to grow. In the early 2000s, there was much debate about the ECB's independence. Some nations such as Germany and the Netherlands were staunch advocates of the ECB's acting in complete independence, while France argued there should be greater political control over it.

When eurozone nations' public debt levels started to skyrocket in 2009 due to a severe recession, coupled with some governments' decisions to spend large sums to bail out banks, the ECB began to deploy additional instruments from its toolbox to try to contain the debt crisis. It started buying up government bonds to boost investors' confidence that the most indebted nations were not about to default on their debts. It also propped up Europe's shaky financial sector by injecting capital into banks. For example, in December 2011 and February 2012, it authorized Long-Term Refinancing Operations (LTROs), which were essentially 1.3 trillion dollars' worth of cheap loans to banks.

Many European governments welcomed these interventions as a necessary complement to the actions that EU political leaders were taking simultaneously to strengthen supervision of banking and to force governments to balance their budgets. But there were grumblings in some quarters, most notably Germany's central bank, the Bundesbank, whose management felt that the ECB interventions were sending the wrong signal to indebted nations—namely, that the ECB would always be there to bail them out. Similar criticisms were leveled at Europe's political leaders when they set up a $648 billion permanent bailout fund to prevent indebted nations from defaulting. That fund, the European Stability Mechanism (ESM), had received the political green light back in 2010 and become operational in September 2012. EU leaders in June 2012 agreed, in principle, to allow ESM funds to be injected directly into banks instead of having to be channeled to government coffers first. By early 2013, they were working on the precise modalities of how to do this.

Meanwhile, the crisis had persuaded Europe's political leaders that they needed a more unitary system for supervising the banking industry. Consequently, in September 2012, the EU's executive branch, the European Commission, proposed entrusting the ECB with the role of supervising 6,000 banks in the European Union. The Commission also proposed empowering the ECB to issue or withdraw banking licenses and to investigate banks. By the end of 2012, these proposals were being considered by the EU's two lawmaking branches, the Council of Ministers and European Parliament. While the details still needed to be ironed out, there was strong political momentum to adopt these "banking union" proposals, which would drastically enhance the ECB's role and powers. The managing director of the International Monetary Fund (IMF), Christine Lagarde, a former French finance minister, was effusive in praising the European Union for taking such steps.

SIGNS OF DEBT STABILIZATION

Although debt and deficit levels in the eurozone remained high throughout 2012, there were signs that the debt crisis was beginning to abate. Two of the three countries that received EU-IMF bailout loans because of the crisis, Ireland and Portugal, were showing signs of recovery by early 2013. Ireland was the stronger of the two, having registered modest economic growth for two successive years and meeting structural reform targets set by the so-called troika—the ECB, Commission, and the IMF—which oversees disbursement of the bailout loans. The Irish government hopes to return to the markets to sell its bonds by the end of 2013, which it must do if the troika is to give it back full sovereignty over economic policy. In January 2013, Portugal borrowed $3.33 billion from the medium-term loan market, the first time it had done so since entering an EU-IMF bailout program in May 2011.

The situation remained dire for the third bailout recipient, Greece. The Greek economy shrank by 6 percent in 2012, its fifth successive year of contraction, and unemployment topped 25 percent, although the government continued to implement the structural reforms demanded by the troika. The Greek situation had a secondary negative impact on its Mediterranean neighbor and fellow eurozone nation, Cyprus, due to their economies being so interlinked. The Cypriot government applied for an EU-IMF bailout loan in June 2012, but by early 2013, it had still not been approved. Having been forced to write off much of Greece's debt over the previous two years, EU governments were wary of loaning Cyprus the $22.65 billion it requested, fearful that the small nation would not be able to pay the money back. A Cyprus bailout was likely to be made conditional upon the country's government tackling the problem of the Russian mafia, which was laundering money through Cypriot banks.

Greece, Ireland, and Portugal were forced to cede a great deal of control over their economies when they agreed to being supervised by the troika as a condition to receiving their bailout loans. However, the euro debt crisis has also resulted in an expanded EU role in coordinating economic policies of all eurozone members, even those who have not received a bailout. For instance, the EU has agreed that henceforth national parliaments must submit draft budgets to the European Commission for vetting and that structural budget deficits should not exceed 0.5 percent of gross domestic product (GDP).

FEARS FOR ITALY AND SPAIN

The EU market's greatest concern was directed toward Italy and Spain because of the sheer size of their economies, the third and fourth largest in the eurozone, respectively. Many doubted the EU's financial capacity to bail Italy and Spain out even if the political will existed. The concerns about Italy peaked in late 2011, as the government of Prime Minister Silvio Berlusconi crumbled and Moody's rating agency downgraded the nation's credit rating. On July 13, 2012, Moody's further reduced Italy's rating two notches from A3 to Baa2, or two notches above junk status. The fears about Italy centered on its chronically low productivity and inefficient public sector, coupled with the economy having slid back into recession in 2012. Some confidence was restored when Mario Monti became prime minister in November 2011 and embarked on radical structural reforms of Italy's economy. Italy's reputation was also buoyed by the high level of private savings among its citizens and its relatively modest public deficit.

As for Spain, its problems were more acute. Unlike Italy, Spain experienced a massive property market bubble in the early 2000s followed by an equally precipitous crash when the global economy tanked in late 2008. By 2012, many of Spain's banks were teetering on the brink of bankruptcy. In response, Spain requested that $48 billion of ESM funds be used to rescue four Spanish banks: Bankia, Catalunya Banc, NCG Banco, and Banco de Valencia. It requested a further $5 billion from various private investors for a new "bad bank," which it planned to set up to siphon off foreclosed property and unrecoverable loans made to developers. In December 2012, Spain's eurozone colleagues agreed to the request but attached various financing conditions, such as requiring the banks to stop lending to the real estate sector and to limit wholesale banking activities to focus instead on small businesses and retail clients.

With shrinking tax revenues due to the economic slowdown, Spain's Prime Minister Mariano Rajoy fell short of his goal of reducing the public deficit from 9 percent to 6.4 percent of GDP in 2012, registering a deficit of 7 percent instead. His government made billions of dollars in spending cuts, triggering street protests and a surge in secessionist sentiment in the Catalonia region, where pro-independence parties won a majority in parliamentary elections in November 2012. Spain's political and economic turmoil—unemployment stood at 25 percent, and the economy shrank by 1.5 percent—translated into higher interest rates on Spanish bonds. Bond yields peaked at 7.5 percent in mid-2012, before falling back to 5.4 percent by the end of the year.

—Brian Beary

Following is the text of the July 5, 2012, press release announcing the European Central Bank's (ECB) decision to cut interest rates; and the edited text of a press conference given on July 5, 2012, by the president of the ECB responding to questions about the rate cuts.

ECB Announces Monetary Policy Decisions

July 5, 2012

At today's meeting the Governing Council of the ECB took the following monetary policy decisions:

1. The interest rate on the main refinancing operations of the Eurosystem will be decreased by 25 basis points to 0.75%, starting from the operation to be settled on 11 July 2012.

2. The interest rate on the marginal lending facility will be decreased by 25 basis points to 1.50%, with effect from 11 July 2012.

3. The interest rate on the deposit facility will be decreased by 25 basis points to 0.00%, with effect from 11 July 2012. . . .

SOURCE: European Central Bank. Press Releases. "Monetary Policy Decisions." July 5, 2012. http://www.ecb.int/press/pr/date/2012/html/pr120705.en.html.

ECB President Responds to Questions Concerning Interest Rate Cuts

July 5, 2012

Ladies and gentlemen, the Vice-President and I are very pleased to welcome you to our press conference. We will now report on the outcome of today's meeting of the Governing Council, which was also attended by the Commission Vice-President, Mr Rehn.

Based on our regular economic and monetary analyses, we decided to cut the **key ECB interest rates** by 25 basis points. Inflationary pressure over the policy-relevant horizon has been dampened further as some of the previously identified downside risks to the euro area growth outlook have materialised. Consistent with this picture, the underlying pace of monetary expansion remains subdued. Inflation expectations for the euro area economy continue to be firmly anchored in line with our aim of maintaining inflation rates below, but close to, 2% over the medium term. At the same time, economic growth in the euro area continues to remain weak, with heightened uncertainty weighing on confidence and sentiment.

We have implemented both standard and non-standard monetary policy measures. This combination of measures has supported the transmission of our monetary policy. All our non-standard monetary policy measures are temporary in nature and we maintain our full capacity to ensure medium-term price stability by acting in a firm and timely manner. Let me also remind you of the decision taken by the Governing Council on 22 June 2012 concerning further measures to increase collateral availability for counterparties.

Let me now explain our assessment in greater detail, starting with the **economic analysis**. On a quarterly basis, euro area real GDP growth was flat in the first quarter of 2012, following a decline of 0.3% in the previous quarter. Indicators for the second quarter of 2012 point to a renewed weakening of economic growth and heightened uncertainty. Looking beyond the short term we expect the euro area economy to recover gradually, although with momentum dampened by a number of factors. In particular, tensions in some euro area sovereign debt markets and their impact on credit conditions, the process of balance sheet adjustment in the financial and non-financial sectors and high unemployment are expected to weigh on the underlying growth momentum.

The risks surrounding the economic outlook for the euro area continue to be on the downside. They relate, in particular, to a renewed increase in the tensions in several euro area financial markets and their potential spillover to the euro area real economy. Downside risks also relate to possibly renewed increases in energy prices over the medium term.

Euro area annual HICP inflation was 2.4% in June 2012, according to Eurostat's flash estimate, unchanged from the previous month. On the basis of current futures prices for oil, inflation rates should decline further in the course of 2012 and be again below 2% in 2013. Over the policy-relevant horizon, in an environment of modest growth in the euro area and well-anchored long-term inflation expectations, underlying price pressures should remain moderate.

Taking into account today's decisions, risks to the outlook for price developments continue to be broadly balanced over the medium term. The main downside risks relate to the impact of weaker than expected growth in the euro area. Upside risks pertain to further increases in indirect taxes, owing to the need for fiscal consolidation, and higher than expected energy prices over the medium term.

Turning to the **monetary analysis**, the underlying pace of monetary expansion has remained subdued, with short-term developments displaying some volatility. The increase in the annual growth rate of M3 to 2.9% in May, up from 2.5% in April and close to the 3.0% observed in March, mainly reflected a reversal of the outflows in April from overnight deposits belonging to non-monetary financial intermediaries (particularly investment funds). In addition to an increased preference for deposits with shorter maturities, these factors have also shaped M1 developments, with the annual growth rate increasing from 1.8% in April to 3.3% in May.

The annual growth rate of loans to the private sector (adjusted for loan sales and securitisation) declined to 0.4% in May (from 0.8% in April). Annual growth rates for loans to both non-financial corporations and households (adjusted for loan sales and securitisation) also decreased in May, to 0.2% and 1.3% respectively, with negative monthly loan flows to non-financial corporations. To a large extent, subdued loan growth reflects the current cyclical situation, heightened risk aversion, and the ongoing adjustment in the balance sheets of households and enterprises which weigh on credit demand.

Looking ahead, it is essential for banks to continue to strengthen their resilience where it is needed. The soundness of banks' balance sheets will be a key factor in facilitating both an appropriate provision of credit to the economy and the normalisation of all funding channels.

To sum up, taking into account today's decisions, the economic analysis indicates that price developments should remain in line with price stability over the medium term. A **cross-check** with the signals from the monetary analysis confirms this picture.

Let me now make a few remarks relating to **other policies**. We welcome the European Council conclusions of 29 June 2012 to take action to address financial market tensions, restore confidence and revive growth. We agree that Economic and Monetary Union needs to be put on a more solid basis for the future and that sustainable growth, sound public finances and structural reforms to boost competitiveness remain key economic priorities. We welcome the decision to develop a specific and time-bound road map for the achievement of a genuine Economic and Monetary Union. We also welcome the euro area summit initiative towards a single supervisory mechanism, the possibility—with appropriate conditionality—to recapitalise banks directly, and the use of existing EFSF/ESM instruments in a flexible and efficient manner in order to stabilise markets. Finally, the ECB is ready to serve as an agent to the EFSF/ESM in conducting market operations.

We are now at your disposal for questions.

* * *

Question: *Mr Draghi, two questions, first of all about the deposit rate: you cut the deposit rate to zero. How exasperated are you with the fact that banks still do not use the money you are pumping into the market sufficiently either to lend it to each other or indeed to lend it to the economy, because clearly in some countries we are still in kind of credit crunch territory?*

And secondly, in terms of other non-standard measures, there is lots of speculation in the market that we might see further LTROs—I know, I know, you are not going to tell us anything about that—but how temporary is temporary in terms of some of the measures that we have seen?

Draghi [President, ECB]: I am sorry, I cannot answer the second question because we have always said that our non-standard measures are temporary and we do not want to pre-commit with regard to future decisions.

On the first question, we have dealt with this now several times. The answer is we need time to see this. The size and the complexity of these two LTROs are such that we cannot expect to see immediate action, and especially as far as the transmission of the LTROs into higher credit flows goes. But certainly now a few months have passed and we see that credit flows are actually weak and remain weak. Several observations: one is that, as I have said many times, there are at least three sets of reasons why banks may not lend. One is risk aversion, another is a lack of capital, and the third is a lack of funding. We have removed only the third, not the other two. The second reason is that this lack of transmission between the LTROs and a further enhancement of credit flows is not the same in all countries. You have countries like France, where credit flows actually continue to be moderately sustained, and you have other countries where credit flows are actually decreasing, which leads us to think that the transmission mechanism is also linked to national factors. They have to do with the way banks lend, special contracts, the contractual arrangements of different countries. But there is a third consideration, and that is that credit is now led predominantly by demand, and if demand is weak, you would not expect strong credit growth.

Question: *Mr Draghi, last month you told us that price signals were not particularly effective in the current environment. Can you tell us a bit about what has changed and about the debate in the Governing Council about this?*

And my second question is: China also cut rates today and we had further stimulus from the Bank of England. We were just kind of wondering about, you know, how much coordination was involved. Was there any sort of contact between you and the People's Bank of China and the Bank of England?

Draghi: On the first question: in a highly fragmented economy, as the euro area is, certainly price changes have a more limited effect than selective quantity changes. However, in this case, the lowering of the short-term rate and the contemporaneous lowering of the rate on the deposit facility has several effects. One is the immediate effect on the pricing of the €1 trillion already allotted in LTROs. The second one is a lowering in the pricing of emergency liquidity assistance. The third effect has more to do with the expectations generated by having brought the rate on the deposit facility to zero. Expectations of a further easing of monetary policy in the event that price stability considerations were to warrant it by themselves have a positive effect, a stimulus effect. But there is a fourth reason, and that is that when we were discussing it a month ago, we could not say that we had the same picture for the whole of the euro area as we do today. We now see a weakening of growth essentially in the whole of the euro area, including countries that were not experiencing that before. So, in a sense, we can now say that this measure is addressed to the whole of the euro area[;] it is not addressed to specific countries. These are the main reasons, and the reason why this price signal has a more powerful effect than was previously deemed to be the case is obviously that it has been accompanied by a reduction in the rate on the deposit facility.

On your question on coordination: no, there was not any coordination that went beyond the normal exchange of views on the state of the business cycle, on the state of the economy and on the state of global demand.

Question: *In June when the last staff economic forecasts were released there was a caveat that some of the more recent data which reflected lower growth and possibly inflation was not included in that. I am wondering whether those staff economic forecasts have been updated, at least internally, to reflect that lower growth and possible inflation path, and in particular whether the HICP inflation for next year, which was at a mid-point of 1.6%, was also possibly reduced and if that for you signals a possible deflationary risk already emerging?*

Draghi: What we said is basically that downside risks are materialising for the economic outlook, and that this would dampen price behaviour in the short and medium term. We now see that the objective of having an inflation rate for the whole euro area that is close to but below 2% will be met in 2013, or perhaps even before then, but do not ask me the exact date, day and time when this will happen. So right now we are pretty safe in saying what I said in the introductory statement, namely that on the basis of current and future oil prices, inflation rates should decline further in the course of 2012 and return to below 2% in 2013. Now, let's define deflation. Deflation is a protracted and generalised drop in the price level, so protracted and so strong and so generalised that it could disanchor inflationary expectations. It has to be generalised across countries and across products and sectors. And we see no sign of this in any country. But something to keep in mind for the future is that we always have to be careful in distinguishing movements in the price level and the inflation rate from movements in relative price adjustments. We can see some prices falling, but that is actually part of a good rebalancing of the situation within the euro area.

Question: *You quite rightly pointed out that we have got a divergence in the euro zone in terms of bank lending. Is there anything you can do to prevent the credit crunch that seems to be emerging in places like Italy and Spain?*

And the second question is also on the EFSF and the ESM fund. We know that if it does come to a situation where Spain does need extra aid, it will probably cover it, but what will happen if Italy also needs aid?

Draghi: What happens if everybody needs it? It is a big question.

On the first question, generally speaking, the idea that the ECB could channel funds via the bank lending channel to a specific category of firms or households is as wrong as the idea that the ECB should make sure banks don't buy government bonds as otherwise it is monetary financing. "Wrong" is probably too strong, but certainly both ideas are very, very hard to implement, requiring us to make sure that the banks do certain things or don't do certain things. We have to remember that their decisions are basically business decisions. What we could do and what we have done with respect to this is broaden the eligibility rules of collateral so as to attract the greatest number of banks, including those banks of a small/medium size which we believe are closest to the SMEs. But we have also done another thing, recently, at the last Governing Council meeting. We broadened the collateral eligibility so that banks can actually use the assets they create in lending to the real economy as collateral in borrowing from the ECB. So they are not only using government bonds, they are now also using credit claims and asset-backed securities of a lower rating, which means that for the banks in a sense it is now very useful to lend to the real economy because that way they also generate collateral that they can use for funding themselves. And we want to do this to keep the risk for the ECB balance sheet—and I have said this many times—very, very low.

As regards your second question, I do not have an answer on the ESM.

Question: *We've just had a question about EU banking supervision. First, do you see a pan-European banking union as a system only for the largest systemically important financial institutions or for all banks?*

And second, would the ECB do the supervising itself or would it outsource it to a separate body?

Draghi: I would say that it is far too early to respond to these questions, as the European Council meeting only took place a few days ago. However, let me give you a few messages of a general, albeit very important, nature.

First, with its decision to introduce a unified supervision of banks in the euro area, the European Council has made a very important step towards creating a "financial markets union" rather than a banking union. Furthermore, the leaders have committed substantial political capital to this decision. We expect that the proposal of the European Commission—after all, it is the competence of the Commission—in consultation with the European Parliament and the ECB, will be as strong as the commitment that the leaders have made in taking this decision. And we are confident that this will be the case.

Second, whatever the proposal may be, it should be such that the ECB can carry out any tasks assigned to it in an *effective, rigorous* and *independent way, without risk to its reputation.*

Third, any new tasks in terms of supervision should be strictly separate from monetary policy tasks. There should be no contamination between the two areas and we will certainly find ways to make it sure that this is the case.

Fourth, the ECB should remain independent in carrying out these tasks.

Fifth, it is essential that we work together with the national supervisors. I myself was a supervisor for six years when I was Governor of the Banca d'Italia, where supervision is one of the bank's areas of competence. Therefore, I know only too well that the knowledge, the skills, the competence, the history and the traditions are at the national level, and we plan to make full use of this fortunate situation.

Finally, there is an issue that is, in a sense, broader: new tasks will entail a higher level of democratic accountability. The Governing Council started to discuss this today, and we basically all agree on all the principles that I have just mentioned, especially the last one. We stand ready to meet higher standards of democratic accountability, as they will be asked of us by the citizens of Europe and especially those of the euro area.

Question: *I would like to go back to the question on the ESM. You mentioned before that you welcomed the fact that it was more flexible and efficient: do you think it is big enough for the tasks that it is being asked to do, from recapitalising banks to buying bonds in the secondary market?*

And in relation to this, there has been an idea out there for a couple of years that the ECB could maybe play a role in increasing the firepower of the ESM, by giving it a bank licence, for example. Would you be open to this or would you rule it out as one of the legal tricks circumventing the spirit of the Treaty that you have warned about in the past?

Draghi: How big is big enough? We know what we have and so we have to make it do! And frankly, I think that, right now, the ESM and the EFSF with the new modalities are big enough to cope with the contingencies that we can envisage now.

With regard to the ECB, I have said on numerous occasions that we are certainly supporting the euro area economy by achieving our objective of price stability in the medium term, and we want to act within the limits of our mandate. I don't think there is anything to gain by asking the institution to act outside the limits of its mandate, thereby destroying its credibility.

Question: *Two questions in relation to the outcome of the euro zone summit last week. There was a specific reference to the rescue of Ireland's banks in the euro zone communiqué. I wonder what in your opinion is the significance of that reference?*

And when it says that there will be an examination of the situation in Ireland's banks, what in your view would be the optimal outcome of that examination?

Draghi: Ireland is a euro area country that, through extraordinary efforts, has run a programme which is on track—so much so that Ireland returned to the markets today, if I am not mistaken. This is much earlier than anybody could have expected until two or three months ago. Even though this might not yet be part of a regular extended programme for a long period of time, I think that this success should be properly celebrated, and it is a testament to the determination of the Irish government and the capacity of the Irish people to understand and "own" this programme and make the needed sacrifices. I think this is very important. Actually, it is so important that an event like this could be one of the factors that are making the financial environment nowadays a little less tense than it was a month ago. I think this ought to be taken into account.

Question: *You said that you can only act within the limits of your mandate. Is there scope to change the mandate?*

Secondly, you have mentioned democratic accountability as one of the principles for this new financial markets union. Could you give some examples? Would you see extra scrutiny powers for the European Parliament? What exactly do you mean by "more democratic accountability"?

Draghi: On your first point, the mandate is the pursuit of price stability in the medium term with well-anchored inflation expectations. That is the mandate and we will use any tool within that mandate.

On the second point, I said that we stand ready and we are very aware that this is an essential requirement that is concomitant with more powers—even more so given that ours is a non-elected institution. We are waiting for the European Commission, the Eurogroup, the European Parliament, and the citizens of the euro area countries to tell us how we can comply with their certain desire for us to be democratically accountable with standards even higher than in the past.

Question: *One question on the monetary policy decision. Was the decision unanimous or were there people arguing either for keeping rates at 1.0% or for lowering them further to 0.5%? And was there discussion about the further loosening of the collateral framework—such as exempting government bonds from any rating requirements?*

On the banking union, you avoided the question of which banks should be subject to the banking supervision. I think that is a very crucial question. There seems to be a disagreement within the Governing Council: Mr Noyer argued for all banks, whereas Mr Nowotny said just a few—the systemic banks. What is your view? Does it make sense to have a supervisor who is only responsible for a few banks, where banks like Bankia, or others who may not be in the league of the systemic banks, may not be subject to that?

Draghi: The decision was unanimous on all grounds. This in itself I think demonstrates the strength of this decision.

On the second question, we are just at the beginning. We have been discussing this new concept for only two days. With a new concept—how to build this supervisory mechanism in the euro area countries—it is natural that people discuss different views. But there are no really diverging views within the Governing Council.

Regarding the principles I spoke of before, the Governing Council is absolutely united. There is no disagreement at all. Of course, it is natural for us to ask if it will apply to only the globally systemically important financial institutions or to all systemically important financial institutions—we are well aware that there are domestic banks that are systemically important. Or, to minimise distortionary situations in the competition among banks, should we extend it to all banks? These are natural questions. There are pros and cons for each one of these options, and we are now working all together on trying to find the right perimeter for this. But we should not forget that ultimately any proposal will come from the Commission, with the consultation of the ECB and the European Parliament.

Question: *Mr. Draghi, I have only one question. On the same day three central banks cut their interest rates. So some experts said the current situation is even worse than when the crisis began in 2007 and 2008. My question is: what do you think about this?*

Draghi: Definitely not. Well, more serious than 2007/2008 I would pick 2009 as the trough of the recession and I think we are not there at all. We have a situation for the euro area where growth is basically hovering around zero. We still expect a gradual, slow recovery around the end of the year. And so, in a sense, the baseline scenario of the ECB has not changed, although the downside risks to that baseline scenario are now materialising. Now I should stop you because I know what your next question will be: where does this recovery come from? You have asked your question, so you are not going to ask this one, but I am sure that one of your colleagues will certainly do so! The answer is basically that we should not forget that nominal rates are very, very low; real rates are negative and certainly the expectation of a recovery by the turn of the year—although muted, although slow, although very gradual and so on—is based on an improvement in the general sentiment, an abating in the sovereign debt crisis and in a somewhat improving market sentiment on the financial markets. Furthermore I would not exclude—I would not say a "strengthening," but a situation for global external demand which would stabilise rather than fall. These are the assumptions on which our expectation of this slow, gradual recovery by the turn of the year is predicated.

Question: *You have mentioned Ireland. Can I ask you about Portugal? As you know, the last troika mission to Portugal identified some growing risks in terms of budget execution this year due to the impact of the recession. Given the general goal of returning to the markets next year, as in the case of Ireland, do you think that the government, the authorities in Portugal should stand ready to take any additional measures necessary to achieve the given target? Or do you see a risk that, at this stage, further cuts will be counterproductive to the economy and to the target as well?*

Draghi: Vítor, the floor is yours.

Constâncio [Vice President of the ECB]: The conclusions of the review were that the programme was still on track in Portugal. There were some risks highlighted but the conclusion was positive. Also positive was the IMF's analysis. So we have to wait and see how the economy will perform in the near future. But certainly all the conditions seem to be there for compliance with the programme[,] which is, of course, a very important objective. The country has been assessed generally now in international markets as being on the right path[,] and that should continue to be the case.

Question: *What do you expect the impact of the rate cut to be? I mean, will banks lend more to the economy or will they lend at a lower price? Or is it just that they have a higher margin?*

And the second question is: do you still see any shortage of collateral in the banking system?

Draghi: On the second question, the situation of collateral changes country by country and so nowadays we have several countries that have plenty of funding and so need less collateral. And there are some local, specific situations where countries are short of funding and need more collateral. I would rather not give names, but you can easily find out for yourselves.

Question: *But it would be interesting to hear your point of view which countries...*

Draghi: You can see where the strains, the funding strains, are in Europe; I am thinking of one country in particular where you can imagine they need collateral. You see, in a normally functioning euro area when a bank is short of funding, they simply borrow from other banks. But in a highly fragmented situation, when a bank is short of funding, they only can go to the ECB. And if the bank is solvent, the ECB stands ready to provide all the liquidity they need. That is important. We should not forget that. I have been saying this on and on and on since the beginning. The ECB is providing liquidity and will keep all liquidity lines open to solvent banks. Of course, the collateral they give should be acceptable and should not increase the risk of the balance sheets of the ECB. And that is what we have done so far. You have doubts, but that is what we have done so far.

We had announced this decision on 22 June and we do not pre-commit, but at the same time we think that the collateral framework will have to be revisited and this is not something we can come out with soon because it is highly complicated, but as I have said many times we should again present a well thought-out, well-organised framework for collateral eligibility.

On the first question, one could ask this question every time we change interest rates: what is the situation? It is clear that when demand is weak, the transmission of these price signals to the aggregate economy is muted. If you had strong demand, you have immediately passed through from the policy rate to bank lending rates. But if the credit demand is low, then we will look at it. But it certainly is a signal, it is encouraging, it should make entrepreneurs think that their investment decisions, trade-offs, are now better. So this is ceteris paribus. Of course, if the risk premium is high, then this will be less effective. If it is low, it will be more effective. But I think that this is a question that actually one should ask every time interest rates are changed. And unfortunately the answer is that this very much depends on demand for credit.

Question: *I have two questions. You have cut the deposit rate to 0.00%. Could you talk us through the risks that you discussed on that? How do you make sure that you are not sowing the seeds for the next bubble?*

My second question is: Given all the discussion about the ECB taking on banking supervision, what would the ECB have done to prevent the attempts to rig the LIBOR/ EURIBOR rate?

Draghi: On the question of bubbles, one of the reasons for taking the decision that we have taken today is that we do not really see any risks for inflation expectations, on either side, certainly not on the upside in the short or medium term. And that has a lot to do with the weakening of the general economy, but also with the behaviour of oil prices, as we have to bear in mind, of course, that they could go either way. So, we had to take that into account. But the rest of the economy does not seem to be inclined to generate upward pressure on inflation.

As regards the LIBOR, I believe there is an enquiry taking place at this very moment. It does show that this process, which was considered fair and pivotal for the functioning of financial markets, was not fair. I therefore think that considerable action ought to be undertaken to improve the governance of this process at both levels. Both the level at which figures are contributed and the level at which the benchmark is produced. It is quite clear that governance at these two levels was weak—if not faulty. And frankly, I do not know what the ECB would have done, but I hope we would have done better.

Question: *I have two questions. Apart from the interest rate decision, were there any other options that you discussed, such as other non-conventional measures, like a new LTRO?*

And another question: A recent survey revealed that ECB staff feels overworked because of the many years of crisis. Especially now that the ECB is being given new tasks, such as banking supervision, do you share ECB staff's worries that there may be an operational risk to the ECB? Does the ECB plan to hire more staff, and to what extent?

Draghi: On the first question, we did not discuss any other non-standard measures. And fairly unusually for me, I will also tell you why we did not discuss that—because we have to have non-standard measures which are effective, and they have to be effective in an area which is fragmented. So, that is why it is not obvious that there are measures that can be effective in a highly fragmented area. Even though, as I have said, market sentiment seems to be improving slightly. For example, one of the remaining benefits of the LTROs is, I think, that we have not seen signs of outflows from the euro area. And this is actually quite important. I think one of the reasons why the euro summit was such a success is that leaders showed that this is a monetary union that is meant to last. They showed their commitment to making it a success. They started identifying an end point—a goal. They started, through the Van Rompuy report, drafting a pact in order to achieve this goal and started identifying conditions that had to be satisfied in order to undertake this journey together. I think this is why the euro summit was viewed so positively by markets and by everybody.

On your second point, let me say that we are all—and I am especially—impressed by the extraordinary commitment that our staff show every day in undertaking tasks that have become more and more numerous, difficult and psychologically demanding. So, I would say that it is no surprise that they see themselves as overworked, and our assessment is exactly the same. The ECB has taken some steps to alleviate that stress and the Executive Board has discussed a proposal to increase the resources of the ECB—in a very modest way—in order to undertake some of the new tasks that have been given to the ECB in the course of the last two or three years.

Question: *I wonder if you have a timeline in mind for when the ECB would be ready to assume this unified banking supervision, considering that there has been talk of the Commission's proposal coming by the end of the year, but also given that fact that it is quite essential for this to be done quickly, as direct lending from the ESM to banks depends on it. I wonder if you have a date in mind when this would be fully operational?*

My other question is: what is your interpretation of the EFSF/ESM bond-buying? Some leaders have said that this new "anti-spread" mechanism will work effectively, i.e.[,] it will curb spreading to countries in difficulty, whereas other leaders have said that nothing has really changed from the agreements that were reached last year. I wonder what your view is on that.

Draghi: On the first point, we do not have a date, because, as I have said, the final proposal is a Commission proposal drawn up in consultation with the ECB and the European

Parliament. I am sure that this will be done as speedily as possible. I would not dramatise too much the need for doing things fast. It is better to do things well. It has been said that this supervisory proposal and the eventual agreement should come very soon because this would enable the ESM to recapitalise banks directly. So, the two things have been linked with each other. But what happens if the proposal is not ready? Well, the public debt of an individual country will increase temporarily, because they will borrow from the EFSF. But we all know that this will occur with the expectation of a decrease later on, once the supervision mechanism is in place. So it is a temporary blip in public debt which can be easily absorbed by markets. We all want to have everything "well done" and "now." But if I had to choose, I would rather focus on it being "well done," because, if it is well done, we can then cope with whatever else occurs and we know that a delay of two or three months will not cause a drama.

On the EFSF/ESM, the agreement at the European summit was that purchases on the markets would be carried out in a flexible and effective way. This was the agreement. We should not forget, and some of the statements tend to forget, that everything—the ESM recapitalisation, the stepping-in of the EFSF or the ESM in the primary or secondary markets—is subject to conditionality. There is nothing without conditionality. Conditionality is what gives credibility to these measures.

Question: *The labour reform has passed through in Italy. Do you have any comments on this? Are you happy with that?*

And second, in lowering the deposit rates to zero, do you think this might accelerate the restitution of LTROs from banks—in some countries, not from others—to within one year, instead of three years?

Draghi: Well, on the first question, I have no comments.

On the second point, it is difficult to foresee how banks might behave. Frankly[,] I do not expect banks' behaviour to change dramatically in any way. Banks might have an incentive to return what they had in the deposit facility earlier if they were sure that, for most scenarios, they would not need that liquidity any time soon. At the same time, it is clear that currently it is a little more expensive for them. But let us not forget that they are also paying less on the LTRO exposure: so, they get less on the deposit, but they pay less on the other side. How this is going to affect their business decisions or their convenience decisions is very hard to predict.

Question: *Is the Governing Council concerned about the impact of negative carry via negative yields for bonds and such, especially for non-banks? And does the Governing Council not think that a negative deposit rate could be risky and, if so, does that mean that the Governing Council rules out negative rates?*

Draghi: We have not discussed this and, as usual, we will not commit to any further measures.

Question: *My first question probably paraphrases what my colleague has just asked. In principle, would you consider operating under negative deposit rates?*

And my second question is this: you have repeatedly stated that credit has mainly been driven by demand in recent months. Does that mean that the ECB is operating close to, or under, a liquidity trap?

Draghi: No, we do not think we are in that situation. And, frankly, on the other part of your question and your colleague's question, I would say that, at this point in time, we are not really elaborating on various non-standard situations in which we may find ourselves. So, at this point in time we are not actually thinking about that.

Question: *Is there any concern on the Governing Council that the ECB is now running low on policy options and that, if there is not an improvement as expected or hoped, there will be a need to turn to some more unconventional measures?*

Draghi: No, there is no such feeling that we are running low on policy options. We still have all our artillery ready to contain inflationary risk in order to pursue the objective of price stability. Let me say one thing: when I say pursue the objective of price stability, I mean on both sides or in both directions. As I was saying, we still have all our tools to continue to pursue our objectives within our mandate and, as I said before, I do not think I want to elaborate on further non-standard measures at this point in time.

Question: *I am getting a number of emails from market participants who wish for some clarification on a comment that you made earlier when you talked about the effect of this rate cut. You talked about the third effect that it had, i.e., that there were expectations of further easing of monetary policy in case price stability considerations were warranted and that this by itself has a positive effect, a stimulus effect. So, people want to know or are debating whether you are keeping the options open to cut rates further or introduce quantitative easing or whatever else. As I said, you will always have those kind of debates, but could you clarify exactly what you meant by this so that people will know?*

Draghi: People are reading too much into this. You can translate what I said into this: whenever the bank pursues the objective of price stability in the medium term, that in itself has a positive effect on the economy.

SOURCE: European Central Bank. Press Conferences. "Introductory Statement to the Press Conference (with Q&A)." July 5, 2012. http://www.ecb.int/press/pressconf/2012/html/is120705.en.html.

OTHER HISTORIC DOCUMENTS OF INTEREST

FROM THIS VOLUME

FROM PREVIOUS *HISTORIC DOCUMENTS*

United Nations on Libyan Elections and a New Government

JULY 9 AND NOVEMBER 1, 2012

After the October 2011 fall of longtime Libyan leader Col. Muammar el-Qaddafi during the Arab Spring uprising of 2011, the North African nation was thrown into a state of uncertainty as the interim government tried to set up elections and maintain security. It was not until July 2012 that Libyans finally went to the polls to elect a new government that would oversee the process of drafting a constitution. Although the vote was an overall success, the prime minister chosen by the new government was unable to seat his cabinet and, shortly after being installed, was ousted and replaced by a new leader. When the new cabinet was finally seated, the prime minister turned his attention to the daunting task of determining how best to fairly represent the diverse Libyan population on the constitutional panel, which was supposed to deliver a draft to voters by 2013.

Revolution Topples Dictator, Brings First Free Election in Fifty Years

The Arab Spring movement that swept across Africa and the Middle East in 2011 forced major changes in Libya, where a revolution against Qaddafi's government began in February. The ruler, who had been in power for four decades, defied the increasingly powerful rebel movement and remained in his position throughout the spring and summer of 2011, using any force necessary to do so. With the backing of the United Nations and the North Atlantic Treaty Organization (NATO), the rebels were eventually able to end Qaddafi's ruthless campaign and bring down his government by August. In October, Qaddafi was captured and killed by a group of Libyans.

During the revolution, rebels formed the Transitional National Council, which was eventually recognized by the international community as the legitimate government of Libya prior to Qaddafi's fall. The council declared Libya liberated on October 23, paving the way for the election of a new government and drafting of a constitution. The body faced significant questions about its legitimacy and was largely unable to maintain order in a nation where hundreds of disparate, well-armed rebel groups remained following the revolution.

The Transitional National Council set up an election for the country's parliamentary body, the 200-member General National Congress, to be held on June 19, 2012. However, due to voter registration problems, the slow pace of adopting election laws, and appeals filed by candidates who had been deemed ineligible to run, the vote was postponed until July 7. Of the 200 available seats, 80 would be for candidates from party lists (through which seats are allocated proportionally to those chosen internally by each political party) while the remaining 120 would be constituency seats. A total of 374 party lists were registered for the vote, as well as more than 2,600 individual candidates.

Prior to the July 7 election, Libya's last fully free parliamentary vote was held shortly after it won independence from Italy in 1952. When Qaddafi came to power in 1969, he ended all direct elections. Approximately 1.7 million Libyans turned out to vote on July 7. When the results were announced on July 17, the National Forces Alliance, a liberal coalition created by Transitional National Council Prime Minister Mahmoud Jibril, won thirty-nine of the eighty party list seats. Jibril himself did not run in the election. Seventeen party seats were awarded to the Justice and Construction Party, the political arm of the Muslim Brotherhood in Libya, and the National Front Party, an anti-Qaddafi group first formed in the 1980s, gained three party seats.

The vote was deemed an overall success by international election observers and the High National Election Commission (HNEC), even though there were some reports of gunmen at polling locations and burning and stealing of ballot boxes. "It is remarkable that nearly all Libyans cast their ballot free from fear or intimidation," said Alexander Graf Lambsdorff, a member of the European Union Assessment Team. U.S. President Barack Obama called the vote "another milestone on their extraordinary transition to democracy," while UN Secretary-General Ban Ki-moon celebrated those who conducted the "election in a peaceful, democratic spirit."

PRIME MINISTER DISMISSED, NEW GOVERNMENT SWORN IN

In September 2012, the new Libyan parliament chose Mustafa Abu Shagour to lead the government as prime minister. Shagour, however, faced difficulties from the start. Parliament was wrought with infighting among its many blocs, and Shagour only narrowly won the seat over Jibril, who was eligible for the position as leader of the National Forces Alliance. Only four weeks into his term, Shagour faced a vote of no confidence after parliament was unable to accept his new cabinet. Shagour was ousted from his position on October 7.

Facing increasing international pressure to seat a stable government—especially in light of the September terrorist attack on the U.S. Consulate in Benghazi that killed four Americans including the ambassador—on October 15, the two largest blocs in parliament choose Ali Zeidan, a former human rights lawyer with the European Court of Human Rights, as the new prime minister. Zeidan presented his proposal for a cabinet on October 30, saying, "I tried to feel the pulse of the nation from all aspects and avoid anything that could provoke controversy, taking in mind the geographical issue, which is very important in order for the nation to be present in government with all its parts." The new prime minister attempted to include members of all the political parties in his government. The initial vote on his cabinet selection was postponed as protesters stormed parliament, arguing that all regions of the country were not fairly represented and that some cabinet posts were to be given to those who had ties to Qaddafi's government. When the vote took place the next day, October 31, under the watchful eye of Libyan militia who kept demonstrators at bay, 105 members of parliament voted for the cabinet, 9 voted against it, and the remainder were absent or abstained.

The new cabinet was sworn in on November 14 and noted the importance of the revolution that overthrew Qaddafi in its oath: "I swear to God that I will fulfill my duties with all dedication to be loyal to the goals of the 17th of February Revolution, and to respect the constitution and its rules and its articles and to completely care for the needs of Libyans and to protect the Libya and the unity of its lands." Although the installment of

Zeidan's cabinet marked the end of the confusion that had engulfed the country since the fall of Qaddafi over who was truly in charge of the government, there were still remaining questions as four ministers—those in charge of electricity, higher education, congressional relations, and the interior—were rejected by the state integrity commission for issues including ties to Qaddafi. The ministers of foreign affairs, agriculture, social affairs, and religious affairs were also under investigation. In total, nineteen of the twenty-seven ministers were sworn in on November 14.

Zeidan's new government will face a number of challenges, including what impact Islamic law will have in Libyan society given the significant bloc of seats in parliament held by members of the Muslim Brotherhood, how to rebuild the nation after more than a year of rebellion and upheaval, and how to maintain relationships with the countries that aided Libya during the overthrow of Qaddafi's regime.

Zeidan will also face the challenge of working with his new government to determine the best method for drafting the country's constitution. Initially, parliament was to be in charge of creating the document. However, those in the oil-rich eastern part of the country, who were allotted only sixty seats in the new parliament, expressed concern that the nation's main export would not receive proper recognition in the constitution if it were developed by parliament. To allay concerns, before the new parliament had been elected, the Transitional National Council decided that Libyans would instead be able to vote for sixty members of a constitutional panel. However, Zeidan has suggested that it might be better if his government appointed the members of the panel. A decision has not yet been made, and it will likely be well into 2013 before the panel convenes.

QADDAFI INNER CIRCLE FACES TRIAL

Because he was killed during the revolution, Libyans were unable to bring Qaddafi to trial for his alleged crimes against the country. However, his son, Seif al-Islam el-Qaddafi, who prior to the revolution had been a spot of hope for ending the country's authoritarian regime and bringing economic change, was captured in November 2011 for his own role in the treatment of the Libyan rebel movement. According to Libyan lawyers, as of October 2012, a team of investigators was collecting evidence in an effort to try Seif Qaddafi for murder, torture, violence against demonstrators, and recruitment of mercenaries.

The International Criminal Court (ICC) in The Hague, the Netherlands, has urged Libya to send Seif Qaddafi and Libya's former intelligence chief, Abdullah al-Senussi, to it for prosecution. Libyan officials have refused, insisting that both should be tried by their own people in their own country. The ICC said that it would not rescind its indictments against the two men until the Libyan government can prove that it will conduct a free trial as necessary under international law. By the close of 2012, no progress had been made in the trials against either man as the nation still lacks stability in its legal system.

—Heather Kerrigan

Following is a statement by the UN envoy to Libya on July 9, 2012, praising the nation's first free election in nearly fifty years; and a press release from the United Nations Support Mission in Libya (UNSMIL) on November 1, 2012, welcoming the formation of Libya's new post-Qaddafi government.

UN Envoy Praises Free Election

July 9, 2012

The top United Nations envoy in Libya today said the country's weekend election—its first free poll in almost half a century—was an "extraordinary achievement" and praised electoral authorities for organizing them efficiently, while also highlighting challenges an incoming government will face, foremost among them building security institutions.

"The mood in Libya is extremely positive with people taking enormous pride in having voted after nearly half a century and in how well they organized this vote for themselves," the Secretary-General's Special Representative and head of the UN Support Mission in Libya (UNSMIL), Ian Martin, told reporters at UN Headquarters in a video-conference.

Speaking from Tripoli, the Libyan capital, Mr. Martin highlighted the fact that the African Union, European Union, and Carter Centre, which fielded election observers, all made positive preliminary statements praising Libya's High National Election Commission, not just for its transparency but for its flexibility given some security threats in eastern parts of the country.

"It was really the will of the people that prevailed in the determination of voters to protect their own polling centres, and the Commission then kept them open to allow people an opportunity to vote," Mr. Martin said.

Some 2.7 million people in the North African nation registered to vote for members of the new National Congress, which will be tasked with drafting a new constitution for Libya. More than 3,000 candidates ran for office, including more than 600 women.

The polls were the first free elections in decades in Libya, where Muammar al-Qadhafi ruled for more than 40 years until a pro-democracy uprising last year—similar to the protests in other countries in the Middle East and North Africa—led to civil war and the end of his regime.

Mr. Martin's words echoed those of Secretary-General Ban Ki-moon, who congratulated the Libyan people earlier for Saturday's election. Mr. Ban also expressed his appreciation to the candidates and political groups that contested the election in a peaceful and democratic spirit, stressing that the UN looks forward to working with the country's new leaders as they address the challenges of drafting a constitution and building a secure and accountable state.

In his remarks to the media, Mr. Martin noted that the elections "must not blind any of us to the enormous challenges that still lie ahead," particularly that of building security institutions.

The envoy has previously voiced concern over incidents of renewed fighting throughout Libya, and called on the authorities to address the causes of the conflicts and protect civilians.

In a briefing to the Security Council in May, he said that armed clashes in recent months between various groups have tested the reach and authority of the Government's security apparatus and ability to impose the rule of law.

He added that other public security matters, such as the integration or demobilization of revolutionary fighters and the control of weapons, in addition to human rights, transitional justice and national reconciliation, are among the other issues that need to be addressed during the North African country's ongoing democratic transition.

SOURCE: United Nations. News Centre. "UN Envoy Praises Libyan Election, Highlights Challenges Faced by New Government." July 9, 2012. http://www.un.org/apps/news/story.asp?NewsID=42428# .USKD3qVBcRx.

UN Mission Welcomes Formation of Post-Qaddafi Government

DOCUMENT

November 1, 2012

The Special Representative of the Secretary-General (SRSG) and Head of the United Nations Support Mission in Libya (UNSMIL), Mr. Tarek Mitri, welcomes the formation of the new Libyan Government, and extends his congratulations to Prime Minister Ali Zeidan and members of his Cabinet.

SRSG Mitri congratulates the General National Congress, the legitimately elected body chosen to represent the will of the Libyan people for moving forward in the process of their democratic transition.

He wishes the new government success in addressing the many challenges new Libya is facing, including the building of security institutions, promoting national reconciliation as well as upholding the rule of law, securing human rights and implementing transitional justice. In meeting these challenges, the support of the Libyan people to its democratically elected State institutions is essential.

SRSG Mitri notes that the recent events in Bani Walid highlight the urgent need for Libyans to foster dialogue, work together towards national reconciliation and strengthen State civilian and security institutions to affirm the authority of the Libyan State over its national territory and ensure protection of all citizens and stability in the country.

SRSG Mitri takes this opportunity to reiterate the commitment of the United Nations to a democratic and prosperous Libya and to fully support the new government and the Libyan people in accordance with its mandate under Security Council resolution 2040 (2012).

He further reiterates that UNSMIL and the whole of the United Nations will continue to work closely with the Government and the National General Congress in support of Libya.

SOURCE: United Nations Support Mission in Libya. Press Releases. "UN Special Representative Welcomes Formation of New Libyan Government." November 1, 2012. http://unsmil.unmissions.org/Default .aspx?tabid=3561&ctl=Details&mid=8549&ItemID=671488&language=en-US.

OTHER HISTORIC DOCUMENTS OF INTEREST

FROM THIS VOLUME

- State Department Responds to Benghazi Consulate Attack, p. 424

FROM PREVIOUS *HISTORIC DOCUMENTS*

- Arab Spring: NATO and President Obama on the Death of Muammar Qaddafi, *2011,* p. 555

Penn State Releases Report on Sandusky Child Sexual Abuse Allegations

JULY 12, 2012

The Pennsylvania State University is revered around the country for its strong football program. But in November 2011, the program was sidelined when a former coach was accused of sexually abusing children. The coach, Jerry Sandusky, was tried and convicted on more than forty counts of sexual abuse and will likely spend the rest of his life in prison. But it was the fallout that shook the campus to its core—its longtime, storied football coach, Joe Paterno, and the school's president, Graham Spanier, were fired by the board of trustees.

In July 2012, an independent panel arranged by the university released its findings about the sex abuse case, reporting that the university and football officials were at fault for not taking action to ensure that Sandusky no longer had access to young boys and for not reporting his crimes to the proper authorities. Following the release of the report, the National Collegiate Athletic Association (NCAA) placed stiff penalties on the Penn State football program, revoking its past championships, withdrawing some scholarships, and disqualifying the school from postseason play for four years.

ALLEGATIONS AGAINST SANDUSKY

In 1977, Sandusky founded The Second Mile, a charity dedicated to helping disadvantaged youth. It was through this organization that Sandusky met each of the ten boys who accused him of sexual abuse. During the period from 1994, when he met the person known as Victim 7, through 2009, at which point the mother of Victim 1 had Sandusky barred from the boy's high school, Sandusky subjected the boys to varying degrees of abuse.

Allegations that Sandusky was sexually abusing young boys were first made in 1998, when Victim 6, who was eleven at the time, arrived home with wet hair after a shower with Sandusky in Penn State's locker rooms. The incident was reported to university police, who worked with the State College Police Department to listen in on conversations between Sandusky and Victim 6's mother, during which Sandusky admitted to showering with other underage boys but would not promise to stop this activity. Victim 6's mother told Sandusky not to contact her son anymore, and according to court testimony, Sandusky responded, "I was wrong. I wish I could get forgiveness. I know I won't get it from you. I wish I were dead." Following the incident, Sandusky admitted to the state Department of Public Welfare that he had showered naked with Victim 6, but the Centre County district attorney chose not to file criminal charges.

Sandusky retired from his position with the Penn State football program in 1999, but he maintained access to the school's football facilities where many of the assaults are said to have taken place. In the fall of 2000, a Penn State janitor reported to his colleagues and supervisor that he witnessed Sandusky in the locker room showers performing oral sex on a boy. The janitor never made a formal report to the university or police, and the identity of that victim, known as Victim 8, remains unknown. The next year, a graduate assistant coach witnessed Sandusky in the locker room showers performing anal sex on Victim 2, estimated to be ten years old. The graduate assistant, Mike McQueary, reported the incident to Paterno on February 10, and Paterno reported the incident to Athletic Director Tim Curley. Later that month, McQueary was informed that Sandusky no longer had locker room privileges. No investigation was conducted into this matter at that time.

The last known incident involving abuse by Sandusky took place in the spring of 2007, when Victim 1 began staying overnight at Sandusky's house. By spring of 2009, Victim 1's mother had Sandusky barred from the victim's high school after reporting a sexual assault on her son. The school reported the assault to local law enforcement. The following year, the Pennsylvania attorney general began investigating Sandusky after another person told law enforcement that he had been abused by Sandusky over a four-year period. A grand jury was convened in 2009, but its existence was not made public until March 2011, when the Harrisburg *Patriot-News* reported that both Paterno and Curley had been called to testify. On November 5, 2011, Sandusky was arrested and arraigned on forty counts of child sexual abuse and released after posting $100,000 bail.

Penn State's board of trustees took a number of actions after Sandusky was arrested as public outcry grew when the state attorney general announced she would also be investigating Paterno and reported that a ninth victim had come forward (only eight were included in the initial arraignment and a tenth came forward later). Most notably, the university chose to fire head coach Paterno on November 9, 2011, after forty-six years on the job because his "decision to do his minimum legal duty and not to do more to follow up constituted a failure of leadership." Paterno had announced earlier that day that he would retire at the end of the season, but the board chose to remove him immediately. The board also fired University President Spanier. Senior Vice President Gary Schultz resigned, while Curley asked to be placed on temporary leave. McQueary, by that time a Penn State assistant coach, was placed on administrative leave.

TRIAL AND SENTENCING

Sandusky's trial opened on June 11, 2012, and throughout, the prosecution alleged that Sandusky had used his influence as a member of the Penn State football coaching team and founder of his charity to target disadvantaged boys to sexually abuse. The defense maintained that Sandusky had a solid record of helping children in unfortunate situations, pointing to his adoption of six children, and said the supposed victims were motivated by money to testify and that they had been coached by police on what to say. In total, eight of the ten alleged victims and one of the victims' mothers took the stand, giving graphic testimony about the abuses. Sandusky's wife spoke in defense of her husband, recounting many pleasant evenings spent with the boys, and said she could remember only one instance of inappropriate contact that she witnessed but that it was the boy who had made an advance on Sandusky.

On June 22, Sandusky was convicted on forty-five counts of child sexual abuse against ten young boys. He was later sentenced in October to thirty to sixty years in prison. Following his sentencing, Sandusky said, "They can take away my life, they can make me out as a monster, they can treat me as a monster, but they can't take away my heart. In my heart, I know I did not do these alleged, disgusting acts. My wife has been my only sex partner and that was after marriage."

Spanier, Schultz, and Curley faced varying charges, including perjury, obstruction of justice, endangering the welfare of children, criminal conspiracy, and failure to report suspected child abuse to the proper authorities. No charges were brought against Paterno, who died of lung cancer on January 22, 2012.

Freeh Report

Penn State set up an independent investigation to look into any wrongdoing on the part of the university and provide recommendations to avoid such incidents in the future. The investigation was led by former Federal Bureau of Investigation (FBI) director Louis Freeh, who over the course of eight months led his team through 430 witness interviews and the review of countless documents and e-mails.

On July 21, Freeh released his findings in a 267-page report. "The most saddening finding by the Special Investigative Counsel is the total and consistent disregard by the most senior leaders at Penn State for the safety and welfare of Sandusky's child victims," the report read. Freeh's findings singled out four officials as the center of the cover-up: Paterno, Spanier, Curley, and Schultz. According to the report, these four officials covered up Sandusky's crimes in an effort to avoid bad publicity for the university and its football program.

In his report, Freeh painted a picture of Paterno, a man he said could bend university officials to his will, and a president who attempted to cover up what he knew to protect himself and the university's image. The board of trustees was largely left in the dark throughout the time of Sandusky's actions. This, the report states, "reveals numerous individual failings, but it also reveals weaknesses of the university's culture, governance, administration, compliance policies and procedures for protecting children." It is common practice at a university for the president to report to the board of trustees on any legal issues or problems facing the university. Spanier did not report any information on Sandusky to the board; nor did the board request such information, according to the report. In fact, Freeh's report found, once it came to light that Spanier and other university officials had been called to testify before a grand jury investigation into Sandusky, Spanier assured the board that the problem was minor.

The investigation panel also found multiple instances of failure to follow state and federal law. A federal law enacted in 1990, known as the Jeanne Clery Act, requires higher education institutions to regularly put together information on threats or crimes on campus and report that information to the university community. This information is supposed to be compiled by a number of college officials, including coaches; however, the Freeh report found that the university assumed it was up to campus police to cull and distribute such information. Although the university developed a plan to properly comply with the Clery Act in 2009, it had not been implemented by 2011.

According to the Freeh report, a law that requires university officials to report suspected child abuse to the state was also violated. The episode in question occurred in 2001, when McQueary reported that he witnessed Sandusky sexually assaulting a boy in a locker room shower. E-mails reviewed by the Freeh panel show that the university president, along with Curley and Schultz, had agreed that the incident would be reported to police. However, instead of following through on that course of action, they decided that "talking it over with Joe [Paterno]," as Curley suggested in an e-mail, would be the best plan.

The board of trustees accepted responsibility for all of the findings addressed by the Freeh report on behalf of the university. "We, the Penn State board of trustees, failed in our obligation to provide proper oversight of the university's operations," said Kenneth Frazier, one of the trustees. "Our hearts remain heavy, and we are deeply ashamed," he continued. The trustees said the information in the report would serve as a guide "to strengthen Penn State's role as a leading academic institution and ensure that what occurred will never be allowed to happen again." The trustees stopped short, however, of claiming that allegations of Sandusky's activity were overlooked or covered up because of the reverence given to the football program.

FALLOUT

Following the release of the Freeh report, the NCAA announced penalties against Penn State, including a $60 million fine, a ban on participation in postseason games for four years, the loss of approximately ninety scholarships, and removal of all team victories from 1998 to 2011. Although the NCAA has the power to shut down a football program—the harshest penalty available to it—in the case of Penn State, it decided the four penalties were significant enough. NCAA President Mark Emmert called the situation the most painful "chapter in the history of intercollegiate athletics."

In response to the NCAA ruling, Pennsylvania Governor Tom Corbett filed a lawsuit against the NCAA in January 2013, alleging that the punishment amounted to a violation of antitrust laws and would have a significant impact on the state's economy. "These sanctions did not punish Sandusky," Corbett said, "nor did they punish the others who have been criminally charged. Rather, they punished the past, the present, the local businesses and the citizens of Pennsylvania." Penn State is not party to the lawsuit.

—Heather Kerrigan

Following are excerpts from the Freeh report released on July 12, 2012, on the actions taken by Penn State University in response to allegations of child sexual abuse committed by Jerry Sandusky.

 ## *Freeh Report on Response to Sandusky Child Abuse Allegations*

July 12, 2012

[The title page, table of contents, scope and methodology, and a note on the independence of the investigation have been omitted.]

[All footnotes have been omitted.]

EXECUTIVE SUMMARY

On November 4, 2011 the Attorney General of the Commonwealth of Pennsylvania ("Attorney General") filed criminal charges against Gerald A. Sandusky ("Sandusky") that included multiple counts of involuntary deviate sexual intercourse, aggravated indecent assault, corruption of minors, unlawful contact with minors and endangering the welfare of minors. Several of the offenses occurred between 1998 and 2002, during which time Sandusky was either the Defensive Coordinator for The Pennsylvania State University ("Penn State" or "University") football team or a Penn State professor Emeritus with unrestricted access to the University's football facilities. On November 4, 2011, the Attorney General filed criminal charges against the University's Athletic Director ("AD") Timothy M. Curley ("Curley") and Senior Vice President Finance and Business ("SVP-FB"), [sic] Gary C. Schultz ("Schultz") for failing to report allegations of child abuse against Sandusky to law enforcement or child protection authorities in 2002 and for committing perjury during their testimony about the allegations to the Grand Jury in Dauphin County, Pennsylvania, in January 2011.

On June 22, 2012, a Centre County jury in Bellefonte, Pennsylvania[,] found Sandusky guilty of 45 counts of the criminal charges against him. As of the date of this report, the charges against Curley and Schultz have not been heard by the court.

The criminal charges filed against these highly respected University and community leaders are unprecedented in the history of the University. Several senior University leaders who had knowledge of the allegations did not prepare for the possibility that these criminal charges would be filed. In the days and weeks surrounding the announcement of the charges, University leaders (referred to on campus as "Old Main") and the University's Board of Trustees ("Board" or "Trustees"), struggled to decide what actions the University should take and how to be appropriately transparent about their actions. The high degree of interest exhibited by members of the University community, alumni, the public and the national media put additional pressure on these leaders to act quickly.

On November 11, 2011, the Trustees formed the "Special Investigations Task Force ("Task Force") of the Board of Trustees of The Pennsylvania State University" and selected Trustees Kenneth C. Frazier and Ronald J. Tomalis to lead its efforts. On November 21, 2011 the Task Force engaged the law firm of Freeh Sporkin & Sullivan, LLP ("FSS") as Special Investigative Counsel, to conduct an investigation into the circumstances surrounding the criminal charges of sexual abuse of minors in or on Penn State facilities by Sandusky; the circumstances leading to the criminal charges of failure to report possible incidents of sexual abuse of minors; and the response of University administrators and staff to the allegations and subsequent Grand Jury investigations of Sandusky. In addition, the Special Investigative Counsel was asked to provide recommendations regarding University governance, oversight and administrative procedures that will better enable the University to effectively prevent and respond to incidents of sexual abuse of minors in the future.

The Pennsylvania State University is an outstanding institution nationally renowned for its excellence in academics and research. There is a strong spirit of community support and loyalty among its students, faculty and staff. Therefore it is easy to understand how the University community was devastated by the events that occurred.

FINDINGS

The most saddening finding by the Special Investigative Counsel is the total and consistent disregard by the most senior leaders at Penn State for the safety and welfare of Sandusky's child victims. As the Grand Jury similarly noted in its presentment, there was no "attempt to investigate, to identify Victim 2, or to protect that child or any others from similar conduct except as related to preventing its re-occurrence on University property."

Four of the most powerful people at The Pennsylvania State University—President Graham B. Spanier, Senior Vice President–Finance and Business Gary C. Schultz, Athletic Director Timothy M. Curley and Head Football Coach Joseph V. Paterno—failed to protect against a child sexual predator harming children for over a decade. These men concealed Sandusky's activities from the Board of Trustees, the University community and authorities. They exhibited a striking lack of empathy for Sandusky's victims by failing to inquire as to their safety and well-being, especially by not attempting to determine the identity of the child who Sandusky assaulted in the Lasch Building in 2001. Further, they exposed this child to additional harm by alerting Sandusky, who was the only one who knew the child's identity, of what McQueary saw in the shower on the night of February 9, 2001.

These individuals, unchecked by the Board of Trustees that did not perform its oversight duties, empowered Sandusky to attract potential victims to the campus and football events by allowing him to have continued, unrestricted and unsupervised access to the University's facilities and affiliation with the University's prominent football program. Indeed, that continued access provided Sandusky with the very currency that enabled him to attract his victims. Some coaches, administrators and football program staff members ignored the red flags of Sandusky's behaviors and no one warned the public about him.

By not promptly and fully advising the Board of Trustees about the 1998 and 2001 child sexual abuse allegations against Sandusky and the subsequent Grand Jury investigation of him, Spanier failed in his duties as President. The Board also failed in its duties to oversee the President and senior University officials in 1998 and 2001 by not inquiring about important University matters and by not creating an environment where senior University officials felt accountable.

Once the Board was made aware of the investigations of Sandusky and the fact that senior University officials had testified before the Grand Jury in the investigations, it should have recognized the potential risk to the University community and to the University's reputation. Instead, the Board, as a governing body, failed to inquire reasonably and to demand detailed information from Spanier. The Board's overconfidence in Spanier's abilities to deal with the crisis, and its complacent attitude left them unprepared to respond to the November 2011 criminal charges filed against two senior Penn State leaders and a former prominent coach. Finally, the Board's subsequent removal of Paterno as head football coach was poorly handled, as were the Board's communications with the public.

Spanier, Schultz, Paterno and Curley gave the following reasons for taking no action to identify the February 9, 2001 child victim and for not reporting Sandusky to the authorities:

- Through counsel, Curley and Schultz stated that the "humane" thing to do in 2001 was to carefully and responsibly assess the best way to handle vague but troubling allegations. According to their counsel, these men were good people trying to do their best to make the right decisions.
- Paterno told a reporter that "I didn't know exactly how to handle it and I was afraid to do something that might jeopardize what the university procedure was. So I backed away and turned it over to some other people, people I thought would have a little more expertise than I did. It didn't work out that way."

- Spanier said, in his interview with the Special Investigative Counsel, that he never heard a report from anyone that Sandusky was engaged in any sexual abuse of children. He also said that if he had known or suspected that Sandusky was abusing children, he would have been the first to intervene.

Taking into account the available witness statements and evidence, the Special Investigative Counsel finds that it is more reasonable to conclude that, in order to avoid the consequences of bad publicity, the most powerful leaders at the University—Spanier, Schultz, Paterno and Curley—repeatedly concealed critical facts relating to Sandusky's child abuse from the authorities, the University's Board of Trustees, the Penn State community, and the public at large.

The avoidance of the consequences of bad publicity is the most significant, but not the only, cause for this failure to protect child victims and report to authorities. The investigation also revealed:

- A striking lack of empathy for child abuse victims by the most senior leaders of the University.
- A failure by the Board to exercise its oversight functions in 1998 and 2001 by not having regular reporting procedures or committee structures in place to ensure disclosure to the Board of major risks to the University.
- A failure by the Board to make reasonable inquiry in 2011 by not demanding details from Spanier and the General Counsel about the nature and direction of the grand jury investigation and the University's response to the investigation.
- A President who discouraged discussion and dissent.
- A lack of awareness of child abuse issues, the Clery Act, and whistleblower policies and protections.
- A decision by Spanier, Schultz, Paterno and Curley to allow Sandusky to retire in 1999, not as a suspected child predator, but as a valued member of the Penn State football legacy, with future "visibility" at Penn State and ways "to continue to work with young people through Penn State," essentially granting him license to bring boys to campus facilities for "grooming" as targets for his assaults. Sandusky retained unlimited access to University facilities until November 2011.
- A football program that did not fully participate in, or opted out [of,] some University programs, including Clery Act compliance. Like the rest of the University, the football program staff had not been trained in their Clery Act responsibilities and most had never heard of the Clery Act.
- A culture of reverence for the football program that is ingrained at all levels of the campus community.

RECOMMENDATIONS FOR UNIVERSITY GOVERNANCE, ADMINISTRATION, AND THE PROTECTION OF CHILDREN IN UNIVERSITY FACILITIES AND PROGRAMS

From the results of interviews with representatives of the University's Office of Human Resources, Office of Internal Audit, Office of Risk Management, Intercollegiate Athletics, Commonwealth Campuses, Outreach, the President's Council, Faculty Senate representatives and the Board of Trustees, and benchmarking similar practices at other large universities, the Special Investigative Counsel developed 120 recommendations for consideration by University administrators and the Board in the following eight areas:

- The Penn State Culture
- Administration and General Counsel: Structure, Policies and Procedures
- Board of Trustees: Responsibilities and Operations
- Compliance: Risk and Reporting Misconduct
- Athletic Department: Integration and Compliance
- University Police Department: Oversight, Policies and Procedures
- Programs for Non-Student Minors and Access to Facilities
- Monitoring Change and Measuring Improvement

These recommendations are detailed in Chapter 10 of this report, and include several that the Special Investigative Counsel recommended to the Board in January 2012. The recommendations made at that time were designed to assist the University in preparing for its upcoming summer programs for children.

These steps should assist the University in improving structures, policies and procedures that are related to the protection of children. Some of these recommendations will help the University more fully comply with federal and state laws and regulations dealing with the protection of children. Other recommendations support changes in the structure and operations of the Board, or promote enhancements to administrative processes and procedures. Most importantly, the recommendations should create a safer environment for young people who participate in its programs and use its facilities.

One of the most challenging of the tasks confronting the Penn State community is transforming the culture that permitted Sandusky's behavior, as illustrated throughout this report, and which directly contributed to the failure of Penn State's most powerful leaders to adequately report and respond to the actions of a serial sexual predator. It is up to the entire University community—students, faculty, staff, alumni, the Board, and the administration—to undertake a thorough and honest review of its culture. The current administration and Board of Trustees should task the University community, including students, faculty, staff, alumni, and peers from similar institutions and outside experts in ethics and communications, to conduct such a review. The findings from such a review may well demand further changes.

[The remainder of the report, including a timeline of events, further details on the findings and recommendations described in the Executive Summary, and the appendices, has been omitted.]

SOURCE: The Pennsylvania State University. "Report of the Special Investigative Child Sexual Abuse Committed by Gerald A. Sandusky." July 12, 2012. http://progress.psu.edu/assets/content/REPORT_FINAL_071212.pdf.

OTHER HISTORIC DOCUMENTS OF INTEREST

FROM PREVIOUS *HISTORIC DOCUMENTS*

Interior Department on the Impact of a National Helium Shortage

JULY 20, 2012

Helium, the second most abundant element on Earth, is running out. And contrary to what many know, it is used in more than just balloons, including anything from military operations to magnetic resonance imaging (MRI) machines. The U.S. government controls and provides a majority of the world's helium needs, but demand has quickly outpaced supply, and a 1996 congressional decision to sell off the nation's helium reserves and privatize the industry has met with little response from interested investors. Without new plants coming online to keep up with demand, a worldwide helium shortage could raise health care prices and slow technological advancements in a number of key areas. Although awareness of the severity of the issue has been growing, it peaked in 2012 when the federal government labeled the shortage a "crisis."

NOT JUST FOR BALLOONS

Helium's properties, including extreme melting and boiling points and an inability to react with other elements, makes it crucial in a number of scientific and technical applications. But most people recognize its use only in balloons, which make up less than one percent of the helium market. "Pretty much anything that's a high-tech industry," said Samuel Burton of the Federal Helium Reserve, "there's probably helium in its manufacture somewhere." Helium is used in arc welding for shipbuilding and aerospace manufacturing, air-to-air missiles, nuclear reactor cooling, particle accelerators that contribute to cutting-edge physics research, deep-sea diving, cryogenics, document preservation, liquid fuel rockets, LCD screens, and military surveillance blimps. On the latter, because it is not flammable, helium replaced hydrogen as a medium for filling blimps after the Hindenburg disaster.

And although helium is the second most abundant element in the universe, behind hydrogen, most of it escapes into space before it can be captured and used. Today's helium supply is largely made as a by-product of natural gas production. Producing and storing the gas isn't as easy as opening up a natural gas facility—only certain areas of the world have helium-rich natural gas fields, including parts of Kansas, Texas, and Wyoming. Worldwide, there are helium operations in Algeria, Australia, Canada, Qatar, and Russia.

The shortage that began in 2012 can be attributed to a number of factors, including a delay in bringing a new Wyoming helium plant online because of wildfires, decreasing demand for natural gas because of the recession, a warm winter that decreased the use of natural gas in heating homes, and plant problems in Algeria, Australia, and Qatar.

FEDERAL HELIUM RESERVES

The U.S. government got into the helium business back in the early 1900s because the gas was critical for military operations and, eventually, space exploration. It was the U.S. Navy that first began storing helium in Amarillo, Texas, for use in dirigibles and barrage balloons. In 1920, the Mineral Leasing Act ensured that the government would maintain control of all helium produced on federal lands. The Bureau of Mines officially established the Amarillo Helium Plant in 1929. Today, the helium reserve in Amarillo supplies 30 percent of the world's helium. In total, the United States produces 75 percent of the world's helium supply.

In 1960, Congress passed the Helium Amendment Act, calling for the Bureau of Mines to buy crude helium from private natural gas producers. The proceeds the Bureau of Mines made from subsequently selling the purchased helium would be used to pay down the cost of funds borrowed from the U.S. Treasury to purchase the crude helium in the first place. The funds were initially required to be paid back by 1985, but that deadline was extended to 1995. When the loan came due, the Bureau of Mines owed a total of $1.3 billion. Because the Bureau was well short of being able to pay its debt, then-president Bill Clinton made it a goal of his administration to privatize the government's helium program.

In 1996, in an effort to shore up the debt, Congress passed the Helium Privatization Act. This gave the Bureau of Land Management (BLM) authority over the reserves when the Bureau of Mines ceased to exist, and it directed them to sell the helium to private companies and stop any helium production. The goal was that by 2015, the federal government would no longer be in charge of the helium supplies, and the industry would become privatized. Unfortunately, few companies have come forward to take on that role. "The hope was by 2015, by the time the reserve was sold down, that new sources of helium would be online and take up the demand. However, it has not happened yet," said Joe Peterson, the Bureau of Land Management's assistant field manager for helium in Amarillo. Current estimates indicate that the helium reserve will no longer be financially able to operate as early as mid-2013.

Given the magnitude of how much helium the government owns, it has been able to set the world price. It was initially sold below its market value, giving little incentive for conservation or recycling of the gas; but with a need to pay off the debt, in April 2012, the government announced that the price would rise from $75.75 to $84.00 per thousand cubic feet in fiscal year 2013. Critics argue such price fluctuations hit a number of industries that pass their higher costs on to consumers. "Because the original base pricing of federal helium started at below market levels, the BLM, at the recommendation of the National Academy of Sciences, is now making unpredictable increases to adjust for the base pricing up to market levels and to incorporate additional fees for costs that are specific only to the operation of the BLM reserve," said David Joyner, president of Liquide Helium America. This structure, he criticized, "drives up the price of helium for all consumers, not only here in the United States, but also around the world."

IMPACT

The 2012 helium shortage wasn't the world's first. Back in 1958, a worldwide shortage meant that the balloons in the Macy's Thanksgiving Day parade were filled with air instead of helium and driven along the route on trucks. But federal officials said that the 2012 shortage is the worst to this point, partly because of how long it is anticipated to last. "Typically in the past, there's been enough helium in the distribution system that the end consumer never saw the problem," said Burton. "This has been an extended shortage, and all of the helium that's been in the supply chain has been expended," he continued.

Right now, Burton anticipates that the shortage will continue through at least 2013 as the world waits for new plants to come online. A plant in Wyoming was expected to open in 2011, and would supply 10 percent of the world's helium, but a number of issues are continuing to cause delays.

In the long run, the reduction in helium supply could impact many different industries. Currently, helium distribution is based on the necessity of an operation. For example, when supplies are low, hospitals get what they need before a party store does. As supplies continue to dwindle and the cost rises, it is likely that the health care and science industries will feel the greatest impact. Forty million MRI exams are conducted each year, and the helium used to cool the magnet in the machine is vital. If not enough helium is available, the magnet can be permanently damaged and, according to Tom Rauch, a health care supply-chain manager for General Electric, "Replacing an MRI often involves a crane, street closures and knocking down ceilings and walls of a care facility," all of which comes at a significant cost that will be passed on to consumers.

The party supply industry has begun researching new techniques for air-filled balloons, which it is calling "the new helium." The spotty availability in some areas has caused economic disruption. At Arkansas's largest party store, The Party Place, the owner estimated losing approximately $50,000 in sales because of the shortage.

In May 2012, Congress took note of the problem. "If Congress does not act," Sen. Jeff Bingaman, D-N.M., told a meeting of the Senate Energy and Natural Resources Committee, "the helium program will disappear altogether in less than three years, leaving our hospitals, national labs, domestic manufacturers and helium producers without an adequate supply." In a congressional testimony, Timothy R. Spisak, deputy assistant director of Minerals and Realty Management at the U.S. Department of the Interior's BLM, said the 2015 sale deadline "could pose a threat to the availability of this resource for future U.S. scientific, technical, biomedical, and national security users of helium." Seeking to prevent such an occurrence, Bingaman cosponsored a bill called the Helium Stewardship Act of 2012 with Sen. John Barrasso, R-Wyo., that would change how the government sells its helium in an effort to prevent future shortages and shore up the current one. The bill would not close the reserve as is currently intended in 2015; rather, it would preserve it and sell off helium at market prices, thus encouraging conservation and recycling of the gas until a new domestic or international source can be developed, and making up any loss that would be experienced by closing the U.S. reserve in Amarillo. However, even if Congress were able to delay the closing of the federal reserve, it would be able to produce helium only through 2018 or 2020 before it runs out. As of the end of 2012, Bingaman's bill had not made it out of committee and will need to be reintroduced in the next Congress.

—Heather Kerrigan

Following is the text of a testimony delivered on July 20, 2012, by Timothy R. Spisak, deputy assistant director of Minerals and Realty Management at the U.S. Department of the Interior's Bureau of Land Management, before the House of Representatives Subcommittee on Energy and Mineral Resources, detailing the nationwide impact of the helium shortage.

Testimony on the Federal Helium Program

July 20, 2012

Statement of

Timothy R. Spisak

Deputy Assistant Director, Minerals and Realty Management

U.S. Department of the Interior

Bureau of Land Management

Before the

U.S. House of Representatives

Committee on Natural Resources

Subcommittee on Energy and Mineral Resources

Oversight Hearing

Helium: Supply Shortages Impacting our Economy,

National Defense and Manufacturing

July 20, 2012

Mr. Chairman and members of the Subcommittee, thank you for the opportunity to testify on the Federal helium program. As indicated by a National Academy of Sciences (NAS) report published in early 2010, the market for helium has proven more volatile than expected over the last 15 years and current law's requirement that the Bureau of Land Management (BLM) offer for sale nearly all of the Federal Helium Reserve by 2015 could pose a threat to the availability of this resource for future U.S. scientific, technical, bio-medical, and national security users of helium.

BACKGROUND

Helium is a critical, non-renewable natural resource that plays an important role in medical imaging, space exploration, military reconnaissance, fiber optics manufacturing, welding and commercial diving. According to the NAS, helium's best known property, being lighter than air, means "that every unit of helium that is produced and used today will eventually escape the Earth's atmosphere and become one less unit available for use tomorrow."

The most common and economical way of capturing helium is by stripping it from natural gas during gas production. Geologic conditions in Texas, Oklahoma, and Kansas make the natural gas in these areas some of the most helium-rich in the United States, ranging from 0.5 to 1.5 percent of the gas extracted during production. The BLM plays a key role in the careful management and stewardship of the only significant long-term storage facility for crude helium in the world, known as the Federal Helium Reserve.

THE FEDERAL HELIUM PROGRAM

Because of helium's potential to lift military reconnaissance devices high above battle-fields, the Federal government's interest in the resource dates back to World War I. Recognizing this key military use for helium, the Mineral Leasing Act of 1920 reserved to the Federal government all helium produced on Federal lands—a reservation that remains in effect today. After World War I, recognition of the potential for helium recovery in the Texas Panhandle, Western Oklahoma, and Kansas area (collectively, the "Hugoton" field) led to the development of the Federal helium program focused in that area. In 1929, the Bureau of Mines built the Amarillo Helium Plant and Cliffside Gasfield Facility near Amarillo, Texas, to produce helium-bearing natural gas from a naturally occurring geo-logic field known as the Bush Dome Reservoir.

After World War II, Federal use of helium shifted towards space exploration, and in 1960 Congress passed the Helium Amendment Act. This Act changed the program's man-date from exclusive government production of helium to conservation of the resource by encouraging private natural gas producers to sell extracted crude helium to the Federal government for storage in the Bush Dome Reservoir. The Act granted the Bureau of Mines the authority to borrow funds from the U.S. Treasury to purchase the helium, with the expectation that the proceeds from future sales of helium would allow the Bureau of Mines to repay the debt. This borrowing authority, established by Congress in lieu of a direct appropriation, required the Bureau of Mines to repay the loan by 1985. Subsequent legisla-tion extended the deadline to 1995.

Federal demands for helium rarely, if ever, met the expectations underlying the terms of the Treasury's loan to the Bureau of Mines. When the 1995 deadline to pay off the debt arrived, the $252 million the Bureau had spent on privately-produced helium had increased to $1.3 billion (principal and interest), and the Bureau of Mines appeared to have little prospect of ever repaying the debt. In his 1995 State of the Union address, President Bill Clinton stated that it was his Administration's goal to privatize the Federal helium program.

Congress subsequently passed the Helium Privatization Act of 1996 (HPA), which required the BLM (which assumed jurisdiction over the program after the termination of the Bureau of Mines) to make available for sale the vast majority of the stockpile of crude helium. The mandate directed the BLM to begin selling helium as late as 2005, in order to avoid market disruption. The BLM was to make a consistent amount of helium available every year at a price based on the amount of remaining helium debt and the amount of helium in storage. When Congress passed the HPA, there was approximately 30.5 billion standard cubic feet (scf) of helium in storage in the Bush Dome Reservoir. The HPA man-dated the BLM to make available for sale all of the helium in excess of a 600 million scf permanent reserve.

Additionally, the HPA required the BLM to cease all helium production, refining, and marketing activities to effectively privatize the refined helium market in the United States. Finally, the Act provided for the NAS to review the impacts of the 1996 Act. The NAS published its first study in 2000, and released a follow-up report in 2010.

The BLM's Helium Operations

The BLM currently operates the Federal helium program with a primary goal of paying off the "helium debt." To this end, the BLM has paid over $1.1 billion to the U.S. Treasury since 1995, a substantial step towards eliminating the helium debt, which the HPA froze at approximately $1.3 billion. During FY 2011, $210 million was paid toward the helium debt from reserve sales. The BLM anticipates full repayment of the helium debt in FY 2013. According to the HPA, once the helium debt is retired, the Helium Fund (used to fund the BLM's helium program operational expenses) would be dissolved and all future receipts would be deposited directly into the general fund of the U.S. Treasury.

The BLM's current helium program, with a workforce of 51 full-time equivalents (FTE), operates not only the original storage and pipeline system, but also a crude helium enrichment unit, owned by private industry refiners, that facilitates transmission of helium to private helium operations on the BLM's helium pipeline. The BLM is responsible for administering helium extracted from Federal resources, including management of fees and royalty contracts. These operations are not limited to the Hugoton gas field, but also occur in fields in Colorado, Wyoming, Utah, and any other state where producers extract helium from the Federal mineral estate. Additionally, the BLM is responsible for administering the sell-off of crude helium to private refiners. These sales make the most significant contributions toward paying off the helium debt. The agency also conducts domestic and, to a lesser extent, international helium resource evaluation and reserve tracking to determine the extent of available helium resources.

Another major part of BLM's helium program is the "In-Kind" program, which supplies helium to Federal agencies (e.g., the Department of Energy and NASA) for operations and/or research. Before the Helium Privatization Act, Congress required Federal agencies to purchase their helium supplies from the Bureau of Mines. Under the current In-Kind program, Federal agencies purchase all of their refined helium from private suppliers who, in turn, are required to purchase an equivalent amount of crude helium from the Federal Helium Reserve. In 2011, Federal agencies purchased $11 million of helium through the In-Kind program, up slightly from $10.8 million in 2010.

The National Academy of Sciences Reports

In 2000, the NAS published its first analysis of the impacts of the HPA. Its general finding was that the Act would not have an impact on helium users. Additionally, the NAS report concluded that because the price-setting mechanism was based on the amount of the helium debt, and not the market for helium, the government's significantly higher price would mean the helium refining industry would buy crude helium from the BLM only as a last resort for fulfilling private contracts. However, private helium refiners would still be required to purchase crude helium from the BLM under the In-Kind program.

Over the course of the last decade, however, it has become apparent that assumptions underlying the 2000 NAS report were not accurate. First, the NAS's assumption that "[t]he price of helium [would] probably remain stable through at least 2010" has proven faulty. The market for helium has seen significant fluctuations on both the demand side—which dropped significantly in 2008 after peaking the prior year—and on the supply side, which experienced a significant decline in private supplies between 2006 and 2008. In the face of this volatility, prices for helium rose steadily over the course of the decade. By 2008, the market price for helium began to hover near the BLM's price, leading to greater withdrawals from the Federal Reserve than the 2000 NAS [r]eport anticipated.

Another market impact that the 2000 NAS [r]eport did not address was international supply and demand for helium. According to the U.S. Department of Commerce, domestic consumption of helium decreased 2.7 percent per year from 2000–2007, while exports to the Pacific Rim grew 6.8 percent annually, exceeding the 5.1 percent growth rate in Europe. The international market also experienced supply issues because of refining capacity problems at plants in Qatar and Algeria, which would normally help supply both Europe and Asia.

In early 2010, the NAS released a follow-up report on the BLM's management of the Helium Reserve. The report, entitled "Selling the Nation's Helium Reserve," focused on "whether the interests of the United States have been well served by the [HPA] and, in particular, whether selling off the helium reserve has had any adverse effect on U.S. scientific, technical, biomedical, and national security users of helium."

The 2010 NAS report, which identified some shortcomings of the 2000 report, takes a markedly different tone than the 2000 report. This change in approach reflects the volatility of the helium market over the last decade. The NAS report analyzes the relationship between supply and demand for helium on a domestic and international basis, as well as the BLM's management of the Federal Helium Reserve under the HPA. The report concludes that the HPA mandated sell-off is negatively impacting the needs of both current and future users of helium in the United States. This conclusion is the driving force behind a series of recommendations in the report directed at the BLM and the United States Congress.

CONCLUSION

The BLM welcomes further discussion about the Federal helium program and the BLM's role in meeting future helium needs for the country, especially for Federal agencies that depend on helium for scientific research, aerospace projects, and defense purposes. Since its formal discovery almost 120 years ago, helium has proven to be an increasingly important natural resource. The expansion of helium-related technology and declining domestic reserves means the importance of helium as a strategic resource is likely to increase. The BLM continues to serve the country by effectively managing the Federal Helium Reserve, and working with natural gas producers to efficiently extract helium from natural gas. I would be happy to answer any questions the Subcommittee may have.

SOURCE: U.S. Department of the Interior. Bureau of Land Management. "Statement of Timothy R. Spisak, Deputy Assistant Director, Minerals and Realty Management, U.S. Department of the Interior, Bureau of Land Management, Before the U.S. House of Representatives Committee on Natural Resources Subcommittee on Energy and Mineral Resources." July 20, 2012. http://www.blm.gov/pgdata/etc/medialib/blm/wo/Communications_Directorate/2012_congressional.Par.99035.File.dat/BLM%20Helium%20Testimony%20(FINAL).pdf.

Nasdaq Proposes $62 Million Concession for Difficulties Related to Facebook's IPO Debut

JULY 26, 2012

Facebook, a popular social networking site with more than a billion active monthly users, became a publicly traded company in May 2012. The site was founded in 2004, by then–college student Mark Zuckerberg. By 2012, the company grew so large that federal law required it to begin disclosing certain financial information, and Zuckerberg seized this opportunity to make Facebook a publicly traded entity. The initial public offering (IPO) was successful in the interest it drew but also marred with technical problems that stemmed from the valuation of the stock price and how the orders for buying and selling the stock were handled. Nasdaq took responsibility for the technical errors and proposed a concession for stock buyers for losses attributable to the system difficulties in an amount not to exceed $62 million, but it would not take responsibility for other issues relating to the IPO.

THE DECISION TO GO PUBLIC

By some measures, Facebook is the most popular social network today and is also one of the fastest-growing and best-known sites on the Internet. The social network, led by twenty-eight-year-old Zuckerberg, was the first company to complete a U.S. IPO in one week. The IPO price of $38 was the third highest in U.S. history.

The decision for Facebook to go public came from necessity. Because of its relatively small investor base, for nearly eight years, Facebook was able to keep its advertising revenues and overall bottom line relatively secret. Those who did hold shares of the company prior to 2012 traded them on a secondary market, but firms and hedge funds were becoming increasingly interested in associating their names with the site. In early 2011, Facebook sent a 100-page document to potential buyers, detailing its plans to increase its number of shareholders to more than 500. Any company—even those that are not publicly traded—with more than $10 million in funds that also has more than 500 investors is regulated under the U.S. Securities Exchange Act. Under the act, these firms are required to disclose certain financial information to protect shareholders.

Although the company had plenty of private capital, because they knew they would soon be regulated under the Securities Exchange Act, Facebook executives decided to cash in on the speculation while they could. If Facebook had not gone public when it did, it would face regulatory costs while giving its competitors insight into the financial dealings of the company, without the benefits of being a publicly traded company. Facebook's IPO occurred on May 18, 2012, thus falling within the 120 days that companies have from their year end to register with the Securities and Exchange Commission (SEC), after they cross the 500 investor mark.

IPO Faces Problems

From the outset, the IPO faced a number of difficulties, including a Nasdaq computer malfunction on the morning the stock went public, causing tens of millions of dollars in trades to be incorrectly placed. The Facebook IPO underwriter, Morgan Stanley, was accused of setting the initial stock price too high and allowing too many shares to be offered. Meanwhile, some Facebook executives were accused of alerting industry insiders to Facebook's earnings before they were released to the public. All three parties involved in the IPO faced litigation because of these issues. The problems with the IPO caused the stock to lose over a quarter of its value in less than a month, although it did go on to regain some of these losses.

A majority of the cases against Facebook and its underwriters were brought by investors claiming they had not been clearly informed in disclosures that Facebook was suffering as its customers migrated from desktop computers to mobile devices. Because mobile users did not see advertisements, other potential advertisers had become wary. In a securities filing, Facebook said the lawsuits were "without merit" and noted that on May 9, 2012, it had updated its stock-sale document with a warning about the mobile device impact. Morgan Stanley backed this claim, stating that the revised filing was "widely publicized" and that "a significant number of research analysts" reduced their earnings views to reflect the "impact of the new information."

Some analysts reported that the value of the stock was simply overestimated and overhyped. Facebook had been a media giant for so long and was so inaccessible to investors that people jumped at the opportunity to buy stock when it was first available, resulting in its selling for more money than it was probably worth because of the personal attachment to the brand. Some interpreted the stock's drop in value as a devaluation, while others saw it as a return to its proper value.

Technical Difficulties

The earlier problems of stock valuation and the dissemination of information occurred in combination with a major technological failing. The biggest problem of the Facebook IPO occurred because of computer error. On May 18, Nasdaq experienced system difficulties during its halt and imbalance cross process, the system designed to give traders the fairest possible opening price for each stock. The cross process utilizes a computer program that analyzes all the orders that have come in for a stock. Based on those orders, the program chooses the best opening price and also looks for any trade imbalance. Nasdaq then sends this information to its network of dealers in an effort to offset the imbalance. Dealers can then place orders, and those orders are factored into the opening price. By combining all of this information, the computer system sets the stock's opening price.

During the Facebook IPO, the computer system was not taking in or sending out this information. These difficulties delayed the completion of the Nasdaq cross from 11:05 a.m. until 11:30 a.m. According to the SEC, when Nasdaq noticed that confirmations were not being delivered, it chose not to "suspend trading in FB stock because at that time price discovery was occurring in an orderly fashion in the continuous market . . . active, deep, and liquid trading was taking place in FB stock on Nasdaq and trading in FB stock was proceeding as well on ten other markets and in over-the-counter trading."

In admitting to the technology glitches that kept investors from buying and selling Facebook stock for a few hours on May 18, Nasdaq proposed compensating members for any losses attributable to these problems for no more than $62 million. Nasdaq also said it should not be held responsible for all Facebook investor losses but only those affected by Nasdaq system difficulties, which according to Nasdaq's own analysis were only a small percentage of the Facebook orders received during the IPO.

More than fifty lawsuits were filed against Facebook, Nasdaq, and the underwriters of Facebook's IPO. About thirty lawsuits named Facebook as a defendant; the rest focused on the other parties. In addition, securities lawyers who represented Facebook investors said they expected hundreds of other claims against firms that worked to sell the company's shares. It would take time for investors to prove that they were entitled to recover losses, and some legal experts said the defendants would likely take a large financial hit because of the significant drop in stock price after the IPO, which erased approximately $38 billion in Facebook's stock market value.

MONETIZING FACEBOOK

Despite the problems that occurred in the IPO, Facebook was doing well in late 2012. It was significantly profitable, but its revenue stream was heavily dependent on display ads, and the company faced hurdles in traditional web advertising. Facebook was trying to adapt as more users accessed its site via mobile phones instead of the web. The company said it would add mobile advertising along with ads to reach users when they log off the company's website as a new method of advertisement.

Facebook has a history of success in adapting advertisements and its advertising platform to meet the needs of advertisers. The new mobile method came on the heels of other successful web advertising campaigns, including a 2007 initiative called Facebook Platform, which invited third-party software developers to create programs for Facebook and make money on advertising alongside such programs. The initiative led to the development of hundreds of new applications, including games and photo sharing tools, which helped increase both activity on the site and estimation of Facebook's value.

At the end of 2012, Facebook was at a juncture, poised to become an even bigger technology company. All the personal information that users willingly gave Facebook was an untapped resource, and Facebook recognized that it must continue working on ways to monetize this information. The anonymous days of the Internet were numbered, with Facebook seeking to become the middleman for everything people did online.

—Jessica Heffner

Following are excerpts from Nasdaq's filing with the Securities and Exchange Commission (SEC) on July 26, 2012, proposing a rule change to allow the company to pay no more than $62 million in damages arising from Facebook's IPO debut.

 **DOCUMENT** *Nasdaq Proposed Rule Change*

July 26, 2012

[All footnotes have been omitted.]

[The opening text containing information on the section of the Securities Exchange Act of 1934 being addressed in the proposal has been omitted.]

A. Self-Regulatory Organization's Statement of the Purpose of, and Statutory Basis for, the Proposed Rule Change

1. Purpose

I. INTRODUCTION

The Proposal

Nasdaq is seeking the SEC's approval of a voluntary accommodation policy for claims arising from system difficulties that Nasdaq experienced during the initial public offering ("IPO") of Facebook, Inc. ("Facebook" or "FB") on May 18, 2012. In the weeks since the Facebook IPO, Nasdaq has reviewed the events of May 18 with the goal of proposing a fair and equitable accommodation policy that is consistent with the Exchange Act and Nasdaq's self-regulatory obligations. This proposal reflects Nasdaq's effort (i) to identify the categories of investors and members that Nasdaq's system difficulties caused objective, discernible harm, and the type and scope of such harm, and (ii) to propose an objectively reasonable and regulatorily balanced plan for accommodating Exchange members and their investor customers for such harm. Nasdaq has undertaken this effort notwithstanding the liability protections afforded by its contractual limitations of liability, common law immunity, and Rule 4626—the rule that Nasdaq proposes to modify.

Rule 4626 limits the liability of Nasdaq and its affiliates with respect to any losses, damages, or other claims arising out of the Nasdaq Market Center or its use and provides for limited accommodations under the conditions specified in the rule. Subsection (b)(1) provides that for the aggregate of all claims made by market participants related to the use of the Nasdaq Market Center during a single calendar month, Nasdaq's payments under Rule 4626 shall not exceed the larger of $500,000 or the amount of the recovery obtained by Nasdaq under any applicable insurance policy. Subsection (b)(2) states that for the aggregate of all claims made by market participants related to systems malfunctions or errors of the Nasdaq Market Center concerning locked/crossed compliance, trade through protection, market maker quoting, order protection, or firm quote compliance, during a single calendar month Nasdaq's payments under Rule 4626 shall not exceed the larger of $3,000,000 or the amount of the recovery obtained by Nasdaq under any applicable insurance policy.

On May 18, 2012, Nasdaq experienced system difficulties during the Nasdaq Halt and Imbalance Cross Process (the "Cross") for the FB IPO. These difficulties delayed the completion of the Cross from 11:05 a.m. until 11:30 a.m. Based on its assessment of the information available at the time, Nasdaq concluded that the system issues would not have any effects beyond the delay itself. In an exercise of its regulatory authority, Nasdaq determined to proceed with the IPO at 11:30 a.m. rather than postpone it.

As a result of the system difficulties, however, certain orders for FB stock that were entered between 11:11:00 a.m. and 11:30:09 a.m. in the expectation of participating in the Cross—and that were not cancelled prior to 11:30:09—either did not execute or executed after 1:50 p.m. at prices other than the $42.00 price established by the Cross. (Other orders entered between 11:11:00 a.m. and 11:30:09 a.m., including cancellations, buy orders below $42.00, and sell orders above $42.00, were handled without incident.) System issues also delayed the dissemination of Cross transaction reports from 11:30 a.m. until 1:50 p.m. At 1:50 p.m., Nasdaq system difficulties were completely resolved. Nasdaq's analysis indicates that only a small percentage of the FB orders received by Nasdaq on May 18 were directly affected by Nasdaq system difficulties.

In the period between 11:30 a.m. and 1:50 p.m., although system issues had prevented Nasdaq from disseminating Cross transaction reports, Nasdaq determined not to halt trading in FB stock. Nasdaq believed that the system issues would be resolved promptly. Moreover, after 11:30 a.m. there was an orderly, liquid, and deep market in FB stock, with active trading on all markets. Halting trading on a market-wide basis in these circumstances would have been unprecedented, and, in Nasdaq's view, unjustified. In any event, in Nasdaq's regulatory judgment, the conditions after 11:30 a.m. did not warrant a halt of trading.

As a result of these unique circumstances, Nasdaq is proposing to accommodate members for losses attributable to the system difficulties on May 18, 2012 in an amount not to exceed $62 million. Nasdaq also proposes standards for orders to qualify for accommodation. For the reasons explained below, Nasdaq proposes to make accommodation payments in respect of:

1. SELL Cross orders that were submitted between 11:11 a.m. and 11:30 a.m. on May 18, 2012, that were priced at $42.00 or less, and that did not execute;

2. SELL Cross orders that were submitted between 11:11 a.m. and 11:30 a.m. on May 18, 2012, that were priced at $42.00 or less, and that executed at a price below $42.00;

3. BUY Cross orders priced at exactly $42.00 and that were executed in the Cross but not immediately confirmed; and

4. BUY Cross orders priced above $42.00 and that were executed in the Cross but not immediately confirmed, but only to the extent entered with respect to a customer that was permitted by the member to cancel its order prior to 1:50 p.m. and for which a request to cancel the order was submitted to Nasdaq by the member, also prior to 1:50 p.m.

The modifications proposed in this rule change are not intended to and do not affect the limitations of liability set forth in Nasdaq's agreements or SEC-sanctioned rules, or those limitations or immunities that bar claims for damages against Nasdaq as a matter of law. Rather, as noted above, they reflect Nasdaq's determination to adopt a fair and equitable accommodation policy that takes into account the impacts of Nasdaq's system issues on the investing public and members.

In the two sections that follow, Nasdaq provides: (i) background information concerning Nasdaq's IPO process generally, the system difficulties Nasdaq experienced with the Facebook IPO process on May 18, 2012, and the impacts that those system difficulties had on certain orders; and (ii) Nasdaq's accommodation proposal, including the standards to be applied to claims for accommodation, the rationale for those standards, the proposed procedure for the submission and evaluation of claims, and the proposed payment process.

[The background section, containing information on the IPO Cross process, has been omitted.]

III. ACCOMMODATION PROPOSAL

Accommodation Standards

Nasdaq's proposal is to provide accommodation within a framework that seeks to replicate what the expected execution prices of orders would have been had the Cross not experienced unexpected and unprecedented difficulties, limited by the expectation that members would exercise reasonable diligence to respond and mitigate losses once made aware that their Cross orders had not executed, or had executed at unexpected prices. Thus, Nasdaq proposes to make accommodation payments in respect of:

(i)   SELL Cross orders that were submitted between 11:11 a.m. and 11:30 a.m. on May 18, 2012, that were priced at $42.00 or less, and that did not execute;

(ii) SELL Cross orders that were submitted between 11:11 a.m. and 11:30 a.m. on May 18, 2012, that were priced at $42.00 or less, and that executed at a price below $42.00;

(iii) BUY Cross orders priced at exactly $42.00 and that were executed in the Cross but not immediately confirmed; and

(iv) BUY Cross orders priced above $42.00 and that were executed in the Cross but not immediately confirmed, but only to the extent entered with respect to a customer that was permitted by the member to cancel its order prior to 1:50 p.m. and for which a request to cancel the order was submitted to Nasdaq by the member, also prior to 1:50 p.m.

These are the situations in which Nasdaq has concluded that its systems issues could have impacted market participants' reasonable expectations in an objectively discernible manner. In these situations, Nasdaq proposes to offer as an accommodation the loss differential for a qualified order—that is, the difference between the price that was reasonably expected and the subsequent execution price actually obtained, or the price available at the point when the market participant could have taken steps to mitigate its losses or otherwise adjust its position.

As described above, Nasdaq believes that it reasonably determined not to suspend the IPO or halt trading in FB stock, and Nasdaq's FB-related systems issues were fully resolved at 1:50 p.m., when Nasdaq disseminated all delayed Cross execution confirmation messages. At that point, Nasdaq believes that member firms were in possession of all the information needed to evaluate their positions and obligations to customers, and take steps accordingly.

Accordingly, for the orders described in (i), (iii), and (iv) above, Nasdaq proposes to establish a uniform benchmark price of $40.527, the price at which Nasdaq has concluded a reasonably diligent member could have obtained shares to mitigate any unexpected losses or to liquidate unanticipated positions coming out of the Cross. Nasdaq calculated this price using the volume-weighted average price of FB stock during the first 45 minutes of trading after execution reports were delivered to firms (i.e., 1:50 p.m. to 2:35 p.m.). Using $40.527 as the uniform benchmark price results in a maximum loss of $1.473 per share per order.

For the orders described in (ii) above, Nasdaq proposes to offer as an accommodation the difference between the price that was reasonably expected (i.e., $42.00) and the execution price actually obtained, because the immediate execution of these orders precluded a member from taking reasonable actions to mitigate losses.

Nasdaq believes that this method provides a reasonable time period for firms to have taken actions to mitigate losses after receiving the Cross transaction reports, as well as a reasonable maximum loss price parameter for determining accommodation payments. Additional alleged losses incurred beyond that benchmark price, regardless of their cause, will remain the responsibility of the member. If a member suffered a lesser loss than that calculated based on the foregoing method, based on the difference between the expected execution price of the order in the Cross process establishing an opening print of $42.00 and the actual execution price received, the member shall not receive more than the lesser actual loss suffered. A member's direct trading losses, as calculated in accordance with these parameters, are referred to in the proposed rule as the "Member's Share."

Alleged losses from other causes shall not be considered eligible for accommodation payments under the proposed rule change. Thus, for example, Nasdaq does not propose to make accommodation payments in respect of alleged losses attributable to: orders received after the commencement of continuous regular trading in FB; individual member firm technology issues or system failures, or member firm operational issues or operational failures; affirmative trading actions taken by member firms on their own behalf or to accommodate their customers after the Cross, except as otherwise provided in the proposed rule; alleged or speculative lost trading opportunities or alleged or speculative lost business profits of any description; non-marketable Cross orders for which, based on their price, there was no reasonable expectation that orders had been executed; and a member firm's failure to adequately and appropriately mitigate losses or adjust trading positions. . . .

Examples of how the accommodation standards would apply are below.

Example 1: A member submitted an IPO Cross order to SELL 1000 shares priced at market (*i.e.,* willing to sell at any price or otherwise equivalent to $0.01) with a Time in Force (TIF) of Immediate or Cancel (IOC), entered at 11:15 a.m. Because the order was priced lower than the opening price, it should have been filled at $42.00 in the Cross, but failed to execute because it was entered after 11:11 a.m. Nasdaq transmitted the order confirmation of the failure to the member at 1:50 p.m., at which time the member covered its position (*i.e.,* sold the 1000 shares it had expected to sell in the Cross) at a price of $41.15. Because the member was able to sell its shares at a higher price than the benchmark price Nasdaq has established ($40.527), the member will be accommodated for the difference between the opening price and the covering execution's price. The amount of loss is 1000 × ($42.00–$41.15) = $850.00.

Example 2: A member submitted an IPO Cross order to SELL 1000 shares priced at market with a TIF of IOC, entered at 11:15 a.m. Because the order was priced lower than the opening price, it should have been filled at $42.00 in the Cross, but failed to execute because it was entered after 11:11 a.m. Nasdaq transmitted the order confirmation message noting the failure to execute to the member at 1:50 p.m., but the member did not cover its position until later in the day at an average price of $39.00. Because the member's covering execution price was lower than the benchmark price Nasdaq has established ($40.527), the member will be accommodated for the difference between the opening price and the benchmark price. The amount of loss is 1000 × ($42.00–$40.527) = $1,473.00.

Example 3: A member submitted an IPO Cross order to SELL 1000 shares priced at market with a TIF of DAY, entered at 11:15 a.m. Because the order was priced lower than the opening price, it should have been filled at $42.00 in the Cross, but failed to execute in the Cross because it was entered after 11:11 a.m. The order was entered into the continuous book at 1:50 p.m., at which time it executed at a price of $41.05. Nasdaq transmitted the order confirmation message to the member at 1:50 p.m. Because the order executed at an inferior price to the opening price, the member will be accommodated for the difference between the opening price and the actual execution price. The amount of loss is 1000 x ($42.00–$41.05) = $950.00.

Example 4: A member submitted an IPO Cross order to SELL 1000 shares priced at market with a TIF of DAY, entered at 11:15 a.m. Because the order was priced lower than the opening price, it should have been filled at $42.00 in the Cross, but failed to execute in the Cross because it was entered after 11:11 a.m. The order was entered into the continuous book at 1:50 p.m., at which time it executed at a price of $40.00. Nasdaq transmitted the order confirmation message to the member at 1:50 p.m. Because the order executed at an inferior price to the opening price, the member will be accommodated for the difference between the opening price and the actual execution price. The amount of loss is 1000 x ($42.00–$40.00) = $2,000.00.

Example 5: A member submitted an IPO Cross order to SELL 1000 shares priced at market with a TIF of DAY, entered at 11:15 a.m. Because the order was priced lower than the opening price, it should have been filled at $42.00 in the Cross, but failed to execute in the Cross because it was entered after 11:11 a.m. The member cancelled the order at 12:30 p.m., after the Cross had taken place at 11:30:09 a.m. but before the order was delivered to the continuous book or a confirmation message was delivered. The order cancelled back to the member at 1:50 p.m. based on the request sent at 12:30 p.m. Because the member's order should have been executed in the Cross, the fact that the member cancelled the order at 12:30 p.m. is not relevant for purposes of determining that the order was directly disadvantaged, and the member will be accommodated for the difference between the opening price and the benchmark price. The amount of loss is 1000 x ($42.00–$40.527) = $1,473.00.

Example 6: A member submitted an IPO Cross order to BUY 1000 shares priced at $42.00 with a TIF of DAY, entered at 11:00 a.m. The order was filled at $42.00, but because the order's price was exactly the opening price, the member could not have reasonably known that the order was filled until 1:50 p.m. As a result, the member acquired an unexpected long position of 1000 shares that resulted in a loss when the position was covered at a price of $40.15. Because the member's covering execution price was worse than the benchmark price Nasdaq has established ($40.527), the member will be accommodated for the difference between the opening price and the benchmark price. The amount of loss is 1000 x ($42.00–$40.527) = $1,473.00.

Example 7: A member submitted an IPO Cross order to BUY 1000 shares at $42.00 with a TIF of IOC, entered at 11:15 a.m. The order was not filled at $42.00 because it was entered after 11:11 a.m., but because the order's price was exactly the opening price, the member could not have reasonably known that the order was not filled until 1:50 p.m. As a result, the member discovered it unexpectedly lacked 1000 shares at 1:50 p.m. At that time, the member could have purchased shares at prices lower than the opening price.

Consequently, the member was not directly disadvantaged by Nasdaq's system error and there is no loss amount.

Example 8: A member submitted an IPO Cross order to BUY 1000 shares at $42.50 with a TIF of IOC, entered at 11:15 a.m. The order was not filled at $42.00 because it was entered after 11:11 a.m., but because the order's price was higher than the opening price, the member should have expected the order was filled until it received a confirmation to the contrary at 1:50 p.m. As a result, the member discovered it unexpectedly lacked 1000 shares at 1:50 p.m. At that time, the member could have purchased shares at prices lower than the opening price. Consequently, the member was not directly disadvantaged by Nasdaq's system error and there is no loss amount.

Example 9: A member submitted an IPO Cross order for a customer to BUY 1000 shares at $42.50 with a TIF of IOC, entered at 11:05 a.m. and a cancel request was submitted by the member before 1:50 p.m. for the order. The order was filled at $42.00 as expected. Because it was priced higher than the opening price, the member should have expected that the order was filled, which was confirmed electronically at 1:50 p.m. In light of the confirmation delay, however, the member received a request to cancel the order from the customer prior to 1:50 p.m., accommodated that request by allowing the customer to cancel the order, and sent a cancellation request for the order to Nasdaq before 1:50 p.m. When confirmation of the customer's order execution in the Cross was received by the member at 1:50 p.m., the member held a long position of shares for which it no longer had a recipient. Although the decision to accommodate the customer's cancellation request was exclusively that of the member, Nasdaq has determined to provide a limited accommodation amount equaling 70% of the member's loss up to maximum loss amount of $0.70 \times 1000 \times (\$42.00 - \$40.527) = \$1,031.10$.

Example 10: A member submitted an IPO Cross order to BUY 1000 shares at $42.50 with a TIF of IOC, entered at 11:05 a.m. The order was filled at $42.00 as expected. Because it was priced higher than the opening price, the member should have expected that the order was filled, which was confirmed electronically at 1:50 p.m. As a result of the delay in confirmation, however, the member purchased additional shares before the confirmations arrived. This resulted in an unintended long position of 1000 shares. Although the member incurred a loss when covering the unintended position, Nasdaq correctly executed the member's order and the member should have expected the original IPO Cross order to be filled because of its price. Consequently, the member was not directly disadvantaged by Nasdaq's system error and there is no loss amount.

Example 11: A member submitted an IPO Cross order to BUY 1000 shares at $42.50 with a TIF of IOC, entered at 11:05 a.m. The order was filled at $42.00 as expected. Because it was priced higher than the opening price, the member should have expected that the order was filled, which was confirmed electronically at 1:50 p.m. Later in the day, the member sold the position at $40.00. The member claims that it would have been able to sell at a higher price if [it] had received the confirmation sooner. Nasdaq correctly executed the member's order. The claim of loss is premised on an alleged or speculative lost trading opportunity rather than the actual failure by Nasdaq to process an order correctly. Consequently, the member was not directly disadvantaged by Nasdaq's system error and there is no loss amount.

[Information on how Nasdaq would evaluate claims and make payments, and Section IV, containing information on the acceptance of public comments on the proposed rule change, have been omitted.]

SOURCE: Securities and Exchange Commission. "Self-Regulatory Organizations; The NASDAQ Stock Market LLC; Notice of Filing of Proposed Rule Change to Amend Rule 4626—Limitation of Liability." July 26, 2012. http://www.sec.gov/rules/sro/nasdaq/2012/34-67507.pdf.

OTHER HISTORIC DOCUMENTS OF INTEREST

FROM PREVIOUS *HISTORIC DOCUMENTS*

2012 Summer Olympic Games Open in London

JULY 27, 2012

The 2012 Summer Olympic Games were launched amid great fanfare in London on July 27, 2012. Hosting the games for an unprecedented third time, London received widespread acclaim for its organizational accomplishments. Despite early concerns about a possible terrorist attack, no security incident occurred, the opening and closing ceremonies proceeded without any major glitch, and new world records were set in some of the most widely watched events. The games were wedged between two royal occasions that generated a similarly warm glow of publicity for the United Kingdom in 2012: Queen Elizabeth's Diamond Jubilee and the announcement that Prince William and his wife, the Duchess of Cambridge, were expecting their first child, who would be third in line to the throne.

LONDON BESTS PARIS

London had previously hosted the games in 1908 and 1948. On this occasion, one of the world's oldest cities found itself nestled between two hosts from emerging economies: Beijing, China, in 2008, and Rio de Janeiro, Brazil, in 2016. London had seven years to carry out the herculean task of organizing the world's largest sporting event, having won the competition to host the games in July 2005. The selection of London was something of a surprise when the news filtered out from an International Olympic Committee (IOC) meeting in Singapore on July 6, as Paris had been favored to win. However, after four rounds of voting, in which first Moscow, then New York, and then Madrid were eliminated, London beat out Paris by fifty-four votes to fifty. Britain's prime minister at the time, Tony Blair, had made a forty-eight-hour visit to Singapore to curry support for London's bid. Within twenty-four hours Londoners' tears of joy at having been bestowed this illustrious honor turned to sorrow as the city was hit by a wave of lethal attacks on its bus and underground train system. The al Qaeda–perpetrated suicide bombings claimed the lives of fifty-two people. The Olympics celebratory party was postponed by two months because of the terrorist attacks.

The leading figure in the games' organization was Sebastian Coe, a former middle-distance runner and four-time Olympic medalist. Coe notably oversaw the construction of the Olympic Park, which contained the main Olympic stadium, the aquatics center, Olympic Village, and the Velodrome (cycling track). The Olympic Park was developed in a rundown part of East London with the goal of rehabilitating and regenerating the neighborhood. The construction project involved large-scale land purchases and relocation of scores of businesses, some of which protested the eviction. The organizers developed an environmental plan to limit carbon dioxide emissions, which met with mixed success. Measures such as installing insulation in local housing and schools helped to limit emissions, but targets on use of renewable energy sources were missed. Efforts were made to construct permanent venues only if there was a long-term use for them.

A minor controversy erupted in the buildup to the games when the official logo was unveiled on June 4, 2007. Designed by the firm Wolff Olins, the logo was a jagged emblem, based on the date 2012. It marked a departure from previous Olympic logos, which tended to feature an iconic image from the host city. The logo received much negative commentary in the British press, with detractors comparing it to a broken swastika or "some sort of comical sex act between the Simpsons." London's Mayor Ken Livingstone criticized the $800,000 bill for designing and developing it. In addition, an animated version of the logo had to be removed from a website after complaints were made that it was causing seizures in epilepsy sufferers. Coe defended the logo and noted that it was designed to reach out to young people.

OPENING CEREMONY

In his speech for the opening ceremony, IOC Chair Jacques Rogge paid tribute to Britain's historic role in developing modern sport by helping to codify rules and regulations for sportsmanship and fair play. He urged athletes to "reject doping. Respect your opponents. Remember that you are all role models." The artistic director of the opening pageant was the British filmmaker Danny Boyle, whose past credits include *Slumdog Millionaire* and *Trainspotting*. The pageant was well received overall, although some U.S. commentators drew attention to its quirky features such as tributes to Britain's National Health Service and children's literature. The pageant began with the depiction of an idyllic countryside setting, replete with sheep, horses, chickens, ducks, and geese. This scene was then transformed into a gritty industrial landscape, with steelworkers forging materials that turned into golden Olympic rings. There was a comical sketch, involving James Bond actor Daniel Craig and Queen Elizabeth, which gave the (false) impression of the queen being flown by helicopter from Buckingham Palace and parachuting into the Olympic stadium. Musical bands that performed included the Clash, the Rolling Stones, and the Sex Pistols.

In the parade of nations, 204 national teams were represented. The inclusion of female athletes in the Saudi Arabian delegation, following pressure placed on the Saudi government by the IOC, meant that for the first time ever, there were female athletes competing from every participating nation. The queen declared the games open. In a break with tradition, the Olympic flame was lit not by a single individual but by a group of seven teenage athletes, who received the torch from established athletes, thereby symbolizing the "passing of the torch" to the next generation. The teenage athletes each lit a single flame on the ground, which ignited 204 copper petals, one for each national team. The long stems of the petals then rose toward one another to form a cauldron.

The 2012 games lasted seventeen days. In terms of athletic feats, U.S. swimmer Michael Phelps became the most decorated competitor in the history of the games, earning a total of twenty-two Olympic medals in his lifetime by the games' close, surpassing the previous record of eighteen medals set by Soviet gymnast Larisa Latynina. The Jamaican sprinter Usain Bolt was another star of the games after he became the first man to retain the 100- and 200-meter Olympic sprint titles. Bolt also helped his national team to shatter the world record in the 4 x 100-meter men's relay with a time of 36.84 seconds. Kenya's David Rudisha set a world record in the men's 800-meter run, registering a time of 1:40:91. In the final medal count, the United States was at the top of the league table, winning 104 medals, followed by China with 88. The United Kingdom won 65. The host nation performed particularly well, with gold medals earned by Mo Farah in the 5,000 and 10,000 meters, Jessica Ennis in the heptathlon, Bradley Wiggins in cycling, and Andy Murray in tennis. South African sprinter Oscar Pistorius made history by becoming the first runner with amputated legs to compete in the games' track and field events. Pistorius's participation was not without controversy, as he had to counter claims that the artificial limbs he used gave him an unfair advantage over able-bodied runners.

The closing ceremony included a symphony of British music from the past fifty years, with performers such as Annie Lennox, the Spice Girls, Madness, and One Direction. At the close of the ceremony, the games were "handed over" to the next host, Rio de Janeiro, and the Olympic flame was extinguished.

London then hosted the Paralympics from August 29 to September 9, in which 4,000 athletes from 164 teams competed. The icon of the games was double-amputee Pistorius, who followed up his Olympic performance by winning a gold medal in the 400-meter run. Pistorius would make even bigger headlines—for the wrong reasons—in February 2013 after he was charged with fatally shooting his girlfriend at his home on Valentine's Day. Wheelchair athlete David Weir was another star of the Paralympics: He won gold medals in the 800-, 1,500-, and 5,000-meter runs and marathon. China finished at the top of the medals league table. The opening ceremony was officiated by Queen Elizabeth, while the musical lineup at the closing ceremony included Coldplay, Rihanna, and Jay-Z.

Ticketing Controversy

In the aftermath of the games, IOC Chair Rogge declared that "nothing fundamental" had gone wrong but that the IOC would review its system for allocating tickets ahead of the 2016 games in Rio. The right balance needed to be struck, he said, between allocating tickets for the home country and for the rest of the world. Images of empty seats at various venues, including basketball and tennis, relayed during the events, evoked comment and criticism in the media. The blame for the no-shows was placed on multiple shoulders: sponsors, federations, athletes, and the media. At one point, British troops and schoolchildren were given free tickets to events such as swimming and gymnastics to quell the controversy over the empty seats. In total, 7 million tickets had been sold for the games, using a complex lottery system, with an estimated million without tickets lining course routes to view the cycling competition.

In light of the London underground bombings of 2005, as well as the riots that erupted in cities across the United Kingdom in August 2011, including in London, there had been fears of the games becoming marred by violence or terrorism. However, in the end, there was no specific terrorist threat, and the games proceeded without any major security incident. The total cost of organizing the games was estimated at $14.3 billion. In the subsequent months, discussion focused on "legacy" issues that Olympic hosts invariably face, such as what to do with all the custom-built facilities. The basketball and field hockey arenas were being dismantled and the aquatics center reconfigured as a new public sports center. As for the Olympic Stadium, despite neighborhood objections, local soccer club West Ham United will move into the facility in 2016.

Momentous Year for Royals

The success of the London Olympics gave a much-needed boost to the spirits of the British people, which had been flagging somewhat as a result of the country's economic recession and austerity-induced public spending cuts. Britons found two other causes for celebration in 2012: the commemoration of Queen Elizabeth's sixtieth year on the throne and the announcement of a future heir to that throne. Elizabeth is one of only two British monarchs to have reigned for sixty years, the other being Queen Victoria, whose reign spanned nearly sixty-four years. While the eighty-six-year-old monarch confined her Diamond Jubilee tours to the United Kingdom, she dispatched other royal family members across the globe to various parts of the British Commonwealth to celebrate the milestone. The celebrations climaxed in a long weekend of festivities from June 2 to June 5, which included 9,500 street parties. The weekend's highlight was a flotilla of approximately 1,000 boats from around the world, which sailed along London's Thames River from Chelsea to Tower Bridge, the largest flotilla since the reign of Charles II some 350 years ago. Despite heavy rain, millions lined the banks of the Thames to catch a glimpse of the queen as she sailed in a royal barge, the *Spirit of Chartwell*.

The year ended on a high note too. On December 3, it was announced that the queen's grandson and second in line to the throne, Prince William, and his wife, Katherine, Duchess of Cambridge, were expecting their first child. The announcement was forced upon the royals prematurely after the Duchess had to be admitted to the hospital with acute morning sickness. Regardless of whether the child is a boy or girl, it will be in the direct line of succession after its grandfather, Prince Charles, and father, Prince William, following a recent change in the Commonwealth's laws of succession.

—Brian Beary

Following is the text of International Olympic Committee (IOC) President Jacques Rogge's speech marking the opening of the 2012 Summer Olympic Games on July 27, 2012.

IOC President Marks Start of 2012 Summer Olympic Games

July 27, 2012

Your Majesty,
Your Majesties,
Your Royal Highnesses,
Distinguished Guests,
Ladies and Gentlemen

In just a few moments, the Olympic Games will officially return to London for the third time, setting an unmatched record for hosting the Games that spans more than a century.

Thank you, London, for welcoming the world to this diverse, vibrant, cosmopolitan city yet again!

It has taken a lot of hard work by many people to get us to this point.

I want to thank the entire team at the London Organising Committee—superbly led by Lord Coe—for their excellent and hard work.

I also want to thank all the public authorities who have helped ensure that these Games will leave a lasting positive legacy long after the Closing Ceremony.

And, of course, we are all grateful to the thousands of dedicated volunteers who are being so generous with their time, their energy and their welcoming smiles.

For the first time in Olympic history all the participating teams will include female athletes. This is a major boost for gender equality.

In a sense, the Olympic Games are coming home tonight.

This great, sports-loving country is widely recognised as the birthplace of modern sport.

It was here that the concepts of sportsmanship and fair play were first codified into clear rules and regulations.

It was here that sport was included as an educational tool in the school curriculum.

The British approach to sport had a profound influence on Pierre de Coubertin, our founder, as he developed the framework for the modern Olympic Movement at the close of the 19th century.

The values that inspired de Coubertin will come to life over the next 17 days as the world's best athletes compete in a spirit of friendship, respect and fair play.

I congratulate all of the athletes who have earned a place at these Games.

And to the athletes, I offer this thought: Your talent, your dedication and commitment brought you here.

Now you have a chance to become true Olympians.

That honour is determined not by whether you win, but by how you compete.

Character counts far more than medals.

Reject doping. Respect your opponents. Remember that you are all role models. If you do that, you will inspire a generation.

Ces Jeux sont porteurs de beaucoup d'espoirs.

Espoir d'entente et de paix entre les 204 Comités Nationaux Olympiques.

Espoir de voir les jeunes générations s'inspirer des valeurs du sport.

Espoir que ces Jeux puissent contribuer au développement durable.

Chers athlètes, faites-nous rêver! Make us dream!

I now have the honour to ask Her Majesty the Queen to open the Games of the XXX Olympiad.

SOURCE: International Olympic Committee. "Opening Ceremony of the Games of the XXX Olympiad." July 27, 2012. http://www.olympic.org/Documents/Games_London_2012/London_2012_Opening_ceremony_Speech_Jacques_Rogge.pdf.

OTHER HISTORIC DOCUMENTS OF INTEREST

FROM PREVIOUS *HISTORIC DOCUMENTS*

- Prime Minister Cameron on the Royal Wedding and Succession Law Changes, *2011,* p. 220
- Concerns Over the 2008 Beijing Summer Olympic Games, *2008,* p. 296

August

NASA Rover Lands on Mars

AUGUST 5 AND DECEMBER 3, 2012

In August 2012, just over a year after the historic space shuttle program ended, the National Aeronautics and Space Administration (NASA) celebrated a new achievement in unmanned spaceflight—landing the largest and most advanced rover to date on Mars. Dubbed Curiosity, the rover would expand upon the work of previous unmanned missions and continue to explore whether Mars had once and could again support life. The mission's early successes were heralded as a major accomplishment both for NASA and the future of space exploration. Curiosity is expected to lay the groundwork for two additional unmanned missions to Mars.

MISSION TO MARS

First conceived in 2000 and formally approved in 2006 by then-president George W. Bush, the Mars Science Laboratory (MSL) mission is part of NASA's broader Mars Exploration Program, a series of expeditions intended to determine whether life ever arose on Mars, characterize the geology and climate of the planet, and prepare for future human exploration. The MSL mission followed on the heels of the Mars Exploration Rover mission, which involved the Spirit and Opportunity rovers. Both vehicles had found evidence of environments on Mars that were at one time habitable; the MSL mission would add to this research by looking for evidence of carbon-based molecules, such as methane, that scientists regard as the building blocks of life.

MSL's rover was given the name Curiosity through a public contest won by sixth-grade Kansas student Clara Ma. In her winning essay, Clara wrote, "Curiosity is the passion that drives us through our everyday lives. We have become explorers and scientists with our need to ask questions and to wonder." The start of the rover mission was a major step forward for Mars surface science and exploration capabilities, helping to demonstrate both the ability to land a larger, heavier rover more precisely and the vehicle's long-range mobility on the planet's surface. During its twenty-three-month mission, the equivalent of one Martian year, Curiosity would study rocks, soil, and other geologic characteristics to determine whether Mars ever "offered conditions favorable for microbial life" and to assess the planet's atmospheric and environmental history. This included examining the present state, distribution, and cycling of water and carbon dioxide.

More than 100 scientists considered more than thirty possible rover landing sites, ultimately selecting a location inside Mars's Gale Crater near Mount Sharp. Scientists had determined from orbital observations of the 18,000-foot-high mountain that it contained many layers of different rock and minerals, including clay and sulfate, which form in water and can preserve organic matter. They also suspected the mountain may have been formed by the remains of sediment that had once completely filled the crater, meaning it could potentially provide a valuable record of Mars's geologic history. The mission plan called for Curiosity to first survey its landing site to configure itself for future tasks and to check the performance of its various mechanisms. It would chemically analyze the soil at its landing site and conduct several sample tests at other locations to ensure that its scoop, drill, and other instruments—ranging from cameras to chemical sensors—were working properly, all the while taking thousands of photos that would help NASA chart the rover's ultimate path to Mount Sharp's base.

The director of NASA's Mars Exploration Program, Doug McCuistion, characterized the MSL mission as "the most challenging planetary mission that's ever been flown," adding, "We're pushing the envelope in a number of areas, and it just kind of built up." The ambitious nature of the mission led to a number of technical setbacks and engineering issues, causing delays and major budget overruns. For example, engineers determined in 2007 that the material originally selected for the rover's heat shield, a critical design element that protects the vehicle as it enters Mars's atmosphere, would no longer be sufficient, forcing them to restart their work. Engineers also spent considerable time developing ninety cutting-edge motors needed to drive the rover's moving parts, but they abandoned them a year into the build after deciding the motors would take too much time and money to construct, opting instead for heavier, more traditional models. Furthermore, development of the rover's advanced scientific instrumentation continually ran over budget, prompting NASA to remove two instruments from the rover until it received funding help from corporate, foreign, and federal sponsors. NASA officials attempted to cover budget shortfalls by trimming funding for other projects, but by the spring of 2008, the MSL mission was already $235 million, or 24 percent, over budget. The program's final cost was roughly $2.5 billion. These glitches also caused the mission to be delayed from its original 2009 launch date until November 26, 2011, the next earliest window of opportunity for a Mars launch.

A New Kind of Rover

Despite these challenges, Curiosity's final design and research capabilities are what distinguished the rover from its predecessors. Designed, developed, and assembled at NASA's Jet Propulsion Laboratory in Pasadena, California, the finished rover was ten feet long and weighed nearly 2,000 pounds—twice as long and five times as heavy as previous rovers. It had a greater travel range than other rovers, with the ability to roll over obstacles up to twenty-five inches high and travel up to 660 feet per day for a total lifetime driving distance of twelve miles. It also relied on nuclear power rather than solar, using a radioisotope power generator supplied by the U.S. Department of Energy that creates electrical power from the decay of plutonium.

Perhaps the most notable component of the rover was its ten different scientific instruments. These included the first-of-its-kind Chemistry and Camera, or ChemCam, instrument, which sat high atop the rover's mast. The ChemCam could direct a concentrated laser beam with the energy equivalent of one million light bulbs at rocks up to twenty-three feet away. The laser would heat the surface of a rock, creating a spark that ChemCam would observe with its telescope. The colors within the light would then tell scientists which atomic elements were in the rock. Also important among Curiosity's tools was the Sample Analysis at Mars (SAM), a suite of instruments that could analyze material and atmospheric samples the rover gathered. SAM had the capability to identify a wide range of organic compounds and determine the ratios of different isotopes of key elements—important clues to detecting a past presence of water and understanding the history of Mars's atmosphere.

Other instruments included the CheMin, an X-ray tool that could identify and quantify the minerals in rocks and soils; the MSL Mast Camera, which could capture high-resolution images and high-definition video of the rover's surroundings; and the Mars Hand Lens Imager, which could take extreme close-up pictures showing details smaller than the width of a human hair. Still other tools were provided by international agencies, such as the Canadian Space Agency, Russian Federal Space Agency, and Spain's Ministry of Education and Science. Curiosity also had a drill and scoop at the end of its seven-foot robotic arm with which it could gather soil and powdered rock samples before sieving and sorting them into its analytical instruments.

"Seven Minutes of Terror"

The innovative landing system NASA devised to deliver Curiosity safely to the Martian surface also made the MSL mission unique. Previous rovers had been small enough to use an airbag-assisted landing, but Curiosity used a new, four-stage system to land. Once the spacecraft carrying the rover entered the Martian atmosphere, traveling at seventeen times the speed of sound, it would use a "guided entry" system of jet thrusters to slow and steer itself as it fell, greatly reducing its downward speed. A giant, supersonic parachute would then deploy, slowing the craft further. Next, the "powered descent" phase would use more rockets to further slow and control the spacecraft's descent until the rover, attached to a jet thruster–propelled sky crane, separated from the rest of the craft. The sky crane would then lower Curiosity, with its wheels down, the last mile to the planet's surface.

The entire process was expected to take seven minutes, a period NASA officials termed the "seven minutes of terror," given the possibility that one small error could disrupt the entire chain of events, and those back on Earth would be unable to fix it. "We've got literally seven minutes to get from the top of the atmosphere to the surface of Mars, going from 13,000 miles an hour to zero," said NASA engineer Tom Rivellini. "If any one thing doesn't work just right, it's game over." Adding to the suspense, NASA officials were not expected to know the outcome of Curiosity's landing until almost fourteen minutes later, as communications were relayed from the rover through the Mars Odyssey orbiter to NASA's Deep Space Network of antennae back on Earth.

At 10:32 p.m. Pacific Daylight Time on August 5, after a thirty-six-week flight, Curiosity landed flawlessly on the surface of Mars. The rover landed within 1.5 miles of its intended target, an exceptionally high degree of accuracy attributable to the multistage landing system. NASA's mission control erupted in cheers upon receiving the news. "This is an amazing achievement, made possible by a team of scientists and engineers from around the world and led by the extraordinary men and women of NASA and our Jet Propulsion Laboratory," said NASA Administrator Charles Bolden. "President Obama has laid out a bold vision for sending humans to Mars in the mid-2030s, and today's landing marks a significant step toward achieving this goal." President Barack Obama called the mission an "unprecedented feat of technology" and congratulated the NASA employees "who made this remarkable accomplishment a reality." John Holdren, the president's science advisor, added, "If anybody has been harboring doubts about the status of U.S. leadership in space, well, there's a one-ton, automobile-size piece of American ingenuity, and it's sitting on the surface of Mars right now."

Seven minutes after the Canberra, Australia, antenna station of the Deep Space Network confirmed Curiosity's landing, NASA received an image from the rover, showing one of its wheels on the planet surface. Shortly thereafter, Curiosity relayed six additional sample pictures to Earth, as well as the results of several health checks of its instruments before shutting down for the planetary night. Later that evening, NASA received approximately 200 more pictures that the rover had taken as it was being lowered to the ground.

CURIOSITY'S FINDINGS

Curiosity spent its first four days on Mars installing operational software to give it full movement and analytic capabilities. It would not move from its landing site until about two weeks later, when it tested its ChemCam on a nearby rock. Following the successful test, Curiosity began examining the exposed rock immediately surrounding its landing site and also tested its forward and backward motion.

Then, on September 27, the rover sent images to NASA of bedrock that suggested an ancient, fast-moving stream, possibly waist deep, once flowed on the planet. The photos showed rounded-off pebbles and gravel that mission scientists said could indicate that rocks had been transported long distances and smoothed out by water. Some of the rocks were as large as a golf ball, prompting scientists to dismiss the possibility that they may have been carried by wind.

More than a month later, on October 30, NASA announced that the rover had completed initial experiments that showed the mineralogy of Martian soil is similar to weathered basaltic soils found near Hawaiian volcanoes, further suggesting that the planet had transitioned from a wet to dry environment. On December 3, NASA revealed that the rover had fully analyzed its first soil sample, finding water and sulfur and chlorine-containing substances among the soil's components.

By the end of the year, Curiosity had returned more than 23,000 raw images of Mars and had traveled more than 0.4 miles. The MSL mission's plans for most of 2013 will focus on driving Curiosity toward Mount Sharp.

—Linda Fecteau

Following is a press release from August 5, 2012, announcing the successful landing of the Curiosity rover on Mars by the National Aeronautics and Space Administration (NASA); and a press release from NASA on December 3, 2012, announcing the successful completion of Curiosity's first soil sample analysis.

DOCUMENT   ## *NASA Announces Rover Landing*

August 5, 2012

NASA's most advanced Mars rover Curiosity has landed on the Red Planet. The one-ton rover, hanging by ropes from a rocket backpack, touched down onto Mars Sunday to end a 36-week flight and begin a two-year investigation.

The Mars Science Laboratory (MSL) spacecraft that carried Curiosity succeeded in every step of the most complex landing ever attempted on Mars, including the final severing of the bridle cords and flyaway maneuver of the rocket backpack.

"Today, the wheels of Curiosity have begun to blaze the trail for human footprints on Mars. Curiosity, the most sophisticated rover ever built, is now on the surface of the Red Planet, where it will seek to answer age-old questions about whether life ever existed on Mars—or if the planet can sustain life in the future," said NASA Administrator Charles Bolden. "This is an amazing achievement, made possible by a team of scientists and engineers from around the world and led by the extraordinary men and women of NASA and our Jet Propulsion Laboratory. President Obama has laid out a bold vision for sending humans to Mars in the mid-2030's, and today's landing marks a significant step toward achieving this goal."

Curiosity landed at 10:32 p.m. Aug. 5, PDT, (1:32 a.m. EDT Aug. 6) near the foot of a mountain three miles tall and 96 miles in diameter inside Gale Crater. During a nearly two-year prime mission, the rover will investigate whether the region ever offered conditions favorable for microbial life.

"The Seven Minutes of Terror has turned into the Seven Minutes of Triumph," said NASA Associate Administrator for Science John Grunsfeld. "My immense joy in the success of this mission is matched only by overwhelming pride I feel for the women and men of the mission's team."

Curiosity returned its first view of Mars, a wide-angle scene of rocky ground near the front of the rover. More images are anticipated in the next several days as the mission blends observations of the landing site with activities to configure the rover for work and check the performance of its instruments and mechanisms.

"Our Curiosity is talking to us from the surface of Mars," said MSL Project Manager Peter Theisinger of NASA's Jet Propulsion Laboratory in Pasadena, Calif. "The landing takes us past the most hazardous moments for this project, and begins a new and exciting mission to pursue its scientific objectives."

Confirmation of Curiosity's successful landing came in communications relayed by NASA's Mars Odyssey orbiter and received by the Canberra, Australia, antenna station of NASA's Deep Space Network.

Curiosity carries 10 science instruments with a total mass 15 times as large as the science payloads on the Mars rovers Spirit and Opportunity. Some of the tools are the first of their kind on Mars, such as a laser-firing instrument for checking elemental composition of rocks from a distance. The rover will use a drill and scoop at the end of its robotic arm to gather soil and powdered samples of rock interiors, then sieve and parcel out these samples into analytical laboratory instruments inside the rover.

To handle this science toolkit, Curiosity is twice as long and five times as heavy as Spirit or Opportunity. The Gale Crater landing site places the rover within driving distance of layers of the crater's interior mountain. Observations from orbit have identified clay and sulfate minerals in the lower layers, indicating a wet history.

The mission is managed by JPL for NASA's Science Mission Directorate in Washington. The rover was designed, developed and assembled at JPL. JPL is a division of the California Institute of Technology in Pasadena.

For more information on the mission, visit: http://www.nasa.gov/mars and http://marsprogram.jpl.nasa.gov/msl.

Follow the mission on Facebook and Twitter at: http://www.facebook.com/marscuriosity and http://www.twitter.com/marscuriosity.

SOURCE: National Aeronautics and Space Administration. "NASA Lands Car-Size Rover Beside Martian Mountain." August 5, 2012. http://www.nasa.gov/mission_pages/msl/news/msl20120805c.html.

Mars Rover Finishes Analyzing Soil Samples

DOCUMENT

December 3, 2012

NASA's Mars Curiosity rover has used its full array of instruments to analyze Martian soil for the first time, and found a complex chemistry within the Martian soil. Water and sulfur and chlorine-containing substances, among other ingredients, showed up in the samples Curiosity's arm delivered to an analytical laboratory inside the rover.

Detection of the substances during this early phase of the mission demonstrates the laboratory's capability to analyze diverse soil and rock samples over the next two years. Scientists also have been verifying the capabilities of the rover's instruments.

The specific soil sample came from a drift of windblown dust and sand called "Rocknest." The site lies in a relatively flat part of Gale Crater still miles away from the rover's main destination on the slope of a mountain called Mount Sharp. The rover's laboratory includes the Sample Analysis at Mars (SAM) suite and the Chemistry and Mineralogy (CheMin) instrument. SAM used three methods to analyze gases given off from the dusty sand when it was heated in a tiny oven. One class of substances SAM checks for is organic compounds—carbon-containing chemicals that can be ingredients for life.

"We have no definitive detection of Martian organics at this point, but we will keep looking in the diverse environments of the Gale Crater," said SAM Principal Investigator Paul Mahaffy of NASA's Goddard Space Flight Center in Greenbelt, Md.

Curiosity's APXS instrument and the Mars Hand Lens Imager (MAHLI) camera on the rover's arm confirmed Rocknest has chemical-element composition and textural appearance similar to sites visited by earlier NASA Mars rovers Pathfinder, Spirit and Opportunity.

Curiosity's team selected Rocknest as the first scooping site because it has fine sand particles suited for scrubbing interior surfaces of the arm's sample-handling chambers. Sand was vibrated inside the chambers to remove residue from Earth. MAHLI close-up images of Rocknest show a dust-coated crust one or two sand grains thick, covering dark, fine sand.

"Active drifts on Mars look darker on the surface," said MAHLI Principal Investigator Ken Edgett of Malin Space Science Systems in San Diego. "This is an older drift that has had time to be inactive, letting the crust form and dust accumulate on it."

CheMin's examination of Rocknest samples found the composition is about half common volcanic minerals and half non-crystalline minerals such as glass. SAM added information about ingredients present in much lower concentrations and about ratios of isotopes. Isotopes are different forms of the same element and can provide clues about environmental changes. The water seen by SAM does not mean the drift was wet. Water molecules bound to grains of sand or dust are not unusual, but the quantity seen was higher than anticipated.

SAM tentatively identified the oxygen and chlorine compound perchlorate. This is a reactive chemical previously found in arctic Martian soil by NASA's Phoenix Lander. Reaction with other chemicals heated in SAM formed chlorinated methane compounds—one-carbon organics that were detected by the instrument. The chlorine is of Martian origin, but it is possible the carbon may be of Earth origin, carried by Curiosity and detected by SAM's high sensitivity design.

"We used almost every part of our science payload examining this drift," said Curiosity Project Scientist John Grotzinger of the California Institute of Technology in Pasadena. "The synergies of the instruments and richness of the data sets give us great promise for using them at the mission's main science destination on Mount Sharp."

NASA's Mars Science Laboratory Project is using Curiosity to assess whether areas inside Gale Crater ever offered a habitable environment for microbes. NASA's Jet Propulsion Laboratory in Pasadena manages the project for NASA's Science Mission Directorate in Washington.

SOURCE: National Aeronautics and Space Administration. "NASA Mars Rover Fully Analyzes First Martian Soil Samples." December 3, 2012. http://www.nasa.gov/mission_pages/msl/news/msl20121203.html.

OTHER HISTORIC DOCUMENTS OF INTEREST

FROM PREVIOUS *HISTORIC DOCUMENTS*

Indian Enquiry Committee Releases Report on Power Grid Failure

AUGUST 16, 2012

For two days at the end of July, more than 650 million residents of India experienced the world's worst electricity outage on record, which caused millions of dollars in economic losses. While it did not reach the business centers of Mumbai, Bangalore, and Hyderabad, in the northern and eastern parts of the country, the outage caused trains and subways to stop running, trapped miners underground, stalled traffic, and ground to a halt much of daily life. The blackout focused a spotlight on key development issues in a nation eager to improve its image and economic prospects on the world stage. Infrastructure is of particular concern for businesses that seek to move to the country that is the world's second largest in terms of population and fourth-largest consumer of electricity. In August, a report into the power outages was released, with blame placed on the overloading of certain transmission lines and system operators who were unable to respond quickly enough to surging power demands.

Two Days of Outages

The July 30 and July 31 outages left 10 percent of the world's population without power. The July 30 outage affected approximately 350 million people in northern India, and it was the nation's worst blackout in a decade. To help restore power, India bought energy from its small neighbor, Bhutan. July 31's larger power outage hit 620 million Indians. The impact was widespread outside of major cities, but even in the capital of New Delhi, subway train service was stopped. More than 200 coal miners were stranded in the West Bengal region for several hours until power was restored and they could be rescued. In terms of the number of people affected, the July 31 outage was the largest in world history. The July 30 outage was the second worst, followed by an outage in Indonesia in 2005 that cut power to 100 million. By the evening of July 31, India's power utility reported that a majority of the electricity had been restored.

Major cities in India were largely unaffected by the outages, mainly because many businesses, homes, offices, and hospitals have diesel backup generators to use during power outages. "It's a very common problem," said Dr. Sachendra Raj, who runs a private hospital in India's most populous state, Uttar Pradesh. He continued, "It's part and parcel of our daily life."

One theory as to the cause of the power outages was a drop in the year's monsoon rains, which decreased the availability of hydroelectric power and also forced farmers to irrigate their fields with pumped water, thus drawing more energy from the power grid in certain places. These rains also act as a natural coolant and relieve humidity in the air. Without them, more Indians used air conditioning units, placing further strain on the system. Others blamed the outages on outdated infrastructure, including power lines unable to transmit enough electricity to meet demand.

LONG-STANDING POWER GENERATION PROBLEMS

Power outages are common in India, where nearly 300 million citizens live entirely without electricity. A growing middle class and an increase in modern appliances means that at peak hours across the nation, demand outweighs supply by more than 10 percent. To avoid blackouts, the government has a system in which each region reports, on a daily basis, how much electricity it intends to use. Once that amount is exceeded, the region is fined, and it is up to the power company to stop the flow of electricity to that region to avoid blacking out other areas of the country. According to the nation's former electricity regulator, Surendra Rao, the circuit breaker system is set up in such a way that it should automatically prevent a blackout. But he said that those who control the system and are in charge of shutting off power to areas that draw more than their quota are beholden to elected officials who demand more power for their regions. "The dispatchers at both the state and the regional level should have cut off the customers who were overdrawing, and they didn't," Rao said of the July incident. Others claim the fault lies with the penalty system, which does not levy fines high enough to be a deterrent to overusing energy.

When blackouts occur in India, public anger is typically directed at the government for failing to live up to promises to improve the power grid and provide a more reliable source of energy for Indians. A majority of India's power is nationalized, with less than 25 percent coming from private companies, leaving Indians reliant on the policies of what many consider a dysfunctional government incapable of action. "This is a huge failure," Prakash Javadekar, a spokesperson for the opposition Bharatiya Janata Party, said of the July blackout. "It is a management failure as well as a failure of policy. It is policy paralysis in the power sector," Javadekar continued.

Since the 1950s, the Indian government has promised to increase power generation and update transmission lines, but it has largely failed to live up to expectations. A plan to add 78,000 megawatts of electricity generation by 2012 met only 64 percent of its goal, while a proposal to put $1 trillion toward infrastructure projects by 2017 was scaled back to compensate for the flagging economy, which at the time of the blackouts was experiencing its slowest growth in nine years. Further affecting the government's ability to invest in power generation is an agreement with businesses and farmers who receive subsidized diesel to run backup generators. It is politically difficult for the government to end these subsidies, especially at a time of low monsoon rains.

Some new power plants have recently come online in India; however, the nation derives most of its energy from coal, and production of it has barely increased, leaving power plants idle. Natural gas is also lacking, and plans to bring nuclear plants online have been hampered by vendor concerns and environmental protests. Getting existing and new power plants working at full capacity will require outside investment, but that has been a hard sell for the government, given the deep debt the utilities find themselves in because of a financing structure that charges less for electricity than it costs to generate. Elected officials have been largely unwilling to raise electricity rates to help shore up the debt, but recently, leaders in West Bengal, Tamil Nadu, Rajasthan, and Punjab have implemented policies to raise electricity rates, which they hope will provide more money to invest in additional power generation while subsequently depressing demand.

The July outage was further proof that the burgeoning nation still needs a number of infrastructure improvements if it wants to expand its economic base. International corporations have cited inadequate roads, ports, and power supply as some of the reasons for not doing business in the South Asian nation. The U.S. State Department's report on India echoes this sentiment, finding that "economic growth is constrained by inadequate infrastructure." According to government estimates, the power outages regularly experienced across the country cause a 1.2 percentage point decrease in annual economic growth. The July outages would be no exception, according to N. Bhanumurthy, a senior economist at the National Institute of Public Finance and Policy, who said the blackouts are "going to have a substantial adverse impact on the overall economic activity. Power failure for two consecutive days hits sentiment very badly."

Report Faults an Overloaded System

Following the July power failure, the government appointed a three-member committee, which was tasked with finding the reasons behind the outages and making recommendations to avoid a future crisis. A week before the report was made public, Rabindra Nath Nayak, the head of the national Power Grid Corp. of India Ltd., gave his first public interview since the blackout and cited the role the outdated infrastructure played in the crisis in addition to increased demand from farmers. He noted that one of two major transmission lines was down for service in northern India, thus overloading the other line. "The entire load fell on one line and that led to the cascading effect," he said. He also said that the company planned to invest $18 billion into the network over the next five years to update it to meet demand that grows by 20 percent each year. But, he argued, "We have the best infrastructure in the world. It is not due to our infrastructure." He continued, "Nobody is having a better electricity transmission infrastructure than us."

On August 16, the committee released its report and cited four leading causes of the blackout. These included weak power transmission, overloading a major power line, little to no response from power centers to reduce power being transmitted to those states that were overdrawing electricity, and poor operation of the energy protection system. Taking steps such as regulating power overuse, coordinating planned outages, and taking faster corrective action when a region overdraws electricity "might have saved the system from collapse," the report states. The committee urged the nation to develop protocol for bringing the power grid back online after a failure, stating it "observed that on both the days unduly long time was taken by some of the generating units in starting the units after start up power was made available." A recommendation was also made to form a follow-up task force to review the current state of the grid and anything that might impact its future function to identify improvements that may be necessary.

—Heather Kerrigan

Following are excerpts from a report by the Indian Enquiry Committee, released on August 16, 2012, detailing the causes of the nation's power grid failure.

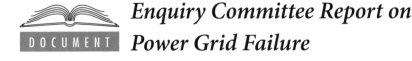

Enquiry Committee Report on Power Grid Failure

August 16, 2012

[The title page, acknowledgments, table of contents, and glossary have been omitted.]

EXECUTIVE SUMMARY

There was a major grid disturbance in Northern Region at 02.33 hrs on 30-07-2012. Northern Regional Grid load was about 36,000 MW at the time of disturbance. Subsequently, there was another grid disturbance at 13.00 hrs on 31-07-2012 resulting in collapse of Northern, Eastern and North-Eastern regional grids. The total load of about 48,000 MW was affected in this black out. On both the days, few pockets survived from black out. Ministry of Power constituted an Enquiry Committee, to analyse the causes of these disturbances and to suggest measures to avoid recurrence of such disturbance in future.

The Committee analysed the output of Disturbance Recorders (DR), Event loggers (EL), PMUs, WAFMS, SCADA data and reports submitted by various SLDCs, RLDCs/ NLDC, POWERGRID and generation utilities to arrive at the sequence of events leading to the blackouts on 30th July, 2012 and 31st July 2012. The Committee also interacted with POWERGRID and POSOCO on various aspects of these grid disturbances. Some teams also made field visits to sub-stations, generating stations, NRLDC, NLDC, UPSLDC and Haryana SLDC.

The Committee is of the opinion that no single factor was responsible for grid disturbances on 30th and 31st July, 2012. After careful analysis of these grid disturbances, the Committee has identified several factors, which led to the collapse of the power systems on both the days, as given below:

Factors that led to the initiation of the Grid Disturbance on 30th July, 2012

a. <u>Weak Inter-regional Corridors due to multiple outages</u>: The system was weakened by multiple outages of transmission lines in the WR-NR interface. Effectively, 400 kV Bina-Gwalior-Agra (one circuit) was the only main AC circuit available between WR-NR interface prior to the grid disturbance.

b. <u>High Loading on 400 kV Bina-Gwalior-Agra link</u>: The overdrawal by some of the NR utilities, utilizing Unscheduled Interchange (UI), contributed to high loading on this tie line.

c. Inadequate response by SLDCs to the instructions of RLDCs to reduce overdrawal by the NR utilities and underdrawal/excess generation by the WR utilities.

d. <u>Loss of 400 kV Bina-Gwalior link</u>: Since the interregional interface was very weak, tripping of 400 kV Bina-Gwalior line on zone-3 protection of distance relay caused the NR system to separate from the WR. This happened due to load encroachment (high loading of line resulting in high line current and low bus voltage). However, there was no fault observed in the system.

Factors that led to the initiation of the Grid Disturbance on 31st July, 2012

(i) *Weak Inter-regional Corridors due to multiple outages:* The system was weakened by multiple outages of transmission lines in the NR-WR interface and the ER network near the ER-WR interface. On this day also, effectively 400 kV Bina-Gwalior-Agra (one circuit) was the only main circuit available between WR-NR.

(ii) *High Loading on 400 kV Bina-Gwalior-Agra link:* The overdrwal [*sic*] by NR utilities, utilizing Unscheduled Interchange (UI), contributed to high loading on this tie line. Although real power flow in this line was relatively lower than on

30th July, 2012, the reactive power flow in the line was higher, resulting in lower voltage at Bina end.

(iii) Inadequate Response by SLDCs to RLDCs' instructions on this day also to reduce overdrawl [*sic*] by the NR utilities and underdrawal by the WR utilities.

(iv) *Loss of 400 kV Bina-Gwalior link:* Similar to the initiation of the disturbance on 30th July, 2012, tripping of 400 kV Bina-Gwalior line on zone-3 protection of distance relay, due to load encroachment, caused the NR system to separate from the WR system. On this day also the DR records do not show occurrence of any fault in the system.

Brief Sequence of Events leading to the Grid Collapse on 30th and 31st July 2012

(i) On 30th July, 2012, after NR got separated from WR due to tripping of 400 kV Bina-Gwalior line, the NR loads were met through WR-ER-NR route, which caused power swing in the system. Since the center of swing was in the NR-ER interface, the corresponding tie lines tripped, isolating the NR system from the rest of the NEW grid system. The NR grid system collapsed due to under frequency and further power swing within the region.

(ii) On 31st July, 2012, after NR got separated from the WR due to tripping of 400 kV Bina-Gwalior line, the NR loads were met through WR-ER-NR route, which caused power swing in the system. On this day the center of swing was in the ER, near ER-WR interface, and, hence, after tripping of lines in the ER itself, a small part of ER (Ranchi and Rourkela), along with WR, got isolated from the rest of the NEW grid. This caused power swing in the NR-ER interface and resulted in further separation of the NR from the ER+NER system. Subsequently, all the three grids collapsed due to multiple tripping attributed to the internal power swings, under frequency and overvoltage at different places.

(iii) The WR system, however, survived due to tripping of few generators in this region on high frequency on both the days.

(iv) The Southern Region (SR), which was getting power from ER and WR, also survived on 31st July, 2012 with part loads remained fed from the WR and the operation of few defense mechanism[s], such as AUFLS and HVDC power ramping.

(v) On both the days, no evidence of any cyber attack has been found by the Committee.

Measures that could have saved the system from collapse:

In an emergency system operating condition, such as on 30th and 31st July 2012, even some of the corrective measures out of the list given below might have saved the system from the collapse.

(i) Better coordinated planning of outages of state and regional networks, specifically under depleted condition of the inter-regional power transfer corridors.

(ii) Mandatory activation of primary frequency response of Governors i.e. the generator's automatic response to adjust its output with variation in the frequency.

(iii) Under-frequency and df/dt based load shedding relief in the utilities' networks.

(iv) Dynamic security assessment and faster state estimation of the system at load despatch centers for better visualization and planning of the corrective actions.

(v) Adequate reactive power compensation, specifically Dynamic Compensation.

(vi) Better regulation to limit overdrawal/underdrawl [*sic*] under UI mechanism, specifically under insecure operation of the system.

(vii) Measures to avoid mal-operation of protective relays, such as the operation of distance protection under the load encroachment on both the days.

(viii) Deployment of adequate synchrophasor based Wide Area Monitoring System and System Protection Scheme.

Restoration of the system

The Committee observed that on both the days unduly long time was taken by some of the generating units in starting the units after start up power was made available.

Recommendations of the Committee

Detailed recommendations of the committee are given in the main report, which are summarized below.

(i) An extensive review and audit of the Protection Systems should be carried out to avoid their undesirable operation.

(ii) Frequency Control through Generation reserves/Ancillary services should be adopted, as presently employed UI mechanism is sometimes endangering the grid security. The present UI mechanism needs a review in view of its impact on recent disturbances.

(iii) Primary response from generators and operation of defense mechanisms, like Under Frequency & df/dt based load shedding and Special Protection Schemes, should be ensured in accordance with provisions of the grid code so that grid can be saved in case of contingencies.

(iv) A review of Total Transfer Capability (TTC) procedure should be carried out, so that it can also be revised under any significant change in system conditions, such as forced outage. This will also allow congestion charges to be applied to relieve the real time congestion.

(v) Coordinated outage planning of transmission elements need to be carried out so that depletion of transmission system due to simultaneous outages of several transmission elements could be avoided.

(vi) In order to avoid frequent outages/opening of lines under over voltages and also providing voltage support under steady state and dynamic conditions, installation of adequate static and dynamic reactive power compensators should be planned.

(vii) Penal provisions of the Electricity Act, 2003 need to be reviewed to ensure better compliance of instructions of Load Desptach [*sic*] Centres and directions of Central Commission.

(viii) Available assets, providing system security support such as HVDC, TCSC, SVC controls, should be optimally utilized, so that they provide necessary support in case of contingencies.

(ix) Synchrophasor based WAMS should be widely employed across the network to improve the visibility, real time monitoring, protection and control of the system.

(x) Load Desptach [*sic*] Centres should be equipped with Dynamic Security Assessment and faster State Estimation tools.

(xi) There is need to plan islanding schemes to ensure supply to essential services and faster recovery in case of grid disruptions.

(xii) There is need to grant more autonomy to all the Load Despatch Centres so that they can take and implement decisions relating to operation and security of the grid

(xiii) To avoid congestion in intra-State transmission system, planning and investment at State level need to be improved.

(xiv) Proper telemetry and communication should be ensured to Load Despatch Centres from various transmission elements and generating stations. No new transmission element/generation should be commissioned without the requisite telemetry facilities.

(xv) Start up time of generating stations need[s] to be shortened to facilitate faster recovery in case of grid disruptions.

(xvi) There is a need to review transmission planning criteria in view of the growing complexity of the system.

(xvii) System study groups must be strengthened in various power sector organizations.

(xviii) It was also felt that a separate task force may be formed, involving experts from academics, power utilities and system operators, to carry out a detailed analysis of the present grid conditions and anticipated scenarios which might lead to any such disturbances in future. The committee may identify medium and long term corrective measures as well as technological solutions to improve the health of the grid.

[The remainder of the report, which offers further details on the causes and recommendations outlined in the Executive Summary, has been omitted.]

SOURCE: Government of India. Ministry of Power. "Report of the Enquiry Committee on Grid Disturbance in Northern Region on 30th July 2012 and in Northern, Eastern & North-eastern Region on 31st July 2012." August 16, 2012. http://www.powermin.nic.in/pdf/GRID_ENQ_REP_16_8_12.pdf.

OTHER HISTORIC DOCUMENTS OF INTEREST

FROM PREVIOUS *HISTORIC DOCUMENTS*

- India's New Prime Minister on Programs and Priorities, *2004*, p. 348

Wife of Chinese Politician Sentenced to Death With Reprieve for Murder

AUGUST 20, 2012

The death of a British businessman, Neil Heywood, in the city of Chongqing, China, in November 2011 sparked a political scandal that brought down one of the country's rising political stars, Bo Xilai. The case unfolded ahead of the eighteenth National Congress of the Communist Party of China, which heralded a once-in-ten-years leadership change. Heywood was murdered by Gu Kailai, the wife of Bo, and by an orderly working for the family, Zhang Xiaojun, following a reported dispute between Gu and Heywood over financial matters. The story came to light after the Chongqing police chief, Wang Lijun, informed Bo in January 2012 that there was an investigation into his family, to which the latter responded angrily and demoted the police chief. Wang subsequently fled Chongqing, reportedly out of fear for his safety, and sought political asylum at the U.S. consulate in Chengdu. It was reportedly during his overnight stay at the consulate that Wang revealed that the British businessman had not died of alcohol poisoning, as previously believed, but was poisoned by Gu. An investigation ensued, and within months Bo was dismissed from his posts and his wife was tried for "intentional murder" and later convicted, along with Zhang. Bo is currently awaiting trial on charges of abuse of power in relation to the cover-up of Heywood's death and of taking bribes, among other charges.

A Scandal Unfolds

In mid-November 2011, forty-one-year-old Heywood, a British businessman living in China, was found dead in his hotel room in the southwestern city of Chongqing, China. Initial reports suggested that Heywood died of alcohol poisoning and his body was cremated within days of his death. The businessman had reportedly lived in China since the 1990s, where he married a Chinese woman with whom he had two children. Heywood worked as a consultant for foreign firms interested in investing in the Chinese market.

On February 2, 2012, state-run Chinese news media announced that the popular Chongqing police chief, Wang, had been demoted to a position of looking after education, environment, and cultural policies. Speculation was rife that the police chief had a falling out with the party secretary and one of China's top politicians, Bo. Four days later, Wang spent the night at the U.S. consulate in Chengdu. When he emerged, the Chinese authorities announced that he would undergo "holiday-style treatment" for extreme work stress. However, later reports indicated that Wang was instead being detained and was under investigation.

Less than a month later, Bo traveled to Beijing for the annual parliamentary session. He reportedly kept a low profile, and speculation mounted that his image had been badly tarnished by his association with Wang. Indeed, it had been widely expected that the party secretary would be promoted to the Politburo's Standing Committee, the body that effectively governs China, in late 2012, but doubts began to grow about his future prospects. On March 14, China's premier, Wen Jiabao, indirectly criticized Bo over the Wang incident. At the same press conference, Wen said that "the mistakes of the Cultural Revolution . . . have yet to be fully eliminated," which was seen as a criticism of Bo's left-wing policies and espousement of economic equality. Just a day later, Chinese news media reported that Bo had been removed from his position as party secretary of Chongqing because of the scandal.

At the time of his removal, observers speculated that Bo's spectacular fall from grace was tied to power struggles at the highest echelons of the Communist Party's leadership. Bo, who is often described as charismatic and ambitious, came to prominence as the mayor of the city of Dalian and then as the governor of the province of Liaoning. He subsequently served as the minister of commerce before his posting to Chongqing. His position as party chief made him one of the twenty-five most influential politicians in the country. Bo Xilai is the son of Bo Yibo, one of the eight elders of the Communist Party of China. Owing to his parentage, Bo was referred to as a "princeling" of Chinese politics—one of a number of powerful sons of party pioneers. But Bo's egalitarian political views, espoused in his "Chongqing model" of development, raised concerns with some of the political elite. Bo's development policies were rooted in the use of state funds to encourage consumption and pumping investment dollars into social welfare programs and infrastructure development. Prior to the scandal, he had openly sought a position on the Politburo's Standing Committee.

In late March, an audio recording surfaced on the Internet that reportedly captured senior Chongqing officials being told of Bo's anger when Wang informed him in January of an investigation into his family. According to the tape, Bo promptly demoted the police chief. After this incident, Wang reportedly feared for his safety and subsequently fled to the U.S. consulate, where he asked for political asylum. A preliminary government report into the scandal did not elaborate on why Wang or his deputies would pursue an investigation into someone of Bo's rank. High-level corruption investigations are typically authorized and overseen by the political elite in the Chinese capital city of Beijing.

Gu Kailai Arrested

Meanwhile, in late March the United Kingdom's government confirmed reports that it had requested that the Chinese government reinvestigate Heywood's death. U.S. and foreign news media reported that during his stay at the U.S. consulate, Wang told officials that Heywood had not died of alcohol poisoning but instead had been poisoned. There was widespread media speculation that Heywood had links to the British government's intelligence services. The *New York Times* reported in November 2012 that the Chinese government had suspected Heywood of being a spy prior to his death. He reportedly met with an operative of the UK's spy agency, MI6, and provided information on the Bo family. The UK's foreign secretary, William Hague, stated that Heywood "was not an employee of the British government in any capacity."

On April 10, Chinese authorities announced that Bo had been stripped of his Communist Party positions and was under investigation for disciplinary violations. Around the same time, it emerged that Wang and Bo ran an extensive wire-tapping operation in Chongqing and reportedly tapped a conversation between a visiting party official and President Hu Jintao. The tapping was said to have been discovered in mid-2011 and seen as a direct challenge to the central Chinese leadership. One Chinese official was quoted as saying, "Not everyone dares to monitor party central leaders."

MURDER CONVICTION

It was also revealed on April 10 that Bo's wife, Gu, a successful lawyer, and an orderly were under investigation for involvement in the death of Heywood. Bo and Heywood had reportedly met when the former was the mayor of Dalian and the British expatriate was working at a local school. The extent of the relationship between Heywood and Bo has not been made public. Gu and Zhang, the family's orderly, were formally charged with "intentional homicide" on July 26. Gu's trial began in August, and she was swiftly convicted of murder, which she was said to have committed because of a conflict over financial interests. Gu did not contest the charges against her and blamed her actions on a "mental breakdown." Gu received a suspended death sentence on August 20. Zhang was also convicted of murder and sentenced to nine years in prison.

In early September, Chinese news media announced that Wang would face charges of defection, abuse of power, and bribe taking. The authorities accused him of purposefully neglecting to investigate Gu's involvement into the death of Heywood. He also stood accused of attempting to defect to the United States when he fled to the consulate in Chengdu. Moreover, it was alleged that Wang had taken bribes and forged documents. The authorities referred to the evidence against him as "concrete and abundant." Wang's trial took place on September 17 and September 18, and on September 24 he was sentenced to fifteen years in prison. The sentence was shorter than many had expected, supposedly reflecting his cooperation with the police during the investigations of Gu and her husband.

BO XILAI FACES PROSECUTION

Just four days later, it was announced that Bo was expelled from the Communist Party and would face criminal charges. Among other things, the disgraced politician stood accused of abuse of power in relation to the cover-up of Heywood's death and of taking bribes. The public airing of the list of crimes he stood accused of, including sordid accusations of inappropriate sexual relationships, underlined the party's decision to take a hard stance against Bo. The timing of the announcement, which settled the issue of how the scandal would be handled, coincided with the announcement that the Communist Party's once-in-a-decade leadership transition would begin on November 8. Bo was also expelled from parliament and, as a result, was no longer immune to prosecution.

Bo's trial could take place as early as March 2013, although rumors swirled in the fall of 2012 that it may begin even earlier, as Bo's Oxford-and-Harvard-educated son, Bo Guagua, came to his father's defense in a public statement in September and returned to China from the United States. The trial is expected to be the most important legal event in recent Chinese history.

—Hilary Ewing

Following is the text of a Chinese media report released on August 20, 2012, pertaining to the sentencing of Gu Kailai, wife of a Chinese politician, following her conviction of killing a British businessman.

DOCUMENT   *Gu Kailai Sentenced to Death*

August 20, 2012

A Chinese court sentenced Bogu Kailai to death with a two-year reprieve for intentional homicide on Monday.

She was deprived of political rights for life, said the court verdict announced by the Hefei City Intermediate People's Court in east China's Anhui Province.

Zhang Xiaojun, an accessory in the case, was sentenced to nine years in prison.

More than 100 people were present for the court session, including relatives and friends of the two defendants, diplomats from the British embassy and consulates in China, representatives from the media, deputies to China's legislature, members of China's political advisory body, as well as people from all walks of life.

Legal representatives of the family of Neil Heywood, the victim in the case, were also at present.

The proceeding started at 9 a.m. Monday. Hu Quanming, chief judge of the court, announced the verdict after confirming the identities of the defendants.

The court found that, in the latter half of 2011, Bogu Kailai and her son surnamed Bo had conflicts with Heywood over economic interests. Heywood had threatened Bo in e-mails, which made Bogu Kailai fear for her son's personal safety and decide to murder Heywood.

She asked Zhang Xiaojun, then an employee of the general office of the Chongqing Municipal Committee of the Communist Party of China (CPC) and a family assistant for Bogu Kailai, to invite and accompany Heywood to Chongqing Municipality in southwest China.

On Nov. 13, 2011, Heywood checked into Room No. 1605 of the 16th building of a vacation resort called the Lucky Holiday Hotel in Chongqing.

That evening, Bogu Kailai and Zhang visited Heywood's hotel, bringing along the poison containing cyanide compound which Bogu Kailai had prepared beforehand.

After entering Heywood's hotel room, Bogu Kailai drank wine and tea with him while Zhang waited outside. Later, Heywood became drunk and fell in the hotel bathroom, and then Bogu Kailai called Zhang into the hotel room and took from Zhang the poison he had brought.

Zhang helped Heywood to the hotel bed. After Heywood vomited and asked for water, Bogu Kailai poured the poison into his mouth, which caused his death.

The forensic lab under the Ministry of Public Security confirmed through toxicology tests that the reason for the death of Heywood accords with cyanide poisoning.

According to the court verdict, Bogu Kailai and Zhang Xiaojun poisoned an individual to death, constituting the crime of intentional homicide.

The court ruled that Bogu Kailai's criminal offense was odious and led to serious consequences. She played the main role in the joint offense and was the principal criminal. The circumstances of her crime warrant the death penalty.

Seeing that the victim Neil Heywood had used threatening language toward the son of Bogu Kailai, this aggravated the dispute between the two sides.

Expert testimony showed that Bogu Kailai had the capacity to assume full criminal responsibility but suffers from a mental disorder. She fully realized the nature and consequences of her crime, but her power of self-control was weakened.

After she was arrested, Bogu Kailai provided to authorities clues regarding other people's violations of the law and discipline and played a positive role in the investigation and handling of relevant cases; in court, Bogu Kailai pleaded guilty and showed remorse for the crime.

Therefore, the court decided to sentence Bogu Kailai to death with reprieve.

Zhang Xiaojun acted on Bogu Kailai's instructions in this joint crime, serving as an accessory. After he was arrested, Zhang accurately recounted the main criminal facts, pleaded guilty and showed repentance in the trial, which led to the mitigation of Zhang's punishment.

The court meted out the penalty according to law, after full consideration of the comments of both the prosecution and defense, according to a court statement.

After the verdict was delivered, both Bogu Kailai and Zhang Xiaojun said they would not lodge appeals. The court was adjourned at 9:20 a.m.

In another development, the Hefei Municipal Intermediate's People's Court on Monday announced the verdict in the case of bending the law for personal gain involving Guo Weiguo, former deputy chief of Chongqing's Public Security Bureau, Li Yang, former chief of the bureau's criminal section, Wang Pengfei, former chief of the bureau's technical detection team and also former chief of the Public Security Sub-bureau of Chongqing's Yubei District, and Wang Zhi, former executive deputy chief of the Public Security Sub-bureau of the municipality's Shapingba District.

The court said in the verdict that clearly knowing there was great suspicion that Bogu Kailai had committed the crime, the four defendants, Guo Weiguo, Li Yang, Wang Pengfei and Wang Zhi, tried to help Bogu Kailai avoid prosecution by fabricating, hiding and destroying evidence, as well as convincing the family members of Neil Heywood to decide not to have an autopsy performed. All of their conduct constituted the crime of bending the law for personal gain.

The crimes committed by the four individuals caused Bogu Kailai's homicidal behavior to be covered up and Bogu Kailai not to be investigated for criminal liability, creating an extremely baneful influence upon society. Therefore, the circumstances of their crimes are especially serious.

The verdict said the crime was a joint offense, with Guo Weiguo acting as the principal, and Li Yang, Wang Pengfei and Wang Zhi as accessories, while Wang Pengfei and Wang Zhi's roles were less important than that of Li Yang.

The four individuals all truthfully confessed the major criminal facts after being apprehended and brought to justice. Guo Weiguo and Li Yang pleaded guilty and showed remorse in court, and Li Yang did not carry out Guo Weiguo's request to destroy key material evidence. In objective terms, this made an important contribution to investigating and solving the case of Neil Heywood's death. Nor did Wang Pengfei and Wang Zhi carry out Guo Weiguo's request to destroy key material evidence, playing a certain role in the investigation and solution of the case.

According to the facts, the nature and the circumstances of the four individuals' crimes, the court, based on the law, sentenced Guo Weiguo and Li Yang to prison terms of 11 years and seven years, respectively, while both Wang Pengfei and Wang Zhi were sentenced to prison terms of five years for their crime of bending the law for personal gain.

The four individuals said in court they will not appeal the sentences.

Yin Chunli, an associate law professor at Anhui University who attended today's court session, said the verdict documents read by the court amply revealed the criminal actions, evidence, as well as legal basis for the rulings.

She said the court ruling was based on law, and the criminals received just punishment for their crimes.

"Legal justice is being upheld," said Wang Xiuqin, a member of the provincial political advisory body of Anhui, who attended the trial and the delivery of the verdict and sentence.

"Everyone is equal before the law. The judicial authorities have made known their stance of safeguarding the dignity of the law," she said.

"These two cases have taught us to revere the law as well as to observe discipline and obey the law," said Yan Lulu, a Hefei resident.

SOURCE: Xinhau. "Bogu Kailai Sentenced to Death With Reprieve for Intentional Homicide." August 20, 2012. http://news.xinhuanet.com/english/china/2012-08/20/c_131796197.htm.

OTHER HISTORIC DOCUMENTS OF INTEREST

FROM PREVIOUS *HISTORIC DOCUMENTS*

Chicago Teachers Union and Mayor Address Strike

AUGUST 29 AND SEPTEMBER 18, 2012

In 2012, only 7 percent of the private sector but nearly 36 percent of the public sector was unionized. Since a wave of Republican governors swept into office in 2010, public sector labor union rights had come under fire, and various proposals had been made to decrease their power. In 2012, Indiana and Michigan became the twenty-third and twenty-fourth states to pass so-called right-to-work laws that bar employees from being forced to join or pay dues to a union as a condition of employment. These laws were just two recent examples in a string of legislation seeking a reduction of union rights in the historically pro-union Midwest. But in Illinois, the Chicago Teachers Union sought to flex its might and prove that all was not lost for union influence when it went on strike for seven days, leaving 350,000 students out of the classroom.

TEACHERS ON STRIKE

Chicago Mayor Rahm Emanuel, formerly President Barack Obama's chief of staff and a Democratic member of Congress, came to office in 2011 promising big changes, especially in the city's struggling public school system. He wanted to see the school day, currently one of the shortest in the nation, lengthened, and to change the student evaluation and teacher pay systems. The mayor quickly butted heads with Karen Lewis, president of the powerful Chicago Teachers Union (CTU), and CTU members who wanted more pay, smaller class sizes, and better job security. The 26,000-strong union was facing not only the mayor's proposed changes but also the impending closure of what could be more than 100 failing schools, some of which would be replaced by an increase in nonunion public charter schools.

Contract negotiations with the CTU dragged on for months, and by midsummer 2012, it was believed that an agreement was close. But on August 29, the union announced its intent to strike if an agreement could not be reached within ten days. On September 10, without a new contract in place, the strike began, keeping 350,000 of the city's school children—many of whom were from low-income neighborhoods—out of classes. The strike was the first for the CTU in twenty-five years and the first teacher strike in a major city in the United States in six years.

The strike continued into a second school week when teachers delayed a vote on September 16 to consider a potential contract, but the union still enjoyed strong support from Chicagoans. "As much as we want our kids back in school, teachers need to make sure they have dotted all their i's and crossed their t's," said Becky Malone, a parent of two Chicago school children. "What's the point of going on strike if you don't get everything you need out of it?" Malone continued. The union issued a letter thanking the public for its support. "We would like to express our profound gratitude for your support in our fight for quality public education and a fair contract," it read in part.

On September 17, with the city and CTU still at an impasse, Emanuel asked the Cook County Circuit Court to stop the strike and force teachers back to work on the grounds that it violated state law, which prohibits striking over noneconomic issues. Emanuel, after learning that a tentative agreement had not passed muster with the union, said, "This was a strike of choice and is now a delay of choice that is wrong for our children." He accused the union of using school students as "pawns in an internal dispute" and said the strike endangered the health and safety of students. The court said it would not take up the case until September 19, a day after the CTU was set to reconvene to consider the potential contract.

The union called the lawsuit "a vindictive act instigated by the mayor" and an attempt to "trample our collective bargaining rights and hinder our freedom of speech and right to protest." Lewis called the inability to agree to a tentative deal an issue of trust. "The trust level is not there," she said. "You have a population of people who are frightened of never being able to work for no fault of their own." Emanuel remained unapologetic. "I did not come to the office of mayor at this point in my career so I get the glory of running for re-election," he said in an interview. "I came here to use this office to bring change. And I want to make sure that the kids of the city of Chicago get the opportunity to have reading and writing, not choose between them."

On September 18, the union's 800 delegates, who represent the full union, voted 98 percent to 2 percent to approve a new contract and end the strike. Students could immediately return to school, but final approval would be required of each member of the union. That came in October, when 79.1 percent approved the contract. "We said that it was time—that we couldn't solve all the problems of the world with one contract, and that it was time to suspend the strike," said Lewis. Emanuel called the deal "an honest compromise" and said, "In this contract, we gave our children a seat at the table. In past negotiations, taxpayers paid more, but our kids got less. This time, our taxpayers are paying less, and our kids are getting more."

There were a number of compromises in the final contract. In terms of pay, Chicago school teachers, who are already some of the highest paid in the nation, will receive, on average, a 7 percent raise over three years. This was less than the 30 percent the union had asked for and less than the 16 percent initially proposed by Emanuel. Teachers will continue to receive bonuses based on seniority. The raises are expected to cost the school district an extra $74 million each year. Emanuel's plan to increase the length of the school day from five hours and forty-five minutes to seven hours at elementary schools and from seven to seven-and-a-half hours at high schools was included in the contract, but the extra high school time will not involve instruction—students will instead spend this time in study hall. Emanuel was also able to extend the school year from 170 days to 180 days.

The teacher evaluation plan, perhaps the biggest point of contention in the negotiations, was also changed in the new contract. A 2010 state law requires public school teachers to be judged at least partially on student performance, a controversial move pushed by President Obama. Supporters of the law said it would keep good teachers in the classroom. Opponents, including the CTU, said there are many factors influencing student performance that are outside of a teacher's control, such as homelessness and a student's home life. In the new contract, standardized tests—on which Chicago students routinely perform poorly—will eventually make up 30 percent of a teacher's evaluation.

A complicated hiring and firing system was also set up in the new contract. Teachers employed at a school that ends up closing will be given priority for any open positions at the schools that their students move to, taking away many of the hiring decisions from principals. And when layoffs are deemed necessary, teachers will be let go based on a combination of seniority and performance. However, once underperforming teachers are let go, those with the most seniority will be kept over newer teachers even if the newer teacher has a better performance evaluation.

RIGHT-TO-WORK

Federal labor law allows employers to require that employees be members of a union as a condition of employment, an arrangement known as a "closed shop." However, that same federal law gives states the ability to ban this practice by passing right-to-work legislation that bars employers from requiring participation in a union or payment of union dues. By the end of 2012, twenty-four states had passed right-to-work legislation.

Unsurprisingly, labor unions, such as the American Federation of Labor and Congress of Industrial Organizations (AFL-CIO), oppose right-to-work laws, arguing that because all employees benefit from negotiations in union shops, those workers who do not pay dues are financially hampering the work of the union. Those who support such laws, including a number of Republican elected officials, say that employees should have the ability to decide whether or not to financially support a union. These supporters argue that by implementing the legislation, states can attract more business and thus improve the overall economy. Critics say that this increase is never passed on to workers, who end up experiencing lower wages. A 2007 study by Hofstra University's Lonnie Stevans concluded, "Although right-to-work states may be more attractive to business, this does not necessarily translate into enhanced economic verve in the right-to-work state if there is little 'trickle-down' from business owners to the non-unionized workers." While business may increase in a state with a right-to-work law, analysts have a difficult time discerning whether the economic effect is in fact caused by that law or other factors.

It is generally agreed that right-to-work laws weaken labor unions, because if employees aren't forced to pay dues, they will choose not to but still benefit from union bargaining. As the union loses money, it also loses influence. One exception to this is what is considered to be the most powerful local union in the country, Culinary Union Local 226, which represents hotel housekeepers in Las Vegas. Nevada has a right-to-work law in place, but this union has nearly 100 percent of its members paying dues. This success has not been replicated in most other right-to-work states.

BIRTHPLACE OF UAW PASSES RIGHT-TO-WORK LEGISLATION

Despite the continual decrease of union participation, the state of Michigan remains one of the most heavily unionized states, at 17.5 percent. The state is also the birthplace of one of the nation's most powerful unions, the United Autoworkers (UAW). Even so, in 2012, the Republican-controlled House and Senate considered a right-to-work bill that drew thousands of protesters to the state capitol in Lansing. Given the bill's unpopularity with unions, the legislature added an appropriation to the bill to ensure it would fall under a Michigan law that bans spending bills from being overturned by legislative referendum. Republican Governor Rick Snyder eventually signed the legislation into law on December 11. Opponents of the law said they plan to consider circulating petitions to recall

Republican legislators and the governor. The law made Michigan the twenty-fourth state in the country to pass right-to-work legislation and the fourth Midwestern state to attempt to weaken labor rights in two years, following Indiana's 2012 right-to-work law, Wisconsin's 2011 collective bargaining legislation, and Ohio's collective bargaining law, which was overturned by voters in 2011.

—Heather Kerrigan

Following is the text of a press release from the Chicago Teachers Union on August 29, 2012, announcing its intent to strike; and a statement by Chicago Mayor Rahm Emanuel on September 18, 2012, marking the end of the teacher strike.

DOCUMENT

Chicago Teachers Union Files Intent to Strike

August 29, 2012

Today, the Chicago Teachers Union (CTU) filed a 10-day notice with the Illinois Education Labor Relations Board indicating more than 26,000 public school teachers, clinicians and paraprofessionals may go on strike in coming days. The notice is a legal requirement defined by state law. No date for a strike has been set by [u]nion leaders. The House of Delegates will meet Thursday at 4:30 p.m. to talk next steps.

Should CTU members call for a work stoppage, this will be the first "teachers' strike" in Chicago since 1987. "This is a difficult decision for all of us to make," said union President Karen Lewis. "But this is the only way to get the Board's attention and show them we are serious about getting a fair contract which will give our students the resources they deserve."

"CPS seems determined to have a toxic relationship with its employees," Lewis said. "They denied us our 4 percent raises when there was money in the budget to honor our agreement; they attempted to ram a poorly thought out longer school day down our throats; and, on top of that they want us to teach a new curriculum and be ready to be evaluated based on how well our students do on a standardized test. It has been insult after insult after insult. Enough is enough."

CTU has been in contract negotiations with the Chicago Public Schools (CPS) since November 2011. Teachers have been without a contract since June of this year after its five-year agreement with the District expired without a new agreement in place. Labor leaders have said they are negotiating for a "better day, job security and fair compensation for employees."

Labor talks have been productive on some fronts such as winning provisions for nursing mothers, ensuring textbooks will be available on day one, teachers will have access to functioning computers and counselors and social workers will have appropriate, private workspaces to serve students. But the bigger issues such as wages, job security and evaluations are on the table and the two sides remain far apart. "We will have a contract," Lewis said, "and it will come the easy way or the hard way. If our members are on the picket-line, we will still be at the negotiating table trying to hammer out an equitable agreement. There's a larger picture here."

Teachers, paraprofessionals and school clinicians have been vocal in their opposition to CPS' draconian policies. In May, nearly 10,000 of them marched in downtown in preparation for a strike authorization vote which drew a 98 percent approval from CTU membership. Only 1.82 percent of CTU members voted against authorizing a strike. Member angst was driven by CPS' overly aggressive push for a longer school day without indicating how the District would staff and pay for the program. Educators were angry that the Board made no commitments to offering students the much needed art, music, physical education and world language classes they needed.

In July, and much to CPS' chagrin, a much anticipated "Fact Finder's Report" recommended, in part, that CPS's longer school day amounts to a 19.4% increase on average that teachers will have to work, and he determined that CPS cannot expect its employees to work nearly 20% more for free or without fair compensation. Accordingly, the Fact-Finder's report recommends both a general wage increase and an additional increase due to the length of the school day: A general wage increase of 2.25% for School Year 2012—essentially a cost of living increase—without any changes to existing steps and lanes. He also recommends an additional increase of 12.6% to compensate teachers for working a longer school day and year representing a combined first-year increase of 14.85%, plus existing step and lane adjustments. Both the CTU and the Board rejected the findings.

"We have chronic underfunding and misplaced priorities in the system," said high school teacher Jen Johnson. "CPS would rather shut down schools . . . than give them the resources they need. Thousands of students have been displaced by CPS' school actions. Teachers are losing their jobs and parents have no choice but to keep their child in an under-resourced neighborhood school or ship them off to a poor-performing charter operation."

Lewis said members are also concerned about the Board's plan to close over 100 neighborhood schools and create a half public–half charter school district. "This education crisis is real especially if you are Black or Brown in Chicago," she explained. "Whenever our students perform well on tests, CPS moves the bar higher, tells them they are failures and blames their teachers. Now they want to privatize public education and further disrupt our neighborhoods. We've seen public housing shut down, public health clinics, public libraries and now public schools. There is an attack on public institutions, many of which serve, [sic] low-income and working-class families."

SOURCE: Chicago Teachers Union, Department of Communications. "Breaking News: CTU Files Notice of Intent to Strike." August 29, 2012. http://www.ctunet.com/media/press-releases/breaking-news-ctu-files-notice-of-intent-to-strike.

Chicago Mayor on End of Teacher Strike

DOCUMENT

September 18, 2012

Remarks as Prepared

I want to start by thanking all the people who volunteered—all the parents, grandparents and administrators—at the 147 schools we kept open during this strike. I want to thank everyone at all the faith based and neighborhood sites who provided our children safe places during the strike. I want to thank everyone for showing who we are as a city: we take care of our children first.

This settlement is an honest compromise. It means returning our schools to their primary purpose: the education of our children. It means a new day and a new direction for Chicago Public Schools.

In this contract, we gave our children a true seat at the table. In past negotiations, taxpayers paid more but our kids got less—this time, our taxpayers are paying less and our kids are getting more. Because of past contracts, teachers and principals had to make false choices about where they spent their time, because there was so little of it. This contract is a break with past practices and brings a fundamental change that benefits our children.

We have been discussing the need for more time for over a decade, but lacked the ability to achieve our primary educational goal. We have been discussing the need for more reading and recess, for more science and sports, for more math and music, for as long as I can remember. Each time it was postponed or rejected because the changes were too difficult. Today, that era and those false choices come to an end.

Our elementary students will gain an extra hour and 15 minutes every day and two additional weeks every year. Our high school students will be in front of a great teacher for an extra thirty minutes each day and two additional weeks each year. For students entering [k]indergarten this year, they will have an extra 2 ½ years in the classroom by the time they graduate high school. That 2 ½ years of additional education is a new day and a new direction for Chicago's children.

We have seen already how great principals and great teachers have designed the full school day to make the most of this additional time. At Spencer Academy, students have been getting 20 more minutes a day in reading, 15 more minutes a day in math, and a new 30-minute period that links technology with student learning. That is time for learning that students did not have just last year.

At Beidler Elementary, students have 60 minutes per week in a new writing lab and 45 minutes for specialized reading at the end of each day—that is learning they didn't have before this year. At Greene Elementary, students have 90 minutes of reading and 60 minutes of writing each day—additional time they did not have before. And those are just a few examples of how this additional time is transforming our classrooms and our children's lives.

This full day gives our kids more quality time for learning and teachers more opportunity to provide quality instruction. The agreement also provides our principals the freedom they need to lead their teams. Principals will have the responsibility they deserve and the accountability for results that we demand.

Third, for the first time, teachers will have a meaningful evaluation based on a system designed by their fellow teachers. Our evaluation system has not changed in 40 years—while our students, and the world, have. This is in the best interest of our students, who need the very best teachers. It is in the best interest of our teachers, who always strive to achieve the best results they can for their students and want to develop as professionals, as every professional does.

Fourth, since a child gets one chance at an education, parents deserve a choice. That's why we have added five new STEM high schools, five new IB high schools, neighborhood schools, magnet schools, schools of excellence, as well as 6,000 more kindergarten seats, and 2,000 more spots for early childhood education. This year, for the first time in a decade, our parents will have more school choices and our children will have more educational time. That is what it means to have a new day and a new direction for Chicago's children.

With this agreement, our teachers will receive higher pay and our students will have a higher standard of education. Chicago is a national leader in putting in place a Common Core Curriculum to raise standards in math and reading. We are making college attendance the expectation, not the exception, for all our students.

We have taken a half-a-billion dollars out of the central office and put that money back into the classroom where it belongs. We will save where we can so that we can invest where we must: in the classroom and in the future of our children.

We are also providing parents more tools to be partners in their children's schools. For the first time, parents get the same report card the principal receives on a school's performance. Parents need to use that information to demand improvement and educational excellence. For the first time, they will see their school's budget online. Teachers need parents as partners—as much as they need principals who are willing to be held accountable. In short, parents must step up and do their part as a true partner.

We all know our teachers do remarkable work in our classrooms. We have seen our students achieve great things against difficult odds. If they can turn obstacles into opportunities, so can we. For every child to have a world-class education, each of us has a responsibility and no one gets a pass: the future of our children demands no less.

So I want to thank the negotiators on both sides, who worked hard to forge this agreement. I want to thank parents and taxpayers for their patience. I want to thank again all the parents, non-profits, principals, religious leaders, and concerned citizens who worked together to support our students during the strike. We showed that we are not just a city of big shoulders, we are a city of big hearts.

Now our students and teachers can return to classrooms across our City, where Chicago's future is being shaped. Now that the negotiations are over, our most important work begins: providing every child in every community of Chicago an education to match their potential.

There are moments, both as Mayor and on the campaign, that leave a lasting impression on you as a person. Too many times I have met kids, whether on the [El] or on the street walking to school, who have a look of emptiness in their eyes that no one would accept in their own child. Downtown, with all its opportunities and possibilities, may only be a few miles away, but for too many kids it seems like a world-apart [sic]. For them, downtown may as well be in a different city, not their own hometown. There is a gulf between what they see downtown and what they see in their own future. The classroom is the only way to bridge that gulf. The classroom is where they learn that not only do they have a place in the future of this city; they are the future of this city. We as adults have to live up to our responsibilities so that those kids can live up to their future. That is what this was about.

Source: City of Chicago. Press Releases. "Statement by Mayor Rahm Emanuel on the End of the Chicago Teachers Union Strike." September 18, 2012. http://www.cityofchicago.org/city/en/depts/mayor/press_room/press_releases/2012/september_2012/statement_by_mayorrahmemanuelontheend ofthechicagoteachersunionst.html.

OTHER HISTORIC DOCUMENTS OF INTEREST

FROM THIS VOLUME

- Wisconsin Governor Survives Recall Election, p. 250

FROM PREVIOUS *HISTORIC DOCUMENTS*

- Wisconsin Passes Anti–Collective Bargaining Bill, *2011,* p. 103
- Report on the Future of Labor-Management Relations, *1995,* p. 15
- Republican Party Platform, *1988,* p. 615
- Democratic Platform, *1972,* p. 527

District Court Rules on Texas Voter ID Law

AUGUST 30, 2012

The Voting Rights Act was first passed in 1965 to ensure that all of-age Americans have an unobstructed chance to vote. Since passage, a number of states have approved their own legislation to implement certain rules to prevent voter fraud. One common method is a voter identification law, which requires voters to present an acceptable form of identification, as determined by the state, to allow poll workers to verify that the person voting is who he or she claims to be. In advance of the 2012 presidential elections, a number of states attempted to pass voter ID laws. Opponents viewed these laws as politicized attempts to suppress the votes of minorities and the poor, groups that often vote Democratic and are less likely to have government-issued identification. A number of these laws landed before federal courts that were tasked with deciding whether the laws were discriminatory or a valid attempt at preventing voter fraud.

VOTER ID LAWS NATIONWIDE

Indiana was the first state to enact a strict voter ID law in 2006, which was upheld by the U.S. Supreme Court in 2008. Prior to Indiana, no state required voters to produce a government-issued photo ID to vote. In 2012, voter ID legislation was introduced in thirty-two states. This included fourteen new laws, ten efforts to strengthen existing laws, and ten instances to amend earlier legislation. Previously proposed legislation met with varying degrees of success—a federal court struck down Texas's law while North Carolina, Pennsylvania, and South Carolina were able to maintain theirs. Wisconsin's voter ID law was declared unconstitutional, and in Minnesota, state voters rejected an ID law on the November ballot.

Although supporters of voter ID laws argue that they prevent fraud, the impact and existence of voter fraud is debatable. A CBS News survey of the ten states that enacted voter ID laws in the past year found less than seventy convictions for voter fraud during the past decade. A joint study by the Knight Foundation and Carnegie Corporation of all fifty states found "infinitesimal" instances of voter fraud, about one in every 15 million registered voters. Rick Hasen, an election law specialist at the University of California, Irvine, said, "When you do see election fraud, it invariably involves election officials taking steps to change election results or it involves absentee ballots which voter ID laws can't prevent." But, he said, "There's no question that in a very close election [voters turned away by the laws] could be enough to make a difference in the outcome."

How voter ID laws impact registered voters varies by state. In Pennsylvania, where a voter ID law was upheld by a state court, the Department of State said about 9 percent of voters didn't have the proper state-issued ID required to vote but that 22 percent of those voters were considered inactive and hadn't voted within the past five years. A study by researchers at the University of Chicago and Washington University in St. Louis estimated that anywhere between 9 and 25 percent of voters nationwide could be demobilized by voter ID laws, which one study author, Cathy Cohen, called a "conservative" estimate. Young minority voters face the biggest potential impact from these laws, according to the study, because they are more likely to be poor, transient, or have suspended licenses. The new ID requirements passed in 2012, the researchers estimated, would disenfranchise up to 475,000 young black voters and between 68,000 and 250,000 young Hispanic voters. Whereas some have insisted that voter ID laws wouldn't have a significant impact on an election outcome, the authors of the study reported that in Florida, where a 537-vote margin separated George W. Bush and Al Gore in the 2000 presidential election, 100,000 young minority voters might be turned away at the polls because of improper ID.

Conservative lawmakers are traditionally the drivers behind voter ID laws, arguing that they are necessary to prevent voter fraud, which supporters believe goes undetected but would be prevented by more restrictive laws. Opponents, on the other hand, argue that because the cases of voter impersonation fraud are rare, voter ID laws are a veiled attempt at reducing turnout among voters more likely to support Democrats. A poll by CBS News and the *New York Times* in early September 2012 revealed that 70 percent of voters support photo ID requirements.

Texas Law Struck Down

Nine states, mainly those in the South, are required under Section 5 of the Voting Rights Act to seek approval from the Justice Department before making any changes to state election laws, while seven other states including Florida and California are partially covered by Section 5. These states are required to receive preclearance because they have a history of racial electoral discrimination.

In May 2011, Texas Governor Rick Perry signed Senate Bill 14 into law, requiring voters to present one of five acceptable forms of identification—a driver's license, U.S. passport, concealed carry permit, U.S. military identification, or a personal ID issued by the state's Department of Public Safety—before they would be allowed to cast a ballot. Anyone unable to produce one of these forms of identification was required to apply for an election identification certificate with a state Department of Public Safety office. These certificates would be given to voters at no cost; however, voters would have to provide a birth certificate in order to prove their identity, which can cost more than $20. Before it could take effect, the new law required preclearance.

The Justice Department responded by asking for additional information on how the law would ensure the right to vote was not abridged for any citizen of the state. Specifically, the department wanted demographic information on the estimated 600,000 Texans who are registered to vote but who do not have an acceptable form of identification, as well as information on how the state planned to educate the public about the new law. Ultimately, the Justice Department determined in March 2012 that Texas had not provided enough evidence to prove that its law would not have a discriminatory effect and denied preclearance.

Seeking approval to put the law into effect, Texas filed a lawsuit against the Justice Department to have preclearance denial reversed. On August 30, a three-judge panel of the U.S. District Court for the District of Columbia decided unanimously that the law, the strictest of its kind, should be struck down. The court found that the time and money required to obtain a voter identification card would disproportionally affect minorities and the poor by imposing "strict, unforgiving burdens." And because many counties in Texas lack a Department of Public Safety office, the court found that "while a 200- to 250-mile trip to and from a D.P.S. office would be a heavy burden for any prospective voter, such a journey would be especially daunting for the working poor." U.S. Attorney General Eric Holder, who had previously called the law the equivalent of a poll tax, celebrated the ruling stating, "The court's decision today . . . not only reaffirm[s]—but help[s] protect—the vital role the Voting Rights Act plays in our society to ensure that every American has the right to vote and to have that vote counted." Governor Perry called the ruling a "victory for fraud," saying in a statement, "Today, federal judges subverted the will of the people of Texas and undermined our effort to ensure fair and accurate elections. The Obama Administration's claim that it's a burden to present a photo ID to vote simply defies common sense." The governor vowed to continue working to gain federal approval for a Texas voter ID law.

South Carolina and Pennsylvania Seek Approval

In December 2011, the Justice Department blocked South Carolina's voter ID law, which would require registered voters to present a driver's license, state-issued ID card, U.S. passport, or military ID, finding that it would disenfranchise African American voters because they are 20 percent more likely to lack one of the acceptable forms of ID than their white counterparts. Those in South Carolina who support the law said that it was necessary to protect the integrity of elections, pointing to evidence that hundreds of people have been recorded as voting after their death. Evidence, however, has suggested that this information is the result of a clerical error rather than an actual vote.

South Carolina appealed the ruling, and in August 2012, the federal circuit court in Washington, D.C., took up the case. A three-judge panel ruled in October that the law could go into effect. "In sum, our comparison of South Carolina's act to some other states' voter ID laws," wrote Judge Brett Kavanaugh, "strongly buttresses the conclusion that South Carolina's law has neither a discriminatory effect nor a discriminatory purpose." Although approved, the law was enjoined from going into effect prior to the 2012 presidential election because there was limited time for voters to obtain the necessary identification.

In Pennsylvania, a group of voters brought a lawsuit to a state court, alleging that the new voter ID law was akin to a poll tax and would place an unfair burden in both cost and time on those who did not have the proper state-issued identification to vote. One ninety-four-year-old plaintiff said she was too sick to travel to receive a driver's license, while another, aged ninety-three, said that she never had a driver's license and that the state would not accept her Social Security card as proof of her identity. In a sixty-eight-page ruling, the state court decided that the law was "a reasonable, non-discriminatory, non-severe burden when viewed in the broader context of the widespread use of photo ID in daily life. The Commonwealth's asserted interest in protecting public confidence in elections is a relevant and legitimate state interest sufficiently weighty to justify the burden." The new law was set to go into effect following the state's May 2013 primary; however, a new challenge was brought against the law, and a trial is tentatively set for July 2013.

SUPREME COURT TO MAKE ULTIMATE DECISION

On November 9, the U.S. Supreme Court announced that it would take up a case on whether Congress was within its right to renew Section 5 of the Voting Rights Act in 2006, leaving the law in place until 2031. This will not be the first time in recent history when the Court reviewed this section of the act. In 2008, the Court upheld Section 5 but encouraged Congress to modernize the law to better reflect the realities of today as being different from those in 1965. Congress has yet to make any changes. A decision in the case, which was brought by Shelby County, Alabama, is expected in June 2013, and could impact those states that have had their voter ID laws blocked.

—Heather Kerrigan

Following are excerpts from the U.S. District Court for the District of Columbia's opinion in State of Texas v. Holder, *in which a three-judge panel ruled unanimously on August 30, 2012, to strike down Texas's voter ID law.*

DOCUMENT *Texas v. Holder*

August 30, 2012

[Footnotes and most legal citations have been excerpted from this opinion.]

UNITED STATES DISTRICT COURT FOR THE DISTRICT OF COLUMBIA

STATE OF TEXAS, Plaintiff

v.

ERIC H. HOLDER, JR., Defendant.

**Civil Action No. 12-cv-128
(DST, RMC, RLW)**

Opinion

Before: TATEL, *Circuit Judge,* and COLLYER and WILKINS, *District Judges.*

Opinion for the Court filed by *Circuit Judge* TATEL.

TATEL, *Circuit Judge:* Pursuant to section 5 of the Voting Rights Act of 1965, Texas seeks a declaratory judgment that Senate Bill 14 (SB 14), a newly-enacted law requiring in-person voters to present a photo ID, "neither has the purpose nor will have the effect of denying or abridging the right to vote on account of race[,] color," or "member[ship] [in] a language minority group." To satisfy section 5's effect requirement, Texas must demonstrate that SB 14 will not "lead to a retrogression in the position of racial minorities with respect to their effective exercise of the electoral franchise." For the reasons set forth in this opinion, we find that Texas has failed to make this showing—in fact, record evidence demonstrates that, if implemented, SB 14 will likely have a retrogressive effect. Given this, we have no need to consider whether Texas has satisfied section 5's purpose element. Accordingly, we deny the state's request for a declaratory judgment.

I.

Under Texas's current election code, i.e., pre-SB 14, any Texan who wishes to vote must file a registration application with the county elections registrar. That application must include the voter's name, date of birth, and a sworn affirmation of U.S. citizenship. If the application is approved, the registrar delivers a "voter registration certificate" to the applicant, either in person or via U.S. mail. This "certificate"—actually a paper postcard—has no photograph, but does include a voter's name, gender, year of birth, and a unique voter ID number. When presented at the polls, a voter registration certificate entitles the registrant to cast an in-person ballot.

Registered voters who fail to present a voter registration certificate may nonetheless cast an in-person ballot if they (1) execute an affidavit stating that they do not have their certificate, and (2) present an alternate "acceptable" form of identification. In addition to a voter registration certificate, Texas's current election code recognizes eight broad categories of documents as "acceptable" voter ID. These include birth certificates, expired and non-expired driver's licenses, U.S. passports, U.S. citizenship papers, utility bills, "official mail addressed to the person . . . from a governmental entity," any "form of identification containing the person's photograph that establishes the person's identity," and "any other form of identification prescribed by the secretary of state." All in-person voters are subject to these ID requirements regardless of age or physical condition. But certain voters—including those who are 65 or older, disabled, or expect to be absent or in jail on Election Day—may choose to vote by mail without presenting identification.

Senate Bill 14, enacted in 2011, is more stringent than existing Texas law. If implemented, SB 14 will require in-person voters to identify themselves at the polls using one of five forms of government-issued photo identification, two state and three federal: (1) a driver's license or personal ID card issued by the Texas Department of Public Safety (DPS); (2) a license to carry a concealed handgun, also issued by DPS; (3) a U.S. military ID card; (4) a U.S. citizenship certificate with photograph; or (5) a U.S. passport. Unlike Texas's current code, which allows voters to present either photographic or non-photographic ID, SB 14 requires every form of acceptable ID to include a photograph of the voter. Also unlike the current code, SB 14 prohibits the use of IDs that have expired more "than 60 days before the date of presentation" at the polls. Finally, SB 14 will prohibit voters from identifying themselves using only the pictureless "voter registration certificate" issued by a county registrar.

Prospective voters lacking one of the forms of photo ID listed in SB 14 will be able to obtain a photographic "election identification certificate" (EIC) for use at the polls. A pocket-sized card "similar in form to . . . a driver's license," an EIC, like a driver's license, will be distributed through the DPS, and prospective voters will have to visit a DPS office to get one.

Although SB 14 prohibits DPS from "collect[ing] a fee for an [EIC]," EICs will not be costless.

[Additional background on SB 14, lower court opinions, and information on the District Court discovery and trial periods have been omitted.]

Based on this extensive record, Texas argues that SB 14 was enacted to prevent voter fraud, and denies that race was a motivating factor. Texas also argues that record evidence affirmatively proves that SB 14 will have no discriminatory effect. For their part, the United States and Defendant-Intervenors argue that the specter of in-person voter fraud is a chimera meant to mask the discriminatory purpose behind SB 14. According to these parties, the record contains virtually no evidence of in-person voter fraud in Texas and this, combined with certain procedural irregularities that occurred during the passage of SB 14, the state's history of racial discrimination, and other evidence, proves that the bill's purpose was to disenfranchise minorities. Moreover, the United States and Defendant-Intervenors argue that SB 14 will have a discriminatory effect—that is, it will "lead to a retrogression in the position of racial minorities with respect to their effective exercise of the electoral franchise." . . .

II.

[Section A, containing the legal framework governing the case, and Section B, outlining Texas's argument, have been omitted.]

III.

With these principles in mind, we turn to the record. Because "courts have no need to find discriminatory intent once they find [retrogressive] effect," and because evidence that a law which "bears more heavily on one race than another"—i.e., has disproportionate effect—is itself "the important starting point for assessing discriminatory intent," we begin with section 5's effect element.

This discussion proceeds as follows. We begin with Texas's argument that, as a general proposition, voter ID laws have little effect on turnout—an argument that relies on social science literature and the experiences of Georgia and Indiana following enactment of their photo ID laws. Next, we consider evidence submitted by Texas, the United States, and Defendant-Intervenors analyzing whether minorities disproportionately lack the forms of ID permitted by SB 14. For the reasons given below, we reject all of this evidence and, because Texas has submitted nothing more, conclude that the state has failed to meet its burden of demonstrating that SB 14 lacks retrogressive effect. As we shall explain, however, this case does not hinge solely on the burden of proof. Undisputed record evidence demonstrates that racial minorities in Texas are disproportionally likely to live in poverty and, because SB 14 will weigh more heavily on the poor, the law will likely have retrogressive effect.

A.

Texas begins with a broad argument: that social science evidence demonstrates voter turnout is generally unaffected by the stringency of a state's voter ID laws. In other words, Texas contends that voters vote regardless of the identification requirements imposed on them at the polls and that SB 14 will thus have "no significant effect at all." And because ID requirements have no bearing on whether voters—minorities or otherwise—turn out on Election Day, Texas concludes that SB 14 will have no retrogressive effect.

We are unable to credit this line of argument because the effect of voter ID laws on turnout remains a matter of dispute among social scientists. Texas relies heavily on a 2009 paper by Dr. Stephen Ansolabehere, a Harvard political scientist who (as discussed *infra*) happens to be one of the United States's expert witnesses in this case. In his paper, Dr. Ansolabehere concludes, based on a telephone survey of eligible voters nationwide, that "almost no one . . . stay[s] away from the polls for want of appropriate identification." But the United States introduced into evidence a 2011 paper by Dr. Michael Alvarez of the California Institute of Technology which reaches precisely the opposite conclusion. Applying a statistical regression model to voting data from all 50 states, Dr. Alvarez concludes that photo ID requirements impose "significant negative burdens on voters." The Alvarez study predicts that imposition of a photo ID requirement in any given state will depress overall voter turnout by approximately 10%. Texas—which bears the burden of proof—has failed to produce any evidence undermining the validity of the Alvarez study. Instead, it focuses entirely on Dr. Ansolabehere's 2009 paper. Yet Dr. Ansolabehere himself testified that "other published research disagrees with me," specifically pointing out that Dr. Alvarez's study found that some photo ID laws have "quite a big effect" on turnout. We thus have no basis for finding that Dr. Ansolabehere's 2009 paper represents any sort of academic consensus about the impact of voter ID laws.

Turning from national studies to state-specific data, Texas next focuses on the experiences of Indiana and Georgia—two states that recently implemented photo ID laws. Relying on expert testimony from University of Texas political scientist Daron Shaw, Texas argues that its population is demographically "similar to" Georgia's and Indiana's, and that these states' experiences with photo ID requirements suggest that SB 14 will have "no significant effect at all" on turnout in Texas. At trial, Dr. Shaw testified that survey data from the 2008 Presidential primaries showed that virtually no Georgia or Indiana voters reported being turned away from the polls because of a lack of photo ID. Moreover, this finding remained constant across racial lines: in Indiana "0 percent of whites, 0 percent of blacks, 0 percent of Hispanics report that they were not allowed to vote"; in Georgia, "0 percent of whites, 1 percent of blacks, 0 percent of Hispanics said they were not allowed to vote" because they lacked photo ID. These figures were particularly notable, Dr. Shaw emphasized, because social scientists had previously concluded that "there were [disparate ID] possession rates by race" in both Georgia and Indiana. From this, Texas urges us to draw three conclusions: (1) photo ID laws ultimately prevent very few people from voting; (2) photo ID laws have no disproportionate effect on racial minorities; and (3) disparate ID possession rates have little effect on turnout. We reject these proposed findings because the circumstances in Georgia and Indiana are significantly different from those in Texas.

First, and most important, SB 14 is far stricter than either Indiana's or Georgia's voter ID laws. Indiana allows voters to use any photo ID that has "expired after the date of the most recent general election." Georgia allows voters to present any expired driver's license at the polls. By contrast, SB 14 prohibits the use of an ID which has expired "more than 60 days before the date of presentation" at the polls.

Moreover, the burdens associated with obtaining a purportedly "free" voter ID card will be heavier under SB 14 than under either Indiana or Georgia law. This is true for at least two reasons. The first relates to out-of-pocket cost. Under SB 14, EIC applicants will have to present DPS officials with a government-issued form of ID, the cheapest of which, a certified copy of a birth certificate, costs $22. By contrast, Georgia residents may present a wide range of documents to obtain a voter ID card, including a student ID, paycheck stub, Medicare or Medicaid statement, or certified school transcript. The diverse range of documents accepted by Georgia (24 categories in all) means that few voters are likely to incur out-of-pocket costs to obtain a voter ID. And although Indiana law, like SB 14, requires voters to present a government-issued document (such as a birth certificate) to obtain a "free" photo ID, in Indiana the "fee for obtaining a copy of one's birth certificate" is significantly lower than in Texas, ranging from $3 to $12, depending on the county.

The second cost SB 14 will impose on EIC applicants is the burden associated with traveling to a DPS office. The United States submitted unrebutted evidence showing that "81 Texas counties have no [DPS] office, and 34 additional counties have [DPS] offices open two days per week or less." This means that in at least one-third of Texas's counties, would-be voters will have to travel out-of-county merely to apply for an EIC. Georgia and Indiana voters face no such burdens. Indeed, Georgia law requires each county to "provide at least one place in the county at which it shall accept applications for and issue [free] Georgia voter identification cards." Similarly, every Indiana county has a BMV office that is required by law to disperse "free" photo IDs.

Given all this, we have little trouble finding that SB 14 will be far more burdensome than either Indiana's or Georgia's voter ID laws. And because the laws are so different, we place very little stock in Dr. Shaw's comparisons among these three states.

[Additional reaction to Dr. Shaw's findings and information on studies pertaining to ID possession rates have been omitted.]

C.

We pause to summarize the evidentiary findings we have made so far. Contrary to Texas's contentions, nothing in existing social science literature speaks conclusively to the effect of photo ID requirements on voter turnout. Moreover, scant lessons, if any, can be drawn from Indiana and Georgia, largely because SB 14 is more restrictive than the photo ID laws adopted by either of those states. Finally, no party has submitted reliable evidence as to the number of Texas voters who lack photo ID, much less the rate of ID possession among different racial groups.

Given this, we could end our inquiry here. Texas bears the burden of proving that nothing in SB 14 "would lead to a retrogression in the position of racial minorities with respect to their effective exercise of the electoral franchise." Because all of Texas's evidence on retrogression is some combination of invalid, irrelevant, and unreliable, we have little trouble concluding that Texas has failed to carry its burden.

Significantly, however, this case does not hinge merely on Texas's failure to "prove a negative." To the contrary, record evidence suggests that SB 14, if implemented, would in fact have a retrogressive effect on Hispanic and African American voters. This conclusion flows from three basic facts: (1) a substantial subgroup of Texas voters, many of whom are African American or Hispanic, lack photo ID; (2) the burdens associated with obtaining ID will weigh most heavily on the poor; and (3) racial minorities in Texas are disproportionately likely to live in poverty. Accordingly, SB 14 will likely "lead to a retrogression in the position of racial minorities with respect to their effective exercise of the electoral franchise."

[Additional evidence supporting the three aforementioned facts has been omitted.]

IV.

To sum everything up: section 5 prohibits covered states from implementing voting laws that will have a retrogressive effect on racial minorities. Texas, seeking to implement its voter ID law, bears the burden of proof and must therefore show that SB 14 lacks retrogressive effect. But as we have found, everything Texas has submitted as affirmative evidence is unpersuasive, invalid, or both. Moreover, uncontested record evidence conclusively shows that the implicit costs of obtaining SB 14–qualifying ID will fall most heavily on the poor and that a disproportionately high percentage of African Americans and Hispanics in Texas live in poverty. We therefore conclude that SB 14 is likely to lead to "retrogression in the position of racial minorities with respect to their effective exercise of the electoral franchise." Given this, and given that Texas must show that SB 14 lacks both discriminatory purpose and effect, we have no need to examine whether the law was enacted with discriminatory purpose. Accordingly, we shall deny Texas's request for declaratory relief.

In reaching this conclusion, we emphasize the narrowness of this opinion. Specifically, we have decided nothing more than that, in this particular litigation and on this particular record, Texas has failed to demonstrate that its particular voter ID law lacks retrogressive effect. Nothing in this opinion remotely suggests that section 5 bars all covered jurisdictions from implementing photo ID laws. To the contrary, under our reasoning today, such laws might well be precleared if they ensure (1) that all prospective voters can easily obtain free photo ID, and (2) that any underlying documents required to obtain that ID are truly free of charge. Indeed, Georgia's voter ID law was precleared by the Attorney General— and probably for good reason. Unlike SB 14, the Georgia law requires each county to provide free election IDs, and further allows voters to present a wide range of documents to obtain those IDs. The contrast with Senate Bill 14 could hardly be more stark.

Finally, during closing arguments, Texas's counsel complained that they had been shouldered with an "impossible burden" in this litigation. This may well be correct, but Texas's lawyers have only their client to blame. The State of Texas enacted a voter ID law that—at least to our knowledge—is the most stringent in the country. That law will almost certainly have retrogressive effect: it imposes strict, unforgiving burdens on the poor, and racial minorities in Texas are disproportionately likely to live in poverty. And crucially, the Texas legislature defeated several amendments that could have made this a far closer case. . . .

V.

For the foregoing reasons, we deny Texas's request for a declaratory judgment. The parties are hereby ordered to meet and confer as to a schedule to govern the constitutional issue and to file an advisory within 14 days with a proposed schedule. A separate order has been filed on this date.

SOURCE: U.S. District Court for the District of Columbia. *State of Texas v. Holder.* Civil Action No. 12-cv-128. August 30, 2012. https://ecf.dcd.uscourts.gov/cgi-bin/show_public_doc?2012cv0128-340.

OTHER HISTORIC DOCUMENTS OF INTEREST

FROM PREVIOUS *HISTORIC DOCUMENTS*

September

Census Bureau Reports on Poverty in the United States

SEPTEMBER 12 AND NOVEMBER 14, 2012

The 2011 U.S. poverty rate did not record a statistically significant change over the 2010 rate, according to a U.S. Census Bureau report released on September 12, 2012, marking the first time the rate had not increased in four years. The official poverty rate, or the percentage of Americans falling below the poverty line, was 15 percent in 2011, or 46.2 million Americans. Although no significant year-over-year change was recorded, the Census Bureau report did show the growing gap between the rich and poor and the significant financial impact experienced mainly by those in the middle class. These data came at a particularly poignant moment in the 2012 presidential campaign as President Barack Obama and Republican contender Mitt Romney argued over who could best bolster the middle class and strengthen the overall economy.

No Significant Poverty Level Change

Prior to the Census Bureau's release of its annual *Income, Poverty, and Health Insurance Coverage in the United States* report, analysts had been anticipating a rise in the number of those considered impoverished given the continuing high rate of unemployment. The Brookings Institution predicted a rise from 15.1 percent in 2010 to 15.5 percent in 2011, which would have put an additional 1.5 million Americans below the poverty line ($23,021 for a family of four in 2011). But when the official rate was released on September 12, 2012, it showed a statistically insignificant decrease from 15.1 percent to 15.0 percent, meaning one in six Americans lived in poverty in 2011. Those considered extremely poor, earning less than half of the official poverty threshold, also remained stable at 6.6 percent.

The Census Bureau attributed the stability in the rate to a greater number of people moving from part-time to full-time employment. Working-age men saw an increase of full-time employed of 1.7 million from 2010 to 2011, while women's part- to full-employment figure increased around half a million. Those making up the lowest-income group saw full-time employment increase 17.3 percent.

Across the country, decreases in the poverty rate were seen in a number of sectors. Hispanics experienced a decrease from 26.5 percent in 2010 to 25.3 percent, and were the only non-white racial group to register a decrease. Nearly 750,000 fewer people residing in U.S. suburbs were living below the poverty line in 2011 as compared to 2010, largely due to an increase of 1.5 million suburbanites finding full-time employment.

The Obama administration was able to chalk up a public relations win for its Affordable Care Act—the 2011 Census report showed a decline in the number of those without health insurance, bolstered by a 2.2 percent drop in the number of those aged nineteen to twenty-five without insurance. "Obamacare," as it has been dubbed, included a provision allowing young people to remain on their parents' health insurance until age twenty-six. Overall, from 2010 to 2011, the number of uninsured Americans fell from 16.3 percent to 15.7 percent.

The report was not entirely positive, however. While the poverty level remained steady, median household income fell to $50,054, a decrease in real terms of 1.5 percent. Since the start of the Great Recession in 2007, median income has fallen 8.1 percent.

SUPPLEMENTAL REPORT PAINTS BLEAKER PICTURE

Since its inception, the annual Census Bureau report has faced criticism for not capturing a complete picture of the state of poverty in the United States. The official report does not consider living expenses, such as medical, child care, and commuting, in its calculations; nor does it consider a variety of government support systems, such as food stamps and tax credits. These expenses and supports could have a significant impact on the number of Americans deemed to be in poverty. In fact, the calculations that go into the official report set the poverty threshold at a number devised in the 1960s that calculated the amount a family of three would need to bring in to spend approximately one-third of that amount on food; today, Americans spend closer to one-seventh on food. Since that time, the government has made adjustments only for inflation in its calculations but still does not include other real costs such as health insurance, job expenses like transportation, and housing.

In November, the Census Bureau released its second annual supplemental poverty estimate, a report meant to take into account some living expenses and government benefits and present a more detailed look at poverty in America. That report put the poverty rate at 16.1 percent overall, not a statistically significant change from 2010. And much the same as the 2010 report, the supplemental rate was lower for children and African Americans than in the official report. But for those aged sixty-five and older, the poverty rate is actually much higher at 15.1 percent in the supplemental versus 8.7 percent in the official measure. A main reason for this is that the supplemental measure takes into account medical expenses, considered to be a leading contributor to poverty across the board. State-wise, California was the most impoverished state, followed by the District of Columbia, Arizona, Florida, and Georgia. California's distinction as the most impoverished state is largely caused by the difficulty residents face in qualifying for food stamps and other government benefits and its percentage of Hispanic residents, who generally have a higher rate of poverty.

Prior to the release of the supplemental measure, a study by researchers at the University of Chicago and the University of Notre Dame found that the most accurate depiction of poverty in the United States could be derived from a measure based on consumption. "Few economic indicators are more closely watched or more important for policy than the official poverty rate," the authors wrote in the summer edition of the *Journal of Economic Prospectives*. And while they recognized the importance of including after-tax income and noncash benefits in the supplemental measure, they found that this could actually be counterproductive to an accurate depiction of poverty. "The new poverty measure that many people thought was going to be an improvement, in terms of figuring out who we should call 'poor' doesn't seem to be an improvement," said report coauthor Bruce Meyer, the McCormick Foundation Professor at the University of Chicago. "It doesn't seem to capture people who are worse off in many dimensions than the official measure. Our consumption measure seems to do better in terms of capturing people who have many different types of disadvantage." The measure promoted by Meyer and his coauthor, James Sullivan of the University of Notre Dame, would take into account factors such as usage of any money in savings, ownership of goods, and access to credit, as well as any participation in government antipoverty programs.

MIDDLE CLASS HARD HIT

In 2011, the Gini index, a measure of inequality used by the Census Bureau, marked its first annual increase since 1993, rising 1.6 percent since 2010. Although the measure had been increasing for some time, it generally changes so slowly that it is difficult to discern a significant year-over-year increase. The 2010 to 2011 change was largely due to declining income in the middle class while income rose for top earners. In 2011, those in the middle 60 percent saw their income fall between 1.6 percent and 1.9 percent, while those in the top one percent experienced 6 percent income growth. Those in the lowest income brackets did not experience a significant change.

"The big story is the squeeze in the middle- and lower-middle classes," said Tim Smeeding, the director of the Institute for Research on Poverty at the University of Wisconsin–Madison. "They got whacked," he continued, noting that the second and third quintile of Americans have only 23.8 percent of the nation's total income. "You're really struck by the unevenness of the recovery," said Lawrence Katz, a Harvard University economics professor. "The top end took a whack in the recession, but they've gotten back on their feet. Everyone else is still down for the count."

BEST POLICIES FOR THE MIDDLE CLASS?

A central argument in the 2012 presidential campaign revolved around how to safeguard the middle class from further economic hardship in an effort to rebuild the economy. Romney used the Census Bureau report as evidence that Obama's economic policies had failed and pointed to what he considered the president's attempts to undo the welfare-to-work system, painting him the "entitlement president." Republicans in the House and Senate, in an effort to reduce the nation's fiscal burden, have proposed limiting entitlement and safety net programs including a Medicaid overhaul that could turn the program into a block grant, placing an increasing amount of financial burden on states.

During the Democratic National Convention in August, former president Bill Clinton spoke at length about the work Democrats have done to help both the poor and the middle class. Clinton took on Republican critics who said the president was trying to allow low-income Americans to live off government welfare programs indefinitely, rather than helping them move successfully from public assistance to employment. He spoke specifically about waivers that the Obama administration had given a handful of states to allow them to change some work requirements, such as allowing job training to qualify a person for continued public assistance. However, Clinton said, these waivers required the states to make a greater effort to help welfare recipients find work. Clinton was also critical of Republican proposals to cut money from school loan programs and early childhood education. These programs, he said, "empower middle-class families and help poor kids."

The Obama administration used the Census Bureau reports and Gini index to continue to put pressure on Congress to pass job legislation and continue the payroll tax cut that impacts 98 percent of Americans. The growing inequality "underscores the fact [that] we must enact policies that help rebuild our economy not from the top down, but from the middle out," said acting U.S. Commerce Secretary Rebecca Blank. There are some indications that 2012 might prove better for the middle class than 2011. Initial job growth, unemployment, and wage data from 2012 indicate that median income is growing. A study of the Census Bureau's Current Population Survey by Sentier Research showed an increase of $1,176 in median household income during the twelve months from July 2011 to July 2012.

—Heather Kerrigan

Following are excerpts from the U.S. Census Bureau report on the poverty level in the United States, released on September 12, 2012; and a press release detailing the findings of a supplemental poverty report released by the U.S. Census Bureau on November 14, 2012.

Census Bureau Report on Poverty in the United States

September 12, 2012

[All portions of the report not corresponding to poverty have been omitted.]

[Tables, graphs, and footnotes, and references to them, have been omitted.]

POVERTY IN THE UNITED STATES

Highlights

- In 2011, the official poverty rate was 15.0 percent. There were 46.2 million people in poverty.
- After 3 consecutive years of increases, neither the official poverty rate nor the number[s] of people in poverty were statistically different from the 2010 estimates.
- The 2011 poverty rates for most demographic groups examined were not statistically different from their 2010 rates. Poverty rates were lower in 2011 than in 2010 for six groups: Hispanics, males, the foreign-born, noncitizens, people living in the South, and people living inside metropolitan statistical areas but outside principal cities. Poverty rates went up between 2010 and 2011 for naturalized citizens.
- For most groups, the number of people in poverty either decreased or did not show a statistically significant change. The number of people in poverty decreased for noncitizens, people living in the South, and people living inside metropolitan statistical areas but outside principal cities between 2010 and 2011. The number of naturalized citizens in poverty increased.
- The poverty rate in 2011 for children under age 18 was 21.9 percent. The poverty rate for people aged 18 to 64 was 13.7 percent, while the rate for people aged 65 and older was 8.7 percent. None of the rates for these age groups were statistically different from their 2010 estimates.

Race and Hispanic Origin

The poverty rate for non-Hispanic Whites was 9.8 percent in 2011, lower than the poverty rates for other racial groups. Non-Hispanic Whites accounted for 63.2 percent of the total population but 41.5 percent of the people in poverty. For non-Hispanic Whites, neither the poverty rate nor the number of people in poverty experienced a statistically significant change between 2010 and 2011.

For Blacks, the 2011 poverty rate was 27.6 percent, which represents 10.9 million people in poverty. Neither estimate was statistically different from its 2010 estimate. For Asians, the 2011 poverty rate was 12.3 percent, which represents 2.0 million people in poverty, not statistically different from the 2010 estimates. Among Hispanics, the poverty rate declined from 26.5 percent in 2010 to 25.3 percent in 2011. The number of Hispanics in poverty in 2011 was 13.2 million, not statistically different from the 2010 estimate.

Sex

In 2011, 13.6 percent of males and 16.3 percent of females were in poverty. Between 2010 and 2011, the male poverty rate decreased from 14.0 percent to 13.6 percent. The female poverty rate did not show a statistically significant change.

Gender differences in poverty rates were more pronounced for the older age group. The poverty rate for women aged 65 and older was 10.7 percent, while the poverty rate for men aged 65 and older was 6.2 percent. The poverty rate for women aged 18 to 64 was 15.5 percent, while the poverty rate for men aged 18 to 64 was 11.8 percent. For children under 18, the poverty rates for girls (22.2 percent) and boys (21.6 percent) were not statistically different from each other.

Age

In 2011, 13.7 percent of people aged 18 to 64 (26.5 million) were in poverty compared with 8.7 percent of people aged 65 and older (3.6 million) and 21.9 percent of children under 18 (16.1 million). None of these age groups experienced a statistically significant change in the number or rates of people in poverty between 2010 and 2011.

Related children are people under age 18 related to the householder by birth, marriage, or adoption who are not themselves householders or spouses of householders. The poverty rate and the number in poverty for related children under age 18 were 21.4 percent and 15.5 million in 2011, not statistically different from the 2010 estimates. For related children in families with a female householder, 47.6 percent were in poverty, compared with 10.9 percent of related children in married-couple families.

The poverty rate and the number in poverty for related children under age 6 were 24.5 percent and 5.8 million in 2011, not statistically different from the 2010 estimate. About 1 in 4 of these children were in poverty in 2011. More than half (57.2 percent) of related children under age 6 in families with a female householder were in poverty. This was more than four and a half times the rate of their counterparts in married-couple families (12.1 percent).

Nativity

The 2011 estimates of the poverty rate and the number in poverty for the native-born population were 14.4 percent and 38.7 million, not statistically different from the

2010 estimates. Among the foreign-born population, the poverty rate decreased from 19.9 percent in 2010 to 19.0 percent in 2011. About 7.6 million foreign-born people lived in poverty in 2011, not statistically different from the 2010 estimate.

Within the foreign-born population, 44.9 percent were naturalized U.S. citizens. For naturalized U.S. citizens, the 2011 poverty rate rose from 11.3 percent in 2010 to 12.5 percent in 2011, and the number of naturalized citizens in poverty increased from 2.0 million to 2.2 million. On the other hand, the poverty rate for those who were not U.S. citizens decreased from 26.8 percent in 2010 to 24.3 percent in 2011, and the number of noncitizens in poverty fell from 5.9 million to 5.4 million.

Region

The South was the only region to show changes in both the poverty rate and the number in poverty between 2010 and 2011. The poverty rate fell from 16.8 percent to 16.0 percent, while the number in poverty fell from 19.1 million to 18.4 million. In 2011, the poverty rates and the number in poverty for the Northeast (13.1 percent and 7.2 million), the Midwest (14.0 percent and 9.2 million), and the West (15.8 percent and 11.4 million) were not statistically different from the 2010 estimates.

Residence

Inside metropolitan statistical areas, the poverty rate and the number of people in poverty were 14.6 percent and 38.2 million in 2011, not statistically different from 2010. Among those living outside metropolitan areas, the poverty rate and the number in poverty were 17.0 percent and 8.0 million in 2011, not statistically different from 2010.

Between 2010 and 2011, for those living inside metropolitan areas but not in principal cities, both the poverty rate and the number in poverty decreased from 11.9 percent and 18.9 million to 11.3 percent and 18.2 million. The 2011 poverty rate and the number of people in poverty for people in principal cities were 20.0 percent and 20.0 million, not statistically different from 2010.

Within metropolitan areas, people in poverty were more likely to live in principal cities in 2011. While 38.4 percent of all people living in metropolitan areas lived in principal cities, 52.4 percent of poor people in metropolitan areas lived in principal cities.

Work Experience

In 2011, 7.2 percent of workers aged 18 to 64 were in poverty. The poverty rate for those who worked full time, year round was 2.8 percent, while the poverty rate for those working less than full time, year round was 16.3 percent. None of these rates were statistically different from the 2010 poverty rates.

Among those who did not work at least 1 week last year, the poverty rate and the number in poverty were 32.9 percent and 16.1 million in 2011, not statistically different from the 2010 estimates. Those who did not work in 2011 represented 61.0 percent of people aged 18 to 64 in poverty, compared with 25.4 percent of all people aged 18 to 64.

Disability Status

In 2011, for people aged 18 to 64 with a disability, the poverty rate and number in poverty were 28.8 percent and 4.3 million. For people aged 18 to 64 without a disability, the poverty rate and number in poverty were 12.5 percent and 22.1 million. None of these estimates were statistically different from the 2010 estimates. Among people aged 18 to 64, those with a disability represented 16.3 percent of people in poverty, compared with 7.7 percent of all people in this age group.

Families

In 2011, the poverty rate and the number of families in poverty were 11.8 percent and 9.5 million, both not statistically different from the 2010 estimates.

In 2011, 6.2 percent of married-couple families, 31.2 percent of families with a female householder, and 16.1 percent of families with a male householder lived in poverty. Neither the poverty rates nor the estimates of the number of families in poverty for these three family types showed any statistically significant change between 2010 and 2011.

Depth of Poverty

Categorizing a person as "in poverty" or "not in poverty" is one way to describe his or her economic situation. The income-to-poverty ratio and the income deficit or surplus describe additional aspects of economic well-being. While the poverty rate shows the proportion of people with income below the appropriate poverty threshold, the income-to-poverty ratio gauges the depth of poverty and shows how close a family's income is to its poverty threshold. The income-to-poverty ratio is reported as a percentage that compares a family's or an unrelated person's income with the appropriate poverty threshold. For example, a family with an income-to-poverty ratio of 110 percent has income that is 10 percent above its poverty threshold.

The income deficit or surplus shows how many dollars a family's or an unrelated person's income is below (or above) their poverty threshold. For those with an income deficit, the measure is an estimate of the dollar amount necessary to raise a family's or a person's income to their poverty threshold.

Ratio of Income to Poverty

. . . In 2011, 20.4 million people had income below one-half of their poverty threshold. They represented 6.6 percent of all people and 44.0 percent of those in poverty. One in 5 people (19.8 percent) had income below 125 percent of their threshold, 1 in 4 people (24.8 percent) had income below 150 percent of their poverty threshold, while approximately 1 in 3 (34.4 percent) had income below 200 percent of their threshold.

Of the 20.4 million people with income below one-half of their poverty threshold, 7.3 million were children under age 18, 12.2 million were aged 18 to 64, and 940,000 were aged 65 years and older. The percentage of people aged 65 and older with income below 50 percent of their poverty threshold was 2.3 percent, less than one-half the percentage of the total population at this poverty level (6.6 percent).

The demographic makeup of the population differs at varying degrees of poverty. In 2011, children represented 23.9 percent of the overall population; 35.6 percent of the people with income below 50 percent of their poverty threshold; 27.7 percent of the people with income between 100 percent and 200 percent of their poverty threshold; and 20.3 percent of the people with income above 200 percent of their poverty threshold. By comparison, people aged 65 and older represented 13.5 percent of the overall population; 4.6 percent of the people with income below 50 percent of their poverty threshold; 17.3 percent of the people with income between 100 percent and 200 percent of their poverty threshold; and 13.6 of the people with income above 200 percent of their poverty threshold.

Income Deficit

The income deficit for families in poverty (the difference in dollars between a family's income and its poverty threshold) averaged $9,576 in 2011, which was not statistically different from the inflation-adjusted 2010 estimate. The average income deficit was larger for families with a female householder ($10,317) than for married-couple families ($8,887).

The average income deficit per capita for families with a female householder ($3,069) was higher than for married-couple families ($2,334). The income deficit per capita is computed by dividing the average deficit by the average number of people in that type of family. Since families with a female householder were smaller on average than married-couple families, the larger per capita deficit for female-householder families reflects their smaller average family size as well as their lower average family income.

For unrelated individuals in poverty, the average income deficit was $6,401 in 2011. The $6,169 deficit for women was lower than the $6,697 deficit for men.

Shared Households

While poverty estimates are based on income in the previous calendar year, estimates of shared households reflect household composition at the time of the survey, which is conducted during the months of February, March, and April of each year. The number and percentage of shared households and additional adults was higher in 2012 than in 2007, prior to the recession. In 2007, there were 19.7 million shared households, representing 17.0 percent of all households; by 2012, there were 22.3 million shared households, representing 18.4 percent of all households. The number of adults in shared households grew from 61.7 million (27.7 percent) in 2007 to 69.5 million (29.6 percent) in 2012.

There was no change in household sharing between 2011 and 2012. Although the total number of households increased by 1.2 million (2.5 percent), the changes in the number and percentage of total households that were shared were not statistically significant.

In 2012, an estimated 9.7 million adults aged 25 to 34 (23.6 percent) were additional adults in someone else's household. Between 2011 and 2012, the changes in the number and percentage of additional adults in this age group residing in someone else's household were not statistically significant. The number and percent of young adults in the same age group residing with their parents did not change between 2011 and 2012.

It is difficult to assess the precise impact of household sharing on overall poverty rates. In 2012, adults aged 25 to 34 living with their parents had an official poverty rate of 9.0 percent (when the entire family's income was compared with the threshold which includes the young adult as a member of the family). However, if poverty status were determined using only the additional adult's own income, 43.7 percent of those aged 25 to 34 would have been below the poverty level for a single person under age 65 ($11,702). . . .

SOURCE: U.S. Census Bureau. "Income, Poverty, and Health Insurance Coverage in the United States: 2011." September 12, 2012. http://www.census.gov/prod/2012pubs/p60-243.pdf.

Census Bureau Releases Supplemental Poverty Report

DOCUMENT

November 14, 2012

The Census Bureau, with support from the Bureau of Labor Statistics, today released its second annual report, *The Research Supplemental Poverty Measure: 2011,* describing research on a new supplemental poverty measure. This measure extends information provided by the official poverty measure, released Sept. 12, by explicitly including benefits from many of the government programs designed to assist low-income families and individuals.

Today's report compares 2011 supplemental poverty estimates to 2011 official poverty estimates for numerous demographic groups at the national level. In addition, for the first time, the report presents supplemental poverty estimates for states, using three-year averages. At the national level, the report also compares 2010 supplemental poverty estimates with 2011 estimates and examines the effect of excluding individual resource or expenditure elements.

According to the report, the supplemental poverty measure rate was 16.1 percent last year, which was higher than the official measure of 15.0 percent. Neither the supplemental measure nor the official poverty rate was significantly different from the corresponding rate in 2010.

There has been a continuing debate about the best approach to measure income and poverty in the United States since the publication of the first official U.S. poverty estimates in 1964. In 2009, an interagency group asked the Census Bureau, in cooperation with the Bureau of Labor Statistics, to develop a new, supplemental measure to allow for an improved understanding of the economic well-being of American families and how federal policies affect those living in poverty.

"There are several important differences between the official and supplemental poverty measures," said Kathleen Short, a U.S. Census Bureau economist and the report's author. "For instance, the supplemental measure uses new poverty thresholds that represent a dollar amount spent on a basic set of goods adjusted to reflect geographic differences in housing costs. The official poverty thresholds are the same no matter where you live."

There are two other major differences as well. The official measure includes only pretax money income. Income for the supplemental measure adds the value of in-kind benefits such as the Supplemental Nutrition Assistance Program, school lunches, housing assistance and refundable tax credits like the earned income tax credit. Additionally, supplemental poverty measure resources deduct from income necessary expenses for critical goods and services such as taxes, child care and other work-related expenses, and contributions toward the cost of medical care and health insurance premiums or medical out-of-pocket costs.

ESTIMATES FOR STATES

Using three-year averages (2009–2011), the U.S. poverty rate was 15.8 percent using the supplemental poverty measure and 15.0 percent using the official measure. However, the picture in individual states varied considerably.

There are 15 states or equivalents for which the supplemental rates were higher than the official statewide poverty rates: California, Colorado, Connecticut, Delaware, the District of Columbia, Florida, Hawaii, Illinois, Maryland, Massachusetts, Nevada, New Hampshire, New Jersey, New York and Virginia.

For another 26 states, supplemental rates were lower than the official statewide poverty rates: Alabama, Arkansas, Idaho, Indiana, Iowa, Kansas, Kentucky, Louisiana, Maine, Michigan, Mississippi, Missouri, Montana, New Mexico, North Carolina, North Dakota, Ohio, Oklahoma, South Carolina, South Dakota, Tennessee, Texas, Vermont, West Virginia, Wisconsin and Wyoming. Rates in the remaining 10 states were not statistically different using the two measures.

Comparing Poverty Rates for Different Demographic Groups

Unlike the current official poverty measure, the supplemental poverty measure can show the effects of tax and transfer policies on various subgroups. According to the report:

- Including in-kind benefits results in lower poverty rates for some groups. For instance, the supplemental poverty rate was lower for children than the official rate: 18.1 percent compared with 22.3 percent.
- Subtracting necessary expenses from income results in higher poverty rates for other groups. The supplemental poverty rate for those 65 and older was 15.1 percent compared with only 8.7 percent using the official measure. Medical out-of-pocket expenses were an important element for this group.
- Even though supplemental poverty rates were lower for children and higher for those 65 and older than under the official measure, the rates for children were still higher than the rates for 18- to 64-year-olds and people 65 and older. The 15.5 percent supplemental rates for 18- to 64-year-olds was not statistically different from the 15.1 percent rate for people 65 and older.
- Supplemental poverty rates were higher than the official measure for all race groups and for Hispanics, with one exception: blacks, who had a supplemental poverty rate of 25.7 percent and an official rate of 27.8 percent.
- Primarily because of geographically adjusted poverty thresholds, supplemental poverty rates differed by region. Supplemental poverty rates were higher than official rates for the Northeast and West, lower in the Midwest and not statistically different from the official measure in the South. These results reflect differences in housing costs.

The measures presented in this report used the 2012 Current Population Survey Annual Social and Economic Supplement with income information that referred to calendar year 2011 to estimate supplemental poverty measure resources.

Source: U.S. Census Bureau. "Census Bureau Releases 2011 New Supplemental Poverty Measure Research Findings." November 14, 2012. http://www.census.gov/newsroom/releases/archives/poverty/cb12-215.html.

OTHER HISTORIC DOCUMENTS OF INTEREST

FROM THIS VOLUME

FROM PREVIOUS *HISTORIC DOCUMENTS*

State Department Responds to Benghazi Consulate Attack

SEPTEMBER 12 AND DECEMBER 18, 2012

On the eleventh anniversary of the September 11, 2001, terrorist attacks on the United States, Islamic militants attacked the U.S. consulate compound in Benghazi, Libya, killing the ambassador and three other personnel. The attack marked the first time an American ambassador had been killed since 1979 and set off a firestorm of questions and allegations about who exactly was responsible, whether they had ties to al Qaeda, and whether the State Department had ignored security warnings. U.S. government agencies struggled in the aftermath to work with the weak transitional Libyan government to investigate the attack and bring those responsible to justice. In December, a scathing report was released criticizing the State Department for failing to offer more security to the ambassador and other Americans working at the consulate.

U.S. Ambassador to Libya Killed in Attack

Details of the lead-up to the attack on the U.S. Consulate in Benghazi were slowly pieced together in the weeks and months after the incident. What is known is that on the evening of September 11, 2012, U.S. Ambassador to Libya Chris Stevens met with a Turkish diplomat. When their meeting concluded, Stevens walked him to the gate of the compound at approximately 8:30 p.m. At that time, there were no observed gatherings or demonstrations. However, approximately one hour later, American security officials tasked with protecting the nearby consulate saw a group of armed men enter the compound as gunfire and explosions were heard. The nearby base from which the local Libyan militia protected the compound was set on fire, as was the consulate itself. In the aftermath of the attack, Stevens, who had suffered severe smoke inhalation, was pulled from the remains of the consulate by Libyan civilians and rushed to a Benghazi hospital, where doctors tried unsuccessfully to resuscitate him. Three other Americans—Foreign Service officer Sean Smith and two security guards, Tyrone Woods and Glen Doherty—were also killed in the attack. "We condemn this vicious and violent attack that took their lives, which they had committed to helping the Libyan people reach for a better future," remarked Secretary of State Hillary Rodham Clinton.

Responsibility

Initially, American officials linked the deadly attack with protests occurring in mid-September in other Middle Eastern nations in response to a trailer released on YouTube for a movie titled *Innocence of Muslims*. The film, produced by a Coptic Christian filmmaker in California, who claimed he had been influenced by radical anti-Islam leaders, portrayed the Prophet Muhammad in a derogatory fashion, painting him as a womanizer who enjoyed killing people. A fourteen-minute trailer of the video drew strong response from the Muslim world and resulted in anti-American protests in nations including Afghanistan, Azerbaijan, Egypt, the Gaza Strip, Indonesia, Iran, Iraq, Lebanon, Libya, Nigeria, Pakistan, Sudan, Tunisia, and Yemen. Secretary of State Clinton called the film "disgusting and reprehensible." Egypt's new leader, Mohamed Morsi, said he did not believe the U.S. government should be blamed for the film, but he did urge the government to stop those who attack religion.

On September 15, al Qaeda's branch in Yemen praised the embassy attack and claimed that it was not a response to *Innocence of Muslims* but rather revenge for the June killing of Sheikh Abu Yahya al Libi, the number two leader of the terrorist organization. That same day, the Libyan government determined that the attack had been preplanned and was not a spontaneous outburst of violence in response to the trailer. It was initially believed that al Qaeda was behind the attack; however, it was later discovered that a radical Islamic group, Ansar al Sharia, was responsible and that any link to al Qaeda was minimal.

The attack in Libya came less than two months before the 2012 presidential election, and it quickly became a point of contention between President Barack Obama and his Republican challenger, former Massachusetts governor Mitt Romney. The partisan bickering between the two candidates over the handling of security abroad came to a head on October 16, when the pair met for the second of three presidential debates. Romney attacked Obama for failing to immediately call the attack an act of terror. In an exchange between the two, Obama held firm that he labeled the attack an act of terror on September 12 in a statement from the Rose Garden. Romney contended, "I want to make sure we get that for the record because it took the president fourteen days before he called the attack in Benghazi an act of terror." The debate's moderator, Candy Crowley, corrected the governor, noting that Obama had in fact used the word *terror* in his speech the day after the attack. While the reference to terror did exist, it was indirect. "No acts of terror will ever shake the resolve of this great nation," Obama said on September 12. It was not until one week later, on September 19, that the administration began using the term regularly to describe the attacks. This followed testimony before a Senate hearing given by Matthew Olsen, director of the National Counterterrorism Center, who said, "Yes, they were killed in the course of a terrorist attack on our embassy." The Obama administration said the change in terms reflected constantly updating information about the situation in Libya.

WEAK LIBYAN GOVERNMENT SLOWS INVESTIGATION PROGRESS

After the September 11 attack, President Obama vowed that those responsible would be brought to justice. And on September 16, Libya's transitional government announced that it had arrested fifty suspects linked to the attack. However, the government failed to charge any of the detained, and they were eventually all released. Months after the attack, the Federal Bureau of Investigation (FBI), the agency leading the charge to detain and try those responsible, still had little evidence of who was involved. And although it had initially promised assistance, Libya's weak government did little to take action against the Islamic extremists thought to be involved, mainly because they were believed to belong to one of the powerful militias that control much of the security in the country.

Frustrated, the FBI issued a global appeal in November 2012 asking for any information that might lead to the capture of those responsible. Libyan residents, including those who witnessed the attack, reported sending in multiple tips, and the attack itself was caught on surveillance video. In addition, consulate guards from both Libya and the

United States who survived the attack saw those responsible and could identify at least some of those involved. One key participant is assumed to be Ahmed Abu Khattala, who remains at large. Information about any others suspected to be involved with the attack has not been released by the Libyan government.

As of January 2013, only one person thought to be involved in the attack, Ali Harzi, was actually jailed in relation to the attack. However, he was released from a jail in Tunisia, where he was being held after his lawyer argued that there was no evidence against him.

SCATHING REPORT PLACES BLAME

Following the attack in Benghazi, the State Department formed an independent commission to look into the cause of the attack and any failings on the part of the State Department. The report was released on December 18, 2012, and sharply criticized the State Department for ignoring warnings from Ambassador Stevens on the need for additional security for Americans serving in Libya.

According to the report, it was clear as the investigation began that warnings had been issued to the State Department from Americans in Libya for months preceding the attack, regarding the deteriorating security situation. Intelligence reports sent to the Obama administration before the attacks indicated that training camps had been set up around Libya by Ansar al Sharia for Islamic extremists and that the training mimicked the tactics used by al Qaeda. In August, Ambassador Stevens sent an e-mail to supervisors in Washington, D.C., saying that since the fall of Col. Muammar el-Qaddafi's government in October 2011, the nation was experiencing "a security vacuum" that was hitting Benghazi particularly hard. One week before the attack, officials at the consulate warned of a Libyan declaration of a "state of maximum alert."

The report also cited the mishandled decision to replace trained U.S. military or other security personnel to protect the compound with members of local Libyan militias. Prior to the fall of Qaddafi's government, the United States did not have an official presence in Benghazi. In 2012, the United States sent a small security force to protect a new consulate it intended to leave open for only one year. As additional security, the United States relied largely on Libyan personnel, fearful that putting American troops in Libya would be politically dangerous for relations between the two governments. At times, there were only two security personnel protecting the compound and the ambassador.

In response to the report, three State Department officials were removed from their positions while another resigned. During a Senate hearing following the release of the report, Deputy Secretary of State William Burns admitted that there may have been errors in how the department responded to reports of security failings in Libya and that the response, or lack thereof, was "unacceptable." Burns was joined in his testimony by Thomas Nides, also a deputy secretary of state, who said that the department would accept all of the twenty-nine recommendations made by the commission, including increasing security personnel in high-risk locations and focusing more on security threats abroad, and had in fact already begun to implement some changes to fix the "serious, systemic problems" that the report uncovered.

Senator John Kerry, D-Mass., who had recently been nominated to replace Clinton as secretary of state, noted during the hearing that the State Department could not properly operate if Congress continued to ignore requests for funding for diplomatic security. Congress, he said, "also bears some responsibility." The commission report on Benghazi said $2.2 billion per year would be needed to provide adequate security to State Department missions abroad.

In January 2013, Secretary Clinton delivered an emotional testimony during a Senate hearing on the attacks. Republicans on the panel sharply criticized the State Department for failing to respond to reports from American personnel of increased threats in Libya. Senators also accused the Obama administration of misleading the public as to what the reason behind the attack was. "With all due respect, the fact is that we had four dead Americans," Clinton said. "Was it because of a protest or was it because of guys out for a walk one night decided they'd go kill some Americans? What difference, at this point, does it make?"

President Obama expressed his own discontent with the findings of the commission, saying that the "huge problems" reflected "sloppiness" in the way the State Department protects embassies and consulates abroad.

POTENTIAL NEXT STEPS

Other than expressing a desire to bring those involved in the attack to justice, by the end of 2012, the Obama administration had few concrete plans to respond to the Benghazi attacks, which drew strong criticism from Republicans in Congress. The Joint Special Operations Command, a top-secret unit, has reportedly been putting together a list of suspects in cooperation with the Central Intelligence Agency (CIA), including detailed information on their whereabouts that could be used for possible action if Obama calls for it. The administration will have to tread carefully, however, as continuing instability in Libya and its weak national government might mean that a unilateral attack on any targets by the United States would foster anti-American sentiment in one of the few Middle Eastern nations that has recently had a relatively positive relationship with Washington.

—Heather Kerrigan

Following is the text of a statement delivered by Secretary of State Hillary Rodham Clinton on September 12, 2012, responding to the death of American personnel at the U.S. Consulate in Benghazi; and excerpts from the State Department Accountability Review Board report on the Benghazi Consulate attack, released on December 18, 2012.

Secretary of State Clinton on Benghazi Attack

DOCUMENT

September 12, 2012

It is with profound sadness that I share the news of the death of four American personnel in Benghazi, Libya yesterday. Among them were United States Ambassador to Libya Chris Stevens and Foreign Service Information Management Officer, Sean Smith. We are still making next of kin notifications for the other two individuals. Our hearts go out to all their families and colleagues.

A 21 year veteran of the Foreign Service, Ambassador Stevens died last night from injuries he sustained in the attack on our office in Benghazi.

I had the privilege of swearing in Chris for his post in Libya only a few months ago. He spoke eloquently about his passion for service, for diplomacy and for the Libyan people. This assignment was only the latest in his more than two decades of dedication to advancing closer ties with the people of the Middle East and North Africa which began as a Peace Corps Volunteer in Morocco. As the conflict in Libya unfolded, Chris was one of the first Americans on the ground in Benghazi. He risked his own life to lend the Libyan people a helping hand to build the foundation for a new, free nation. He spent every day since helping to finish the work that he started. Chris was committed to advancing America's values and interests, even when that meant putting himself in danger.

Sean Smith was a husband and a father of two, who joined the Department ten years ago. Like Chris, Sean was one of our best. Prior to arriving in Benghazi, he served in Baghdad, Pretoria, Montreal, and most recently The Hague.

All the Americans we lost in yesterday's attacks made the ultimate sacrifice. We condemn this vicious and violent attack that took their lives, which they had committed to helping the Libyan people reach for a better future.

America's diplomats and development experts stand on the front lines every day for our country. We are honored by the service of each and every one of them.

SOURCE: U.S. Department of State. "Statement on the Death of American Personnel in Benghazi, Libya." September 12, 2012. http://www.state.gov/secretary/rm/2012/09/197630.htm.

Accountability Review Board Report on Benghazi Consulate Attack

December 18, 2012

[The introduction, outlining the mission of the Accountability Review Board, has been omitted.]

[All footnotes have been omitted.]

EXECUTIVE OVERVIEW

A series of terrorist attacks in Benghazi, Libya, on September 11–12, 2012, resulted in the deaths of four U.S. government personnel, Ambassador Chris Stevens, Sean Smith, Tyrone Woods, and Glen Doherty; seriously wounded two other U.S. personnel and injured three Libyan contract guards; and resulted in the destruction and abandonment of the U.S. Special Mission compound and Annex.

FINDINGS

In examining the circumstances of these attacks, the Accountability Review Board for Benghazi determined that:

1. The attacks were security related, involving arson, small arms and machine gun fire, and the use of RPGs, grenades, and mortars against U.S. personnel at two separate facilities—the SMC and the Annex—and en route between them. Responsibility for the tragic loss of life, injuries, and damage to U.S. facilities and property

rests solely and completely with the terrorists who perpetrated the attacks. The Board concluded that there was no protest prior to the attacks, which were unanticipated in their scale and intensity.

2. Systemic failures and leadership and management deficiencies at senior levels within two bureaus of the State Department (the "Department") resulted in a Special Mission security posture that was inadequate for Benghazi and grossly inadequate to deal with the attack that took place.

Security in Benghazi was not recognized and implemented as a "shared responsibility" by the bureaus in Washington charged with supporting the post, resulting in stove-piped discussions and decisions on policy and security. That said, Embassy Tripoli did not demonstrate strong and sustained advocacy with Washington for increased security for Special Mission Benghazi.

The short-term, transitory nature of Special Mission Benghazi's staffing, with talented and committed, but relatively inexperienced, American personnel often on temporary assignments of 40 days or less, resulted in diminished institutional knowledge, continuity, and mission capacity.

Overall, the number of Bureau of Diplomatic Security (DS) security staff in Benghazi on the day of the attack and in the months and weeks leading up to it was inadequate, despite repeated requests from Special Mission Benghazi and Embassy Tripoli for additional staffing. Board members found a pervasive realization among personnel who served in Benghazi that the Special Mission was not a high priority for Washington when it came to security-related requests, especially those relating to staffing.

The insufficient Special Mission security platform was at variance with the appropriate Overseas Security Policy Board (OSPB) standards with respect to perimeter and interior security. Benghazi was also severely under-resourced with regard to certain needed security equipment, although DS funded and installed in 2012 a number of physical security upgrades. These included heightening the outer perimeter wall, safety grills on safe area egress windows, concrete jersey barriers, manual drop-arm vehicle barriers, a steel gate for the Villa C safe area, some locally manufactured steel doors, sandbag fortifications, security cameras, some additional security lighting, guard booths, and an Internal Defense Notification System.

Special Mission Benghazi's uncertain future after 2012 and its "non-status" as a temporary, residential facility made allocation of resources for security and personnel more difficult, and left responsibility to meet security standards to the working-level in the field, with very limited resources.

In the weeks and months leading up to the attacks, the response from post, Embassy Tripoli, and Washington to a deteriorating security situation was inadequate. At the same time, the SMC's dependence on the armed but poorly skilled Libyan February 17 Martyrs' Brigade (February 17) militia members and unarmed, locally contracted Blue Mountain Libya (BML) guards for security support was misplaced.

Although the February 17 militia had proven effective in responding to improvised explosive device (IED) attacks on the Special Mission in April and June 2012, there were some troubling indicators of its reliability in the months and weeks preceding the September attacks. At the time of Ambassador Stevens' visit, February 17 militia members had stopped accompanying Special Mission vehicle movements in protest over salary and working hours.

Post and the Department were well aware of the anniversary of the September 11, 2001 terrorist attacks but at no time were there ever any specific, credible threats against the mission in Benghazi related to the September 11 anniversary. Ambassador Stevens and Benghazi-based DS agents had taken the anniversary into account and decided to hold all meetings on-compound on September 11.

The Board found that Ambassador Stevens made the decision to travel to Benghazi independently of Washington, per standard practice. Timing for his trip was driven in part by commitments in Tripoli, as well as a staffing gap between principal officers in Benghazi. Plans for the Ambassador's trip provided for minimal close protection security support and were not shared thoroughly with the Embassy's country team, who were not fully aware of planned movements off compound. The Ambassador did not see a direct threat of an attack of this nature and scale on the U.S. Mission in the overall negative trendline of security incidents from spring to summer 2012. His status as the leading U.S. government advocate on Libya policy, and his expertise on Benghazi in particular, caused Washington to give unusual deference to his judgments.

Communication, cooperation, and coordination among Washington, Tripoli, and Benghazi functioned collegially at the working-level but were constrained by a lack of transparency, responsiveness, and leadership at the senior levels. Among various Department bureaus and personnel in the field, there appeared to be very real confusion over who, ultimately, was responsible and empowered to make decisions based on both policy and security considerations.

3. Notwithstanding the proper implementation of security systems and procedures and remarkable heroism shown by American personnel, those systems and the Libyan response fell short in the face of a series of attacks that began with the sudden penetration of the Special Mission compound by dozens of armed attackers.

The Board found the responses by both the BML guards and February 17 to be inadequate. The Board's inquiry found little evidence that the armed February 17 guards offered any meaningful defense of the SMC, or succeeded in summoning a February 17 militia presence to assist expeditiously.

The Board found the Libyan government's response to be profoundly lacking on the night of the attacks, reflecting both weak capacity and near absence of central government influence and control in Benghazi. The Libyan government did facilitate assistance from a quasi-governmental militia that supported the evacuation of U.S. government personnel to Benghazi airport. The Libyan government also provided a military C-130 aircraft which was used to evacuate remaining U.S. personnel and the bodies of the deceased from Benghazi to Tripoli on September 12.

The Board determined that U.S. personnel on the ground in Benghazi performed with courage and readiness to risk their lives to protect their colleagues, in a near impossible situation. The Board members believe every possible effort was made to rescue and recover Ambassador Stevens and Sean Smith.

The interagency response was timely and appropriate, but there simply was not enough time for armed U.S. military assets to have made a difference.

4. The Board found that intelligence provided no immediate, specific tactical warning of the September 11 attacks. Known gaps existed in the intelligence community's understanding of extremist militias in Libya and the potential threat they posed to U.S. interests, although some threats were known to exist.

5. The Board found that certain senior State Department officials within two bureaus demonstrated a lack of proactive leadership and management ability in their responses to security concerns posed by Special Mission Benghazi, given the deteriorating threat environment and the lack of reliable host government protection. However, the Board did not find reasonable cause to determine that any individual U.S. government employee breached his or her duty.

KEY RECOMMENDATIONS

With the lessons of the past and the challenges of the future in mind, the Board puts forward recommendations in six core areas: Overarching Security Considerations; Staffing High Risk, High Threat Posts; Training and Awareness; Security and Fire Safety Equipment; Intelligence and Threat Analysis; and Personnel Accountability.

OVERARCHING SECURITY CONSIDERATIONS

1. The Department must strengthen security for personnel and platforms beyond traditional reliance on host government security support in high risk, high threat posts. The Department should urgently review the proper balance between acceptable risk and expected outcomes in high risk, high threat areas. While the answer cannot be to refrain from operating in such environments, the Department must do so on the basis of having: 1) a defined, attainable, and prioritized mission; 2) a clear-eyed assessment of the risk and costs involved; 3) a commitment of sufficient resources to mitigate these costs and risks; 4) an explicit acceptance of those costs and risks that cannot be mitigated; and 5) constant attention to changes in the situation, including when to leave and perform the mission from a distance. The United States must be self-reliant and enterprising in developing alternate security platforms, profiles, and staffing footprints to address such realities. Assessments must be made on a case-by-case basis and repeated as circumstances change.

2. The Board recommends that the Department re-examine DS organization and management, with a particular emphasis on span of control for security policy planning for all overseas U.S. diplomatic facilities. In this context, the recent creation of a new Diplomatic Security Deputy Assistant Secretary for High Threat Posts could be a positive first step if integrated into a sound strategy for DS reorganization.

3. As the President's personal representative, the Chief of Mission bears "direct and full responsibility for the security of [his or her] mission and all the personnel for whom [he or she is] responsible," and thus for risk management in the country to which he or she is accredited. In Washington, each regional Assistant Secretary has a corresponding responsibility to support the Chief of Mission in executing this duty. Regional bureaus should have augmented support within the bureau on security matters, to include a senior DS officer to report to the regional Assistant Secretary.

4. The Department should establish a panel of outside independent experts (military, security, humanitarian) with experience in high risk, high threat areas to support DS, identify best practices (from other agencies and other countries), and regularly evaluate U.S. security platforms in high risk, high threat posts.

5. The Department should develop minimum security standards for occupancy of temporary facilities in high risk, high threat environments, and seek greater flexibility for the use of Bureau of Overseas Buildings Operations (OBO) sources of funding so that they can be rapidly made available for security upgrades at such facilities.

6. Before opening or re-opening critical threat or high risk, high threat posts, the Department should establish a multi-bureau support cell, residing in the regional bureau. The support cell should work to expedite the approval and funding for establishing and operating the post, implementing physical security measures, staffing of security and management personnel, and providing equipment, continuing as conditions at the post require.

7. The Nairobi and Dar es Salaam ARBs' report of January 1999 called for collocation of newly constructed State Department and other government agencies' facilities. All State Department and other government agencies' facilities should be collocated when they are in the same metropolitan area, unless a waiver has been approved.

8. The Secretary should require an action plan from DS, OBO and other relevant offices on the use of fire as a weapon against diplomatic facilities, including immediate steps to deal with urgent issues. The report should also include reviews of fire safety and crisis management training for all employees and dependents, safehaven standards and fire safety equipment, and recommendations to facilitate survival in smoke and fire situations.

9. Tripwires are too often treated only as indicators of threat rather than an essential trigger mechanism for serious risk management decisions and actions. The Department should revise its guidance to posts and require key offices to perform in-depth status checks of post tripwires.

10. Recalling the recommendations of the Nairobi and Dar es Salaam ARBs, the State Department must work with Congress to restore the Capital Security Cost Sharing Program at its full capacity, adjusted for inflation to approximately $2.2 billion in fiscal year 2015, including an up to ten-year program addressing that need, prioritized for construction of new facilities in high risk, high threat areas. It should also work with Congress to expand utilization of Overseas Contingency Operations funding to respond to emerging security threats and vulnerabilities and operational requirements in high risk, high threat posts.

11. The Board supports the State Department's initiative to request additional Marines and expand the Marine Security Guard (MSG) Program—as well as corresponding requirements for staffing and funding. The Board also recommends that the State Department and DoD identify additional flexible MSG structures and request further resources for the Department and DoD to provide more capabilities and capacities at higher risk posts.

STAFFING HIGH RISK, HIGH THREAT POSTS

12. The Board strongly endorses the Department's request for increased DS personnel for high- and critical-threat posts and for additional Mobile Security Deployment teams, as well as an increase in DS domestic staffing in support of such action.

13. The Department should assign key policy, program, and security personnel at high risk, high threat posts for a minimum of one year. For less critical personnel, the temporary duty length (TDY) length should be no less than 120 days. The ARB suggests a comprehensive review of human resources authorities with an eye to using those authorities to promote sending more experienced officers, including "When Actually Employed" (WAE) personnel, to these high risk, high threat locations, particularly in security and management positions for longer periods of time.

14. The Department needs to review the staffing footprints at high risk, high threat posts, with particular attention to ensuring adequate Locally Employed Staff (LES) and management support. High risk, high threat posts must be funded and the human resources process prioritized to hire LES interpreters and translators.

15. With increased and more complex diplomatic activities in the Middle East, the Department should enhance its ongoing efforts to significantly upgrade its language capacity, especially Arabic, among American employees, including DS, and receive greater resources to do so.

TRAINING AND AWARENESS

16. A panel of Senior Special Agents and Supervisory Special Agents should revisit DS high-threat training with respect to active internal defense and fire survival as well as Chief of Mission protective detail training.

17. The Diplomatic Security Training Center and Foreign Service Institute should collaborate in designing joint courses that integrate high threat training and risk management decision processes for senior and mid-level DS agents and Foreign Service Officers and better prepare them for leadership positions in high risk, high threat posts. They should consult throughout the U.S. government for best practices and lessons learned. Foreign Affairs Counter Threat training should be mandatory for high risk, high threat posts, whether an individual is assigned permanently or in longer-term temporary duty status.

SECURITY AND FIRE SAFETY EQUIPMENT

18. The Department should ensure provision of adequate fire safety and security equipment for safehavens and safe areas in non-Inman/SECCA2 facilities, as well as high threat Inman facilities.

19. There have been technological advancements in non-lethal deterrents, and the State Department should ensure it rapidly and routinely identifies and procures additional options for non-lethal deterrents in high risk, high threat posts and trains personnel on their use.

20. DS should upgrade surveillance cameras at high risk, high threat posts for greater resolution, nighttime visibility, and monitoring capability beyond post.

INTELLIGENCE AND THREAT ANALYSIS

21. Post-2001, intelligence collection has expanded exponentially, but the Benghazi attacks are a stark reminder that we cannot over-rely on the certainty or even likelihood of warning intelligence. Careful attention should be given to factors

showing a deteriorating threat situation in general as a basis for improving security posture. Key trends must be quickly identified and used to sharpen risk calculations.

22. The DS Office of Intelligence and Threat Analysis should report directly to the DS Assistant Secretary and directly supply threat analysis to all DS components, regional Assistant Secretaries and Chiefs of Mission in order to get key security-related threat information into the right hands more rapidly.

PERSONNEL ACCOUNTABILITY

23. The Board recognizes that poor performance does not ordinarily constitute a breach of duty that would serve as a basis for disciplinary action but is instead addressed through the performance management system. However, the Board is of the view that findings of unsatisfactory leadership performance by senior officials in relation to the security incident under review should be a potential basis for discipline recommendations by future ARBs, and would recommend a revision of Department regulations or amendment to the relevant statute to this end.

24. The Board was humbled by the courage and integrity shown by those on the ground in Benghazi and Tripoli, in particular the DS agents and Annex team who defended their colleagues; the Tripoli response team which mobilized without hesitation; those in Benghazi and Tripoli who cared for the wounded; and the many U.S. government employees who served in Benghazi under difficult conditions in the months leading up to the September 11–12 attacks. We trust that the Department and relevant agencies will take the opportunity to recognize their exceptional valor and performance, which epitomized the highest ideals of government service.

POLITICAL AND SECURITY CONTEXT PRIOR TO THE ATTACKS

On April 5, 2011, then Special Envoy to the Libyan Transitional National Council (TNC) Chris Stevens arrived via a Greek cargo ship at the rebel-held city of Benghazi to reestablish a U.S. presence in Libya. The State Department had been absent from Libya since the Embassy in Tripoli suspended operations and evacuated its American personnel on February 25, 2011, amidst an escalating campaign by Muammar Qaddafi to suppress violently a popular uprising against his rule.

Benghazi, the largest city and historical power center in eastern Libya, was the launching point for the uprising against Qaddafi and a long time nexus of anti-regime activism. It also served as the rebel-led Transitional National Council's base of operations. Eastern Libya (Cyrenaica) had long felt neglected and oppressed by Qaddafi, and there had been historic tensions between it and the rest of the country. Throughout Qaddafi's decades-long rule, eastern Libya consistently lagged behind Tripoli in terms of infrastructure and standard of living even as it was responsible for the vast majority of Libya's oil production. Stevens' presence in the city was seen as a significant sign of U.S. support for the TNC and a recognition of the resurgence of eastern Libya's political influence.

Benghazi was the seat of the Senussi monarchy until 1954, the site of a U.S. consulate, which was overrun by a mob and burned in 1967, and the place where Qaddafi began his 1969 revolution against the monarchy. Qaddafi's subsequent combination of oppression and neglect enhanced the city's sense of marginalization, and its after-effects were felt more widely in the eastern region where a Salafist jihadist movement took root. Jihadis from Benghazi engaged in Afghanistan against the Soviets and took up arms against U.S. forces in the post-2003 Iraq insurgency. Many of them reemerged in 2011 as leaders of anti-Qaddafi militias in eastern Libya.

Stevens initially operated from the Tibesti Hotel in downtown Benghazi. He was accompanied by a security contingent of 10 Diplomatic Security agents whose primary responsibilities were to provide personal protective services. Stevens' mission was to serve as the liaison with the TNC in preparation for a post-Qaddafi democratic government in Libya. By all accounts, he was extremely effective, earned the admiration of countless numbers of Libyans, and personified the U.S. government commitment to a free and democratic Libya.

Benghazi, however, was still very much a conflict zone. On June 1, 2011, a car bomb exploded outside the Tibesti Hotel, and shortly thereafter a credible threat against the Special Envoy mission prompted Stevens to move to the Annex. On June 21, 2011, he and his security contingent moved to what would become the Special Mission Benghazi compound (SMC). By the end of August 2011, the walled compound consisted of three sections (Villas A, B, and C) on 13 acres. (Use of Villa A was discontinued in January 2012, when the SMC footprint was consolidated into the Villas B and C compounds, some eight-acres total.)

On July 15, 2011, the United States officially recognized the TNC as Libya's legitimate governing authority although Qaddafi and his forces still retained control over significant portions of the country, including Tripoli. The TNC continued attacking the remaining Qaddafi strongholds, and Tripoli fell earlier than expected at the end of August. The TNC immediately began moving the government from Benghazi to Tripoli. By early September, 21 members of State Department Mobile Security Deployment teams were in Tripoli with the Deputy Chief of Mission (DCM) in preparation for the resumption of operations of the U.S. Embassy, which Ambassador Gene Cretz officially re-opened on September 22, 2011. From September 2011 onwards, Embassy Tripoli was open with a skeleton staff built on temporary duty (TDY) assignments, to include the DCM and Regional Security Officer (RSO). (The fall of Tripoli took place shortly after Embassy Tripoli lost its assigned staff and bureaucratically ceased to exist, pursuant to Department regulations regarding the length of time a post can remain open in evacuation status.)

Although the TNC declared that Tripoli would continue to be the capital of a post-Qaddafi Libya, many of the influential players in the TNC remained based in Benghazi. Stevens continued as Special Envoy to the TNC in Benghazi until he departed Libya on November 17, 2011, after which the Special Envoy position was not filled. Stevens was replaced by an experienced Civil Service employee who served for 73 days in what came to be called the "principal officer" position in Benghazi. After November 2011, the principal officer slot became a TDY assignment for officers with varying levels of experience who served in Benghazi anywhere from 10 days to over two months, usually without transiting Tripoli. In December 2011, the Under Secretary for Management approved a one-year continuation of the U.S. Special Mission in Benghazi, which was never a consulate and never formally notified to the Libyan government. Stevens arrived in Tripoli on May 26, 2012, to replace Cretz as Ambassador.

Throughout Libya, the security vacuum left by Qaddafi's departure, the continued presence of pro-Qaddafi supporters, the prevalence of and easy access to weapons, the inability of the interim government to reestablish a strong security apparatus, and the resulting weakness of those security forces that remained led to a volatile situation in which militias previously united in opposition to Qaddafi were now jockeying for position in the new Libya. Frequent clashes, including assassinations, took place between contesting militias. Fundamentalist influence with Salafi and al Qaeda connections was also growing, including notably in the eastern region. Public attitudes in Benghazi continued to be positive toward Americans, and it was generally seen as safer for Americans given U.S. support of the TNC during the war. However, 2012 saw an overall deterioration of the security environment in Benghazi, as highlighted by a series of security incidents involving the Special Mission, international organizations, non-governmental organizations (NGOs), and third-country nationals and diplomats:

- March 18, 2012—Armed robbery occurs at the British School in Benghazi.
- March 22, 2012—Members of a militia searching for a suspect fire their weapons near the SMC and attempt to enter.
- April 2, 2012—A UK armored diplomatic vehicle is attacked after driving into a local protest. The vehicle was damaged but occupants uninjured.
- April 6, 2012—A gelatina bomb (traditional homemade explosive device used for fishing) is thrown over the SMC north wall.
- April 10, 2012—An IED (gelatina or dynamite stick) is thrown at the motorcade of the UN Special Envoy to Libya in Benghazi.
- April 26, 2012—Special Mission Benghazi principal officer is evacuated from International Medical University (IMU) after a fistfight escalated to gunfire between Tripoli-based trade delegation security personnel and IMU security.
- April 27, 2012—Two South African nationals in Libya as part of U.S.-funded weapons abatement, unexploded ordnance removal and demining project are detained at gunpoint by militia, questioned and released.
- May 22, 2012—Benghazi International Committee of the Red Cross (ICRC) building struck by rocket propelled grenades (RPGs).
- May 28, 2012—A previously unknown organization, Omar Abdurrahman group, claims responsibility for the ICRC attack and issues a threat against the United States on social media sites.
- June 6, 2012—IED attack on the SMC. The IED detonates with no injuries but blows a large hole in the compound's exterior wall. Omar Abdurrahman group makes an unsubstantiated claim of responsibility.
- June 8, 2012—Two hand grenades target a parked UK diplomatic vehicle in Sabha (800 km south of Benghazi).
- June 11, 2012—While in Benghazi, the British Ambassador's convoy is attacked with an RPG and possible AK-47s. Two UK security officers are injured; the UK closes its mission in Benghazi the following day.
- June 12, 2012—An RPG attack is made on the ICRC compound in Misrata (400 km west of Benghazi).
- June 18, 2012—Protestors storm the Tunisian consulate in Benghazi.
- July 29, 2012—An IED is found on grounds of the Tibesti Hotel.
- July 30, 2012—Sudanese Consul in Benghazi is carjacked and driver beaten.
- July 31, 2012—Seven Iranian-citizen ICRC workers abducted in Benghazi.
- August 5, 2012—ICRC Misrata office is attacked with RPGs. ICRC withdraws its representatives from Misrata and Benghazi.

- August 9, 2012—A Spanish-American dual national NGO worker is abducted from the Islamic Cultural Center in Benghazi and released the same day.
- August 20, 2012—A small bomb is thrown at an Egyptian diplomat's vehicle parked outside of the Egyptian consulate in Benghazi.

It is worth noting that the events above took place against a general backdrop of political violence, assassinations targeting former regime officials, lawlessness, and an overarching absence of central government authority in eastern Libya. While the June 6 IED at the SMC and the May ICRC attack were claimed by the same group, none of the remaining attacks were viewed in Tripoli and Benghazi as linked or having common perpetrators, which were not viewed as linked or having common perpetrators. This also tempered reactions in Washington. Furthermore, the Board believes that the longer a post is exposed to continuing high levels of violence the more it comes to consider security incidents which might otherwise provoke a reaction as normal, thus raising the threshold for an incident to cause a reassessment of risk and mission continuation. This was true for both people on the ground serving in Libya and in Washington.

While the June IED attack and the RPG attack targeting the UK convoy in Benghazi prompted the Special Mission to reduce movements off compound and have a one-week pause between principal officers, the successful nature of Libya's July 7, 2012, national elections—which exceeded expectations—renewed Washington's optimism in Libya's future. Nevertheless, the immediate period after the elections did not see the central government increase its capacity to consolidate control or provide security in eastern Libya, as efforts to form a government floundered and extremist militias in and outside Benghazi continued to work to strengthen their grip. At the time of the September attacks, Benghazi remained a lawless town nominally controlled by the Supreme Security Council (SSC)—a coalition of militia elements loosely cobbled into a single force to provide interim security—but in reality run by a diverse group of local Islamist militias, each of whose strength ebbed and flowed depending on the ever-shifting alliances and loyalties of various members. There was a notional national police presence, but it was ineffectual. By August 2012, Special Mission Benghazi would evaluate the worsening security situation and its implications. . . .

[A timeline on the attack has been omitted.]

FINDINGS AND DISCUSSION

1. **The attacks in Benghazi were security-related, resulting in the deaths of four U.S. personnel after terrorists attacked two separate U.S. government facilities—the Special Mission compound (SMC) and the Annex.**

Identification of the perpetrators and their motivations are the subject of an ongoing FBI criminal investigation. The Board concluded that no protest took place before the Special Mission and Annex attacks, which were unanticipated in their scale and intensity.

ADEQUACY OF SECURITY SYSTEMS AND PROCEDURES PRIOR TO SEPTEMBER 11, 2012

2. **Systemic failures and leadership and management deficiencies at senior levels within two bureaus of the State Department resulted in a Special Mission**

security posture that was inadequate for Benghazi and grossly inadequate to deal with the attack that took place.

Through the course of its inquiry, the Board interviewed over 100 individuals, reviewed thousands of pages of documents, and viewed hours of video footage. On the basis of its comprehensive review of this information, the Board remains fully convinced that responsibility for the tragic loss of life, injuries, and damage to U.S. facilities and property rests solely and completely with the terrorists who perpetrated the attack.

Overriding Factors

This is not to say, however, that there are no lessons to be learned. A recurring theme throughout the Board's work was one also touched upon by the Nairobi and Dar es Salaam ARBs in 1999. Simply put, in the months leading up to September 11, 2012, security in Benghazi was not recognized and implemented as a "shared responsibility" in Washington, resulting in stove-piped discussions and decisions on policy and security. Key decisions, such as the extension of the State Department presence in Benghazi until December 2012, or non-decisions in Washington, such as the failure to establish standards for Benghazi and to meet them, or the lack of a cohesive staffing plan, essentially set up Benghazi as a floating TDY platform with successive principal officers often confined to the SMC due to threats and inadequate resources, and RSOs resorting to field-expedient solutions to correct security shortfalls.

Communication, cooperation, and coordination between Washington, Tripoli, and Benghazi occurred collegially at the working-level but were constrained by a lack of transparency, responsiveness, and leadership at senior bureau levels. The DS Bureau's action officers who worked on Libya are to be commended for their efforts within DS and across the Department to provide additional security resources to Benghazi. Action officers in the Bureau of Near Eastern Affairs' (NEA) Office of Maghreb Affairs and Executive Office showed similar dedication in collaborating on solutions with their DS counterparts and responding to TDY staffing demands. However, in DS, NEA, and at post, there appeared to be very real confusion over who, ultimately, was responsible and empowered to make decisions based on both policy and security considerations.

The DS Bureau showed a lack of proactive senior leadership with respect to Benghazi, failing to ensure that the priority security needs of a high risk, high threat post were met. At the same time, with attention in late 2011 shifting to growing crises in Egypt and Syria, the NEA Bureau's front office showed a lack of ownership of Benghazi's security issues, and a tendency to rely totally on DS for the latter. The Board also found that Embassy Tripoli leadership, saddled with their own staffing and security challenges, did not single out a special need for increased security for Benghazi.

Further shortfalls in Washington coordination were manifested by the flawed process by which Special Mission Benghazi's extension until the end of December 2012 was approved, a decision that did not take security considerations adequately into account. The result was the continuation of Special Mission Benghazi with an uncertain future and a one-year expiration date that made allocations of resources for security upgrades and personnel assignments difficult.

Another key driver behind the weak security platform in Benghazi was the decision to treat Benghazi as a temporary, residential facility, not officially notified to the host government, even though it was also a full time office facility. This resulted in the Special Mission compound being excepted from office facility standards and accountability under the Secure Embassy Construction and Counterterrorism Act of 1999 (SECCA) and the Overseas Security Policy Board (OSPB). Benghazi's initial platform in November 2011 was far short of OSPB standards and remained so even in September 2012, despite multiple field-expedient upgrades funded by DS. (As a temporary, residential facility, SMC was not eligible for OBO-funded security upgrades.) A comprehensive upgrade and risk-mitigation plan did not exist, nor was a comprehensive security review conducted by Washington for Benghazi in 2012. The unique circumstances surrounding the creation of the mission in Benghazi as a temporary mission outside the realm of permanent diplomatic posts resulted in significant disconnects and support gaps.

Personnel

The Board found the short-term, transitory nature of Benghazi's staffing to be another primary driver behind the inadequate security platform in Benghazi. Staffing was at times woefully insufficient considering post's security posture and high risk, high threat environment. The end result was a lack of institutional knowledge and mission capacity which could not be overcome by talent and hard work alone, although the Board found ample evidence of both in those who served there. The situation was exacerbated by the lack of Locally Employed Staff (LES) who would normally provide a backstop of continuity, local knowledge, and language ability. This staffing "churn" had significant detrimental effects on the post's ability to assess adequately both the political and security environment, as well as to provide the necessary advocacy and follow-through on major, essential security upgrades.

The Board determined that DS staffing levels in Benghazi after Embassy Tripoli re-opened were inadequate, decreasing significantly after then–Special Envoy Stevens' departure in November 2011. Although a full complement of five DS agents for Benghazi was initially projected, and later requested multiple times, Special Mission Benghazi achieved a level of five DS agents (not counting DoD-provided TDY Site Security Team personnel sent by Embassy Tripoli) for only 23 days between January 1–September 9, 2012.

As it became clear that DS would not provide a steady complement of five TDY DS agents to Benghazi, expectations on the ground were lowered by the daunting task of gaining approvals and the reality of an ever-shifting DS personnel platform. From discussions with former Benghazi-based staff, Board members concluded that the persistence of DS leadership in Washington in refusing to provide a steady platform of four to five DS agents created a resignation on the part of post about asking for more. The TDY DS agents resorted to doing the best they could with the limited resources provided.

Furthermore, DS's reliance on volunteers for TDY positions meant that the ARSOs in Benghazi often had relatively little or no prior DS program management or overseas experience. For a time, more experienced RSOs were sent out on longer term TDYs, but even that appeared to diminish after June 2012, exactly at the time the security environment in Benghazi was deteriorating further. It bears emphasizing, however, that the Board found the work done by these often junior DS agents to be exemplary. But given the threat environment and with very little operational oversight from more experienced, senior colleagues, combined with an under-resourced security platform, these agents were not well served by their leadership in Washington. The lack of Arabic-language skills among most American personnel assigned to Benghazi and the lack of a dedicated LES interpreter and sufficient local staff also served as a barrier to effective communication and situational awareness at the Special Mission.

Required security training for DS agents prior to service in Benghazi consisted of the High Threat Training Course (HTTC). However, domestically-based DS agents who had not served abroad did not have the opportunity to receive RSO training before serving in Benghazi. In addition, after April 2012 all personnel scheduled to serve in Libya for over 30 days were required to take the Foreign Affairs Counter Threat (FACT) training. IMOs, who also served as the "management officer" at post, did not, as a prerequisite, receive any basic management or General Services Officer (GSO) training to prepare them for their duties.

The Board determined that reliance on February 17 for security in the event of an attack was misplaced, even though February 17 had been considered to have responded satisfactorily to previous, albeit less threatening, incidents. The four assigned February 17 guards were insufficient and did not have the requisite skills and reliability to provide a reasonable level of security on a 24/7 basis for an eight-acre compound with an extended perimeter wall. In the days prior to the attack and on September 11, 2012, one was absent. Over the course of its inquiry, the Board also learned of troubling indicators of February 17's loyalties and its readiness to assist U.S. personnel. In the weeks preceding the Ambassador's arrival, February 17 had complained about salaries and the lack of a contract for its personnel. At the time of the attacks, February 17 had ceased accompanying Special Mission vehicle movements in protest. The Blue Mountain Libya (BML) unarmed guards, whose primary responsibilities were to provide early warning and control access to the SMC, were also poorly skilled.

Physical Security

Given the threat environment, the physical security platform in Benghazi was inadequate. It is incumbent upon the Board, however, to acknowledge that several upgrades and repairs took place over 2012. DS provided additional funding for the Local Guard Force (LGF), February 17, and residential security upgrades, including heightening the outer perimeter wall, safety grills on safe area egress windows that helped save the life of ARSO 1 on the night of September 11, concrete jersey barriers, manual drop-arm vehicle barriers, a steel gate for the Villa C safe area, some locally manufactured steel doors, sandbag fortifications, security cameras, some additional security lighting, guard booths, and an Internal Defense Notification System. Because OBO does not fund security upgrades for "temporary" facilities, DS also identified non-traditional funding streams to fund physical security upgrades and worked with the IMOs, NEA and Embassy Tripoli to move funds and supplies to Benghazi. The Engineering Security Office (ESO) in Cairo provided strong technical support and regularly visited. Following the June 2012 IED incident, which blew a large hole in the compound wall, DS, OBO, Tripoli, NEA and ESO Cairo immediately responded to Benghazi's request for assistance. Tripoli identified OBO funds that could be used to fix the wall, and ESO Cairo traveled to Benghazi on June 8 to provide technical support. The TDY IMOs worked tirelessly with the RSOs, Tripoli procurement and financial management staff, and Libyan professionals on statements of work, contracts and funding for the emergency repair of the SMC wall and for the other physical security upgrades, as well as ongoing electrical repairs. New upgrades remained a challenge, however, due to a lack of cash reserves and contract and procurement expertise, which meant Benghazi had to rely on Tripoli for further processing.

The Board found, however, that Washington showed a tendency to overemphasize the positive impact of physical security upgrades, which were often field-expedient improvements to a profoundly weak platform, while generally failing to meet Benghazi's repeated requests to augment the numbers of TDY DS personnel. The insufficient Special Mission compound security platform was at variance with the appropriate Overseas Security

Policy Board (OSPB) standards with respect to perimeter, interior security, and safe areas. Benghazi was also under-resourced with regard to certain needed security equipment.

Security Planning

Post and the Department were well aware of the anniversary of the September 11, 2001, terrorist attacks, although DS did not issue a worldwide caution cable to posts related to the anniversary. Ambassador Stevens and his DS agents had taken the anniversary into account by deciding to hold all meetings at the SMC that day rather than making any moves outside.

The Ambassador chose to travel to Benghazi that week, independent of Washington, as per standard practice. Timing for his trip was driven in part by commitments in Tripoli, as well as a staffing gap between principal officers in Benghazi. His trip had been put off earlier in the summer, and the September 10–14 dates were not decided upon well in advance. The Board found that plans for the Ambassador's trip provided for minimal close protection security support, and that Embassy country team members were not fully aware of planned movements off compound. The Ambassador did not see a direct threat of an attack of this nature and scale on the U.S. Mission in the overall negative trendline of security incidents from spring to summer 2012. His status as the leading U.S. government advocate on Libya policy, and his expertise on Benghazi in particular, caused Washington to give unusual deference to his judgments.

IMPLEMENTATION OF SECURITY SYSTEMS AND PROCEDURES ON SEPTEMBER 11–12, 2012

3. **Notwithstanding the proper implementation of security systems and procedures and remarkable heroism shown by American personnel, those systems themselves and the Libyan response fell short in the face of a series of attacks that began with the sudden penetration of the Special Mission compound by dozens of armed attackers.** In short, Americans in Benghazi and their Tripoli colleagues did their best with what they had, which, in the end, was not enough to prevent the loss of lives of Ambassador Stevens, Sean Smith, Tyrone Woods, and Glen Doherty. At the same time, U.S. security professionals prevented a further loss of life and helped ensure the safe evacuation of remaining American personnel in Benghazi 12 hours after the attacks began.

As noted in the preceding section, physical security at the Special Mission was insufficient. The SMC perimeter was breached immediately, providing no reaction time to the five DS agents on compound. There was no advance warning regarding the group of attackers approaching outside the SMC prior to the attack, and no sign of them on surveillance cameras outside the C1 gate until the attack was underway. The Board learned that, as of the time of the attacks, the Special Mission compound had received additional surveillance cameras, which remained in boxes uninstalled, as technical support to install them had not yet visited post. In addition, the camera monitor in the local guard force booth next to the C1 gate was inoperable on the day of the attacks, a repair which also awaited the arrival of a technical team.

Some aspects of physical security upgrades did perform as intended—in particular, the safe area in Villa C, which prevented intruders from entering and the TOC door, which protected the DS agents from attackers trying to enter. Also, the installation of exits in the window grates of the Villa C safe area allowed ARS01 to escape the fire, and those exits were the entry point for him and other DS agents and Annex personnel to make multiple attempts to rescue and recover Sean Smith and Ambassador Stevens.

The Board found the responses by both BML and February 17 to be inadequate. No BML guards were present outside the compound immediately before the attack ensued, although perimeter security was one of their responsibilities, and there is conflicting information as to whether they sounded any alarms prior to fleeing the C1 gate area to other areas of the SMC. Although the unarmed BML guards could not be expected to repel an attack, they had core responsibility for providing early warning and controlling access to the compound, which they had not always performed well in the past. In the final analysis, the Board could not determine exactly how the C1 gate at the Special Mission compound was breached, but the speed with which attackers entered raised the possibility that BML guards left the C1 pedestrian gate open after initially seeing the attackers and fleeing the vicinity. They had left the gate unlatched before.

The Board's inquiry found little evidence that the armed February 17 guards alerted Americans at the SMC to the attack or summoned a February 17 militia presence to assist expeditiously once the attack was in progress—despite the fact that February 17 members were paid to provide interior security and a quick reaction force for the SMC and the fact that February 17 barracks were in the close vicinity, less than 2 km away from the SMC. A small number of February 17 militia members arrived at Villa C nearly an hour after the attack began. Although some February 17 members assisted in efforts to search for Ambassador Stevens in the smoke-filled Villa C building, the Board found little evidence that February 17 contributed meaningfully to the defense of the Special Mission compound, or to the evacuation to the airport that took place on the morning of September 12.

In contrast, DS and Annex personnel on the ground in Benghazi performed with courage and an overriding desire to protect and rescue their colleagues, in a near impossible situation. The multiple trips that the DS agents and Annex security team members made into a burning, smoke-filled building in attempts to rescue Sean Smith and Ambassador Stevens showed readiness to risk life and limb to save others. They ultimately were unable to save Sean Smith and Ambassador Stevens, due to the intensity of the heat and smoke and a lack of resources, including breathing apparatus. The DS agents' decision to depart the SMC without the Ambassador came after they had all suffered smoke inhalation due to multiple rescue attempts, and amidst a renewed attack that continued as they departed the compound. The Board members believe every possible effort was made to protect, rescue, and recover Ambassador Stevens and Sean Smith, and that the bravery of the DS agents present in Benghazi helped prevent a further loss of life, particularly given their assistance in defending the Annex.

The Board found that the lack of non-lethal crowd control options also precluded a more vigorous defense of the SMC. The Board also determined that the lack of fire safety equipment severely impacted the Ambassador's and Sean Smith's ability to escape the deadly smoke conditions. On the other hand, the DS agents' tactical driving training, as well as their fully-armored vehicle, saved their lives when they were attacked by weapons fire en route from the SMC to the Annex. In addition, the DS emergency medical training and the DS-issued personal medical kit saved an ARSO's life after he was severely injured by a mortar attack at the Annex.

The Board found the Libyan government's response to be profoundly lacking on the night of the attacks, reflecting both weak capacity and a near total absence of central government influence in Benghazi. The Libyan government did facilitate assistance from a quasi-governmental militia that supported the evacuation of U.S. government personnel to Benghazi airport. It also facilitated the departure of the charter plane carrying the Tripoli rescue team to Benghazi, and provided a Libyan Air Force C-130 that was used to evacuate remaining personnel and the bodies of the deceased from Benghazi on the morning of September 12.

Washington-Tripoli-Benghazi communication, cooperation, and coordination on the night of the attacks were effective, despite multiple channels of communication among Washington, Tripoli, Benghazi, and AFRICOM headquarters in Stuttgart, as well as multiple channels of communication within Washington itself. Embassy Tripoli served as a lifeline to Benghazi throughout the attacks, marshalling support from Washington, Stuttgart and elsewhere, including quickly organizing the charter plane that sent the seven-person reinforcement team to Benghazi. At the direction of AFRICOM, DoD moved a remotely piloted, unarmed surveillance aircraft to Benghazi, which arrived over the SMC shortly before the DS team departed. A second remotely piloted, unarmed surveillance aircraft relieved the first, and monitored the eventual evacuation of personnel from the Annex to Benghazi airport later on the morning of September 12.

Embassy Tripoli staff showed absolute dedication and teamwork in mobilizing to respond to the crisis, with the DCM, DATT, Political, and other country team sections reaching out to a wide range of contacts in Tripoli and Benghazi to secure support; the Public Affairs team monitoring social media sites and recording a log of Mission calls; the Embassy nurse providing invaluable guidance on caring for the wounded evacuated from Benghazi; and a Consular officer donating blood that helped save the life of a wounded colleague. Throughout the crisis, the Acting NEA Assistant Secretary provided crucial leadership guidance to Embassy Tripoli's DCM, and Embassy Tripoli's RSO offered valuable counsel to the DS agents in Benghazi.

The interagency response was timely and appropriate, but there simply was not enough time given the speed of the attacks for armed U.S. military assets to have made a difference. Senior-level interagency discussions were underway soon after Washington received initial word of the attacks and continued through the night. The Board found no evidence of any undue delays in decision making or denial of support from Washington or from the military combatant commanders. Quite the contrary: the safe evacuation of all U.S. government personnel from Benghazi twelve hours after the initial attack and subsequently to Ramstein Air Force Base was the result of exceptional U.S. government coordination and military response and helped save the lives of two severely wounded Americans. In addition, at the State Department's request, the Department of Defense also provided a Marine FAST (Fleet Antiterrorism Security Team) as additional security support for Embassy Tripoli on September 12.

Overall, communication systems on the night of the attacks worked, with a near-constant information flow among Benghazi, Tripoli, and Washington. Cell phones were the main method of contact, but lacked redundancy. Radio communications between the Annex and the SMC also worked well, thanks to prior coordination between the two.

Shortly after receiving the initial notification from Embassy Tripoli at approximately 1545 EST, the State Department Operations Center notified the interagency, including the White House, of the Special Mission attack by secure conference call and email alerts. The Operations Center and the Diplomatic Security Command Center (DSCC) were exemplary in eliciting information from Tripoli- and Benghazi-based colleagues without overloading them.

IMPACT OF INTELLIGENCE AND INFORMATION AVAILABILITY

4. **The Board found that intelligence provided no immediate, specific tactical warning of the September 11 attacks. Known gaps existed in the intelligence community's understanding of extremist militias in Libya and the potential threat they posed to U.S. interests, although some threats were known to exist.**

Terrorist networks are difficult to monitor, and the Board emphasizes the conclusion of previous accountability review boards that vulnerable missions cannot rely on receiving specific warning intelligence. Similarly, the lack of specific threat intelligence does not imply a lessening of probability of a terrorist attack. The Board found that there was a tendency on the part of policy, security and other U.S. government officials to rely heavily on the probability of warning intelligence and on the absence of specific threat information. The result was possibly to overlook the usefulness of taking a hard look at accumulated, sometimes circumstantial information, and instead to fail to appreciate threats and understand trends, particularly based on increased violence and the targeting of foreign diplomats and international organizations in Benghazi. The latter information failed to come into clear relief against a backdrop of the lack of effective governance, widespread and growing political violence and instability and the ready availability of weapons in eastern Libya. There were U.S. assessments that provided situational awareness on the persistent, general threat to U.S. and Western interests in eastern Libya, including Benghazi. Board members, however, were struck by the lack of discussion focused specifically on Benghazi.

Benghazi's threat environment had been generally deteriorating since the "gelatina" bomb was thrown over the SMC fence on April 6, but was not judged to have reached a critical point before September 11. The July 7 elections, about which there had been some trepidation regarding the security situation, passed with less violence than expected and were followed by Ramadan, when incidents are usually lower. Before September 11, a patchwork of militias in Benghazi had assumed many, if not all, of the security functions normally associated with central government organs, as the government had little authority or reach in Benghazi. There seemed to be no attempt, however, to link formally the many anti-Western incidents in Benghazi, the general declarations of threat in U.S. assessments and a proliferation of violence prone and little understood militias, the lack of any central authority and a general perception of a deteriorating security environment to any more specific and timely analysis of the threat to U.S. government facilities.

Board members found that there was little understanding of militias in Benghazi and the threat they posed to U.S. interests. One prime factor behind this knowledge gap was that eastern Libya is home to many militias, which are constantly dissolving, splitting apart and reforming. Furthermore, many individuals are associated with more than one militia. Understanding of February 17, in particular, was further limited by the fact that it is an umbrella organization, made up of many different militias with differing ideologies, some of which are extremist in nature.

The Board determined there were no warnings from Libyan interlocutors.

ACCOUNTABILITY OF PERSONNEL

5. **The Board found that certain senior State Department officials within two bureaus in critical positions of authority and responsibility in Washington demonstrated a lack of proactive leadership and management ability** appropriate for the State Department's senior ranks in their responses to security concerns posed by Special Mission Benghazi, given the deteriorating threat environment and the lack of reliable host government protection. However, the Board did not find that any individual U.S. Government employee engaged in misconduct or willfully ignored his or her responsibilities, and, therefore did not find reasonable

cause to believe that an individual breached his or her duty so as to be the subject of a recommendation for disciplinary action.

SOURCE: U.S. Department of State. "Accountability Review Board (ARB) Report (Unclassified)." December 18, 2012. http://www.state.gov/documents/organization/202446.pdf.

OTHER HISTORIC DOCUMENTS OF INTEREST

FROM THIS VOLUME

FROM PREVIOUS *HISTORIC DOCUMENTS*

China and Japan Dispute Island Territory

SEPTEMBER 19 AND 25, 2012

Tension increased between Asia's two largest economies, Japan and China, in mid-2012, following Japan's purchase of a portion of a chain of islands northeast of Taiwan and west of Okinawa in the East China Sea. Over time, the islands, known as Diaoyu Dao in China and Senkaku in Japan, have been claimed separately by each nation. The debate over the islands extended into public life in the two countries, leading to protests and economic disruptions. The islands are of particular interest to each nation because they are situated in important shipping lanes and near an abundance of fishing resources, and it was recently discovered that there might be oil and gas deposits in the waters surrounding the islands, which could be lucrative for whichever nation controls the land.

International law provides no assistance in determining which country is the rightful owner of the islands: The UN Convention on the Law of the Sea, to which both China and Japan are party, gives countries territorial control of anything 12 nautical miles from its coastline and exclusive economic rights to anything within 200 nautical miles from its coastline. The disputed islands are within 200 nautical miles of both China and Japan.

JAPANESE CLAIM

Japan claims it has owned the string of uninhabited, rocky islands in the East China Sea since it incorporated them into its territory in January 1895. Before that time, the Japanese government asserts there was no official owner of the islands. Four months after Japanese inclusion of the territory, China and Japan ended the Sino-Japanese War by signing the Treaty of Shimonoseki, under which China ceded Taiwan "together with all the islets appertaining or belonging to the said island" to Japan. Although the Senkaku Islands were not specifically named in the treaty, Japan argued that they were at that time considered a part of Taiwan and that no objection was raised as to the ownership of the Senkakus by China when the treaty was signed. In 1945, following the end of World War II, Japan gave control of Taiwan back to China but did not mention the Senkakus in the transfer and, therefore, maintained control of the islands.

From 1953 to 1971, the United States administered the islands as part of its occupation of Okinawa. In 1971, the United States and Japan signed the Okinawa Reversion Treaty, in which the United States returned "all territories with their territorial waters" that had been administered by it during the preceding two decades. Because the United States considered the Senkaku Islands to be one of the Okinawa territories, it was assumed by Japan that the Reversion Treaty included them, although the islands were not expressly named.

The Senkaku Islands had long been privately owned by the family of a Japanese businessman who ran a fish processing plant there in the early 1900s. Shortly after the Senkaku

Islands were returned to Japan in 1972, the Kurihara family purchased the islands from the businessman's descendants. The Japanese government rents the land from the private owners and keeps it tightly controlled, allowing almost no landing access. The islands are considered a part of the Okinawa prefecture, and are administered by that local government. "There can be no doubt that the Senkaku Islands are part of Japanese territory, both under international law and from a historical point of view," said then–prime minister Yoshihiko Noda on July 7. "The Senkakus are under the effective control of our nation, and there is no territorial issue with any country over the islands."

In April 2012, the heavily nationalist mayor of Tokyo, Ishihara Shintaro, announced that his prefecture would purchase the islands from the private owner with intent to solidify Japanese ownership by building a port, telecommunications base, and meteorological station on them. Shintaro raised approximately $20 million toward the purchase. The proposal drew a strong response from China, and in an effort to diffuse the situation and prevent development—the latter of which the Japanese thought would increase tension with China—in September, the Japanese government purchased three of the five islands from the private owner for $26 million.

Since the signing of the Reversion Treaty, the United States has maintained a neutral position in the dispute, except to note that because Japan is currently responsible for administration of the islands, they therefore fall under the U.S.-Japan Mutual Defense Treaty. This means, if China chose to attack Japan because of the island dispute, the United States may be required to assist the Japanese.

CHINESE CLAIM

China says that the islands were discovered by ancient Chinese people and appeared on Chinese maps for centuries before the Japanese claimed them. The government believes the islands fall under the administration of the province of Taiwan, which China considers its sovereign territory. According to a report released by the Chinese State Council Information Office, "Diaoyu Dao and its affiliated islands are an inseparable part of the Chinese territory. Diaoyu Dao is China's inherent territory in all historical, geographical and legal terms, and China enjoys indisputable sovereignty over Diaoyu Dao."

China argues that Japan used brutal tactics against the Chinese people to win the Sino-Japanese War that resulted in the transfer of Taiwan to Japan and claims that the treaty that ended the war was forced upon them. Because Japan took the islands by force, China says the Cairo Declaration and Potsdam Proclamation of World War II require Japan to return to China any land it had illegally annexed. When Japan returned Taiwan to China under the Treaty of San Francisco, it did not mention the Senkaku Islands; nor did the Chinese government dispute the islands' ownership. The Chinese government has noted that it was dependent on the United States for support following World War II, and because the islands were under U.S. trusteeship, it did not want to inflame tensions with Washington.

In 1972, when Japan and China normalized relations, Chinese Premier Zhou Enlai proposed that the issue of island ownership be set aside until the time "was ripe" for a resolution. This sentiment was echoed six years later by Chinese leader Deng Xiaoping, who said the issue should be settled by "our children and grandchildren."

Following Japan's September 2012 actions, the Chinese government called for the revocation of the purchase. "We strongly urge the Japanese side to stop making repeated mistakes, and immediately halt any move that violates China's sovereignty. Japan should return to the existing consensus and dialogue framework between the two sides. China will take necessary measures to safeguard sovereignty according to how the situation develops," Chinese Foreign Ministry spokesperson Hong Lei said. Japanese Foreign Minister Koichiro Gemba rejected that idea, stating, "There is no way we would reconsider the transfer, acquisition and possession of their ownership right." China responded that it "has the unshakable resolve and will to uphold the nation's territorial sovereignty," adding, "It has the confidence and ability to safeguard China's state sovereignty and territorial integrity."

Escalating Dispute

Since the 1990s, tensions flared periodically with regard to the disputed islands, but actions by each nation in 2012 reached a new height. In mid-August, fourteen Chinese activists arrived on the islands from Hong Kong and were detained upon their arrival and returned to Hong Kong. In response, a group of Japanese nationalists sailed to the Senkakus, which further incensed the Chinese and resulted in a "strong protest" being filed with the Japanese government. On September 14, China sent six patrol boats into the waters near the Senkakus. The nation's Foreign Ministry said the boats were conducting a maritime surveillance exercise and providing "law enforcement over its maritime rights." The Japanese government asked the ships to leave. "It is deplorable that the invasion of the territorial waters happened at this time and we strongly request that the Chinese authorities leave our territory," said Osamu Fujimura, the chief government spokesperson. The Chinese government retorted, calling the patrol a "rights defense law enforcement action, to reflect the Chinese government's jurisdiction over the Diaoyu Islands and safeguard China's maritime rights and interests." Approximately four hours after their entry into the waters surrounding the disputed islands, the boats left.

Sino-Japanese relations were significantly impacted by the dispute both on economic and personal levels. In one case, a Japanese man had hot noodles thrown at him by a Chinese citizen. Japanese auto manufacturers, including Honda, Mazda, and Nissan, whose market share makes up a significant portion of the Japanese economy, were forced to close plants and dealerships in China for fear that the escalating tension would put employees at risk. In Shanghai, a man set his Honda Civic on fire in front of a local dealership, unfurling banners that read "Japanese devils return home." Large-scale, anti-Japanese protests broke out across China, but they were closely monitored by state police seeking to avoid devolution into violent protests similar to those that occurred in 2005, when rioters stormed the Japanese embassy in Beijing. Japanese Foreign Minister Gemba warned that any violent acts committed over ownership of the islands could result in economic sanctions. "Investments in China, not only from Japanese companies but from others, might be withheld, and that would be a loss to China as well. Given today's mutual interdependence between Japan and China, we should try to make efforts to minimize the impact, especially on the economy."

Some Chinese travel companies stopped selling tour packages to Japan, while airlines in both nations reported canceling flights and routes due to decreasing demand. A welcoming ceremony in Kobe, Japan, for 3,000 Chinese tourists was canceled, as were a number of concerts and events set to mark the fortieth anniversary of the establishment of diplomatic relations between China and Japan.

The escalation in tension between China and Japan came at a particularly poignant moment for China, as the ruling Communist Party was preparing for a transition of power—a once-in-a-decade occurrence. Although the party sought to maintain calm during the transition process, it was not politically viable in China for leaders to appear weak on the issue of the islands. "I sincerely worry that a maritime incident before the Party Congress could force the hand of Beijing's leadership team to be tougher in its response than it would be once Xi Jinping has entrenched himself in power," said Linda Jakobson, the East Asia program director at the Lowy Institute.

This delicate transition raised the concern of many international observers about the possibility that the 2012 island dispute could turn into an armed conflict. In the fall, China sent a number of law enforcement and surveillance boats to the islands in an effort to establish its ownership of the land. "The presence of Chinese law enforcement vessels in the area will increase the chances that the Japanese coast guard feels it needs to respond. If there is an incident it will be extremely difficult to walk back given the current state of diplomatic relations, the delicate Chinese transition and the high-pitched nationalist sentiment in China," said Stephanie Kleine-Ahlbrandt, the North East Asia project director for the International Crisis Group. After filing baselines—or the land points from which its maritime claims originate—with the United Nations and thus marking its intent to defend such claims, China announced in January 2013 that it would produce a geological survey of the islands, which it claimed was part of its "program to safeguard its maritime rights and interests." The Japanese government filed its own baselines with the United Nations and formally submitted an objection to the Chinese claims.

—Heather Kerrigan

Following is the edited text of a press conference on September 19, 2012, held by Japanese Minister of Foreign Affairs Koichiro Gemba, regarding the rising tensions between China and Japan over the Senkaku/Diaoyu Dao Islands; and excerpts from a report released by China's State Council Information Office on September 25, 2012, detailing China's claim on the Senkaku/Diaoyu Dao Islands.

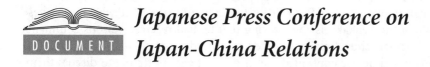

Japanese Press Conference on Japan-China Relations

September 19, 2012

Murat, Turkish National Broadcasting Agency: I have two questions to ask, one is that whether Japan have any intention of strengthening [*sic*] the military considering pressure from surrounding countries regarding territory? Question number two is related to the Senkaku Islands. Is there any impact on the Japan-China economic relationship?

Minister Gemba: First I would like to respond to your latter, the second question with regard to the situation surrounding the Senkaku Islands and others—whether there is any impact on the economy. As you know, there are anti-Japanese protests occurring recently. Some of them have become rampant. There are damages on Japanese companies, so in that sense, there is an impact as a matter of course. Having said that, however, I think both sides should make efforts so that there is as few impacts on economy as possible. With regard to the recent anti-Japanese demonstrations with some becoming vandalism causing damage to Japanese companies, essentially speaking, this should have been avoided. There should be no resort to violence for any reason. This is reported by the press and disseminated to the international community. As a consequence, investments in China, not only from Japanese companies but from others, might be withheld, and that would be a loss to China as well. Given today's mutual interdependence between Japan and China, we should try to make efforts to minimize the impact, especially on the economy. Naturally speaking, we must make mutual effort on both sides.

I would now like to respond to defense capability development raised in your first question. Setting aside the territorial issues, as far as I am concerned, the defense of Japan should be primarily conducted by itself, and then comes the alliance. Therefore, from the standpoint that Japan should defend itself, it is necessary that we develop appropriate defense capabilities in order to defend ourselves, because we have strictly defensive forces and do not resort to the use of force against other countries.

Yokota, Mainichi Shimbun: I wish to reconfirm your basic recognition with regard to the Senkaku Islands. According to the Chinese government's argument, [i]n the press conference on the visit to Japan of the then deputy premier Deng Xiaoping in 1978, he said that based on the normalization of Japan-China diplomatic relations and the negotiations of the Treaty of Peace and Friendship, the two countries had promised not to touch upon the issue. And the Chinese government insists that, judging by the fact above, there is an agreement between the two governments that they shelve the issue. One of the grounds that China criticizes Japan is that the agreement has been broken by the acquisition by the Japanese government. My question is that if the Japanese government is of the view that the two governments agreed during the negotiations to put the issue aside, and if you are not, what is the Japanese government's recognition of the treatment of the Senkaku Islands during the past negotiations and of what gave rise to the historical uncertainties?

Minister Gemba: I have at hand a record of the Japan-China diplomatic relations normalization negotiations, which relates to your question. The document, which has already been made public, says that Prime Minister Kakuei Tanaka asked what the Chinese side thought about the Senkaku Islands, saying that he had received various comments and inquiries. Premier Zhou Enlai responded that he did not want to talk about the Senkaku Islands this time. He continued that it was not a good timing to discuss them, that they became an issue because oil is produced there, and that otherwise, neither Taiwan nor the U.S. would make it an issue. He turned to the next topic then. The question is whether this constitutes an agreement. Needless to say, our position is that there is no agreement, while on the Chinese side, they claim that there is an agreement. As I mentioned before, the position of Japan is that there is no agreement.

Matsumura, Asahi Shimbun: Anti-Japanese demonstrations are occurring in China, and they are taking countermeasures. At the same time, China is activating its diplomatic activities such as depositing a chart with the United Nations that depicts the waters around the Senkaku Islands within its borders. Under the circumstances, Director-General of the Asian and Oceanian Affairs Bureau Shinsuke Sugiyama said at yesterday's Liberal Democratic Party meeting that Japan must send out messages more strongly. More specifically, how do you intend to assert Japan's position to the international community?

Minister Gemba: First, as you pointed out, in terms of the chart, the Chinese side has submitted one to the UN. I am aware of such moves, and under such circumstances the Japanese government will officially submit our objection to the UN. We would do the same about the issue of the continental shelf too. On top of that, during this time period, as has been raised earlier on, in the case of anti-Japanese protests, we have repeatedly requested the protection of the Japanese citizens as well as the immediate suspension of violent acts. As I said before, violence would not do any good for China either. Violence should not be condoned for any reason.

We are sending out our messages to the international community more strongly. First, starting from a few days ago, under my instructions to the Japanese embassies in the capitals of various countries around the world, we have strengthened sending out Japan's position. As Japan's position has been that there is no territorial issue with regard to the Senkaku Islands, [i]t has been the case that we present our position when the other country presents its original position. This time, with China presenting its own position in various places, Japan has to strengthen sending out ours to the international community, and we are doing so through our embassies abroad. Also, to the embassies here in Tokyo, we are to conduct briefing sessions on Japan's position this afternoon.

[Two questions regarding an upcoming visit to the United Nations have been omitted.]

Nakai, Kyodo News: You said that you would be promoting the messages to be sent out. Up until now, some people on the Chinese side [have] been making statements indicating that the responsibility for all of the situations lies only on the Japanese side. I think that the Japanese government is, while making objections, stressing that the Japan-China relationship calls for a calm-headed, broad perspective. Do you recognize that the position of Japan is, at this point in time, being supported by Asian countries, European countries, the U.S. and the international community as a whole?

Minister Gemba: First of all, toward the international community, the position of Japan that the islands are undoubtedly an inherent part of our territory in light of historical facts and based on international law should be explained based on the past background. Having said that, related to your question, as the Chief Cabinet Secretary has commented, Japan has taken the realistic and best possible measures in the aim of ensuring a peaceful and stable maintenance and management in the long term. That, with backgrounds and details, is what I try to explain to different countries through overseas establishments under my instruction. In that regard, there still remain some aspects that haven't been well-known, which I intend to explain.

Nakai Kyodo News: Regarding the peaceful and stable maintenance and management of the islands, to continue the dissemination of Japan's position—would it be a contribution or how could it be a contribution to the peaceful and stable maintenance and management, or could it produce a backfire? What do you think?

Minister Gemba: I don't think it would pose any counter effects.

Koyama, Freelance Journalist: You are sending out messages to the international community. What about messages to be sent to the Japanese public? Do you think you are providing proper explanations to them? . . .

Koyama: Things like why the islands are Japanese territory. And one more question, you said that there was no agreement to shelve the issue. Have you provided such explanations to China through diplomatic channels?

Minister Gemba: Starting with the latter question. Explanations have been provided every time when necessary, of course. As for explaining to the Japanese public, I recall earlier questions from you. In light of historical facts and based on international law, the islands are an inherent part of Japan's territory. When it comes to the contents and the reasons, indeed, more detailed, more comprehensible explanation could have been provided. I agree. When I had your question before, I talked about occupation of terra nullius. It was in January 1895, when the government of Japan made the cabinet decision to formally incorporate the islands into Okinawa Prefecture. The incorporation was implemented after detailed on-site surveys before the Sino-Japan War, even ten years before 1895, and they confirmed that the islands were not attributable to any country. At the same time, looking into the San Francisco Peace Treaty as well as other treaties, the Senkaku Islands were not included in the territory that was to be abandoned by Japan. Also looking at the process of the Reversion of Okinawa, I think it is obvious. Having said that, as has been pointed out, this has to be explained in a more comprehensible manner. After all, our position has been that no territorial dispute exists, so, the same sorts of efforts as in the Takeshima Island and the Northern Territories cases, including publishing leaflets, have not been made. Therefore, in that regard, I do agree that more could be done. Therefore, more comprehensible explanation has to be provided at home.

Kaku, Xinhua: Related to the territorial issue, once again the question about the position of the Japanese government. At the 1972 diplomatic relation normalization negotiations, Prime Minister Kakuei Tanaka posed the before mentioned question on his own. Doesn't that contradict Japan's position that territorial issues do not exist? Why did Prime Minister Tanaka refer to the Senkaku Islands from his side?

Minister Gemba: Frankly speaking, as you have pointed out, I think it is a fact that Prime Minister Tanaka said that he had received various comments and inquiries as to how to think about the Senkaku Islands. Premier Zhou Enlai, on the other hand, said that he did not want to talk about the Senkaku Islands this time, and that it was not a good timing to discuss them at that point in time, etc. Whether that constitutes an agreement or not, that is the question. Meanwhile, not only recently, but whenever we discuss this matter with China, Japan has conveyed that there was no such agreement as I answered to the earlier question. Interpretation differs between Japan and China on this, and that is the situation where we are in.

Kaku, Xinhua: According to some major Japanese newspapers' reports and editorials, the position of Japan that there is no territorial issue can pose a barrier in the sense that it closes a window for diplomatic dialogues between Japan and China. What do you think of this?

Minister Gemba: The islands are undoubtedly an inherent part of the territory of Japan both in light of historical facts and based on international law. There is no doubt that any territorial issues do not exist in the first place. I am aware that a variety of opinions exist on the unexistence of the territorial issue, while I think what we face now is a diplomatic issue. However, the territorial issue does not exist. That is the position of Japan.

[The remaining questions on defense issues and Chinese protests have been omitted.]

SOURCE: Ministry of Foreign Affairs of Japan. "Press Conference by Minister of Foreign Affairs Koichiro Gemba." September 19, 2012. http://www.mofa.go.jp/announce/fm_press/2012/9/0919_01.html.

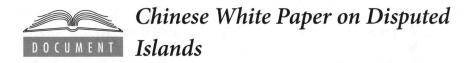

Chinese White Paper on Disputed Islands

September 25, 2012

[The table of contents has been omitted.]

FOREWORD

Diaoyu Dao and its affiliated islands are an inseparable part of the Chinese territory. Diaoyu Dao is China's inherent territory in all historical, geographical and legal terms, and China enjoys indisputable sovereignty over Diaoyu Dao.

Japan's occupation of Diaoyu Dao during the Sino-Japanese War in 1895 is illegal and invalid. After World War II, Diaoyu Dao was returned to China in accordance with such international legal documents as the Cairo Declaration and the Potsdam Proclamation. No matter what unilateral step Japan takes over Diaoyu Dao, it will not change the fact that Diaoyu Dao belongs to China. For quite some time, Japan has repeatedly stirred up troubles on the issue of Diaoyu Dao. On September 10, 2012, the Japanese government announced the "purchase" of Diaoyu Dao and its affiliated Nanxiao Dao and Beixiao Dao and the implementation of the so-called "nationalization." This is a move that grossly violates China's territorial sovereignty and seriously tramples on historical facts and international jurisprudence.

China is firmly opposed to Japan's violation of China's sovereignty over Diaoyu Dao in whatever form and has taken resolute measures to curb any such act. China's position on the issue of Diaoyu Dao is clear-cut and consistent. China's will to defend national sovereignty and territorial integrity is firm and its resolve to uphold the outcomes of the World Anti-Fascist War will not be shaken by any force.

I. DIAOYU DAO IS CHINA'S INHERENT TERRITORY

Diaoyu Dao and its affiliated islands, which consist of Diaoyu Dao, Huangwei Yu, Chiwei Yu, Nanxiao Dao, Beixiao Dao, Nan Yu, Bei Yu, Fei Yu and other islands and reefs, are located to the northeast of China's Taiwan Island, in the waters between 123°20'–124°40'E (East Longitude) and 25°40'–26°00'N (North Latitude), and are affiliated to the Taiwan Island. The total landmass of these islands is approximately 5.69 square kilometers. Diaoyu Dao, situated in the western tip of the area, covers a landmass of about 3.91 square kilometers and is the largest island in the area. The highest peak on the island stands

362 meters above the sea level. Huangwei Yu, which is located about 27 kilometers to the northeast of Diaoyu Dao, is the second largest island in the area, with a total landmass of about 0.91 square kilometers and a highest elevation of 117 meters. Chiwei Yu, situated about 110 kilometers to the northeast of Diaoyu Dao, is the easternmost island in the area. It covers a landmass of approximately 0.065 square kilometers and stands 75 meters above the sea level at its peak.

1. Diaoyu Dao was first discovered, named and exploited by China

Ancient ancestors in China first discovered and named Diaoyu Dao through their production and fishery activities on the sea. In China's historical literatures, Diaoyu Dao is also called Diaoyu Yu or Diaoyu Tai. The earliest historical record of the names of Diaoyu Dao, Chiwei Yu and other places can be found in the book *Voyage with a Tail Wind* (Shun Feng Xiang Song) published in 1403 (the first year of the reign of Emperor Yongle of the Ming Dynasty). It shows that China had already discovered and named Diaoyu Dao by the 14th and 15th centuries.

In 1372 (the fifth year of the reign of Emperor Hongwu of the Ming Dynasty), the King of Ryukyu started paying tribute to the imperial court of the Ming Dynasty. In return, Emperor Hongwu (the first emperor of the Ming Dynasty) sent imperial envoys to Ryukyu. In the following five centuries until 1866 (the fifth year of the reign of Emperor Tongzhi of the Qing Dynasty), the imperial courts of the Ming and Qing Dynasties sent imperial envoys to Ryukyu 24 times to confer titles on the Ryukyu King, and Diaoyu Dao was exactly located on their route to Ryukyu. Ample volume of records about Diaoyu Dao could be found in the reports written by Chinese imperial envoys at the time. For example, the *Records of the Imperial Title-conferring Envoys to Ryukyu* (Shi Liu Qiu Lu) written in 1534 by Chen Kan, an imperial title-conferring envoy from the Ming court, clearly stated that "the ship has passed Diaoyu Dao, Huangmao Yu, Chi Yu. . . . Then Gumi Mountain comes into sight, that is where the land of Ryukyu begins." The Shi Liu Qiu Lu of another imperial envoy of the Ming Dynasty, Guo Rulin, in 1562 also stated that "Chi Yu is the mountain that marks the boundary of Ryukyu." In 1719, Xu Baoguang, a deputy title-conferring envoy to Ryukyu in the Qing Dynasty, clearly recorded in his book *Records of Messages from Chong-shan* (Zhong Shan Chuan Xin Lu) that the voyage from Fujian to Ryukyu passed Huaping Yu, Pengjia Yu, Diaoyu Dao, Huangwei Yu, Chiwei Yu and reached Naba (Naha) port of Ryukyu via Gumi Mountain (the mountain guarding the southwest border of Ryukyu) and Machi Island.

In 1650, the *Annals of Chong-shan* (Zhong Shan Shi Jian), the first official historical record of the Ryukyu Kingdom drafted under the supervision of Ryukyu's prime minister Xiang Xiangxian (Kozoken), confirmed that Gumi Mountain (also called Gumi Mountain, known as Kume Island today) is part of Ryukyu's territory, while Chi Yu (known as Chiwei Yu today) and the areas to its west are not Ryukyu's territory. In 1708, Cheng Shunze (Tei Junsoku), a noted scholar and the Grand Master with the Purple-Golden Ribbon (Zi Jin Da Fu) of Ryukyu, recorded in his book *A General Guide* (Zhi Nan Guang Yi) that "Gumi Mountain is the mountain guarding the southwest border of Ryukyu."

These historical accounts clearly demonstrate that Diaoyu Dao and Chiwei Yu belong to China and Kume Island belongs to Ryukyu, and that the separating line lies in Hei Shui Gou (today's Okinawa Trough) between Chiwei Yu and Kume Island. In 1579, Xie Jie, a deputy imperial title-conferring envoy of the Ming Dynasty, recorded in his book, *Addendum to Summarized Record of Ryukyu* (Liu Qiu Lu Cuo Yao Bu Yi) that he entered

Ryukyu from Cang Shui to Hei Shui, and returned to China from Hei Shui to Cang Shui. Xia Ziyang, another imperial envoy of the Ming court, wrote in 1606 that "when the water flows from Hei Shui back to Cang Shui, it enters the Chinese territory." *Miscellaneous Records of a Mission to Ryukyu* (Shi Liu Qiu Za Lu), a book written in 1683 by Wang Ji, an imperial envoy of the Qing Dynasty, stated that "Hei Shui Gou," situated outside Chi Yu, is the "boundary between China and foreign land." In 1756, Zhou Huang, a deputy imperial envoy of the Qing Dynasty, recorded in his book, the *Annals of Ryukyu* (Liu Qiu Guo Zhi Lue), that Ryukyu "is separated from the waters of Fujian by Hei Shui Gou to the west."

The waters surrounding Diaoyu Dao are traditionally Chinese fishing ground. Chinese fishermen have, for generations, engaged in fishery activities in these waters. In the past, Diaoyu Dao was used as a navigation marker by the Chinese people living on the southeast coast.

2. Diaoyu Dao had long been under China's jurisdiction

In the early years of the Ming Dynasty, China placed Diaoyu Dao under its coastal defense to guard against the invasion of Japanese pirates along its southeast coast. In 1561 (the 40th year of the reign of Emperor Jiajing of the Ming Dynasty), *An Illustrated Compendium on Maritime Security* (Chou Hai Tu Bian) compiled by Zheng Ruozeng under the auspices of Hu Zongxian, the supreme commander of the southeast coastal defense of the Ming court, included the Diaoyu Dao Islands on the "Map of Coastal Mountains and Sands" (Yan Hai Shan Sha Tu) and incorporated them into the jurisdiction of the coastal defense of the Ming court. The Complete Map of Unified Maritime Territory for Coastal Defense (Qian Kun Yi Tong Hai Fang Quan Tu), drawn up by Xu Bida and others in 1605 (the 33rd year of the reign of Emperor Wanli of the Ming Dynasty) and the Treatise on Military Preparations. Coastal Defense II. Map of Fujian's Coastal Mountains and Sands (Wu Bei Zhi.Hai Fang Er.Fu Jian Yan Hai Shan Sha Tu), drawn up by Mao Yuanyi in 1621 (the first year of the reign of Emperor Tianqi of the Ming Dynasty), also included the Diaoyu Dao Islands as part of China's maritime territory.

The Qing court not only incorporated the Diaoyu Dao Islands into the scope of China's coastal defense as the Ming court did, but also clearly placed the islands under the jurisdiction of the local government of Taiwan. Official documents of the Qing court, such as *A Tour of Duty in the Taiwan Strait* (Tai Hai Shi Cha Lu) and *Annals of Taiwan Prefecture* (Tai Wan Fu Zhi) all gave detailed accounts concerning China's administration over Diaoyu Dao. Volume 86 of *Recompiled General Annals of Fujian* (Chong Zuan Fu Jian Tong Zhi), a book compiled by Chen Shouqi and others in 1871 (the tenth year of the reign of Emperor Tongzhi of the Qing Dynasty), included Diaoyu Dao as a strategic location for coastal defense and placed the islands under the jurisdiction of Gamalan, Taiwan (known as Yilan County today).

3. Chinese and foreign maps show that Diaoyu Dao belongs to China

The Roadmap to Ryukyu (Liu Qiu Guo Hai Tu) in the Shi Liu Qiu Lu written by imperial title-conferring envoy Xiao Chongye in 1579 (the seventh year of the reign of Emperor Wanli of the Ming Dynasty), the Record of the Interpreters of August Ming (Huang Ming Xiang Xu Lu) written by Mao Ruizheng in 1629 (the second year of the reign of Emperor Chongzhen of the Ming Dynasty), the Great Universal Geographic Map (Kun Yu Quan

Tu) created in 1767 (the 32nd year of the reign of Emperor Qianlong of the Qing Dynasty), and the Atlas of the Great Qing Dynasty (Huang Chao Zhong Wai Yi Tong Yu Tu) published in 1863 (the second year of the reign of Emperor Tongzhi of the Qing Dynasty) all marked Diaoyu Dao as China's territory.

The book *Illustrated Outline of the Three Countries* written by Hayashi Shihei in 1785 was the earliest Japanese literature to mention Diaoyu Dao. The Map of the Three Provinces and 36 Islands of Ryukyu in the book put Diaoyu Dao as being apart from the 36 islands of Ryukyu and colored it the same as the mainland of China, indicating that Diaoyu Dao was part of China's territory.

The Map of East China Sea Littoral States created by the French cartographer Pierre Lapie and others in 1809 colored Diaoyu Dao, Huangwei Yu, Chiwei Yu and the Taiwan Island as the same. Maps such as A New Map of China from the Latest Authorities published in Britain in 1811, Colton's China published in the United States in 1859, and A Map of China's East Coast: Hongkong to Gulf of Liao-Tung compiled by the British Navy in 1877 all marked Diaoyu Dao as part of China's territory.

II. Japan Grabbed Diaoyu Dao From China

Japan accelerated its invasion and external expansion after the Meiji Restoration. Japan seized Ryukyu in 1879 and changed its name to Okinawa Prefecture. Soon after that, Japan began to act covertly to invade and occupy Diaoyu Dao and secretly "included" Diaoyu Dao in its territory at the end of the Sino-Japanese War of 1894–1895. Japan then forced China to sign the unequal Treaty of Shimonoseki and cede to Japan the island of Formosa (Taiwan), together with Diaoyu Dao and all other islands appertaining or belonging to the said island of Formosa.

1. Japan's covert moves to seize Diaoyu Dao

In 1884, a Japanese man claimed that he first landed on Diaoyu Dao and found the island to be uninhabited. The Japanese government then dispatched secret facts-finding missions to Diaoyu Dao and attempted to invade and occupy the island. The above-mentioned plots by Japan triggered China's alert. On September 6, 1885 (the 28th day of the 7th month in the 11th year of the reign of Emperor Guangxu of the Qing Dynasty), the Chinese newspaper *Shen-pao (Shanghai News)* reported: "Recently, Japanese flags have been seen on the islands northeast to Taiwan, revealing Japan's intention to occupy these islands." But the Japanese government did not dare to take any further action for fear of reaction from China.

After the secret facts-finding missions to Diaoyu Dao, the governor of Okinawa Prefecture sent a report in secrecy to the Minister of Internal Affairs Yamagata Aritomo on September 22, 1885, saying that these uninhabited islands were, in fact, the same Diaoyu Tai, Huangwei Yu and Chiwe Yu that were recorded in the *Records of Messages from Chong-shan* (Zhong Shan Chuan Xin Lu) and known well to imperial title-conferring envoys of the Qing court on their voyages to Ryukyu, and that he had doubts as to whether or not sovereignty markers should be set up and therefore asked for instruction. The Minister of Internal Affairs Yamagata Aritomo solicited opinion from the Foreign Minister Inoue Kaoru on October 9. Inoue Kaoru replied in a letter to Yamagata Aritomo on October 21, "At present, any open moves such as placing sovereignty markers are bound to alert the Qing imperial court. Therefore, it is advisable not to go beyond field surveys and detailed reports on the shapes of the bays, land and other resources for future development. In the meantime, we will wait for a better time to engage in such activities as putting up sovereignty markers and embarking on development on the islands." Inoue Kaoru also made a special emphasis that "it is inappropriate to publicize the missions on official gazette or newspapers." As a result, the Japanese government did not approve of the request of Okinawa Prefecture to set up sovereignty markers.

The governor of Okinawa Prefecture submitted the matter for approval to the Minister of Internal Affairs once again on January 13, 1890, saying that Diaoyu Dao and other "above-mentioned uninhabited islands have remained under no specific jurisdiction," and that he "intends to place them under the jurisdiction of the Office of Yaeyama Islands." On November 2, 1893, the governor of Okinawa Prefecture applied once again for setting up sovereignty markers to incorporate the islands into Japan's territory. The Japanese government did not respond. On May 12, 1894, two months before the Sino-Japanese War, the secret facts-finding missions to Diaoyu Dao by Okinawa Prefecture came to a final conclusion, "Ever since the prefecture police surveyed the island in 1885 (the 18th year of the Meiji period), there have been no subsequent investigations. As a result, it is difficult to provide any specific reports on it. . . . In addition, there exist no old records related to the said island or folklore and legends demonstrating that the island belongs to our country."

Japan's attempts to occupy Diaoyu Dao were clearly recorded in Japan Diplomatic Documents compiled by the Japanese Foreign Ministry. Relevant documents evidently show that the Japanese government intended to occupy Diaoyu Dao, but refrained from acting impetuously as it was fully aware of China's sovereignty over these islands.

Japan waged the Sino-Japanese War in July 1894. Towards the end of November 1894, Japanese forces seized the Chinese port of Lushun (then known as Port Arthur), virtually securing defeat of the Qing court. Against such backdrop, the Japanese Minister of Internal Affairs Yasushi Nomura wrote to Foreign Minister Mutsu Munemitsu on December 27 that the "circumstances have now changed," and called for a decision by the cabinet on the issue of setting up sovereignty markers in Diaoyu Dao and incorporating the island into Japan's territory. Mutsu Munemitsu expressed his support for the proposal in his reply to Yasushi Nomura on January 11, 1895. The Japanese cabinet secretly passed a resolution on January 14 to "place" Diaoyu Dao under the jurisdiction of Okinawa Prefecture.

Japan's official documents show that from the time of the facts-finding missions to Diaoyu Dao in 1885 to the occupation of the islands in 1895, Japan had consistently acted in secrecy without making its moves public. This further proves that Japan's claim of sovereignty over Diaoyu Dao does not have legal effect under international law.

2. Diaoyu Dao was ceded to Japan together with the Taiwan Island

On April 17, 1895, the Qing court was defeated in the Sino-Japanese War and forced to sign the unequal Treaty of Shimonoseki and cede to Japan "the island of Formosa (Taiwan), together with all islands appertaining or belonging to the said island of Formosa." The Diaoyu Dao Islands were ceded to Japan as "islands appertaining or belonging to the said island of Formosa." In 1900, Japan changed the name of Diaoyu Dao to "Senkaku Islands."

III. BACKROOM DEALS BETWEEN THE UNITED STATES AND JAPAN CONCERNING DIAOYU DAO ARE ILLEGAL AND INVALID

Diaoyu Dao was returned to China after the Second World War. However, the United States arbitrarily included Diaoyu Dao under its trusteeship in the 1950s and "returned" the "power of administration" over Diaoyu Dao to Japan in the 1970s. The backroom deals between the United States and Japan concerning Diaoyu Dao are acts of grave violation of China's territorial sovereignty. They are illegal and invalid. They have not and cannot change the fact that Diaoyu Dao belongs to China.

1. Diaoyu Dao was returned to China after the Second World War

In December 1941, the Chinese government officially declared war against Japan together with the abrogation of all treaties between China and Japan. In December 1943, the Cairo Declaration stated in explicit terms that "all the territories Japan has stolen from the Chinese, such as Manchuria, Formosa [Taiwan] and the Pescadores, shall be restored to the Republic of China. Japan will also be expelled from all other territories which she has taken by violence and greed." In July 1945, the Potsdam Proclamation stated in Article 8: "The terms of the Cairo Declaration shall be carried out and Japanese sovereignty shall be limited to the islands of Honshu, Hokkaido, Kyushu, Shikoku and such minor islands as we determine." On September 2, 1945, the Japanese government accepted the Potsdam Proclamation in explicit terms with the Japanese Instrument of Surrender and pledged to faithfully fulfill the obligations enshrined in the provisions of the Potsdam Proclamation. On January 29, 1946, the Supreme Commander for the Allied Powers Instruction (SCAPIN) No. 677 clearly defined Japan's power of administration to "include the four main islands of Japan (Hokkaido, Honshu, Kyushu and Shikoku) and the approximately 1,000 smaller adjacent islands, including the Tsushima Islands and the Ryukyu Islands north of the 30th parallel of North Latitude." On October 25, 1945, the ceremony for accepting Japan's surrender in Taiwan Province of the China War Theater was held in Taipei, and the Chinese government officially recovered Taiwan. On September 29, 1972, the Japanese government committed with all seriousness in the China-Japan Joint Statement that "the Government of Japan fully understands and respects this stand of the Government of the People's Republic of China [Taiwan is an inalienable part of the territory of the People's Republic of China], and it firmly maintains its stand under Article 8 of the Potsdam Proclamation."

These facts show that in accordance with the Cairo Declaration, the Potsdam Proclamation and the Japanese Instrument of Surrender, Diaoyu Dao, as affiliated islands of Taiwan, should be returned, together with Taiwan, to China.

2. The United States illegally included Diaoyu Dao under its trusteeship

On September 8, 1951, Japan, the United States and a number of other countries signed the Treaty of Peace with Japan (commonly known as the Treaty of San Francisco) with China being excluded from it. The treaty placed the Nansei Islands south of the 29th parallel of North Latitude under United Nations' trusteeship, with the United States as the sole administering authority. It should be pointed out that the Nansei Islands placed under the administration of the United States in the Treaty of Peace with Japan did not include Diaoyu Dao.

The United States Civil Administration of the Ryukyu Islands (USCAR) issued Civil Administration Ordinance No. 68 (Provisions of the Government of the Ryukyu Islands) on February 29, 1952 and Civil Administration Proclamation No. 27 (defining the "geographical boundary lines of the Ryukyu Islands") on December 25, 1953, arbitrarily expanding its jurisdiction to include China's Diaoyu Dao. However, there were no legal grounds whatsoever for the US act, to which China has firmly opposed.

3. The United States and Japan conducted backroom deals concerning the "power of administration" over Diaoyu Dao

On June 17, 1971, Japan and the United States signed the Agreement Concerning the Ryukyu Islands and the Daito Islands (Okinawa Reversion Agreement), which provided that any and all powers of administration over the Ryukyu Islands and Diaoyu Dao would be "returned" to Japan. The Chinese people, including overseas Chinese, all condemned such a backroom deal. On December 30, 1971, the Chinese Ministry of Foreign Affairs issued a solemn statement, pointing out that "it is completely illegal for the government of the United States and Japan to include China's Diaoyu Dao Islands into the territories to be returned to Japan in the Okinawa Reversion Agreement and that it can by no means change the People's Republic of China's territorial sovereignty over the Diaoyu Dao Islands." The Taiwan authorities also expressed firm opposition to the backroom deal between the United States and Japan.

In response to the strong opposition of the Chinese government and people, the United States had to publicly clarify its position on the sovereignty over Diaoyu Dao. In October 1971, the US administration stated that "the United States believes that a return of administrative rights over those islands to Japan, from which the rights were received, can in no way prejudice any underlying claims. The United States cannot add to the legal rights Japan possessed before it transferred administration of the islands to us, nor can the United States, by giving back what it received, diminish the rights of other claimants. . . . The United States has made no claim to Diaoyu Dao and considers that any conflicting claims to the islands are a matter for resolution by the parties concerned." In November 1971, when presenting the Okinawa Reversion Agreement to the US Senate for ratification, the US Department of State stressed that the United States took a neutral position with regard to the competing Japanese and Chinese claims to the islands, despite the return of administrative rights over the islands to Japan.

IV. Japan's Claim of Sovereignty Over Diaoyu Dao Is Totally Unfounded

On March 8, 1972, Japan's Ministry of Foreign Affairs issued the Basic View on the Sovereignty over the Senkaku Islands in an attempt to explain the Japanese government's claims of sovereignty over Diaoyu Dao. First, Japan claims that Diaoyu Dao was "terra nullius" and not part of Pescadores, Formosa [Taiwan] or their affiliated islands which were ceded to Japan by the Qing government in accordance with the Treaty of Shimonoseki. Second, Japan claims that Diaoyu Dao was not included in the territory which Japan renounced under Article 2 of the Treaty of San Francisco, but was placed under the administration of the United States as part of the Nansei Islands in accordance with Article 3 of the said treaty, and was included in the area for which the administrative rights were reverted to Japan in accordance with the Okinawa Reversion Agreement. Third, Japan claims that China didn't regard Diaoyu Dao as part of Taiwan and had never challenged the inclusion of the islands in the area over which the United States exercised administrative rights in accordance with Article 3 of the Treaty of San Francisco.

Such claims by Japan fly in the face of facts and are totally unfounded.

Diaoyu Dao belongs to China. It is by no means "terra nullius." China is the indisputable owner of Diaoyu Dao as it had exercised valid jurisdiction over the island for several hundred years long before the Japanese people "discovered" it. As stated above, voluminous

Japanese official documents prove that Japan was fully aware that according to international law, Diaoyu Dao has long been part of China and was not "terra nullius." Japan's act to include Diaoyu Dao as "terra nullius" into its territory based on the "occupation" principle is in fact an illegal act of occupying Chinese territory and has no legal effect according to international law.

Diaoyu Dao has always been affiliated to China's Taiwan Island both in geographical terms and in accordance with China's historical jurisdiction practice. Through the unequal Treaty of Shimonoseki, Japan forced the Qing court to cede to it "the island of Taiwan, together with all islands appertaining or belonging to it," including Diaoyu Dao. International legal documents such as the Cairo Declaration and the Potsdam Proclamation provide that Japan must unconditionally return the territories it has stolen from China. These documents also clearly define Japan's territory, which by no means includes Diaoyu Dao. Japan's attempted occupation of Diaoyu Dao, in essence, constitutes a challenge to the post-war international order established by such legal documents as the Cairo Declaration and the Potsdam Proclamation and seriously violates the obligations Japan should undertake according to international law.

Diaoyu Dao was not placed under the trusteeship established by the Treaty of San Francisco, which was signed between the United States and other countries with Japan and is partial in nature. The United States arbitrarily expanded the scope of trusteeship to include Diaoyu Dao, which is China's territory, and later "returned" the "power of administration" over Diaoyu Dao to Japan. This has no legal basis and is totally invalid according to international law. The government and people of China have always explicitly opposed such illegal acts of the United States and Japan.

V. CHINA HAS TAKEN RESOLUTE MEASURES TO SAFEGUARD ITS SOVEREIGNTY OVER DIAOYU DAO

China has, over the past years, taken resolute measures to safeguard its sovereignty over Diaoyu Dao.

China has, through the diplomatic channel, strongly protested against and condemned the backroom deals between the United States and Japan over Diaoyu Dao. On August 15, 1951, before the San Francisco Conference, the Chinese government made a statement: "If the People's Republic of China is excluded from the preparation, formulation and signing of the peace treaty with Japan, it will, no matter what its content and outcome are, be regarded as illegal and therefore invalid by the central people's government." On September 18, 1951, the Chinese government issued another statement stressing that the Treaty of San Francisco is illegal and invalid and can under no circumstances be recognized. In 1971, responding to the ratifications of the Okinawa Reversion Agreement by the US Congress and Japanese Diet, the Chinese Foreign Ministry issued a stern statement which pointed out that the Diaoyu Dao Islands have been an indivisible part of the Chinese territory since ancient times.

In response to Japan's illegal violation of China's sovereignty over Diaoyu Dao, the Chinese government has taken active and forceful measures such as issuing diplomatic statements, making serious representations with Japan and submitting notes of protest to the United Nations, solemnly stating China's consistent proposition, principle and position, firmly upholding China's territorial sovereignty and maritime rights and interests, and earnestly protecting the safety of life and property of Chinese citizens.

China has enacted domestic laws, which clearly provide that Diaoyu Dao belongs to China. In 1958, the Chinese government released a statement on the territorial sea, announcing that Taiwan and its adjacent islands belong to China. In light of Japan's repeated violations of China's sovereignty over Diaoyu Dao since the 1970s, China adopted the Law of the People's Republic of China on the Territorial Sea and the Contiguous Zone in 1992, which unequivocally prescribes that "Taiwan and the various affiliated islands including Diaoyu Dao" belong to China. The 2009 Law of the People's Republic of China on the Protection of Offshore Islands establishes the protection, development and management system of offshore islands and prescribes the determination and announcement of the names of offshore islands, on the basis of which China announced the standard names of Diaoyu Dao and some of its affiliated islands in March 2012. On September 10, 2012, the Chinese government issued a statement announcing the baselines of the territorial sea of Diaoyu Dao and its affiliated islands. On September 13, the Chinese government deposited the coordinates table and chart of the base points and baselines of the territorial sea of Diaoyu Dao and its affiliated islands with the Secretary-General of the United Nations.

China has maintained routine presence and exercised jurisdiction in the waters of Diaoyu Dao. China's marine surveillance vessels have been carrying out law enforcement patrol missions in the waters of Diaoyu Dao, and fishery administration law enforcement vessels have been conducting regular law enforcement patrols and fishery protection missions to uphold normal fishing order in the waters of Diaoyu Dao. China has also exercised administration over Diaoyu Dao and the adjacent waters by releasing weather forecasts and through oceanographic monitoring and forecasting.

Over the years, the issue of Diaoyu Dao has attracted attention from Hong Kong and Macao compatriots, Taiwan compatriots and overseas Chinese. Diaoyu Dao has been an inherent territory of China since ancient times. This is the common position of the entire Chinese nation. The Chinese nation has the strong resolve to uphold state sovereignty and territorial integrity. The compatriots across the Taiwan Straits stand firmly together on matters of principle to the nation and in the efforts to uphold national interests and dignity. The compatriots from Hong Kong, Macao and Taiwan and the overseas Chinese have all carried out various forms of activities to safeguard China's territorial sovereignty over Diaoyu Dao, strongly expressing the just position of the Chinese nation, and displaying to the rest of the world that the peace-loving Chinese nation has the determination and the will to uphold China's state sovereignty and territorial integrity.

Conclusion

Diaoyu Dao has been an inherent territory of China since ancient times, and China has indisputable sovereignty over Diaoyu Dao. As China and Japan were normalizing relations and concluding the Sino-Japanese Treaty of Peace and Friendship in the 1970s, the then leaders of the two countries, acting in the larger interest of China-Japan relations, reached important understanding and consensus on "leaving the issue of Diaoyu Dao to be resolved later." But in recent years, Japan has repeatedly taken unilateral measures concerning Diaoyu Dao and conducted in particular the so-called "nationalization" of Diaoyu Dao. This severely infringed upon China's sovereignty and ran counter to the understanding and consensus reached between the older generation of leaders of the two countries. It has not only seriously damaged China-Japan relations, but also rejected and challenged the outcomes of the victory of the World Anti-Fascist War.

China strongly urges Japan to respect history and international law and immediately stop all actions that undermine China's territorial sovereignty. The Chinese government has the unshakable resolve and will to uphold the nation's territorial sovereignty. It has the confidence and ability to safeguard China's state sovereignty and territorial integrity.

SOURCE: Government of the People's Republic of China. State Council Information Office. "Diaoyu Dao, an Inherent Territory of China." September 25, 2012. http://english.gov.cn/official/2012-09/25/content_2232763.htm.

OTHER HISTORIC DOCUMENTS OF INTEREST

FROM PREVIOUS *HISTORIC DOCUMENTS*

- China-Japan Accord, *1972*, p. 827

October

President Obama Issues Executive Order Sanctioning Iran; IAEA and Iran Continue Nuclear Talks

OCTOBER 9, NOVEMBER 16, AND DECEMBER 14, 2012

In October 2012, the United States once again imposed additional sanctions on Iran, expanding the list of targeted individuals and entities, closing loopholes in some existing sanctions, and enhancing penalties for violators. The move followed two rounds of sanctions imposed earlier in the year and occurred at a time when diplomatic talks between Iran and the international community had stalled. Later that fall, the UN's International Atomic Energy Agency (IAEA) announced a resumption of its talks with Iran, even as it continued reporting on Iran's progress in constructing uranium enrichment facilities and the country's alleged efforts to cover up its activities at one site.

WHY SANCTIONS?

International sanctions of Iran are driven by concerns among the international community that Iran is attempting to build nuclear weapons, a violation of the Nuclear Non-Proliferation Treaty (NPT), which was designed to prevent the spread of nuclear weapons and promote peaceful uses of nuclear energy. Iran has long sought to develop technology that would enable it to build a nuclear bomb, but it has a history of attempting to conceal these activities and their possible military applications from the international community. Although Iran's former president Mohammad Khatami agreed in 2003 to suspend uranium enrichment, a key component in developing nuclear fuel, President Mahmoud Ahmadinejad reversed that decision in 2006 and significantly restricted the IAEA's access to information on the country's nuclear activities. Iran has traditionally claimed that its nuclear program is peaceful in nature and is only intended to generate electricity for its citizens.

Through sanctions, the United Nations, Europe, and the United States have attempted to push Iran to cooperate with the IAEA and to participate in multiparty talks aimed at finding a diplomatic solution to the nuclear dispute. The United States has imposed a variety of sanctions on the country since Iranian students stormed and seized the U.S. Embassy in Tehran in 1979 during the Islamic Revolution. U.S. officials have cited Iran's support for terrorism, human rights violations, failure to cooperate with IAEA inspectors, and suspected ambitions to acquire weapons of mass destruction as reasons for the sanctions, which broadened under former president Bill Clinton in the mid-1990s and have continued to expand since 2005. Today, U.S. sanctions prohibit almost all trade with Iran, except for specific instances that are "intended to benefit the Iranian people," such as providing humanitarian assistance.

Throughout 2012, the U.S. Congress and President Barack Obama implemented several new rounds of sanctions, including a February freeze of all U.S. property owned by the Central Bank of Iran, other Iranian financial institutions, and the Iranian government. In June, measures intended to punish foreign countries for buying Iranian oil went into effect. The following month, President Obama signed an executive order aimed at preventing Iran from creating different payment mechanisms for its oil and energy products in order to circumvent existing sanctions, and the U.S. Treasury Department announced sanctions against Chinese and Iraqi banks that it claimed had "facilitated transactions worth millions of dollars on behalf of Iranian banks that are subject to sanctions for their links to Iran's illicit proliferation activities."

EXECUTIVE ORDER 13628

Building on these actions, President Obama signed Executive Order 13628 on October 9, 2012. The order created a framework for implementing the Iran Threat Reduction and Syria Human Rights Act of 2012, passed by the Senate on August 1, which approved new sanctions on Iran's energy, shipping, and financial industries. In light of the Central Bank of Iran and other Iranian banks' efforts to conceal transactions made by sanctioned parties, a key goal of the legislation was to close loopholes that made it possible for some companies to circumvent existing sanctions. It also sought to prevent the return to Iran of any revenue from purchases of Iranian oil that are still legally allowed and to impose sanctions on those responsible for or complicit in human rights abuses committed against Iranian citizens.

The president's order delegated enforcement authority of the new law to the secretaries of state and the Treasury and instructed them to prevent any Iranian assets deemed to be in U.S. control, including foreign branches of American banks, from being transferred, paid, exported, or withdrawn. In addition to other restrictions, the order instructed the secretaries to prohibit any U.S. financial institutions from making loans or providing credit to a sanctioned person; prohibit U.S. citizens from investing in or purchasing equity or debt of a sanctioned person; prohibit any transfers of credit or payments between financial institutions, or by, through, or to any financial institution, that involve the interest of a sanctioned person; and restrict or prohibit imports of goods, technology, or services directly or indirectly into the United States. The order also prohibited the provision of goods, services, technology, information, or other support of a certain market value that could facilitate Iran's production and refinement of refined petroleum products. Furthermore, it suspended entry to the United States for immigrants or nonimmigrants who had supported the Iranian government in committing human rights abuses or limiting Iranians' freedom of expression. The order did make exceptions for extending loans or credit to those "engaged in activities to relieve human suffering" as long as the funds were used for such activities.

"The onus is on Iran to abide by its international obligations with respect to its nuclear program," said Tommy Vietor, National Security Council spokesperson, in a statement following the order's signing. "If the Iranian government continues its defiance, there should be no doubt that the United States and our partners will continue to tighten our sanctions and impose increasing consequences." Indeed, on December 13, the United States imposed sanctions on seven companies and five individuals that officials said had provided support to Iran's nuclear program, freezing assets they held in the United States and prohibiting them from conducting business with U.S. firms or citizens.

RETURNING TO THE NEGOTIATING TABLE

Exactly one month after President Obama's executive order, IAEA and Iranian officials announced that they would resume their bilateral talks, on hold since August, in Tehran on December 13. They had been meeting throughout the year to discuss the IAEA's concerns, outlined in a November 2011 report, that there are military dimensions to Iran's nuclear activities. While the report did not provide evidence of a fully constructed nuclear weapon, it cited activities such as high explosives testing and the development of atomic bomb triggers as indicators of possible ongoing weapons research. The IAEA also hoped to reach an agreement with Iran on where and how agency inspectors could further investigate whether the country was taking steps to create nuclear weapons, or had done so in the past, and the actions Iran could take to meet its obligations under the NPT. For its part, Iran sought an agreement that would limit the extent of the IAEA's investigation and its right to ask further questions about Iran's nuclear activities.

One issue of particular focus during the talks was the IAEA's desire for an agreement that would allow it to inspect Parchin, a military facility at which the IAEA believed Iran had been conducting certain tests that could have nuclear applications. Inspectors had previously been allowed to visit Parchin in January 2005 but were only given access to five buildings in one of the site's four sectors and did not see evidence of nuclear activities. Iran had so far denied the IAEA's request to return to Parchin, offering instead to let inspectors visit a different site about which the agency had no information; IAEA officials declined. Following a meeting with Iran in May, IAEA Director General Yukiya Amano said that Iranian officials had indicated some willingness to allow inspections of the Parchin facility, though they had not offered a specific timeline or other details, and expressed optimism that the two sides would be able to reach an agreement. Yet in June, IAEA officials emerged from their latest discussions with Iran saying that they had made "no progress" in gaining access to restricted nuclear sites. Additional meetings yielded no further results.

Meanwhile, separate six-party talks between the United States, Russia, China, Britain, France, Germany, and Iran had resumed in April after a fifteen-month suspension. This group sought an agreement with Iranian officials to stop enriching uranium to 20 percent purity, a level at which it is easy to convert the material into weapons-grade fuel, and to consider exporting whatever stockpile of such uranium it already had. The six-party talks had also been unsuccessful in achieving results, causing some to suspect that Iran was delaying diplomatic progress on purpose in order to buy time to continue enriching uranium and possibly hide evidence of its activities.

The lack of progress led some to be skeptical that a new round of talks between the IAEA and Iran would be productive. "We will see how this round goes," said Victoria Nuland, U.S. State Department spokesperson. "In the past Iran has been unwilling to do what it needs to do despite the best efforts of the IAEA. But we commend the IAEA for keeping at it and we call on Iran to do what it needs to do to meet the international community's concerns."

Potentially complicating matters, Fereydoon Abbasi-Davani, Iran's vice president and head of the country's Atomic Energy Organization, made several pointed criticisms of the IAEA during a September 17 speech at a conference hosted by the agency. Abbasi-Davani claimed the IAEA was filled with "terrorists and saboteurs" and suggested the agency may have been responsible for past explosions that had occurred at two of Iran's main uranium enrichment facilities. He also told the newspaper *Al Hayat* that the Iranian government had sometimes given false information about its nuclear program to international officials in an effort to protect itself from foreign espionage. "We presented false information sometimes in order to protect our nuclear position and our achievements, as there is no other choice but to mislead foreign intelligence," Abbasi-Davani said, though he did not specify which government statements had been false.

IAEA Reports

As IAEA officials prepared for their meeting in Iran, the agency released a new report on November 16 on the country's most recent nuclear activities. The report found that Iran had made significant progress in completing its underground uranium enrichment facility, Fordow, noting that it had installed all of the centrifuges it would need to run the plant, though not all of them were operational. It also affirmed that "extensive activities" at the Parchin facility have likely "seriously undermined" the IAEA's ability to effectively verify what nuclear activities might have taken place there, pointing to satellite pictures showing that earth had been moved and equipment removed from the site. The agency called on Iran to provide access to Parchin and substantive answers to its questions regarding the site "without further delay."

Unclear Results

No major details emerged immediately following the December 13 meeting between IAEA and Iranian officials. Iran's ambassador to the IAEA, Ali Asghar Soltanieh, told the Islamic Republic News Agency, "Intensive negotiations were held. . . . There was good progress made. The two sides agreed to hold the next round of talks on January 16 in Tehran." The following day, IAEA Deputy Director General for Safeguards Herman Nackaerts issued a statement echoing the sentiment that officials made progress in coming up with an approach "to resolving the outstanding issues on possible military dimensions of Iran's nuclear programme," though he acknowledged to reporters that the IAEA had not yet been granted access to Parchin. He also noted that officials expected to finalize an agreement at their January meeting and to begin implementing the plan shortly thereafter.

—Linda Fecteau

Following is the text of an executive order issued on October 9, 2012, by President Barack Obama, imposing additional sanctions on Iran; the edited text of a report from the International Atomic Energy Agency (IAEA) on nuclear activities in Iran, issued on November 16, 2012; and the text of a statement from the IAEA on December 14, 2012, regarding ongoing nuclear talks with Iran.

DOCUMENT   *Executive Order Sanctions Iran*

October 9, 2012

By the authority vested in me as President by the Constitution and the laws of the United States of America, including the International Emergency Economic Powers Act

(50 U.S.C. 1701 et seq.) (IEEPA), the National Emergencies Act (50 U.S.C. 1601 et seq.), the Iran Sanctions Act of 1996 (Public Law 104–172) (50 U.S.C. 1701 note), as amended (ISA), the Comprehensive Iran Sanctions, Accountability, and Divestment Act of 2010 (Public Law 111–195) (22 U.S.C. 8501 et seq.), as amended (CISADA), the Iran Threat Reduction and Syria Human Rights Act of 2012 (Public Law 112–158) (ITRSHRA), section 212(f) of the Immigration and Nationality Act of 1952, as amended (8 U.S.C. 1182(f)), and section 301 of title 3, United States Code, and in order to take additional steps with respect to the national emergency declared in Executive Order 12957 of March 15, 1995,

I, *Barack Obama,* President of the United States of America, hereby order:

Section 1. (a) When the President, or the Secretary of State or the Secretary of the Treasury pursuant to authority delegated by the President and in accordance with the terms of such delegation, has determined that sanctions shall be imposed on a person pursuant to ISA, CISADA, or ITRSHRA and has, in accordance with those authorities, selected one or more of the sanctions set forth in section 6 of ISA to impose on that person, the Secretary of the Treasury, in consultation with the Secretary of State, shall take the following actions with respect to the sanctions selected and maintained by the President, the Secretary of State, or the Secretary of the Treasury:

  (i)   with respect to section 6(a)(3) of ISA, prohibit any United States financial institution from making loans or providing credits to the sanctioned person consistent with that section;

  (ii) with respect to section 6(a)(6) of ISA, prohibit any transactions in foreign exchange that are subject to the jurisdiction of the United States and in which the sanctioned person has any interest;

  (iii) with respect to section 6(a)(7) of ISA, prohibit any transfers of credit or payments between financial institutions or by, through, or to any financial institution, to the extent that such transfers or payments are subject to the jurisdiction of the United States and involve any interest of the sanctioned person;

  (iv) with respect to section 6(a)(8) of ISA, block all property and interests in property that are in the United States, that come within the United States, or that are or come within the possession or control of any United States person, including any foreign branch, of the sanctioned person, and provide that such property and interests in property may not be transferred, paid, exported, withdrawn, or otherwise dealt in;

  (v)   with respect to section 6(a)(9) of ISA, prohibit any United States person from investing in or purchasing significant amounts of equity or debt instruments of a sanctioned person;

  (vi) with respect to section 6(a)(11) of ISA, impose on the principal executive officer or officers, or persons performing similar functions and with similar authorities, of a sanctioned person the sanctions described in sections 6(a)(3), 6(a)(6), (6)(a)(7), 6(a)(8), 6(a)(9), or 6(a)(12) of ISA, as selected by the President, Secretary of State, or Secretary of the Treasury, as appropriate; or

  (vii) with respect to section 6(a)(12) of ISA, restrict or prohibit imports of goods, technology, or services, directly or indirectly, into the United States from the sanctioned person. . . .

Sec. 2. (a) All property and interests in property that are in the United States, that hereafter come within the United States, or that are or hereafter come within the possession or control of any United States person, including any foreign branch, of the following persons are blocked and may not be transferred, paid, exported, withdrawn, or otherwise dealt in: any person determined by the Secretary of the Treasury, in consultation with or at the recommendation of the Secretary of State:

(i)   to have knowingly, on or after August 10, 2012, transferred, or facilitated the transfer of, goods or technologies to Iran, any entity organized under the laws of Iran or otherwise subject to the jurisdiction of the Government of Iran, or any national of Iran, for use in or with respect to Iran, that are likely to be used by the Government of Iran or any of its agencies or instrumentalities, or by any other person on behalf of the Government of Iran or any of such agencies or instrumentalities, to commit serious human rights abuses against the people of Iran;

(ii)   to have knowingly, on or after August 10, 2012, provided services, including services relating to hardware, software, or specialized information or professional consulting, engineering, or support services, with respect to goods or technologies that have been transferred to Iran and that are likely to be used by the Government of Iran or any of its agencies or instrumentalities, or by any other person on behalf of the Government of Iran or any of such agencies or instrumentalities, to commit serious human rights abuses against the people of Iran;

(iii) to have materially assisted, sponsored, or provided financial, material, or technological support for, or goods or services to or in support of, the activities described in subsection (a)(i) or (a)(ii) of this section or any person whose property and interests in property are blocked pursuant to this section; or

(iv)   to be owned or controlled by, or to have acted or purported to act for or on behalf of, directly or indirectly, any person whose property and interests in property are blocked pursuant to this section. . . .

Sec. 3. (a) All property and interests in property that are in the United States, that hereafter come within the United States, or that are or hereafter come within the possession or control of any United States person, including any foreign branch, of the following persons are blocked and may not be transferred, paid, exported, withdrawn, or otherwise dealt in: any person determined by the Secretary of the Treasury, in consultation with or at the recommendation of the Secretary of State:

(i)   to have engaged in censorship or other activities with respect to Iran on or after June 12, 2009, that prohibit, limit, or penalize the exercise of freedom of expression or assembly by citizens of Iran, or that limit access to print or broadcast media, including the facilitation or support of intentional frequency manipulation by the Government of Iran or an entity owned or controlled by the Government of Iran that would jam or restrict an international signal;

(ii)   to have materially assisted, sponsored, or provided financial, material, or technological support for, or goods or services to or in support of, the activities described in subsection (a)(i) of this section or any person whose property and interests in property are blocked pursuant to this section; or

(iii) to be owned or controlled by, or to have acted or purported to act for or on behalf of, directly or indirectly, any person whose property and interests in property are blocked pursuant to this section. . . .

Sec. 4. (a) No entity owned or controlled by a United States person and established or maintained outside the United States may knowingly engage in any transaction, directly or indirectly, with the Government of Iran or any person subject to the jurisdiction of the Government of Iran, if that transaction would be prohibited by Executive Order 12957, Executive Order 12959 of May 6, 1995, Executive Order 13059 of August 19, 1997, Executive Order 13599 of February 5, 2012, section 5 of Executive Order 13622 of July 30, 2012, or section 12 of this order, or any regulation issued pursuant to the foregoing, if the transaction were engaged in by a United States person or in the United States.

(b) Penalties assessed for violations of the prohibition in subsection (a) of this section, and any related violations of section 12 of this order, may be assessed against the United States person that owns or controls the entity that engaged in the prohibited transaction.

(c) Penalties for violations of the prohibition in subsection (a) of this section shall not apply if the United States person that owns or controls the entity divests or terminates its business with the entity not later than February 6, 2013. . . .

Sec. 5. The Secretary of State, in consultation with the Secretary of the Treasury, the Secretary of Commerce, and the United States Trade Representative, and with the President of the Export-Import Bank of the United States, the Chairman of the Board of Governors of the Federal Reserve System, and other agencies and officials as appropriate, is hereby authorized to impose on a person any of the sanctions described in section 6 or 7 of this order upon determining that the person:

(a) knowingly, between July 1, 2010, and August 10, 2012, sold, leased, or provided to Iran goods, services, technology, information, or support with a fair market value of $1,000,000 or more, or with an aggregate fair market value of $5,000,000 or more during a 12-month period, and that could directly and significantly facilitate the maintenance or expansion of Iran's domestic production of refined petroleum products, including any direct and significant assistance with respect to the construction, modernization, or repair of petroleum refineries;

(b) knowingly, between July 1, 2010, and August 10, 2012, sold or provided to Iran refined petroleum products with a fair market value of $1,000,000 or more, or with an aggregate fair market value of $5,000,000 or more during a 12-month period;

(c) knowingly, between July 1, 2010, and August 10, 2012, sold, leased, or provided to Iran goods, services, technology, information, or support with a fair market value of $1,000,000 or more, or with an aggregate fair market value of $5,000,000 or more during a 12-month period, and that could directly and significantly contribute to the enhancement of Iran's ability to import refined petroleum products;

(d) is a successor entity to a person determined by the Secretary of State in accordance with this section to meet the criteria in subsection (a), (b), or (c) of this section;

(e) owns or controls a person determined by the Secretary of State in accordance with this section to meet the criteria in subsection (a), (b), or (c) of this section, and had knowledge that the person engaged in the activities referred to in that subsection; or

(f) is owned or controlled by, or under common ownership or control with, a person determined by the Secretary of State in accordance with this section to meet the criteria in subsection (a), (b), or (c) of this section, and knowingly participated in the activities referred to in that subsection.

Sec. 6. (a) When the Secretary of State, in accordance with the terms of section 5 of this order, has determined that a person meets any of the criteria described in section 5 and has selected any of the sanctions set forth below to impose on that person, the heads of relevant agencies, in consultation with the Secretary of State, shall take the following actions where necessary to implement the sanctions imposed by the Secretary of State:

   (i)   the Board of Directors of the Export-Import Bank shall deny approval of the issuance of any guarantee, insurance, extension of credit, or participation in an extension of credit in connection with the export of any goods or services to the sanctioned person;

   (ii)   agencies shall not issue any specific license or grant any other specific permission or authority under any statute that requires the prior review and approval of the United States Government as a condition for the export or reexport of goods or technology to the sanctioned person;

   (iii) with respect to a sanctioned person that is a financial institution:

      (1) the Chairman of the Board of Governors of the Federal Reserve System and the President of the Federal Reserve Bank of New York shall take such actions as they deem appropriate, including denying designation, or terminating the continuation of any prior designation of, the sanctioned person as a primary dealer in United States Government debt instruments; or

      (2) agencies shall prevent the sanctioned person from serving as an agent of the United States Government or serving as a repository for United States Government funds; or

   (iv)   agencies shall not procure, or enter into a contract for the procurement of, any goods or services from the sanctioned person. . . .

Sec. 7. (a) When the Secretary of State, in accordance with the terms of section 5 of this order, has determined that a person meets any of the criteria described in section 5 and has selected any of the sanctions set forth below to impose on that person, the Secretary of the Treasury, in consultation with the Secretary of State, shall take the following actions where necessary to implement the sanctions imposed by the Secretary of State:

   (i)   prohibit any United States financial institution from making loans or providing credits to the sanctioned person totaling more than $10,000,000 in any 12-month period, unless such person is engaged in activities to relieve human suffering and the loans or credits are provided for such activities;

   (ii)   prohibit any transactions in foreign exchange that are subject to the jurisdiction of the United States and in which the sanctioned person has any interest;

   (iii) prohibit any transfers of credit or payments between financial institutions or by, through, or to any financial institution, to the extent that such transfers or payments are subject to the jurisdiction of the United States and involve any interest of the sanctioned person;

(iv)   block all property and interests in property that are in the United States, that come within the United States, or that are or come within the possession or control of any United States person, including any foreign branch, of the sanctioned person, and provide that such property and interests in property may not be transferred, paid, exported, withdrawn, or otherwise dealt in; or

(v)   restrict or prohibit imports of goods, technology, or services, directly or indirectly, into the United States from the sanctioned person. . . .

Sec. 8. I hereby determine that, to the extent that section 203(b)(2) of IEEPA (50 U.S.C. 1702(b)(2)) may apply, the making of donations of the types of articles specified in such section by, to, or for the benefit of any person whose property and interests in property are blocked pursuant to this order would seriously impair my ability to deal with the national emergency declared in Executive Order 12957, and I hereby prohibit such donations as provided by subsections 1(a)(iv), 2(a), 3(a), and 7(a)(iv) of this order.

Sec. 9. The prohibitions in subsections 1(a)(iv), 2(a), 3(a), and 7(a)(iv) of this order include but are not limited to:

(a) the making of any contribution or provision of funds, goods, or services by, to, or for the benefit of any person whose property and interests in property are blocked pursuant to this order; and

(b) the receipt of any contribution or provision of funds, goods, or services from any such person.

Sec. 10. I hereby find that the unrestricted immigrant and nonimmigrant entry into the United States of aliens who meet one or more of the criteria in subsections 2(a) and 3(a) of this order would be detrimental to the interests of the United States, and I hereby suspend the entry into the United States, as immigrants or nonimmigrants, of such persons. . . .

Sec. 11. The Secretary of the Treasury, in consultation with the Secretary of State, is hereby authorized to take such actions, including the promulgation of rules and regulations, and to employ all powers granted to the President by IEEPA and sections 6(a)(6), 6(a)(7), 6(a)(8), 6(a)(9), 6(a)(11), and 6(a)(12) of ISA, and to employ all powers granted to the United States Government by section 6(a)(3) of ISA, as may be necessary to carry out the purposes of this order. The Secretary of the Treasury may redelegate any of these functions to other officers and agencies of the United States Government consistent with applicable law.

Sec. 12. (a) Any transaction that evades or avoids, has the purpose of evading or avoiding, causes a violation of, or attempts to violate any of the prohibitions set forth in this order or in Executive Order 12957, Executive Order 12959, Executive Order 13059, or Executive Order 13599 is prohibited.

(b) Any conspiracy formed to violate any of the prohibitions set forth in this order or in Executive Order 12957, Executive Order 12959, Executive Order 13059, or Executive Order 13599 is prohibited.

[The following page has been omitted. It contains definitions of several terms used in the executive order.]

Sec. 14. For those persons whose property and interests in property are blocked pursuant to this order who might have a constitutional presence in the United States, I find that because of the ability to transfer funds or other assets instantaneously, prior notice to such persons of measures to be taken pursuant to this order would render those measures ineffectual. I therefore determine that for these measures to be effective in addressing the national emergency declared in Executive Order 12957, there need be no prior notice of an action taken pursuant to subsections 1(a)(iv), 2(a), 3(a), and 7(a)(iv) of this order. . . .

Sec. 16. The Secretary of the Treasury, in consultation with the Secretary of State, is hereby authorized to take such actions, including the promulgation of rules and regulations, and to employ all powers granted to the President by IEEPA, as may be necessary to carry out section 104A of CISADA (22 U.S.C. 8514). The Secretary of the Treasury may redelegate any of these functions to other officers and agencies of the United States Government consistent with applicable law.

Sec. 17. All agencies of the United States Government are hereby directed to take all appropriate measures within their authority to carry out the provisions of this order. . . .

BARACK OBAMA

The White House,
October 9, 2012.

SOURCE: Executive Office of the President. "Executive Order 13628—Authorizing the Implementation of Certain Sanctions Set Forth in the Iran Threat Reduction and Syria Human Rights Act of 2012 and Additional Sanctions With Respect to Iran." October 9, 2012. *Compilation of Presidential Documents* 2012, no. 00795 (October 9, 2012). http://www.gpo.gov/fdsys/pkg/DCPD-201200795/pdf/DCPD-201200795.pdf.

DOCUMENT   *IAEA Releases Nuclear Report on Iran*

November 16, 2012

[All footnotes have been omitted.]

[Sections A–C, including the introduction, an explanation of resolutions and unresolved issues, and the nuclear facilities monitored under the Safeguards Agreement, have been omitted.]

D. ENRICHMENT RELATED ACTIVITIES

8. Contrary to the relevant resolutions of the Board of Governors and the Security Council, Iran has not suspended its enrichment related activities in the declared facilities referred to below. All of these activities are under Agency safeguards, and all of the nuclear material, installed cascades and the feed and withdrawal stations at those facilities are subject to Agency containment and surveillance.

9. Iran has stated that the purpose of enriching UF6 up to 5% U-235 is the production of fuel for its nuclear facilities and that the purpose of enriching UF6 up to 20% U-235 is the manufacture of fuel for research reactors.

10. Since Iran began enriching uranium at its declared facilities, it has produced at those facilities approximately:

   - 7611 kg (+735 kg since the Director General's previous report) of UF6 enriched up to 5% U-235, of which: 5303 kg is presently in storage; 1226 kg has been fed into the Pilot Fuel Enrichment Plant (PFEP) and 1029 kg has been fed into the Fordow Fuel Enrichment Plant (FFEP) for enrichment up to 20% U-235; and 53 kg has been fed into the Uranium Conversion Facility (UCF) for conversion to UO_2; and
   - 232.8 kg (+43.4 kg since the Director General's previous report) of UF6 enriched up to 20% U-235, of which: 134.9 kg is presently in storage; 1.6 kg has been down-blended; and 96.3 kg has been fed into the Fuel Plate Fabrication Plant (FPFP) for conversion to U308.

[A listing of each individual facility and the enrichment activities occurring there has been omitted.]

D.3. Other Enrichment Related Activities

26. The Agency is still awaiting a substantive response from Iran to Agency requests for further information in relation to announcements made by Iran concerning the construction of ten new uranium enrichment facilities, the sites for five of which, according to Iran, have been decided. Iran has not provided information, as requested by the Agency, in connection with its announcement on 7 February 2010 that it possessed laser enrichment technology. As a result of Iran's lack of cooperation on those issues, the Agency is unable to verify and report fully on these matters.

E. REPROCESSING ACTIVITIES

27. Pursuant to the relevant resolutions of the Board of Governors and the Security Council, Iran is obliged to suspend its reprocessing activities, including R&D. Iran has stated that it "does not have reprocessing activities." The Agency has continued to monitor the use of hot cells at the Tehran Research Reactor (TRR) and the Molybdenum, Iodine and Xenon Radioisotope Production (MIX) Facility. The Agency carried out an inspection and design information verification (DIV) at TRR on 11 November 2012, and a DIV at the MIX Facility on 12 November 2012. It is only with

respect to TRR, the MIX Facility and the other facilities to which the Agency has access that the Agency can confirm that there are no ongoing reprocessing related activities in Iran.

F. Heavy Water Related Projects

28. Contrary to the relevant resolutions of the Board of Governors and the Security Council, Iran has not suspended work on all heavy water related projects, including the ongoing construction of the heavy water moderated research reactor at Arak, the Iran Nuclear Research Reactor (IR-40 Reactor), which is under Agency safeguards.

29. On 10 November 2012, the Agency carried out a DIV at the IR-40 Reactor at Arak and observed that the installation of cooling and moderator circuit piping was continuing. During the DIV, Iran stated that the operation of the IR-40 Reactor was now expected to commence in the first quarter of 2014.

30. Since its visit to the Heavy Water Production Plant (HWPP) on 17 August 2011, the Agency has not been provided with further access to the plant. As a result, the Agency is again relying on satellite imagery to monitor the status of HWPP. Based on recent images, the plant appears to continue to be in operation. To date, Iran has not permitted the Agency to take samples from the heavy water stored at UCF.

G. Uranium Conversion and Fuel Fabrication

31. Although Iran is obliged to suspend all enrichment related activities and heavy water related projects, it is conducting a number of activities at UCF, the Fuel Manufacturing Plant (FMP) and FPFP at Esfahan, as indicated below, which are in contravention of those obligations, notwithstanding that the facilities are under Agency safeguards. Iran has stated that it is conducting these activities in order to make fuel for research reactors.

32. According to the latest information available to the Agency:

  * Iran has produced at UCF: 550 tonnes of natural UF6, 99 tonnes of which has been sent to FEP; and
  * Iran has transferred to TRR the following fuel items produced at FMP and FPFP: ten containing uranium enriched up to 20% U-235, four containing uranium enriched to 3.34% U-235 and five containing natural uranium.

33. **Uranium Conversion Facility**: As previously reported, the Agency carried out a PIV at UCF in March 2012. In order to finalise its evaluation of the PIV results, the Agency has requested that Iran provide further information.

34. In the DIQ for UCF dated 13 October 2012, Iran informed the Agency of an increase in its capacity to produce natural UO_2 at UCF from 10 tonnes per year to 14 tonnes per year.

35. The Agency has verified that, as of 5 November 2012, Iran had produced 24 kg of uranium in the form of UO_2 during R&D activities involving the conversion of UF6 enriched up to 3.34% U-235. Iran subsequently transferred 13.6 kg of uranium in the form of UO_2 to FMP. As of 6 November 2012, Iran had resumed these R&D activities, but had not produced additional uranium in the form of UO_2 from the

conversion of UF6 enriched to 3.34% U-235. As of the same date, Iran, through the conversion of uranium ore concentrate, had produced about 6231 kg of natural uranium in the form of UO_2, of which the Agency has verified that Iran transferred 3100 kg to FMP.

36. During a DIV carried out at UCF on 6 November 2012, Iran informed the Agency that, due to the rupture of a storage tank, a large quantity of liquid containing natural uranium scrap material had spilled onto the floor of the facility. Agency inspectors confirmed that the spillage had taken place. The Agency is discussing with Iran the accountancy of the nuclear material that has spilled from the tank.

37. **Fuel Manufacturing Plant**: Between 4 and 6 September 2012, the Agency carried out a PIV at FMP, the results of which it is still evaluating. On 7 November 2012, the Agency carried out a DIV and an inspection at FMP and confirmed that the manufacture of pellets for the IR-40 Reactor using natural UO_2 was ongoing. Iran informed the Agency that it had completed the manufacture of dummy fuel assemblies for the IR-40 Reactor. As of 7 November 2012, Iran had not commenced the manufacture of fuel assemblies containing nuclear material. On the same date, the Agency also verified two prototype fuel rods made of UO_2 enriched to 3.34% U-235 prior to their transfer to TRR.

38. **Fuel Plate Fabrication Plant**: The Agency carried out a PIV at FPFP on 29 September 2012 and verified that, between the start of conversion activities on 17 December 2011 and 26 September 2012, 82.7 kg of UF6 enriched up to 20% U-235 had been fed into the conversion process and 38 kg of uranium had been produced in the form of U308 powder and fuel items. Iran has declared that, between 27 September 2012 and 10 November 2012, it did not convert any more of the UF6 enriched up to 20% U-235 contained in the cylinder attached to the process. On 11 November 2012, the Agency verified a new fuel assembly prior to its transfer to TRR and verified the presence of 46 fuel plates. On 12 November 2012, the Agency and Iran agreed to an updated safeguards approach for FPFP.

H. Possible Military Dimensions

39. Previous reports by the Director General have identified outstanding issues related to possible military dimensions to Iran's nuclear programme and actions required of Iran to resolve these. Since 2002, the Agency has become increasingly concerned about the possible existence in Iran of undisclosed nuclear related activities involving military related organizations, including activities related to the development of a nuclear payload for a missile.

40. The Annex to the Director General's November 2011 report (GOV/2011/65) provided a detailed analysis of the information available to the Agency, indicating that Iran has carried out activities that are relevant to the development of a nuclear explosive device. This information, which comes from a wide variety of independent sources, including from a number of Member States, from the Agency's own efforts and from information provided by Iran itself, is assessed by the Agency to be, overall, credible. The information indicates that, prior to the end of 2003 the activities took place under a structured programme; that some continued after 2003; and that some may

still be ongoing. Since November 2011, the Agency has obtained more information which further corroborates the analysis contained in the aforementioned Annex.

41. In resolution 1929 (2010), the Security Council reaffirmed Iran's obligations to take the steps required by the Board of Governors in its resolutions GOV/2006/14 and GOV/2009/82, and to cooperate fully with the Agency on all outstanding issues, particularly those which give rise to concerns about the possible military dimensions to Iran's nuclear programme, including by providing access without delay to all sites, equipment, persons and documents requested by the Agency. In its resolution GOV/2011/69, the Board of Governors, inter alia, expressed its deep and increasing concern about the unresolved issues regarding the Iranian nuclear programme, including those which need to be clarified to exclude the existence of possible military dimensions. As indicated above, in its resolution GOV/2012/50, the Board of Governors decided, inter alia, that Iranian cooperation with Agency requests aimed at the resolution of all outstanding issues was essential and urgent to restore international confidence in the exclusively peaceful nature of Iran's nuclear programme.

42. As indicated in Section B above, since the November 2011 Board, the Agency, through several rounds of formal talks and numerous informal contacts with Iran, has made intensive efforts to seek to resolve all of the outstanding issues related to Iran's nuclear programme, especially with respect to possible military dimensions, but without concrete results. Specifically, the Agency has:

- Sought agreement with Iran on a structured approach to the clarification of all outstanding issues (referred to in paragraph 4 above), focusing on the issues outlined in the Annex to GOV/2011/65. Agreement has yet to be reached;
- Requested that Iran provide the Agency with an initial declaration in connection with the issues identified in Section C of the Annex to GOV/2011/65. Iran's subsequent declaration dismissed the Agency's concerns in relation to these issues, largely on the grounds that Iran considered them to be based on unfounded allegations;
- Identified, as part of the structured approach, thirteen topics, consistent with those identified in the Annex to GOV/2011/65, which need to be addressed;
- Provided Iran with clarification of the nature of the Agency's concerns, and the information available to it, about Parchin and the foreign expert, and presented Iran with initial questions in this regard, to which Iran has not responded; and
- Requested on several occasions, from January 2012 onwards, access to the Parchin site. Contrary to Board resolution GOV/2012/50, Iran has still not provided the Agency with access to the site.

43. **Parchin**: As stated in the Annex to the Director General's November 2011 report, information provided to the Agency by Member States indicates that Iran constructed a large explosives containment vessel in which to conduct hydrodynamic experiments; such experiments would be strong indicators of possible nuclear weapon development. The information also indicates that the containment vessel was installed at the Parchin site in 2000. As previously reported, the location at the Parchin site of the vessel was only identified in March 2011, and the Agency notified Iran of that location in January 2012. Iran has stated that "the allegation of nuclear activities in Parchin site is baseless."

44. As previously reported, satellite imagery available to the Agency for the period from February 2005 to January 2012 shows virtually no activity at or near the building housing the containment vessel. Since the Agency's first request for access to this location, however, satellite imagery shows that extensive activities and resultant changes have taken place at this location. Among the most significant developments observed by the Agency at this location since February 2012 are:

- Frequent presence of, and activities involving, equipment, trucks and personnel;
- Run off of large amounts of liquid from the containment building over a prolonged period;
- Removal of external pipework from the containment vessel building;
- Razing and removal of five other buildings or structures and the site perimeter fence;
- Reconfiguration of electrical and water supply infrastructure;
- Shrouding of the containment vessel building and another building; and
- Initial scraping and removal of considerable quantities of earth at the location and its surrounding area, covering over 25 hectares, followed by further removal of earth to a greater depth at the location and the depositing of new earth in its place.

45. In light of the extensive activities that have been, and continue to be, undertaken by Iran at the aforementioned location on the Parchin site, when the Agency gains access to the location, its ability to conduct effective verification will have been seriously undermined. While the Agency continues to assess that it is necessary to have access to this location without further delay, it is essential that Iran also provide without further delay substantive answers to the Agency's detailed questions regarding the Parchin site and the foreign expert, as requested by the Agency in February 2012.

[Sections I–K, containing information on the design of nuclear facilities, Additional Protocol contained in the Safeguards Agreement, and other matters reviewed by the IAEA, have been omitted.]

L. Summary

53. While the Agency continues to verify the non-diversion of declared nuclear material at the nuclear facilities and LOFs declared by Iran under its Safeguards Agreement, as Iran is not providing the necessary cooperation, including by not implementing its Additional Protocol, the Agency is unable to provide credible assurance about the absence of undeclared nuclear material and activities in Iran, and therefore to conclude that all nuclear material in Iran is in peaceful activities.

54. Contrary to the Board resolutions of November 2011 and September 2012, and despite the intensified dialogue between the Agency and Iran since January 2012, no concrete results have been achieved in resolving the outstanding issues, including Iran having not concluded and implemented the structured approach. The Director General is, therefore, unable to report any progress on clarifying the issues relating to possible military dimensions to Iran's nuclear programme.

55. It is a matter of concern that the extensive and significant activities which have taken place since February 2012 at the location within the Parchin site to which the Agency

has requested access will have seriously undermined the Agency's ability to undertake effective verification. The Agency reiterates its request that Iran, without further delay, provide both access to that location and substantive answers to the Agency's detailed questions regarding the Parchin site and the foreign expert.

56. Given the nature and extent of credible information available, the Agency continues to consider it essential for Iran to engage with the Agency without further delay on the substance of the Agency's concerns. In the absence of such engagement, the Agency will not be able to resolve concerns about issues regarding the Iranian nuclear programme, including those which need to be clarified to exclude the existence of possible military dimensions to Iran's nuclear programme.

57. The Director General continues to urge Iran, as required in the binding resolutions of the Board of Governors and mandatory Security Council resolutions, to take steps towards the full implementation of its Safeguards Agreement and its other obligations, and to urge Iran to engage with the Agency to achieve concrete results on all outstanding substantive issues.

58. The Director General will continue to report as appropriate.

SOURCE: International Atomic Energy Agency. "Implementation of the NPT Safeguards Agreement and Relevant Provisions of Security Council Resolutions in the Islamic Republic of Iran." November 16, 2012. http://www.iaea.org/Publications/Documents/Board/2012/gov2012-55.pdf.

DOCUMENT   *IAEA Official on Iran Talks*

December 14, 2012

The following is a transcript of remarks made on 14 December 2012 by Herman Nackaerts, Deputy Director General for Safeguards, upon returning to Vienna, after talks between senior International Atomic Energy Agency officials and Iranian representatives in Tehran on 13 December 2012:

"We had a long day of meetings and we were able to make progress on the text of the structured approach to resolving the outstanding issues on possible military dimensions of Iran's nuclear programme. We have agreed to meet again on the 16th of January of next year where we expect to finalize the structured approach and start implementing the plan shortly after that."

In response to questions from reporters about access to Parchin, the atmosphere of the talks, and expectations for the agreed to meeting in January 2013, Deputy Director General Nackaerts replied:

"We have not been given access to Parchin this time but as you know access to Parchin is part of the structured approach and we hope as I said that we will implement that shortly after agreeing on the approach.

"We had a good meeting.

"We expect to finalize it [the structured approach] next time."

SOURCE: International Atomic Energy Agency. IAEA Press Statements. "Statement on IAEA-Iran Talks." December 14, 2012. https://www.iaea.org/newscenter/mediaadvisory/2012/ma201218.html.

OTHER HISTORIC DOCUMENTS OF INTEREST

President Obama and Former Gov. Romney Meet in Second Presidential Debate

OCTOBER 16, 2012

During the 2012 general election season, President Barack Obama and Republican challenger Mitt Romney met for a series of three debates. The first debate covered domestic politics and the third foreign affairs, while the second debate featured a town hall format that resulted in the candidates more directly confronting each other as they answered audience questions. The vice presidential candidates, Democrat Joe Biden and Republican Representative Paul Ryan of Wisconsin, also met for one debate. In each debate, regardless of the overarching topic, the focus was on the economy and how each candidate would bolster the middle class while shoring up the federal deficit.

FIRST PRESIDENTIAL DEBATE

The first presidential debate was held on Wednesday, October 3, at the University of Denver in Colorado. Jim Lehrer, the executive editor of the *PBS NewsHour*, moderated the domestic policy–focused event.

There was consensus among analysts, and even the Obama campaign, that the president was outperformed. Prior to the debate, his advisers said Obama had little time to prepare, and his aloof, preoccupied behavior reflected that. While Romney smiled and engaged Obama, Obama spent most of the debate looking down at his notes or speaking directly to Lehrer, only briefly looking into the camera. The president attacked Romney only during the final minutes of the debate, when he complained that the former governor had failed to release specifics about his tax plan and how it would help the middle class. Obama claimed that an independent study proved that Romney's plan would hurt the middle class because there would not be enough savings to avoid raising taxes. Romney went on the defensive, saying, "I will not, under any circumstances, raise taxes on middle-income families," and claimed, "there are six other studies that looked at the study you describe and say it's completely wrong." Romney did make one mention early in the debate of how to achieve his planned savings, which included cutting funding for PBS, the network that airs shows like *Sesame Street*. "I love Big Bird," the former governor said, but added, "I'm not going to keep on spending money on things to borrow money from China to pay for." Democrats jumped on the comment, and Twitter accounts for @sadbigbird and @firedbigbird collected thousands of followers. Romney stuck to his bipartisan theme, heard in his stump speech across the country, stating that he would use his framework proposals to work with Congress to formulate the specifics of an agenda if elected. "I had the great experience—it didn't seem like it at the time—of being elected in a state where my legislature was 87 percent Democrat and that meant I figured out from day one I had to get along and I had to work across the aisle to get anything done," Romney said.

According to polls after the debate, Romney was the clear winner, boosting enthusiasm for his candidacy. Prior to the debate, only 37 percent of Republicans polled by Reuters/Ipsos had a "very favorable" opinion of Romney, but after the debate, that number grew to 51 percent. About 60 percent of those polled by CNN said the president did worse than they had expected, while 82 percent said Romney did better than expected. Romney made big gains on the economy, the major focus of the debate. The CNN poll, with a sampling error of plus or minus 4.5 percentage points, found that 55 percent of watchers thought Romney would be better at handling the economy, 53 percent thought he would be better on taxes, and 57 percent said he could better handle the budget deficit. Overall, Romney's debate performance improved his standing with American voters. A Gallup poll before the debate gave Obama a 5-percentage-point lead nationwide, but after the debate, the electorate was evenly split, 47–47.

VICE PRESIDENTIAL DEBATE

Although there is generally little weight placed on the vice presidential debate in terms of election outcomes, Vice President Biden seized the opportunity to repair the Obama campaign's footing on October 11 after President Obama's widely panned performance during his first face-off with Romney. Vice President Biden is well known for his straight-talking demeanor, which sometimes leads to public gaffes, and he didn't change his tone when debating the House Budget Committee chair. Biden smirked and scoffed at Ryan's remarks and frequently interrupted when the seven-term congressman spoke, and Ryan rarely fought back. When Ryan criticized the Obama administration's response to the attack in Libya, noting that the president did not label it a "terrorist attack" until two weeks later, Biden flatly responded, "With all due respect, that's a bunch of malarkey." Biden in turn accused Republicans in Congress of cutting security funding for embassies abroad, noting, "These guys bet against America all the time."

"Mr. Ryan," as he asked the debate moderator to call him, used the event as a way to introduce himself to the American people. Ryan is well known within the Republican Party as a rising star, but he is new to the national stage (with the exception of his widely covered budget plan). Ryan was pressed by the moderator to defend his plan to change Medicare into a voucher-type program, something unpopular with Democrats and some Republicans. "We will be no part of a voucher program or the privatization of Social Security," said Biden, to which Ryan responded, "They got caught with their hands in the cookie jar turning Medicare into Obamacare." Ryan further accused the Obama administration of failing to put together a comprehensive plan to shore up the underfunded Medicare program.

On taxes, Ryan defended Romney's plan to lower taxes across the board in an effort to both boost the middle class and lower the deficit. Ryan claimed that a number of economic studies have been done to prove that the Romney plan would achieve its goal, but Biden questioned how it would be mathematically possible to find $5 trillion in savings without getting rid of the mortgage deduction for middle-class families. "Jack Kennedy lowered tax rates and increased growth," Ryan told Biden. "Oh, now you're Jack Kennedy," Biden said, rolling his eyes.

Ryan spent a fair portion of the debate addressing detractors, specifically those in the Obama campaign, who have accused Romney of offering only a framework for his economic policies as president, rather than giving the American public concrete plans. Ryan said it was the intent of the Romney campaign to work out the specifics through congressional negotiations. "Different than this administration, we actually want to have big bipartisan agreements," Ryan said.

In their closing statements, both Biden and Ryan made a play for middle-class voters. "My whole life has been devoted to leveling the playing field for middle-class people," Biden said. "The president and I are not going to rest until the playing field is leveled," he continued. Ryan said that to help the middle class, the country needed to elect "people who, when they see problems, fix those problems." He continued, "Mitt Romney and I will not duck the tough issues, and we will not blame others for the next four years. We will take responsibility."

Postdebate analysis rated the event a tie, but, said David Steinberg, a debate coach and communications professor at the University of Miami, "a tie goes to the incumbent." According to a Reuters/Ipsos poll, Biden helped boost Democratic enthusiasm for the Obama campaign, after it fell from 63 percent to 51 percent following the first debate. Biden did lose some points, however, for grinning when attacked and covering up some of his arguments with too many talking points. Ryan, on the other hand, lost points for failing to give clear arguments as to how some of Romney's policies differed from Obama's, specifically in the area of foreign policy in Syria and Iran.

SECOND PRESIDENTIAL DEBATE

The presidential candidates met for a town hall–style debate on October 16 at Hofstra University in Hempstead, New York. Candy Crowley, the chief political correspondent for CNN, became the first female to moderate a presidential debate since 1992. The second debate offered President Obama a chance to reassure voters after the first debate that he could make a convincing case for another term. Romney had challenges of his own—to keep his momentum going and to connect with the undecided voters in the audience who would be asking the questions. Obama excelled in the town hall setting, making a personal connection with audience members and seemingly transforming himself into the energetic candidate he was in 2008. Although some of his answers were long or even off topic, he managed to make a number of point-by-point arguments as to why he deserved a second chance. Romney, on the other hand, was unable to make as much of an audience connection, often following questions with phrases like "I appreciate that" rather than directly addressing the audience member who asked the question. Debate analysts said Romney sometimes came off as petulant as he demanded more time or the final word on a topic, which did not appeal to the audience.

From the start, Obama came out confident and swinging, attacking Romney's business record, tax rate, and campaign promises. The two went toe-to-toe, pointing fingers at each other over a number of contentious issues. Attempting to paint himself as better on the economy, Obama criticized Romney's $8 trillion tax cut and spending increase proposal, arguing that his opponent had not explained how he would pay for it: "We haven't heard from the governor any specifics beyond Big Bird and eliminating funding for Planned Parenthood in terms of how he pays for that." Although the president commanded much of the debate, Romney did not shy away from Obama's attacks, landing some blows of his own by giving concise one-liners to sum up what he considered Obama's four years of failed promises. "This is a president who has not been able to do what he said he'd do," Romney noted. "He said that he'd cut in half the deficit. He hasn't done that. . . .

In fact, he doubled it. He said by now middle-income families would have a reduction in their health insurance premiums by $2,500 a year. It's gone up by $2,500 a year. And if Obamacare is passed or implemented—it's already been passed—if it's implemented fully, it'll be another $2,500 on top."

In one area that Romney should have fared far better—U.S. policy in Libya following the attack on the embassy there and death of Ambassador Chris Stevens—the governor faltered, getting caught up in an argument over semantics and when Obama used the word *terror* to describe the attack. Moderator Crowley stepped in to correct the governor, stating that Obama had in fact used the word *terror,* although indirectly, in a speech in the White House Rose Garden the day after the attack, contrary to Romney's claim that it had taken the administration two weeks to use such a label. Obama used Libya as a moment to profile the foreign policy successes his administration had accomplished. "I said that we'd go after al Qaeda and bin Laden, we have. I said we'd transition out of Afghanistan, and start making sure that Afghans are responsible for their own security, that's what I'm doing. And when it comes to this issue, when I say that we are going to find out exactly what happened, everybody will be held accountable. And I am ultimately responsible for what's taking place there because these are my folks, and I'm the one who has to greet those coffins when they come home. You know that I mean what I say," Obama said.

Romney faced significant criticism after the debate for a comment he made regarding a search for female candidates to fill his cabinet during his time as Massachusetts governor, remarking that he had been given "whole binders full of women." The phrase instantly lit up social media sites and generated Twitter feeds and Tumblr pages devoted to Romney's binders. Emma Keller, a writer for Britain's *The Guardian,* called the comment a reflection of what many women fear—"that a president Romney would be sexist and set women back." Keller continued, "The phrase objectified and dehumanized women." Obama went on the attack the day after the debate, telling a crowd in Iowa, "We should make sure all our young people, our daughters as well as our sons, are thriving" in the fields of science, technology, engineering, and mathematics. "We don't have to collect a bunch of binders to find qualified, talented, driven young women ready to learn and teach in these fields right now," the president said.

Postdebate polls gave Obama the win, but, only by a slight margin. Obama improved his standing in the CBS News poll on who would be better on the economy—prior to the debate, 27 percent said Obama would be better, while 34 percent said the same after the debate. Fifty-six percent of undecided or uncommitted voters polled by CBS after the debate said Obama would be better for the middle class, while only 43 percent said the same about Romney.

Final Presidential Debate

The final presidential debate, focused on foreign policy, was held on October 22 in Boca Raton, Florida, and moderated by Bob Schieffer, the chief Washington correspondent for CBS News. On the heels of a strong performance in New York, Obama came into the third debate confident in his answers and his success as president. Arguably, Obama had the upper hand with more foreign policy experience than his opponent and could easily play the "commander-in-chief" card, which he did a number of times. Romney, on the other hand, did not give the clear, concise answers he had delivered in the first two debates, instead giving vague ideas as to his own foreign policy stance, using phrases such as "kill the bad guys." However, Romney had the advantage of being able to deliver his vision for future U.S. foreign policy, rather than defending his record. Both candidates seemed to agree on a number of larger issues—for example, that Iran should be kept from developing nuclear weapons. And although the candidates would certainly have different methods for achieving these goals, Romney seemed to have a difficult time articulating how his administration would differ from current Obama policy.

The debate did stray into domestic issues a number of times, as both candidates made their final push two weeks before the election to remind voters of their economic policies. Romney said the economy was a national security issue and again laid out his five-point framework proposal for continuing the economic recovery and helping the middle class.

With the economy first on the minds of voters, the third and final debate was viewed as the least important and least likely to sway undecided voters. A CNN poll conducted immediately following the debate gave the president a slight edge, with 48 percent of registered voters polled saying Obama had won, while only 40 percent said the same of Romney.

—Heather Kerrigan

Following is the edited text of the town hall debate that took place on October 16, 2012, and featured President Barack Obama and the Republican challenger, former Massachusetts governor Mitt Romney.

President Obama and Gov. Romney Town Hall Debate Transcript

October 16, 2012

PRESIDENT BARACK OBAMA AND FORMER GOV. MITT ROMNEY PARTICIPATE IN A CANDIDATES DEBATE, HOFSTRA UNIVERSITY, HEMPSTEAD, NEW YORK

OCTOBER 16, 2012

SPEAKERS: FORMER GOV. MITT ROMNEY, R-MASS.

PRESIDENT BARACK OBAMA

CANDY CROWLEY, MODERATOR
[*]

CROWLEY: Good evening from Hofstra University in Hempstead, New York. I'm Candy Crowley from CNN's "State of the Union." We are here for the second presidential debate, a town hall, sponsored by the Commission on Presidential Debates.

CROWLEY: The Gallup organization chose 82 uncommitted voters from the New York area. Their questions will drive the night. My goal is to give the conversation direction and to ensure questions get answered. . . .

QUESTION: Mr. President, Governor Romney, as a 20-year-old college student, all I hear from professors, neighbors and others is that when I graduate, I will have little chance to get employment. What can you say to reassure me, but more importantly my parents, that I will be able to sufficiently support myself after I graduate?

ROMNEY: . . . Your question—your question is one that's being asked by college kids all over this country. I was in Pennsylvania with someone who had just graduated—this was in Philadelphia—and she said, "I've got my degree. I can't find a job. I've got three part-time jobs. They're just barely enough to pay for my food and pay for an apartment. I can't begin to pay back my student loans."

So what we have to do is two things. We have to make sure that we make it easier for kids to afford college.

ROMNEY: And also make sure that when they get out of college, there's a job. . . .

And likewise you've got more and more debt on your back. So more debt and less jobs. I'm going to change that. I know what it takes to create good jobs again. I know what it takes to make sure that you have the kind of opportunity you deserve. And kids across this country are going to recognize, we're bringing back an economy.

It's not going to be like the last four years. The middle-class has been crushed over the last four years, and jobs have been too scarce. I know what it takes to bring them back, and I'm going to do that, and make sure that when you graduate. . . . I'm going to make sure you get a job.

CROWLEY: Mr. President?

OBAMA: . . . [T]he fact that you're making an investment in higher education is critical. Not just to you, but to the entire nation. Now, the most important thing we can do is to make sure that we are creating jobs in this country. But not just jobs, good paying jobs. Ones that can support a family.

OBAMA: And what I want to do, is build on the five million jobs that we've created over the last 30 months in the private sector alone. And there are a bunch of things we can do to make sure your future is bright.

Number one, I want to build manufacturing jobs in this country again. . . .

Number two, we've got to make sure that we have the best education system in the world. . . .

Number three, we've got to control our own energy. Now, not only oil and natural gas, which we've been investing in; but also, we've got to make sure we're building the energy source of the future, not just thinking about next year, but ten years from now, 20 years from now. That's why we've invested in solar and wind and biofuels, energy efficient cars.

We've got to reduce our deficit, but we've got to do it in a balanced way. Asking the wealthy to pay a little bit more along with cuts so that we can invest in education like yours.

And let's take the money that we've been spending on war over the last decade to rebuild America, roads, bridges schools. . . .

CROWLEY: Let me ask you for [a] more immediate answer and begin with Mr. Romney just quickly what—what can you do? We're looking at a situation where 40 percent of the unemployed have been unemployed have been unemployed for six months or more. . . .

ROMNEY: Well what you're seeing in this country is 23 million people struggling to find a job. And a lot of them, as you say, Candy, have been out of work for a long, long, long time. The president's policies have been exercised over the last four years and they haven't put Americans back to work.

We have fewer people working today than we had when the president took office. . . .

We have not made the progress we need to make to put people back to work. That's why I put out a five-point plan that gets America 12 million new jobs in four years and rising take-home pay. . . . It's going to help people across the country that are unemployed right now. . . .

OBAMA: . . . Governor Romney says he's got a five-point plan? Governor Romney doesn't have a five-point plan. He has a one-point plan. And that plan is to make sure that folks at the top play by a different set of rules. . . .

QUESTION: Your energy secretary, Steven Chu, has now been on record three times stating it's not [the] policy of his department to help lower gas prices. Do you agree with Secretary Chu that this is not the job of the Energy Department?

OBAMA: The most important thing we can do is to make sure we control our own energy. So here's what I've done since I've been president. We have increased oil production to the highest levels in 16 years.

Natural gas production is the highest it's been in decades. We have seen increases in coal production and coal employment. . . . We've also got to look to the future. That's why we doubled fuel efficiency standards on cars. . . . That's why we doubled clean—clean energy production like wind and solar and biofuels.

And all these things have contributed to us lowering our oil imports to the lowest levels in 16 years. Now, I want to build on that. And that means, yes, we still continue to open up new areas for drilling. We continue to make it a priority for us to go after natural gas. . . .

And we can do it in an environmentally sound way. But we've also got to continue to figure out how we have efficiency energy, because ultimately that's how we're going to reduce demand and that's what's going to keep gas prices lower.

Now, Governor Romney will say he's got an all-of-the-above plan, but basically his plan is to let the oil companies write the energy policies. . . .

CROWLEY: Governor, on the subject of gas prices?

ROMNEY: . . . [T]he president's right in terms of the additional oil production, but none of it came on federal land. As a matter of fact, oil production is down 14 percent this year on federal land, and gas production was down 9 percent. Why? Because the president cut in half the number of licenses and permits for drilling on federal lands, and in federal waters. . . .

Look, I want to make sure we use our oil, our coal, our gas, our nuclear, our renewables. I believe very much in our renewable capabilities; ethanol, wind, solar will be an important part of our energy mix. . . .

Let's take advantage of the energy resources we have, as well as the energy sources for the future. . . . I'll get America and North America energy independent. I'll do it by more drilling, more permits and licenses. . . .

This is about bringing good jobs back for the middle class of America, and that's what I'm going to do.

CROWLEY: . . . Is it within the purview of the government to bring those prices down, or are we looking at the new normal?

OBAMA: Candy, there's no doubt that world demand's gone up, but our production is going up, and we're using oil more efficiently. And very little of what Governor Romney just said is true. We've opened up public lands. We're actually drilling more on public lands than in the previous administration. . . .

And the proof is our oil imports are down to the lowest levels in 20 years. Oil production is up, natural gas production is up, and, most importantly, we're also starting to build cars that are more efficient.

And that's creating jobs. That means those cars can be exported, 'cause that's the demand around the world, and it also means that it'll save money in your pocketbook.

OBAMA: That's the strategy you need, an all-of-the-above strategy, and that's what we're going to do in the next four years.

ROMNEY: But that's not what you've done in the last four years. That's the problem. In the last four years, you cut permits and licenses on federal land and federal waters in half.

OBAMA: Not true, Governor Romney.

ROMNEY: So how much did you cut (inaudible)?

OBAMA: Not true.

ROMNEY: How much did you cut them by, then?

OBAMA: Governor, we have actually produced more oil—

ROMNEY: No, no. How much did you cut licenses and permits on federal land and federal waters?

OBAMA: Governor Romney, here's what we did. There were a whole bunch of oil companies.

(CROSSTALK)

ROMNEY: No, no, I had a question and the question was how much did you cut them by?

OBAMA: You want me to answer a question—

ROMNEY: How much did you cut them by?

OBAMA: I'm happy to answer the question.

ROMNEY: All right. And it is—

OBAMA: Here's what happened. You had a whole bunch of oil companies who had leases on public lands that they weren't using. So what we said was you can't just sit on this for

10, 20, 30 years, decide when you want to drill, when you want to produce, when it's most profitable for you. These are public lands. So if you want to drill on public lands, you use it or you lose it.

ROMNEY: OK, (inaudible)—

OBAMA: And so what we did was take away those leases. And we are now reletting them so that we can actually make a profit.

ROMNEY: And production on private—on government land—

OBAMA: Production is up.

ROMNEY:—is down.

OBAMA: No, it isn't.

ROMNEY: Production on government land of oil is down 14 percent.

OBAMA: Governor—

ROMNEY: And production on gas—

(CROSSTALK)

OBAMA: It's just not true.

ROMNEY: It's absolutely true. . . .

ROMNEY: . . . If you're paying less than you paid a year or two ago, why, then, the strategy is working. But you're paying more. When the president took office, the price of gasoline here in Nassau County was about $1.86 a gallon. Now, it's $4.00 a gallon. The price of electricity is up. . . .

CROWLEY: Mr. President, could you address, because we did finally get to gas prices here, could you address what the governor said, which is if your energy policy was working, the price of gasoline would not be $4 a gallon here. Is that true?

OBAMA: . . . He said when I took office, the price of gasoline was $1.80, $1.86. Why is that? Because the economy was on the verge of collapse, because we were about to go through the worst recession since the Great Depression, as a consequence of some of the same policies that Governor Romney's now promoting. . . .

QUESTION: Governor Romney, you have stated that if you're elected president, you would plan to reduce the tax rates for all the tax brackets and that you would work with the Congress to eliminate some deductions in order to make up for the loss in revenue.

Concerning the—these various deductions, the mortgage deductions, the charitable deductions, the child tax credit and also. . . .

The education credits, which are important to me, because I have children in college. What would be your position on those things, which are important to the middle class?

ROMNEY: Thank you very much. And let me tell you, you're absolutely right about part of that, which is I want to bring the rates down, I want to simplify the tax code, and I want to get middle-income taxpayers to have lower taxes.

The middle-income families in America have been crushed over the last four years. So I want to get some relief to middle-income families. That's part—that's part one.

Now, how about deductions? 'Cause I'm going to bring rates down across the board for everybody, but I'm going to limit deductions and exemptions and credits, particularly for people at the high end, because I am not going to have people at the high end pay less than they're paying now.

The top 5 percent of taxpayers will continue to pay 60 percent of the income tax the nation collects. So that'll stay the same.

Middle-income people are going to get a tax break.

And so, in terms of bringing down deductions, one way of doing that would be say everybody gets—I'll pick a number—$25,000 of deductions and credits, and you can decide which ones to use. . . .

And I will not—I will not under any circumstances, reduce the share that's being paid by the highest income taxpayers. And I will not, under any circumstances increase taxes on the middle-class. . . .

CROWLEY: Thanks, Governor.

OBAMA: My philosophy on taxes has been simple. And that is, I want to give middle-class families and folks who are striving to get into the middle class some relief. Because they have been hit hard over the last decade. . . .

So four years ago I stood on a stage just like this one. Actually it was a town hall, and I said I would cut taxes for middle-class families, and that's what I've done, by $3,600.00. I said I would cut taxes for small businesses, who are the drivers and engines of growth. And we've cut them 18 times. . . .

But what I've also said is, if we're serious about reducing the deficit, if this is genuinely a moral obligation to the next generation, then in addition to some tough spending cuts, we've also got to make sure that the wealthy do a little bit more.

So what I've said is, your first $250,000.00 worth of income, no change. And that means 98 percent of American families, 97 percent of small businesses, they will not see a tax increase. I'm ready to sign that bill right now. The only reason it's not happening is because Governor Romney's allies in Congress have held the 98 percent hostage because they want tax breaks for the top 2 percent. . . .

[The remainder of the answers from Obama and Romney on tax cuts and the federal deficit have been omitted.]

[Questions about pay equity for women, the differences between former president George W. Bush and former governor Romney, and President Obama's record over the past four years, and the answers from Obama and Romney, have been omitted.]

QUESTION: Mr. Romney, what do you plan on doing with immigrants without their green cards that are currently living here as productive members of society?

ROMNEY: . . . I want our legal system to work better. I want it to be streamlined. I want it to be clearer. I don't think you have to—shouldn't have to hire a lawyer to figure out how to get into this country legally. I also think that we should give visas to people—green cards, rather, to people who graduate with skills that we need. People around the world with accredited degrees in science and math get a green card stapled to their diploma, come to the U.S. of A. We should make sure our legal system works.

Number two, we're going to have to stop illegal immigration. There are 4 million people who are waiting in line to get here legally. Those who've come here illegally take their place. So I will not grant amnesty to those who have come here illegally.

What I will do is I'll put in place an employment verification system and make sure that employers that hire people who have come here illegally are sanctioned for doing so. . . . I would not give driver's licenses to those that have come here illegally as the president would.

The kids of those that came here illegally, those kids, I think, should have a pathway to become a permanent resident of the United States and military service, for instance, is one way they would have that kind of pathway to become a permanent resident. . . .

OBAMA: . . . So what I've said is we need to fix a broken immigration system and I've done everything that I can on my own and sought cooperation from Congress to make sure that we fix the system.

The first thing we did was to streamline the legal immigration system, to reduce the backlog, make it easier, simpler and cheaper for people who are waiting in line, obeying the law to make sure that they can come here and contribute to our country and that's good for our economic growth. . . .

Number two, we do have to deal with our border so we put more border patrol on the—any time in history and the flow of undocumented works across the border is actually lower than it's been in 40 years.

What I've also said is if we're going to go after folks who are here illegally, we should do it smartly and go after folks who are criminals, gang bangers, people who are hurting the community, not after students, not after folks who are here just because they're trying to figure out how to feed their families. . . .

CROWLEY: Let me get the governor in here, Mr. President. Let's speak to, if you could. . . .

CROWLEY: . . . the idea of self-deportation?

ROMNEY: . . . Now, let me mention one other thing, and that is self-deportation says let people make their own choice. What I was saying is, we're not going to round up 12 million people, undocumented illegals, and take them out of the nation. Instead let people make their own choice. . . .

[The remainder of the answers on immigration has been omitted.]

QUESTION: We were sitting around, talking about Libya, and we were reading and became aware of reports that the State Department refused extra security for our embassy in Benghazi, Libya, prior to the attacks that killed four Americans.

Who was it that denied enhanced security and why?

OBAMA: . . . So as soon as we found out that the Benghazi consulate was being overrun, I was on the phone with my national security team and I gave them three instructions.

Number one, beef up our security and procedures, not just in Libya, but at every embassy and consulate in the region.

Number two, investigate exactly what happened, regardless of where the facts lead us, to make sure folks are held accountable and it doesn't happen again.

And number three, we are going to find out who did this and we're going to hunt them down, because one of the things that I've said throughout my presidency is when folks mess with Americans, we go after them.

OBAMA: Now Governor Romney had a very different response. While we were still dealing with our diplomats being threatened, Governor Romney put out a press release, trying to make political points, and that's not how a commander in chief operates. . . .

ROMNEY: . . . There were other issues associated with this—with this tragedy. There were many days that passed before we knew whether this was a spontaneous demonstration, or actually whether it was a terrorist attack.

ROMNEY: And there was no demonstration involved. It was a terrorist attack and it took a long time for that to be told to the American people. Whether there was some misleading, or instead whether we just didn't know what happened, you have to ask yourself why didn't we know five days later when the ambassador to the United Nations went on TV to say that this was a demonstration. How could we have not known?

But I find more troubling than this, that on—on the day following the assassination of the United States ambassador, the first time that's happened since 1979, when—when we have four Americans killed there, when apparently we didn't know what happened, that the president, the day after that happened, flies to Las Vegas for a political fund-raiser, then the next day to Colorado for another event, other political event. . . .

And this calls into question the president's whole policy in the Middle East. Look what's happening in Syria, in Egypt, now in Libya. Consider the distance between ourselves and—and Israel, the president said that—that he was going to put daylight between us and Israel.

We have Iran four years closer to a nuclear bomb. Syria—Syria's not just a tragedy of 30,000 civilians being killed by a military, but also a strategic—strategically significant player for America.

The president's policies throughout the Middle East began with an apology tour and—and—and pursue a strategy of leading from behind, and this strategy is unraveling before our very eyes. . . .

OBAMA: . . . The day after the attack, governor, I stood in the Rose Garden and I told the American people in the world that we are going to find out exactly what happened. That this was an act of terror and I also said that we're going to hunt down those who committed this crime. . . .

ROMNEY: I—I think interesting the president just said something which—which is that on the day after the attack he went into the Rose Garden and said that this was an act of terror.

OBAMA: That's what I said.

ROMNEY: You said in the Rose Garden the day after the attack, it was an act of terror.

It was not a spontaneous demonstration, is that what you're saying?

OBAMA: Please proceed governor.

ROMNEY: I want to make sure we get that for the record because it took the president 14 days before he called the attack in Benghazi an act of terror.

OBAMA: Get the transcript.

CROWLEY: It—it—it—he did in fact, sir. . . .

[Questions about limiting the availability of assault weapons, outsourcing American jobs, and misperceptions about each candidate, and the Obama and Romney responses, have been omitted.]

SOURCE: Commission on Presidential Debates. "October 16, 2012 Debate Transcript." October 16, 2012. http://www.debates.org/index.php?page=october-1-2012-the-second-obama-romney-presidential-debate.

OTHER HISTORIC DOCUMENTS OF INTEREST

FROM THIS VOLUME

FROM PREVIOUS *HISTORIC DOCUMENTS*

FBI Report on Crime in the United States

OCTOBER 29, 2012

The Federal Bureau of Investigation (FBI) released its annual statistical report, *Crime in the United States, 2011,* on October 29, 2012. The document compiles the number of crimes committed in the United States from January 1 through December 31, 2011, in a variety of categories including violent crime and property crime. The 2011 report shows that the number of violent crimes declined for the fifth consecutive year. Since 2007, violent crime has decreased 15.4 percent, and since 2002, it's down 15.5 percent. Between 2010 and 2011, violent crime fell 3.8 percent. The volume of property crimes also decreased in 2011, by 0.5 percent, making 2011 the ninth straight year in which the volume of property crime had fallen. The volumes of the four types of violent crimes—murder and nonnegligent manslaughter, aggravated assault, robbery, and forcible rape, a category that includes assaults, attempt to commit rape, and forcing a female to have sex against her will but does not include nonforcible rape (i.e., statutory)—all declined from 2010 to 2011. Murder and nonnegligent manslaughter declined by 0.7 percent, aggravated assault by 3.9 percent, robbery by 4 percent, and forcible rape by 2.5 percent.

The 2011 report was accompanied by a warning against using the crime statistics presented by the FBI to rank cities, counties, and states. "These rankings . . . are merely a quick choice made by the data user; they provide no insight into the many variables that mold the crime in a particular town, city, county, state, region, or other jurisdiction. Consequently, these rankings lead to simplistic and/or incomplete analyses that often create misleading perceptions adversely affecting cities and counties, along with their residents," according to the report. The FBI wrote that a clear analysis of any area is possible only after looking at a number of factors that impact law enforcement in each locality, including population density, composition of the population, economic conditions, family conditions, the strength of law enforcement agencies, and citizens' attitudes toward crime.

The FBI also cautioned that the annual *Uniform Crime Report* includes only crimes that are reported to law enforcement. In addition, if multiple crimes are committed during one incident, only the most serious offense is included in the FBI report; this practice obviously has an effect on the overall numbers associated with certain crimes. Each year, the U.S. Department of Justice, Bureau of Justice Statistics, conducts the National Crime Victimization Survey, which estimates unreported crimes. When the two studies are considered together, they give the most accurate representation of the actual crime rate in the United States. The version of the National Crime Victimization Survey released in October 2012 showed an increase in both violent crime and property crime victimization, of 17 percent and 11 percent, respectively, for U.S. residents aged twelve and older. The FBI and Bureau of Justice Statistics caution against comparing the two reports because each uses a different methodology for establishing a crime rate.

CRIME RATES

The FBI does not include reasons for the rise and fall of crime rates in its annual report, but criminologists speculated that reasons for the continuing drops in violent and property crime might include a more settled cocaine market, an aging population, an increase in the number of incarcerations, and technological advances that lead to better surveillance and data-driven policing. But according to James Alan Fox, a criminologist at Northeastern University, these factors have a limited impact. "I call it the limbo stick effect," said Fox. "You can only go so low. You're never going to get down to zero crime." And although the National Crime Victimization Survey seemed at odds with the FBI data, according to Fox, the Justice Department's data in 2010 reported an all-time low in the crime rate, so the jump does not indicate a drastic increase in the number of crimes and is actually below the average year-over-year changes seen in the past. According to the Justice Department, the increase in violent crime can be attributed to a larger number of interviewees reporting simple assaults, which do not result in an injury and are generally never reported to police.

Despite the generally positive report, FBI Director Robert Mueller cautioned, "Many communities are still confronting crime, drugs, violence, and domestic terrorism." This is especially true in large, urban areas—for example, New York City and Chicago, where 514 and 431 murders were committed in 2011, respectively. Nationwide, there were 14,612 murders in 2011, or one every thirty-six minutes. On a positive note, that marks a nearly 17 percent decrease over the past decade.

In each violent crime category—murder and nonnegligent manslaughter, forcible rape, robbery, and aggravated assault—the number of offenses declined from 2010 to 2011. The violent crime rate in 2011 was 386.3 offenses per 100,000 people. Aggravated assaults made up the greatest portion of all violent crimes, at 62.4 percent, while robbery accounted for 29.4 percent, forcible rape for 6.9 percent, and murder for 1.2 percent.

The rate of property crime, including burglary, larceny-theft, motor vehicle theft, and arson, fell 0.5 percent from 2010 to 2011 to a rate of 2,908.7 offenses committed per 100,000 people. The property crime rate in 2011 was 11.2 percent lower than in 2007. The FBI estimates that in 2011, $15.6 billion in losses were caused by property crime, of which larceny-theft accounted for 68 percent, burglary for 24.1 percent, and motor vehicle theft 7.9 percent.

Nationwide, 52,333 arsons were reported in 2011, of which 45.9 percent involved structures, including houses, storage units, and office buildings; 23.9 percent involved mobile property; and 30.2 percent involved other forms of property, such as crops and fences. Per event, the average dollar amount lost was estimated at $13,196. Arson decreased 4.7 percent from 2010 to 2011.

In 2011, the FBI reported 12,408,899 arrests for all offenses, excluding traffic violations. Of those, more than 530,000 were for violent crime, while more than 1.6 million were for property crime. Most of the arrests were for drug abuse, driving under the influence, and larceny-theft. From 2010 to 2011, the number of violent crime arrests declined 4.9 percent; arrests for property crime decreased 0.1 percent; arrests of juveniles decreased 11.1 percent; and arrests of adults decreased 3.6 percent. Males were more likely to be arrested than females, accounting for more than 74 percent of all those arrested in 2011. Arrests of white citizens accounted for 69.2 percent of all arrests, while the arrest of black citizens was 28.4 percent.

HATE CRIMES

Nationwide, law enforcement agencies experienced a number of successes investigating and prosecuting hate crime offenders in 2011. In April, three men in Houston,

Texas, were sentenced to prison for their roles in a racially motivated attack against a man at a bus stop. A man in Detroit pled guilty in August to assaulting someone he thought was gay, and in September, sixteen people were convicted on federal hate crimes charges in Cleveland, Ohio, for cutting the beards of members of an Amish community. In each instance, the perpetrators were in violation of the Matthew Shepard and James Byrd, Jr., Hate Crimes Prevention Act, passed in October 2009 to expand on an earlier hate crimes law. The act, which had its first conviction in May 2011, gave the federal government authority to prosecute hate crimes in states with inadequate hate crime laws, or where authorities are unwilling or unable to prosecute suspected offenders. It also granted the government greater authority to investigate and prosecute hate crimes based on actual or perceived sexual orientation, gender, gender identity, or disability.

On December 10, 2012, the FBI released its annual publication on hate crimes in the United States, which like the overall *Crime in the United States* report looked at data collected in 2011. The number of hate crimes decreased slightly from 2010 to 2011, from 6,628 to 6,222. The number of reported victims was 7,713. Reporting hate crimes statistics to the FBI is voluntary, but of the nearly 14,600 law enforcement agencies that participated in 2011, 86.7 percent reported no hate crimes. According to the Southern Poverty Law Center, which tracks hate crime statistics nationwide, because of the voluntary reporting procedure, the number of hate crime incidents in 2011 is likely closer to 200,000. "The unfortunate reality is these numbers only give us some kind of indication of what's going on," said Mark Potok, a senior fellow with the organization.

As defined by the FBI, victims of hate crimes can be individuals, businesses, institutions, or even society as a whole. In 2011, 63.7 percent of hate crimes were carried out against people, while 36 percent were committed against property. More than 46 percent of the reported hate crimes were motivated by racial bias. Religion bias hate crimes accounted for 19.8 percent of reported hate crimes. Nearly 21 percent of hate crimes committed were motivated by sexual orientation, 11.6 percent dealt with ethnicity or national origin, and 0.9 percent were because of a person's disability.

A majority of hate crimes, 32 percent, took place in or near the victim's home, while another 18 percent took place on highways, roads, alleys, or streets. More than 9 percent happened at a school or college, 5.9 percent in a parking lot or garage, and 4.4 percent in a place of worship.

A majority of the 5,731 known hate crime offenders were white, and 20.9 percent were black. More than 10 percent of offenders were of unknown race. More than 4,600 hate crimes were committed against individuals, with 45.6 percent involving intimidation, 34.5 percent simple assaults, and 19.4 percent aggravated assault; four murders and seven forcible rapes were classified as hate crimes.

Gun Ownership

Guns continue to play a large role in crime in the United States. In 2011, guns were used in two thirds of the nation's murders, 41 percent of robberies, and 21 percent of aggravated assaults. But even as the level of violent crime continues to decrease, gun ownership, and with it attempts at gun laws, are on the rise. "This is not a one-year anomaly," said Andrew Arulanandam, spokesperson for the National Rifle Association (NRA). "It would be disingenuous for anyone to not credit increased self-defense laws to account for this decline." Arulanandam cited statistics that when violent crime peaked a quarter of a century ago, less than a dozen states had concealed-carry laws on the books, but today, more than forty states have laws that allow carrying firearms without a permit or make it easy for noncriminals to receive a permit.

According to gun-rights advocacy groups, when President Barack Obama came to office promising tougher restrictions on gun ownership, firearm sales increased. The number of buyers leveled off around 2010, but in late 2012, following the shooting at Sandy Hook Elementary School in Newtown, Connecticut, a renewed call for heavier gun control laws resulted in another surge in sales.

The call for more gun control reignites the debate between gun rights and gun restriction advocates over whether tougher gun laws actually have an impact on violent crime. Rep. Louie Gohmert, R-Texas, was one of the first gun supporters to speak publicly after the Newtown shooting in opposition to tighter regulation, stating instead that if the Sandy Hook principal had been armed, she may have been able to stop the shooter. Furthermore, he said, "The facts are every time guns have been allowed, concealed-carry has been allowed, the crime rate has gone down." The causal relationship between these laws and violent crime is heavily disputed. According to a 2012 paper by Stanford law professor John Donohue, "aggravated assault rises when RTC [right to carry] laws are adopted. For every other crime category, there is little or no indication of any consistent RTC impact on crime." Two schools of thought have emerged on the topic—those who believe, like NRA CEO Wayne LaPierre, that "the best way to stop a bad guy with a gun is a good guy with a gun," and those who think that the greater the number of concealed weapons, the higher the number of disputes that will escalate to the use of guns and therefore cause more violent crime.

Studies have long shown a statistical relationship between the number of gun owners in a geographic location and the number of gun homicides. As one goes up, the other tends to as well. However, academic studies have been unable to show a causal relationship because there are a number of factors that go into the number of gun homicides such as climate and economics. The Annenberg Public Policy Center at the University of Pennsylvania, a nonpartisan consumer advocate for voters, calls it a chicken-and-egg scenario: "Did the violence come first, and then the guns followed, or the other way around?"

—Heather Kerrigan

Following are excerpts from the FBI's annual report, Crime in the United States, 2011, *released on October 29, 2012.*

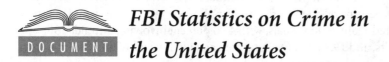 ## FBI Statistics on Crime in the United States

October 29, 2012

Definition

In the FBI's Uniform Crime Reporting (UCR) Program, violent crime is composed of four offenses: murder and nonnegligent manslaughter, forcible rape, robbery, and aggravated assault. Violent crimes are defined in the UCR Program as those offenses which involve force or threat of force.

Data Collection

The data presented in *Crime in the United States* reflect the Hierarchy Rule, which requires that only the most serious offense in a multiple-offense criminal incident be counted. The descending order of UCR violent crimes are murder and nonnegligent manslaughter, forcible rape, robbery, and aggravated assault, followed by the property crimes of burglary, larceny-theft, and motor vehicle theft. Although arson is also a property crime, the Hierarchy Rule does not apply to the offense of arson. In cases in which an arson occurs in conjunction with another violent or property crime, both crimes are reported, the arson and the additional crime.

Overview

- In 2011, an estimated 1,203,564 violent crimes occurred nationwide, a decrease of 3.8 percent from the 2010 estimate.
- When considering 5- and 10-year trends, the 2011 estimated violent crime total was 15.4 percent below the 2007 level and 15.5 percent below the 2002 level.
- There were an estimated 386.3 violent crimes per 100,000 inhabitants in 2011.
- Aggravated assaults accounted for the highest number of violent crimes reported to law enforcement at 62.4 percent. Robbery comprised 29.4 percent of violent crimes, forcible rape accounted for 6.9 percent, and murder accounted for 1.2 percent of estimated violent crimes in 2011.
- Information collected regarding type of weapon showed that firearms were used in 67.7 percent of the nation's murders, 41.3 percent of robberies, and 21.2 percent of aggravated assaults. (Weapons data are not collected for forcible rape.) . . .

MURDER

Definition

The FBI's Uniform Crime Reporting (UCR) Program defines murder and nonnegligent manslaughter as the willful (nonnegligent) killing of one human being by another.

The classification of this offense is based solely on police investigation as opposed to the determination of a court, medical examiner, coroner, jury, or other judicial body. The UCR Program does not include the following situations in this offense classification: deaths caused by negligence, suicide, or accident; justifiable homicides; and attempts to murder or assaults to murder, which are scored as aggravated assaults.

Overview

- In 2011, an estimated 14,612 persons were murdered in the United States. This was a 0.7 percent decrease from the 2010 estimate, a 14.7 percent decline from the 2007 figure, and a 10.0 percent decrease from the 2002 estimate.
- There were 4.7 murders per 100,000 inhabitants, a 1.5 percent decrease from the 2010 rate. Compared with the 2007 rate, the murder rate declined 17.4 percent, and compared with the 2002 rate, the murder rate decreased 16.8 percent. . . .
- Nearly 44 percent (43.6) of murders were reported in the South, the most populous region, 21.0 percent were reported in the West, 20.6 percent were reported in the Midwest, and 14.8 percent were reported in the Northeast. . . .

Forcible Rape

Definition

Forcible rape, as defined in the FBI's Uniform Crime Reporting (UCR) Program, is the carnal knowledge of a female forcibly and against her will. Attempts or assaults to commit rape by force or threat of force are also included; however, statutory rape (without force) and other sex offenses are excluded.

Overview

- There were an estimated 83,425 forcible rapes reported to law enforcement in 2011. This estimate was 2.5 percent lower than the 2010 estimate and 9.5 percent and 12.4 percent lower than the 2007 and 2002 estimates, respectively. . . .
- The rate of forcible rapes in 2011 was estimated at 52.7 per 100,000 female inhabitants.
- Rapes by force comprised 93.0 percent of reported rape offenses in 2011, and attempts or assaults to commit rape accounted for 7.0 percent of reported rapes. . . .

Robbery

Definition

The FBI's Uniform Crime Reporting (UCR) Program defines robbery as the taking or attempting to take anything of value from the care, custody, or control of a person or persons by force or threat of force or violence and/or by putting the victim in fear.

Overview

- In 2011, there were an estimated 354,396 robberies nationwide.
- The 2011 estimated number of robberies decreased 4.0 percent from the 2010 estimate and 20.8 percent from the 2007 estimate.
- When compared with the 2010 rate, the 2011 estimated robbery rate of 113.7 per 100,000 inhabitants showed a decrease of 4.7 percent. . . .
- Robberies accounted for an estimated $409 million in losses in 2011. . . .
- The average dollar value of property stolen per reported robbery was $1,153. . . . Banks experienced the highest average dollar loss at $4,704 per offense. . . .
- Among the robberies for which the UCR Program received weapon information in 2011, strong-arm tactics were used in 42.3 percent, firearms were used in 41.3 percent, and knives and cutting instruments were used in 7.8 percent of robberies. Other dangerous weapons were used in 8.7 percent of robberies in 2011. . . .

Aggravated Assault

Definition

The FBI's Uniform Crime Reporting (UCR) Program defines aggravated assault as an unlawful attack by one person upon another for the purpose of inflicting severe or aggravated bodily injury. The UCR Program further specifies that this type of assault is usually accompanied by the use of a weapon or by other means likely to produce death or great bodily harm. Attempted aggravated assault that involves the display of—or threat to use—a gun, knife, or other weapon is included in this crime category because serious personal injury would likely result if the assault were completed. When aggravated assault and larceny-theft occur together, the offense falls under the category of robbery.

Overview

- In 2011, there were an estimated 751,131 aggravated assaults in the nation.
- The estimated number of aggravated assaults in 2011 declined 3.9 percent when compared with data from 2010 and 15.7 percent when compared with the estimate for 2002.
- In 2011, the estimated rate of aggravated assaults was 241.1 offenses per 100,000 inhabitants.
- A 10-year comparison of data from 2002 and 2011 showed that the rate of aggravated assaults in 2011 dropped 22.1 percent. . . .
- Of the aggravated assault offenses in 2011 for which law enforcement agencies provided expanded data, 26.9 percent were committed with personal weapons such as hands, fists, or feet. Slightly more than 21 percent (21.2) of aggravated assaults were committed with firearms, and 19.1 percent were committed with knives or cutting instruments. The remaining 32.8 percent of aggravated assaults were committed with other weapons. . . .

PROPERTY CRIME

Definition

In the FBI's Uniform Crime Reporting (UCR) Program, property crime includes the offenses of burglary, larceny-theft, motor vehicle theft, and arson. The object of the theft-type offenses is the taking of money or property, but there is no force or threat of force against the victims. The property crime category includes arson because the offense involves the destruction of property; however, arson victims may be subjected to force. Because of limited participation and varying collection procedures by local law enforcement agencies, only limited data are available for arson. Arson statistics are included in trend, clearance, and arrest tables throughout *Crime in the United States,* but they are not included in any estimated volume data. The arson section in this report provides more information on that offense.

Data Collection

The data presented in *Crime in the United States* reflect the Hierarchy Rule, which requires that only the most serious offense in a multiple-offense criminal incident be counted. In descending order of severity, the violent crimes are murder and nonnegligent manslaughter, forcible rape, robbery, and aggravated assault, followed by the property crimes of burglary, larceny-theft, and motor vehicle theft. Although arson is also a property crime, the Hierarchy Rule does not apply to the offense of arson. In cases in which an arson occurs in conjunction with another violent or property crime, both crimes are reported.

Overview

- In 2011, there were an estimated 9,063,173 property crime offenses in the nation.
- The 2-year trend showed that property crime decreased 0.5 percent in 2011 compared with the 2010 estimate. The 5-year trend, comparing 2011 data with that of 2007, showed an 8.3 percent drop in property crime.
- In 2011, the rate of property crime was estimated at 2,908.7 per 100,000 inhabitants, a 1.3 percent decrease when compared with the rate in 2010. The 2011 property crime rate was 11.2 percent lower than the 2007 rate and 19.9 percent below the 2002 rate. . . .
- Larceny-theft accounted for 68.0 percent of all property crimes in 2011. Burglary accounted for 24.1 percent and motor vehicle theft for 7.9 percent. . . .
- Property crimes in 2011 resulted in losses estimated at $15.6 billion. . . .

BURGLARY

Definition

The FBI's Uniform Crime Reporting (UCR) Program defines burglary as the unlawful entry of a structure to commit a felony or theft. To classify an offense as a burglary, the use of force to gain entry need not have occurred. The UCR Program has three subclassifications for burglary: forcible entry, unlawful entry where no force is used, and attempted forcible entry. The UCR definition of "structure" includes apartment, barn, house trailer or houseboat when used as a permanent dwelling, office, railroad car (but not automobile), stable, and vessel (i.e., ship).

Overview

- In 2011, there were an estimated 2,188,005 burglaries—an increase of 0.9 percent when compared with 2010 data.
- The number of burglaries increased 1.7 percent in 2011 when compared with the 2002 estimate. . . .
- Of the estimated number of property crimes committed in 2011, burglary accounted for 24.1 percent. . . .
- By subcategory, 60.6 percent of burglaries involved forcible entry, 33. 1 percent were unlawful entries (without force), and 6.3 percent were forcible entry attempts. . . .
- Victims of burglary offenses suffered an estimated $4.8 billion in lost property in 2011; overall, the average dollar loss per burglary offense was $2,185. . . .
- Burglaries of residential properties accounted for 74.5 percent of all burglary offenses. . . .

LARCENY-THEFT

Definition

The FBI's Uniform Crime Reporting (UCR) Program defines larceny-theft as the unlawful taking, carrying, leading, or riding away of property from the possession or constructive possession of another. Examples are thefts of bicycles, motor vehicle parts and accessories, shoplifting, pocket-picking, or the stealing of any property or article that is not taken by force and violence or by fraud. Attempted larcenies are included. Embezzlement, confidence games, forgery, check fraud, etc., are excluded.

Overview

- In 2011, there were an estimated 6,159,795 larceny-thefts nationwide.
- The number of estimated larceny-thefts dropped 0.7 percent in 2011 when compared with the 2010 estimate. The 2011 figure was 6.6 percent lower than the 2007 estimate.
- The rate of estimated larceny-thefts in 2011 was 1,976.9 per 100,000 inhabitants.
- From 2010 to 2011, the rate of estimated larceny-thefts declined 1.4 percent, and from 2002 to 2011, the rate decreased 19.3 percent. . . .
- Larceny-thefts accounted for an estimated 68.0 percent of property crimes in 2011. . . .
- The average value of property taken during larceny-thefts was $987 per offense. Applying this average value to the estimated number of larceny-thefts showed that the loss to victims nationally was more than $6 billion. . . .
- Over 24 percent (24.8) of larceny-thefts were thefts from motor vehicles. . . .

MOTOR VEHICLE THEFT

Definition

In the FBI's Uniform Crime Reporting (UCR) Program, motor vehicle theft is defined as the theft or attempted theft of a motor vehicle. In the UCR Program, a motor vehicle is a self-propelled vehicle that runs on land surfaces and not on rails. Examples of motor vehicles include sport utility vehicles, automobiles, trucks, buses, motorcycles, motor scooters, all-terrain vehicles, and snowmobiles. Motor vehicle theft does not include farm equipment, bulldozers, airplanes, construction equipment, or water craft such as motorboats, sailboats, houseboats, or jet skis. The taking of a motor vehicle for temporary use by persons having lawful access is excluded from this definition.

Overview

- There were an estimated 715,373 thefts of motor vehicles nationwide in 2011. The estimated rate of motor vehicle thefts was 229.6 per 100,000 inhabitants.
- The estimated number of motor vehicle thefts declined 3.3 percent when compared with data from 2010, 35.0 percent when compared with 2007 figures, and 42.6 percent when compared with 2002 figures. . . .
- More than $4.3 billion was lost nationwide to motor vehicle thefts in 2011. The average dollar loss per stolen vehicle was $6,089. . . .
- Of all motor vehicles reported stolen in 2011, 73.9 percent were automobiles. . . .

ARSON

Definition

The FBI's Uniform Crime Reporting (UCR) Program defines arson as any willful or malicious burning or attempting to burn, with or without intent to defraud, a dwelling house, public building, motor vehicle or aircraft, personal property of another, etc.

Data Collection

Only the fires that investigation determined to have been willfully set are included in this arson data collection. Fires labeled as suspicious or of unknown origin are excluded from these data. . . .

Overview

- In 2011, 15,640 law enforcement agencies provided 1–12 months of arson data and reported 52,333 arsons. Of the participating agencies, 14,887 provided expanded offense data regarding 43,412 arsons.
- Nearly 46 percent (45.9) of all arson offenses involved structures (e.g., residential, storage, public, etc.). Mobile property was involved in 23.9 percent of arsons, and other types of property (such as crops, timber, fences, etc.) accounted for 30.2 percent of reported arsons.
- The average dollar loss per arson was $13,196.
- Arsons of industrial/manufacturing structures resulted in the highest average dollar losses (an average of $68,349 per arson).
- Arson offenses decreased 4.7 percent in 2011 when compared with arson data reported in 2010. . . .
- Nationwide, there were 18.2 arson offenses for every 100,000 inhabitants. . . .

OFFENSES CLEARED

In the FBI's Uniform Crime Reporting (UCR) Program, law enforcement agencies can clear, or "close," offenses in one of two ways: by arrest or by exceptional means. Although an agency may administratively close a case, that does not necessarily mean that the agency can clear the offense for UCR purposes. To clear an offense within the UCR Program's guidelines, the reporting agency must adhere to certain criteria, which are outlined in the following text. *(Note: The UCR Program does not distinguish between offenses cleared by arrest and those cleared by exceptional means in collecting or publishing data via the traditional Summary Reporting System.)*

CLEARANCES INVOLVING ONLY PERSONS UNDER 18 YEARS OF AGE

When an offender under the age of 18 is cited to appear in juvenile court or before other juvenile authorities, the UCR Program considers the incident for which the juvenile is being held responsible to be cleared by arrest, even though a physical arrest may not have occurred. When clearances involve both juvenile and adult offenders, those incidents are classified as clearances for crimes committed by adults. Because the clearance percentages for crimes committed by juveniles include only those clearances in which no adults were involved, the figures in this publication should not be used to present a definitive picture of juvenile involvement in crime.

Overview

- In the nation in 2011, 47.7 percent of violent crimes and 18.6 percent of property crimes were cleared by arrest or exceptional means.

- When considering clearances of violent crimes, 64.8 percent of murder offenses, 41.2 percent of forcible rape offenses, 28.7 percent of robbery offenses, and 56.9 percent of aggravated assault offenses were cleared.
- Among property crimes, 21.5 percent of larceny-theft offenses, 12.7 percent of burglary offenses, and 11.9 percent of motor vehicle theft offenses were cleared.
- 18.8 percent of arson offenses were cleared by arrest or exceptional means in 2011.
- 32.7 percent of arson offenses cleared involved juveniles (persons under age 18); this was the highest percentage of all offense clearances involving only juveniles. . . .

ARRESTS

Definition

The FBI's Uniform Crime Reporting (UCR) Program counts one arrest for each separate instance in which a person is arrested, cited, or summoned for an offense. The UCR Program collects arrest data on 28 offenses, as described in Offense Definitions. (Please note that, beginning in 2010, the UCR Program no longer collected data on runaways.) Because a person may be arrested multiple times during a year, the UCR arrest figures do not reflect the number of individuals who have been arrested; rather, the arrest data show the number of times that persons are arrested, as reported by law enforcement agencies to the UCR Program.

Data Collection—Juveniles

The UCR Program considers a juvenile to be an individual under 18 years of age regardless of state definition. The program does not collect data regarding police contact with a juvenile who has not committed an offense, nor does it collect data on situations in which police take a juvenile into custody for his or her protection, e.g., neglect cases.

Overview

- Nationwide, law enforcement made an estimated 12,408,899 arrests in 2011. Of these arrests, 534,704 were for violent crimes, and 1,639,883 were for property crimes. *(Note: The UCR Program does not collect data on citations for traffic violations.)*
- The highest number of arrests were for drug abuse violations (estimated at 1,531,251 arrests), larceny-theft (estimated at 1,264,986), and driving under the influence (estimated at 1,215,077).
- The estimated arrest rate for the United States in 2011 was 3,991.1 arrests per 100,000 inhabitants. The arrest rate for violent crime (including murder and non-negligent manslaughter, forcible rape, robbery, and aggravated assault) was 172.3 per 100,000 inhabitants, and the arrest rate for property crime (burglary, larceny-theft, motor vehicle theft, and arson) was 531.3 per 100,000 inhabitants.
- Two-year arrest trends show violent crime arrests declined 4.9 percent in 2011 when compared with 2010 arrests, and property crime arrests decreased 0.1 percent when compared with the 2010 arrests.
- Arrests of juveniles for all offenses decreased 11.1 percent in 2011 when compared with the 2010 number; arrests of adults declined 3.6 percent.

- Over 74 percent (74.1) of the persons arrested in the nation during 2011 were males. They accounted for 80.4 percent of persons arrested for violent crime and 62.9 percent of persons arrested for property crime.
- In 2011, 69.2 percent of all persons arrested were white, 28.4 percent were black, and the remaining 2.4 percent were of other races. . . .

SOURCE: U.S. Department of Justice. Federal Bureau of Investigation. "Crime in the United States, 2011." October 29, 2012. http://www.fbi.gov/about-us/cjis/ucr/crime-in-the-u.s/2011/crime-in-the-u.s.-2011/index-page.

OTHER HISTORIC DOCUMENTS OF INTEREST

FROM THIS VOLUME

FROM PREVIOUS *Historic Documents*

State and Federal Officials on Hurricane Sandy Damage and Recovery

OCTOBER 31, DECEMBER 18, AND DECEMBER 27, 2012

On October 29, 2012, a hurricane made landfall near Atlantic City, New Jersey, packing eighty-mile-per-hour winds and causing record storm surges along the East Coast. Superstorm Sandy, as it came to be known, was the second costliest hurricane in U.S. history, causing more than $70 billion in damage and killing more than 100 people. The storm impacted a total of twenty-four states, with the greatest amount of damage done in New Jersey and New York, where millions lost power and tens of thousands of homes and businesses were destroyed. The storm forged an unlikely partnership between Democrat Barack Obama and New Jersey's Republican Governor Chris Christie, who just two months before the storm delivered a scathing review of the president's record at the 2012 Republican presidential convention.

PREPARATIONS

As the days to Sandy's U.S. landfall drew closer, meteorologists painted numerous pictures of the possible paths the storm could take and its potential impact. Some U.S. forecasts showed Sandy petering out in the Atlantic Ocean before it could hit the East Coast, but the European weather model, which some meteorologists argue is more advanced than forecasting in the United States, showed the storm on a direct northward track that would undoubtedly cause heavy damage. What was certain was that a number of weather forces were coming together in an unprecedented way. "We are dealing with categories here that we don't normally see," said Dr. Louis Uccellini, the director of the National Centers for Environmental Prediction, describing a tropical storm moving west rather than east, combined with a powerful winter storm from the Midwest, and a full moon, the latter of which had the potential to increase the storm surge along the East Coast. Three days before Sandy made landfall, U.S. forecasters were nearly certain that it would hit southern New Jersey hard, with the epicenter estimated to be near Atlantic City, causing coastal flooding and record storm surges. "There is no avoiding a significant storm surge event over a large area," said Rick Knabb, the director of the National Hurricane Center.

In anticipation of the storm, governors in Connecticut, Delaware, Maryland, New Jersey, New York, North Carolina, Rhode Island, and Virginia issued both mandatory and voluntary evacuation orders for various portions of their coasts, and states of emergency were declared in order to activate the National Guard. "Everyone's saying, 'This is crap, it isn't going to happen. The weathermen always get it wrong, so I'm just going to hang out here,'" said Governor Christie. "Please don't, OK? We have to be prepared for the worst here."

STATE-BY-STATE IMPACT

Superstorm Sandy started in the Caribbean Sea as a tropical depression on October 22, then formed into a tropical storm hitting Jamaica, Cuba, and the Bahamas before moving up the East Coast of the United States on October 29 and 30. As it moved toward Canada and eventually back out to sea, the storm affected a total of twenty-four states with a mix of devastating rain, wind, and snow.

In North Carolina, a number of homes on the state's barrier islands, known as the Outer Banks, were damaged, and the main highway connecting the islands with the mainland was nearly destroyed. A tall ship sank off the coast of the Outer Banks while trying to avoid the storm. The U.S. Coast Guard made a daring rescue attempt to save the sixteen crewmembers, but two were killed.

Although Sandy's epicenter was hundreds of miles off its coast, Maryland's Ocean City, a popular tourist destination, lost its main fishing pier and hundreds of thousands across the state lost power. Commuter rail lines were shut down during and briefly after the storm. In Delaware, where mandatory evacuations were issued for most of the low-lying coastal areas, thousands lost power and heavy flooding temporarily closed some highways. Connecticut, a state with a densely populated coastline, had hundreds of thousands of residents without power, but it escaped without too much damage. Even though it doesn't have a coastline, wide swaths of Pennsylvania were without power following Sandy, and regional transit systems were halted. Rhode Island's biggest problem was power outages as well, but its main hurricane wall withstood the storm surge.

New York and New Jersey bore the brunt of the storm. In New Jersey, the state hardest hit and the first place where Sandy made landfall, millions of residents lost power, and tens of thousands of homes and businesses were destroyed. The historic boardwalk in Atlantic City, where the casinos had been shuttered in anticipation of the storm, was partially washed away, as was the boardwalk in Seaside Heights, providing what would become an iconic image of the storm: a damaged wooden roller coaster now in the ocean just off the coast. Portions of the New Jersey Turnpike were closed, and residents were encouraged to drive only when necessary. Public transportation systems, including those linking New Jersey to New York, were shut down. More than 30,000 homes and businesses were destroyed or structurally damaged, while another 42,000 homes had other damage. In total, Christie estimated that the damage sustained by the storm cost $36.9 billion, which included nearly $30 billion in repair and restoration. "We have a long way to go to rebuild and restore our communities, but the people of New Jersey have already shown that we are ready to meet the challenge," he said.

New York City was the hardest-hit section of New York, where 750,000 citizens lost electricity. Approximately 100,000 homes on Long Island were damaged or destroyed. In Lower Manhattan, the financial district lost power, shutting down the New York Stock Exchange trading floor on October 29 and October 30, marking the first time since 1888 that the stock market had been unexpectedly closed for two consecutive days. Mayor Michael Bloomberg decided to cancel the New York Marathon just days before it was set to be held, saying, "While holding the race would not require diverting resources from the recovery effort, it is clear that it has become the source of controversy and division." Bloomberg estimated the total damage to the city to be approximately $19 billion, while Governor Andrew Cuomo estimated that New York State's total cost would be $42 billion.

Transportation Stalled

Power outages across the Northeast left drivers struggling to find gas stations with functioning pumps. Lines at some stations in New York and New Jersey stretched for up to three miles, and drivers waited for up to sixteen hours to reach a pump. The Defense Department worked to get fuel directly to gas stations in New York and New Jersey and also sent generators to help power those stations that closed when the power went out. Governor Cuomo announced that state residents would be able to get ten gallons of gas for free from fuel trucks provided by the federal government. On November 2, Governor Christie enacted a gas-rationing plan in some areas to prevent a fuel shortage, which was followed on November 9 by a similar program in New York City. Mayor Bloomberg said he hoped the system would keep at bay the fistfights and arrests that had cropped up across the city. New Jersey's gas rationing ended on November 13, while New York City's extended to November 24.

New York's subway system, which moves millions of riders each day, was paralyzed by the storm. At 108 years old, "it has never faced a disaster as devastating as what we experienced last night," said Metropolitan Transit Authority chair Joseph Lhota, the day after Sandy made landfall. Seven subway tunnels were flooded and required extensive repair. Partial operation of the New York subway system resumed on November 1, and the system was running at 80 percent by November 5. Within two weeks of Sandy, all New York–area transit was running close to normal operation.

Airlines canceled tens of thousands of flights both in anticipation of Sandy and afterward. Luckily, Sandy hit at slow travel season, meaning that the number of travelers stranded was minimized. Train travel was also affected, and Amtrak canceled routes along its Northeast Corridor, sending a ripple effect throughout the southern United States and Canada.

Federal Response

Members of Congress left Washington, D.C., in late December without reaching a conclusion on the fiscal cliff, but more important for those along the storm-battered East Coast, the House failed to approve Senate legislation to send billions of dollars in aid to the states hit by Hurricane Sandy. It was ultimately House Speaker John Boehner, R-Ohio, who decided not to hold the vote because the most fiscally conservative in his party wanted to offset any spending increase, but members could not reach a quick decision on how to do so. There was additional disagreement about whether the package total was too large. New Jersey and New York officials on both sides of the aisle lambasted Boehner and GOP leadership. "Our people were played last night as a pawn, and that's why people hate Washington, D.C.," said Christie. Calling for the Speaker to directly face the families who had their homes and businesses destroyed, Sen. Kirsten Gillibrand, D-N.Y., said she doubted Boehner "has the dignity nor the guts to do it."

On January 2, Boehner announced that he would let a vote come to the floor to provide more than $50 billion to the region affected by Sandy. The bill passed 241–180 on January 15. On January 28, the Senate took up consideration of the bill. An amendment was proposed by Sen. Mike Lee, R-Utah, to offset the total cost of the relief package by decreasing federal discretionary spending by 0.49 percent for nine years. "We have to consider that we are more than $16 trillion in debt," said Lee, noting that his "heart goes out" to those affected by the storm. The amendment was handily defeated, 35–62. With the final bill before them, Sen. Charles Schumer, D-N.Y., said in a floor speech, "Sandy's wrath was wide and it was deep. Nearly 300,000 families had their homes damaged. . . . We can't wait any longer, because nothing about this was a game for those families." The Senate ultimately passed the bill 62–36, with all 36 "no" votes cast by Republicans. Overall, the recovery package from the federal government for areas affected by Hurricane Sandy was more than $60 billion, and included $9.7 billion for the National Flood Insurance Program to assist in handling claims from the storm. Despite its wide reach, no states outside of the Northeast received federal funding for Sandy disaster assistance.

STRANGE BEDFELLOWS

During the 2012 Republican presidential primary, conservatives unhappy with their choice of candidates urged Christie to enter the race, hoping that the straight-talking, rising star who is best known for berating his opponents would breathe new life into the race. Christie ultimately chose not to run, but he was picked to give a keynote address at the Republican convention in August. In his speech, the governor was tough on President Obama and said, "It's time to end this era of absentee leadership in the Oval Office and send real leaders back to the White House."

Two months later, after Sandy had crippled his state, Christie and Obama forged a partnership and appeared together multiple times. Christie praised Obama's leadership at the federal level, saying, "I cannot thank the President enough for his personal concern and compassion for our state and the people of our state." Obama, too, saw past the politics of the moment, and pledged to do anything in his power to help the recovery. "We are here for you, and we will not forget; we will follow up and make sure that you get all the help that you need until you've rebuilt," Obama said at a joint press conference with Christie. The president said he had expedited emergency declarations to allow state residents to register for federal emergency assistance as soon as possible, and he told his team that everyone's phone calls should be answered within fifteen minutes. "If they need something," the president said, "we figure out a way to say yes."

Christie faced immediate backlash from his party, but the outspoken governor responded, "I've got a job to do here in New Jersey that's much bigger than presidential politics, and I couldn't care less about any of that stuff." Conservative radio pundit Rush Limbaugh called the governor a "fool" for his behavior toward the president, while Robert Kuttner, a writer for the right-wing publication *The American Prospect*, said, "If Christie thinks he has a snowball's chance of being the [2016] Republican nominee, he is delusional." Christie's change of heart toward the president was speculated to be the reason he was kept off the speakers' list at the annual Conservative Political Action Committee conference in early 2013.

—Heather Kerrigan

Following is the text of two statements delivered on October 31, 2012—one by New Jersey Governor Chris Christie and the other by President Barack Obama— on the damage caused by Hurricane Sandy; the text of a floor statement made on December 18, 2012, by Sen. Robert Menendez, D-N.J., imploring his colleagues to vote in favor of a $60 billion relief package for Hurricane Sandy cleanup; and the text of a floor statement delivered on December 27, 2012, by Sen. Daniel Coats, R-Ind., requesting a reduction in the amount of funds immediately made available through a Hurricane Sandy recovery bill.

Christie and Obama Remarks on Hurricane Sandy

October 31, 2012

GOVERNOR CHRISTIE: Good afternoon, everybody. And thank you all for coming today. I want to thank the members who are here as well. And obviously, I want to thank the President.

We spent a significant afternoon together surveying the damage up and down the New Jersey coastline; we were on *Marine One* together to be able to show the President that personally. I had an opportunity to see it, and we had an opportunity to discuss it at length. And then, going over to the shelter here, being able to meet with folks to have them see the President and his concern, and the concern that all of us have for making sure that things get back to normal as quickly as possible.

We have lots of challenges. One of our challenges now is to get back to normalcy. And so the things we need to do is to make sure that we get power restored as quickly as possible; make sure that people have clean drinking water, and waste water treatment plants are working; hospitals are taken care of the way they need to; and that we get kids back to school.

And so, I discussed all those issues today with the President, and I'm pleased to report that he has sprung into action immediately to help get us those things while we were in the car riding together. So I want to thank him for that. He has worked incredibly closely with me since before the storm hit. I think this is our sixth conversation since the weekend, and it's been a great working relationship to make sure that we're doing the jobs that people elected us to do.

And I cannot thank the President enough for his personal concern and compassion for our state and for the people of our state. And I heard it on the phone conversations with him, and I was able to witness it today personally.

And so we're going to continue to work. The state government is here. We're doing what we need to do. We're coordinating with FEMA, and I want to thank Administrator Fugate for being here and for the input he's already had in helping to make our operation even better. And we will move on from here.

What I said yesterday I really mean. I know there has got to be sorrow, and you see that and the President has seen that today in the eyes—the faces of a lot of the folks he's met. And that sorrow is appropriate; we've suffered some loss. Luckily, we haven't suffered that much loss of life and we thank God for that. But we have suffered losses, and this is the worst storm that I've seen in my lifetime in this state. But we cannot permit that sorrow to replace the resilience that I know all New Jerseyans have. And so we will get up and we'll get this thing rebuilt, and we'll put things back together, because that's what this state is all about and always has been all about.

And so for all of you who are here—and I met a bunch of you today at Brigantine who disregarded my admonition—to get the hell out of here—you're forgiven this time. You are forgiven this time, but not for much longer. We've got to make sure when all of you look around and you see all this destruction, that's fine—but you know what, all that stuff can be replaced. You look to your right and to your left, to your husband or wife, your son or your daughter—those are the things that can't be replaced. So I'm glad that we don't have that kind of loss of life to have to deal with.

So I want to thank him for being here today, for bringing his personal attention to it. And it's my honor to introduce to all of you the President of the United States.

THE PRESIDENT: Thank you, everybody. Let me just make sure that I acknowledge the folks who are here, because they've played an important role in this.

First of all, your congressional delegation—Senator Bob Menendez, Senator Frank Lautenberg, Congressman Frank LoBiondo, Atlantic County Executive Dennis Levinson, and Brigantine Mayor Philip Guenther.

Obviously, this is a federal, state, and local effort. And the first thing I want to do is just to thank everybody who has been involved in the entire rescue and recovery process. At the top of my list, I have to say that Governor Christie throughout this process has been responsive; he has been aggressive in making sure that the state got out in front of this incredible storm. And I think the people of New Jersey recognize that he has put his heart and soul into making sure that the people of New Jersey bounce back even stronger than before. So I just want to thank him for his extraordinary leadership and partnership.

I want to thank the congressional delegation because part of the reason we're going to be able to respond quickly to all this is because they helped to make sure that FEMA financing was in place, and we're very appreciative of those efforts. And I want to thank Craig Fugate; sometimes people just think FEMA and they don't think the people behind them, but Craig lives and breathes this stuff, making sure that we're providing the help that people so desperately need in these situations.

I want to thank all the first responders who have been involved in this process—the linesmen, the firefighters, the folks who were in here shuttling out people who were supposed to "get the hell out" and didn't. You've helped to save a lot of lives and a lot of property. And one of the things that you learn in these tragedies is, the first responders—keep in mind their homes usually are underwater too, or their families have been affected in some way, and yet they make those personal sacrifices to help other people. So we really appreciate them.

I'm just going to make a couple of comments. Number one, and most important, our hearts go out to the families who have lost loved ones. It's true that because of some good preparation, the loss of life was kept lower than it might have been, but for those individual families, obviously their world has been torn apart. And we need to make sure that everybody who has lost a loved one knows they're in our thoughts and prayers—and I speak for the whole country there.

For those like the people I just had the chance to meet on this block and throughout New Jersey and throughout the region whose lives have been upended, my second message is we are here for you, and we will not forget; we will follow up to make sure that you get all the help that you need until you've rebuilt.

At this point, our main focus is on the states of New Jersey, which got hit harder than anybody; the state of New York, particularly lower Manhattan and Long Island. We are very concerned about some situations in Connecticut as well, and we're still monitoring West Virginia where there are heavy snows in some inaccessible areas. But for the most part, those four states are really bearing the brunt of this incredible storm.

What we've been able to do is to pre-position and stage commodities—water, power generators, ambulances in some cases, food, medical supplies, emergency supplies—and we have over 2,000 FEMA personnel that are on the ground right now. Their job, now that we're moving out of the search-and-rescue phase, is to make sure that they are going out and talking to individual communities so that people know exactly how they can get the help that they need.

We expedited our emergency declarations for the state of New Jersey and local counties that have been affected. What that means is, is that people can immediately start registering for emergency assistance. And one of the things I want to emphasize to the people of New Jersey and throughout the region: Now that you're safe, your family is safe, but you're trying to figure out where you're going to stay for the next couple of days, et cetera, it's very important that you know that there is help available to you right now, for example, to find rental housing or to be able to pay for some groceries. Over at the community center we saw a young woman who had a newborn, or I guess probably an eight-month old, still needs diapers and formula, and has run out. Those are the kinds of basic supplies and help that we can provide.

If you call 800–621-FEMA—800–621-FEMA—or DisasterAssistance.gov—if you've got access to the Internet, you can go to DisasterAssistance.gov. What that allows you to do is to register right now so that you can immediately start receiving help. We want to make sure that you get everything that you need.

Just a couple of final points. Obviously, our biggest priority right now is getting power turned back on. We were very pleased that Newark got power yesterday; Jersey City is getting power we believe today. But there are still big chunks of the community, including this community right here, that don't have power. And so it's hard enough cleaning up debris and dealing with boats that have been upended and roads that are blocked; when people don't have power, though, obviously they're disabled in all sorts of ways and it's hard to get back to normal.

So yesterday, I had a chance to speak to the CEOs of the utilities from all across the country. And a lot of the states that were spared, that were not hard hit, or some states as far away as California, they have pledged to start getting equipment crews, et cetera, here into New Jersey and New York and Connecticut as quickly as possible.

And one of the things that we've been able to do—just to give you a sense of how this is an all-hands-deck approach—we're able to get C-17s and C-130s, military transport planes, potentially, to move assets, personnel to speed up the process of getting power up and running as soon as possible.

Our first priority is water filtration plants and some other critical infrastructure in the state; for that, we've got emergency generators. We've got a Navy ship that has some helicopters that can help to move assets around the state as well. And so we're going to be working with Governor Christie's office and local officials to identify what are those critical infrastructure, how can we get what's needed as quickly as possible.

Just a couple of other things that we're concerned about—one is, as power starts coming back on, we want to make sure that people can also get to work. Obviously, there are a lot of folks in Jersey who work in New York, in the city, and in other places where transportation may be hobbled. One of the things I mentioned to the Governor is the possibility of us using federal assets, military assets, as well as taking inventory of assets from around the country that can be brought in so that we can help people get to their work.

And Governor Christie also mentioned the importance of schools. The sooner we can get our kids back into school, the sooner they're back into a routine; that obviously helps the families and helps the kids as well.

So we're going to have a lot of work to do. I don't want anybody to feel that somehow this is all going to get cleaned up overnight. We want to make sure that people have realistic expectations.

But what I can promise you is that the federal government will be working as closely as possible with the state and local officials, and we will not quit until this is done. And the directive that I have given—and I said this yesterday, but I will repeat; and I think Craig and others who are working with me right now know I mean it—we are not going to tolerate red tape. We're not going to tolerate bureaucracy. And I've instituted a 15-minute rule, essentially, on my team: You return everybody's phone calls in 15 minutes, whether it's the mayors,' the governors,' county officials.' If they need something, we figure out a way to say yes.

As I was just gathering around, I had a chance to talk to some of the young people here who have been volunteering, going up and down the block cleaning up debris. And when we were over at the community center, there was a restaurant owner who, for the last 18 hours, had been cooking meals, just as his contribution to the recovery process. And some of the folks were saying the food was better than they got at home. [*Laughter.*] You had a 15-year-old young man whose mother was disabled, and he was making sure that she was okay, and taking on extraordinary responsibilities for himself but also for his mom.

And when you see folks like that respond with strength and resilience, when you see neighbors helping neighbors, then you're reminded about what America is all about. We go through tough times, but we bounce back. And the reason we bounce back is because we look out for one another and we don't leave anybody behind.

And so my commitment to the people on this block, the people in this community, and the people of this state is that that same spirit will carry over all the way through until our work is done. All right?

Thank you very much, everybody.

SOURCE: State of New Jersey. Office of the Governor. "Remarks by President Barack Obama and Governor Chris Christie After Surveying Damage from Hurricane Sandy in Brigantine, New Jersey." October 31, 2012. http://www.state.nj.us/governor/news/news/552012/approved/20121031q.html.

Sen. Menendez on Funding for Hurricane Sandy Relief

December 18, 2012

Mr. MENENDEZ. Mr. President, I rise to respond to some of the comments I heard from my colleagues with reference to the Hurricane Sandy emergency supplemental. Hopefully I can give all of our colleagues—who will be casting a vote here at some point—an understanding as to why we hold a different view than some of the comments that have been made.

One of those comments I will generally put under the rubric we can wait and do something small. Various comments have been referenced in that respect. Some seem to be questioning whether this emergency is worthy of a robust Federal response. They say the cost to help families rebuild and recover is too much and should be reduced. I have heard that in this emergency it is not necessary, and unlike many other similar emergencies in the past, we should do something smaller and wait to do the rest later.

I think those who suggest or make that argument don't seem to understand that a piecemeal recovery is a failed recovery. We cannot rebuild half of a bridge unless we know the entirety of the money that is necessary is committed, like the Mantoloking Bridge in New Jersey, which I have shown many pictures of. We cannot hire a contractor to ultimately replace an entire sewage treatment system that had enormous amounts of sewage dispersing directly into the Hudson River because it was overcome if we only have half of the funding. We cannot hire a contractor to rebuild half a home or restore half of a community unless we know the money is there and that they can depend upon it in order to finish the project. We need the money in place to rebuild entire projects and entire areas to ensure that families and businesses devastated by the storm can recover.

Right now there are literally tens of thousands of small business owners trying to decide whether to reopen or pack it in. They are in a limbo. They are waiting to see what we, their Federal Government, do to respond to their tragedy. They are making decisions in their lives, their businesses, and everyone who is hired by those businesses. They are frozen and waiting to make those decisions based on whether the government is going to offer them a small business loan at low rates that are competitive with the marketplace and have longer term payments. Will they give them a grant toward rebuilding? What type of other benefits will they be able to derive in order to make a determination of whether they can open their business again? Having just a sense that there is only some emergent money and not the moneys to be able to do that doesn't allow them to open their business. It doesn't allow them to make that decision, and it freezes them in time.

The same thing is true for the person who, as winter is biting in the Northeast, faces the challenges of deciding what they might get from the government as it relates to rebuilding their home. Should they go forth or not? It is as if some of our colleagues don't believe when we describe this tragedy—and I welcome any one of our colleagues who wants to visit us in New Jersey to come with me to see the breadth, depth, and scope of our devastation. I have already taken a number of Members who were willing to go.

I ask my colleagues: Do you think Governor Christie is making this up? Do you think this fiscal hawk of the Republican Party is looking for Federal aid that is not desperately needed? Do you think we made up these photos of the damage? I can assure everyone we did not.

This is a picture taken just at one small part of the Jersey shore. If I could have a continuum that would bring us around this Chamber, it would look exactly like this. This is Ortley Beach. It shows blocks and blocks of homes that have been totally destroyed. It is an image that can be seen up and down the New Jersey coast.

Here is another example in Union Beach. It is half a home, but that whole community was significantly devastated. If we were to see this community, there would be rows and rows of houses reduced to rubble. I think that is the reality of what we have as a continuation of those neighborhoods in Union Beach.

I was talking to the mayor today—as part of a group of mayors—about their challenges, and this is an example of what he is facing throughout his community.

The storm damage is real and the Governor's request for funding is actually $20 billion higher than the supplemental we are debating. It is significant that it is $20 billion higher than the amount we are debating. These requests were scrubbed by OMB from the Governor's original request and gone over with a fine-tooth comb by the Appropriations

Committee. Everything in this bill, whether it is about Sandy or something else, is about declared disasters. Now is the time to come to our neighbors' help.

Secondly, there are those who come to the floor and say they are upset about the Army Corps element of this disaster bill and that the budget in this bill is too rigorous. They say that planning and rebuilding for the future is a waste, and that we can have another legislative opportunity to deal with the future. I would submit to those Members who very much care about fiscal responsibility that it is neither efficient, effective, nor fiscally responsible. What should we do, have the Army Corps go back to exactly what existed before? In many cases, what existed before did not sustain those communities, did not withhold the consequence of the surge, and created enormous losses.

We lost over 40 lives. The storm affected over 300,000 homes—30,000 permanently gone.

It seems to me, if we want to be smart fiscally, planning for the future means rebuilding well and rebuilding smart. It means rebuilding in a way that protects us from future storms.

We learned a lot from this superstorm. We know Army Corps coastal defenses work. Where we had them in place, the damage was minimal; where we didn't, there was more devastation, there was more damage, there was more destruction, and more recovery costs.

Stockton College did a study of the Army Corps beach engineering projects before and after the storm, and what it found was unambiguous. Where the Army Corps was able to complete a beach engineering project recently, the dunes helped and damage to communities behind the project was manageable.

Here is a picture taken at Surf City, NJ, right after the storm. This beach received beach engineering in 2007 as part of the Army Corps Long Beach Island Shore Protection Project, and my colleagues can see that despite damage being done to the dune, the dune held and saved lives, saved property, and saved money.

Alternatively, the pictures of Union Beach, which I previously referred to—it is a working-class town that couldn't afford the local match for the Army Corps project, and as my colleagues can see, we have an entirely devastated neighborhood. So we see the fundamental difference: Engineered beaches by the Army Corps, minimal destruction: Those that weren't engineered, maximum destruction; costs, and consequences. Rebuilding the defenses only to the standard that existed before the storm will just give us more of the same in the next storm. If we don't do things differently, we shouldn't expect a different outcome.

In this photo, we also see the homes destroyed by the storm surge. Yes, we can help these homeowners rebuild, but if we don't rebuild smarter, better, and with stronger coastal protections, we will be paying again after the next storm, both in terms of human suffering and Federal funds. The storm crews with the Army Corps of Engineers, academic studies, and local community officials have been telling us for years that beach engineering works. It protects lives. It protects properties. It saves us money in the long run.

Time is of the essence. The severe storm damage caused by Sandy has left New Jersey defenseless. As we enter what is our most vulnerable storm season—the winter Nor'easters—we don't need a Superstorm Sandy to have major consequences all the way up and down the communities throughout New Jersey.

Right now, the Jersey shore is similar to a person with a weak immune system. The storm has destroyed our defenses, and that is why we need to rebuild them quickly. If we don't, a relatively mild storm can cause catastrophic damage.

This is a challenge to us right now—right now. Suggesting the Army Corps budget is not one we need right now and it can wait—these communities can't wait. These communities can't wait. In fact, it will be far more costly to us.

I think we have close to anywhere between $750 million and $1 billion in Army Corps of Engineers projects that have been approved—passed and been approved—but they have not had the funding. So when we add those that would ensure we don't end up like Ortley Beach and that we can recover those like Ortley Beach that have been battered and shattered, then I think it makes critical sense.

Finally, I know there are some who suggest mitigation is not worthy of this disaster. I think I have made the case, in the case of the Army Corps, although the Army Corps is not the only form of mitigation. Mitigation means rebuilding smarter and stronger. Whether it is through a flexible CDBG account that will allow the hardening of our electrical grid or elevating homes or via traditional Army Corps or FEMA programs, mitigation has long been a part of supplemental appropriations.

In the gulf coast, we spent $16 billion building a world-class storm protection system in Louisiana—$16 billion. In Alabama and Texas, we used CDBG funding to raise homes and improve infrastructure. So much of the public infrastructure in our region that was damaged as a result of the superstorm is eligible for reimbursement from FEMA. There is no disputing that.

The Stafford Act has now been the law of the land for many years, and it says the Federal Government will assume the cost of repairs to critical infrastructure after an event such as Sandy. These communities, when we talk to mayors in Little Ferry and Moonachie—not the Jersey Shore but northern New Jersey and other places that were dramatically hit—when I was visiting them soon after the storm, one mayor said to me, Mayor Vaccaro, I lost my police department, my fire department, and city hall is underwater.

They need to be protecting their citizens. They need to be able to fully depend upon the resources to get back their public safety efforts. It does not make good fiscal sense for Congress to pay to fix our broken infrastructure, which we are legally required to do, without looking to protect our investment and prevent similar costly damage in the future. To me, that makes a lot more fiscal sense at the end of the day. So we will look forward to coming back to the floor again and again as we deal with these issues, but I hope our colleagues understand the urgency of now.

Final point. After Katrina, in 10 days the Congress passed two emergency supplementals that totaled a little over $62 billion for Louisiana, Alabama, Mississippi. It has been 6 weeks—6 weeks, not 10 days, 6 weeks—since the storm hit New Jersey, New York, and the Northeast, and there hasn't been any action. The urgency of now is incredibly important and the urgency of doing this robustly is incredibly important to the recovery of a region that is so important to the economic engine of this country.

SOURCE: Sen. Robert Menendez. "Disaster Relief." December 18, 2012. *Congressional Record* 2012, pt. 158, S8133-S8135. http://www.gpo.gov/fdsys/pkg/CREC-2012-12-18/pdf/CREC-2012-12-18-pt1-PgS8133.pdf.

Sen. Coats on Decrease in Immediate Hurricane Sandy Funding

December 27, 2012

Mr. COATS. Mr. President, I am cognizant of the fact that we will have a series of votes beginning in just 15 minutes, and so even though the unanimous consent request on this amendment is for 30 minutes equally divided, I am going to try to judiciously use this time between myself and Senator Alexander to explain why we are offering this amendment, and hopefully our colleagues will be persuaded to support us when we vote on this probably tomorrow.

We are all, of course, sensitive to the pain and damage inflicted by Mother Nature in the Northeast. In fact, some of the Northeast is getting some more of that pain with a storm up there today.

No State or region in our country should be left to fend for itself after a storm as devastating as Hurricane Sandy. It is important to understand that many things have overwhelmed the ability of the States and local communities to deal with some of the effects of this, and that is why the Sandy emergency supplemental is before us attached to H.R. 1 and why we will be voting on that, I assume, tomorrow.

There are two versions before us; one is the Senate Democrats' emergency supplemental proposal. That totals $60.4 billion. It includes nearly $13 billion in mitigation funding. That goes for the next storm, not this storm. There is $3.46 billion for Army Corps of Engineers, $500 million of which is projects from previous disasters; $3 billion to repair or replace Federal assets that do not fall into the category of emergency need. There is $56 million for tsunami cleanup on the west coast, which, of course, does not relate to Sandy. There is a lot of new authorizing language for reform of disaster relief programs, which I would support through the regular process. But without having gone through the authorizing committee, I don't think that is a good idea.

Our proposed alternative provides $23.8 billion in funding for the next 3 months. We are not saying this is the be-all and end-all of what Congress will ultimately fund to meet the needs of those who have been impacted by Sandy. We are simply saying that before rushing to a number, which has not been fully scrubbed, fully looked at, plans haven't been fully developed yet—and that is understandable—we think it most important we provide emergency funding for those in immediate need over the next 3 months.

We have carefully worked with FEMA Director Fugate and we have worked with Secretary Donovan at HUD. We have worked through the Appropriations Committee to identify those specific needs that get to the emergency situations under which this bill is titled. It provides funding for States to allow them to begin to rebuild but also leaves us time to review what additional funds might be needed.

So rather than throwing out a big number and simply saying let us see what comes in under that number, let us look at the most immediate needs that have to be funded now and provide a sufficient amount of funds in order to do that. In fact, the amount we are providing would extend, in terms of outlays, far beyond March 27, but we want those mayors and we want those Governors to be able to begin the planning process of looking how they would go forward. We also want, in respect to our careful need, to carefully look at how we extend taxpayer dollars.

We want to allow this 3-month period of time for which the relevant committees in the Senate and the House of Representatives can look at these plans, can document the request, can examine the priorities that might be needed and then put a sensible plan in place that hopefully will be an efficient and effective use of taxpayer dollars. Therefore, we have struck from the Democratic proposal all moneys that would go to mitigation funding, not saying mitigation funding isn't necessary but simply saying it doesn't meet the emergency need this first 3-month proposal addresses. This will give States time to begin to rebuild but also allow us time to review what additional funds are needed for that rebuilding.

We don't allow authorizing language because we don't believe in authorizing something on an emergency appropriations bill that ought to go through the authorizing committee. We focus specifically on Sandy-related needs. There are a number of other needs, as I have just addressed, that are perhaps legitimate, that ought to come through the regular process.

With that, let me turn to my colleague from Tennessee who has been working with me. I would say our Appropriations Committee, our Republican staff, has gone through this very carefully and tried to identify how we can get money for the essential needs to those people, to those communities that need them now. We want to be responsible in terms of spending taxpayer dollars by having a period of time in which we can look at the plans for the future and see what additional funds might be needed. . . .

SOURCE: Sen. Dan Coats. "Department of Defense Appropriations Act." December 27, 2012. *Congressional Record* 2012, pt. 158, S8425-S8426. http://www.gpo.gov/fdsys/pkg/CREC-2012-12-27/pdf/CREC-2012-12-27-pt1-PgS8425.pdf.

OTHER HISTORIC DOCUMENTS OF INTEREST

FROM PREVIOUS *HISTORIC DOCUMENTS*

November

Colorado and Washington State Officials Respond to Marijuana Referenda

NOVEMBER 7 AND DECEMBER 10, 2012

On November 6, Colorado and Washington became the first two states in the country to legalize the possession and sale of marijuana for personal, recreational use. Although the two ballot initiatives violated federal law, the administration of President Barack Obama did not appear poised to make an all-out effort to track down users in the two states. The new laws in Colorado and Washington follow a nationwide trend that shows Americans becoming increasingly more tolerant of decriminalizing recreational marijuana use. A 2011 Gallup poll found that 50 percent of Americans support legalizing marijuana, while only 46 percent oppose. Opponents of legalizing marijuana say that it has the potential to cause a decline in economic productivity as well as increase the number of traffic and workplace accidents. Supporters, however, argue that the anticipated tax revenue would greatly outweigh any harm, and the laws would also free up law enforcement, offer some relief to strained jails and prisons, and deal a blow to drug traffickers.

AMENDMENT 64

Colorado already had a law in place for medical marijuana use, allowing those with a prescription to possess up to two ounces, and more in some cases. The medical marijuana law also allowed for the creation of state-regulated dispensaries to serve these clients. In 2006, Colorado marijuana supporters made their first attempt at legalizing recreational use, and the measure was defeated by 59 percent of voters. The 2012 referendum was more successful, winning 55 percent to 45 percent. Some law enforcement personnel came out in support of the initiative, arguing that marijuana arrests hampered their already stretched-thin personnel and benefited only drug cartels, but some cautioned that if not implemented properly, the new law could undermine the efforts of public safety officials. Opponents included a panel of state legislators who said that to generate large sums of revenue, the tax on marijuana would need to increase to as much as 25 percent, but because this would be a new tax, it would have to be approved by voters, which is unlikely.

Amendment 64 would allow anyone over the age of twenty-one in the state of Colorado to possess up to one ounce of marijuana for personal, recreational use. Nonresidents can purchase up to one-quarter ounce. Residents would also be permitted to grow, in their own homes, up to six marijuana plants; however, only three could be mature and flowering at one time. The individual could keep any marijuana produced by these plants, even if it was more than an ounce; however, this marijuana was prohibited from leaving the grower's residence. Starting in 2014, businesses would be allowed to apply for licenses from the state to sell marijuana for recreational use. Because marijuana will be subject to state and local taxes and an excise tax, it is estimated that one ounce, the maximum amount that can be sold to one person, will cost approximately $185.

There would be consequences for those found in possession of more than one ounce of marijuana, and users were not necessarily immune from federal prosecution. Additionally, anyone with more than five nanograms of tetrahydrocannabinol (THC) per milliliter of blood, or the equivalent of having used marijuana within the past two hours, while behind the wheel of a moving motor vehicle would receive a ticket for driving under the influence (DUI). Cities were given the opportunity to ban recreational marijuana stores, businesses, and commercial cultivation farms in their jurisdictions and could also require additional licensing on top of state requirements.

Supporters of the amendment celebrated its passage. "Colorado will no longer have laws that steer people toward using alcohol, and adults will be free to use marijuana instead if that is what they prefer. And we will be better off as a society because of it," said Mason Tvert, codirector of the Colorado pro-legalization campaign.

Governor John Hickenlooper, an opponent of the amendment, said he would respect the will of the voters. "This will be a complicated process, but we intend to follow through," the governor said in a statement. However, he cautioned, "Federal law still says marijuana is an illegal drug, so don't break out the Cheetos or gold fish too quickly." On December 10, the governor signed an executive order officially making Amendment 64 a part of Colorado's constitution. "We will begin working immediately with the General Assembly and state agencies to implement Amendment 64," Hickenlooper said. He also announced the creation of a task force that would help with the implementation of Amendment 64. According to the governor's office, the task force would address which state and local laws would need to be amended, whether security would be required for marijuana sellers, the potential impact on the economy, and the best method for educating the public about the health consequences of long-term marijuana use or use by minors.

The new Colorado law would be enforced by the state Medical Marijuana Enforcement Division. As part of its regulation program, the division announced that it intended to track marijuana production through radio frequency ID tags in seeds. The state estimates about $50 million in new revenue to be generated each year by Amendment 64. The first $40 million in tax revenue will go toward school construction, while any remaining revenue will go to the state's general fund. An additional $12 million in savings in criminal costs is anticipated in the year after the law goes into effect, and local governments in the state are expecting an extra $14 million in sales tax revenue per year.

INITIATIVE 502

A pro-marijuana group, New Approach Washington, circulated the petition that helped put Initiative 502 on the ballot, asking voters whether they wanted to amend Washington's constitution to allow for recreational use of marijuana. Like Colorado, Washington already had a medical marijuana law. A number of current and former law enforcement and judicial officials came out in support. In a November 2011 op-ed in the *Seattle Times*, a former U.S. attorney, retired State Superior Court judge, former deputy mayor of Seattle, and former Municipal Court judge wrote, "Decriminalizing marijuana would allow our state and local governments to refocus limited police and court resources on more important priorities than arresting, jailing and trying adult marijuana users. It would redirect hundreds of millions of dollars that are currently flowing to criminal organizations each year to legitimate businesses." The voters agreed and on November 6 passed the initiative 56 percent to 44 percent.

Initiative 502 officially became law on December 6. Like Colorado, the law allows for one ounce of marijuana for personal use, but unlike Colorado, Washington does not permit anyone other than state-licensed farmers to grow marijuana (unless a person is a medical-marijuana patient). It will not be until 2014 that stores will be able to apply for licenses to sell marijuana for recreational use. Any drivers with more than five nanograms of THC per milliliter of blood will receive a DUI, and marijuana consumption in public will remain illegal; however, doing so will result in only a fine and no arrest. The state's Liquor Control Board will largely be in charge of implementing the new law, and will look to law enforcement, public policy experts, and medical marijuana distributors for recommendations on how best to regulate the industry.

Washington, which already has one of the nation's highest liquor taxes and fifth-highest tobacco taxes, would impose a 25 percent tax three times in the marijuana, distribution process—when a grower sells to a processor, when a processor sells to a retailer, and when a retailer sells to a customer—and will also impose a regular sales tax. Given the high taxation rate, it is expected that after 2014, buyers will pay $467 per ounce of marijuana when purchasing from a retail outlet. These taxes are expected to raise $564 million in 2015; $214 million will go toward the State Health Plan, $198 million to the general fund, and $43 million will be set aside for marijuana education and public health programs.

OTHER STATE ATTEMPTS AT LEGALIZATION

On November 6, six states had marijuana initiatives on the ballot—half regarded the decriminalization of personal possession and recreational cultivation of marijuana, while the other half dealt with medical marijuana. In Oregon, voters turned down a measure to allow for recreational use of marijuana by a vote of 54 percent to 46 percent. The failure was largely blamed on poor organization. Peter Buckley, the cochair of the state legislature's budget committee, said he would continue to push for legalization. "There's a source of revenue that's reasonable, that is rational, that is the right policy choice for our state," he said.

California, the first state to legalize medical marijuana back in 1996, tried to legalize recreational use in 2010 with Proposition 19. However, when the Obama administration threatened to crack down, the state legislature acted before the initiative hit the ballot and reclassified marijuana possession as an infraction with no more than a $100 fine. Proposition 19 ultimately failed 53 percent to 47 percent. Supporters in the state are unlikely to bring another referendum to the ballot until 2016, because they claim they need the increased youth vote that turns out during presidential election years. There is some indication, however, that the state government might act first. Governor Jerry Brown, a Democrat, has long been a supporter of legalizing personal marijuana use, and his party holds a supermajority in the state legislature.

Alaska is one of the nation's most open states in terms of marijuana use because of a 1975 state supreme court decision that law enforcement could not prohibit small amounts of marijuana in citizens' homes. This allowed for up to four ounces and twenty-four plants to be grown by an individual at any one time. However, when supporters attempted to fully legalize personal use in 2004, it failed at 56 percent to 44 percent. The state attempted to outlaw marijuana in 2006, but a state judge upheld the 1975 decision.

The Rhode Island and Maine legislatures have moved toward legalizing recreational marijuana in the past few years. In Rhode Island in June 2012, personal marijuana possession was changed from a misdemeanor to a simple civil fine. Analysts have estimated that the state stands to bring in $30 million per year if it decriminalizes personal marijuana use. Rep. Edith Ajello, a sponsor of a bill to do just that, said, "Our prohibition has failed," so "legalizing and taxing it, just as we did to alcohol, is the way to do it." A few states away, in Maine, the legislature estimates it could bring in $8 million in new revenue each year by moving to a "legalize and regulate" plan for personal marijuana use.

Of the three states that had medical marijuana initiatives on the ballot, Massachusetts passed its legalization referendum, while voters in Arkansas rejected a similar proposal. In Montana, voters added restrictions to their current medical marijuana laws. After November 2012, eighteen states and Washington, D.C., allow for cannabis to be used for medical purposes.

CONFLICT WITH FEDERAL LAW

Under the 1970 Controlled Substances Act, the federal government classifies marijuana as a Schedule I controlled substance, meaning that it has no accepted medical use. The Americans for Safe Access pro-marijuana group challenged this classification in early 2013, but the U.S. Court of Appeals for the D.C. Circuit upheld the current classification.

Following the approval of the Colorado initiative, the Department of Justice said it was "reviewing the ballot initiative" and had "no additional comment at this time." In an effort to protect the state's law, representatives from Colorado, including Reps. Diana DeGette, Jared Polis, Mike Coffman, and Ed Perlmutter, introduced the "Respect States' and Citizens' Rights Act" to exempt states with marijuana laws from federal enforcement.

The federal government has had a mixed response to past marijuana laws. In California, the federal government has cracked down on dispensaries and greenhouses thought to be fronts for the illegal drug trade. Still, no individual has been prosecuted under federal law in any state where medical marijuana use has been legalized. Some experts agree that this has a lot to do with how tough in-state regulations are. In California, for example, the state left most regulation up to the cities, and that has resulted in an atmosphere in which almost anyone, even those with minor aches and pains, can receive a permit for medical marijuana. In the summer of 2012, the city of Los Angeles voted to close down most medical marijuana dispensaries, noting that at nearly 1,000 shops, it had become too difficult for the city to regulate. Lawsuits led city leaders to reverse their decision, but they are now asking the state to step in and pass stricter regulations.

In an interview with Barbara Walters in December, President Obama said of drug enforcement against individuals in states such as Colorado and Washington, "We've got bigger fish to fry. It would not make sense for us to see a top priority as going after recreational users in states that have determined that it's legal." But according to the *New York Times,* discussions have taken place among federal officials that arrests of personal users in Colorado and Washington could set a precedent that may be beneficial in future marijuana cases. According to Kevin Sabet, a former senior adviser at the White House Office of National Drug Control Policy, "How [federal law is] enforced, given resource constraints, is that small-scale users will likely not be targeted. But you're going to see efforts by the Justice Department against large commercial grows or retail sales or states making money off the new laws." Because the Colorado and Washington laws are still in the implementation stage, Ethan Nadelmann, the executive director of the Drug Policy Alliance, a group backing recreational marijuana use laws, said there was no reason for the federal government to take action immediately. "There is time right now for consultation and deliberation for how to best proceed and for the states to persuade the federal government to give this time to develop," Nadelmann said.

—Heather Kerrigan

Following is the text of a press release from the Washington State Liquor Control Board on November 7, 2012, announcing its intent to begin implementing Initiative 502 regarding personal marijuana use; a statement from the Colorado Attorney General on November 7, 2012, clarifying the marijuana referendum passed by voters; and a statement from the Office of Colorado Governor John Hickenlooper on December 10, 2012, officially enacting the voters' marijuana legalization referendum.

Washington Liquor Control Board on Legalization of Marijuana

November 7, 2012

Washington State Liquor Control Board (WSLCB) issued the following statement regarding the passage of Initiative 502.

The Washington State Liquor Control Board will move forward to carry out the will of the voters who Tuesday passed Initiative 502.

I-502 establishes precedent for growing, processing, retailing and possessing marijuana. Essentially, a system will be built from the ground up. The initiative provides the WSLCB until December 1, 2013 to craft rules for implementation. We expect that it will take the full year to craft the necessary rules which will provide the framework for the new system. As we develop the rules we will keep in mind our top priority, public safety.

Questions remain ahead as we work to implement I-502. Chief among them is the issue that marijuana remains illegal at the federal level.

We will reach out to the federal Department of Justice in the coming weeks for clarification. We will also communicate with our state partners such as the Washington State Patrol, the Department of Health, the Department of Agriculture, and others affected by I-502. . . .

SOURCE: Washington State Liquor Control Board. "Liquor Control Board Statement Following Passage of Initiative 502." November 7, 2012. http://www.liq.wa.gov/publications/Marijuana/I-502/11-7-12-Board-Statement-I502.pdf.

Colorado Attorney General Responds to Voter Passage of Marijuana Referendum

November 7, 2012

Despite my strongly held belief that the "legalization" of marijuana on a state level is very bad public policy, voters can be assured that the Attorney General's Office will move forward in assisting the pertinent executive branch agencies to implement this new provision in the Colorado Constitution.

Coloradans should be cognizant of two caveats, however. First the ability of the federal government to criminally sanction possession, use and distribution of marijuana, even if grown, distributed and used in a single state, was recognized by the U.S. Supreme Court in *Gonzales v. Raich* (545 US.1,2005). Therefore, absent action by Congress, Coloradans should not expect to see successful legal challenges to the ability of the federal government to enforce its marijuana laws in Colorado. Accordingly, I call upon the United States Department of Justice to make known its intentions regarding prosecution of activities sanctioned by Amendment 64 (particularly large wholesale grow operations) as soon as possible in order to assist state regulators and the citizens of Colorado in making decisions about the implementation of Amendment 64.

Secondly, the proponents of Amendment 64 told voters that it imposed a surtax of up to 15 percent on marijuana sale that would result in up to $40 million each year going to K–12 schools in the state. In fact Amendment 64 did not comply with required language under the Taxpayers Bill of Rights and no such tax will be imposed. Instead it will be up to the Colorado Legislature whether to refer such a tax to the voters and up to the voters of Colorado whether to actually impose the tax. Therefore, such revenue is speculative and will not be forthcoming when Amendment 64 begins to be implemented.

SOURCE: Office of the Attorney General of Colorado. "Attorney General Releases Statement on Passage of Amendment 64." November 7, 2012. http://www.coloradoattorneygeneral.gov/sites/default/files/press_releases/2012/11/07/110712_passage_amendment_64_statement_final.pdf.

Gov. Hickenlooper Signs Executive Order on Amendment 64

December 10, 2012

Gov. John Hickenlooper today signed an Executive Order that makes an "official declaration of the vote" related to Amendment 64. That declaration formalizes the amendment as part of the state Constitution and makes legal the personal use, possession and limited home-growing of marijuana under Colorado law for adults 21 years of age and older.

It is still illegal under state law to buy or sell marijuana in any quantity and to consume marijuana in public or in a way that endangers others.

"Voters were loud and clear on Election Day," Hickenlooper said. "We will begin working immediately with the General Assembly and state agencies to implement Amendment 64."

To help inform the upcoming legislative process, the governor today also signed an Executive Order to create a Task Force on the Implementation of Amendment 64. The task force will consider and resolve a number of policy, legal and procedural issues, involving various interests and stakeholders, to implement the new constitutional amendment.

"All stakeholders share an interest in creating efficient and effective regulations that provide for the responsible development of the new marijuana laws," the Executive Order says. "As such, there is a need to create a task force through which we can coordinate and create a regulatory structure that promotes the health and safety of the people of Colorado."

The Task Force will be co-chaired by Jack Finlaw, the Governor's Chief Legal Counsel, and Barbara Brohl, the Executive Director of the Colorado Department of Revenue. There will be 24 total members:

Rep. Dan Pabon, appointed by the incoming Speaker of the House;

Sen. Cheri Jahn, appointed by the incoming President of the Senate;

Rep.-elect Dan Nordberg, appointed by the incoming House Minority Leader;

Sen.-elect Vicki Marble, appointed by the incoming Senate Minority Leader;

David Blake, representing the Colorado Attorney General;

Kevin Bommer, representing the Colorado Municipal League;

Eric Bergman, representing Colorado Counties Inc.;

Chris Urbina, the Executive Director of the Colorado Department of Public Health and Environment;

James Davis, the Executive Director of the Colorado Department of Public Safety;

John Salazar, the Colorado Commissioner of Agriculture;

Ron Kammerzell, the Senior Director responsible for the Colorado Medical Marijuana Enforcement Division;

Christian Sederberg, representing the campaign to pass Amendment 64;

Meg Sanders, representing the medical marijuana dispensary and cultivation industry;

Craig Small, representing marijuana consumers;

Sam Kamin, a person with expertise in legal issues related to the legalization of marijuana;

Dr. Christian Thurstone, a person with expertise in the treatment of marijuana addiction;

Charles Garcia, representing the Colorado Commission on Criminal & Juvenile Justice;

Larry Abrahamson, representing the Colorado District Attorney's Council;

Brian Connors, representing the Colorado State Public Defender;

Daniel Zook, an at-large member from outside of the Denver area;

Tamra Ward, representing the interests of employers; and

Mike Cerbo, representing the interests of employees.

The co-chairs of the Task Force expect to form working groups, chaired by one or more members of the Task Force and comprised of persons with subject matter expertise, to aid in the group's work.

Issues that will be addressed include: the need to amend current state and local laws regarding the possession, sale, distribution or transfer of marijuana and marijuana products to conform them to Amendment 64's decriminalization provisions; the need for new regulations for such things as security requirements for marijuana establishments and for labeling requirements; education regarding long-term health effects of marijuana use and harmful effects of marijuana use by those under the age of 18; and the impact of Amendment 64 on employers and employees and the Colorado economy.

The Task Force will also work to reconcile Colorado and federal laws such that the new laws and regulations do not subject Colorado state and local governments and state and local government employees to prosecution by the federal government.

"Task Force members are charged with finding practical and pragmatic solutions to the challenges of implementing Amendment 64 while at all times respecting the diverse perspectives that each member will bring to the work of the task force," the Executive Order says. "The Task Force shall respect the will of the voters of Colorado and shall not engage in a debate of the merits of marijuana legalization or Amendment 64."

All meetings of the Task Force and any working groups will be open to the public. The Task Force will also endeavor to solicit public comment as part of its consideration of the policy, legal and procedural issues that need to be resolved to implement Amendment 64.

The Task Force will hold its first meeting at noon Dec. 17 in the Department of Revenue Gaming Conference Room, 17301 W. Colfax Ave., Suite 135, in Golden.

The Task Force is expected to report its recommendations and findings to the Governor, the General Assembly and the Attorney General no later than Feb. 28, 2013, unless it is either earlier terminated or extended beyond that date by further Executive Order.

Hickenlooper and Colorado Attorney General John Suthers sent a letter on Nov. 14 to U.S. Attorney General Eric Holder seeking clarity on the federal government's position related to Amendment 64. Colorado has not yet received a response.

"As we move forward now with implementation of Amendment 64, we will try to maintain as much flexibility as possible to accommodate the federal government's position on the amendment," Hickenlooper said. . . .

SOURCE: Office of the Governor of Colorado. "Gov. Hickenlooper Signs Amendment 64 Proclamation, Creates Task Force to Recommend Needed Legislative Actions." December 10, 2012. http://www.colorado.gov/cs/Satellite?c=Page&childpagename=GovHickenlooper%2FCBONLayout&cid=1251634887823&pagename=CBONWrapper.

OTHER HISTORIC DOCUMENTS OF INTEREST

FROM PREVIOUS *HISTORIC DOCUMENTS*

President Obama Remarks on 2012 Reelection Victory

NOVEMBER 7, 2012

The 2012 presidential election—which began in earnest in early 2011 as Republican contenders vied for the opportunity to challenge President Barack Obama—focused primarily on the economy. Both Obama and his ultimate opponent, former Massachusetts governor Mitt Romney, struggled to portray themselves as the person who would be better to continue the economic recovery and, more specifically, benefit the middle class. Both men were aided throughout the process by super PACs, new political action committees born out of the 2010 Supreme Court decision *Citizens United v. Federal Election Commission* that gave nearly unlimited spending capabilities to individuals, corporations, and labor unions.

REPUBLICAN NATIONAL CONVENTION

Despite the Republican National Committee (RNC) announcing in late April that Romney was the presumed nominee, the general election campaign did not technically start until Romney was officially chosen to take on Obama at the Republican National Convention in August. The Republican convention was held from August 28–30 in Tampa, Florida. The keynote speaker lineup for the Republicans included Romney's wife, Anne, who was tasked with helping voters see a more personal side of her husband. She strived to make him appear more in touch with America's middle class, something his campaign had been struggling to do. Mrs. Romney, who opened her speech noticeably nervous, spoke about the struggles she and her husband had faced, including her battle with multiple sclerosis, tying it to how he would treat his job as president. "This is the man America needs," she said. "This is the man who will wake up every day with the determination to solve the problems that others say can't be solved, to fix what others say is beyond repair." Mrs. Romney's performance was followed by a fiery speech delivered by New Jersey Governor Chris Christie, a rising star in the Republican Party and potential future presidential contender. Well known as boisterous and free speaking, Christie delivered his argument as to why Romney was the man for the job and why conservatives needed to take back the White House. "I know this simple truth and I'm not afraid to say it. Our ideas are right for America and their ideas have failed America," Christie said.

Night two of the Republican convention featured the vice presidential nominee, Rep. Paul Ryan, R-Wis., chair of the powerful House Budget Committee. Although popular within the GOP, Ryan was not well known on the national scene until being chosen as Romney's running mate on August 10. Given his background, Ryan's speech focused primarily on fiscal issues, including Obama's health care law, the federal deficit, and stimulus spending. During his speech, Ryan used a much-debated number: that Obama pulled $700 billion out of Medicare to fund his health care law. That figure comes from a Congressional Budget Office report detailing savings if Obamacare, as it is dubbed, was repealed; however, an accompanying letter indicated that if the law was maintained, Medicare would not experience a more than $700 billion decrease in its budget.

Primetime on the third night of the convention, during which Romney officially accepted the nomination, opened with what some deemed a bizarre and unexpected speech by actor Clint Eastwood. Eastwood spent a majority of his time on stage improvising and speaking to an empty chair that was supposed to represent Obama. In two separate instances, Eastwood indicated that Obama had directed profane remarks at the actor and Romney. Although he was given talking points by the campaign, he ignored a majority of them and also ignored a flashing red light indicating that his five minutes were up (he went on to speak for twelve). According to the *New York Times,* unnamed Romney advisers referred to the speech, which was arranged by Romney himself, as "strange," "weird," and "theater of the absurd."

When Romney did take the stage, his thirty-seven-minute speech aimed squarely at influencing swing voters. He attempted to make inroads with Hispanics, African Americans, women, and the middle class. Drawing on Obama's 2008 campaign theme, Romney expressed regret that Americans had not witnessed the change they expected. "You know there's something wrong with the kind of job he's done as president when the best feeling you had was the day you voted for him," Romney said. He promised to correct the mistakes of the past administration by creating new jobs, reducing the unemployment rate, and lowering the deficit. Romney said in closing that it was time to "put the disappointments of the last four years behind us. To put aside the divisiveness and the recriminations. To forget about what might have been and to look ahead to what can be. Now is the time to restore the promise of America."

Democratic Convention

The Democrats held their convention from September 4–6 in Charlotte, North Carolina. The first night featured speakers including First Lady Michelle Obama, who reminded the audience of how her husband had struggled in the past and how he understood the problems of everyday Americans. "Barack knows what it means when a family struggles," she said. "He knows what it means to want something more for your kids and grandkids. Barack knows the American dream because he's lived it, and he wants everyone in this country to have the same opportunity." Preceding the first lady was Julián Castro, the young mayor of San Antonio and the first Latino to deliver a keynote address at a Democratic convention. Comparisons were quickly drawn between Castro and Obama. Castro's grandmother came to the United States from Mexico as an orphan at age six, teaching herself to read and write. Castro's mother was taught in school to disregard her heritage, but she instead went on to fight for reforms in the Mexican American community. Castro said it was his mother who inspired him and his twin brother to enter politics. "My family's story isn't special. What's special is the America that makes our story possible. Ours is a nation like no other—a place where great journeys can be made in a single generation. No matter who you are or where you come from, the path is always forward."

Former president Bill Clinton took the stage on the second night of the convention, delivering an impassioned argument for why Obama deserved a second term. He praised the president for having helped bring the country out of the depths of a recession, making clear that no president could fix everything in one term. And he took hard hits at Republicans who criticized Obama for changes in the welfare to work program, specifically vouchers for states that Republicans claim allowed more Americans to forgo any work requirement. "This is personal to me," said Clinton, who signed welfare reform legislation into law in 1996. "But I am telling you, the claim that President Obama weakened welfare reform's work requirement is just not true. But they keep on running ads claiming it. You want to know why? Their campaign pollster said, 'We're not going to let our campaign be dictated by fact-checkers.'"

The final night of the debate featured the president and Vice President Joe Biden. Prior to the final night, Obama was slated to speak to a crowd of 75,000 in an outdoor venue. However, citing potential thunderstorms, the speech was moved back to the 20,000-seat convention hall. Political analysts questioned whether the event was moved due to an inability to fill the seats. In introducing the president, Biden had the challenge of giving an insider's perspective of Obama's four years in office, and did so on topics ranging from the economy to the assassination of Osama bin Laden. The often gaffe-prone vice president was panned by critics for incorrectly and repeatedly using the word *literally*. When Obama took the stage, he addressed the difficulties the country was still facing head on, and asked for another term to continue the work he had started. "I won't pretend the path I'm offering is quick or easy; I never have," the president said. "But know this, America: Our problems can be solved. Our challenges can be met. The path we offer may be harder, but it leads to a better place. And I'm asking you to choose that future."

The Rise of Super PACs

During his first run for office, Obama and his challenger, Sen. John McCain, R-Ariz., were beholden to campaign finance regulations that left little wiggle room for even the wealthiest donors. But in 2010, the U.S. Supreme Court ruled in the landmark case of *Citizens United v. Federal Election Commission* that because political donations are a form of free speech, corporations and labor unions cannot be stopped from spending money in support of or against certain candidates. Although they were still prohibited from giving money directly to candidates, they were able to offer indirect support through television advertisements and other means. This decision ushered in the era of a new political action committee (PAC) known as super PACs.

Although super PACs did have some clout in the 2010 midterm elections, it was during the 2012 race that they truly took off, spending more than $567 million during the campaign season, according to Federal Election Commission data. Since their arrival on the political scene, super PACs have been hotly contested by those who support them and believe voters gain additional information, and opponents who think they take away the power of the individual.

During the 2012 election season, super PACs primarily benefited Republicans, and specifically Romney as the presidential candidate. The biggest spender was Restore Our Future, which spent more than $142 million in support of Romney and in opposition to his competitors. The next biggest spender was Priorities USA Action, which spent more than $64 million opposing Romney. Postelection analysis questioned whether super PACs actually have the clout that some feared they would after the 2010 ruling, especially in light of Romney's defeat. A variety of super PACs backed Romney's primary challengers, whose campaigns were nearly bankrupt early in 2012, providing such support as scathing ads about Romney's time as the head of the investment firm Bain Capital. The outside financial support may have hurt Romney by extending the primary season by keeping his opponents' campaigns alive. Romney, who had been criticized by mainstream Republicans for his more moderate stance on some issues, moved increasingly to the right as the primary season dragged on and proposed more conservative spending and deficit reduction packages, something that appealed to mainstream Republican voters but was a hard sell with the crucial segment of uncommitted swing voters.

FORTY-SEVEN PERCENT AND WHO BUILT WHAT

Both the Obama and Romney campaigns made a number of missteps throughout 2012, but perhaps the biggest on the Republican side was a line in a speech delivered by Romney during a closed-door fund-raiser in May 2012 in which he said 47 percent of voters would choose Obama because they are people "who are dependent upon government, who believe that they are victims, who believe the government has a responsibility to care for them, who believe that they are entitled to health care, to food, to housing, to you-name-it. That that's an entitlement. And the government should give it to them. And they will vote for this president no matter what. . . . These are people who pay no income tax." Romney went on to say, "My job is not to worry about these people. I'll never convince them they should take personal responsibility and care for their lives." The comment, caught on tape by a bartender at the event, was released in September. Following the comment, a poll by Gallup revealed that it made 36 percent of voters less likely to support Romney. Romney refused to back down from the remark, instead trying to turn the tables on Obama after a video was released of a speech the president gave in 1998 about "redistribution" as a key to making government more effective. The Obama campaign used the "47 percent" comment as a talking point moving forward and featured it in numerous television ads.

Obama's cringe-worthy moment came in July, when he told those gathered at a campaign rally, "If you've got a business, you didn't build that. Somebody else made that happen." Obama was attempting to explain the importance of government investment and working together to rebuild America and went on to close his speech saying, "We rise or fall together as one nation and as one people, and that's the reason I'm running for president. . . . You're not on your own, we're in this together." Republicans quickly went on the attack, calling Obama antibusiness and in favor of increasing the size of government. The Republican convention slogan was "We Built It," and numerous speakers at the event focused on the president's ill will toward business. "We need a president who will say to a small businesswoman, 'Congratulations,'" said Governor Bob McDonnell of Virginia. The Obama campaign argued that the comment was taken out of context, and Obama himself admitted that he regretted the way in which he made the statement. The president's campaign noticeably toned down its "necessary government" rhetoric following the remark.

ELECTION DAY AND REACTION

On November 6, Obama and Romney watched and waited to see which candidate would reach the 270 electoral votes needed to win the presidency. Although Florida didn't announce an official winner until November 10, Obama was declared victorious, with an eventual 332 electoral votes to Romney's 206, a 51 percent to 47 percent victory in the popular vote. Of the ten states considered battlegrounds, Obama won all but one—North Carolina. Obama was successful in capturing the most important battleground state, Ohio, where he successfully drew working-class voters to his message about the importance of the auto bailout. The president also claimed a victory in Virginia, a former

Republican stronghold, for the second time. Young and Hispanic voters overwhelmingly supported the president, despite attempts made throughout election season by the Romney campaign to make headway with these groups. Those places facing higher unemployment generally favored Romney.

In his concession speech, which he had not drafted until after Obama was declared victorious, Romney thanked his supporters and noted, "This is a time of great challenge for America, and I pray that the president will be successful in guiding our nation." He encouraged all Americans to reach across the aisle and work toward bipartisan solutions to combat the problems currently facing the country. "We look to Democrats and Republicans in government at all levels to put the people before the politics," Romney said.

Obama delivered his victory speech in his hometown of Chicago, Illinois, telling a crowd of some 10,000 people about the hard work to be done in the coming four years, and promising a more bipartisan approach to making the changes necessary to move forward. "We are not as divided as our politics suggest," the president said. "We're not as cynical as the pundits believe. We are greater than the sum of our individual ambitions, and we remain more than a collection of red states and blue states. We are and forever will be the United States of America."

—Heather Kerrigan

Following is the text of the speech delivered by President Barack Obama on November 7, 2012, upon his reelection victory.

DOCUMENT *Obama Delivers Victory Speech*

November 7, 2012

Thank you so much. Tonight, more than 200 years after a former colony won the right to determine its own destiny, the task of perfecting our Union moves forward.

It moves forward because of you. It moves forward because you reaffirmed the spirit that has triumphed over war and Depression; the spirit that has lifted this country from the depths of despair to the great heights of hope; the belief that while each of us will pursue our own individual dreams, we are an American family, and we rise or fall together, as one Nation and as one people.

Tonight, in this election, you, the American people, reminded us that while our road has been hard, while our journey has been long, we have picked ourselves up, we have fought our way back, and we know in our hearts that for the United States of America, the best is yet to come.

I want to thank every American who participated in this election. Whether you voted for the very first time or waited in line for a very long time—by the way, we have to fix that. Whether you pounded the pavement or picked up the phone, whether you held an Obama sign or a Romney sign, you made your voice heard, and you made a difference.

I just spoke with Governor Romney, and I congratulated him and Paul Ryan on a hard-fought campaign. We may have battled fiercely, but it's only because we love this country deeply, and we care so strongly about its future. From George to Lenore, to their son Mitt, the Romney family has chosen to give back to America through public service, and that is a legacy that we honor and applaud tonight.

In the weeks ahead, I also look forward to sitting down with Governor Romney to talk about where we can work together to move this country forward.

I want to thank my friend and partner of the last 4 years, America's happy warrior, the best Vice President anybody could ever hope for, Joe Biden.

And I wouldn't be the man I am today without the woman who agreed to marry me 20 years ago. Let me say this publicly: Michelle, I have never loved you more. I have never been prouder to watch the rest of America fall in love with you too, as our Nation's First Lady. Sasha and Malia, before our very eyes, you're growing up to become two strong, smart, beautiful young women, just like your mom. And I'm so proud of you guys. But I will say that for now, one dog is probably enough.

To the best campaign team and volunteers in the history of politics—the best, the best ever: Some of you were new this time around, and some of you have been at my side since the very beginning. But all of you are family. No matter what you do or where you go from here, you will carry the memory of the history we made together, and you will have the lifelong appreciation of a grateful President. Thank you for believing all the way, through every hill, through every valley. You lifted me up the whole way. And I will always be grateful for everything that you've done and all the incredible work that you put in.

I know that political campaigns can sometimes seem small, even silly. And that provides plenty of fodder for the cynics who tell us that politics is nothing more than a contest of egos or the domain of special interests. But if you ever get the chance to talk to folks who turned out at our rallies and crowded along a rope line in a high school gym or saw folks working late at a campaign office in some tiny county far away from home, you'll discover something else.

You'll hear the determination in the voice of a young field organizer who's working his way through college and wants to make sure every child has that same opportunity. You'll hear the pride in the voice of a volunteer who's going door to door because her brother was finally hired when the local auto plant added another shift. You'll hear the deep patriotism in the voice of a military spouse who's working the phones late at night to make sure that no one who fights for this country ever has to fight for a job or a roof over their head when they come home.

That's why we do this. That's what politics can be. That's why elections matter. It's not small, it's big. It's important.

Democracy in a nation of 300 million can be noisy and messy and complicated. We have our own opinions. Each of us has deeply held beliefs. And when we go through tough times, when we make big decisions as a country, it necessarily stirs passions, stirs up controversy. That won't change after tonight, and it shouldn't. These arguments we have are a mark of our liberty, and we can never forget that as we speak, people in distant nations are risking their lives right now just for a chance to argue about the issues that matter, the chance to cast their ballots like we did today.

But despite all our differences, most of us share certain hopes for America's future. We want our kids to grow up in a country where they have access to the best schools and the best teachers, a country that lives up to its legacy as the global leader in technology and discovery and innovation, with all the good jobs and new businesses that follow.

We want our children to live in an America that isn't burdened by debt, that isn't weakened by inequality, that isn't threatened by the destructive power of a warming planet.

We want to pass on a country that's safe and respected and admired around the world, a nation that is defended by the strongest military on Earth and the best troops this world has ever known, but also a country that moves with confidence beyond this time of war to shape a peace that is built on the promise of freedom and dignity for every human being.

We believe in a generous America, in a compassionate America, in a tolerant America, open to the dreams of an immigrant's daughter who studies in our schools and pledges to our flag. To the young boy on the South Side of Chicago who sees a life beyond the nearest street corner. To the furniture worker's child in North Carolina who wants to become a doctor or a scientist, an engineer or an entrepreneur, a diplomat or even a President. That's the future we hope for. That's the vision we share. That's where we need to go. Forward. [*Applause*] That's where we need to go.

Now, we will disagree, sometimes fiercely, about how to get there. As it has for more than two centuries, progress will come in fits and starts. It's not always a straight line. It's not always a smooth path. By itself, the recognition that we have common hopes and dreams won't end all the gridlock or solve all our problems or substitute for the painstaking work of building consensus and making the difficult compromises needed to move this country forward. But that common bond is where we must begin.

Our economy is recovering. A decade of war is ending. A long campaign is now over. And whether I earned your vote or not, I have listened to you. I have learned from you. And you've made me a better President. And with your stories and your struggles, I return to the White House more determined and more inspired than ever about the work there is to do and the future that lies ahead.

Tonight you voted for action, not politics as usual. You elected us to focus on your jobs, not ours. And in the coming weeks and months, I am looking forward to reaching out and working with leaders of both parties to meet the challenges we can only solve together: reducing our deficit, reforming our Tax Code, fixing our immigration system, freeing ourselves from foreign oil. We've got more work to do.

But that doesn't mean your work is done. The role of citizen in our democracy does not end with your vote. America has never been about what can be done for us, it's about what can be done by us, together, through the hard and frustrating, but necessary work of self-government. That's the principle we were founded on.

This country has more wealth than any nation, but that's not what makes us rich. We have the most powerful military in history, but that's not what makes us strong. Our university, our culture are all the envy of the world, but that's not what keeps the world coming to our shores.

What makes America exceptional are the bonds that hold together the most diverse nation on Earth: the belief that our destiny is shared, that this country only works when we accept certain obligations to one another and to future generations so that the freedom which so many Americans have fought for and died for comes with responsibilities as well as rights, and among those are love and charity and duty and patriotism. That's what makes America great.

I am hopeful tonight because I have seen this spirit at work in America. I've seen it in the family business whose owners would rather cut their own pay than lay off their neighbors and in the workers who would rather cut back their hours than see a friend lose a job.

I've seen it in the soldiers who reenlist after losing a limb and in those SEALs who charged up the stairs into darkness and danger because they knew there was a buddy behind them watching their back.

I've seen it on the shores of New Jersey and New York, where leaders from every party and level of government have swept aside their differences to help a community rebuild from the wreckage of a terrible storm.

And I saw it just the other day in Mentor, Ohio, where a father told the story of his 8-year-old daughter, whose long battle with leukemia nearly cost their family everything, had it not been for health care reform passing just a few months before the insurance company was about to stop paying for her care. I had an opportunity to not just talk to the father, but meet this incredible daughter of his. And when he spoke to the crowd, listening to that father's story, every parent in that room had tears in their eyes because we knew that little girl could be our own. And I know that every American wants her future to be just as bright.

That's who we are. That's the country I'm so proud to lead as your President. And tonight, despite all the hardship we've been through, despite all the frustrations of Washington, I've never been more hopeful about our future. I have never been more hopeful about America. And I ask you to sustain that hope.

I'm not talking about blind optimism: the kind of hope that just ignores the enormity of the tasks ahead or the roadblocks that stand in our path. I'm not talking about the wishful idealism that allows us to just sit on the sidelines or shirk from a fight. I have always believed that hope is that stubborn thing inside us that insists, despite all the evidence to the contrary, that something better awaits us, so long as we have the courage to keep reaching, to keep working, to keep fighting.

America, I believe we can build on the progress we've made and continue to fight for new jobs and new opportunity and new security for the middle class. I believe we can keep the promise of our founding: the idea that if you're willing to work hard, it doesn't matter who you are or where you come from or what you look like or [who] you love, it doesn't matter whether you're Black or White, or Hispanic or Asian, or Native American, or young or old, or rich or poor, abled, disabled, gay or straight, you can make it here in America if you're willing to try.

I believe we can seize this future together, because we are not as divided as our politics suggests, we're not as cynical as the pundits believe, we are greater than the sum of our individual ambitions, and we remain more than a collection of red [s]tates and blue [s]tates. We are and forever will be the United States of America. And together, with your help and God's grace, we will continue our journey forward and remind the world just why it is that we live in the greatest nation on Earth.

Thank you, America. God bless you. God bless these United States.

SOURCE: Executive Office of the President. "Remarks at a Victory Celebration in Chicago, Illinois." November 7, 2012. *Compilation of Presidential Documents* 2012, no. 00873 (November 7, 2012). http:// www.gpo.gov/fdsys/pkg/DCPD-201200873/pdf/DCPD-201200873.pdf.

OTHER HISTORIC DOCUMENTS OF INTEREST

FROM THIS VOLUME

FROM PREVIOUS *HISTORIC DOCUMENTS*

Gen. Petraeus Resigns as CIA Director Amid Scandal

NOVEMBER 9, 2012

On the heels of a terrorist attack at a U.S. embassy in Libya that was criticized by many as a failure of intelligence, Central Intelligence Agency (CIA) Director Gen. David Petraeus found himself embroiled in personal scandal that led to his resignation. Through a matter of routine investigation into potential cybercrime, the Federal Bureau of Investigation (FBI) linked Petraeus to a woman who was sending harassing e-mails and had obtained classified government documents. Over the months, agents slowly pieced together information that led them to the conclusion that Petraeus was having an affair with his biographer, Paula Broadwell. Because of his personal digressions, Petraeus chose to step down, and the fallout from the event brought down a second military leader and opened investigations on Capitol Hill into why the investigation had not been disclosed to the president or congressional intelligence leaders sooner.

SOCIAL PLANNER BRINGS DOWN POWERFUL GENERAL

In May 2012, Jill Kelley, the de facto social events organizer at MacDill Air Force Base in Tampa, Florida, informed the FBI that she was receiving harassing e-mails. The FBI pursued the case as a possible cybercrime, believing that, based on the language in the e-mails, there was a possibility that classified government documents had been breached. Starting with about five to ten e-mails, the investigators tried to piece together who was sending them, some of which accused Kelley of having an affair with an unnamed person. Agents were eventually able to determine, through metadata footprints left by the e-mails, that they were being sent by Broadwell, who lived in North Carolina. Once they had linked the e-mails with a name, the FBI obtained a warrant to watch Broadwell's e-mail accounts.

While monitoring Broadwell, agents learned that she had set up a secret e-mail account to communicate, often in a sexually explicit manner, with another person. By late summer, the agents monitoring Broadwell learned that the man Broadwell was communicating with was CIA Director Petraeus. Agents did not monitor Petraeus's accounts directly but did alert senior officials at the Justice Department and FBI of their discovery. In September, agents worked with prosecutors to decide whether anything illegal was taking place and whether charges should be brought. Both Broadwell and Petraeus were brought in for interviews in September and October, at which time both admitted to the extramarital affair. Broadwell willingly gave her computer to investigators, who found classified documents stored on its hard drive. Petraeus denied giving the documents to Broadwell. As of the end of 2012, the source of the documents has not been found, and the Justice Department has not released details as to what was contained in the documents.

Shortly before Election Day, November 6, FBI investigators determined that they had no basis to bring charges against Broadwell or Petraeus over the classified documents.

James Clapper, the director of National Intelligence, was informed of the decision, and although there would be no further action taken against Petraeus, he quietly urged the CIA director to resign. President Barack Obama learned about the investigation two days after his reelection victory, the same day Petraeus offered his resignation. The president, who according to advisers was shocked by the news, asked for a night to think about it, but ultimately, he accepted Petraeus's resignation. According to those with knowledge of the situation, an affair would not disqualify Petraeus from continuing to serve in his position, but he believed that a lower-level CIA employee would be disciplined for such improper behavior; therefore, he needed to set an example.

Petraeus announced his resignation in a letter to CIA employees on November 9, 2012, noting that his behavior was "unacceptable, both as a husband and as the leader of an organization such as ours." President Obama, in accepting the resignation, said, "By any measure, through his lifetime of service, David Petraeus has made our country safer and stronger." Mike Morrell, deputy CIA director, was tapped as acting director for the second time in his career, following Petraeus's resignation. Morell started at the CIA as an international energy issues and East Asia analyst. He became director of the Office of Asian Pacific and Latin American Analysis in 1999 before serving as a presidential briefer to then-president George W. Bush and executive assistant to former CIA Director George Tenet. Following a brief tour overseas, Morell served as deputy director for intelligence at the National Counterterrorism Center before becoming associate deputy director at the CIA.

The investigation into how Broadwell obtained classified files is continuing, but Petraeus is not being investigated, and the FBI said there is no reason to believe that he compromised national security.

SHOULD CONGRESS HAVE BEEN INFORMED?

Throughout its investigation, the FBI largely kept its findings quiet, but shortly before Petraeus announced his resignation to Obama, facts began to leak to some members of Congress. Lawmakers reacted with outrage that they had not been informed about the event sooner. "This is something that could have had an effect on national security," said Sen. Dianne Feinstein, D-Calif., chair of the Senate Select Committee on Intelligence. "I think we should have been told." The FBI stuck by its decision, citing a policy to keep the details of ongoing criminal investigations quiet. Some lawmakers, who learned that Attorney General Eric Holder knew about the investigation well before its details were made public, argued that the investigation was kept secret because of the upcoming presidential election. "The FBI has a lot of explaining to do, and so does the White House," said Rep. Peter King, R-N.Y.

According to congressional officials, by law, chairs and ranking members of intelligence panels are required to be told about important developments in intelligence. As such, Feinstein announced that she would launch an investigation into why congressional intelligence committees were not informed of the investigation and whether the National Security Act of 1947 was violated. Rep. King, the chair of the House Homeland Security Committee, called for a separate House investigation into why the FBI failed to disclose its investigation to the president or National Security Council sooner.

STORIED CAREER

Petraeus spent more than thirty years rising through the ranks of the military before taking over as director of the CIA in April 2011 to replace Leon Panetta, who moved into the position of secretary of the Department of Defense. Throughout his career, Petraeus made a name for himself as someone with a keen understanding of battlefield strategy and tactics, but he also understood how to navigate Washington politics and the media. "He was controversial; a lot of people didn't like him. But everybody looked at him as the model of what a modern general was to be," said Stephen Biddle, a military scholar at The George Washington University and adviser to Petraeus.

Petraeus credits his father, a Dutch immigrant, for his confidence and will to succeed. Petraeus told *Newsweek* in 2011 that his father would never accept anything but a win from his son and that he would constantly yell, "Results, boy, results!" Petraeus attended the U.S. Military Academy at West Point, where he graduated in 1974 in the top 5 percent of his class. He entered the army that same year and later went on to earn a doctorate in international relations in 1987 from Princeton University's Woodrow Wilson School of Public and International Affairs.

Petraeus had a distinguished army career. In 2003, he led the 101st Airborne Division during the invasion of Iraq and was eventually appointed by then-president Bush to oversee the "surge" strategy and strengthen Iraqi security forces. During his confirmation hearing before the Senate Armed Services Committee, Petraeus defended Bush's surge strategy, noting, "We face a determined, adaptable, barbaric enemy. He will try to wait us out." In 2008, President Bush appointed him head of U.S. Central Command. After President Obama came to office, Petraeus was assigned in 2010 to oversee North Atlantic Treaty Organization (NATO) troops in Afghanistan after the resignation of Gen. Stanley McChristal.

Republicans and Democrats alike celebrated Petraeus's military and intelligence records. Calling Petraeus one of "America's greatest military heroes," Sen. John McCain, R-Ariz., said Petraeus's "inspirational leadership and his genius were directly responsible—after years of failure—for the success of the surge in Iraq." Sen. Feinstein said she "would have stood up for" Petraeus if he had decided to keep his position. "I wanted him to continue. He was good, he loved the work, and he had a command of intelligence issues second to none."

PAULA BROADWELL

The woman at the center of the scandal that led to Petraeus's resignation was Broadwell, the four-star general's biographer. Broadwell started her career in the military, graduating from West Point before turning her pursuits to purely scholarly activities, in which she studied the military. Broadwell met Petraeus in 2006 when he spoke at the Harvard Kennedy School, where Broadwell was working on her master's degree. During their first encounter, Broadwell explained to Petraeus that she was researching the military, and he gave her his card. When she began work on her PhD dissertation, Broadwell reached out again to Petraeus, who by 2010 had taken over as commander of allied troops in Afghanistan. The commander gave Broadwell unprecedented access to the work he was doing in the country, and Broadwell decided to turn the research she was doing into a book about Petraeus. It is not unusual for top military commanders to offer various opportunities to journalists who represent top media outlets or those they know well. Petraeus's staff, however, raised concern that he was giving access to someone who was neither a journalist nor a historian. But they never assumed that the two had engaged in an extramarital affair. Broadwell's book, *All In: The Education of David Petraeus*, was released on November 21, 2012. Broadwell currently serves as a research associate at Harvard University's Center for Public Leadership while she continues work on her dissertation for King's College London on innovation in the 101st Airborne Division in northern Iraq in 2003.

Gen. Allen Investigated

On November 13, the Department of Defense announced that its inspector general had launched an investigation into whether there was any improper communication between Marine Gen. John Allen, the U.S. commander in Afghanistan, and Kelley. The two reportedly exchanged hundreds of e-mails, and, like Petraeus, had met during Allen's time at U.S. Central Command in Florida. The FBI discovered the e-mails during its investigation into the harassing e-mails sent by Broadwell, and the inspector general was trying to determine whether any military law or government regulations had been violated. Agents with knowledge of the e-mails described some as being sexually explicit, and the Department of Defense said that some were embarrassing; however, Allen's defenders said there was no offensive language of any sort contained in the e-mails. On January 22, 2013, the inspector general, who is not in charge of determining guilt or innocence, announced that the allegations against Allen were unsubstantiated.

Because of the investigation, Obama put on hold Allen's nomination to assume the position as supreme allied commander for NATO forces in Europe. Allen was replaced in Afghanistan during the course of a normal military rotation by Gen. Joseph Dunford Jr. and ultimately resigned from the military upon his return to the United States. In February 2013, the Department of Defense announced, in response to numerous Freedom of Information Act requests from media outlets, that it would keep the details of the Allen investigation and any e-mails secret, saying that divulging the records would "constitute a clearly unwarranted invasion of personal privacy."

—Heather Kerrigan

Following is the text of a statement to employees from General David Petraeus on November 9, 2012, announcing his resignation as Central Intelligence Agency director; and a statement by President Barack Obama on November 9, 2012, accepting the resignation.

Gen. Petraeus Resigns as CIA Director

November 9, 2012

Yesterday afternoon, I went to the White House and asked the President to be allowed, for personal reasons, to resign from my position as D/CIA. After being married for over 37 years, I showed extremely poor judgment by engaging in an extramarital affair. Such behavior is unacceptable, both as a husband and as the leader of an organization such as ours. This afternoon, the President graciously accepted my resignation.

As I depart Langley, I want you to know that it has been the greatest of privileges to have served with you, the officers of our Nation's Silent Service, a work force that is truly exceptional in every regard. Indeed, you did extraordinary work on a host of critical missions during my time as director, and I am deeply grateful to you for that.

Teddy Roosevelt once observed that life's greatest gift is the opportunity to work hard at work worth doing. I will always treasure my opportunity to have done that with you and I will always regret the circumstances that brought that work with you to an end.

Thank you for your extraordinary service to our country, and best wishes for continued success in the important endeavors that lie ahead for our country and our Agency.

With admiration and appreciation,

David H. Petraeus

SOURCE: Central Intelligence Agency. "Message from General David H. Petraeus (US Army Retired)." November 9, 2012. https://www.cia.gov/news-information/press-releases-statements/2012-press-release-statements/statement-to-employees-from-petraeus.html.

President Obama Accepts Petraeus Resignation

November 9, 2012

David Petraeus has provided extraordinary service to the United States for decades. By any measure, he was one of the outstanding general officers of his generation, helping our military adapt to new challenges and leading our men and women in uniform through a remarkable period of service in Iraq and Afghanistan, where he helped our Nation put those wars on a path to a responsible end. As Director of the Central Intelligence Agency, he has continued to serve with characteristic intellectual rigor, dedication, and patriotism. By any measure, through his lifetime of service, David Petraeus has made our country safer and stronger.

Today I accepted his resignation as Director of the Central Intelligence Agency. I am completely confident that the CIA will continue to thrive and carry out its essential mission, and I have the utmost confidence in Acting Director Michael Morell and the men and women of the CIA, who work every day to keep our Nation safe.

Going forward, my thoughts and prayers are with Dave and Holly Petraeus, who has done so much to help military families through her own work. I wish them the very best at this difficult time.

SOURCE: Executive Office of the President. "Statement on the Resignation of David H. Petraeus as Director of Central Intelligence." November 9, 2012. *Compilation of Presidential Documents* 2012, no. 00877 (November 9, 2012). http://www.gpo.gov/fdsys/pkg/DCPD-201200877/pdf/DCPD-201200877.pdf.

OTHER HISTORIC DOCUMENTS OF INTEREST

FROM PREVIOUS *HISTORIC DOCUMENTS*

China Unveils New Leadership

NOVEMBER 15, 2012

Once every five years, the People's Republic of China holds a National Congress to announce policy and personnel changes within the Communist Party, which has controlled the nation's government for the past sixty years. Once each decade, that meeting features a full leadership transition. On November 15, 2012, the eighteenth National Congress came to a conclusion when the new slate of leaders was revealed, with Xi Jinping at its helm. Xi was chosen to lead the seven-member Politburo Standing Committee, the group that sits atop the government and controls foreign and domestic politics, and would assume the position of president in March 2013. Xi was also given the position of chair of the powerful Central Military Commission. The carefully choreographed ceremony capped off months of political bargaining, but it is unlikely to have significant impact on the policies in China moving forward. The new leaders are mainly conservative, and party elders will continue to exert great influence on the Standing Committee. Xi and the other new leaders are facing growing calls for more political and economic openness as China continues its march toward global economic dominance.

PEACEFUL POWER TRANSFER

Unlike power transfers in the West, in China, there is no campaigning for the top seats in government—everything takes place behind closed doors. And although the nation of more than one billion people has slowly opened up its political system, the Communist Party has maintained its complete control of power and, as such, is also able to tightly control who leads the nation. In theory, a new central committee is selected during the National Congress. It is then the job of this committee to choose members of the Politburo and its powerful Standing Committee. But in practice, closed-door negotiations take place among the various factions in Chinese politics with the aim of choosing the leaders before the National Congress convenes.

President Hu Jintao opened the week-long meeting, warning the more than 2,000 delegates gathered that if the Communist Party did not tackle its internal corruption and the nation's economic challenges, it could spell the end of Communist rule in China. On corruption, the president noted, "If we fail to handle this issue well, it could prove fatal to the party, and even cause the collapse of the party and the fall of the state." Prior to the National Congress, state-run media outlets launched websites dedicated to its proceedings and received thousands of comments calling on the party not only to fight corruption but also improve the environment, especially the polluted air and waterways, and deal with China's growing wealth gap. "We must aim higher and work harder and continue to pursue development in a scientific way, promote social harmony and improve the people's lives," Hu said. He urged the new leaders to develop a better model for economic growth in line with changing domestic and global priorities, with a goal of doubling gross domestic product (GDP) and per capita income by 2020.

The eighteenth National Congress brought a sigh of relief to those across China who had witnessed political infighting as the power transfer drew near. The past two power transfers had not been smooth, with the outgoing head of the Politburo Standing Committee holding onto the position of head of the Central Military Commission and thus continuing to exercise a significant amount of influence in Chinese politics. In this instance, however, Xi took over both positions from Hu, giving Xi a greater ability to consolidate his power at the top of the party.

"Princeling" Takes the Top Spot

Xi's family has long held a position in the Communist Party's leadership, going back to Chairman Mao Zedong, the founder of modern China, who chose Xi's father to be one of his top lieutenants. Because of his standing in the party aristocracy, Xi's rise through the political ranks was expected and largely unchallenged. Xi joined the party in 1974 after studying chemical engineering and worked in a variety of local positions before being tapped as party chief in Shanghai in 2007. He is well known in China for tackling problems of corruption, in 2004 telling officials, "Rein in your spouses, children, relatives, friends and staff, and vow not to use power for personal gain." Xi, aged fifty-nine, is married to a popular folk singer and is thought to have close ties to the nation's military, the People's Liberation Army.

Despite his entering politics at a young age, there is still a lot of mystery surrounding what changes Xi might make or how he will lead China in the coming years. "Xi Jinping is in many ways an unknown commodity," said Mike Chinoy, a senior fellow at the University of Southern California's U.S.-China Institute. "He's risen to the top of the Chinese system by being very careful not to disclose what he really thinks."

Xi's right-hand man will be Li Keqiang. Although a protégé of Hu, once thought to be a given for the Standing Committee's top post, Li was chosen to be second in command and will take the position of premier in 2013, replacing Wen Jiabao. It is widely believed that Xi was the more favorable candidate among the various parties, while Li did not garner as much support. Li studied law and was a manual laborer before joining the Communist Party. He was named deputy party secretary in 1998 for Henan Province and one year later became the youngest provincial governor in modern Chinese history.

The other five members of the committee include Zhang Dejiang, head of the National People's Congress; Yu Zhengsheng, head of an advisory body; Liu Yunshan, vice president of propaganda; Wang Qishan, head of an anticorruption agency; and Zhang Gaoli, executive vice premier, who assists in overseeing the economy. Xi and Li were the only two returning members of the Standing Committee from the previous National Congress.

At the start of 2012, there was some indication that a couple of reformists might be chosen as members of the Standing Committee. Two top contenders were Liu Yuanchao, head of the Organization Department, and Wang Yang, the party chief in Guangdong. Bo Xilai, the former party leader in Chongqing once considered a likely contender for a position on the committee, lost his chance after he was expelled from the Communist Party, following the conviction of his wife for murder of a British businessman. Bo will face his own corruption charges in early 2013.

Challenges for the New Leadership

Although the power transfer was relatively smooth, Xi and the other new leaders now face a number of challenges in both foreign and domestic politics. Chinese elites have increasingly called for opening up the political system and economic market. Xi acknowledged in his address before the National Congress that the Communist Party faces "many severe challenges," including internal disputes corruption, and a detachment from Chinese citizens. "Many ordinary people don't feel so excited or joyful about what's happening," said Beijing author Lijia Zhang. "People say, 'Oh, it's the party's business, nothing to do with us—and we do not have a say in selecting the leader or the policy.'"

The new, streamlined format of the Standing Committee—it dropped from nine members to seven during this National Congress—makes it more likely that there will be unity among the top leaders, who may in turn be able to govern more efficiently. There are some ideological differences among the seven Standing Committee members, but each comes from the elite class of Chinese citizens who made their wealth mostly from China's political economy. It is still a largely conservative body, heavily influenced by party elders who control much of the nation's wealth. Five of the seven members of the body have expressed loyalty to Jiang Zemin, an eighty-six-year-old former party chief who held the Standing Committee's top spot prior to Hu. Jiang's continued clout, according to some observers, makes political reform unlikely. According to Willy Lam, a history professor at the Chinese University of Hong Kong, the new leaders are "in favor of staying the course, maintaining political stability, and defusing challenges to the party's authority."

In his speech on November 15, Xi struck an optimistic tone. "Our people have great enthusiasm in life," Xi said. "They hope for better education, more stable jobs, more satisfactory income, more reliable social security, medical services with higher standards, more comfortable living conditions and a more beautiful environment." He noted that Chinese people "hope that their children can grow up better, work better and live better," and said those goals will become the government's goals. Xi made a rare decision to chastise the Communist Party for failing to combat corruption within its ranks. "Our party faces many severe challenges," Xi said, "and there are many pressing problems within the party that need to be resolved, especially problems such as corruption and bribe-taking by some party members and cadres, being out of touch with the people, placing undue emphasis on formality and bureaucracy must be addressed with great effort."

The economy is likely to be the biggest challenge facing Xi and the new leaders. Thirty-five years ago, China had an economy smaller than Italy's, and today, it is home to one million millionaires. However, its meteoric rise is slowing, and the 10 percent per year growth seen in the past dropped to 7.8 percent in 2012. China's growth has been driven by an economy based largely on exports and investment, and successive governments have recognized the importance of becoming a more consumption-driven country moving forward. Xi may turn to Li's expertise in this area, because during his time in Henan, Li changed the province from one of the lowest in per capita GDP to the nation's number one grain- and meat-processing province. Although still a party conservative, Li is open to making changes in how the government and market are tied to each other, believing that the allocation of resources across the country should be increasingly driven by market forces rather than the government. "Those who refuse to reform may not make mistakes," Li told the state-run *People's Daily*, "but they will be blamed for not assuming their historical responsibility."

IMPORTANCE ABROAD

As the second-largest economy and an ever-present voice on the world stage, China's power transfer was closely watched by international observers around the globe. Japan, which as of mid-2012 was at a standoff with China over ownership of a group of islands in the East China Sea, said it hoped "the mutually beneficial relationship based on common strategic interest will be further developed and enhanced with the new leadership."

One area of particular interest for the international community is how the new government will respond to North Korea. China has long been the reclusive nation's primary ally, supplying economic and diplomatic support, but after a new North Korean leader, Kim Jong-un, came to power in December 2011 and launched two missiles in violation of international agreements, China expressed concern. Prior to the power transition in China, however, the Chinese government had been unwilling to work with the United Nations Security Council to sanction North Korea for its actions, leaving the body incapable of a tough response. After the National Congress, Kim reasserted his intent to maintain the "friendship" between his nation and China, according to the Korean Central News Agency.

Xi's opinion of China's relationship with the United States is largely unknown, although his daughter is a student at Harvard, and Xi himself has made many trips to the United States. He has made indications that he wants to maintain the current bilateral relationship, but he has not yet indicated how he might respond to U.S. criticism of Chinese human rights violations and the devaluation of its currency. In early 2013, the United States sharply criticized the Communist nation for hacking computer networks. The Chinese government denied any responsibility.

—Heather Kerrigan

Following is the text of a release from the Chinese government on November 15, 2012, announcing the election of new leaders of the Central Committee of the Communist Party.

DOCUMENT   *New Chinese Leaders Announced*

November 15, 2012

A new generation of top Chinese leaders took the stage on Thursday in one of the world's most important power transitions, taking the helm of the ruling party of the world's second-largest economy and the most populous country.

Xi Jinping was sworn in as general secretary of the Central Committee of the Communist Party of China (CPC), leading the seven-seat Political Bureau Standing Committee.

The other six members of the top leadership of the Party's central leading organ are Li Keqiang, Zhang Dejiang, Yu Zhengsheng, Liu Yunshan, Wang Qishan and Zhang Gaoli.

They were elected at the first plenum of the 18th CPC Central Committee following the CPC's 18th National Congress. Their election marked a smooth top leadership transition following the 16th national congresses of the Party in 2002.

The smooth transition suggests that the Party is moving steadily towards an established norm regarding the handing over of power, which will be crucial for sustained stability and development of the country, analysts observed.

"The new leaders are not ossified or conservative. Their election will ensure that China will continue with both reforms and the socialist path with Chinese characteristics, as they have witnessed, participated in and benefited from reform and opening-up," said Xie Chuntao, a professor of the Party School of the CPC Central Committee.

The leaders made their debut upon their election at the Great Hall of the People under the spotlight of hundreds of reporters from across the world.

Xi said they will take "the relay baton passed on to us by history" and make continued efforts to achieve the renewal of the Chinese nation.

"We will rally and lead the whole Party and the people in making continued efforts to free our minds, carry out reform and open up," Xi said.

Xi noted that the Party faces many severe challenges and that there are many pressing problems within the Party, citing corruption, a separation from the people and bureaucracy.

Amid global economic uncertainties and domestic complaints over the wealth gap, corruption and environmental woes with rising calls for deepened reform, analysts said China will face more challenges in the years to come.

From the People

The seven Standing Committee members of the Political Bureau have witnessed and endured China's vicissitudes and hardships over the last six decades, including the Cultural Revolution (1966–1976).

Xi and Li were born in the 1950s, while the other five were born in the mid- to late 1940s.

Xi, Li, Zhang Dejiang and Wang toiled in communes and villages during the Cultural Revolution, when millions of high school graduates were sent to rural areas to receive "re-education" from peasants and help with rural development.

It was during their re-education that Xi and Li received their first official titles. Acting as the Party branch secretaries of their respective production brigades, they got the chance to learn administration at the grassroots level.

Yu worked as a technician at a radio factory in the city of Zhangjiakou in north China's Hebei province for a few years, while Liu was a teacher before becoming a reporter at the Xinhua News Agency. Zhang Gaoli was a craneman and loader at an oil company in south China's Guangdong province after graduating from university.

Such experiences, analysts observed, gave them keen insight into China's situation and helped them understand the people's woes and expectations.

Xi previously said that he received a great deal of guidance from two groups of people: the old generation of revolutionaries and the village people in Shaanxi, his ancestral home where he received seven years of "re-education."

Governance Experience

As observed by Professor Xie, the new generation of leaders have shown "capacity in controlling overall situations and tackling complicated emergencies" and "are well prepared for challenges and ready to take opportunities."

All of them boast rich governance experience, climbing the Party cadre echelon step by step.

Over his 40-year-long career, Xi left his footprint in both the comparatively underdeveloped inland and rural areas, such as a commune in Shaanxi province and Zhengding county in Hebei province, as well as the more prosperous coastal Fujian and Zhejiang provinces and the country's financial and economic hub of Shanghai.

Most of the new leaders have experience in governing frontier regions for reform, while others are familiar with the situation in underdeveloped central and west regions.

Analysts said the lineup will help the collective leadership to consider matters from an overall perspective when making decisions.

In addition, as a result of long years of experience as local governors, they have also cultivated a down-to-earth work style.

"Do it now" is Xi's motto. He always warns officials to perform services while keeping in mind that their official titles are in the hands of the people, instead of within their own grasp.

THEORETICAL GROUNDING, GLOBAL VISION

Unlike their predecessors, the new leaders grew up in a peaceful time, which offered them a chance to receive better education than previous generations.

Notably, they received a complete and systematic education on the mainstream ideology of socialism, which had a formative effect on their views and values, said Dai Yanjun, a professor with the Party School of the CPC Central Committee.

The seven leaders have diverse higher learning backgrounds, varying from engineering to humanities.

Xi holds a doctorate of law from the prestigious Qinghua University, where he also received education in chemical engineering after he returned to Beijing from Shaanxi.

Li studied law at the elite Beijing University after he ended "re-education" in Anhui province. He later received a doctoral degree of economics from the university.

These education opportunities equipped the leaders with a firm theoretical grounding.

Xi has urged officials at various levels to "read some history" and learn to "seek the correct orientation and path from history."

As witnesses and participants in ongoing globalization, the new leaders also have a broad vision and know how to deal with the international community.

Xi Jinping made a successful visit to the United States in Feburary this year. In a written interview with the *Washington Post* before his tour, the vice president said, "The vast Pacific Ocean has ample space for China and the United States."

As vice premier, Li Keqiang visited the three European nations of Spain, Germany and Britain in January 2011. Prior to his visits, he wrote three articles that were published in influential newspapers in the countries, stating China's development orientation.

Another vice premier, Wang Qishan was described by former U.S. Secretary of the Treasury Henry Paulson as a man who "enjoys philosophical debates and has a wicked sense of humor."

RIGHT FORMULA

According to the CPC's constitution, a Central Committee is elected at a national congress, which is held every five years. The Central Committee, usually with more than 300 full and alternate members, then elects its Political Bureau and the bureau's Standing Committee.

More than 2,300 delegates to the national congress on Wednesday elected the 18th CPC Central Committee through secret ballots, who then voted on the Political Bureau and its Standing Committee on Thursday.

Previously, a meeting of leading cadres was held in Beijing in May to nominate candidates of the Political Bureau and its Standing Committee.

In the eyes of Huang Yebin, a delegate to the Party congress, the new generation of leadership are "energetic, trustworthy and with both integrity and capacity."

"I'm sure they will lead the nation to a prosperous society," Huang said.

The CPC's National Congress was a widely watched agenda this year for "one of the world's most important power transitions" that followed it, as some foreign media said.

Two authors co-published a comment in the *Financial Times* on Monday, which said that China "has developed the right formula for choosing political rulers that is consistent with China's culture and history and suitable for modern circumstances."

Daniel Bell and Eric Li, a professor of political theory at Qinghua University in Beijing and a Shanghai-based venture capitalist, wrote in the British newspaper, "The Chinese political system has undergone significant change over the past three decades and it comes close to the best formula for governing a large country.

"It (Chinese regime) should be improved on the basis of this formula, not western style democracy," they observed.

NEW FACES IN POLITICAL BUREAU

In addition to the seven Standing Committee members, the Political Bureau has another 18 members. Among them, Liu Yandong, Li Yuanchao and Wang Yang are serving their second term in the central leading organ.

Liu, 67, is also a state councilor. She holds a doctoral degree of law.

Li is also a doctor of law. He was previously a member of the Secretariat of the CPC Central Committee. He is 62.

Wang, 57, is Party chief of Guangdong Province. He previously worked in Chongqing. He is a master of engineering.

The new members of the bureau are: Ma Kai, Wang Huning, Liu Qibao, Xu Qiliang, Sun Chunlan, Sun Zhengcai, Li Jianguo, Zhang Chunxian, Fan Changlong, Meng Jianzhu, Zhao Leji, Hu Chunhua, Li Zhanshu, Guo Jinlong and Han Zheng.

Among the new faces, eight were born around 1949, the founding year of New China. State Councilor Ma Kai is 66. The master of economics previously led the National Development and Reform Commission.

Sun Chunlan from Fujian Province is currently the only woman Party chief in the 31 provinces, autonomous regions and municipalities. Her entry added one more woman member to the Political Bureau. Liu Yandong was the only woman in the central leading body. Sun is 62.

Li Jianguo, 66, is vice chairman of the Standing Committee of the National People's Congress. The senior legislator is a Chinese language and literature graduate.

Meng Jianzhu, 65, is a state councilor and also minister of public security. He holds a master's degree of engineering.

Li Zhanshu is director of the General Office of the CPC Central Committee. He was previously Party chief of Guizhou Province. He is 62.

Beijing Party chief Guo Jinlong received a physics education in university, and previously worked in Tibet for 11 years. He is 65.

Fan Changlong, 65, and Xu Qiliang, 62, are two members from the army. The two generals are both vice chairmen of the Central Military Commission. They began service in the 1960s.

Seven new faces are under the age of 60. Wang Huning, 57, was previously a member of the Central Committee's Secretariat. Before he started a political career, he was a professor of the prestigious Fudan University in Shanghai.

Sichuan Province Party chief Liu Qibao, 59, is a master of economics. He previously worked at the Communist Youth League of China, served as deputy secretary-general of the State Council and deputy editor-in-chief of the *People's Daily*. He has also worked in Guangxi Zhuang Autonomous Region.

Zhang Chunxian, 59, is Party chief of Xinjiang Uygur Autonomous Region. He holds a master's degree in management. He worked in Hunan Province before he was transferred to Xinjiang.

Zhao Leji, party chief of Shaanxi Province, previously worked in Qinghai, a plateau province with adverse natural condition, for 27 years. The philosophy graduate from Beijing University is 55.

Shanghai Mayor Han Zheng is a master of economics. He is 58.

Notably, the Political Bureau has two members who were born in the 1960s—Sun Zhengcai and Hu Chunhua.

Sun, also 49, is a doctor of agronomy. The Party chief of Jilin Province was previously minister of agriculture.

Hu, 49, is Party chief of Inner Mongolia Autonomous Region. He volunteered to work in Tibet after graduating from university, and stayed there for about 20 years. He worked at the Communist Youth League of China before going to Inner Mongolia.

The plenum also elected the Secretariat of the Central Committee, which includes Liu Yunshan, Liu Qibao, Zhao Leji, Li Zhanshu, Du Qinglin, Zhao Hongzhu and Yang Jing.

It is observed that the new leading echelon has rich governance experience at provincial levels, and they also boast good education backgrounds, with more than 10 doctors and masters, whose majors vary from economics, politics and law to agronomy and management.

Their experience and education backgrounds will help push China towards greater progress, observers said.

Liu Xiangting, a resident at Dashilan, a community near Tian'anmen in downtown Beijing, said the emergence of a new leading team indicates that China will enjoy greater development momentum.

"I hope the new leaders will care for our livelihoods, boost development and keep themselves clean," said Liu.

Source: Xinhau. "Xinhau Insight: China's New Helmsmen." November 15, 2012. http://news.xinhuanet.com/english/special/18cpcnc/2012-11/15/c_131977176.htm.

OTHER HISTORIC DOCUMENTS OF INTEREST

FROM THIS VOLUME

FROM PREVIOUS *HISTORIC DOCUMENTS*

Federal Court Strikes Down Michigan Affirmative Action Ban

NOVEMBER 15, 2012

On November 15, 2012, the Sixth Circuit Court of Appeals addressed the constitutionality of a 2006 statewide voter referendum that added a flat ban to the Michigan state constitution on the use of race in the admissions decisions of Michigan's state colleges and universities. By an 8–7 decision, the court in *Coalition to Defend Affirmative Action v. Regents of the University of Michigan* held that the ban on the use of affirmative action in state admissions decisions violated the Equal Protection Clause of the federal Constitution. The court concluded, therefore, that the voter-approved ban must be struck down as unconstitutional. The decision did not say anything about the constitutionality of affirmative action itself; that is an issue currently before the U.S. Supreme Court in another case, *Fisher v. University of Texas*. Instead, the Sixth Circuit voided the Michigan ban on affirmative action based on the finding that the ban made it harder for black students to change the school admissions policy than for other students, creating what the court called "a comparative structural burden" that "undermines the Equal Protection Clause's guarantee that all citizens ought to have equal access to the tools of political change." The voters, according to the majority, had made it harder for underrepresented minorities to even get the state government to consider adopting race-conscious programs, and this, they concluded, makes the political process itself unequal. As could be expected, the case has been appealed to the U.S. Supreme Court, which will likely hear the appeal in the term that starts in the fall of 2013.

LEGAL BACKGROUND

The U.S. Supreme Court first addressed the issue of race-conscious admissions decisions in the 1978 landmark case, *Regents of the University of California v. Bakke*. A white student, Allan P. Bakke, had challenged a special admissions program at the Davis campus of the University of California's medical school. He claimed that the admissions program had discriminated against him on the basis of his race. The Supreme Court, in a 5–4 decision, agreed with him and held that it was unconstitutional for a state to reserve a specific and limited number of slots for qualified minority applicants. While this decision clearly outlawed the use of numerical racial quotas, the Court also held that race could be taken into consideration as a "plus factor" in admissions decisions. This decision allowed the majority of affirmative action plans at public universities to continue; however, it also marked the beginning of a period of increased political debate and lawsuits about how to structure an admissions program that takes race into account.

The Supreme Court again weighed in on affirmative action in 2003 in the combined cases *Gratz v. Bollinger* and *Grutter v. Bollinger*. In these cases, the Court reemphasized that "universities cannot establish quotas for members of certain racial groups" and struck down the University of Michigan's undergraduate admissions program in which students, evaluated on a 150-point scale, were granted 20 points for being a member of an underrepresented minority group. However, the Court upheld Michigan's law school admissions program, which took race into account without a numerical scale—allowing universities to continue to "consider race or ethnicity more flexibly as a 'plus' factor in the context of individualized consideration." As long as schools do not use numerical quotas, the justices, by a 5–4 majority, allowed schools to take race into account as just one factor among many.

After the Supreme Court declined to reject all affirmative action programs on federal constitutional grounds, Ward Connerly, a wealthy African American Republican from California, joined with Jennifer Gratz, the plaintiff in the Supreme Court case, to put on the November 2006 Michigan ballot a statewide referendum to amend the Michigan constitution to ban affirmative action programs. Similar to Proposition 209, which Connerly had successfully championed in California, the Michigan version, known as Proposal 2, states, "The state shall not discriminate against, or grant preferential treatment to any individual or group on the basis of race, sex, color, ethnicity, or national origin in the operation of public employment, public education or public contracting." Michigan voters passed the proposal by a margin of 58 percent to 42 percent.

A collection of interest groups and individuals brought suit in federal district court, arguing that the newly passed part of the Michigan constitution violates the U.S. Constitution. The judge rejected these arguments and upheld Proposal 2. On appeal, a panel of judges from the Sixth Circuit Court of Appeals overturned the district court judge, concluding that Proposal 2 impermissibly alters the political process in violation of the Equal Protection Clause. The attorney general of Michigan petitioned for an en banc review of this decision—that is, a review by all the judges of the Sixth Circuit together. The Sixth Circuit agreed to give *Coalition to Defend Affirmative Action v. Regents of the University of Michigan* an en banc review, and by a narrow margin, again found Proposal 2 to be unconstitutional.

VIOLATION OF THE EQUAL PROTECTION CLAUSE

In reaching its decision that Proposal 2 is unconstitutional, the ruling by eight of the fifteen judges on the Sixth Circuit asked us to imagine two different prospective university students in Michigan. The first one is a nonminority applicant who wants the university admissions office to give greater weight to his family's alumni connections. This student could lobby the admissions committee, petition the leadership of the university, seek to influence the school's governing board, or, if necessary, even campaign and vote for new members of the board who are more amenable to his position. By contrast, the second imagined student, a black student who wants race factored into her application in a constitutionally permissible way, does not initially have any of these avenues open to her. This student must first attempt to amend the Michigan constitution, a process that is, as the court describes, "lengthy, expensive and arduous." Only after successfully altering the state constitution "would our now-exhausted citizen reach the starting point of his neighbor who sought a legacy-related admissions policy change." This added burden placed only on racial minorities seeking the opportunity to get the state government to even consider a policy change in their favor, the court concludes, makes the political process itself unequal.

The majority opinion, written by Circuit Judge R. Guy Cole Jr., found that the Michigan Proposal 2 violated the "political process doctrine" of the Fourteenth

Amendment's Equal Protection Clause. This doctrine, the court explained, "hews to the unremarkable notion that when two competitors are running a race, one may not require the other to run twice as far or to scale obstacles not present in the first runner's course." The court based this doctrine on two Supreme Court cases, *Hunter v. Erickson*, a 1969 case striking down a move by Akron, Ohio, voters to amend their city's charter to require a citywide majority to change fair housing laws only when they involve policy that benefits racial minorities; and *Washington v. Seattle School District No. 1*, a 1982 decision to strike down a voter-approved statewide law to bar busing when used to achieve racial integration, but not for any other purpose. Together, Judge Cole wrote, these two cases stand for the rule that a law will unconstitutionally deprive minority groups of equal protection of the laws when (1) its focus is a program that primarily benefits minorities and (2) it reallocates political power or reorders the decision-making process to put special burdens on the minority group's ability to achieve its goals through that process. Because Michigan's law put a formidable obstacle before those advocating for the consideration of race in college admissions that does not exist for those advocating consideration of any other nonracial factors, this court held it to be unconstitutional.

A bare majority of the fifteen justices signed on to this opinion, and there were five separate dissenting opinions, several of which accused the majority of conflating policies that make it hard for minorities to defend themselves against discrimination with policies that seek racial preferences. Michigan Attorney General Bill Schuette filed a petition for review by the Supreme Court, arguing that the appellate court had misinterpreted the Equal Protection Clause. He wrote that it is "exceedingly odd to say that a statute which bars a state from discriminating on the basis of race violates the Equal Protection Clause because it discriminates on the basis of race." The Sixth Circuit issued a stay on its ruling that the voter-approved mandate is unconstitutional until the Supreme Court addresses its appeal.

IMPACT OF THE SIXTH CIRCUIT'S RULING

The last time the Supreme Court addressed affirmative action in college admissions, it concluded that universities are allowed to use racial preferences if considered as one factor among many. It did not rule that states are required to do so. Michigan, along with seven other states—Arizona, California, Florida, Nebraska, New Hampshire, Oklahoma, and Washington—passed laws or amended their constitutions to ban the use of racial preferences in admissions. The Court of Appeals for the Ninth Circuit upheld California's ban, while the Sixth Circuit has now struck down the same ban in Michigan. This split in the circuits on an issue of such importance, and the closeness of the decision in the Sixth Circuit, ensured that the Supreme Court will hear the case.

Before that will happen, however, the Supreme Court is expected to rule again on the merits of affirmative action in public university admissions. On October 10, 2012, the Court heard oral arguments in the case of *Fisher v. University of Texas*. In this case, Abigail Fisher, a young white woman who claims she was denied admission to the University of Texas because of her race, challenged the school's use of race in freshman admissions. Commentators describe four different potential outcomes when the ruling is released. The Supreme Court could decide that Fisher, who has since graduated from another university, did not suffer sufficient injury to bring suit and therefore decline to address the central issue. It could maintain the current law by finding the Texas policy of taking race into account for a small subset of its students to be constitutional. It could uphold the Texas policy as permissible but only in a more narrowed set of circumstances. Or, finally, it could overrule earlier precedent and say that race may not ever be used in university admissions decisions.

Any result in *Fisher* that limits the permissibility of considering race could render the appeal of the Sixth Circuit's decision in *Coalition to Defend Affirmative Action v. Regents of the University of Michigan* moot.

—Melissa Feinberg

Following are excerpts from the Sixth Circuit Court decision in Coalition to Defend Affirmative Action v. Regents of the University of Michigan, *released on November 15, 2012, in which the court ruled 8–7 that Michigan's 2006 affirmative action ban was unconstitutional.*

Coalition to Defend Affirmative Action v. Regents of the University of Michigan

November 15, 2012

[Footnotes and some in-text citations have been omitted.]

Nos. 08-1387/1543

Coalition to Defend Affirmative Action, Integration and Immigrant Rights and Fight for Equality by any Means Necessary (BAMN), et al.,

    Plaintiffs-Appellants (08-1387)/Cross-Appellees,

    v.

Regents of the University of Michigan, Board of Trustees of Michigan State University; Board of Governors of Wayne State University; Mary Sue Coleman; Irvin D. Reid; Lou Anna K. Simon,

    Defendants-Appellees/Cross-Appellants (08-1534),

Bill Schuette, Michigan Attorney General,

            Intervenor-Defendant-Appellee.

Nos. 08-1387/1389/1534; 09-1111

No. 08-1389

Coalition to Defend Affirmative Action, Integration and Immigrant Rights and Fight for Equality by any Means Necessary (BAMN), et al.,

            Plaintiffs,

Chase Cantrell, et al.,

            Plaintiffs-Appellees,

    v.

REGENTS OF THE UNIVERSITY OF MICHIGAN,
BOARD OF TRUSTEES OF MICHIGAN STATE
UNIVERSITY; BOARD OF GOVERNORS OF WAYNE
STATE UNIVERSITY; MARY SUE COLEMAN; IRVIN D.
REID; LOU ANNA K. SIMON,

Defendants,

ERIC RUSSELL,

Intervenor-Defendant-Appellant,

JENNIFER GRATZ,

Proposed Intervenor-Appellant.

No. 09-1111

COALITION TO DEFEND AFFIRMATIVE ACTION,
INTEGRATION AND IMMIGRANT RIGHTS AND FIGHT
FOR EQUALITY BY ANY MEANS NECESSARY
(BAMN), et al.,

Plaintiffs,

CHASE CANTRELL, et al.,

Plaintiffs-Appellants,

v.

REGENTS OF THE UNIVERSITY OF MICHIGAN,
BOARD OF TRUSTEES OF MICHIGAN STATE
UNIVERSITY; BOARD OF GOVERNORS OF WAYNE
STATE UNIVERSITY; MARY SUE COLEMAN; IRVIN D.
REID; LOU ANNA K. SIMON,

Defendants-Appellees/Cross-
Appellants (08-1534),

BILL SCHUETTE, Michigan Attorney General,

Intervenor-Defendant-Appellee.

Appeal from the United States District Court
for the Eastern District of Michigan at Detroit.
No. 06-15024—David M. Lawson, District Judge.

Argued: March 7, 2012

Decided and Filed: November 15, 2012

COLE, J., delivered the opinion of court in which MARTIN, DAUGHTREY, MOORE, CLAY, WHITE, STRANCH, and DONALD, JJ., joined; and BATCHELDER, C. J., and GIBBONS, ROGERS, SUTTON, COOK, and GRIFFIN, JJ., joined in Part II.B and C. BOGGS, J., delivered a separate dissenting opinion, in which BATCHELDER, C. J., joined. GIBBONS, delivered a separate dissenting opinion, in which BATCHELDER, C. J., and ROGERS, SUTTON, and COOK, JJ., joined, and GRIFFIN, J., joined with the exception of Part III. ROGERS delivered a separate dissenting opinion, in which COOK, J., joined. SUTTON, delivered a separate dissenting opinion in which BATCHELDER, C. J., and BOGGS and COOK, JJ., joined. GRIFFIN, J., delivered a separate dissenting opinion.

OPINION

A student seeking to have her family's alumni connections considered in her application to one of Michigan's esteemed public universities could do one of four things to have the school adopt a legacy-conscious admissions policy: she could lobby the admissions committee, she could petition the leadership of the university, she could seek to influence the school's governing board, or, as a measure of last resort, she could initiate a statewide campaign to alter the state's constitution. The same cannot be said for a black student seeking the adoption of a constitutionally permissible race-conscious admissions policy. That student could do only one thing to effect change: she could attempt to amend the Michigan Constitution—a lengthy, expensive, and arduous process—to repeal the consequences of Proposal 2. The existence of such a comparative structural burden undermines the Equal Protection Clause's guarantee that all citizens ought to have equal access to the tools of political change. We therefore REVERSE the judgment of the district court on this issue and find Proposal 2 unconstitutional. We AFFIRM the denial of the University Defendants' motion to be dismissed as parties, and we AFFIRM the grant of the Cantrell Plaintiffs' motion for summary judgment as to Russell.

[Section I, containing the factual and procedural background in the case, has been omitted.]

II.

A. Constitutionality of Proposal 2

The Equal Protection Clause provides that "[n]o state shall . . . deny to any person . . . the equal protection of the laws." The Plaintiffs argue that Proposal 2 violates this provision in two distinct ways. Both Plaintiff groups argue that Proposal 2 violates the Equal Protection Clause by impermissibly restructuring the political process along racial lines (the "political process" argument), and the Coalition Plaintiffs additionally argue that Proposal 2 violates the Equal Protection Clause by impermissibly classifying individuals on the basis of race (the "traditional" argument).

In addressing the Plaintiffs' arguments, we are neither required nor inclined to weigh in on the constitutional status or relative merits of race-conscious admissions policies as such. This case does not present us with a second bite at *Gratz* and *Grutter*—despite the best efforts of the dissenters to take one anyway. This case instead presents us with a challenge to the constitutionality of a state amendment that alters the process by which supporters of permissible race-conscious admissions policies may seek to enact those policies. In other words, the sole issue before us is whether Proposal 2 runs afoul of the constitutional guarantee of equal protection by removing the power of university officials to even consider using race as a factor in admissions decisions—something they are specifically allowed to do under *Grutter*.

1. Equal Protection Within the Political Process

The Equal Protection Clause "guarantees racial minorities the right to full participation in the political life of the community. It is beyond dispute . . . that given racial or ethnic groups may not be denied the franchise, or precluded from entering into the political process in a reliable and meaningful manner." But the Equal Protection Clause reaches even further, prohibiting "a political structure that treats all individuals as equals, yet more subtly distorts governmental processes in such a way as to place special burdens on the ability of minority groups to achieve beneficial legislation." "[T]he State may no more disadvantage any particular group by making it more difficult to enact legislation in its behalf than it may dilute any person's vote or give any group a smaller representation than another of comparable size."

The Supreme Court's statements in *Hunter* and *Seattle* emphasize that equal protection of the laws is more than a guarantee of equal treatment under existing law. It is also a guarantee that minority groups may meaningfully participate in the process of creating these laws and the majority may not manipulate the channels of change so as to place unique burdens on issues of importance to them. In effect, the political-process doctrine hews to the unremarkable notion that when two competitors are running a race, one may not require the other to run twice as far or to scale obstacles not present in the first runner's course. Ensuring the fairness of the political process is particularly important because an electoral minority is disadvantaged by definition in its attempts to pass legislation; this is especially true of "discrete and insular minorities," who face unique additional hurdles.

Ensuring a fair political process is nowhere more important than in education. Education is the bedrock of equal opportunity and "the very foundation of good citizenship." Safeguarding the guarantee "that public institutions are open and available to all segments of American society, including people of all races and ethnicities, represents a paramount government objective." Moreover, universities "represent the training ground for a large number of our Nation's leaders.... [T]o cultivate a set of leaders with legitimacy in the eyes of the citizenry, it is necessary that the path to leadership be visibly open to talented and qualified individuals of every race and ethnicity." Therefore, in the high-stakes context of education, we must apply the political-process doctrine with the utmost rigor.

Of course, the Constitution does not protect minorities from political defeat: Politics necessarily produces winners and losers. We must therefore have some way to differentiate between the constitutional and the impermissible. And *Hunter* and *Seattle* provide just that. They set the benchmark for when the majority has not only won, but has rigged the game to reproduce its success indefinitely.

[Information on two past cases has been omitted.]

2. Application of the Hunter/Seattle *Test to Proposal 2*

Hunter and *Seattle* thus expounded the rule that an enactment deprives minority groups of the equal protection of the laws when it: (1) has a racial focus, targeting a policy or program that "inures primarily to the benefit of the minority"; and (2) reallocates political power or reorders the decisionmaking process in a way that places special burdens on a minority group's ability to achieve its goals through that process. Applying this rule here, we conclude that Proposal 2 targets a program that "inures primarily to the benefit of the minority" and reorders the political process in Michigan in a way that places special burdens on racial minorities.

a. Racial Focus

The first prong of the *Hunter/Seattle* test requires us to determine whether Proposal 2 has a "racial focus." This inquiry turns on whether the targeted policy or program, here holistic race-conscious admissions policies at public colleges and universities, "at bottom inures primarily to the benefit of the minority, and is designed for that purpose." The targeted policy need not be for the sole benefit of minorities, for "it is enough that minorities may consider [the now burdened policy] to be 'legislation that is in their interest.'"

[Additional discussion of how past cases apply to Proposal 2 has been omitted.]

Nor do policy arguments attacking the wisdom of race-conscious admissions programs preclude our finding that these programs "inure primarily to the benefit of the minority." Critics of affirmative action maintain that race-conscious admissions policies actually harm minorities by stigmatizing minority students admitted into high-caliber institutions through a perception that they lack sufficient qualifications; by impeding the academic success of minority students admitted to institutions they are not qualified to attend; and by impairing the admissions prospects of traditionally higher-performing minority groups, such as Asian-Americans. But the controversy surrounding the policies that Proposal 2 targets is irrelevant as to whether Proposal 2 itself has a racial focus; rather, this controversy is a "matter to be resolved through the political process."

We find that the holistic race-conscious admissions policies now barred by Proposal 2 inure primarily to the benefit of racial minorities, and that such groups consider these policies to be in their interest. Indeed, we need not look further than the approved ballot language— characterizing Proposal 2 as an amendment "to ban affirmative action programs"—to confirm that this legislation targets race-conscious admissions policies and, insofar as it prohibits consideration of applicants' race in admissions decisions, that it has a racial focus.

b. A Reordering of the Political Process That Burdens Racial Minorities

The second prong of the *Hunter/Seattle* test asks us to determine whether Proposal 2 reallocates political power or reorders the political process in a way that places special burdens on racial minorities. We must first resolve (1) whether the affected admissions procedures lie within the "political process," and then (2) whether Proposal 2 works a "reordering" of this political process in a way that imposes "special burdens" on racial minorities.

i. Proposal 2's Effect on a "Political Process"

The breadth of Proposal 2's influence on a "political process" turns on the role the popularly elected governing boards of the universities play in setting admissions procedures. The key question is whether the boards had the power to alter the universities' admissions policies prior to the enactment of Proposal 2. If the boards had that power and could influence the use (or non-use) of race-conscious admissions policies, then Proposal 2's stripping of that power works a reordering of the political process because minorities can no longer seek to enact a type of legislation that is in their interest at the board level. But if board members lacked such power, because policy decisions are actually under the control of politically unaccountable faculty members or admissions committees, then Proposal 2's effect on the political process is negligible.

This issue—whether the admissions policies affected by Proposal 2 are part of a "political process"—was the subject of stark disagreement between the majority and the dissent when this case was originally before a three-judge panel, and it continues to be here. In supplemental briefing, the University Defendants clarified their admissions practices, undercutting the factual and legal basis of the panel dissent's core contention that Proposal 2 falls outside the political process. We examine the administrative structure of Michigan's public universities and their admissions processes in light of this new information, even though the dissenters choose to look the other way.

The Michigan Constitution establishes three public universities—the University of Michigan, Michigan State University, and Wayne State University—and grants control of each to a governing board. These boards have the same role: to run, with plenary authority, their respective institutions. Michigan law has consistently confirmed this absolute authority. Indeed, the boards are described as "the highest form of juristic person known to the law, a constitutional corporation of independent authority, which, within the scope of its functions, is co-ordinate with and equal to that of the legislature."

Eight popularly elected individuals sit on these boards, and they hold office for eight years. The boards have the "power to enact ordinances, by-laws and regulations for the government of the university." Exercising this power, the boards have enacted bylaws—which they have complete authority to revise or revoke—detailing admissions procedures.

The University of Michigan's bylaws delegate the day-to-day management of undergraduate admissions to the associate vice provost and executive director of undergraduate admissions. Although the board delegates this responsibility, it continues to exercise ultimate decisionmaking authority because it directly appoints the associate vice provost and executive director of undergraduate admissions, and because it retains the power to revoke or alter the admissions framework. Nothing prevents the board from adopting an entirely new framework for admissions decisions if it is so inclined. Indeed, that the board can revise its bylaws is not a mere theoretical possibility, but a reality that occurs with some frequency. Since 2008, the University of Michigan's Board of Regents has revised more than two dozen of its bylaws, two of which fall within Chapter VIII, the section regulating admissions practices.

Of course power in a large university, a vast and highly complex institution, must be delegated. As such, the board fulfills its general supervisory role by conducting monthly public meetings to remain apprised of all university operations and by exercising its power to amend bylaws or revise delegations of responsibility. At these meetings, the board regularly discusses admissions practices, including the use of race-conscious admissions policies. Thus, the elected boards of Michigan's public universities can, and do, change their respective admissions policies, making the policies themselves part of the political process. But even if they did not, the Attorney General provides no authority to support his contention that an unused power is a power abandoned.

Nevertheless, the Attorney General argues, echoed by the dissenters, that admissions decisions lie outside the political process because the governing boards of the universities have "fully delegated" responsibility for establishing admissions standards to politically unaccountable admissions committees and faculty members. But the Michigan Constitution, state statutes, and the universities' bylaws and current practices directly contradict this argument. Article VIII, section 5 of the Michigan Constitution entrusts the board with "general supervision of its institution." Michigan statutes §§ 390.3–.5 vest full governing authority in the board, including the power to enact bylaws and regulations to promote and achieve the university's educational mission. The University of Michigan bylaws unambiguously retain the power to alter or revoke any bylaw, including any delegation of responsibility. This robust legal authority makes the fact of such delegation irrelevant for our purposes, as the board may revoke the delegation at will.

Moreover, to the extent the Attorney General and the dissenters express concern over the degree to which the board has delegated admissions decisions, that delegation does not affect whether admissions decisions should be considered part of the political process. When an elected body delegates power to a non-elected body for the day-to-day implementation of policy, it does not remove the policy from the political process. In the administrative law context, for example, rule-making powers are delegated from the President to appointed cabinet officials, and as a practical matter, further down to civil service professionals.

Regardless of the level at which the rule is drafted, the rulemaking process is at all times under the umbrella of the powers of the President. These rules are often the subject of political debate, lobbying, and electioneering, again without regard to who actually drafted the particular rule in question. Without question, federal rule-making is part of the political process. Similarly, whether it is the board or a delegated body that sets the rules for consideration of race in admissions, these decisions fall under the umbrella of the elected board and are thus part of the political process.

Telling evidence that board members can influence admissions policies—bringing such policies within the political process—is that these policies can, and do, shape the campaigns of candidates seeking election to one of the boards. As the boards are popularly elected, citizens concerned with race-conscious admissions policies may lobby for candidates who will act in accordance with their views—whatever they are. Board candidates have, and certainly will continue, to include their views on race-conscious admissions policies in their platforms. Indeed, nothing prevents Michigan citizens from electing a slate of regents who promise to review admissions policies based on their opposition to affirmative action. Once elected, the new slate may revise the bylaws and change their university's admissions policies—either by entirely revoking the delegation and handling all admissions policies at the board level or by enacting new bylaws giving more explicit direction to admissions committees. Thus, Proposal 2 affects a "political process."

ii. Reordering of a "Political Process"

The next issue is whether Proposal 2 reordered the political process in a way that places special burdens on racial minorities. The Supreme Court has found that both implicit and explicit reordering violates the Fourteenth Amendment. In *Hunter*, the express language of the charter amendment required any ordinance regulating real estate "on the basis of race, color, religion, national origin or ancestry" to be approved by a majority of the electorate and the City Council, as opposed to solely the City Council for other real-estate ordinances. This reallocation of power was directly written into the charter amendment, creating "in effect . . . an 'explicitly racial classification treating racial housing matters differently' " from all other housing matters.

In *Seattle*, however, the reordering was implicit: On its face, Initiative 350 simply prohibited school boards from using mandatory busing, but its practical effect was to force "[t]hose favoring the elimination of de facto school segregation" to "seek relief from the state legislature, or from the statewide electorate" in order to overturn Initiative 350. Nonetheless, "authority over all other student assignment decisions . . . remain[ed] vested in the local school board." Whereas a proponent of smaller class sizes could seek redress at the local level, a proponent of integrative busing had to scale the more onerous hurdle of a successful statewide campaign. The *Seattle* legislation implicitly reallocated power because the "initiative remove[d] the authority to address a racial problem—and only a racial problem—from the existing decisionmaking body. . . ." Similar to the amendment in *Hunter*, Initiative 350 modified "the community's political mechanisms . . . to place effective decisionmaking authority over a racial issue at a different level of government."

The *Seattle* Court then clarified what sort of reordering contravenes the political process doctrine: "[t]he evil condemned by the *Hunter* Court was not the particular political obstacle of mandatory referenda imposed by the Akron charter amendment; it was, rather, the comparative structural burden placed on the political achievement of minority interests." In both *Hunter* and *Seattle*, "the effect of the challenged action was to redraw decisionmaking authority over racial matters—and only over racial matters—in such a way as to place *comparative burdens* on minorities." (emphasis added). Thus, any "comparative structural burden," be it local or statewide or national, satisfies the reordering prong of the *Hunter/Seattle* test.

The comparative structural burden we face here is every bit as troubling as those in *Hunter* and *Seattle* because Proposal 2 creates the highest possible hurdle. This comparative structural burden is most apparent in tracing the channels for change available to a citizen promoting any policy unmodified by Proposal 2 and those available to a citizen promoting constitutionally permissible race-conscious admissions policies.

An interested Michigan citizen may use any number of avenues to change the admissions policies on an issue outside the scope of Proposal 2. For instance, a citizen interested in admissions policies benefitting legacy applicants—sons and daughters of alumni of the university—may lobby the admissions committees directly, through written or in-person communication. He may petition higher administrative authorities at the university, such as the dean of admissions, the president of the university, or the university's board. He may seek to affect the election—through voting, campaigning, or other means—of any one of the eight board members whom the individual believes will champion his cause and revise admissions policies accordingly. And he may campaign for an amendment to the Michigan Constitution.

Each of these methods, respectively, becomes more expensive, lengthy, and complex. Because Proposal 2 entrenched the ban on all race-conscious admissions policies at the highest level, this last resort—the campaign for a constitutional amendment—is the sole recourse available to a Michigan citizen who supports enacting such policies. That citizen must now begin by convincing the Michigan electorate to amend its constitution—an extraordinarily expensive process and the most arduous of all the possible channels for change. Just to place a proposed constitutional amendment repealing Proposal 2 on the ballot would require either the support of two-thirds of both the Michigan House of Representatives and Senate or the signatures of a number of voters equivalent to at least ten percent of the number of votes cast for all candidates for governor in the preceding general election. Once on the ballot, the proposed amendment must then earn the support of a majority of the voting electorate to undo Proposal 2's categorical ban.

Only after traversing this difficult and costly road would our now-exhausted citizen reach the starting point of his neighbor who sought a legacy-related admissions policy change. After this successful constitutional amendment campaign, the citizen could finally approach the university—by petitioning the admissions committees or higher administrative authorities—to request the adoption of race-conscious admissions policies. By amending the Michigan Constitution to prohibit university admissions units from using even modest race-conscious admissions policies, Proposal 2 thus removed the authority to institute any such policy from Michigan's universities and lodged it at the most remote level of Michigan's government, the state constitution. As with the unconstitutional enactment in *Hunter,* proponents of race-conscious admissions policies now have to obtain the approval of the Michigan electorate and, if successful, admissions units or other university powers—whereas proponents of other non-universal admissions factors need only garner the support of the latter.

The "simple but central principle" of *Hunter* and *Seattle* is that the Equal Protection Clause prohibits requiring racial minorities to surmount more formidable obstacles than those faced by other groups to achieve their political objectives. A state may not "allocate[] governmental power nonneutrally, by explicitly using the *racial* nature of a decision to determine the decisionmaking process." As the Supreme Court has recognized, such special procedural barriers to minority interests discriminate against racial minorities just as surely as—and more insidiously than—substantive legal barriers challenged under the traditional equal protection rubric. Because less onerous avenues to effect political change remain open to those advocating consideration of nonracial factors in admissions decisions, Michigan cannot force those advocating for consideration of racial factors to traverse a more arduous road without violating the Fourteenth Amendment. We thus conclude that Proposal 2 reorders the political process in Michigan to place special burdens on minority interests.

[Section 3, concerning objections to the doctrine the court has put forth, has been omitted.]

4. Constitutionality of Proposal 2 Under the Political-Process Doctrine

Proposal 2 modifies Michigan's political process "to place special burdens on the ability of minority groups to achieve beneficial legislation." Because Proposal 2 fails the *Hunter/Seattle* test, it must survive strict scrutiny. Under the strict scrutiny standard, the Attorney General must prove that Proposal 2 is "necessary to further a compelling state interest." In *Seattle,* the Court did not consider whether a compelling state interest might justify a state's enactment of a racially-focused law that restructures the political process, because the government made no such argument. Likewise, because the Attorney General does not assert that Proposal 2 satisfies a compelling state interest, we need not consider this argument. Therefore, those portions of Proposal 2 that affect Michigan's public institutions of higher education violate the Equal Protection Clause.

[The final discussion of the court decision has been omitted.]

III.

Finding those provisions of Proposal 2 affecting Michigan's public colleges and universities unconstitutional, we REVERSE the district court's judgment granting the defendants-Appellees' motion for summary judgment. We further AFFIRM the district court's denial of the University Defendants' motion to be dismissed as parties, and AFFIRM the district court's grant of the Cantrell Plaintiffs' motion for summary judgment as to Russell.

[The dissent of Circuit Judge Danny Boggs has been omitted.]

JULIA SMITH GIBBONS, Circuit Judge, dissenting. Proposal 2 is not unconstitutional under either a political restructuring theory or under traditional equal protection analysis. I therefore respectfully dissent.

I.

Elementary principles of constitutional law tell us that plaintiffs' challenge to Proposal 2 should have little to no chance of success. Plaintiffs argue that Michigan must retain its racial and other preference policies in higher education and that the state's voters cannot make the contrary policy choice that factors like race and gender may not be taken into account in admissions. They make this argument in the face of the core equal protection principle of nondiscrimination—a principle consistent with the choice of the people of Michigan. They make the argument despite the absence of any precedent suggesting that states must employ racial preferences in university admissions. Essentially, the argument is one of constitutional protection for racial and gender preference—a concept at odds with the basic meaning of the Equal Protection Clause, as understood and explained through decades of jurisprudence.

Although it has convinced a majority of this court, plaintiffs' argument must be understood for the marked departure it represents—for the first time, the presumptively invalid policy of racial and gender preference has been judicially entrenched as beyond the political process. In reaching its conclusion, the majority strays from analysis bounded by familiar principles of constitutional law and loses sight of the parameters within which we should operate in deciding this case. To be accurate in characterizing the majority's approach, it relies on two Supreme Court cases, which it deems highly instructive. Yet, when examined carefully, these cases have no application here, and, in emphasizing them, the majority overlooks recent case law providing more relevant guidance.

II.

The political restructuring theory on which the majority relies does not invalidate Proposal 2. Racial preference policies in university admissions—presumptively invalid but permissible under limited circumstances and for a finite period of time—do not receive the same structural protections against statewide popular repeal as other laws that inure to the interest of minorities. To understand why this is the case, it is necessary to view the *Hunter/ Seattle* doctrine in the context of the recent decisional law of race-based classification.

[Additional discussion of previous cases, and how they apply to the Michigan case at hand, has been omitted.]

The majority is quick to conclude that Proposal 2 and Initiative 350 each target policies—affirmative action and integrative busing, respectively—that "inure[] primarily to the benefit of the minority" and therefore each has a "racial focus." But in a political-restructuring challenge, it is not enough to observe that some of the policies affected by the challenged enactment primarily benefit minorities. Nor is it enough to observe that, as here, the challenged enactment was passed in response to a high-profile case permitting racially conscious admissions policies under some circumstances. Though relevant, these observations are alone insufficient: in a political restructuring case, it is imperative to consider the scope of the challenged enactment itself. The majority fails to account for the broad substantive reach of Proposal 2 when compared to the narrow focus of Initiative 350 and, in so doing, improperly stretches the political restructuring doctrine that *Seattle* articulates to the instant case.

There is an additional reason that the political restructuring doctrine should not apply here, a reason that has less to do with *Seattle* itself than with the evolution of equal protection jurisprudence since it was decided. Today, it is plain that a racially conscious student assignment system—such as the one that the Seattle initiative attempted to make more difficult to enact—would be presumptively invalid and subject to strict scrutiny. . . .

Thus, when articulating the reach of the political restructuring doctrine, *Seattle* did not consider that the underlying policy affected by the challenged enactment was presumptively invalid. But we must consider that fact here. And indeed, the circumstance that racially conscious admissions policies are subject to the most exacting judicial scrutiny and limited in time—legal realities that the *Seattle* Court neither confronted nor factored into its decision—counsels heavily against applying the political restructuring doctrine to the enactment of Proposal 2. So while the majority is correct that *Seattle* employs broad language about protecting the "'ability of minority groups to achieve beneficial legislation,'" it must be remembered that the "beneficial" policy that Proposal 2 purportedly makes more difficult to enact is itself "'highly suspect.'" This is exactly the type of "[c]ontext [that] matters when reviewing race-based governmental action under the Equal Protection Clause." In short, equal protection jurisprudence regarding the use of racial classifications has developed markedly since *Seattle* was decided, and this development makes clear that applying the political restructuring doctrine to the enactment of Proposal 2 is hardly appropriate.

[Section B, which discusses other affirmative action court cases, has been omitted.]

[Section III, which includes a review of the school system set up in Michigan, has been omitted.]

IV.

Finally, it is plain that Proposal 2 does not violate the Equal Protection Clause under a traditional approach to equal protection. "The central purpose of the Equal Protection Clause of the Fourteenth Amendment is the prevention of official conduct discriminating on the basis of race."

We apply strict scrutiny to laws that (1) include a facial racial classification or (2) have a discriminatory impact and a discriminatory purpose. Proposal 2, which prohibits racial classifications, a fortiori does not classify facially on the basis of race. As to discriminatory impact and purpose, the district court did find "sufficient evidence to establish a fact question on the disparate impact part of the test" but found no discriminatory purpose. Indeed, it stated that "the demonstration of a discriminatory purpose . . . dooms [the] conventional equal protection argument" because it "cannot [be] sa[id] that the only purpose of Proposal 2 is to discriminate against minorities." The district court's conclusions are correct. "[A]bsent a referendum that facially discriminates racially, or one where although facially neutral, the only possible rationale is racially motivated, a district court cannot inquire into the electorate's motivations in an equal protection clause context." Thus, no heightened level of scrutiny need be applied to Proposal 2, and under rational basis review, Proposal 2 is easily justifiable. Proposal 2 does not violate the Equal Protection Clause under the conventional analysis.

V.

As a last matter, I have no disagreement with the majority's treatment of the procedural issues discussed in Part II.B and C.

VI.

For these reasons, I would conclude that Proposal 2 does not violate the Equal Protection Clause of the United States Constitution under either a political restructuring theory or traditional theory of equal protection. Accordingly, I would affirm the judgment of the district court.

[The dissenting opinions of Circuit Judges Rogers and Sutton, supporting Judge Gibbons's dissent, and the dissent of Circuit Judge Griffin have been omitted.]

SOURCE: U.S. Court of Appeals for the Sixth Circuit. *Coalition to Defend Affirmative Action v. Regents of the University of Michigan.* November 15, 2012. http://www.ca6.uscourts.gov/opinions.pdf/12a0386p-06.pdf.

OTHER HISTORIC DOCUMENTS OF INTEREST

FROM PREVIOUS *HISTORIC DOCUMENTS*

Egypt Announces Presidential Decree, Acceptance of Draft Constitution

NOVEMBER 23 AND DECEMBER 26, 2012

After only five months in office, and at the height of his global popularity for diffusing tension in Gaza between Israel and Hamas, Egyptian President Mohamed Morsi issued a far-reaching decree that put himself and any of his decisions above judicial review until a new constitution was approved at the end of the year. The Morsi government defended the decree, calling it necessary to complete the transition to democracy, while the president's opponents saw it as an attempt to revert the nation back to autocratic rule and impose strict Islamist law across the country.

SWEEPING PRESIDENTIAL DECREE

On November 22, citing the inability of the government to successfully transition Egypt to a constitutional democracy, President Morsi granted himself sweeping powers, noting that any of his past and future decisions could not be overturned by Egypt's courts until a new constitution was passed and a new parliament elected. He also called for a retrial of former president Hosni Mubarak and granted immunity to the Islamist-dominated assembly that was drafting the new constitution, making it immune from legal challenges. Many of the justices who hold top spots in Egypt's court system are Mubarak loyalists, and Morsi saw them as a direct challenge to the constitutional assembly.

Although Morsi attempted to paint his announcement as a mode of respecting the will of the people and the 2011 Arab Spring revolution, Egyptians saw it as another attempt to cement authoritarian rule. In June, the nation's military dissolved parliament and concentrated legislative powers in the presidency, and in August, Morsi assumed that power when he took over all executive affairs from the military. Amr Hamzawy, a member of the dissolved Egyptian parliament, called the move "absolute presidential tyranny." Morsi's spokesperson, Yasser Ali, stressed that the decree was simply "an attempt to end the transitional period as soon as possible," and that it would be immediately rescinded following the ratification of the country's new constitution. The Muslim Brotherhood, with which Morsi is aligned, considered the decision "unprecedented" but "necessary," according to senior Muslim Brotherhood adviser Gehad el-Haddad.

Demonstrations were almost immediately organized following Morsi's decree. The protests reopened the dispute between Islamists in Egypt and their opponents, who had most recently surfaced during the intervening months between the fall of Mubarak in February 2011 and the election of Morsi on June 24, 2012. Egypt's military, which was in charge prior to Morsi's decision in the summer of 2012 to force the resignations of its top leaders and fully take over executive affairs himself, did not become involved in the demonstrations against the president. Peter Jones, a Middle East expert at the University of Ottawa, said that while even those protesting in opposition to Morsi's decree might agree with the principles behind

567

it, like speeding up progress toward new elections, they take issue with the way it was done "because it reminds them of the way Mubarak used to govern."

Protesters camped out in Tahrir Square in Cairo, site of the 2011 demonstrations that brought down Mubarak, to speak out against Morsi's decree, and at one point at least 200,000 were demonstrating against the president. The protesters carried signs accusing Morsi of being a "demigod" and "pharaoh." The Muslim Brotherhood and its more radical supporters issued a call for counterdemonstrations. Protesters from both sides clashed with police, who used tear gas and other means to halt demonstrators. The most violent clashes took place in Alexandria, where the office of the Salafist–Muslim Brotherhood coalition was set on fire.

The most cohesive opposition to Morsi's decree came from the National Salvation Front (NSF), an organization that brought together the various factions that opposed Morsi's rule. Mohamed ElBaradei, a former UN diplomat, heads the group; a former head of the Arab League, Amr Moussa, is also a major player. The NSF called for early presidential elections to replace Morsi and the formation of a new, national salvation government modeled after the reasons behind the 2011 uprising. In December, the NSF was under investigation by Morsi officials for "conspiring to topple" the government.

Only a few days after issuing his decree, Morsi appeared poised to accept a compromise regarding the extent of his powers. The president met with members of the Supreme Judicial Council, the highest court in the nation, to discuss the council's proposal that only "sovereign matters" be outside of judicial review. According to Ali, the president approved the language proposed by the council. This announcement was not enough to diffuse the tension. Opposition movement Popular Current said its protests would continue until the president fully canceled his decree. Legal experts said that even during Mubarak's reign, Egypt's government has used the phrase "sovereign matters" broadly and that it could extend to more than just declarations of war or calling elections and would effectively leave the decree intact.

By the first week of December, protests had grown increasingly violent and Morsi showed no sign of relenting. He appeared in a nationwide televised address to indicate his support for peaceful opposition to his decree but said he would hold accountable anyone using violence as a means of protest.

MORSI BACKS DOWN

On December 8, in an effort to bring the protests to an end and diffuse tension across Egyptian government and society, Morsi announced that he would immediately annul his decree. The annulment would not be retroactive; therefore, any decisions made by Morsi prior to December 8 were left intact. This included the decision to retry Mubarak and his former interior minister, who were sentenced to life in prison in June for their roles in the deaths of protesters during the 2011 revolution. When the demonstrations wound down, Egyptian officials announced that at least seven people had been killed while hundreds were injured. A number of Morsi's closest advisers resigned their positions in the government in response to the protests.

When he initially issued his decree, Morsi gave the 100-member body drafting the constitution a two-month extension on its work, giving it until February 2013 to finalize the document, after which time the draft would be put before voters for approval. But because the Supreme Constitutional Court, which did not respect Morsi's decree, announced that it would rule on whether the constitutional assembly should be dissolved, work sped up, and a proposed draft was completed before the court could meet. This gave Morsi the opportunity to call for a referendum on the draft constitution, which was set for December 15. And because he called for the referendum before December 8, the date stood.

EGYPTIANS APPROVE DRAFT CONSTITUTION

Prior to the public vote, there was opposition to the 234-article document, with critics expressing concern that it did not offer enough protection for minority religious groups and women. Secular representatives of the assembly and those representing the Coptic Church walked out before the document was finalized. ElBaradei wrote on Twitter that the draft "undermines basic freedoms & violates universal values." The biggest point of contention for opponents was that the constitution maintained sharia law as the guiding legislative principle, something unchanged from Mubarak's reign. Despite this, the largest opposition parties urged their supporters to participate in the referendum.

On December 15 and 22, Egyptians voted on the proposed constitution. The voting was held over two days because many judges who opposed Morsi's constitutional assembly refused to oversee the elections, thus making a one-day vote logistically impossible. About one third of eligible voters turned out, according to the Muslim Brotherhood.

With the results of the two-stage referendum showing 64 percent of Egyptians backing the constitution, on December 25, Morsi formally approved the document, paving the way for parliamentary elections to take place about two months later. The new constitution limits presidents to two four-year terms; maintains Islamic, or sharia, law; and says that Islamic authorities will be consulted when necessary on whether sharia law is being violated. The latter point was of concern to Christians and Egypt's other minority religious sects.

Morsi opponents noted some irregularities in the voting, including polling places that opened late and illegal campaigning taking place in favor of the Islamists outside of polling locations. Egyptian officials overseeing the vote did not note any irregularities that would have had a significant impact on the outcome of the vote. The Muslim Brotherhood called the constitution "a historic opportunity to unite all national powers on the basis of mutual respect and honest dialogue for the sake of stabilizing the nation."

While the referendum resulted in some calming of political fervor, Morsi will now face the challenge of building consensus for the new law of the land and paving a way forward that will rebuild Egypt's floundering economy. In his first speech following the formal approval of the constitution, Morsi said he would make Egypt attractive to investors again and would govern with a desire to work with both his supporters and opponents. "Those who said 'no' and those who said 'yes,' I thank you both because we do not want to return to the era of one opinion or fake majorities," Morsi said.

Following the referendum, the NSF announced its intent to form a political party that would take on the Muslim Brotherhood and other Islamists in Egypt in the upcoming parliamentary elections. "The referendum is not the end of the road," said Khaled Dawoud, a spokesperson for the NSF. "It is only the beginning of a long struggle for Egypt's future."

RENEWED PROTESTS

On January 25, 2013, protesters gathered across Egypt to mark the second anniversary of the start of the revolution that brought down the Mubarak government. The gatherings quickly turned into demonstrations against Morsi and his handling of the constitutional process and what protesters claimed was a disregard for the tenets of the 2011 revolution. At their root, the demonstrations recognized the loss of confidence in Morsi's government and, specifically, in his security forces. Morsi imposed states of emergency in three cities and, backed by his cabinet, deployed armed forces "to participate with the police in preserving security and protecting vital establishments." Morsi invited various opposition groups, including the NSF, to his presidential palace for discussions, but the NSF refused the invitation as "empty of content."

—Heather Kerrigan

Following are two press releases from the Egypt State Information Service. The first, from November 23, 2012, details President Mohamed Morsi's presidential decree making all laws instated since he came to office unchallengeable. The second, from December 26, 2012, announces the approval by the Egyptian people of a draft of the new constitution.

Egyptian President Issues Constitutional Declaration

DOCUMENT

November 23, 2012

President Mohamed Morsy on Thursday 22/11/2012 issued a new constitutional declaration that would bring about retrials of suspects involved in killing and attempted killing of protesters of the January revolution.

The new constitutional declaration stipulates holding retrials into crimes pertaining to killing and injuring protesters as well as terror crimes committed against revolutionaries under the former regime, said presidential spokesman Yasser Ali.

All laws, decrees and constitutional declarations issued by the president since coming to office on 30 June 2012 are final and unchallengeable by anyone, Ali said.

A new prosecutor general was appointed for a four-year term, he added.

The new draft constitution will be formed within a maximum period of eight months, instead of six, from the date of the formation of the Constituent Assembly, the president ordered.

According to the declaration, no judicial body is entitled to dissolve the Shura Council or the Constituent Assembly, the presidential spokesman said.

The president has the right to take measures necessary to face any threats posed to the January revolution, national unity or security in accordance with the law, the spokesman added.

SOURCE: Egypt State Information Service. "Morsy Announces New Constitutional Declaration." November 23, 2012. http://www.sis.gov.eg/En/Story.aspx?sid=65185.

Egyptians Vote on New Draft Constitution

December 26, 2012

The High Elections Commission (HEC) has announced on Tuesday 25/12/2012 that the majority of Egyptians voted in favor of the draft constitution.

In a press conference on Tuesday, Head of the HEC Counselor Samir Abu el-Maati said %63.8 of Egyptians said 'yes' against %36.2 said 'no' in the referendum.

He added that the turnout reached up to %32.9 of eligible voters.

The total number of eligible voters is estimated at 51,919,067, out of them 10,755,012 voters said yes and 6,061,101 voters said no in the referendum on the new constitution, he said.

Abu el-Maati noted that the HEC has seriously investigated all the complaints, stressing that it was the HEC that suggested holding the referendum on two stages.

The HEC fully oversaw the two-round referendum, he said, reiterating that the balloting process was conducted under full judicial supervision.

SOURCE: Egypt State Information Service. "HEC: Majority of Egyptians Support Draft Constitution." December 26, 2012. http://www.sis.gov.eg/En/Story.aspx?sid=65865.

OTHER HISTORIC DOCUMENTS OF INTEREST

FROM THIS VOLUME

FROM PREVIOUS *HISTORIC DOCUMENTS*

United Nations Grants Non-Member Observer State Status to Palestine

NOVEMBER 26 AND 29, 2012

Since the creation of Israel in 1948, the disputed area known as Palestine has been a source of tension in the Middle East, pitting those who want to give it greater sovereignty against those who deny that it should exist as a separate entity at all. Palestinians have looked to the United Nations (UN) to settle the dispute by granting it "member state" status, which would mean that in the eyes of the international community, it is a sovereign nation. Previous attempts at such recognition failed to elevate Palestine above its "permanent observer" status, but on November 29, 2012, despite an ongoing dispute in the region, the UN General Assembly voted to upgrade Palestine to "Non-Member Observer State" status.

PALESTINE SOLUTION

The status of Palestine has been controversial since the creation of the state of Israel in 1948. Israel was established following the Holocaust in World War II, but it has its roots in the earlier development of Zionism as a movement in the nineteenth century. The movement, which sought to create a tangible Jewish nation, accelerated with the establishment of settlements in present-day Israel from the 1860s and 1870s, as well as the First Zionist Congress in Basel, Switzerland, in 1897. In 1917, Britain, which had control over Palestine following World War I, issued the Balfour Declaration in which it supported the creation of a "national home" for the Jewish people.

Nevertheless, intercommunal tensions persisted through the 1940s. The announcement of a UN plan to partition the area into two states on November 29, 1947, prompted a civil war between the Jewish and Arab communities, the latter of which objected to living under a Jewish government. Following the declaration of an independent Israel on May 14, 1948, Israel was invaded by Egypt, Lebanon, Iraq, Syria, and Jordan. Jordan captured part of the Old City of Jerusalem, which had theretofore been inhabited by Muslims, Jews, and Christians, while many Palestinians migrated toward the West Bank. Israeli territory was expanded in the Six Day War in 1967 and in the Yom Kippur War in 1973. Israel also temporarily controlled part of the Sinai Peninsula after the 1956 Suez War.

Although Israel subsequently signed peace treaties or ceasefire agreements with many of its neighbors, notably signing a comprehensive peace treaty with Egypt in 1979, internal conflict has persisted. Notwithstanding years of negotiations between Israelis and Palestinians, the peace process has largely failed due to the incompatible objectives of the two parties. Israel habitually demands that new peace talks begin without preconditions, while the Palestinians counter that construction to begin or expand Israeli settlements must stop before negotiations begin. Additionally, the parties are divided over water rights, the scope of national borders, the "right of return" for ethnic Palestinians living elsewhere, and the status of Jerusalem.

Negotiations are further complicated by divisions within the Palestinian leadership. Palestinians are represented by two groups, including the Palestinian Authority (PA), which was established through a series of talks in the 1990s and is led by the more moderate Fatah. Fatah controls the West Bank, which borders Jordan. Fatah is countered by the more militant Hamas, which has links to the Muslim Brotherhood and Iran, and does not recognize the legitimacy of the Israeli state. Hamas controls Gaza, the other Palestinian territory, which borders Egypt. Hamas has governed Gaza since its victory in the 2006 elections and subsequently had a brief civil war with Fatah, which sought to dissolve the Hamas-led government.

International organizations, meanwhile, often propose a two-state solution based on pre-1967 borders, with a Palestinian capital in East Jerusalem. The last proposal is particularly controversial, as East Jerusalem contains the Old City and many sites holy to all the Abrahamic religions.

SEARCHING FOR INTERNATIONAL RECOGNITION

Due to the enduring stalemate between Israeli and Palestinian representatives, in recent years, Palestine has sought to plead its cause with the international community. A bid for UN membership failed in November 2011, due to opposition within the Security Council. Undeterred, the Palestinians changed tack and sought to upgrade their existing status as a Permanent Observer to a Non-Member Observer State. Since the status change would not confer membership, it required only a majority vote in the General Assembly, which is increasingly well disposed toward Palestinian arguments. The upgrade was significant in that it acknowledged Palestine as a state, rather than a generic observer interest.

The vote came fast on the heels of fresh conflict in Palestine. Following a series of Gaza-based rocket attacks toward southern Israel in early November 2012, the Israel Defense Forces initiated Operation Pillar of Defense, which aimed to destroy Hamas's missile capacities and included targeted killings of senior Hamas leaders. Israel also debuted its missile shield, Iron Dome, during the conflict. In the parallel war for international opinion, the Israel Defense Forces highlighted the country's security concerns, while Palestinians appealed to human sympathy for the civilians endangered by the operation. The campaign lasted from November 14 to November 20, ending with a U.S.-backed ceasefire mediated by Egypt that went into effect on November 21. Egypt's role as a mediator has grown since its election of a Muslim Brotherhood government in 2012, which has credibility with the Palestinians, whose cause is supported by the Egyptian public. Conversely, Egypt is also mindful of U.S. interests in Israeli security, as Egypt is reliant on U.S. aid.

Following the ceasefire, security concerns continued to direct Israel's response to the Palestinian proposal at the United Nations. In voting against the initiative, Ron Prosor, Israel's permanent representative to the body, argued that Israel's "vital interests" had not been acknowledged in the resolution that was calling for a change in Palestine's status at the UN. The United States cautioned that there was no "shortcut to peace," but Turkey countered that Palestine was a "bleeding wound" and deserved increased support. Members of the Non-Aligned Movement, which includes anti-Western states such as Iran, generally sided with Palestine. Surprisingly, China endorsed the measure, despite its own problems with separatists. The leader of the PA, Mahmoud Abbas, presented the vote dramatically as a "last chance to save the two-[s]tate solution." The majority of members, however, were focused on prospects for the bilateral peace process after the vote. As shown in the transcript from the forty-fourth and forty-fifth meetings of the General Assembly

Plenary, supporters and detractors of the motion both claimed that they cast their votes to spur fresh negotiations toward a two-state solution.

The declaration on the question of Palestine from the sixty-seventh session emphasized the "urgent need" to resume and advance negotiations. The United Nations supported the status upgrade for Palestine by citing its existing memberships in bodies such as the UN Educational, Scientific and Cultural Organization (UNESCO), the League of Arab States, and the Organization of Islamic Cooperation as de facto recognition of its sovereignty. The United Nations also rejected "the acquisition of territory by force," echoing Palestinian arguments regarding occupation. Finally, the question was closed with a call to support Palestinians in their pursuit of self-determination, albeit with due references to the peace process and security for both states.

On November 29, 2012, the anniversary of the 1947 UN partition proposal and the International Day of Solidarity with Palestine, the motion passed easily, with 138 votes in favor against 9 opposition votes and 41 abstentions. Amid defeat, Israel claimed a "moral majority," citing its support from leading developed democracies.

IMPLICATIONS OF THE UN VOTE

While the status upgrade was met with jubilation in the Palestinian territories, observers cautioned that its value was primarily symbolic and would have little impact on Palestinians' lives. Nevertheless, the upgrade increased the possibility of additional recognition through membership in other organizations, including the International Criminal Court (ICC). Palestine planned to press for investigations of alleged Israeli war crimes and other abuses if it became a member. These charges could potentially limit Israeli leaders' freedom of movement, rendering them subject to arrest warrants in ICC member countries. In January 2013, Israel responded to what it viewed as institutional bias by refusing to participate in the UN's annual review of its human rights practices, complaining that it was the only country to be subject to an annual review. UN officials expressed concern that Israel's noncompliance could set a precedent for other countries.

Israeli and U.S. reactions to the UN vote ranged from outrage on the part of hardline Israeli politicians to concern among dovish U.S. diplomats that the vote would undermine resumption of negotiations. Both countries responded to Palestine with economic sanctions. Israel withheld tax revenues collected for the PA, limiting services in the West Bank. The funds were ostensibly withheld to pay for debts owed to Israeli utility companies, but they were an implicit response to the UN vote. In January 2013, however, Israel relented in the face of increasing economic difficulty for the PA and released taxes withheld for December without promising to do so the following month. The United States, meanwhile, delayed payment of $200 million in aid. The International Monetary Fund (IMF) cautioned in March 2013 that financial strains could destabilize the only moderate force in the territories.

PROSPECTS FOR PEACE

The formation of a center-right government after Israeli elections in January 2013 reduced the likelihood that officials would grant the concessions long sought by Palestinians as precursors to fresh negotiations. The presence in the cabinet of Tzipi Livni, a veteran proponent of peace talks, as justice minister could increase Israeli willingness to release political prisoners or transfer some West Bank areas to Palestinian control. Nevertheless, the government was expected to focus on domestic issues, particularly long-simmering grievances over stagnant living standards and controversy over the proposed integration of Orthodox Jews into the military and civilian workforce. The perceived success of the Iron Dome during the Pillar of Defense operation may have also assuaged some voters' security concerns, giving them space to press the government regarding bread-and-butter issues.

Meanwhile, Fatah was allowed to hold its first rally in Gaza in five years in January 2013, as Hamas and its more moderate counterparts increasingly emphasized the importance of national unity. A unified leadership would allow the Palestinians to speak with one voice in hypothetical negotiations, but it is unlikely that Israel would accept the presence of Hamas in talks, as the latter is viewed by Israel, the European Union, and the United States as a terrorist organization. Hopes for new talks were further undermined by Palestine's view of the new Israeli government as an impediment to a two-state solution.

While the UN resolution on Palestine certainly encouraged Palestinian nationalists, it is not expected to yield any breakthroughs in the peace process or significantly strengthen Palestinian leverage in negotiations. Given recent political developments in both Israel and Palestine, a two-state solution is unlikely in the immediate future.

—Anastazia Clouting

Following is the text of the resolution before the United Nations to upgrade Palestine's UN status, released on November 26, 2012; and the edited text of a press release from the United Nations General Assembly on November 29, 2012, announcing the upgrade of Palestine's UN status to Non-Member Observer State.

DOCUMENT   *UN Resolution on Palestinian Status*

November 26, 2012

[All footnotes have been omitted.]

The General Assembly,
   Guided by the purposes and principles of the Charter of the United Nations, and stressing in this regard the principle of equal rights and self-determination of peoples,
   Recalling its resolution 2625 (XXV) of 24 October 1970, by which it affirmed, inter alia, the duty of every State to promote through joint and separate action the realization of the principle of equal rights and self-determination of peoples,
   Stressing the importance of maintaining and strengthening international peace founded upon freedom, equality, justice and respect for fundamental human rights,
   Recalling its resolution 181 (II) of 29 November 1947,
   Reaffirming the principle, set out in the Charter, of the inadmissibility of the acquisition of territory by force,
   Reaffirming also relevant Security Council resolutions, including, inter alia, resolutions 242 (1967) of 22 November 1967, 338 (1973) of 22 October 1973, 446 (1979) of 22 March 1979, 478 (1980) of 20 August 1980, 1397 (2002) of 12 March 2002, 1515 (2003) of 19 November 2003 and 1850 (2008) of 16 December 2008,

Reaffirming further the applicability of the Geneva Convention relative to the Protection of Civilian Persons in Time of War, of 12 August 1949, to the Occupied Palestinian Territory, including East Jerusalem, including, inter alia, with regard to the matter of prisoners,

Reaffirming its resolution 3236 (XXIX) of 22 November 1974 and all relevant resolutions, including resolution 66/146 of 19 December 2011, reaffirming the right of the Palestinian people to self-determination, including the right to their independent State of Palestine,

Reaffirming also its resolutions 43/176 of 15 December 1988 and 66/17 of 30 November 2011 and all relevant resolutions regarding the Peaceful settlement of the question of Palestine, which, inter alia, stress the need for the withdrawal of Israel from the Palestinian territory occupied since 1967, including East Jerusalem, the realization of the inalienable rights of the Palestinian people, primarily the right to self-determination and the right to their independent State, a just resolution of the problem of the Palestine refugees in conformity with resolution 194 (III) of 11 December 1948 and the complete cessation of all Israeli settlement activities in the Occupied Palestinian Territory, including East Jerusalem,

Reaffirming further its resolution 66/18 of 30 November 2011 and all relevant resolutions regarding the status of Jerusalem, bearing in mind that the annexation of East Jerusalem is not recognized by the international community, and emphasizing the need for a way to be found through negotiations to resolve the status of Jerusalem as the capital of two States,

Recalling the advisory opinion of the International Court of Justice of 9 July 2004,

Reaffirming its resolution 58/292 of 6 May 2004, affirming, inter alia, that the status of the Palestinian territory occupied since 1967, including East Jerusalem, remains one of military occupation and that, in accordance with international law and relevant United Nations resolutions, the Palestinian people have the right to self-determination and to sovereignty over their territory,

Recalling its resolutions 3210 (XXIX) of 14 October 1974 and 3237 (XXIX) of 22 November 1974, by which, respectively, the Palestine Liberation Organization was invited to participate in the deliberations of the General Assembly as the representative of the Palestinian people and was granted observer status,

Recalling also its resolution 43/177 of 15 December 1988, by which it, inter alia, acknowledged the proclamation of the State of Palestine by the Palestine National Council on 15 November 1988 and decided that the designation "Palestine" should be used in place of the designation "Palestine Liberation Organization" in the United Nations system, without prejudice to the observer status and functions of the Palestine Liberation Organization within the United Nations system,

Taking into consideration that the Executive Committee of the Palestine Liberation Organization, in accordance with a decision by the Palestine National Council, is entrusted with the powers and responsibilities of the Provisional Government of the State of Palestine,

Recalling its resolution 52/250 of 7 July 1998, by which additional rights and privileges were accorded to Palestine in its capacity as observer,

Recalling also the Arab Peace Initiative adopted in March 2002 by the Council of the League of Arab States,

Reaffirming its commitment, in accordance with international law, to the two-[s]tate solution of an independent, sovereign, democratic, viable and contiguous State of Palestine living side by side with Israel in peace and security on the basis of the pre-1967 borders,

Bearing in mind the mutual recognition of 9 September 1993 between the Government of the State of Israel and the Palestine Liberation Organization, the representative of the Palestinian people,

Affirming the right of all States in the region to live in peace within secure and internationally recognized borders,

Commending the Palestinian National Authority's 2009 plan for constructing the institutions of an independent Palestinian State within a two-year period, and welcoming the positive assessments in this regard about readiness for statehood by the World Bank, the United Nations and the International Monetary Fund and as reflected in the Ad Hoc Liaison Committee Chair conclusions of April 2011 and subsequent Chair conclusions, which determined that the Palestinian Authority is above the threshold for a functioning State in key sectors studied,

Recognizing that full membership is enjoyed by Palestine in the United Nations Educational, Scientific and Cultural Organization, the Economic and Social Commission for Western Asia and the Group of Asia-Pacific States and that Palestine is also a full member of the League of Arab States, the Movement of Non-Aligned Countries, the Organization of Islamic Cooperation and the Group of 77 and China,

Recognizing also that, to date, 132 States Members of the United Nations have accorded recognition to the State of Palestine,

Taking note of the 11 November 2011 report of the Security Council Committee on the Admission of New Members,

Stressing the permanent responsibility of the United Nations towards the question of Palestine until it is satisfactorily resolved in all its aspects,

Reaffirming the principle of universality of membership of the United Nations,

1. *Reaffirms* the right of the Palestinian people to self-determination and to independence in their State of Palestine on the Palestinian territory occupied since 1967;

2. *Decides* to accord to Palestine non-member observer State status in the United Nations, without prejudice to the acquired rights, privileges and role of the Palestine Liberation Organization in the United Nations as the representative of the Palestinian people, in accordance with the relevant resolutions and practice;

3. *Expresses the hope* that the Security Council will consider favourably the application submitted on 23 September 2011 by the State of Palestine for admission to full membership in the United Nations;

4. *Affirms* its determination to contribute to the achievement of the inalienable rights of the Palestinian people and the attainment of a peaceful settlement in the Middle East that ends the occupation that began in 1967 and fulfils the vision of two States: an independent, sovereign, democratic, contiguous and viable State of Palestine living side by side in peace and security with Israel on the basis of the pre-1967 borders;

5. *Expresses the urgent need* for the resumption and acceleration of negotiations within the Middle East peace process based on the relevant United Nations resolutions, the terms of reference of the Madrid Conference, including the principle of land for peace, the Arab Peace Initiative and the Quartet road map to a permanent two-[s]tate solution to the Israeli-Palestinian conflict for the achievement of a just, lasting and comprehensive peace settlement between the Palestinian and Israeli sides that resolves all outstanding core issues, namely the Palestine refugees, Jerusalem, settlements, borders, security and water;

6. *Urges* all States, the specialized agencies and organizations of the United Nations system to continue to support and assist the Palestinian people in the early realization of their right to self-determination, independence and freedom;

7. *Requests* the Secretary-General to take the necessary measures to implement the present resolution and to report to the Assembly within three months on progress made in this regard.

SOURCE: United Nations. UNISPAL Documents Collection. "Status of Palestine at the United Nations." November 26, 2012. http://unispal.un.org/UNISPAL.nsf/47D4E277B48D9D3685256DDC00612265/181 C72112F4D0E0685257AC500515C6C.

DOCUMENT *UN Approves Palestine Status Upgrade*

November 29, 2012

Voting by an overwhelming majority—138 in favour to 9 against (Canada, Czech Republic, Israel, Marshall Islands, Micronesia (Federated States of), Nauru, Panama, Palau, United States), with 41 abstentions—the General Assembly today accorded Palestine non-Member Observer State status in the United Nations.

"The moment has arrived for the world to say clearly: enough of aggression, settlements and occupation," said Mahmoud Abbas, President of the Palestinian Authority, as he called on the 193-member body to "issue a birth certificate of the reality of the State of Palestine." Indeed, following Israel's latest aggression against the Gaza Strip, the international community now faced "the last chance" to save the long elusive two-[s]tate solution, he said, adding: "the window of opportunity is narrowing and time is quickly running out."

Palestine came before the Assembly because it believed in peace, and because its people were in desperate need of it, he said, speaking ahead of the vote. Its endeavour to seek a change in status at the United Nations did not aim to terminate what remained of the long stagnant peace negotiations; instead, he said, it was aimed at trying to "breathe new life" into the process. Support for the resolution would also send a promising message to millions of Palestinians "that justice is possible and that there is a reason to be hopeful," he stressed.

The text upgraded Palestine's status without prejudice to the acquired rights, privileges and role of the Palestine Liberation Organization in the United Nations as the representative of the Palestinian people, in accordance with the relevant resolutions and practice. The Palestinian Liberation Organization was recognized as an observer entity in 1974. By other terms of the resolution—the adoption of which coincided with the observance of the International Day of Solidarity with the Palestinian People and with the Assembly's annual debate on the Question of Palestine—Member States echoed the "urgent need for the resumption and acceleration" of the peace negotiations.

Israel's representative, also taking the floor before the vote, emphasized that the "one-sided" resolution did not advance peace, but instead pushed the process backward. "There is only one route to Palestinian statehood. There are no shortcuts. No quick fixes," he said. The route to peace ran through direct negotiations between Jerusalem and Ramallah.

"Israel is prepared to live in peace with a Palestinian State, but for peace to endure, Israel's security must be protected," he added.

He said that certain vital interests of his country, including recognition of the Jewish State and an agreement to end the conflict with Israel once and for all, did not appear in the text. Indeed, the only way to achieve peace was through agreements that had been reached by the parties and not through United Nations resolutions. He added that, as long as President Abbas preferred symbolism over reality, as long as he preferred to travel to New York rather than travel to Jerusalem for genuine dialogue, any hope of peace would be out of reach.

"There can be no substitute for negotiations," agreed United Nations Secretary-General Ban Ki-moon, who also addressed the Assembly following the resolution's adoption. The decision to accord Palestine non-Member Observer State status was the prerogative of Member States, he said of the action, reiterating his belief that the Palestinians had a legitimate right to an independent State, and that Israel had the right to live in peace and security. "I call on all those concerned to act responsibly" and intensify efforts towards reconciliation and towards a just and lasting peace, he said.

General Assembly President Vuk Jeremić said that in today's interconnected world, "what happens between the River Jordan and the shores of the Mediterranean has become the key to the security and well-being of [all] mankind." Notwithstanding the efforts of some of the most courageous statesmen of the twentieth century, a negotiated comprehensive settlement that would enable Israel and Palestine to live side by side in peace and security had yet to materialize "[a]nd so we still witness . . . enmity, estrangement, and mistrust—as parents continue to bury their children."

He appealed to both sides to work for peace; to negotiate in good faith; and ultimately, to succeed in reaching a historic settlement. "I have no doubt that history will judge this day to have been fraught with significance—but whether it will come to be looked upon as a step in the right direction on the road to peace will depend on how we bear ourselves in its wake," he declared.

Among speakers who expressed their support for the resolution was Ahmet Davutoğlu, Minister for Foreign Affairs of Turkey, who said that, for 65 years, the whole world had shut its eyes to the plight of the Palestinian people. During that time, no resolution towards a Palestinian State had been honoured. "The reality of Palestine," he said, "is a bleeding wound in the conscience of all humanity."

Further, he said, "our vision for justice, international order and human rights will not be achieved until the moment we . . . see the flag of the State of Palestine side by side with ours, as a full Member of the United Nations." The granting of non-Member Observer State status could act as a "booster" creating the long-needed momentum towards a negotiated, comprehensive solution. Calling today's vote a "first step," he urged all United Nations Members to fulfil their long overdue responsibility towards the Palestinians.

"The eyes of all the children of Palestine are directed towards us," said the representative of Sudan, who introduced the resolution. He called on all States to contribute today "to make history" and to "pave the way for the future" by casting their votes in favour. Doing so would be a victory both for the value of truth and for the Palestinian people themselves, he said.

However, other delegates, explaining their votes against the resolution, agreed with Israel's representative that the text would do nothing to advance positive relations between the two parties to the conflict. In that vein, the representative of the United States said that her delegation had voted against the "unfortunate and counterproductive" resolution as it placed further obstacles in the path to peace.

The United States felt strongly that today's "grand pronouncements would soon fade" and that the Palestinian people would wake up tomorrow "and find out that little about their lives had changed," save that the prospects of peace had receded. Therefore, the United States called on both parties to renew direct negotiations, and continued to urge all parties to avoid all provocative actions in the region, in New York or elsewhere. . . .

BACKGROUND

The General Assembly met this afternoon to take up the question of Palestine. It had before it two reports for consideration.

The report of the Committee on the Exercise of the Inalienable Rights of the Palestinian People (document A/67/35) states that the reporting period, 7 October 2011 to 6 October 2012, was characterized by the deadlocked political process and the deteriorating socio-economic situation in the Occupied Palestinian Territory, including East Jerusalem. According to the report, there has been no breakthrough in efforts towards resuming direct Israeli-Palestinian negotiations, owing to Israel's consistent refusal to freeze its settlement activity and adhere to the long-standing terms of reference of the peace process.

The report states that the Committee continued to work for the realization of the inalienable rights of the Palestinian people, including their right to self-determination, and a negotiated settlement of the Israeli-Palestinian conflict in all its aspects, resulting in an end to the occupation and the independence of a sovereign, viable, contiguous and democratic Palestinian State based on 1967 borders with East Jerusalem as its capital, and a just solution for the Palestine refugees based on General Assembly resolution 194 (III).

A durable settlement of the conflict is a prerequisite for a just and lasting peace in the Middle East. Thus, the report notes that the international community should maintain its focus on the Israeli-Palestinian conflict, uphold its legal obligations in that regard, and present bold initiatives to break the current deadlock. With Palestinian membership in the Organization pending before the Security Council, the Committee believes that progress on Palestinian status at the United Nations will generate a new dynamic in the peace process and help safeguard the two-[s]tate solution.

According to the report, the Committee was also concerned by the ongoing violence and gross violations of humanitarian and human rights law, and reiterated its condemnation of all attacks against civilians, including rocket fire from the Gaza Strip, air strikes on populated areas, and settler violence, and calls upon the Security Council and the High Contracting Parties to the Fourth Geneva Convention to act urgently to guarantee the protection of civilians.

The Palestinian Authority advanced its State-building programme, the report notes, but a serious budget deficit, as well as restrictions and obstacles imposed by Israel on the Occupied Palestinian Territory, including East Jerusalem, prevented the normal movement of persons and goods, economic activity and sustained growth. The Committee calls upon donors to meet their prior commitments and to provide emergency aid to buttress the two-[s]tate solution. Progress towards that goal also requires all Palestinian factions to unite behind the legitimate leadership of President Mahmoud Abbas. The Committee urges the speedy implementation, in good faith, of national reconciliation agreements.

Among numerous other actions urged in the report, the Committee also calls on the international community to take serious and concrete action to compel Israel to stop its illegal settlement activities and to genuinely commit to ending its 45-year military occupation and to making peace, and calls upon the Security Council to undertake a mission to the region to examine the situation first-hand.

The report of the Secretary-General on the peaceful settlement of the question of Palestine (documents A/67/364-S/2012/701 and A/67/364/Add.1), covering the period September 2011 to August 2012, contains replies received from the parties concerned to the notes verbales sent by the Secretary-General, as well as his observations on the current state of the Israeli-Palestinian conflict and on international efforts to move the peace process forward.

It states that there has been little progress towards the peaceful settlement of the issue during the reporting period, and that confidence between the parties and in the political process continued to erode despite efforts by the United Nations, the Quartet and individual Member States. The unwillingness of the parties to engage in direct talks was due to a lack of trust and disagreement over the conditions that would allow them to do so.

The report also notes that the Palestinians had submitted an application for membership in the United Nations and acquired membership in the United Nations Educational, Scientific and Cultural Organization (UNESCO) and that Israel continued to accelerate settlement activities in the West Bank. The situation on the ground remained challenging, in particular for the population living under closure in Gaza, while Israel, for its part, continued to face the threat of rocket fire. The situation on the ground presented a growing cause for concern over the viability of the two-[s]tate solution.

At the same time, the report states, the Palestinians continued to implement an ambitious State-building programme. They also briefly had resumed their efforts towards reuniting the West Bank and Gaza, albeit with limited success at reconciliation.

The report urges Israel to cease all settlement activity in the occupied West Bank, including East Jerusalem, and to take concrete steps to further ease the numerous restrictions in place both in the West Bank and Gaza. It also strongly encourages all Palestinians on the path of non-violence and unity in line with past Palestine Liberation Organization commitments.

In conclusion, the report states that the Secretary-General will continue to ensure that the United Nations works towards the establishment of an independent, democratic, contiguous and viable Palestinian State living side by side in peace with a secure Israel in the framework of a comprehensive regional settlement consistent with relevant Security Council resolutions, and in accordance with the Quartet road map, the Arab Peace Initiative and the principle of land for peace.

STATUS OF PALESTINE AT UNITED NATIONS

[A statement from Daff-Alla Elhag Ali Osman of Sudan, who introduced the draft resolution in support of Palestine's status, has been omitted.]

MAHMOUD ABBAS, Chairman of the Executive Committee of the Palestinian Liberation Organization and President of the Palestinian Authority, said that Palestine came before the Assembly at a time when it was "still tending to its wounds" from the latest Israeli aggression in the Gaza Strip, which had wiped out entire families, murdering men, women and children along with their dreams, their hopes, their futures and their longing to live an ordinary life in freedom and peace. It came before the Assembly because it believed in peace, and because its people were in desperate need of it.

The international community now faced "the last chance to save the two-[s]tate solution," he stressed in that regard. Indeed, the recent Israeli aggression had confirmed, once again, the urgent and pressing need to end the Israeli occupation and for the Palestinian people to gain their freedom and independence.

During the dark days of its past—which included one of the most dreadful campaigns of ethnic cleansing and dispossession in modern history—the Palestinian people had looked to the United Nations as a beacon of hope. It had appealed for an end to injustice, for the achievement of peace and for the realization of its rights, "and our people still believe in this and continue to wait."

Over the last months, the world had heard the "incessant flood" of Israeli threats to Palestine's peaceful, political and diplomatic endeavour to acquire non-Member Observer status in the United Nations. Some of those threats had been carried out in a "horrific and barbaric manner" in the Gaza Strip just days ago. The conviction that Israel was above the law and that it had immunity was bolstered by the failure by some to condemn and demand the cessation of its violations and crimes, and by the position that "equates the victim and the executioner." "The moment has arrived for the world to say clearly: enough of aggression, settlements and occupation," he affirmed.

He went on to say that Palestine did not seek to delegitimize a State established years ago, but rather to affirm the legitimacy of the State that must now achieve its independence. Nor was Palestine's endeavour aimed at terminating what remains of the negotiation process—"which has lost its objectivity and credibility." Instead, it was aimed at trying to breathe new life into the negotiations.

"We will not give up, we will not tire, and our determination will not wane," he emphasized, adding that the Palestinian people would not relinquish their inalienable rights, as defined by United Nations resolutions, including the right to defend themselves against aggression and occupation. They would continue their popular, peaceful resistance and their "epic steadfastness," and they would continue to build on their land. "We will accept no less than the independence of the state of Palestine with East Jerusalem as its capital," on all the Palestinian territory occupied in 1967, he stressed.

However, he warned, "the window of opportunity is narrowing and time is quickly running out." Indeed, "the rope of patience is shortening and hope is withering." It was time for action and time to move forward, he said, calling for support from those present in the Assembly today. That support would send a promising message to millions of Palestinians "that justice is possible and that there is a reason to be hopeful." It would show that the world would not accept the continuation of the occupation.

In its endeavour to acquire non-Member State status today, Palestine reaffirmed that it would always adhere to and respect the Charter and resolutions of the United Nations and international law, uphold equality, guarantee civil liberties, uphold the rule of law, promote democracy and pluralism and uphold and protect the rights of women. Sixty-five years ago on this day, the United Nations General Assembly had adopted resolution 181 (1947), which partitioned the land of Palestine into two States and had become "the birth certificate for Israel." It now had a moral and historic duty, as well as a practical one, to "salvage the chances for peace." In that regard, he asked the Assembly to "issue a birth certificate of the reality of the State of Palestine" on an urgent basis.

RON PROSOR (Israel) said he represented the world's one and only Jewish State; built in the Jewish people's ancient homeland, with its eternal capital Jerusalem as its "beating heart." He declared: "We are a nation with deep roots in the past and bright hopes for the future. We are a nation that values idealism, but acts with pragmatism. Israel is a nation that never hesitated to defend itself, but will always extend its hand for peace." The Bible stated "seek peace and pursue it." It had been the goal of the Israeli people and every Israeli leader since the re-establish[ment] of Israel 64 years ago. This week marked the thirty-fifth anniversary of Egyptian President Anwar Sadat's historic visit to Jerusalem. In a speech just before that visit, that official had famously stood in the Egyptian Parliament and stated that he would go to the "ends of the Earth" to make peace with Israel.

Israel's then–Prime Minister, Menachem Begin, had welcomed President Sadat to Israel and paved the way for peace. This morning, Prime Minister Benjamin Netanyahu had said of the resolution the General Assembly was about to act upon: "Israel is prepared to live in peace with a Palestinian State, but for peace to endure, Israel's security must be protected. The Palestinians must recognize the Jewish State and they must be prepared to end the conflict with Israel once and for all."

None of those vital interests appeared in the resolution, he said, and as such, Israel could not accept it. The only way to achieve peace was through agreements that had been reached by the parties and not through United Nations resolutions that had completely ignored Israel's vital security and national interests. And because the resolution was so one-sided, it did not advance peace, but pushed it backwards. No decision by the United Nations could break the 4,000-year-old bond between the people of Israel and the land of Israel. The people of Israel waited for a Palestinian leader that was willing to follow in the path of President Sadat. For as long as President Abbas preferred symbolism over reality, as long as he preferred to travel to New York for United Nations resolutions, rather than travel to Jerusalem for genuine dialogue, any hope of peace would be out of reach.

He said that President Abbas had described today's proceedings as "historic." But the only thing historic about that official's speech was how much it had ignored history. The truth was that 65 years ago today, the United Nations had voted to partition the British Mandate into two States: a Jewish State and an Arab State—two States for two peoples. Israel had accepted that plan. The Palestinians and Arab nations had rejected it and launched a "war of annihilation" to throw "the Jews into the sea." . . .

The resolution would not confer statehood on the Palestinian Authority, which clearly failed to meet the relevant criteria. The text would not enable the Palestinian Authority to join international treaties, organizations, or conferences as a State. The resolution could not serve as an acceptable term of reference for peace negotiations with Israel. "Let me tell you what his resolution does do," he said, explaining that he believed it violated a fundamental binding commitment. It sent a message that the international community was willing to turn a blind eye to peace agreements. "Why continue to make painful sacrifices for peace, in exchange for pieces of paper that the other side will not honour?" he asked.

"There is only one route to Palestinian statehood. And that route does not run through this chamber in New York," he said, adding that that route ran through direct negotiations between Jerusalem and Ramallah. "There are no shortcuts. No quick fixes. No instant solutions," he said, recalling that United States President Barack Obama had said in 2010: "Peace cannot be imposed from the outside." In closing, he said, "65 years ago the Palestinians could have chosen to live side by side with the Jewish State of Israel. They could have chosen to accept the solution of two States for two peoples. They rejected it then, and they are rejecting it again today." The United Nations had been founded to advance the cause of peace. Today, the Palestinians were turning their back on peace. "Don't let history record that today the world body helped them along on their march of folly."

[The remaining statements pertaining to the resolution have been omitted.]

Source: United Nations General Assembly. Department of Public Information. "General Assembly Votes Overwhelmingly to Accord Palestine 'Non-Member Observer State' Status in United Nations." November 29, 2012. http://www.un.org/News/Press/docs/2012/ga11317.doc.htm.

OTHER HISTORIC DOCUMENTS OF INTEREST

From previous *Historic Documents*

U.S. and Mexican Presidents on the New Mexican Government

NOVEMBER 27 AND DECEMBER 1, 2012

On December 1, 2012, Enrique Peña Nieto was inaugurated as the newest president of Mexico, taking the helm of a country that has struggled to increase its economic standing and is largely losing the war against drug cartels. Peña Nieto won a four-way race to become president, and his victory was at one time called into question and required various investigations into electoral irregularities. When he took office in December, Peña Nieto promised to institute economic reforms that he said would be key to combatting the drug war. Peña Nieto was also tasked with maintaining the close relationship with the United States and working with President Barack Obama on issues including immigration and drug violence and trafficking.

ENRIQUE PEÑA NIETO

A member of the Institutional Revolutionary Party (PRI) that ruled Mexico for seventy-one years until Felipe Calderón's conservative National Action Party (PAN) took office twelve years ago, the forty-six-year-old Peña Nieto was formerly a popular state governor who devoted himself to implementing much-needed public works and infrastructure projects. Peña Nieto governed from 2005 to 2011 and was presented as the new face of his party, a reformer who would tackle the toughest issues.

Peña Nieto is well known in Mexico, mainly because of his ties to the nation's biggest television network, Televisa. During his time as governor, Peña Nieto bought large quantities of airtime to talk about his new policies and the changes he was making. His second marriage was to a Televisa soap opera star—during his first marriage, he admitted to having affairs that led to him fathering two children, but such transgressions did little to hurt his popularity.

While Peña Nieto is called one of Mexico's most handsome politicians, his critics despise his close relationship with media outlets and criticize what they call a lack of substance. In one instance, Peña Nieto was asked about the price of tortillas, a food staple in Mexico, to which he responded he did not know because he was not "the lady of the house." Peña Nieto's opponents also note that despite PRI's attempt to paint him as a reformer, he is closely linked to leaders in the party who have opposed collaboration with PAN and any changes in Mexican political life.

PUSHING ECONOMIC REFORMS

During his campaign, Peña Nieto said that he wanted to shift the government's focus from the drug trade to economic reforms. He would still work to combat the former, according to Peña Nieto, by shoring up the economy and making Mexico an attractive place for international businesses. He claimed that his policies would create more jobs, which would ultimately make working in drug trafficking less attractive. Without this, Peña

Nieto said, "millions of my countrymen have no other option than to dedicate themselves sometimes to criminal activity." The new president will face an uphill battle—although the economy is slowly turning around and unemployment remains low, Mexico's poverty rate grew from 44.5 percent in 2008 to 46.2 percent in 2010, while the economy averaged only 1.9 percent growth per year during Calderón's term. It is Peña Nieto's ultimate goal to get Mexico to an annual economic growth rate of 6 percent.

Peña Nieto does have some solid footing to start on. Manufacturing in Mexico increased in the months before Peña Nieto took office, driven by auto manufacturing, which was moving back to Mexico from China because of competitive wages and lower transportation costs. The auto sector is concentrated in the northern part of the country, which has been hardest hit by the drug war. With free-trade agreements with forty-four countries, Mexico should be able to exploit its growing manufacturing base. The Mexican economy grew by 3.9 percent.

Other proposals made by the new president include reforming the energy sector, generating new tax revenue, and creating a new social security structure. "A series of political and economic reforms will be favored that seek to improve the well-being of the Mexican people . . . that for a long time have been evident and necessary, but which have never been concretized," Peña Nieto said. Mexico is the seventh-largest oil producer in the world and relies heavily on its energy sector, which makes up approximately 40 percent of the federal budget. All of this revenue comes from one state-run company, Pemex. Mexican law prohibits Pemex from accepting private investment, which has hampered the company's ability to pay for new energy exploration. And because it cannot work to find new sources of oil, production has dropped from 3 million barrels to 2.5 million barrels per day, leaving the company with a significant amount of debt. Peña Nieto has not yet made public his plan to reform the energy sector and increase investment, partly because his party is allied with the powerful oil workers' union.

Peña Nieto also wants to tackle Mexico's tax system, which only accounts for less than 10 percent of the country's gross domestic product (GDP)—in contrast, U.S. taxes account for between 15 and 16 percent of GDP, according to the Tax Policy Center. Tax evasion is common, and politicians have been reluctant to change the tax rate, beholden to the richest Mexicans who believe they should receive enormous tax breaks. Mexico's current payroll tax in some sectors can be 30 percent, which in many instances keeps laborers out of the workforce because companies are unwilling to hire. Changes in the tax system will be necessary to support Peña Nieto's other goal of changing the social security plan, which currently offers different programs for private- and public-sector workers. Peña Nieto wants to merge the two systems to allow for more balanced payouts.

Peña Nieto's goals were met with mixed reaction from his party, which typically does not favor tough reform; and because PRI does not hold a majority in either house of Mexico's congress, reaching the agreements necessary for effective reform could be difficult. Additionally, members of congress are heavily influenced by a variety of interest groups that funnel money into party coffers. "There are interest groups involved in all these negotiations," said Nader Nazmi, an economist with BNP Paribas in New York. "So there will be a watering down of reforms. The hope is that the watering down will not be substantial."

RELATIONSHIP WITH THE UNITED STATES

Because they share a long border, the United States and Mexico are closely connected. Each day more than $1 billion in goods cross the border, and a majority of the illegal immigrants in the United States are from Mexico, not to mention the more than 30 million people of Mexican descent who live legally in the country. With a new leader in office, the most pressing issues facing the allies will be the drug trade and immigration. Without a foreign policy track record, it was largely unknown what the new Mexican president would mean for the United States. According to Emilio Lozoya, Peña Nieto's campaign official, "It will mean a stabilization of the situation in Mexico and advancement on many of the issues Americans care about."

When he was reelected in November, President Obama promised to focus on comprehensive immigration legislation in his second term. Following the failure of the U.S. Congress to pass the president's Development, Relief, and Education for Alien Minors (DREAM) Act, in June 2012, Obama used his executive power to institute new immigration regulations that prohibited immigration enforcement agencies from deporting those aged sixteen to thirty-one who were brought to the United States as young children and who met other criteria, including postsecondary study or service in the military. Referred to as "DREAM Act lite," the order would need to be renewed every two years, and because it affected only a portion of illegal immigrants, a more permanent and comprehensive solution was necessary. "We fully support your proposal," Peña Nieto told Obama during a November 27 meeting at the White House between the two leaders. "We want to contribute, we want to be part of this."

The United States was equally—if not more—concerned with how Peña Nieto would handle the drug war, which spills across the U.S. border. In congratulating Peña Nieto on his election in July, Sen. John Kerry, D-Mass., the chair of the Senate Foreign Relations Committee, said, "We've got to make a long-term commitment to ensure that drug-related violence does not become even more dangerous tomorrow." In light of Colorado and Washington legalizing recreational use of marijuana in 2012, some Mexican leaders have pushed Peña Nieto to call on President Obama's Drug Enforcement Agency (DEA) to take a tougher stance on personal drug use, which they believe would decrease demand and be a blow to the Mexican drug cartels. César Duarte Jáquez, the Chihuahua governor and an ally of Peña Nieto, said that he thinks Mexico should legalize marijuana export to the United States in an effort to curb drug cartel influence and raise revenue. Peña Nieto told President Obama that he was not in favor of drug legalization, but he said that Mexico would need to rethink its drug war strategy in light of the Colorado and Washington votes.

Fighting the Drug War

Perhaps the largest challenge facing the new president will be how he responds to Mexico's ongoing drug war that has left more than 60,000 dead over the past six years and hampers economic growth. Mexicans are highly critical of the job former president Calderón did during his time in office to curb the illegal drug trade and have grown wary of images of headless corpses hanging from bridges and trucks full of dismembered bodies. A recent poll by Mexican company GCE found that two-thirds of Mexicans believe the drug cartels are winning the drug war and that the Calderón strategy, comprised mainly of a military show of force, has been overall ineffective. Federico Guevara, the spokesperson for the governor of Chihuahua, the state hit hardest by the drug war, said the former president was trying to "fight fire with fire," and that military solution amounted to more show than actual action.

During his campaign, Peña Nieto gave only vague ideas as to how he hoped to reduce murders and reduce drug crime but made clear that he would not use the same military offensive as his predecessor. Working in Peña Nieto's favor, the number of murders attributed to drug cartels has been falling. Ciudad Juárez, known as Mexico's murder capital, has seen its daily homicide rate fall from ten to one, and nationwide, 8 percent fewer drug-related homicide cases were opened from January to October of 2012. But some analysts say Peña Nieto will have few options for further improvement because he will be bound by past drug war efforts that have become ingrained in local culture. "He's got little margin to maneuver because [drug violence] problems are structural," said Jorge Chabat, a security analyst and author. "It's a problem that has to do with social exclusion, the corruption, and ineffectiveness of institutions that goes back many years."

On December 17, Peña Nieto laid out his official strategy for combating the drug cartels before the country's National Council on Public Security. He said his aim was to reduce crime against citizens rather than going after the leaders of the drug cartels, as his predecessor had. To do this, he said he would unify the state police forces from the country's thirty-one states under federal control and would create a 10,000-person paramilitary security force that would take over drug enforcement from the military. Peña Nieto did not, however, give a timeline for training such a force and said the military would remain the primary drug enforcement arm for the near term. Internal struggles are a frequent problem in Mexico's security forces, and many have expressed skepticism about whether such a plan might work. Peña Nieto also said that he would review Mexico's arrest and trial policies with a goal of imposing harsher punishments to deter crime—currently, only about one in every ten drug-related charges is prosecuted.

—Heather Kerrigan

Following is the text of a press conference on November 27, 2012, featuring U.S. President Barack Obama and the new Mexican president, Enrique Peña Nieto; and three documents written and released by the new president of Mexico on December 1, 2012, detailing the goals of his new administration and announcing proposals submitted to various agencies for consideration.

DOCUMENT

Presidents Obama and Peña Nieto Remark on U.S.-Mexico Partnership

November 27, 2012

President Obama. Well, it is my great pleasure to welcome President-elect Peña Nieto to the Oval Office and to the White House. This is a longstanding tradition where—almost unique, I think, in the relationship between countries—we meet early with the President-elect of Mexico because it symbolizes the extraordinarily close relationship we have between our two countries.

Over the last 4 years, I've been able to work with President Felipe Calderón, and I think we established an excellent working relationship, so I wish him all the best in his new life.

And I'm very confident that I'm going to establish a strong personal, as well as professional, relationship with the President-elect, who, I know, has an outstanding reputation for wanting to get things done.

Now, President Peña Nieto, I think, represents the close ties between our two countries, because I understand that he lived in the United States in Maine for a year, where the winters are even worse than Chicago, my hometown.

But I think that's representative of the strength of the relationship between the United States and Mexico. It's not just a matter of policy, but it's a matter of people, as represented by the many U.S. citizens who travel to Mexico, who live in Mexico, and obviously, the incredible contribution that Mexican Americans make to our economy, our society, and to our politics.

I know that President Peña Nieto has a very ambitious reform agenda, and we are very much looking forward to having a fruitful discussion here today about not only how we can strengthen our economic ties, our trade ties, our coordination along the border, improving our joint competitiveness, as well as common security issues. But I think what I know the President-elect is also interested in is a discussion about both regional and global issues, because Mexico has become not simply an important bilateral partner, but is today a very important multilateral, multinational leader on a whole range of issues from energy to climate change. And we look forward to working with Mexico not only on regional issues, but also on global issues.

And just as President Peña—President-elect Peña Nieto's reform agenda is of great interest to us because what happens in Mexico has an impact on our society, I know he's interested in what we do as well on issues like comprehensive immigration reform. And I'll be sharing with him my interest in promoting some issues that are important to the United States, but ultimately will be important to Mexico as well.

So, Mr. President-elect, I want to welcome you. Congratulations on your outstanding victory. Vice President Biden will be leading our delegation to your Inauguration. We only send the Vice President to Inaugurations when the country is really at the top of the list in importance to us. And so we just want to wish you well, and I look forward to an excellent relationship in the years to come.

Thank you. Thank you very much.

President-elect Peña Nieto. Thank you very much, President Barack Obama. It's truly a great pleasure to be here with you. I feel so happy, and thank you for your hospitality. This is of course my first visit as President-elect of Mexico, and I also want to congratulate you for your victory last November 6 for your second term as President of the United States. I of course wish you great success, and I know you have a great task before you, but I know—I trust—that you will be doing a wonderful job.

And I also want to thank you so much, President Obama, for having Vice President Joseph Biden go to Mexico for my Inaugural ceremony next Saturday, December 1. I feel so pleased to be able to have Vice President Biden represent you in Mexico. And of course, we're waiting for him and your delegation with open arms.

And I find that this is an opportunity we only have every 12 years. We're practically beginning our administration, same that you'll be starting your next 4-year term, I will be starting a 6-year administration in Mexico, as you well know, and I think this is really a great opportunity for all of us to have a closer link of brotherhood, of sister-hood, of collaboration, and of course, of great accomplishments we might both have working together.

Yes, and I believe that we have very important tasks before us that are common, as a matter of fact. For instance, we have many common things: we were both Congressmen—legislators, as we say in Spanish—in our respective Congresses in our own countries. And this means we're very sensitive to the needs of our peoples. And we also share a very important vision; the vision, for instance, of creating more jobs. We know this is very important, not only for the American people, but also for the Mexican people, for both of our nations. These are two very important demands in our countries.

And we do have the opportunity to grow, but not only that; we also have the opportunity to integrate North America, to be participating in this part of the world. And I am so pleased that this is the situation we're in.

And of course, as I've said, to increase the integration of North America, to really take advantage of the open spaces we have for our work, and not only in this part of the world, but also with Asia, of course, and just mentioning, for instance, the TPP, the Trans-Pacific Partnership. And my Government is of course very much interested in strengthening this because we believe that this is going to be a great opportunity for all of us.

Yes, and of course, in terms of security, that's another major challenge we all face. My Government has set out to reduce the violence situation in our country. And for that, of course, we have set out to launch a strategy for this purpose. And I will do everything we can for this. We want to have—we have the will to have cooperation, efficient cooperation, with respect, respect for our sovereign states. And of course, in terms of the border, we want our border to be a safe, modern, connected border, legal border. That's exactly what we've set out to accomplish.

Yes, and in terms of the reform for migration, the migration reform, we do have to tell you that we fully support your proposal, sir, and—for this migration reform. More than demanding what you should do or shouldn't do, we do want to tell you that we want to contribute. We really want to participate with you. We want to contribute towards the accomplishment so that of course we can participate in the betterment and the well-being of so many millions of people who live in your country and who are also participating. So we want to be part of this.

And I trust that we'll be able to have a very close relationship in our work, Mr. President. And that—and of course, I want to invite you to come to Mexico, to make a state visit. And as you know, next year in 2013, we're going to be holding the North American Summit, the leaders' summit. And you're of course invited. And we really hope to see you there. We'll be waiting for you with open arms.

President Obama. Any excuse to go to Mexico, I'm always game. In fact, I'm jealous of Joe Biden. But anyway, thank you very much. Welcome. Thank you, everybody. Appreciate it.

SOURCE: Executive Office of the President. "Remarks Prior to a Meeting With President-Elect Enrique Peña Nieto of Mexico." November 27, 2012. *Compilation of Presidential Documents* 2012, no. 00909 (November 27, 2012). http://www.gpo.gov/fdsys/pkg/DCPD-201200909/pdf/DCPD-201200909.pdf.

New Mexican President Calls for Government Transformation

December 1, 2012

On the cusp of a new government, we Mexicans can make a conscious decision on which future we wish for our country. We must now take the opportunity to build, side by side, the Mexico we aspire to.

All Mexicans want to live in an environment of peace and security[.] Mexico must also reduce poverty.

We deserve a sustained period of growth, with more employment and higher salaries, to reward individual effort, whether at home or in businesses, with better living conditions. Our educational system needs to be modernized, to enhance our children's opportunities when they finish their studies. Mexico must also be a global player.

The transformation we will lead over the next few years will not be the work of a single man or even a single party. Indeed, every Mexican wants his country to improve, and as a result Mexico is ready for a new stage of development.

In this regard, I would like to recall the main lines of my campaign message, which will guide my government for the next six years.

The first line of action consists of restoring peace and tranquility for Mexicans. To this end, we will implement a national crime prevention policy; restructure and professionalize State policies; modernize the legal system; focus efforts on zones with the highest rates of violence and consolidate the penitentiary system.

The second line of action is creating an inclusive Mexico, free of poverty. To achieve this, we will create a new Universal Social Security System, consolidate and create effective programs to combat poverty, promote gender equality, strive to incorporate indigenous Mexicans into the development process and design policies to assist young and disabled persons.

The third line of action is Extending Quality Education to All Mexicans. This involves increasing education quality and coverage, creating a system offering training and permanent support for teachers, investing in more and improved educational infrastructure, innovation and Science and Technology, in addition to encouraging physical activity among students.

We must focus all the country's efforts on growing economically. The fourth line of action is therefore Growth, to create more and better quality employment. I propose ten points to achieve this growth: 1) maintaining macroeconomic stability; 2) encouraging economic competition in all spheres; 3) promoting Mexico as a major energy producer; 4) greater investment in human capital; 5) increasing the credit level to finance strategic areas; 6) increasing investment in infrastructure; 7) promoting the formal economy; 8) designing a new foreign trade strategy; 9) a modern policy to stimulate rural Mexico, tourism and industrial development; and 10) a comprehensive Treasury reform.

Lastly, the fifth line of action is restoring a leading, confident role internationally for Mexico. To this end, we will pursue an active foreign policy, to integrate more effectively with North America, but also increase trade with South America, deepen our relationship with the European Union and create effective links with the Asia-Pacific region.

These five points from my election campaign will be the basis of my government program. There will thus be clear consistency between what I offered the electorate and my government's actions. By working together, we will lay the foundations to give Mexico a brighter future.

SOURCE: Office of the President of the Republic of Mexico. "Mexico Ushers in a New Era." December 1, 2012. http://en.presidencia.gob.mx/nuevos-tiempos-para-mexico.

President Peña Nieto Remarks on His Inaugural Address

December 1, 2012

I addressed the Mexicans for the first time as president from the National Palace, a symbol of Republican history and life.

Today, democracy has become a firm part of our culture.

Thanks to solid institutions, an immutable democracy and robust finances, Mexico is now ready to shine in the 21st century.

From today onwards, my first obligation as president is to comply with the law and ensure that others do the same.

It is also my responsibility to transform the country, and to do so by entirely democratic means.

My government will promote unity, within a plural society. As president, I will respect each and every voice in the Mexican population.

I will work to achieve an effective government guided by the fundamental Human Rights recognized in our Constitution, by basing my work on five strategic lines of action.

We will drive Mexico forward. It is time for us to collectively shatter the myths, paradigms and all other obstacles to our development.

Today all Mexicans must stride forward together.

To transform our country we must defeat backwardness and drive all sectors forward: people, mentalities and institutions.

It is time to enable Mexico to grow.

Let us be the generation that achieves a national transformation.

It is Mexico's moment.

SOURCE: Office of the President of the Republic of Mexico. "It Is Time to Transform Mexico." December 1, 2012. http://en.presidencia.gob.mx/es-momento-de-transformar-a-mexico.

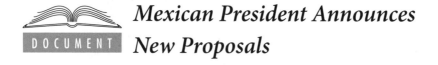

Mexican President Announces New Proposals

DOCUMENT

December 1, 2012

To mark the beginning of a new government, I would like to announce the following presidential decisions, from the National Palace:

1. I have instructed the Interior Secretary and those of Finance, Social Development, Education and Health to create a **National Crime Prevention Program**. This will be reflected in the draft Expenditure Budget 2013 to be submitted to Congress.

2. As promised, I have ordered the Legal Counsel to **waive the Constitutional Controversy on the General Victims' Law**. Once it has been approved by the Supreme Court of Justice, the law will therefore be published exactly as it was approved by Congress. A law must be established as soon as possible to protect this country's victims.

3. I will submit a constitutional reform bill, to establish a **single Criminal Code** and another for **Criminal Procedures**, to be implemented nationwide.

4. I have instructed the Secretariat of Social Development to begin the **National Crusade Against Hunger** in the next 60 days.

5. I have ordered the Secretariat of Social Development and Treasury to create the **Life Insurance Program for Women Heads of Household**, and to include it in the draft **Expenditure Budget 2013**. Once it has been approved by the Chamber of Deputies, it will begin operating in January.

6. I have also instructed the same Secretariats to include a budgetary allocation in order for the 70 and Over Program to be modified and extended to provide pensions for all Mexicans over the age of 65. Once approved by the legislators, it will be the first step towards the creation of the **Universal Social Security System** that I promised the Mexican population.

7. **Educational Reform** is urgently needed in Mexico. I will submit a bill to Congress to reform the Article Three of the Constitution and the subsequent **Reform of the General Education Law**. This educational reform will lay the foundations for the **Professional Teaching Career Service**. Clear, precise laws will enable all aspiring teachers, directors and supervisors to succeed professionally based on their work and merits, and are guaranteed job stability. In addition to this reform, I have instructed the Secretariat of Public Education to request that INEGI carry out a census of schools, teachers and pupils.

8. To reduce the disparity between different regions of Mexico and drive economic growth and competitiveness, this government will considerably increase the country's **road, rail and port infrastructure**. Moreover, infrastructure projects will be considered to connect and incorporate southern Mexico into the global economy.

9. Mexico will see the return of passenger trains to connect its cities. I have ordered the Secretariat of Communication and Transport to begin work on a train between Mexico City and Querétaro. The following projects will also be undertaken: a **train connecting Mexico City and Toluca, a Transpeninsular train connecting Yucatán and Quintana Roo, Line 3 of the Monterrey Metropolitan network**, mass transportation from Chalco to La Paz in Mexico State, and an expansion of the electric train of Guadalajara's Metropolitan Area.

10. It is crucial to stimulate economic competition, in particular in the telecommunications sector. This is why in the next few days I will submit a bill to Congress to recognize **Broadband Internet access** in the Constitution, and a series of reforms to increase competition among telephone, information, television and radio providers. To this end, the government will tender two new open television channels in the next few months.

11. To find an immediate solution to reduce debt in states and municipalities, over the next few days I will submit a **National Bill for Treasury Responsibility and Public Debt** to Congress to put local governments' debt in order.

12. In the next few days I will submit the 2013 **Economic Package** with a zero budgetary deficit to Congress. The solidity of public finances will remain a pillar in the management of the national economy.

13. The government that begins today is committed to reducing current expenditure and **investing more in works, programs and actions of direct benefit to the population**.

These presidential decisions are the first step towards a comprehensive transformation of Mexico.

SOURCE: Office of the President of the Republic of Mexico. "Presidential Decisions Announced on 1 December." December 1, 2012. http://en.presidencia.gob.mx/decisiones-presidenciales-anunciadas-el-1o-de-diciembre.

OTHER HISTORIC DOCUMENTS OF INTEREST

FROM THIS VOLUME

- Secretary of Homeland Security Amends Immigration Policy, p. 255
- Supreme Court Rules on Arizona Immigration Law, p. 275

FROM PREVIOUS *HISTORIC DOCUMENTS*

- U.S.-Mexican Initiative to Fight Drug Violence in Mexico, *2008,* p. 508
- Calderón on His Inauguration as President of Mexico, *2006,* p. 695

December

2012 Doha Climate Change Conference

Delegates meeting in Doha, Qatar, at the eighteenth annual United Nations (UN) climate change summit in late 2012 had a variety of topics on their agenda, most notably the extension of the Kyoto Protocol, which was set to expire at the end of the year. Many nations and climate change scientists view Kyoto as ineffective because it covers only about a quarter of the world's greenhouse gases and does not place any greenhouse gas emissions targets on developing nations like China or nonsignatory nations, such as the United States. The Doha meeting was largely viewed as a means to make procedural advances toward a new climate change agreement that would encompass all 194 nations and could be in place by 2020. No major developments or agreements were expected.

DIRE CLIMATE CHANGE REPORTS SET TONE FOR MEETING

Climate discussions started on controversial footing in late 2012, primarily because of the location chosen for the meeting. Qatar has the highest carbon emissions per capita, largely because of the fossil fuels burned in desalinating water and running air-conditioning units. Qatar's representative to lead the conference, His Excellency Abdullah Bin Hamad Al-Attiyah, was a former president of the Organization of the Petroleum Exporting Countries (OPEC) and was once named the Petroleum Executive of the Year. This was the first UN climate conference to be held in an Arab nation, an oil-rich region that has drawn criticism from the West for failing to make significant commitments to climate change. "Despite expectations from the new civil society movement around climate change in the region, Arab political leadership has so far failed to materialize," said the director of the Climate Action Network–International, Wael Hmaidan.

Ahead of the conference, two reports—one from the World Bank and one from the UN's top climate change body, the UN Environment Programme—were released, detailing the significance of reaching new agreements in Qatar. In 2009, participants at the UN climate change conference in Copenhagen agreed to limit global temperature rise to 2° Celsius, about 3.6° Fahrenheit, by 2100. The report released by the United Nations ahead of the meeting found that global temperatures had already risen 0.8° Celsius over preindustrial levels, and the concentration of carbon dioxide in the atmosphere was up 20 percent since 2000. According to the World Bank report, by the year 2100 on its current trajectory, global temperatures would rise 4° Celsius. "There's no new ambition since Copenhagen, and that's very worrying," said Jennifer Morgan of the World Resources Institute. The UN report also noted that even the most ambitious plans to reduce carbon emissions discussed at earlier conferences would not be enough to avoid global temperature change, but that there may still be a chance of meeting the 2° Celsius target if more investment is made in renewable energy and green transportation and deforestation is stopped.

Both reports cited facts well known to climate change scientists: that smaller islands, mainly those in the developing world, stand to lose the most due to rising sea levels caused by climate change. Over the next century, some islands have the potential to disappear entirely into the oceans. However, the world's largest industrialized nations are not immune, as evidenced by Hurricane Sandy, which caused tens of billions of dollars in damage along the U.S. Eastern Seaboard. Scientists are reluctant to link individual storms to global warming but said that overall higher water levels due to climate change in the region prior to the storm are thought to have made flooding worse. All countries will likely experience rising sea levels, larger deserts, more frequent and severe droughts, fiercer storms, and declining agricultural productivity. "The alarm bells are going off all over the place," said Alden Meyer of the Union of Concerned Scientists. "We are in a crisis and treating it like a process where we can dither away forever."

With the impact of climate change clearly displayed for conference attendees, Christiana Figueres, the executive secretary of the UN Framework Convention on Climate Change (UNFCCC), opened the conference noting, "The door is closing fast because the pace and scale of action is simply not yet enough. So Doha must deliver its part in the longer-term solution."

EXTENDING KYOTO

Delegates gathered at the 1997 UNFCCC in Kyoto, Japan, established an agreement on greenhouse gas emissions, known as the Kyoto Protocol. The agreement required all signatory nations to reduce their carbon emissions, the gases that become trapped in the atmosphere and increase global temperatures, shift weather patterns, and raise sea levels. Nations party to the agreement would be required to meet country-specific reductions in greenhouse gas emissions by the end of the first commitment period in 2012. Those nations exceeding their emissions targets would have additional requirements placed on them or be declared "non-compliant." While that distinction would be embarrassing in the global community, it carried few tangible sanctions.

The Kyoto Protocol has faced international criticism since its inception because of the imbalance between industrialized and developing countries. Nations considered to be "developing" at the time of the agreement, like China and India, were not required to meet any emissions goals, but those countries are now major contributors to greenhouse gas emissions. The United States never ratified the agreement, disagreeing with the lack of regulations for the developing world. Canada left the agreement in 2011, knowing that it would not meet its 2012 reduction commitment and fearful that it would not be able to increase production in its lucrative oil sands if it remained party to Kyoto.

In subsequent UN climate change conferences, delegates worked to map out a process to make Kyoto fairer to all nations, but the solutions that were proposed faced resistance from both the industrial and developing sides of the debate. The impending end of Kyoto forced the delegates at the 2012 conference to act. The extension of Kyoto garnered significant resistance from Russia, Belarus, and Ukraine, which received pollution permits in 1997 to allow new industries to thrive after the fall of communism. Those nations still have an abundance of carbon permits they can either use or sell, and they want them to be carried over into any new climate change agreement.

In the final package of documents that emerged from the conference, called the Doha Climate Gateway, delegates ultimately agreed to extend Kyoto to 2020. No additional climate regulations were placed on signatories, and developing nations remained outside of the agreement's scope. Additionally, some nations such as Russia decided not to sign up for the second commitment period. This left less than 15 percent of the world's carbon emissions being regulated under the Kyoto extension and included only the European Union (EU), Australia, and some smaller countries.

Although the European Union's delegation agreed to the Kyoto extension, which required a 20 percent reduction in carbon emissions, internally the group was struggling to decide whether it should make deeper cuts of 30 percent of 1990 levels. Climate scientists indicate that to have meaningful impact, the European Union would need to make a 40 percent reduction. Resistance came mainly from the Polish government, which wanted assurances that it would be able to burn its vast amounts of coal.

Analysts have questioned how the European Union will respond to a new climate agreement that would go into effect in 2020. Under Kyoto, many EU countries have cap-and-trade carbon permits that they want to carry into the next agreement, which would allow them leeway to produce about 13 billion more tonnes of carbon dioxide than they currently do. Nations without such permits claim that it is unfair treatment, and some also argue that the allowance to increase carbon emissions could render future agreements useless.

Who Is Financially Responsible for Climate Change?

"As we vacillate and procrastinate here, we are suffering," said Naderev Sano, the envoy from the Philippines. Referring to a recent typhoon in his country that left more than 1,000 dead or missing, he said, "There is massive and widespread devastation back home." But, he cautioned, "Heartbreaking tragedies like this are not unique to the Philippines."

In his comments, Sano was directly taking aim at wealthy nations that were, over time, slow to cut their emissions, thus having some of the greatest impact on climate change that disproportionately affects the developing world. The spokesperson for the conference's organization of small island states, Ronald Jumeau, said that if these nations had taken responsibility sooner, the world would be in a very different place. "We're past the mitigation and adaptation eras. We're now right into the era of loss and damage. What's next after that? Destruction? Disappearance of some of our islands?" asked Jumeau.

During the 2012 conference, developing nations pushed the wealthiest countries to recognize the permanent loss and damage caused by climate change and establish a formal mechanism for aiding those countries affected. (Conference participants avoided using the word *compensation* because the United States and other large nations felt that such a term implied guilt.) The United States was strongly opposed to the measure, noting that it could come with an unlimited cost. Without the support of the United States, it was unlikely the loss and damage issue would be closed at the Doha conference. But the U.S. delegation was facing a dilemma—if the action was vetoed, President Barack Obama, who came to office promising to tackle environmental issues, would likely be accused of hypocrisy by his environmental supporters. If the United States instead supported the measure, the president would face backlash from Republicans in Congress for continuing to spend at a time when the nation was already deeply in debt. Ultimately, the United States relented. "We don't like this text, but we can live with it," said Todd Stern, who headed the U.S. delegation to Doha.

By the end of the conference, the loss and damage language was formalized for the first time, and the next conference will likely focus on funding the program. "The term Loss and Damage is in the text—this is a huge step in principle. Next comes the fight for cash," said Martin Khor, executive director of the South Center, an organization of more than fifty developing nations. While developing nations claimed success, they failed to make progress on the funding of the Green Climate Fund, agreed to in 2009 with the goal of providing $100 billion per year by 2020 to developing nations to aid in adapting to climate change and produce clean energy. To date, about $30 billion had been raised.

LOOKING AHEAD TO 2020

The close of the conference brought with it knowledge that delegates were facing a tight deadline to develop a new climate treaty to replace Kyoto. The language of the new document was expected to be completed by 2015, and it would enter into force in 2020. However, the Kyoto Protocol took more than five years to draft, so the slow progress being made at the annual meetings will need to hasten; but that won't be easy, especially as the United States and China remain at odds with each other. The former wants China to be open about what efforts it is making to reduce greenhouse gases, while the latter wants deeper cuts from the United States.

President Obama's environmental policy has differed from that of his predecessor, but some nations still say it does not do enough. As of 2012, the United States, which makes up less than 20 percent of the world's carbon emissions, was on track to meet its goal of reducing its greenhouse gas emissions to 17 percent below 2005 levels by 2020, largely due to a decrease in natural gas demand during the recession and a move toward controversial drilling for shale gas, which has a smaller carbon footprint. China, on the other hand, has agreed to reduce its carbon dioxide emissions per unit of gross domestic product (GDP), a measure known as carbon intensity, by as much as 45 percent. However, experts say greenhouse gas emissions in China will likely not fall until 2030 due to its continuing industrialization.

In 2011, renewable energy investment hit a record $260 billion around the world. Despite this, emissions are expected to be up 2.6 percent in 2012, led by increased industrialization in China and India. While China and the United States bickered over individual targets, UNFCCC delegates stressed the need for working together toward a common goal. "This is a global problem, it has to be addressed globally," said Denmark's Energy Minister Martin Lidegaard. "But obviously, this can't stand alone. Nations can't continue to hide behind the process. There's a direct link between what we deliver at home and here. We desperately need to combine action by regions, municipalities, citizens with this global approach." Britain's minister of state for energy and climate change echoed those remarks. "We need . . . a higher sense of urgency," said Gregory Barkey, adding, "developed countries also need to demonstrate a clear ambition across the board in terms of climate goals."

—Heather Kerrigan

Following is the text of a press release issued on December 8, 2012, by the United Nations Framework Convention on Climate Change, detailing the agreements reached at its eighteenth annual conference in Doha, Qatar.

Agreements Reached at 2012 UN
Climate Change Conference

December 8, 2012

At the UN Climate Change Conference in Doha, Qatar (COP18/CMP8), governments have taken the next essential step in the global response to climate change.

Countries have successfully launched a new commitment period under the Kyoto Protocol, agreed a firm timetable to adopt a universal climate agreement by 2015 and agreed a path to raise necessary ambition to respond to climate change. They also endorsed the completion of new institutions and agreed ways and means to deliver scaled-up climate finance and technology to developing countries.

"Doha has opened up a new gateway to bigger ambition and to greater action—the Doha Climate Gateway. Qatar is proud to have been able to bring governments here to achieve this historic task. I thank all governments and ministers for their work to achieve this success. Now governments must move quickly through the Doha Climate Gateway to push forward with the solutions to climate change," said COP President Abdullah bin Hamad Al-Attiyah.

The Executive Secretary of the UN Framework Convention on Climate Change (UNFCCC), Christiana Figueres, called on countries to swiftly implement what has been agreed in Doha so that the world can stay below the internationally agreed maximum two degrees Celsius temperature rise.

"I congratulate the Qatar Presidency for managing a complex and challenging conference. Now, there is much work to do. Doha is another step in the right direction, but we still have a long road ahead. The door to stay below two degrees remains barely open. The science shows it, the data proves it," said Ms Figueres.

"The UN Climate Change negotiations must now focus on the concrete ways and means to accelerate action and ambition. The world has the money and technology to stay below two degrees. After Doha, it is a matter of scale, speed, determination and sticking to the timetable," she said.

In Doha, governments also successfully concluded work under the Convention that began in Bali in 2007 and ensured that remaining elements of this work will be continued under the UN Climate Change process.

The next major UN Climate Change Conference—COP19/CMP9—will take place in Warsaw, Poland, at the end of 2013.

The results of COP18/CMP8 in more detail

1) Amendment of the Kyoto Protocol

The Kyoto Protocol, as the only existing and binding agreement under which developed countries commit to cutting greenhouse gases, has been amended so that it will continue as of 1 January 2013.

- Governments have decided that the length of the second commitment period will be 8 years.

- The legal requirements that will allow a smooth continuation of the Protocol have been agreed.
- The valuable accounting rules of the protocol have been preserved.
- Countries that are taking on further commitments under the Kyoto Protocol have agreed to review their emission reduction commitments at the latest by 2014, with a view to increasing their respective levels of ambition.
- The Kyoto Protocol's Market Mechanisms—the Clean Development Mechanism (CDM), Joint Implementation (JI) and International Emissions Trading (IET)—can continue as of 2013.
- Access to the mechanisms will be uninterrupted for all developed countries that have accepted targets for the second commitment period.
- JI will continue to operate, with the agreed technical rules allowing the issuance of credits, once a host country's emissions target has been formally established.
- As part of accounting rules, provisions relating to carry-over of assigned amount units from the first to the second commitment period were further developed, aiming to strengthen the environmental integrity of the Kyoto Protocol regime. In addition, Australia, the EU, Japan, Liechtenstein, Monaco, Norway and Switzerland clarified, through declarations attached to the Doha decision on the second commitment period, that they will not purchase such surplus units from other Parties.

2) Time table for the 2015 global climate change agreement and increasing ambition before 2020

Governments have agreed to speedily work toward a universal climate change agreement covering all countries from 2020, to be adopted by 2015, and to find ways to scale up efforts before 2020 beyond the existing pledges to curb emissions so that the world can stay below the agreed maximum 2 degrees Celsius temperature rise.

- A significant number of meetings and workshops are to be held in 2013 to prepare the new agreement and to explore further ways to raise ambition.
- Governments have agreed to submit to the UN Climate Change Secretariat, by 1 March 2013, information, views and proposals on actions, initiatives and options to enhance ambition.
- Elements of a negotiating text are to be available no later than the end of 2014, so that a draft negotiating text is available before May 2015.
- In Doha, the UN Secretary General Ban Ki-moon announced he would convene world leaders in 2014 to mobilize the political will to help ensure the 2015 deadline is met.

3) Completion of new infrastructure

In Doha, governments significantly advanced the completion of new infrastructure to channel technology and finance to developing nations and move toward the full implementation of this infrastructure and support. Most importantly, they have:

- endorsed the selection of the Republic of Korea as the location of the Green Climate Fund and the work plan of the Standing Committee on Finance. The Green Climate Fund is expected to start its work in Sondgo in the second half of 2013, which means that it can launch activities in 2014.

- confirmed a UNEP-led consortium as host of the Climate Technology Center (CTC), for an initial term of five years. The CTC, along with its associated Network, is the implementing arm of the UNFCCCs Technology Mechanism. Governments have also agreed [on] the constitution of the CTC advisory board.

4) Long-term climate finance

- Developed countries have reiterated their commitment to deliver on promises to continue long-term climate finance support to developing nations, with a view to mobilizing 100 billion USD both for adaptation and mitigation by 2020.
- The agreement also encourages developed countries to increase efforts to provide finance between 2013–15 at least to the average annual level with which they provided funds during the 2010–2012 fast-start finance period. This is to ensure there is no gap in continued finance support while efforts are otherwise scaled up.
- Governments will continue a work programme on long-term finance during 2013 under two co-chairs to contribute to the on-going efforts to scale up mobilization of climate finance and report to the next COP on pathways to reach that target.
- Germany, the UK, France, Denmark, Sweden and the EU Commission announced concrete finance pledges in Doha for the period up to 2015, totaling approximately 6 billion USD.

Other key outcomes of COP18/CMP8 in Doha

Review

- Governments have launched a robust process to review the long-term temperature goal. This will start in 2013 and conclude by 2015, and is a reality check on the advance of the climate change threat and the possible need to mobilize further action.

Adaptation

- Governments have identified ways to further strengthen the adaptive capacities of the most vulnerable, also through better planning.
- A pathway has been established towards concrete institutional arrangements to provide the most vulnerable populations with better protection against loss and damage caused by slow onset events such as rising sea levels.
- Ways to implement National Adaptation Plans for least developed countries have been agreed, including linking funding and other support.

Support of developing country action

- Governments have completed a registry to record developing country mitigation actions that seek recognition or financial support. The registry will be a flexible, dynamic, web-based platform. A new work programme to build capacity through climate change education and training, create public awareness and enable the public to participate in climate change decision-making has been agreed in Doha. This is important to create a groundswell of support for embarking on a new climate change regime after 2020.

New market mechanisms

- A work programme has been agreed to further elaborate the new market-based mechanism under the UNFCCC, and also sets out possible elements for its operation.
- A work programme to develop a framework for recognizing mechanisms established outside the UNFCCC, such as nationally-administered or bilateral offset programmes, and to consider their role in helping countries to meet their mitigation targets, has also been agreed.

Actions on forests

- In Doha, governments have further clarified ways to measure deforestation, and to ensure that efforts to fight deforestation are supported.

Carbon [c]apture and [s]torage

- Governments meeting in Doha have looked at ways to ensure the effectiveness and environmental integrity of projects under the Kyoto Protocol's Clean Development Mechanism that capture and store carbon emissions.

Development and transfer of technology

- Countries have taken forward work on enabling the development and transfer of technologies that can help developing countries adapt and curb their emissions.

Avoiding negative consequences of climate action

- In some cases, the implementation of actions that reduce emissions could result in negative economic or social consequences for other countries. In Doha, governments discussed measures to address such consequences in a special forum.

About the UNFCCC

With 195 Parties, the United Nations Framework Convention on Climate Change (UNFCCC) has near universal membership and is the parent treaty of the 1997 Kyoto Protocol. The Kyoto Protocol has been ratified by 192 of the UNFCCC Parties. Under the Protocol, 37 States, consisting of highly industrialized countries and countries undergoing the process of transition to a market economy, have legally binding emission limitation and reduction commitments. The ultimate objective of both treaties is to stabilize greenhouse gas concentrations in the atmosphere at a level that will prevent dangerous human interference with the climate system.

See also: unfccc.int
UNFCCC Executive Secretary Christiana Figueres on Twitter: @CFigueres
Follow UNFCCC on Twitter: @UN_ClimateTalks
UNFCCC on Facebook: facebook.com/UNclimatechange

Source: United Nations. Framework Convention on Climate Change. "At UN Climate Change Conference in Doha, Governments Take Next Essential Step in Global Response to Climate Change." December 8, 2012. http://unfccc.int/files/press/press_releases_advisories/application/pdf/pr20120812_cop18_close.pdf.

OTHER HISTORIC DOCUMENTS OF INTEREST

FROM THIS VOLUME

FROM PREVIOUS *HISTORIC DOCUMENTS*

European Union Awarded
2012 Nobel Peace Prize

DECEMBER 10, 2012

In 2012, the Norwegian Nobel Committee made a controversial decision in awarding the annual Nobel Peace Prize to the European Union (EU). At the time of the announcement, the twenty-seven-member body was continuing its struggle to provide adequate financial backing for members facing fiscal crisis. The committee stressed that its decision was one based on the EU's history of forging bonds through peace and that the cohesion of the group would be vital to seeing it through its current crisis.

Award Announcement

In 2012, the Nobel Committee chose from 231 nominations for its annual Peace Prize, 43 for organizations and the remainder for individuals. Although the committee does not reveal the names of nominees, observers had some guesses about who might be top contenders, based on their own estimates and information from nominators. Among those assumed to be under consideration were American academic Gene Sharp, who is said to have helped influence the Arab Spring uprisings through a number of his writings; Maggie Gobran, who was nominated by five Republican members of the U.S. Congress for her work in giving a voice to the poorest in Egypt; U Thein Sein, the president of Burma (Myanmar), whose administration has overseen the release of hundreds of political prisoners; Radio Echo Moscow, a free-media outlet in Russia that is critical of Kremlin politics; Tunisian blogger and activist Lina Ben Mhenni; and Cuban human rights advocate Oscar Elias Biscet Gonzalez.

On October 12, 2012, the Norwegian Nobel Committee announced that it would award that year's Nobel Peace Prize to the European Union because "the union and its forerunners have for over six decades contributed to the advancement of peace and reconciliation, democracy and human rights in Europe." In its announcement, the committee recognized the ongoing economic struggle currently testing the European Union but said that instead of focusing on social unrest and economic turmoil, it instead wanted to award "the successful struggle for peace and reconciliation and for democracy and human rights." Thorbjørn Jagland, chair of the Norwegian Nobel Committee, said that the 2012 award "could be important in giving a message to the European public of how important it is to secure what they have achieved on this continent."

José Manuel Barroso, the president of the European Commission, and Herman Van Rompuy, the president of the European Council, issued a joint statement expressing "tremendous honour" in having been awarded the Nobel Peace Prize. "This prize is the strongest possible recognition of the deep political motives behind our Union: the unique effort by ever more European states to overcome war and divisions and to jointly shape a continent of peace and prosperity. It is a Prize not just for the project and the institutions embodying a common interest, but for the 500 million citizens living in our Union."

The announcement was met with gasps among members of the media gathered in Oslo, Norway, because they were well aware of the recent pressure the body was under. A number of the EU's twenty-seven member states, including Greece, Spain, and Portugal, were in a financial crisis that required billions of dollars in bailouts from the EU's Central Bank. The countries that accepted financial assistance from the European Union were forced to impose austerity measures that met with widespread protests and further tamped down economic markets. Some countries were also battling anti-EU sentiment. In the United Kingdom, for example, Prime Minister David Cameron was facing growing calls to hold a referendum on whether the non-eurozone country should remain a member of the European Union.

Although the announcement of the award shed light on the recurring historical divisions between the largest economic powers in Europe, which were experiencing low interest rates, and struggling nations, which were facing public resentment of austerity measures at the time the award was announced, some of the European policies aimed at solidifying the Union and bolstering nations in need were paying off. Greek government debt was shrinking, and Spain and Portugal were working toward closing their budget deficits by increasing exports. Bond yields dropped in Spain, Italy, and Portugal, helping to further calm European markets. In Spain, from July to October, bank stocks rose 50 percent. Even some international observers were changing their outlook on the European market. In July, economists at Citigroup had predicted a 90 percent chance of Greece exiting the eurozone by mid-2013, but by late 2012, they said there was only a 60 percent change Greece would leave the eurozone by late 2014. "There is merit in cooperation and there is a need for multilateralism," said Jan Techau, director of the think tank Carnegie Europe.

REACTION

Criticism of the Nobel Committee decision was swift and widespread. In 2009, when the committee chose to award U.S. President Barack Obama only months after he took office, critics said that the committee was veering away from Alfred Nobel's original intent and instead playing politics. Those same criticisms were raised after the 2012 announcement by those who noted that not only were Europe's largest economic powers imposing strict restrictions on struggling markets in countries such as Greece and Italy, in terms of its peace record, the European Union did not always act alone to head off conflict, as in the case when it asked the United States to help settle the Balkans conflict. "Today's award of the Nobel Peace Prize to the EU is an insult to the people of Europe themselves, who currently are experiencing an undeclared war as a result of the barbaric, anti-social austerity policies that are destroying social cohesion and democracy," said Rania Svigkou, a spokesperson for Greece's far-left Syriza party. Marine Le Pen, leader of France's extreme nationalist National Front party, said the award "demonstrates great cynicism toward the millions of Europeans who are suffering mortally" due to the ongoing financial crisis. In Norway, the home of the Peace Prize, where voters twice rejected joining the European Union, only one in four citizens polled had a positive view of the 2012 decision.

Three former Nobel Peace Prize laureates issued an open letter to the Nobel Foundation, saying that the European Union was "clearly not one of the 'champions of peace' Alfred Nobel had in mind" when creating the prize and that the 2012 award would not "realize Nobel's demilitarized global peace order." The trio, including Archbishop

Desmond Tutu of South Africa, Mairead Maguire of Northern Ireland, and Adolfo Perez Esquivel of Argentina, called on the Nobel Committee to rescind the award and not pay out the $1.2 million prize.

European leaders, however, celebrated the prize as an indication that the struggle to bring the continent together over the past sixty years had paid off, and that continued cohesion was necessary. François Hollande, France's new president, said the award "commits us all to continue toward a Europe more united, more just, stronger and more capable of peacemaking." German Finance Minister Wolfgang Schäuble said the prize "reminds us that the EU is endlessly more than [interest-rate] spreads and bailout funds."

Nobel Peace Prize Ceremony

In presenting the award, Jagland spoke of the desire of European leaders post–World War II to bring the continent's nations together by fostering political, commercial, and social links that would help ensure the nations would never go to war with one another again. The foundations for the European Union are rooted in the decision of Germany and France to align their coal and steel industries, which resulted in the formation of the Coal and Steel Community of 1951. "The reconciliation between Germany and France is probably the most dramatic example in history to show that war and conflict can be turned so rapidly into peace and cooperation," Jagland said. By 1957, the west portion of the continent had formed a common market and opened trade with the signing of the Treaty of Rome. It was not until 1993 that this common market officially became the European Union, and in 2000, the common currency, the euro, was introduced. As Western European nations continued to work together toward common social and economic goals, Eastern European nations slowly followed, hastened by the fall of the Berlin Wall in 1989. Surprising many in Europe, divisions between the East and West quickly dissolved. "Events during the months and years following the fall of the Berlin Wall may have amounted to the greatest act of solidarity ever on the European continent," said Jagland.

Jagland called on the EU member states to maintain their togetherness to stand up to the challenges they were facing, from the financial crisis to the still unsettled issue of peace in the Balkans, Kosovo, and Bosnia-Hercegovina. "The Balkans were and are a complicated region. Unresolved conflicts remain. . . . [T]he status of Kosovo is still not finally settled. Bosnia-Hercegovina is a state that hardly functions owing to the veto the three population groups have become entitled to exercise against each other." Jagland concluded,

> We are not gathered here today in the belief that the EU is perfect. We are gathered in the belief that here in Europe we must solve our problems together. For that purpose we need institutions that can enter into the necessary compromises. We need institutions to ensure that both nation-states and individuals exercise self-control and moderation. . . . What this continent has achieved is truly fantastic, from being a continent of war to becoming a continent of peace.

Presidents Van Rompuy and Barroso accepted the award on behalf of the European Union. Van Rompuy took the stage first and said he accepted the award with "humility and gratitude." He continued, "At a time of uncertainty, this day reminds people across Europe and the world of the Union's fundamental purpose: to further the fraternity between European nations, now and in the future." Van Rompuy spoke of the past challenges facing Europe after World War II, as well as the financial and social unrest being experienced today. When Barroso took the stage, he said it was important to recognize that

> as a continent that went from devastation to become one of the world's strongest economies, with the most progressive social systems, being the world's largest aid donor, we have a special responsibility to millions of people in need. My message today is: you can count on our efforts to fight for lasting peace, freedom and justice in Europe and in the world. Over the past sixty years, the European project has shown that it is possible for peoples and nations to come together across borders. That it is possible to overcome the difference between "them" and us."

—Heather Kerrigan

Following is the text of the Nobel Peace Prize presentation speech delivered by Thorbjørn Jagland, chair of the Norwegian Nobel Committee, on December 10, 2012; and the text of the acceptance speech delivered by the president of the European Council, Herman Van Rompuy, and the president of the European Commission, José Manuel Durão Barroso, also on December 10, 2012.

DOCUMENT   *Nobel Peace Prize Presentation Speech*

December 10, 2012

Your Majesties, Your Royal Highnesses, Heads of State, Heads of Government, Excellencies, ladies and gentlemen,

Honourable Presidents of the European Union,

At a time when Europe is undergoing great difficulties, the Norwegian Nobel Committee has sought to call to mind what the European Union means for peace in Europe.

After the two world wars in the last century, the world had to turn away from nationalism and move in the direction of international cooperation. The United Nations were formed. The Universal Declaration of Human Rights was adopted.

For Europe, where both world wars had broken out, the new internationalism had to be a binding commitment. It had to build on human rights, democracy, and enforceable principles of the rule of law. And on economic cooperation aimed at making the countries equal partners in the European marketplace. By these means the countries would be bound together so as to make new wars impossible.

The Coal and Steel Community of 1951 marked the start of a process of reconciliation which has continued right to the present day. Beginning in Western Europe, the process continued across the east-west divide when the Berlin Wall fell, and has currently reached the Balkans, where there were bloody wars less than 15 to 20 years ago.

The EU has constantly been a central driving force throughout these processes of reconciliation.

The EU has in fact helped to bring about both the "fraternity between nations" and the "promotion of peace congresses" of which Alfred Nobel wrote in his will.

The Nobel Peace Prize is therefore both deserved and necessary. We offer our congratulations.

In the light of the financial crisis that is affecting so many innocent people, we can see that the political framework in which the Union is rooted is more important now than ever. We must stand together. We have collective responsibility. Without this European cooperation, the result might easily have been new protectionism, new nationalism, with the risk that the ground gained would be lost.

We know from the inter-war years that this is what can happen when ordinary people pay the bills for a financial crisis triggered by others. But the solution now as then is not for the countries to act on their own at the expense of others. Nor for vulnerable minorities to be given the blame.

That would lead us into yesterday's traps.

Europe needs to move forward.

Safeguard what has been gained.

And improve what has been created, enabling us to solve the problems threatening the European community today.

This is the only way to solve the problems created by the financial crisis, to everyone's benefit.

In 1926, the Norwegian Nobel Committee awarded the Peace Prize to the Foreign Ministers of France and Germany, Aristide Briand and Gustav Stresemann, and the following year to Ferdinand Buisson and Ludwig Quidde, all for their efforts to advance Franco-German reconciliation.

In the 1930s the reconciliation degenerated into conflict and war.

After the Second World War, the reconciliation between Germany and France laid the very foundations for European integration. The two countries had waged three wars in the space of 70 years: the Franco-Prussian war in 1870–71, then the First and Second World Wars.

In the first years after 1945, it was very tempting to continue along the same track, emphasizing revenge and conflict. Then, on the 9th of May 1950, the French Foreign Minister Robert Schuman presented the plans for a Coal and Steel Community.

The governments in Paris and Bonn decided to set history on a completely different course by placing the production of coal and steel under a joint authority. The principal elements of armaments production were to form the beams of a structure for peace. Economic cooperation would from then on prevent new wars and conflicts in Europe, as Schuman put it in his 9th of May speech: "The solidarity in production thus established will make it plain that any war between France and Germany becomes not merely unthinkable, but materially impossible."

The reconciliation between Germany and France is probably the most dramatic example in history to show that war and conflict can be turned so rapidly into peace and cooperation.

The presence here today of German Chancellor Angela Merkel and French President François Hollande makes this day particularly symbolic.

The next step after the Coal and Steel Community was the signing of the Treaty of Rome on the 25th of March 1957. The four freedoms were now established. Borders were to be opened, and the whole economy, not just the coal and steel industry, was to be woven into a whole. The six heads of state, of Germany, France, Italy, the Netherlands, Belgium and Luxembourg, wrote that they "by thus pooling their resources to preserve and strengthen peace and liberty, and calling upon the other peoples of Europe who share their ideal to join in their efforts, have decided to create a European Economic Community. . . ."

In 1973, Great Britain, Ireland and Denmark decided to respond to this call.

Greece joined in 1981, and Spain and Portugal in 1986. Membership of the EEC and EU was the right of all European countries "whose system of government is founded on the principles of democracy" and who accept the conditions for membership. Membership consolidated democracy in these countries, not least through the generous support schemes from which Greece, Portugal and Spain were able to benefit.

The next step forward came when the Berlin Wall fell in the course of a miraculous half year in 1989. Opportunities opened up for the neutral countries Sweden, Finland and Austria to become members.

But the new democracies, too, wished to become parts of the West, militarily, economically and culturally. In that connection membership of the EU was a self-evident objective. And a means, enabling the transition to democracy to be made as painlessly as possible. If they were left to themselves, nobody could be certain how things would turn out.

For history has taught us: freedom comes at a price.

The difference is very marked between what happened after the fall of the Berlin Wall and what is now happening in the countries of the Arab world. The Eastern European countries were quickly able to participate in a European community of values, join in a large market, and benefit from economic support. The new democracies in the vicinity of Europe have no such safe haven to make for. The transition to democracy also looks like being long and painful and has already triggered war and conflict.

In Europe the division between east and west was broken down more quickly than anyone could have anticipated. Democracy has been strengthened in a region where democratic traditions were very limited; the many disputes over ethnicity and nationality that had so troubled the region have largely been settled.

Mikhail Gorbachev created the external conditions for the emancipation of Eastern Europe, and national leaders headed by Lech Walesa took the necessary local initiatives. Both Walesa and Gorbachev received their well-deserved Peace Prizes.

Now at last it is the EU's turn. Events during the months and years following the fall of the Berlin Wall may have amounted to the greatest act of solidarity ever on the European continent.

This collective effort could not have come about without the political and economic weight of the EU behind it.

On this day we must also pay tribute to the Federal Republic of Germany and its Chancellor Helmut Kohl for assuming responsibility and accepting the enormous costs on behalf of the inhabitants of the Federal Republic when East Germany was included practically overnight in a united Germany.

Not everything was settled yet, however. With the fall of communism an old problem returned: the Balkans. Tito's authoritarian rule had kept a lid on the many ethnic conflicts. When that lid was lifted, violent conflicts blazed up again the like of which we had thought we would never see again in a free Europe.

Five wars were in fact fought in the space of a few years. We will never forget Srebrenica, where 8,000 Muslims were massacred in a single day.

Now, however, the EU is seeking to lay the foundations for peace also in the Balkans. Slovenia joined the EU in 2004. Croatia will become a member in 2013. Montenegro has opened membership negotiations, and Serbia and the Former Yugoslav Republic of Macedonia have been given candidate status.

The Balkans were and are a complicated region. Unresolved conflicts remain. Suffice it to mention that the status of Kosovo is still not finally settled. Bosnia-Hercegovina is a state that hardly functions owing to the veto the three population groups have become entitled to exercise against each other.

The paramount solution is to extend the process of integration that has applied in the rest of Europe. Borders become less absolute; which population group one belongs to no longer determines one's security.

The EU must accordingly play a main part here, too, to bring about not only an armistice but real peace.

For several decades Turkey and the EU have been discussing their relations to each other. After the new government, headed by the AKP party, won a clear parliamentary majority, the aim of EU membership has provided a guideline for the process of reform in Turkey. There can be no doubt that this has contributed to strengthening the development of democracy there. This benefits Europe, but success in this respect is also important to developments in the Middle East.

The Norwegian Nobel Committee has time and again presented the Peace Prize to champions of human rights. Now the prize is going to an organization of which one cannot become a member without first having adapted all one's legislation to the Universal Declaration of Human Rights and the European Convention on Human Rights.

But human rights as such are not enough. We can see this now that country after country is undergoing serious social unrest because misplaced policies, corruption and tax evasion have led to money being poured into gaping black holes.

This leads, understandably, to protests. Demonstrations are part of democracy. The task of politics is to transform the protests into concrete political action.

The way out of the difficulties is not to dismantle the European institutions.

We need to maintain solidarity across borders, as the Union is doing by cancelling debts and adopting other concrete support measures, and by formulating the framework for a finance industry on which we all depend. Unfaithful servants must be removed. These are preconditions for the continuing belief of the European masses in the compromises and moderation which the Union is now demanding of them.

Your Majesties, Your Royal Highnesses, Heads of Government and Heads of State, ladies and gentlemen, Honourable Presidents of the European Union,

Jean Monnet said that "nothing can be achieved without people, but nothing becomes permanent without institutions."

We are not gathered here today in the belief that the EU is perfect. We are gathered in the belief that here in Europe we must solve our problems together. For that purpose we need institutions that can enter into the necessary compromises. We need institutions to ensure that both nation-states and individuals exercise self-control and moderation. In a world of so many dangers, compromise, self-control and moderation are the principal needs of the 21st century.

80 million people had to pay the price for the exercise of extremism.

Together we must ensure that we do not lose what we have built on the ruins of the two world wars.

What this continent has achieved is truly fantastic, from being a continent of war to becoming a continent of peace. In this process the European Union has figured most prominently. It therefore deserves the Nobel Peace Prize.

The frescos on the walls here in the Oslo City Hall are inspired by Ambrogio Lorenzetti's frescos from the 1300s in the Siena town hall, named "Allegory of the effects of good government." The fresco shows a living medieval town, with the gates in the wall invitingly wide open to spirited people bringing the harvest in from fruitful fields. But Lorenzetti painted another picture: "Allegory of the effects of bad government." It shows Siena in chaos, closed and ravaged by the plague, destroyed by a struggle for power and war.

The two pictures are meant to remind us that it is up to ourselves whether or not we are to live in well-ordered circumstances.

May good government win in Europe. We are bound to live together on this continent.

Living together

Vivre ensemble

Zusammenleben

Convivencia Birlikte

Yasamak

Git'vemeste

Leve sammen

Congratulations to Europe. In the end we decided to live together.
May other continents follow.
Thank you for your attention.

SOURCE: Nobel Foundation. "Presentation Speech by Thorbjørn Jagland, Chairman of the Norwegian Nobel Committee." December 10, 2012. http://www.nobelprize.org/nobel_prizes/peace/laureates/2012/presentation-speech.html.

DOCUMENT   *EU Leaders Accept Nobel Peace Prize*

December 10, 2012

[President Von Rompuy takes the floor]

Your Majesties, Your Royal Highnesses, Heads of State and Government, Members of the Norwegian Nobel Committee, Excellencies, Ladies and Gentlemen,

It is with humility and gratitude that we stand here together, to receive this award on behalf of the European Union.

At a time of uncertainty, this day reminds people across Europe and the world of the Union's fundamental purpose: to further the fraternity between European nations, now and in the future.

It is our work today. It has been the work of generations before us. And it will be the work of generations after us.

Here in Oslo, I want to pay homage to all the Europeans who dreamt of a continent at peace with itself, and to all those who day by day make this dream a reality. This award belongs to them.

* * *

War is as old as Europe. Our continent bears the scars of spears and swords, canons and guns, trenches and tanks, and more.

The tragedy of it all resonates in the words of Herodotus, 25 centuries ago: *"In peace, sons bury their fathers. In war, fathers bury their sons."*

Yet, after two terrible wars engulfed the continent and the world with it, . . . finally lasting peace came to Europe.

In those grey days, its cities were in ruins, the hearts of many still simmering with mourning and resentment. How difficult it then seemed, as Winston Churchill said, "to regain the simple joys and hopes that make life worth living."

As a child born in Belgium just after the war, I heard the stories first-hand. My grand-mother spoke about the Great War. In 1940, my father, then seventeen, had to dig his own grave. He got away; otherwise I would not be here today.

So what a bold bet it was, for Europe's Founders, to say, yes, we can break this endless cycle of violence, we can stop the logic of vengeance, we can build a brighter future, together. What power of the imagination.

Of course, peace might have come to Europe without the Union. Maybe. We will never know. But it would never have been of the same quality. A lasting peace, not a frosty cease-fire. To me, what makes it so special, is reconciliation.

In politics as in life, reconciliation is the most difficult thing. It goes beyond forgiving and forgetting, or simply turning the page.

To think of what France and Germany had gone through, and then take this step. Signing a Treaty of Friendship. Each time I hear these words—*Freundschaft, Amitié*—I am moved. They are private words, not for treaties between nations.

But the will to not let history repeat itself, to do something radically new, was *so* strong that new words had to be found. For people Europe was a promise, Europe equalled hope.

When Konrad Adenauer came to Paris to conclude the Coal and Steel Treaty, in 1951, one evening he found a gift waiting at his hotel. It was a war medal, *une Croix de Guerre,* that had belonged to a French soldier. His daughter, a young student, had left it with a little note for the Chancellor, as a gesture of reconciliation and hope.

I can see many other stirring images before me. Leaders of six States assembled to open a new future, in Rome, *città eternal.* Willy Brandt kneeling down in Warsaw. The dockers of Gdansk, at the gates of their shipyard. Mitterrand and Kohl hand in hand. Two million people linking Tallinn to Riga to Vilnius in a human chain, in 1989. These moments healed Europe.

But symbolic gestures alone cannot cement peace. This is where the European Union's "secret weapon" comes into play: an unrivalled way of binding our interests so tightly that war becomes materially impossible. Through constant negotiations, on ever more topics, between ever more countries.

It's the golden rule of Jean Monnet: *"Mieux vaut se disputer autour d'une table que sur un champ de bataille."* ("Better fight around a table than on a battle-field.") If I had to explain it to Alfred Nobel, I would say: not just a peace congress, a perpetual peace congress!

Admittedly, some aspects can be puzzling, and not only to outsiders. Ministers from landlocked countries passionately discussing fish-quota. Europarlementarians from Scandinavia debating the price of olive oil. The Union has perfected the art of compromise.

No drama of victory or defeat, but ensuring all countries emerge victorious from talks. For this, boring politics is only a small price to pay. It worked. Peace is now self-evident. War has become inconceivable. Yet "inconceivable" does not mean "impossible."

And that is why we are gathered here today. Europe must keep its promise of peace. I believe this is still our Union's ultimate purpose. But Europe can no longer rely on this promise alone to inspire citizens.

In a way, it's a good thing; war-time memories are fading. Even if not yet everywhere. Soviet rule over Eastern Europe ended just two decades ago. Horrendous massacres took place in the Balkans shortly after. The children born at the time of Srebrenica will only turn eighteen next year. But they already have little brothers and sisters born after that war: the first real post-war generation of Europe. This must remain so.

So, where there was war, there is now peace. But another historic task now lies ahead of us: keeping peace where there *is* peace.

After all, history is not a novel, a book we can close after a Happy Ending: we remain fully responsible for what is yet to come.

This couldn't be more clear than it is today, when we are hit by the worst economic crisis in two generations, causing great hardship among our people, and putting the political bonds of our Union to the test.

Parents struggling to make ends meet, workers recently laid off, students who fear that, however hard they try, they won't get that first job: when they think about Europe, peace is not the first thing that comes to mind. . . .

When prosperity and employment, the bedrock of our societies, appear threatened, it is natural to see a hardening of hearts, the narrowing of interests, even the return of long-forgotten fault-lines and stereotypes. For some, not only joint decisions, but the very fact of deciding jointly, may come into doubt. And while we must keep a sense of proportion—even such tensions don't take us back to the darkness of the past—the test Europe is currently facing is real.

If I can borrow the words of Abraham Lincoln at the time of another continental test, what is being assessed today is *"whether that Union, or any Union so conceived and so dedicated, can long endure."*

We answer with our deeds, confident we will succeed. We are working very hard to overcome the difficulties, to restore growth and jobs.

There is of course sheer necessity. But there is more that guides us: the will to remain masters of our own destiny, a sense of togetherness, and in a way speaking to us from the centuries, the idea of *Europa* itself.

The presence of so many European leaders here today underlines our common conviction: that we will come out of this together, and stronger. Strong enough in the world to defend our interests and promote our values. We all work to leave a better Europe for the children of today and those of tomorrow. So that, later, others might turn and judge: that generation, ours, preserved the promise of Europe.

Today's youth is already living in a new world. For them Europe is a daily reality. Not the constraint of being in the same boat. No, the richness of being able to freely share, travel and exchange. To share and shape a continent, experiences, a future.

Our continent, risen from the ashes after 1945 and united in 1989, has a great capacity to reinvent itself. It is to the next generations to take this common adventure further. I hope they will seize this responsibility with pride. And that they will be able to say, as we here today: *Ich bin ein Europäer. Je suis fier d'être européen. I am proud to be European.*

[*President Barroso takes the floor*]

"Peace is not mere absence of war, it is a virtue," wrote Spinoza: *"Pax enim non belli privatio, sed virtus est."* And he added it is *"a state of mind, a disposition for benevolence,*

confidence, justice." Indeed, there can only be true peace if people are confident. At peace with their political system. Reassured that their basic rights are respected.

The European Union is not only about peace among nations. It incarnates, as a political project, that particular state of mind that Spinoza was referring to. It embodies, as a community of values, this vision of freedom and justice.

I remember vividly in 1974 being in the mass of people, descending the streets in my native Lisbon, in Portugal, celebrating the democratic revolution and freedom. This same feeling of joy was experienced by the same generation in Spain and Greece. It was felt later in Central and Eastern Europe and in the Baltic States when they regained their independence. Several generations of Europeans have shown again and again that their choice for Europe was also a choice for freedom.

I will never forget Rostropovich playing Bach at the fallen Wall in Berlin. This image reminds the world that it was the quest for freedom and democracy that tore down the old divisions and made possible the reunification of the continent. Joining the European Union was essential for the consolidation of democracy in our countries.

Because it places the person and respect of human dignity at its heart. Because it gives a voice to differences while creating unity. And so, after reunification, Europe was able to breathe with both its lungs, as said by Karol Wojtyła. The European Union has become our common house. The "homeland of our homelands" as described by Václav Havel.

Our Union is more than an association of states. It is a new legal order, which is not based on the balance of power between nations but on the free consent of states to share sovereignty.

From pooling coal and steel, to abolishing internal borders, from six countries to soon twenty-eight with Croatia joining the family this has been a remarkable European journey which is leading us to an *"ever closer Union."* And today one of the most visible symbols of our unity is in everyone's hands. It is the Euro, the currency of our European Union. We will stand by it.

Peace cannot rest only on the good will of man. It needs to be grounded on a body of laws, on common interests and on a deeper sense of a community of destiny.

The genius of the founding fathers was precisely in understanding that to guarantee peace in the 20th century nations needed to think beyond the nation-state. As Walter Hallstein, the first President of the European Commission[,] said: *"Das System der Nationalstaaten hat den wichtigsten Test des 20. Jahrhunderts nicht bestanden ("The system of sovereign nation-states has failed the most important test of the 20th century").* And he added *"through two world wars it has proved itself unable to preserve peace."*

The uniqueness of the European project is to have combined the legitimacy of democratic States with the legitimacy of supranational institutions: the European Commission, the European Court of Justice. Supranational institutions that protect the general European interest, defend the European common good and embody the community of destiny. And alongside the European Council, where the governments are represented, we have over the years developed a unique transnational democracy symbolised by the directly elected European Parliament.

Our quest for European unity is not a perfect work of art; it is work in progress that demands constant and diligent tending. It is not an end in itself, but a means to higher ends. In many ways, it attests to the quest for a cosmopolitan order, in which one person's gain does not need to be another person's pain; in which abiding by common norms serves universal values.

That is why despite its imperfections, the European Union can be, and indeed is, a powerful inspiration for many around the world. Because the challenges faced from one region to the other may differ in scale but they do not differ in nature.

We all share the same planet. Poverty, organised crime, terrorism, climate change: these are problems that do not respect national borders. We share the same aspirations and universal values: these are progressively taking root in a growing number of countries all over the world. We share *"l'irréductible humain,"* the irreducible uniqueness of the human being. Beyond our nation, beyond our continent, we are all part of one mankind.

Jean Monnet[] ends his *Memoirs* with these words: *"Les nations souveraines du passé ne sont plus le cadre où peuvent se résoudre les problèmes du présent. Et la communauté elle-même n'est qu'une étape vers les formes d'organisation du monde de demain."* ("The sovereign nations of the past can no longer solve the problems of the present. And the [European] Community itself is only a stage on the way to the organised world of the future.")

This federalist and cosmopolitan vision is one of the most important contributions that the European Union can bring to a global order in the making.

The concrete engagement of the European Union in the world is deeply marked by our continent's tragic experience of extreme nationalism, wars and the absolute evil of the Shoah. It is inspired by our desire to avoid the same mistakes being made again.

That is the foundation of our multilateral approach for a globalisation based on the twin principles of global solidarity and global responsibility; that is what inspires our engagement with our neighbouring countries and international partners, from the Middle East to Asia, from Africa to the Americas.

It defines our stance against the death penalty and our support for international justice embodied by the International Court of Justice and the International Criminal Court[;] it drives our leadership in the fight against climate change and for food and energy security; it underpins our policies on disarmament and against nuclear proliferation.

As a continent that went from devastation to become one of the world's strongest economies, with the most progressive social systems, being the world's largest aid donor, we have a special responsibility to millions of people in need.

In the 21st century it is simply unacceptable to see parents powerless as their baby is dying of lack of basic medical care, mothers compelled to walk all day in the hope of getting food or clean water and boys and girls deprived of their childhood because they are forced to become adults ahead of time.

As a community of nations that has overcome war and fought totalitarianism, we will always stand by those who are in pursuit of peace and human dignity.

And let me say it from here today: the current situation in Syria is a stain on the world's conscience and the international community has a moral duty to address it.

And as today marks the international human rights day, more than any other day our thoughts go to the human rights' defenders all over the world who put their lives at risk to defend the values that we cherish. And no prison wall can silence their voice. We hear them in this room today.

And we also remember that last year on this very podium three women were honoured for their non-violent struggle for the safety of women and for women's rights. As a Union built on the founding value of equality between women and men, enshrined in the Treaty of Rome in 1957, we are committed to protecting women's rights all over the world and supporting women's empowerment. And we cherish the fundamental rights of those who are the most vulnerable, and hold the future in their hands: the children of this world.

As a successful example of peaceful reconciliation based on economic integration, we contribute to developing new forms of cooperation built on exchange of ideas, innovation and research. Science and culture are at the very core of the European openness: they enrich us as individuals and they create bonds beyond borders.

Humbled, and grateful for the award of the Nobel Peace Prize, there is no better place to share this vision than here in Norway, a country which has been giving so much to the cause of global peace.

The *"pacification of Europe"* was at the heart of Alfred Nobel's concerns. In an early version of his will, he even equated it to international peace.

This echoes the very first words of the Schuman Declaration, the founding document of the European Union. *"La paix mondiale."* *"World Peace,"* it says, *"cannot be safeguarded without the making of creative efforts proportionate to the dangers which threaten it."*

My message today is: you can count on our efforts to fight for lasting peace, freedom and justice in Europe and in the world.

Over the past sixty years, the European project has shown that it is possible for peoples and nations to come together across borders. That it is possible to overcome the differences between "them" and "us."

Here today, our hope, our commitment, is that, with all women and men of good will, the European Union will help the world come together.

SOURCE: Council of the European Union. "From War to Peace: A European Tale." December 10, 2012. http://www.consilium.europa.eu/uedocs/cms_data/docs/pressdata/en/ec/134126.pdf.

OTHER HISTORIC DOCUMENTS OF INTEREST

FROM THIS VOLUME

FROM PREVIOUS *HISTORIC DOCUMENTS*

Gov. Malloy and President Obama Remark on Sandy Hook School Shooting

DECEMBER 15 AND 16, 2012

Throughout 2012, the United States experienced a rash of mass shootings that once again brought the long-standing debate between gun control and gun rights advocates to the forefront. On April 2, Oikos University dropout One L. Goh returned to the school's Oakland, California, campus, lined students up against a classroom wall, and shot them, killing seven and injuring three. On August 5, Wade Michael Page, a U.S. Army veteran involved in the white supremacist movement, entered a Sikh temple in Oak Creek, Wisconsin, just before Sunday service and opened fire, killing six people and injuring three before taking his own life. After learning he was being fired from his job at a sign-making company, Andrew Engeldinger shot and killed six people at the business on September 27 then killed himself. Yet perhaps no shootings captured the attention of policymakers, the media, and the general public more than two of the deadliest shootings in U.S. history—one at a Colorado movie theater and one at a Connecticut elementary school. The shootings revived what had been a dormant debate on Capitol Hill over whether tighter regulations of guns and ammunition were needed to stop the violence or whether other measures would be more effective.

AURORA, COLORADO

On July 20, a man dressed in black entered the Century 16 movie theater in Aurora, Colorado, during a midnight showing of the newly released Batman film, *The Dark Knight Rises*. According to police, he wore a gas mask and other protective gear, and he "threw some type of gas or explosive device" before opening fire on the audience. The shooting began about twenty minutes into the movie, leading many patrons to think it was part of the film. Salina Jordan, a patron in the adjacent theater, later said, "We thought it was a special effect because they were trying to do it up big for opening night." The shooter killed twelve people, ten of whom died at the theater, and injured another fifty-eight.

Shortly after the shooting occurred, police took twenty-four-year-old James Eagan Holmes, who had dyed his hair an orange-red color like Batman's archenemy the Joker, into custody in a parking lot behind the theater. Holmes was a PhD candidate at the University of Colorado who had been studying neuroscience, but he was in the process of withdrawing after a poor performance on his spring comprehensive exams. He had no criminal record and had been a gifted student, earning a merit scholarship to the University of California, Riverside, and graduating with honors before receiving funding support from the National Institutes of Health to attend the University of Colorado. Yet Holmes had begun receiving poor test scores during his spring semester, and one professor said school staff had considered putting him on academic probation. One faculty member who had taught Holmes told the *Washington Post* that he was "very quiet, strangely quiet in class," and that he seemed "socially off." Holmes's psychiatrist had reportedly told at least one member of the university's threat assessment team before the shooting that he was concerned Holmes might be dangerous, and Holmes had also been seeing Lynne Fenton, the university's medical director of student mental health services.

Federal officials said Holmes had bought a ticket and entered the theater like other patrons, but he left through an emergency exit at the front of the theater through which he would later return. Police found two Glock pistols, a Remington 12-gauge shotgun, and a Smith & Wesson AR-15 assault rifle at the scene and said there was evidence that the shotgun, assault rifle, and at least one of the pistols had been used during the shooting. All four guns had been legally purchased, along with approximately 6,000 rounds of ammunition.

"This is not only an act of extreme violence, it is also an act of depravity," said Colorado Governor John Hickenlooper. "It is beyond the power of words to fully express our sorrow this morning." Both President Barack Obama and Republican presidential candidate Mitt Romney spoke about the shooting during previously scheduled campaign stops, though they cancelled several other events, and both stopped airing campaign advertisements in Colorado. "There are going to be other days for politics," said President Obama. "This, I think, is a day for prayer and reflection." Neither candidate mentioned gun control issues at the time, though New York City Mayor Michael Bloomberg was among those trying to raise the issue. "No matter where you stand on the Second Amendment, no matter where you stand on guns, we have a right to hear from both of them concretely, not just in generalities—specifically, what are they going to do about guns?" Congressional Democrats were also quiet on the issue.

NEWTOWN, CONNECTICUT

Nearly five months later, another shooting drew even more attention to gun violence in the country. Around 9:30 a.m. on December 14, twenty-year-old Adam Lanza shot his way into Sandy Hook Elementary School in Newtown, Connecticut. Within the next hour, Lanza killed twenty six- and seven-year-old students and six adults before killing himself. During the shooting, teachers tried locking the doors to their classrooms, turning off lights, and closing blinds to prevent Lanza from entering. Some also tried to protect their students by hiding them in closets and in bathrooms. Police later reported that all of Lanza's victims had been shot more than once with a Bushmaster .223 caliber rifle, a semi-automatic weapon, and that some had been shot at close range. Lanza reportedly also brought a Glock 10mm and a Sig-Sauer 9mm handgun into the school. All of the guns were registered to Nancy Lanza, Adam's mother, and had been taken from her gun cabinet. It was later discovered that Lanza had shot his mother at their house before heading to the school. Initial reports suggested Nancy Lanza was or had been a teacher at Sandy Hook, but the school district superintendent later said that was not the case.

Former classmates described Lanza as an awkward student without close friends and told reporters that it was their understanding that he had Asperger's syndrome, a high-functioning form of autism. Lanza had been active in his high school's technology club; the club's adviser noted that Lanza had "some disabilities" and would have "episodes" during which he would completely withdraw from everyone. Lanza dropped out of the Newtown school system during high school, and he was homeschooled for a time by his mother, a gun enthusiast who also took Lanza and his brother to shooting ranges.

Investigators recovered a hard drive from a computer belonging to Lanza, but the device had practically been destroyed, leading some to question whether it could provide any evidence of a motive or Lanza's planning.

The country reacted to the news in horror and disbelief. "Those educators, and those innocent little boys and girls were taken from their families far too soon," said Connecticut Governor Dannel Malloy. "Let us all hope and pray those children are now in a place where that innocence will forever be protected." During an interfaith prayer vigil held in Newtown two days after the shooting, President Obama called for change. "These tragedies must end. And to end them, we must change," he said. "We will be told that the causes of such violence are complex, and that is true. No single law—no set of laws—can eliminate evil from the world or prevent every senseless act of violence in our society. But that can't be an excuse for inaction."

Gun Control and the NRA

Almost immediately following the shooting, politicians and pundits alike began speculating whether the president would pursue new gun regulations in the wake of the tragedy. In particular, many questioned whether he would pursue a renewal of the assault weapons ban that expired in 2004. In his first term, President Obama had signed more relaxed rules for guns into law, such as allowing people to carry concealed guns in national parks and on Amtrak trains, and during the 2012 campaign, he promised that he would not "take guns away" from gun owners. However, he had also expressed support for closing a loophole that did not require background checks for guns purchased at gun shows and for reinstating the assault weapons ban, though he made no effort to push those policies. Romney had signaled his strong support for protecting the Second Amendment earlier in the campaign. The issue also came up during the second presidential debate, two months before the shooting in Newtown, when an audience member asked the candidates about restricting access to assault rifles. President Obama offered some support for such restrictions, but he also said the United States needed to "enforce the laws we've already got" and emphasized the role of communities in preventing gun violence.

Democratic lawmakers and other elected officials quickly called for new gun regulations after the shooting. "The time to talk about it should have been after the last shooting or the shooting before that," said Rep. Carolyn McCarthy, D-N.Y. Mayor Bloomberg also called for immediate action and promised to spend his own money to support political candidates who were willing to oppose the powerful gun lobby. On December 17, Sen. Dianne Feinstein, D-Calif., announced that she would introduce an updated assault weapons ban when Congress reconvened in January 2013. Some who had previously been reluctant to support new gun measures seemed to shift their positions after Newtown. Rep. John Yarmuth, D-Ky., acknowledged that he had been "largely silent on the issue of gun violence over the past six years" and that he was "now as sorry for that as I am for what happened to the families who lost so much in this most recent, but sadly not isolated, tragedy."

Many Republicans, however, said more gun laws were not the answer. "We need real solutions to a significant problem in our country, and I'm not sure passing another law in Washington is going to actually find a real solution," said Sen. John Barrasso, R-Wyo. Sen. Lindsey Graham, R-S.C., said an assault weapons ban "doesn't make sense," adding, "The worst thing we can do is create a false sense of security. Every bad event in the world can't be fixed by government action."

One week after the shootings, the National Rifle Association (NRA) held a press conference at which Executive Vice President Wayne LaPierre laid out the organization's own policy recommendations. Arguing that "the only thing that stops a bad guy with a gun is a good guy with a gun," LaPierre called on Congress to "act immediately to appropriate whatever is necessary to put armed police officers in every single school in this nation." He said the NRA would develop and fund a national model school shield program to arm and train guards, who could include retired police officers and volunteers, in collaboration with schools, and that former congressman Asa Hutchinson would lead a task force to establish the program. During his remarks, LaPierre also blamed violent video games, the news media, and inadequate enforcement of existing laws as causes for mass shootings, but offered no support for gun-related legislative proposals. School administrators, law enforcement officials, and some politicians were critical of the NRA's proposed program. Ernest Logan, president of the Council of School Supervisors and Administrators, said it would "expose our children to far greater risk from gun violence than the very small risk they now face."

On December 19, President Obama announced that he was forming a task force that would be led by Vice President Joe Biden and would examine all possible solutions to gun violence, from gun restrictions to improving mental health programs, and societal factors such as entertainment media. The group would also involve the Departments of Justice, Education, Health and Human Services, and Homeland Security, and would bring outside groups and lawmakers together to discuss options. The president also called on lawmakers to reinstate the assault weapons ban, close loopholes in the nation's background check system, and restrict high-capacity ammunition clips.

The task force is set to announce its policy recommendations and proposals in January 2013.

—Linda Fecteau

Following is the text of remarks delivered by Connecticut Governor Dannel Malloy on December 15, 2012, following the shooting at Sandy Hook Elementary School in Newtown, Connecticut; and the text of a speech delivered by President Barack Obama on December 16, 2012, at a vigil for victims of the Newtown shooting.

DOCUMENT   *Gov. Malloy on Sandy Hook Shooting*

December 15, 2012

Yesterday an unspeakable tragedy occurred in the community of Newtown. 20 beautiful children and 7 wonderful adults lost their lives.

All of Connecticut's people—indeed the people of the world—weep for the immeasurable losses suffered by the families and loved ones of these victims.

Though we could all try, when something as senseless as this occurs, there's precious little anyone can say to the families of the victims that will lessen the horror and sense of loss they feel. We could say we feel their pain, but the truth is we can't.

When tragedies like this occur, people often look for answers, an explanation of how this could have occurred. But the sad truth is, there are no answers. No good ones, anyway.

We have all seen tragedies like this play out in other states and countries. Each time, we wondered how something so horrific could occur, and we thanked God that it didn't happen here in Connecticut. But now it has.

So what can we do? As was no doubt the case last night, we can hug someone we love a little tighter. As has been happening since yesterday, we can show and share with each other the grief we feel for the children and adults who were killed, and for their families and loved ones. We can speak about what's really important, and what can wait for another day.

There will be time soon for a discussion of the public policy issues surrounding yesterday's events, but what's important right now is this: love, courage, and compassion.

Love, as it has poured in from around the world.

Courage, as was demonstrated by the teachers and other adults in the school building, whose actions no doubt saved lives.

Courage on display, as it always is, by all our first-responders.

Compassion, as shown by people around Connecticut who've arrived in Newtown wanting only to help.

Too often, we focus on what divides us as people, instead of what binds us as human beings. What we saw yesterday were those bonds, that sense of community.

In the coming days, we will rely upon that which we have been taught and that which we inherently believe: that there is faith for a reason, and that faith is God's gift to all of us.

Those educators, and those innocent little boys and girls were taken from their families far too soon. Let us all hope and pray those children are now in a place where that innocence will forever be protected.

May God bless you, may God bless those 27 people, may God bless their families and friends, and may the pain their loved ones feel be someday absorbed by the love of mankind.

SOURCE: Office of the Governor of Connecticut. "Remarks of Governor Dannel P. Malloy on the Shooting in Newtown." December 15, 2012. http://www.governor.ct.gov/malloy/cwp/view.asp?A=11&Q=515560.

 **DOCUMENT**

President Obama Remarks at Newtown Vigil

December 16, 2012

Thank you, Governor. To all the families, first-responders; to the community of Newtown, clergy, guests—Scripture tells us: "Do not lose heart. Though outwardly we are wasting away, inwardly we are being renewed day by day. For our light and momentary troubles are achieving for us an eternal glory that far outweighs them all. So we fix our eyes not on what is seen, but on what is unseen, since what is seen is temporary, but what is unseen is eternal. For we know that if the earthly tent we live in is destroyed, we have a building from God, an eternal house in heaven, not built by human hands."

We gather here in memory of 20 beautiful children and 6 remarkable adults. They lost their lives in a school that could have been any school, in a quiet town full of good and decent people that could be any town in America.

Here in Newtown, I come to offer the love and prayers of a nation. I am very mindful that mere words cannot match the depths of your sorrow, nor can they heal your wounded hearts. I can only hope it helps for you to know that you're not alone in your grief; that our world too has been torn apart; that all across this land of ours, we have wept with you and we've pulled our children tight. And you must know that whatever measure of comfort we can provide, we will provide; whatever portion of sadness that we can share with you to ease this heavy load, we will gladly bear it. Newtown, you are not alone.

As these difficult days have unfolded, you've also inspired us with stories of strength and resolve and sacrifice. We know that when danger arrived in the halls of Sandy Hook Elementary, the school's staff did not flinch; they did not hesitate. Dawn Hochsprung and Mary Sherlach, Vicki Soto, Lauren Rousseau, Rachel D'Avino, and Anne Marie Murphy— they responded as we all hope we might respond in such terrifying circumstances: with courage and with love, giving their lives to protect the children in their care.

We know that there were other teachers who barricaded themselves inside classrooms and kept steady through it all and reassured their students by saying: "Wait for the good guys; they're coming." "Show me your smile."

And we know that good guys came: the first-responders who raced to the scene, helping to guide those in harm's way to safety and comfort those in need, holding at bay their own shock and their own trauma because they had a job to do and others needed them more.

And then, there were the scenes of the schoolchildren, helping one another, holding each other, dutifully following instructions in the way that young children sometimes do, one child even trying to encourage a grownup by saying: "I know karate. So it's okay. I'll lead the way out."

As a community, you've inspired us, Newtown. In the face of indescribable violence, in the face of unconscionable evil, you've looked out for each other, and you've cared for one another, and you've loved one another. This is how Newtown will be remembered. And with time and God's grace, that love will see you through.

But we as a nation, we are left with some hard questions. Someone once described the joy and anxiety of parenthood as the equivalent of having your heart outside of your body all the time, walking around. With their very first cry, this most precious, vital part of ourselves—our child—is suddenly exposed to the world, to possible mishap or malice. And every parent knows there is nothing we will not do to shield our children from harm. And yet we also know that with that child's very first step and each step after that, they're separating from us; that we won't—that we can't—always be there for them. They'll suffer sickness and setbacks and broken hearts and disappointments. And we learn that our most important job is to give them what they need to become self-reliant and capable and resilient, ready to face the world without fear.

And we know we can't do this by ourselves. It comes as a shock at a certain point where you realize, no matter how much you love these kids, you can't do it by yourself; that this job of keeping our children safe and teaching them well is something we can only do together, with the help of friends and neighbors, the help of a community, and the help of a nation. And in that way, we come to realize that we bear a responsibility for every child because we're counting on everybody else to help look after ours; that we're all parents; that they're all our children.

This is our first task: caring for our children. It's our first job. If we don't get that right, we don't get anything right. That's how, as a society, we will be judged.

And by that measure, can we truly say, as a nation, that we're meeting our obligations? Can we honestly say that we're doing enough to keep our children—all of them—safe from harm? Can we claim, as a nation, that we're all together there, letting them know that they are loved and teaching them to love in return? Can we say that we're truly doing enough to give all the children of this country the chance they deserve to live out their lives in happiness and with purpose?

I've been reflecting on this the last few days, and if we're honest with ourselves, the answer is no. We're not doing enough. And we will have to change.

Since I've been President, this is the fourth time we have come together to comfort a grieving community torn apart by mass shootings, the fourth time we've hugged survivors, the fourth time we've consoled the families of victims. And in between, there have been an endless series of deadly shootings across the country, almost daily reports of victims, many of them children, in small towns and big cities all across America, victims whose—much of the time, their only fault was being in the wrong place at the wrong time.

We can't tolerate this anymore. These tragedies must end. And to end them, we must change. We will be told that the causes of such violence are complex, and that is true. No single law—no set of laws—can eliminate evil from the world or prevent every senseless act of violence in our society.

But that can't be an excuse for inaction. Surely, we can do better than this. If there is even one step we can take to save another child or another parent or another town from the grief that's visited Tucson and Aurora and Oak Creek and Newtown and communities from Columbine to Blacksburg before that, then surely we have an obligation to try.

In the coming weeks, I will use whatever power this office holds to engage my fellow citizens—from law enforcement to mental health professionals to parents and educators—in an effort aimed at preventing more tragedies like this. Because what choice do we have? We can't accept events like this as routine. Are we really prepared to say that we're powerless in the face of such carnage, that the politics are too hard? Are we prepared to say that such violence visited on our children year after year after year is somehow the price of our freedom?

All the world's religions—so many of them represented here today—start with a simple question: Why are we here? What gives our life meaning? What gives our acts purpose? We know our time on this Earth is fleeting. We know that we will each have our share of pleasure and pain; that even after we chase after some earthly goal, whether it's wealth or power or fame or just simple comfort, we will in some fashion fall short of what we had hoped. We know that no matter how good our intentions, we'll all stumble sometimes, in some way. We'll make mistakes; we will experience hardships. And even when we're trying to do the right thing, we know that much of our time will be spent groping through the darkness, so often unable to discern God's heavenly plans.

There's only one thing we can be sure of, and that is the love that we have: for our children, for our families, for each other. The warmth of a small child's embrace: That is true. The memories we have of them, the joy that they bring, the wonder we see through their eyes, that fierce and boundless love we feel for them, a love that takes us out of ourselves and binds us to something larger—we know that's what matters. We know we're always doing right when we're taking care of them, when we're teaching them well, when we're showing acts of kindness. We don't go wrong when we do that.

That's what we can be sure of. And that's what you, the people of Newtown, have reminded us. That's how you've inspired us. You remind us what matters. And that's what should drive us forward in everything we do, for as long as God sees fit to keep us on this Earth.

"Let the little children come to me," Jesus said, "and do not hinder them—for to such belongs the Kingdom of Heaven."

Charlotte. Daniel. Olivia. Josephine. Ana. Dylan. Madeleine. Catherine. Chase. Jesse. James. Grace. Emilie. Jack. Noah. Caroline. Jessica. Benjamin. Avielle. Allison.

God has called them all home. For those of us who remain, let us find the strength to carry on and make our country worthy of their memory.

May God bless and keep those we've lost in His heavenly place. May He grace those we still have with His holy comfort. And may He bless and watch over this community and the United States of America.

SOURCE: Executive Office of the President. "Remarks at the Sandy Hook Interfaith Prayer Vigil in Newtown, Connecticut." December 16, 2012. *Compilation of Presidential Documents,* 2012, no. 00953 (December 16, 2012). http://www.gpo.gov/fdsys/pkg/DCPD-201200953/pdf/DCPD-201200953.pdf.

OTHER HISTORIC DOCUMENTS OF INTEREST

FROM THIS VOLUME

FROM PREVIOUS *HISTORIC DOCUMENTS*

United Nations Approves Intervention in Mali

DECEMBER 20, 2012

In late 2012, coup attempts in the Democratic Republic of the Congo (DRC), Central African Republic (CAR), and Mali came to a head. The DRC government was able to repel rebel forces that attempted an overthrow, but the CAR and Mali were not as successful, requiring international intervention. As of March 2013, despite a military intervention backed by the United Nations, Islamist rebels still controlled portions of northern Mali, and in the CAR, militant leaders declared themselves the official government.

UN Authorizes Military Intervention in Mali

In January 2012, rebel groups in northern Mali launched a campaign against the government to split the northern region, known as Azawad, from the south in an effort to form its own country. The group leading the effort was the National Movement for the Liberation of Azawad (MNLA), made up mainly of minority ethnic Tuaregs. The Tuaregs have lived in the northern part of the country for hundreds of years, establishing cities such as Timbuktu, but lost their independence when the French colonized the country in 1892. Since Mali declared itself liberated from the French in 1960, the Tuareg people have desired their own independence from the central government.

On March 22, 2012, one month before a presidential election was set to take place, the Tuareg rebel movement overthrew the government of Malian President Amadou Toumani Touré in a military-style coup. The rebels looted the presidential palace, took control of the north's three largest cities—Kidal, Gao, and Timbuktu—and invalidated the Malian constitution. The coup was "unanimously condemned" by United Nations, the Economic Community of West African States (ECOWAS), and the African Union (AU). ECOWAS demanded that the rebels hand control back to the rightful government or the country's borders would be closed and its assets frozen. Development funds to Mali from a variety of international organizations were suspended in response to the coup. On April 6, ECOWAS reached an agreement with the rebels, who announced that they had met their objectives. The MNLA ended its coup and declared the north independent. The AU refused to recognize the declaration of independence.

The Islamist group Ansar Dine initially supported the MNLA in its coup attempt. However, once the MNLA had secured northern Mali and driven out the central government's military, the group broke away and began imposing strict Islamist, or sharia, law. Other Islamist groups operating in the region, including Jihad in West Africa, an offshoot of al Qaeda in the Islamic Maghreb, joined Ansar Dine. Unable to reach a consensus on how northern Mali should be governed, the MNLA split from the Islamists and began fighting its former supporters for control of northern cities.

By midsummer, the Islamist fighters had overtaken most northern cities in Mali, forcing the MNLA to retreat. The MNLA attempted to merge the two groups, and a power-sharing treaty was signed, but violence continued to escalate. In October 2012, facing increasingly deadly attacks from the Islamists and protests from non-Tuareg people, the MNLA retreated to the northeastern city of Ménaka, where their supporters sought refuge from strict Islamist rule. In the fall of 2012, after various attempts to retake some northern cities, the MNLA changed its mission from independence to casting out the Islamists.

On October 12, 2012, the UN Security Council passed a resolution to allow for an African-led security force that would assist the Malian army in stopping the Islamists. This resolution did not give nations the power to use force to combat the militants. On December 20, 2012, however, the UN Security Council passed Resolution 2085, which "authorizes the deployment of an African-led International Support Mission in Mali (AFISMA) for an initial period of one year." The resolution gave the forces the mandate to use "all necessary measures" to take back the northern part of the country from "terrorist, extremist and armed groups."

Although the second resolution approved the use of force, it made clear that such tactics could be used only after all political methods were exhausted. The AFISMA was instructed to form a coalition with the MNLA and train Mali's army to combat the Islamist militants. Before any force would be used, according to the resolution, certain benchmarks would have to be met and military plans would have to be approved under a separate resolution. No UN funding was authorized for the mission, which angered African nations, but member states were called on to pay for the support mission.

On January 11, 2013, the French government sent a military unit to its former colony to help fight the Islamist militants. Support soon followed from the AU and ECOWAS, and the United Nations announced that it would accelerate plans to put the military portion of Resolution 2085 into action. The British, Canadian, Danish, and Belgian governments sent equipment to aid the French-led mission. The United States intensified its own involvement in the region, offering midair refueling to French planes and transport for the international coalition's troops. As of early March 2013, the Islamists had been driven from a number of major northern cities, but the Malian government was not yet fully in control of the region. An estimated 430,000 people have been displaced by the ongoing violence.

CENTRAL AFRICAN REPUBLIC REBELLION

The Central African Republic (CAR) has a long history of rebellions since its independence in 1960 from France. The president who was deposed in a coup in early 2013, François Bozizé, himself took power in 2003 in a coup. The unrest in the country is largely caused by rival ethnic groups and impoverished communities that believe the central government has overlooked their plight. From 2004 to 2007, the CAR was embroiled in a bush war led by the Union for Democratic Forces for Unity (UFDR) in response to Bozizé's power grab. A peace agreement was signed in 2007 that gave amnesty to the UFDR and allowed the militant group to function as a political party. Two other groups that fought alongside the UFDR, the Convention of Patriots for Justice and Peace (CPJP) and Union of Republican Forces (UFR), were also granted amnesty and were integrated into the CAR army.

As part of the agreement, Bozizé said he would release political prisoners and pay the rebels who agreed to end the violence. In late 2012, the three rebel groups from the Bush

War, known collectively as Seleka, took up arms against the government, claiming that it had not followed through on the 2007 agreement. Rebel groups began seizing towns in the northern portion of the country in early December, moving slowly toward the capital city of Bangui.

During the skirmish, citizens of CAR demanded assistance from the French, at one point throwing stones and burning tires in front of the French embassy, accusing their former colonizer of ignoring their calls for help. On December 27, President Bozizé directly appealed to both France and the United States for aid in warding off the rebel attacks. Both nations refused to offer assistance and began evacuating their citizens and other foreign nationals from the country. The United Nations followed suit, removing all non-essential personnel. CAR did receive assistance from some African nations, including Chad and South Africa, and aid from the Economic Community of Central African States (ECCAS), each of which sent a small number of troops to help protect the capital.

On December 30, Bozizé agreed to enter talks with the Seleka rebels with the goal of forming a coalition government to end the fighting. The peace talks opened on January 8 in Gabon, and a ceasefire was reached three days later. The conditions of the ceasefire included Bozizé maintaining his position as president until his term ended but appointing a Seleka leader as prime minister, the dissolution of the National Assembly, a new legislative election to be held within twelve months, the release of all political prisoners, and the end of foreign troop presence. Seleka rebels were also allowed to maintain control of any cities and towns they had occupied during the fighting.

On March 22, the rebels accused Bozizé of not upholding the ceasefire agreement and took up arms against the government. On March 24, the Seleka forces took control of the capital and Bozizé fled the country. The rebels immediately declared themselves the rightful government of the CAR.

DRC Government Faces Overthrow Attempt

Since the end of the Second Congo War in 2003, the government of the DRC has faced numerous mutinies and has managed to stop multiple rebel movements. In April 2012, a group of ethnic Tutsis took up arms against the central government, forming a rebel group called the March 23 Movement (M23), with the intent of "liberating" the Congolese people by overthrowing the government. Throughout the summer of 2012, rebels captured small towns in the North Kivu province, facing little resistance from government troops. On November 20, M23 took control of North Kivu's capital, Goma. UN peacekeepers stayed out of the fray, and the Congolese made little effort to stop the rebel movement. Demanding peace talks with the central government, M23 ordered the people of Goma to return to work, allowed aid workers to enter the region, and gave the UN peacekeeping forces permission to continue their patrols.

DRC president Joseph Kabila called on Goma's residents and military force to resist the takeover, as African organizations scrambled to determine the best method to stop any future fighting that could plunge the region back into a bloody conflict. On November 21, M23 announced that it would begin an effort to overtake South Kivu's capital, Bukavu. A government counterattack failed, and M23 responded that it "warns the government forces against this new military adventure. We must react with vigour to discourage this new war-like initiative." Despite promises to overthrow the government and without much negotiation, M23 withdrew from Goma on December 1, and was never able to fully control Bukavu.

In late February 2013, eleven African nations met to discuss a possible peace agreement for the DRC. The ceasefire was negotiated by the United Nations and called for new security reforms in the DRC and more cooperation from other African governments to increase stability in the region. These governments, however, were encouraged to stay out of the DRC's internal affairs. To date, the rebels remain engaged in on-again, off-again peace talks with the central government.

—Heather Kerrigan

Following is the text of a United Nations resolution, agreed to on December 20, 2012, offering assistance to Mali to combat Islamist extremists that had taken over the northern part of the country.

UN Security Council Passes Resolution Offering Assistance to Mali

December 20, 2012

Resolution 2085 (2012)

Adopted by the Security Council at its 6898th meeting, on 20 December 2012

The Security Council,

Recalling its resolutions 2056 (2012) and 2071 (2012), its Presidential Statements of 26 March 2012 (S/PRST/2012/7), 4 April 2012 (S/PRST/2012/9) as well as its Press Statements of 22 March 2012, 9 April 2012, 18 June 2012, 10 August 2012, 21 September 2012, 11 December 2012 on Mali,

Reaffirming its strong commitment to the sovereignty, unity and territorial integrity of Mali,

Emphasizing that the situation and entrenchment of terrorist groups and criminal networks in the north of Mali continue to pose a serious and urgent threat to the population throughout Mali, and to the stability in the Sahel region, the wider African region and the international community as a whole,

Condemning strongly the continued interference of members of the Malian Defence and Security Forces in the work of the Transitional authorities of Mali, stressing the need to work expeditiously toward the restoration of democratic governance and constitutional order in Mali and taking note of the on-going efforts of the Secretary-General, including through the Special Representative of the Secretary-General for West Africa, to assist the Transitional authorities of Mali in developing a roadmap for the electoral process and national dialogue,

Remaining seriously concerned over the insecurity and the significant ongoing humanitarian crisis in the Sahel region, which is further complicated by the presence of armed groups, including separatist movements, terrorist and criminal networks, and their increased activities, as well as the continued proliferation of weapons from within and outside the region that threaten peace, security, and stability of States in this region,

Condemning strongly all abuses of human rights in the north of Mali by armed rebels, terrorist and other extremist groups, including those involving violence against civilians, notably women and children, killings, hostage-taking, pillaging, theft, destruction of cultural and religious sites and recruitment of child soldiers, reiterating that some of such acts may amount to crimes under the Rome Statute and that their perpetrators must be held accountable and noting that the Transitional authorities of Mali referred the situation in Mali since January 2012 to the International Criminal Court on 13 July 2012,

Recalling the letter of the Transitional authorities of Mali dated 18 September 2012 addressed to the Secretary-General, requesting the authorization of deployment through a Security Council resolution, under Chapter VII as provided by the United Nations Charter, of an international military force to assist the Armed Forces of Mali to recover the occupied regions in the north of Mali and recalling also the letter of the Transitional authorities of Mali dated 12 October 2012 addressed to the Secretary-General, stressing the need to support, including through such an international military force, the national and international efforts to bring to justice the perpetrators of war crimes and crimes against humanity committed in the north of Mali,

Taking note of the endorsement of the Strategic Concept for the Resolution of the Crisis in Mali at the second meeting of the Support and Follow-Up Group on the Situation in Mali in Bamako on 19 October 2012, attended by ECOWAS Member States, countries of the region and other international partners, as well as its adoption by the African Union Peace and Security Council on 24 October 2012,

Taking note of the final communiqué of the Extraordinary Session of the authority of ECOWAS Heads of State and Government held in Abuja on 11 November 2012 and of the subsequent communiqué of the African Union Peace and Security Council on 13 November 2012 endorsing the Joint Strategic Concept of Operations for the International Military Force and the Malian Defence and Security forces,

Welcoming the appointment of Romano Prodi as Special Envoy of the Secretary General for the Sahel, as well as the appointment of Pierre Buyoya as High Representative of the African Union for Mali and the Sahel and encouraging them to work in close coordination with the Special Representative of the Secretary-General for West Africa and the ECOWAS mediator,

Welcoming the efforts of the ECOWAS-led mediation, with the support of the Special Representative of the Secretary-General for West Africa, the Organization of Islamic Cooperation (OIC) and neighbouring countries of Mali,

Taking note of the Secretary-General's report on Mali dated 28 November 2012 (S/2012/894) for continued action on the political and security tracks and a comprehensive solution to the crisis affecting Mali,

Emphasizing that the Malian authorities have primary responsibility for resolving the inter-linked crises facing the country and that any sustainable solution to the crisis in Mali should be Malian-led,

Encouraging the international community to provide support to resolve the crisis in Mali through coordinated actions for immediate and long-term needs, encompassing security, development and humanitarian issues,

Determining that the situation in Mali constitutes a threat to international peace and security,

Acting under Chapter VII of the Charter of the United Nations,

I. Political process

1.   *Urges* the transitional authorities of Mali, consistent with the Framework agreement of 6 April 2012 signed under the auspices of ECOWAS, to finalize a transitional roadmap through broad-based and inclusive political dialogue, to fully restore constitutional order and national unity, including through the holding of peaceful, credible and inclusive presidential and legislative elections, in accordance with the agreement mentioned above which calls for elections by April 2013 or as soon as technically possible, requests the Secretary-General, in close coordination with ECOWAS and the African Union, to continue to assist the transitional authorities of Mali in the preparation of such a roadmap, including the conduct of an electoral process based on consensually established ground rules and further urges the transitional authorities of Mali to ensure its timely implementation;

2.   *Demands* that Malian rebel groups cut off all ties to terrorist organizations, notably Al-Qaida in Islamic Maghreb (AQIM) and associated groups, and take concrete and visible steps to this effect, takes note of the listing of Movement of Unity and Jihad in Western Africa (MUJWA) on the Al-Qaida sanctions list established and maintained by the Committee pursuant to resolutions 1267 (1999) and 1989 (2011) and further reiterates its readiness to continue to adopt further targeted sanctions, under the above-mentioned regime, against those rebel groups and individuals who do not cut off all ties to al-Qaida and associated groups, including AQIM and MUJWA;

3.   *Urges* the transitional authorities of Mali to expeditiously put in place a credible framework for negotiations with all parties in the north of Mali who have cut off all ties to terrorist organizations, notably AQIM and associated groups including MUJWA, and who recognize, without conditions, the unity and territorial integrity of the Malian State, and with a view to addressing the long-standing concerns of communities in the north of Mali, and requests the Secretary-General, through his Special Representative for West Africa, in coordination with the ECOWAS Mediator and the High Representative of the African Union for Mali and the Sahel, and the OIC, to take appropriate steps to assist the transitional authorities of Mali to enhance their mediation capacity and to facilitate and strengthen such a dialogue;

4.   *Condemns* the circumstances that led to the resignation of the Prime Minister and the dismissal of the Government on 11 December 2012, reiterates its demand that no member of the Malian Armed Forces should interfere in the work of the Transitional authorities and expresses its readiness to consider appropriate measures, as necessary, against those who take action that undermines the peace, stability, and security, including those who prevent the implementation of the constitutional order in Mali;

5.   *Calls upon* all Member States to implement their obligations pursuant to resolution 1989 (2011) and 2083 (2012) and strongly condemns incidents of kidnapping and hostage taking by Al-Qaida in Mali and across the Sahel region with the aim of raising funds or gaining political concessions;

II. Security process

Training of Malian forces

6.   *Emphasises* that the consolidation and redeployment of the Malian Defence and Security forces throughout the Malian territory is vital to ensure Mali's long term security and stability and to protect the people of Mali;

7. *Urges* Member States, regional and international organizations to provide coordinated assistance, expertise, training, including on human rights and international humanitarian law, and capacity-building support to the Malian Defence and Security Forces, consistent with their domestic requirements, in order to restore the authority of the State of Mali over its entire national territory, to uphold the unity and territorial integrity of Mali and to reduce the threat posed by terrorist organizations and associated groups, further invites them to regularly inform the Secretariat of their contributions;

8. *Takes note* of the commitment of Member States and international organizations to the rebuilding of the capacities of the Malian Defence and Security forces, including the planned deployment by the European Union of a military mission to Mali to provide military training and advice to the Malian Defence and Security Forces;

Deployment of AFISMA

9. *Decides* to authorize the deployment of an African-led International Support Mission in Mali (AFISMA) for an initial period of one year, which shall take all necessary measures, in compliance with applicable international humanitarian law and human rights law and in full respect of the sovereignty, territorial integrity and unity of Mali to carry out the following tasks:

(a) To contribute to the rebuilding of the capacity of the Malian Defence and Security Forces, in close coordination with other international partners involved in this process, including the European Union and other Member States;

(b) To support the Malian authorities in recovering the areas in the north of its territory under the control of terrorist, extremist and armed groups and in reducing the threat posed by terrorist organizations, including AQIM, MUJWA and associated extremist groups, while taking appropriate measures to reduce the impact of military action upon the civilian population;

(c) To transition to stabilisation activities to support the Malian authorities in maintaining security and consolidate State authority through appropriate capacities;

(d) To support the Malian authorities in their primary responsibility to protect the population;

(e) To support the Malian authorities to create a secure environment for the civilian-led delivery of humanitarian assistance and the voluntary return of internally displaced persons and refugees, as requested, within its capabilities and in close coordination with humanitarian actors;

(f) To protect its personnel, facilities, premises, equipment and mission and to ensure the security and movement of its personnel;

10. *Requests* the African Union, in close coordination with ECOWAS, the Secretary-General and other international organizations and bilateral partners involved in the Malian crisis, to report to the Security Council every 60 days on the deployment and activities of AFISMA, including, before the commencement of offensive operations in the north of Mali, on: (i) the progress in the political process in Mali, including the roadmap for the restoration of constitutional order and negotiations between the Malian authorities and all parties in the north of Mali who have cut off all ties to terrorist organizations;

(ii) the effective training of military and police units of both AFISMA and the Malian defence and security forces in their obligations under international human rights, humanitarian and refugee law; (iii) the operational readiness of AFISMA, including the level of staffing leadership and equipment of the units, their operational adaptation to the climate and terrain conditions and ability to conduct joint armed operations with logistical, air and ground fire support; (iv) the efficiency of the chain of command of AFISMA, including its interaction with that of the Malian Defence and Security Forces and further expresses its willingness to monitor closely these benchmarks before the commencement of offensive operations in the north of Mali;

11. *Emphasizes* that the military planning will need to be further refined before the commencement of the offensive operation and requests that the Secretary-General, in close coordination with Mali, ECOWAS, the African Union, the neighbouring countries of Mali, other countries in the region and all other interested bilateral partners and international organizations, continue to support the planning and the preparations for the deployment of AFISMA, regularly inform the Council of the progress of the process, and requests that the Secretary-General also confirm in advance the Council's satisfaction with the planned military offensive operation;

12. *Requests* the Secretary-General to provide, as and when requested by the Malian authorities, support in critical areas that will be required to accompany or follow a military operation in the north of Mali, with respect to the extension of the Malian State authority, including rule of law and security institutions, mine action, promotion of national dialogue, regional cooperation, security sector reform, human rights and the initial demobilization, disarmament and reintegration of former combatants;

International support

13. *Calls upon* Member States, including from the Sahel region, to contribute troops to AFISMA in order to enable AFISMA to fulfil its mandate, welcomes the troop contributions already pledged by ECOWAS countries and further encourages Member States to cooperate closely with the African Union, ECOWAS, the United Nations, countries contributing troops and other donors to this end;

14. *Urges* Member States, regional and international organizations to provide coordinated support to AFISMA, including military training, provision of equipment, intelligence, logistical support and any necessary assistance in efforts to reduce the threat posed by terrorist organizations, including AQIM, MUJWA and associated extremist groups in accordance with paragraph 9 (b), in close coordination with AFISMA and the Malian authorities;

15. *Calls upon* the transitional authorities of Mali and all other parties in Mali to cooperate fully with the deployment and operations of AFISMA, in particular by ensuring its safety, security and freedom of movement with unhindered and immediate access throughout the territory of Mali to enable it to fully carry out its mandate and further calls upon neighbouring countries of Mali to take appropriate measures to support the implementation of AFISMA mandate;

16. *Demands* that all parties in Mali take appropriate steps to ensure the safety and security of humanitarian personnel and supplies, and further demands that all parties in Mali ensure safe and unhindered access for the delivery of humanitarian aid to persons in

need of assistance across Mali, consistent with international humanitarian, human rights and refugee law and the guiding principles of humanitarian assistance;

Human rights

17.   *Emphasizes* that the Malian authorities have primary responsibility to protect civilians in Mali, further recalls its resolutions 1674 (2006), 1738 (2006) and 1894 (2009) on the protection of civilians in armed conflict, its resolutions 1612 (2005), 1882 (2009) and 1998 (2010) on Children And Armed Conflict and its resolutions 1325 (2000), 1820 (2008), 1888 (2009), 1889 (2009), and 1960 (2010) on Women, Peace and Security, and calls upon all military forces in Mali to take them into account;

18.   *Emphasizes* that any support provided by the United Nations, regional and sub-regional organizations and Member States in the context of the military operation in Mali shall be consistent with international humanitarian and human rights law and refugee law, further requests the Secretary-General to ensure the relevant capacity within the United Nations presence as referred to in paragraph 23 below in order to observe adherence to international humanitarian and human rights law with regards to military operations in the north of Mali and include in his regular reports to the Security Council, as referred to in paragraph 24 below, the situation of civilians in the north of Mali and any violation of human rights law, international humanitarian law and refugee law in the north of Mali, as well as to advise on ways to mitigate any adverse impact of military operations on the civilian population, including on women and children;

19.   *Calls upon* AFISMA, consistent with its mandate, to support national and international efforts, including those of the International Criminal Court, to bring to justice perpetrators of serious human rights abuses and violations of international humanitarian law in Mali;

Funding

20.   *Calls upon* Member States and international organisations, to provide financial support and contributions in kind to AFISMA to enable its deployment and implementation of its mandate and welcomes the willingness of the European Union to provide such financial support to AFISMA through the mobilization of the African Peace Facility;

21.   *Expresses its intention* to consider the provision of a voluntary and a United Nations-funded logistics support packages to AFISMA, including equipment and services for an initial period of one year, takes note of the letter of the Secretary-General (S/2012/926) on the possible deployment of a logistics support package to AFISMA and on the support financial costs and, to this effect, requests the Secretary-General, in coordination with the African Union, ECOWAS and the Malian authorities, to further develop and refine options within 30 days of the adoption of this resolution for such a voluntary and a United Nations–funded logistics support packages, including detailed recommendations for a swift, transparent and effective implementation;

22.   *Requests* the Secretary-General to establish a trust fund through which Member States can provide earmarked and/or non-earmarked financial support to AFISMA and/ or to the training and equipping of Malian Defence and Security forces, also requests the Secretary-General to support, in coordination with the African Union and ECOWAS, the holding of a donors conference to solicit contributions to this trust fund as soon as

possible, calls upon Member States to contribute generously and promptly to the trust fund, while noting that the existence of the trust fund does not preclude the conclusion of direct bilateral arrangements and *further requests* the African Union, in consultation with ECOWAS and the Secretary-General, to submit budgetary request to this trust fund;

United Nations presence and reporting

23.   *Requests* the Secretary-General to establish, in consultation with the Malian authorities, a multidisciplinary United Nations presence in Mali, in order to provide coordinated and coherent support to (i) the on-going political process and (ii) the security process, consistent with paragraph 12 above and including support to the planning, deployment and operations of AFISMA and therefore requests the Secretary-General to submit as soon as possible specific and detailed proposals to the Council for further consideration;

24.   *Requests* the Secretary-General to keep the Council regularly informed of the situation in Mali and to report back to the Council, through the provision of written reports, every 90 days, on the implementation of this resolution, including on the United Nations support to the political and security efforts to solve the crisis in Mali, the deployment and preparation of AFISMA and updated information and recommendations related to a voluntary and United Nations–funded support packages to AFISMA;

25.   *Decides* to remain actively seized of the matter.

SOURCE: United Nations. Security Council. "Resolution 2085 (2012)." December 20, 2012. http://www .un.org/ga/search/view_doc.asp?symbol=S/RES/2085%20%282012%29.

OTHER HISTORIC DOCUMENTS OF INTEREST

FROM THIS VOLUME

- International Organizations Respond to Coup in Guinea-Bissau, p. 176

FROM PREVIOUS *HISTORIC DOCUMENTS*

- United Nations on the Violence in the Democratic Republic of the Congo, *2007*, p. 374
- United Nations on the al Qaeda Terrorist Network and the Taliban, *2004*, p. 534
- UN Secretary General on the Democratic Republic of the Congo, *2004*, p. 505
- UN Security Council on Threats to Peace in Congo, *2003*, p. 288

South Korea Elects First Female President

DECEMBER 28, 2012

On December 19, South Koreans went to the polls to elect a new president to replace Lee Myung-bak, a conservative leader of the Grand National Party who was required by law to leave office after one five-year term. The outgoing president had a mixed record, largely due to the political scandals that overshadowed the final years of his time in office. When the results of the 2012 election were finalized, Park Geun-hye, daughter of a former South Korean president, was the victor. Park became the first female president in South Korean history, a surprise for a country ranked near the bottom in the World Economic Forum's 2012 gender-gap rankings.

FORMER "FIRST LADY"

Park has spent a majority of her life in politics. In 1961, her father, Park Chung-hee, seized control of the country in a military coup. The elder Park was credited with quickly developing South Korea into the world's eleventh-largest economic power but also criticized for doing so at the expense of delaying democratization and suppressing dissidents. Under the president's watch, thousands who criticized his government were arrested and sometimes tortured. In 1974, while Park was studying abroad, her mother was killed by a North Korean sympathizer who was attempting to assassinate Park Chung-hee. Park assumed the position of First Lady, taking appointments with foreign dignitaries and representing the First Family at official functions. In 1979, Park's father was assassinated by his intelligence chief, although the reason behind the murder remains unknown. It has been reported that following her father's death, Park's first question was, "Is the border secure?" fearing a possible invasion from North Korea.

Following Park Chung-hee's death, Park disappeared from public life, only to reemerge in 1998 after being elected to South Korea's National Assembly. Park served four terms in the National Assembly; during a campaign stop in 2006, she was attacked by an ex-convict wielding a box cutter and received a ten-centimeter scar on her cheek. In 2007, Park challenged Lee to be the Grand National Party's nominee for the presidency. In a close vote, Park was edged out, and Lee went on to defeat his opponent, Chung Dong-young.

In 2011, Park was chosen as leader of the Grand National Party. In an effort to remake the party and distance it from some of Lee's far-right policies, Park led a charge to rename the party Saenuri, or New Frontier. The new name was adopted in February 2012. Even as public sentiment for Lee waned, Park was able to lead the Saenuri party to a surprise victory in legislative elections in April 2012, helping the party regain its legislative majority in the National Assembly.

CAMPAIGN AND CANDIDATES

Under party rules, those seeking the presidential nomination for the Saenuri party are chosen by a combination of votes in an electoral college and opinion poll results. There is no open primary system. In 2012, four candidates came forward seeking the nomination, with Park throwing her hat into the ring last. Park's primary challengers included Kim Moon-soo, a former labor activist; Chung Mong-joon, a member of the National Assembly; and Ahn Sang-soo, the former mayor of Incheon. The primary campaign saw the three challengers gang up on Park, attempting to paint her as too closely tied to her father's oppressive regime and forcing Park to make a public apology for the human rights violations that occurred under her father's watch. On August 20, Park was declared the official party nominee, who would face off against the winner of the liberal Democratic Unity Party primary. That primary featured Ahn Cheol-soo, a political novice and information technology (IT) entrepreneur, and Moon Jae-in, who was briefly jailed during Park's father's reign and served as chief of staff to a former president. In November, Ahn dropped out of the race, hoping to help party members unite behind Moon.

The presidential election revolved around two main issues—economic inequality and North Korea. Although a rising economic star—South Korea is the world's sixth-biggest exporter and is set to become the eighth-largest trading nation—South Korea faces a growing gap between its richest and poorest residents and has struggled to deliver on much-needed social welfare programs. Any economic changes moving forward would require addressing the nation's large and powerful conglomerates, like Samsung. These companies and their owners wield a great amount of power and influence in various aspects of Korean life. Historically, the Saenuri party has supported these companies, but as Park has realigned the party toward the center of the political spectrum, that position has been changing.

On North Korea, Moon and Park agreed on opening a dialogue with their northern neighbor but differed in their proposed approaches. Park wanted the North to agree to a number of conditions before the South would reopen communications and assistance programs, and also sought an apology from the North for its aggression over the past few years. Moon, on the other hand, wanted to refocus the dialogue on increasing economic ties without set conditions and said he would hold a summit with North Korean leaders during the five years of his presidency.

The campaign revealed a deep divide in the electorate by age. Park was most popular among those over age fifty who were more likely to recall her father's time in office as having positively transformed the country. Her opponent attracted younger voters who were born into relative affluence. The nation's breadwinners, those aged forty to forty-nine, were considered the deciding swing vote during the December 19 election.

Ultimately, the sixty-year-old conservative, who will lead South Korea for the next five years, won nearly 52 percent of the vote to Moon's 48 percent. The National Election Commission estimated turnout to be nearly 76 percent. Upon learning that she had defeated her challenger, Park did not deliver a formal victory speech, but she did address supporters briefly in Seoul, stating, "This is a victory brought by the people's hope for overcoming crisis and economic recovery." She promised to "definitely open an era of people's happiness in which everyone can enjoy some simple pleasures and their dreams can come true." The election marked the first time in the nation's history that a higher percentage of voters were over the age of fifty than under the age of forty. The Democratic Unity Party placed the blame for its loss on Ahn's late decision to leave the race, thus not giving the party enough time to challenge Park directly.

CHALLENGES FACING PARK

Park was officially sworn in on February 25, 2013, during a turbulent time in Asia when North Korea's new leader was continuing to test his power and defy international agreements. Prior to Lee's election, the North and South were engaged in an era of "sunshine policy," during which two summits were held, the South made economic investments in the North, and families split by the border were reunified. When Lee took office, he had immediately put a stop to these policies because North Korea refused to end its nuclear program. After the 2010 sinking of a South Korean naval vessel by a North Korean torpedo, Lee cut off nearly all trade. Park has tried to distance herself from Lee's policies, calling instead for the "100% completion of Korea," which the new president believes could help persuade North Korea to end or scale back its nuclear program, but said she would "not tolerate any action that threatens the lives of our people and the security of our nation." This completion program could involve reestablishing humanitarian aid and closer economic ties, but North Korea's nullification of the armistice ending the Korean War and declaration of war against the South in early 2013 will likely put these goals on hold.

South Korea was also facing a war of words with Japan over so-called comfort women who were forced to work as sex slaves for the Japanese military during World War II. Many of these women were from South Korea, and Japan's new president, Shinzo Abe, has denied their existence. Unlike North Korea, Japan has sent envoys to South Korea to diffuse tension over the question of sex slaves, as well as a continuing dispute over the ownership of a chain of islands.

How Park decides to engage with her Asian neighbors will have repercussions around the globe. "Korea is one of the most connected countries in the world," said Troy Stangarone of the Korea Economic Institute of America. "Both its role in Northeast Asia and globally will probably be shaped by the next administration."

Domestically, Park faces the challenges of a slowing economy, registering growth of 2 to 3 percent after experiencing decades of growth above 5 percent, and growing welfare costs for the aging population. Household debt in South Korea now accounts for more than 150 percent of disposable income, attributed to the nation's materialistic lifestyle, and among the Organization for Economic Co-operation and Development nations, South Korea spends the least on welfare. "Korea has become a republic of angry citizens," said Lee Chung-min, a professor at Yonsei University and a Park adviser. "Students are under great pressure to pass their exams; young couples struggle to find a home; people in their 40s are scared of losing their job; and seniors feel abandoned."

Unsurprisingly, Park has also promised to tackle gender issues. Although unmarried and childless herself, Park said that she wants to see the low birth rate increase and also wants to stop the flow of females out of the workforce. Many women graduate from top South Korean universities, but they face a male-driven culture that undervalues their work. Women serve in many low-wage jobs, earning on average 39 percent less than men, and are often without benefits. "Women can not only succeed as vibrant social leaders but simultaneously as nurturing mothers," said Park.

—Heather Kerrigan

Following is the text of a release from the South Korean National Election Commission on December 28, 2012, announcing Park Geun-hye as the victor in the 2012 presidential election.

Park Declared Winner in Presidential Election

December 28, 2012

The National Election Commission announced that Ms. Park Geun-hye, the Saenuri party's candidate[,] has won the 18th Presidential Election.

Ms[.] Park Geun-hye has gained 51.55% of the total valid votes, that is, 15,773,128 out of 30,721,459 votes. The Democratic United party's candidate, Moon Jae-in, on the other hand, has gained 48.02%, 14,690,000 votes. In addition, independent candidates Kang Ji-won has obtained 0.17% (53,303 votes) of the entire valid votes, Kim Soon-ja 0.15% (46,017 votes), Kim So-yeon 0.05% (16,687 votes) and Park Jong-sun 0.04% (12,854 votes).

The final voter turnout reached 75.8% with 30,721,459 out of 40,507,842 voters having cast their ballots. The figure has increased by 12.8% . . . from the turnout of 63.0% in the 17th Presidential Election and by 21.6% . . . from the turnout of 54.2% in the 19th National Assembly election.

Meanwhile, the Saenuri party's candidates Hong Jun-pyo has been elected as the governor of Gyeongsangnam-do and Moon Yong-Lin as the Superintendent of Education of Seoul in the Repeat & By-elections held simultaneously with the Presidential Election on December 19.

The election for the head of Gu/Si/Gun Office were also held, where the Saenuri party's candidate Kim Hong-Sub has been elected in Jung-gu Incheon, the Democratic United party's Noh Hee-yong in Dong-gu Gwangju and the independent candidate Choi Young-jo in Gyeongsan-si Gyeongsangbuk-do.

Two candidates of the Saenuri party have won the election for the Si/Do Assembly members held in two areas, while 9 Saenuri party's candidates, 6 Democratic United party's candidates, 2 Unified Progressive party's candidates and 2 independent candidates have been elected in the Gu/Si/Gun Assembly elections.

The list of elected candidates as well as the information on voting and counting for the Presidential Election and repeat & by-elections can be found on the NEC website (www.nec.go.kr).

SOURCE: Republic of Korea National Election Commission. "Ms. Park Geun-hye Wins the 18th Presidential Election." December 28, 2012. http://www.nec.go.kr/engvote_2013/04_news/02_02.jsp?num=271&pg=1&col=&sw=.

OTHER HISTORIC DOCUMENTS OF INTEREST

FROM THIS VOLUME

FROM PREVIOUS HISTORIC DOCUMENTS

Republicans and Democrats Announce Deal to Avert Fiscal Cliff

DECEMBER 31, 2012

In late 2012, the term *fiscal cliff* entered common parlance. It was the phrase used to describe a simultaneous increase in tax rates and decrease in government spending (known as the "sequester") set to take place in January 2013 because Congress had failed to agree on a variety of essential tax and spending packages in 2010 and 2011. According to the Congressional Budget Office (CBO), if Congress allowed the United States to go over the fiscal cliff, it would almost certainly mean another recession, at least in the short term, because 98 percent of Americans would see their taxes increase. In the long term, however, it would reduce the federal deficit by hundreds of billions of dollars. This balancing act played out between Republicans in Congress and Democrats in the White House who alternately offered various fixes to stave off the most significant impacts. It was not until the last moment, shortly before midnight on December 31, 2012, that the Senate announced a compromise and helped avert, at least for a while, the effects of the fiscal cliff.

How the United States Reached the Cliff

The fiscal cliff was precipitated by a number of previous congressional actions. In 2001, and subsequently in 2003, under the administration of then-president George W. Bush, Congress passed two tax cut packages, each of which significantly reduced tax rates for most Americans. These cuts included an income tax rate reduction and made changes to the capital gains tax. The cuts were set to expire in 2010. The Bush tax cuts did not make any changes to the alternative minimum tax (AMT), an Internal Revenue Service (IRS) provision that was meant to ensure wealthy Americans could not take advantage of an overabundance of tax breaks. Because the AMT was not adjusted to reflect the new tax rates, taxes went up for a number of upper-middle-class Americans.

Facing the expiration of the Bush tax cuts, in 2010, Congress passed the Tax Relief, Unemployment Insurance Reauthorization, and Job Creation Act of 2010. The law extended the tax cuts for two years, made some changes to the AMT through 2011 that would help upper-middle-class Americans, and added a one-year reduction of 2 percent in the Social Security payroll tax. In late 2011, a congressional showdown took place over the extension of the Social Security payroll tax. Democrats wanted to raise taxes on the highest income earners to cover some of the bill's spending provisions, while Republicans refused any such increase, arguing that such an increase would have a detrimental impact on the economy. Ultimately, in February 2012, Congress passed the Middle Class Tax Relief and Job Creation Act of 2012 to extend the 2 percent payroll tax. The 2012 legislation also extended unemployment benefits and further delayed a cut in Medicare physician reimbursement rates. There was no provision included to extend the AMT patch.

A decrease in overall revenue from the tax cuts, coupled with a necessary increase in spending to cover the nation's current liabilities, led to a congressional debate as to where the government could make cuts to shore up its deficit. On May 16, 2011, the United States officially reached its debt ceiling, a cap set by Congress that limits the amount the government can borrow. The Department of the Treasury was able to avoid a default until at least August 2 but warned that failing to raise the debt limit, as had been done seventy-eight times since 1960, could result in the government being unable to make necessary payments, including Social Security benefits. A congressional compromise to raise the debt ceiling required that the increase be offset by $1.2 trillion in spending cuts over the next decade. The Budget Control Act of 2011 also created the Joint Select Committee on Deficit Reduction, known as the "super committee," which would be responsible for recommending how cuts should be made and proposing legislation to do so. The super committee was given until November to present its recommendations, a deadline it failed to meet. As such, a provision of the Budget Control Act went into effect, meaning that the required $1.2 trillion in cuts would be automatically distributed evenly between defense and domestic spending. These across-the-board cuts, set to go into effect on January 2, 2013, were known as sequestration.

CBO Projections

Without congressional intervention prior to the end of the 112th Congress on January 3, 2013, the sequestration would automatically go into effect and, at the same time, 98 percent of Americans would see their taxes rise. In August 2012, the CBO released its annual baseline projections on the U.S. budget and economic outlook for fiscal years (FY) 2012 to 2022. The projection estimated a $1.1 trillion federal budget deficit for FY 2012, which ended on September 30, continued economic recovery, and low inflation. However, considering the impending fiscal cliff, the CBO estimated in its baseline what would happen if Congress did not act. The estimate includes a shrinking of the federal deficit to $641 billion in FY 2013, which would likely lead to a recession and rising unemployment.

In an unusual move, the CBO also released an alternative fiscal scenario to note what would happen if all expiring tax cuts were kept indefinitely, the AMT patch was extended, the Medicare reimbursement rates remained stable, and the sequester did not go into effect. Under this scenario, in 2013, the federal deficit would be $1 trillion and the economy would be stronger, resulting in real gross domestic product (GDP) growth of 1.7 percent between the end of 2012 and end of 2013. If this scenario was left intact, by the end of 2017, the U.S. unemployment rate would fall to 5.7. However, the positive economic growth would come at the cost of increasing the federal deficit, which would grow to approximately 5 percent of GDP rather than 1 percent of GDP under the baseline projection.

In its alternative fiscal scenario, the CBO noted that the federal deficit would remain high from 2014 through 2022, while unemployment would remain low. However, debt held by the public would grow and government outlays would also increase. In sum, the CBO said, if Congress followed the alternative path,

> the persistence of large budget deficits and rapidly escalating federal debt would hinder national saving and investment, thus reducing GDP and income relative to the levels that would occur with smaller deficits. In the later part of the projection period, the economy would grow more slowly than in CBO's baseline, and

interest rates would be higher. Ultimately, the policies assumed in the alternative fiscal scenario would lead to a level of federal debt that would be unsustainable from both a budgetary and an economic perspective.

Flurry of Plans

Five proposals were made by Democrats and Republicans to avert the fiscal cliff—three came from President Barack Obama and two from House Speaker John Boehner, R-Ohio. The first Obama plan was laid out to congressional leaders by Treasury Secretary Timothy Geithner on November 29 and included $425 billion in stimulus spending and tax extensions, more than $1.5 trillion in tax increases over ten years, and $350 billion in mandatory cuts to Social Security, Medicare, and Medicaid. The Obama plan would raise the marginal tax rates for top income earners, defer the sequester, and fix the AMT. A number of the proposals contained in the president's plan were featured in his FY 2013 budget proposal, which was rejected by Congress in early 2012.

In response, Republicans, led by Boehner, made a counteroffer on December 3 that included $850 billion in tax increases; more than $1 trillion in mandatory cuts to Social Security, Medicare, and Medicaid; and $300 billion in discretionary cuts. The plan would cut the deficit by $2.2 trillion over the next decade and would not increase most tax rates. Although the Republican plan would offer some tax relief to middle-class Americans, it would not raise taxes on the highest income earners as the president desired. According to White House spokesperson Amy Brundage, "The only thing preventing us from reaching a deal that averts the fiscal cliff and avoids a tax hike on 98 percent of Americans is the refusal of Congressional Republicans to ask the very wealthiest individuals to pay higher tax rates."

During the week of December 10, Obama and Boehner released revised plans. The second Obama plan reflected the first, except that he reduced his tax increase from $1.55 trillion to $1.4 trillion. The Boehner response on December 15 raised tax increases from $850 billion to $1 trillion, but did not indicate a split between discretionary and nondiscretionary spending cuts. In a bid to appease Democrats, some of the spending cuts and new revenue in the Boehner plan would come from allowing tax cuts for millionaires to expire.

Obama's final plan was released on December 17, followed one day later by the Republican proposal known as "Plan B." The two parties were slowly moving closer to an agreement, but a number of factors kept them from reaching a compromise—specifically, which high-income earners would see a tax increase. The final Obama plan reduced the stimulus programs he wanted from $425 billion to $175 billion and increased the mandatory cuts to Social Security, Medicare, and Medicaid from $350 billion to $725 billion. The offer dropped an earlier requirement to raise tax rates for those earning over $250,000, instead requiring a moderate increase for those making over $400,000. Boehner's Plan B was simple—extend the expiring tax cuts for most Americans, while reverting the tax rate for those making over $1 million back to 1990s levels, resulting in an overall increase for high-income earners.

Boehner was confident that his plan would pass the House and would put pressure on Democrats to act, but on December 20, Rep. Eric Cantor, R-Va., the majority leader, announced that the bill would not be brought for a vote. According to Boehner, Republican leadership was not able to gather sufficient support from its members to pass the bill: "Now it is up to the president to work with Senator [Harry] Reid on legislation to avert the fiscal cliff." Democrats had already indicated that they would not vote for Boehner's Plan B.

FINAL AGREEMENT

Unable to reach a compromise of his own, President Obama dispatched Vice President Joe Biden to meet with Senate Republican leaders to reach an agreement. The two sides emerged from meetings each day during the final week of December, indicating that they were nearing an agreement but that there were still many hurdles to overcome.

Shortly before midnight on New Year's Eve, Senate Republicans announced that they had reached an agreement with the White House. At approximately 2 a.m. on January 1, 2013, the compromise package came to a vote before the Senate and passed 89–8. On December 31, House Republican leaders announced that they would not immediately take up the bill after Senate passage, instead waiting to bring the bill to a vote at 11 p.m. on January 1. The measure passed the House by a vote of 257–167 and was signed into law by President Obama on January 2. The American Taxpayer Relief Act of 2012 (ATRA) would result not only in a smaller increase in taxes than Democrats had wanted, but also a smaller reduction in the federal deficit than desired by Republicans.

In the final compromise, individuals earning over $400,000 or couples earning more than $450,000 would see their income and capital gains tax rates increase. Estate taxes rose 5 percent, and the AMT was indexed to inflation to prevent it from affecting middle-class Americans. The Earned Income Tax Credit and college tuition tax credit, important to lower- and middle-income families, were extended for five years, and new limits were imposed on tax deductions and credits for those earning more than $250,000. The reduction in the Medicare reimbursement rate for doctors was delayed for one year, while unemployment benefits were extended for one year. Democrats were not able to reach an agreement with Republicans to continue the 2 percent payroll tax deduction. The ATRA would result in $600 billion in new tax revenue over the next decade and was the first year-to-year income tax rate increase since 1993.

The final compromise did not fix all of the problems leading up to the fiscal cliff and offered only an extension of the sequestration to March 1. Additionally, the bill did not address raising the debt ceiling, thus leaving both issues open for future debate in the next Congress.

—Heather Kerrigan

Following is the text of three statements on December 31, 2012, concerning the fiscal cliff. The first was delivered by President Barack Obama regarding the ongoing negotiations in Congress to avert the fiscal cliff, the second by Senate Minority Leader Mitch McConnell, R-Ky., announcing that the Senate was nearing an agreement, and the third, from House Republican leadership, responding to the Senate agreement.

President Obama Remarks on Fiscal Cliff Negotiations

December 31, 2012

The President. Hello, everybody! Thank you. Please, everybody, have a seat. Well, good afternoon, everybody.

Audience members. Good afternoon!

The President. Welcome to the White House.

Audience members. Thank you!

Audience member. Thank you for having us.

The President. Now, I realize that the last thing you want to hear on New Year's Eve is another speech from me. But I do need to talk about the progress that's being made in Congress today.

For the last few days, leaders in both parties have been working toward an agreement that will prevent a middle class tax hike from hitting 98 percent of all Americans, starting tomorrow. Preventing that tax hike has been my top priority, because the last thing folks like the folks up here on this stage can afford right now is to pay an extra $2,000 in taxes next year. Middle class families can't afford it. Businesses can't afford it. Our economy can't afford it.

Now, today it appears that an agreement to prevent this New Year's tax hike is within sight, but it's not done. There are still issues left to resolve, but we're hopeful that Congress can get it done. But it's not done.

And so part of the reason that I wanted to speak to all of you here today is to make sure that we emphasize to Congress and that members of both parties understand that all across America, this is a pressing concern on people's minds.

Now, the potential agreement that's being talked about would not only make sure that taxes don't go up on middle class families, it also would extend tax credits for families with children. It would extend our tuition tax credit that's helped millions of families pay for college. It would extend tax credits for clean energy companies that are creating jobs and reducing our dependence on foreign oil. It would extend unemployment insurance to 2 million Americans who are out there still actively looking for a job.

Now, I have to say that ever since I took office, throughout the campaign, and over the last couple of months, my preference would have been to solve all these problems in the context of a larger agreement, a bigger deal, a grand bargain—whatever you want to call it—that solves our deficit problems in a balanced and responsible way, that doesn't just deal with the taxes, but deals with the spending in a balanced way so that we can put all this behind us and just focusing on growing our economy.

But with this Congress, that was obviously a little too much to hope for at this time. It may be we can do it in stages. We're going to solve this problem instead in several steps.

Last year, in 2011, we started reducing the deficit through $1 trillion in spending cuts. Those have already taken place. The agreement being worked on right now would further reduce the deficit by asking the wealthiest 2 percent of Americans to pay higher taxes for the first time in two decades, so that would add additional hundreds of billions of dollars to deficit reduction. So that's progress, but we're going to need to do more.

Keep in mind that just last month Republicans in Congress said they would never agree to raise tax rates on the wealthiest Americans. Obviously, the agreement that's currently being discussed would raise those rates and raise them permanently.

Now—but keep in mind, we're going to still have more work to do. We still have deficits that have to be dealt with. We're still going to have to think about how we put our economy on a long-term trajectory of growth, how we continue to make investments in things like education, things like infrastructure that help our economy grow.

And keep in mind that the threat of tax hikes going up is only one part of this so-called fiscal cliff that everybody's been talking about. What we also have facing us starting tomorrow are automatic spending cuts that are scheduled to go into effect. And keep in mind that some of these spending cuts that Congress has said will automatically go into effect have an impact on our Defense Department, but they also have an impact on things like Head Start. And so there are some programs that are scheduled to be cut that—we're using an ax instead of a scalpel—may not always be the smartest cuts. And so that is a piece of business that still has to be taken care of.

And I want to make clear that any agreement we have to deal with these automatic spending cuts that are being threatened for next month, those also have to be balanced. Because remember, my principle has always been let's do things in a balanced, responsible way. And that means that revenues have to be part of the equation in turning off the sequester, in eliminating these automatic spending cuts, as well as spending cuts.

Now, the same is true for any future deficit agreement. Obviously, we're going to have to do more to reduce our debt and our deficit. I'm willing to do more, but it's going to have to be balanced. We're going to have to do it in a balanced, responsible way.

For example, I'm willing to reduce our Government's Medicare bills by finding new ways to reduce the cost of health care in this country. That's something that we all should agree on. We want to make sure that Medicare is there for future generations. But the current trajectory of health care costs is going up so high we've got to find ways to make sure that it's sustainable.

But that kind of reform has to go hand in hand with doing some more work to reform our Tax Code so that wealthy individuals, the biggest corporations can't take advantage of loopholes and deductions that aren't available to most of the folks standing up here, aren't available to most Americans. So there's still more work to be done in the Tax Code to make it fairer, even as we're also looking at how we can strengthen something like Medicare.

Now, if Republicans think that I will finish the job of deficit reduction through spending cuts alone—and you hear that sometimes coming from them, that, sort of, after today we're just going to try to shove only spending cuts down, well—shove spending cuts at us that will hurt seniors or hurt students or hurt middle class families, without asking also equivalent sacrifice from millionaires or companies with a lot of lobbyists, et cetera, if they think that's going to be the formula for how we solve this thing, then they've got another think coming. That's not how it's going to work. We've got to do this in a balanced and responsible way. And if we're going to be serious about deficit reduction and debt reduction, then it's going to have to be a matter of shared sacrifice, at least as long as I'm President. And I'm going to be President for the next 4 years, I hope, so—

So anyway, for now, our most immediate priority is to stop taxes going up for middle class families, starting tomorrow. I think that is a modest goal that we can accomplish. Democrats and Republicans in Congress have to get this done, but they're not there yet. They are close, but they're not there yet. And one thing we can count on with respect to this Congress is that if there's even one second left before you have to do what you're supposed to do—they will use that last second.

So, as of this point, it looks like I'm going to be spending New Year's here in DC.

Audience members. Aww!

The President. It's—you all are going to be hanging out in DC too. I can come to your house? Is that what you said? I don't want to spoil the party.

Audience member. You are the party.

The President. But the people who are with me here today, the people who are watching at home, they need our leaders in Congress to succeed. They need us to all stay focused on them, not on politics, not on special interests. They need to be focused on families, students, grandmas, folks who are out there working really, really hard and are just looking for a fair shot and some reward for that hard work.

They expect our leaders to succeed on their behalf. So do I. And so keep the pressure on over the next 12 hours or so. Let's see if we can get this thing done.

And I thank you all. And if I don't see you, if I don't show up at your house—I want to wish everybody a happy New Year. Thank you very much. All right.

SOURCE: Executive Office of the President. "Remarks on the National Economy." December 31, 2012. *Compilation of Presidential Documents* 2012, no. 00980 (December 31, 2012). http://www.gpo.gov/fdsys/pkg/DCPD-201200980/pdf/DCPD-201200980.pdf.

DOCUMENT *Sen. McConnell on Nearing Agreement*

December 31, 2012

Mr. McCONNELL. Mr. President, yesterday—after days of inaction—I came to the floor and noted the obvious: we need to act but I need a dance partner. So I reached out to the Vice President in an effort to get things done. I am happy to report that the effort has been a successful one, and as the President just said in his television appearance, we are very close to an agreement.

We need to protect American families and job creators from this looming tax hike. Everyone agrees that action is necessary, and I can report that we have reached an agreement on all of the tax issues. We are very close.

As the President just said, the most important piece—the piece that has to be done now—is preventing the tax hikes. The President said, "For now our most immediate priority is to stop taxes going up for middle-class families starting tomorrow." I agree. He suggested that action on the sequester is something we can continue to work on in the coming months.

So I agree, let's pass the tax relief portion now. Let's take what has been agreed to and get moving. This was not easy to get to. The Vice President and I spoke at 12:45 this morning, 6:30 this morning, and multiple times again during this morning. This has clearly been a good-faith negotiation. We all want to protect taxpayers, and we could get it done right now.

So let me be clear: We will continue to work on finding smarter ways to cut spending, but let's not let that hold up protecting Americans from the tax hike that will take place in about 10 hours from now. We can do this; we must do this.

I want my colleagues to know that we will keep everybody updated as we continue to try to wrap this up.

I yield the floor.

SOURCE: Sen. Mitch McConnell. "The Fiscal Cliff." *Congressional Record* 2012, pt. 158, S8570. December 31, 2012. http://www.gpo.gov/fdsys/pkg/CREC-2012-12-31/pdf/CREC-2012-12-31-pt1-PgS8570-2.pdf.

Republican Statement on
Senate Agreement

December 31, 2012

House Speaker John Boehner (R-OH), Majority Leader Eric Cantor (R-VA), Majority Whip Kevin McCarthy (R-CA), and Republican Conference Chair Cathy McMorris Rodgers (R-WA) issued the following statement on the Senate agreement:

"The House will honor its commitment to consider the Senate agreement if it is passed. Decisions about whether the House will seek to accept or promptly amend the measure will not be made until House members—and the American people—have been able to review the legislation."

SOURCE: Office of Representative John Boehner. "House Leadership Statement on Senate Agreement." December 31, 2012. http://boehner.house.gov/news/documentsingle.aspx?DocumentID=316086.

OTHER HISTORIC DOCUMENTS OF INTEREST

FROM THIS VOLUME

- State of the Union Address and Republican Response, p. 60

FROM PREVIOUS *HISTORIC DOCUMENTS*

- House and Senate Debate Temporary Payroll Tax Extension, *2011*, p. 686
- Federal Deficit Reduction Committee Folds Without Conclusion, *2011*, p. 618
- President Obama Remarks on the Debt Ceiling and Credit Downgrade, *2011*, p. 423
- Bush on Signing the Tax Relief Bill, *2001*, p. 400

Index

Names starting with al- or el- are alphabetized by the subsequent part of the name.

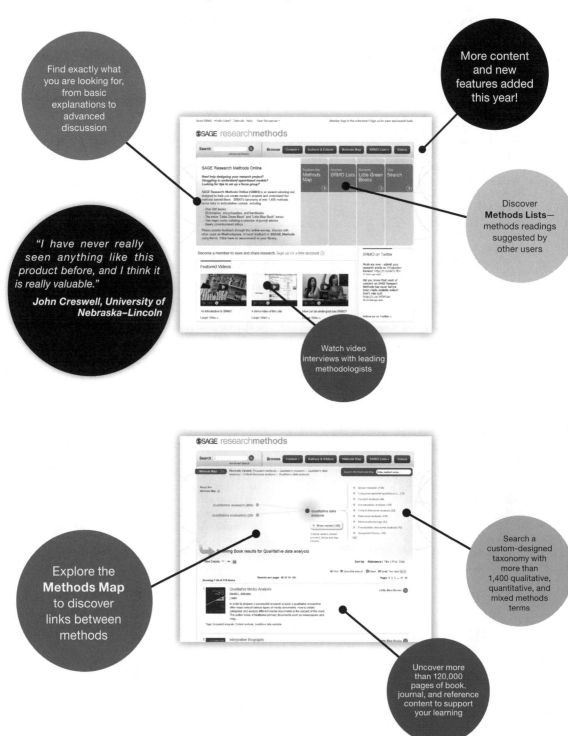